Pathways to Collaboration
Volume 2

Pathways to Collaboration
Volume 2

**Jim Fowler, Roman Holowinsky, Austin Channell,
Otto J Crocomo, Julius P Kreier and William R. Sharp**

Pathways to Collaboration Copyright © 2017 William R Sharp & Jim Fowler &
Roman Holowinsky & Austin Channell & Otto J Crocomo & Julius P Kreier
All Rights Reserved
ISBN: 1973945231
ISBN 13: 9781973945239
Printed in the United States of America

Acknowledgements

The editors are grateful to their colleagues, family members and friends for their contributions and support during the two year book development journey. In particular, the editors thank the following:

Consuelo Baher, Author and One of Four National Content Providers, Named by *Fast Company*

Charlene Brenner J.D., Project Coordinator, The Ohio State University STEAM Factory

Rebecca Butcher Rivera, Production Editor, *Pathways to Collaboration*

Linda Channell, Home School Educator and Speech Therapist

Anna Gawboy, Ph.D. Associate Professor, School of Music, The Ohio State University

Diva Lovadino Crocomo, Educator and Musician

Sally Sharp Holland, Author and Educator

Ashley Miller, Head of the Digital Publishing Program, The Ohio State University Office of Distance Education and eLearning

John Pieper, Administrative Manager, Mathematics Department, The Ohio State University

Edward Ramos Sousa J.D., Attorney and Author

Jeffrey Sharp, Entrepreneur and Film Producer

Mike Shiflet, Educational Technologist, The Ohio State University Office of Distance Education and eLearning

Douglas S. Steinbrech M.D., Surgeon and Author

Cover Design and Photography

The editors provide special thanks to Mike Cairns, Infinite Impact & Aerial Image Solutions for shooting the magnificent cover photograph and Mauricio Diaz, Book Cover Designer, for the brilliant cover design. Mike Cairns resides in Columbus, Ohio and Mauricio Diaz resides in New York City.

Dedication

The Contributors Dedicate *Pathways to Collaboration* to Our Mentors and Successors

Preface

Our Pathway

We began our *Pathways to Collaboration* journey like countless other collaborative efforts – with that magical combination of serendipity, collective brainstorming, and a healthy dose of grassroots support. The origins of *Pathways* can be traced back to September 30, 2014 and the book release party for *Reflections and Connections – Personal Pathways Through the Life Sciences*. The evening was the culmination of a two-year effort, which had yielded a rich collection of twenty-five chapters featuring personal stories of friendship, mentorships and triumphs of the human spirit over adversity in the competitive world of academia. Many of the authors and editors who attended the event were colleagues of mine from The Ohio State University, Rutgers University and University of Sao Paulo, the three members of the collaborative Tripartite Institute. As I looked out at my accomplished colleagues and friends, there was a sense that these personal stories and the lessons they teach might become our true legacies – legacies that would outlast our professional and academic accomplishments.

It was that sense of excitement that inspired us to think beyond the evening's celebration and towards a new challenge: creating a new publishing project around collaboration its many pathways and byways. After several long walks with my son Jeff along the beautiful bluffs of Santa Monica, California, the vision for the new project became clearer in my mind. Fortunately, this vision's inception happened to coincide with several key introductions, which helped take *Pathways* from a vision to a reality.

In early 2014, I was attending a quarterly meeting for The Ohio State University Arts and Sciences Academic Advisory Committee. The Dean of Natural and Mathematical Sciences, who normally attended the meetings, had an out of town engagement. In his absence, we were invited to hear a young mathematician Roman Holowinsky tell us about The STEAM Factory, a groundbreaking organization that he and his colleagues had recently founded at OSU. The STEAM Factory is a non-profit organization dedicated to exploring new collaborative pathways outside of traditional university routes. In listening to Roman speak, I experienced a powerful sense of connection between The STEAM Factory and the collaborative themes we had explored in *Reflections and Connections*. That spark inspired me to introduce myself to Roman at the end of his presentation. Despite a nearly forty-year age gap, our conversation marked the start of an ever-growing warm and rewarding friendship and the beginning of an exciting new chapter in my career, as an advisor and advocate for academic efforts. Following our conversation, Roman encouraged me to join the STEAM Factory Advocacy Committee where I had the unique opportunity to meet an incredible selection of distinguished faculty members in diverse fields and departments. Among these new acquaintances was Jim Fowler, Roman's mathematical colleague, MOOCulus team member, and now senior editor for *Pathways to Collaboration.*

The STEAM Factory's infectious passion for collaboration spread to other universities, resulting in the creation of the Erdős Institute, named after renown mathematician Paul Erdős. The Institute was cofounded by Roman Holowinsky and colleagues from Vanderbilt University for the purpose of fostering inter-institutional collaborations. It was through this network that I met Vanderbilt student Austin Channell, who is in his early twenties, making him our youngest *Pathways* editor. In conversations with Austin, I have had the exciting opportunity to learn about the latest modes of collaboration through social media and in the arts.

Suddenly, I found myself working alongside academics from multiple generations of leadership in an electric, possibility-filled environment. By early 2015, I became sufficiently inspired and emboldened to approach Roman, Jim and Austin about the possibility of joining Otto Crocomo, Julius Kreier and me, the editors of our first publishing project, to create a new book series, *Pathways to Collaboration*. We were moved by an image of OSU's famous Oval, a quadrangle at the heart of the university with pathways that extend out in all directions. Just as the Oval's paths stretch beyond the handsome old academic buildings towards the city of Columbus and beyond, the new book would also extend beyond the halls of academia and into the world of government and private industry. In the midst of all of this, I somehow turned eighty years old on September 13, 2016. This occasion became yet another inspiration to bring this new publication, which you now have in your hands, to life.

The authors in *Pathways to Collaboration* were sourced by the editors from diverse backgrounds, including undergraduates, faculty, retired faculty, government officials, and private sector innovators. The accomplishments of the authors stretch across four corners of the earth and include grassroots intra- and inter-institutional academic collaborations, boundary collaborations with government and the private sector, and collaborative spin-off enterprises.

We hope that *Pathways* will be read by a wide range of people, as these stories of collaboratively navigating life have something to offer everyone. Young people, mid-career professionals, and those of us who are retired may all find comfort in seeing we are not alone in our struggles and may draw inspiration from the passion and successes contained in these pages.

Collaboration is a beautiful, messy experience. The triumphs are often great, the failures are often painful, but the journey is one that is absolutely worth taking. With six editors and 52 authors, *Pathways to Collaboration* has been a truly collaborative endeavor, one which I am enormously grateful to have been a part of. Thank you for joining us on our journey as our final collaborator: the reader.

With gratitude and appreciation.
William Rodney Sharp

Prologue

In the spring of 1986, while deciding where to enroll in a doctoral program in English, I rode the train from Washington, D.C., where I was working as a paralegal, to New Haven, Connecticut, to visit Yale University. As I walked into the Old Campus, I ran into a Yale English graduate student who had been a teaching assistant of mine when I was an undergraduate there. When I told him that I had been admitted into the graduate program, he paused and said, "You will be happy here if you like cliques of one." Having learned to be independent with a high tolerance for solitude, I decided that I could thrive in such an environment and enrolled the next fall.

Five years later I completed my PhD and began my career as an English professor at Ohio State, where I recently celebrated my 25th year of service, eight of which have been in full time administrative service as a vice provost and vice dean. During that time, I have moved from traversing "cliques of one" to working in an administrative team that is, among other things, invested in supporting academic collaboration. As a scholar of American literature, I have also studied and written about the history of authorship in the nineteenth century—a period in which notions of solitary "genius" were ascendant even as publishers, editors, and writers worked in close collaboration to engage readers in what we would now call virtual communities. While most of my publications have been single authored, I have also co-edited an academic journal and a book of essays, served on numerous committees that have produced collaboratively written reports, team-taught courses with an English colleague and an art historian, and served on multiple dissertation committees that worked together to support the original work of PhD students. As an administrator, I have served as a co-principal investigator on a large National Science Foundation Advance grant and written hundreds of letters, memos, policies, and reports that reflect input from multiple stakeholders, many of which were distributed under another administrator's name or with no attribution. In short, even as I have studied the history of authorial collaboration, I have learned to collaborate within the norms of my discipline and the norms of my administrative roles, all the while working to try to ensure that others are appropriately recognized and rewarded for their collaborations.

I come to this project, then, with personal and professional experiences that frame my understanding of the topic. As this collection of essays demonstrates, perspectives on and definitions of collaboration are wide ranging and diverse, and readers will find a variety of ways to engage with the topic. By way of introduction, I would like to offer three overarching considerations to keep in mind when trying to conceptualize, advance, and support collaboration in the academy and beyond. First, it is crucial to remember that collaboration has a history that has shaped our understanding of the term—a history that has not only impacted our conceptions of individual effort and value but has also made it easier for some members of our community to be recognized for collaboration than others. Second, we must attend to the words that we use to describe collaborative activities. As a term, "collaboration" is connected to a host of other terms—most particularly "interdisciplinarity"—that themselves each have a particular history and association and their own specific meaning. And finally, it is important to be attuned to disciplinary context. As the various essays in this volume reveal, each individual brings a different perspective to the subject of collaboration. It is important to be curious and open to these various perspectives as a first point toward moving toward a more complex, nuanced, and inclusive understanding of collaboration's promise as well as of its inherent tensions and contradictions.

Historical conceptions of authorship and collaboration

Contributors to collaborative efforts in academia, particularly those that result in a publication, grant, patent, license, or copyright, often struggle over questions of appropriate reward and recognition for their individual efforts as "investigators" or "authors." Different disciplines have different norms about which collaborators should appropriately be listed as co-authors and which ones should be listed in the acknowledgments. At Ohio State, for example, the university policy on research data underscores these field-specific differences when it describes "the responsibility of the PI [principal investigator] to ensure that all persons listed as authors on publications or presentations meet accepted criteria in their field for authorship credit, and that only such persons are listed as authors." It also states that "the PI is responsible for ensuring that faculty, students, and/or research staff members who do not meet the criteria for authorship, yet have provided special assistance or contributions to the research, be listed in an acknowledgments section, if available in the publication."[1]

The value attached to "authorship credit" is at the heart of peer review in the academy, from manuscript and grant reviews to promotion and tenure reviews to measurements of "excellence" and "distinction" for national awards and titled professorships. In some fields, including my own, single authored works (with appropriate acknowledgments and notes) are the gold standard, leading to seemingly straight-forward accounting of contribution and effort as well as impact through citations. In others, it is more common to have multi-authored works. In 2015, for example, a study in Physics Review Letters listed 5154 authors, demonstrating the multi-institutional scale of research in particle physics.[2] In fields where multi-authorship is common, authorship disputes arise when a lead or first author believes that a collaborator's contributions do not meet the criteria for authorship, while the collaborator—often a student, postdoctoral researcher, or more junior faculty member who has lower institutional standing—believes that

---

1 http://orc.osu.edu/files/ResearchDataPolicy.pdf, pp. 2-3.
2 http://www.sciencemag.org/news/sifter/physics-paper-sets-record-more-5000-authors

they do. They also emerge when the criteria for "credit" are not well defined or are taken for granted but not fully explained.

In most cases, participation in or assistance with a project is not sufficient to receive such credit; it is important to be able to document one's unique contribution as an "intellectual driver" of the project.[3] As former Ohio State provost Joseph Steinmetz recently put it in a different context, "What separates participation from collaboration is a step forward where you join in, take ownership of, and are actively engaged in the process. Collaborators are unique in that they share a unified goal of a more successful outcome and the push to completion."[4] The concept of shared ownership, in this view, is crucial to effective collaboration.

The connection between authorship and ownership as we currently understand it is grounded in Romantic notions of the importance of individual originality and creativity that emerged during the nineteenth century. In the United States, publishers, literary critics, and artists and authors themselves began to promote the value of original and autonomous "genius" as a corollary to American individualism and self-reliance. Walt Whitman, for example, defined the poet as the individual who could "contain multitudes" by himself.[5] With little cultural history and social capital, the United States could nonetheless exercise a form of patriotism that valued scholars and artists who were original, visionary, and autonomous in their ability to address issues of great magnitude. In the "American Scholar," Ralph Waldo Emerson defined the "office of the scholar" as a "private observatory" where he "catalogu[es] obscure and nebulous stars of the human mind, which as yet no man has thought of as such," and "must accept, — how often! poverty and solitude."[6] In this view, a scholarly author is a solitary

---

3 I am grateful to my former colleague Anne McCoy, now a professor of chemistry at the University of Washington, for this phrase.
4 Joseph Steinmetz, Chancellor's Welcome to Campus IT Workshop, University of Arkansas, May 22, 2017, https://www.youtube.com/watch?v=NsYxQvpskkE&sns=em.
5 Walt Whitman, Leaves of Grass, in *Complete Poetry and Prose* (New York: Library of America, 1982), p. 87.
6 Ralph Waldo Emerson, "The American Scholar," in *The Portable Emerson*, ed. Carl Bode (New York: Penguin, 1981), pp. 62-63.

visionary who struggles for financial reward while providing perceptions and innovations that produce new thoughts or concepts.

Over the course of the nineteenth century, there was a concerted effort to provide legal rights and cultural privileges to authorship, culminating in the International Copyright Act of 1891. Amateurs could become writers and get published, but authorship itself was a concept generally associated with individual expertise, originality, and protection of intellectual property.[7] In this context, the concept of collaborative "ownership" co-exists uneasily alongside long-standing notions of authors as having individual rights based on their hard-won originality and exceptional abilities and professional expertise. This is particularly true for authors from groups that have historically found it more difficult to assert their individual rights. Some historians have suggested that by recovering the history of collective endeavors alongside the history of individualist authorship, we can escape the tensions between them. Martha Woodmansee and Peter Jaszi, for example, have argued that we can recognize the collective rights of indigenous peoples in folklore by reconstructing intellectual property law and policy. At the same time, other scholars have pointed out the irony in the fact that the academy started focusing on collaboration at the moment when scholars from underrepresented groups were finally beginning to emerge as distinct voices who could earn individual "authorial credit."[8]

The "clique of one" that I encountered at Yale in the 1980s was a successor to the Romantic notion of the scholar-author as an individual who requires solitude and sacrifice. Ironically, the graduate assistant who shared that phrase with me worked in the "Boswell Factory" in the Sterling Library at Yale, the colloquial title of the Yale Edition of the Private Papers of James Boswell, a collaborative editorial project that has been housed at Yale since 1949. In this "factory," students, staff and faculty from Yale and other institutions have worked for decades

---

[7] For more information on this historical trajectory, see my essay, "Writing, Authorship, and Genius: Literary Women and Modes of Literary Production," in *The Cambridge History of American Women's Literature*, ed. Dale Bauer (Cambridge: Cambridge UP, 2012), pp. 204-31.

[8] June Howard discusses Woodmansee and Jaszi in *Publishing the Family* (Durham: Duke University Press, 2001), p. 26. Lisa Ede and Andrea A. Lunsford discuss the material consequences of the critique of individual authorship in "Collaboration and Concepts of Authorship," *Publications of the Modern Language Association of America* 116.2 (March 2001): 355.

to edit and publish the private papers of James Boswell, a writer who himself is best known for his collaborative work as the biographer of one of the most influential thinkers of the eighteenth century, Samuel Johnson. A 1975 New York Times article on this "thriving industry" describes the factory's "boss," Frederick A. Pottle, as an expert leader whose wife assembles scraps of paper beside him and who received a National Endowment for the Humanities grant only after another colleague, Irma Lustig, wrote the application that he approved before leaving for vacation.[9]

This journalistic description of a collaborative editorial "factory" helps illuminate some of the tensions and contradictions that can be inherent in collaborative work in the academy. Who does the work of assembly and discovery, who writes, and who approves? Who gets the credit? Who stays in the factory and who goes on vacation? The factory "boss," Professor Pottle, is described by the Times reporter as a "perfectly gentle tyrant, taming the smallest clue into relevance, and showing the hand of the master in writing the narrative large." This description draws on the Emersonian definition of the American scholar: the "master" sees what the other workers cannot. It also firmly establishes Professor Pottle as the principal investigator of the project, and in so doing helps establish the "Boswell Factory" as an important scholarly site. About the same time that the Boswell Factory was started, the Ohio State Libraries started supporting a similar editorial "factory" dedicated to publishing a definitive Centenary Edition of all of Nathaniel Hawthorne's works. Unlike the workers described in the Times, the "devoted laborers" in this factory were reviewed in 1963 as being "bibliographic drones" whose work should not be confused "with scholarship."[10] In these cases, institutional prestige, the cultural value of the subject, and the credit given to scholarly practice all bear on the impact and recognition of similar kinds of collaborative work.

---

9 Israel Shenker, "Boswell's Life a Thriving Industry at Yale," *The New York Times*, July 25, 1975. http://www.nytimes.com/1975/07/25/archives/boswells-life-a-thriving-industry-at-yale-boswells-life-provides-a.html?_r=0

10 Jesse H. Shira, review of Hawthorne, Nathaniel. *Centenary Edition Vol. 1, The Scarlet Letter. American Notes and Queries* 10.6 (June 1963): 160.

Today's academic laboratories, collaboratories, sand boxes, maker spaces, and factories put great effort into creating work spaces that intentionally and explicitly diminish hierarchy and facilitate exchange. The complexity and scope of the problems and topics they study call for innovative structures. Yet the scholars who work in them still operate within a culture that bears traces of the Emersonian master scholar. In my work as an administrator, I have often heard frustration from scholars and researchers that collaboration is not sufficiently recognized and rewarded, and from administrators that the scholars and researchers are themselves not sufficiently open to valuing collaborative work. The two views are interrelated, or course. Thinking about the history of authorship and debates about individual and collective agency will not end the frustration on both sides. Yet it is important, I think, to understand the cultural weight that the term "author" has within and beyond academia. Projects like the present collection help to expand our understanding of the differing perspectives on the value of and challenges to collaboration. As these discussions continue, it is important to remember that our questions about "credit" and recognition in collaborative projects themselves have a long history that needs to be understood in order, to affect real change.

Collaboration and Interdisciplinarity

When I came to Ohio State in 1991, I understood that my primary goal as an untenured assistant professor was to publish a single-authored monograph based on my dissertation, which focused on the representation of portraits and photographs in early and mid-nineteenth century American fiction. The dissertation itself had been co-directed by an American literature professor in the English department, Richard Brodhead, and a professor in the interdisciplinary American Studies department, Alan Trachtenberg. I benefitted from their different perspectives, which I received by talking to each one individually: we never met as a group, and I never heard them together in conversation about my work (Yale did not have formal dissertation defenses, instead asking faculty uninvolved in the project to read and comment on it at a faculty meeting). Although my work itself was an interdisciplinary synthesis of different methodologies and fields that linked literary criticism and history, periodical studies, and art history, my advisers modelled for me the importance of individual discussion—of cliques of one. On the job market, aware that there were (and still are) very few jobs in American Studies, I was advised to focus on my literary training in order to be marketable to English departments. At Ohio State, on the other hand, as I began to look for publishers for my book, I was advised to push its interdisciplinary aspects. However, I quickly learned that doing so could complicate the peer review of my work. Literary scholars provided positive readers' reports, but the first art historian that received it was concerned that it did not cover the history of landscape—an issue less important to the authors I was studying but very important in the history of painting. I realized that when an acquisitions editor asked for potential readers, I needed to focus on those in English studies who would be appropriate for vetting my work. Although I thought of my work as interdisciplinary—drawing together methodologies I had learned working with faculty in two distinct departments at Yale—I learned that it was more precise to describe them as intradisciplinary: drawing together different methodologies that could all be subsumed under English studies.

My early scholarly work, then, sought to get the "author credit" by synthesizing a number of different historical and methodological threads; I considered it interdisciplinary but not collaborative, and worked to adapt it to the disciplinary standards expected from my peers in the field. My collaborative endeavors as an assistant professor mostly were in the realm of curricular development and participation in seminars where individuals workshopped their work in progress. The goal of such workshops was to enable the individual scholar to hone his or her own argument, with the role of the participants being to identify gaps, inconsistencies, or other weaknesses in a manuscript. During this time, the Hawthorne "factory" mentioned above was beginning to wind down, and my understanding of its collaborative enterprise was restricted to reports from graduate students who worked on the project. As one later reported, this collaboration involved the graduate student sitting across the desk from the lead editor, reading aloud to catch errors and "puzzle out things that perhaps called for an explanation."[11] Working together to puzzle out things is a hallmark of good collaboration at any level, drawing as it does on the notion that two heads are better than one. Yet this model was and is very rare in English studies, which tends instead to value individual scholars who think and write in solitude and then test their assumptions with readers whose job is to be critical and analytical.

As a beginning faculty member, my greatest exemplar of scholarly collaboration was Andrea Lunsford, a professor of rhetoric and composition whose regular and highly valued publications with Lisa Ede, a collaborator at another institution, paved the way for Lunsford to move to Stanford in 2000. Lunsford and Ede believe strongly that the best way to destabilize a notion of the author as an autonomous individual is to not only critique the historical constructions I briefly outlined above but also to adopt "collaborative writing practices…not only in the classrooms but in scholarly and professional work as well."[12] Lunsford and Ede are particularly interested in adding collaborative practices within English studies such as "invitational rhetoric" (alternatives to traditional argumentative structures in the field) and collaboratively written dissertations that acknowledge "the impossibility of making a truly original contribution to knowledge" (358). For them, collaboration within disciplines—in this case, English—is its own good, and one to which they have both dedicated their careers. Andrea Lunsford underscored for me that collaboration is not necessarily interdisciplinary, and that giving institutional recognition of collaborative work within departments and fields is itself an important goal.

While believing that collaboration within English studies can make it more welcoming, inclusive, and productive for the scholars within it, Ede and Lunsford also acknowledge that it is in some respects easier to produce than interdisciplinary collaboration, which can "bring special challenges" (361). They recognize the growing importance of large-scale interdisciplinary projects that, extending beyond the humanities and beyond the academy, bring together "differing stylistic and methodological assumptions and practices." At the same time, they state

---

11 Paul Eistenstein, "In Memoriam," Thomas Miller Woodson, *Nathaniel Hawthorne Review* 40.2 (Fall 2014): 119.

12 Ede and Lunsford, "Collaboration and Concepts of Authorship," 356.

that such projects risk "conceptual incoherence" (364). This is an important point. Disciplinary collaboration can help drive methodological change and norms and advance particular fields. Interdisciplinary collaboration has the potential to take on larger problems and find more transformative, innovative, and/or translational solutions. Yet in order to address these problems and identify these solutions, interdisciplinary collaborators have to spend time addressing and understanding their "conceptual incoherence." The time and effort involved in this process can interrupt or slow down progress toward the "unified goal of a more successful outcome and the push to completion" that Steinmetz articulates and advocates.

Ohio State historian and English professor Harvey Graff has suggested that the Romantic ideal of the individual author that I outlined above has now been joined by "a sense of the romance of discovery and brilliance of leading researchers who draw from two or more disciplines" in order to address "perceived limitations in theory, practice, or data."[13] This romance leads to a "standard version" of "one true" interdisciplinarity that fails to "appreciate diversity, multiple paths, and different or mixed forms of success" and "stimulates endless dickering over multi-, pluri-, inter-, trans-disciplinarity, [and] even anti- or a-disciplinarity." To address this, he provides historical case studies that remind us that disciplinary clusters sometimes work in parallel without formal interdisciplinary structures and that "there is no single organization, form, pattern of institutionalization, or set of rules that signifies interdisciplinarity" (236). He also points out that some disciplines themselves grew out of collaborations across disciplines—what he terms "interdisciplines." For example, in the early twentieth century, the new discipline of biology emerged as an "interdisciplinary integration of preexisting fields," including botany, zoology and a number, of subfields (21).

Given this history as well as the various connotations of collaboration and interdisciplinarity respectively, it is important to pay attention to these key words in conversations and initiatives dedicated to promoting one or both. At Ohio State, one such initiative is the Discovery

---

13 See Harvey J. Graff, *Undisciplining Knowledge: Interdisciplinarity in the Twentieth Century* (Baltimore: Johns Hopkins University Press, 2015), p. 13.

Themes program, which aims to be "a model of interdisciplinarity and transinstitutionality that promotes and enhances broad university collaboration."[14] In practice, this has meant establishing cluster hires of new faculty (with the goal of 200 by 2020) focused on integrated solutions to significant global challenges, as well as programs and grants geared toward connecting current Ohio State researchers to others doing related work. It is an ambitious and exciting project that seeks nothing less than to change the academic culture at the institution to recognize and reward the importance of large-scale, team-oriented research, often encapsulated under the term "team science." At the same time, its emphasis on collaboration as interdisciplinarity signals the challenges inherent in such culture change. In disciplines whose highest-ranked departments still implicitly or explicitly venerate "cliques of one," culture change might come as much from collaboration within the discipline as across it. For faculty hired in newly expanding fields such as data analytics, culture change might come from being embedded in a department and bringing new methodologies to it rather than working across departments. The terms matter, and differ, according to the perspective of the person who hears it, and these contextual differences can complicate communication between and among different communities and clusters within the university.

Contextual diversity

As I have described, I am first and foremost part of a community of literary scholars who operate within a discipline that has valued single-authored individual work and that has absorbed a number of different methodologies and fields of study over time. At the same time, I have worked both at the university and within Ohio State's College of Arts and Sciences to understand and manage the promotion and tenure process—a process that is rooted above all in disciplinary contexts and differences, with the tenured faculty in, a given department or school having the primary responsibility for making decisions. College and university administrators can overturn their decisions only when they

---

14 https://discovery.osu.edu/about/guiding-principles.html

can show that the department or school has not followed its own processes or upheld its own standards.

Within such an environment, I am aware that discussions about specific models of collaboration will vary greatly according to discipline. While Lisa Ede and Andrea Lunsford are unusual in arguing for the benefits of co-authorship in English, colleagues in physics and astronomy routinely have hundreds if not thousands of collaborators—so much so that a former chair of astronomy once explained to me that everyone in the field was a collaborator. While humanities departments encourage PhD students to write "original" dissertations that can be the basis for a single-authored monograph in the future, engineering departments encourage their graduate students to submit dissertations that consist of several co-authored articles with their advisor. While book departments measure the impact of their research by the quality of the press and the detailed comments of their peer reviewers, medical school faculty measure impact through principal investigator status on R01 grants, impact factors of journals, citation data, invited talks, and invitations by the National Institutes of Health to evaluate grants.

These local differences create challenges in implementing general principles about the importance of collaborative research. For example, the College of Medicine at Ohio State—which is deeply invested in the importance of team and translational science—states in its promotion criteria that "faculty members are encouraged to collaborate with other investigators and are encouraged to meet the requirement for extramural support for their research as a one of several program directors or principal investigators on network-type or center grants (multiple-PD/PI) or, in some circumstances, by serving as a co-investigator on multiple NIH grants." In a related passage, the College of Medicine also states that "participation in collaborative, multidisciplinary research and team science is highly valued, especially to the extent that a faculty member's record of collaborative scholarship includes manuscripts on which authorship is first, senior, or corresponding; or the individual input of the faculty member as a middle author is uniquely contributory and clearly evident." This passage suggests that the scientific, lab-oriented disciplines in medicine both value collaboration and also retain vestiges of the autonomous

American scholar that Emerson identified: the scholar who can define his or her "unique" individual contributions. Other disciplines, on the other hand, are more willing to de-couple collaboration from individual uniqueness. The Department of Design in the College of Arts and Sciences, for example, explicitly values collaborative research as highly as individual research: its criteria for promotion state that "collaborative and/or interdisciplinary work is encouraged, and acknowledged as essential to some types of design inquiry. Evidence of significant contribution to successful and substantive collaborative research is valued equally to individual research accomplishments."[15]

As I have mentioned, in some fields scholars attribute the "value" of contributions through acknowledgments or through participating in seminars or work groups, while in others such contributions receive "credit" as authorship. At the highest levels of university policy, it can be difficult to account for all of these various practices, with the result that some members of the academic community inevitably feel unrecognized or undervalued in relation to others. At an institutional level, collaboration can be held out as a strategic principle, while in a specific lab a young assistant professor can struggle with knowing the right moment to stop collaborating with his or her adviser and start collaborating with his or her own students. At an institutional level, collaboration can be identified as itself a "unique" practice, as Joseph Steinmetz does, while in Ohio State's STEAM Factory, assistant professors worry about how to document their unique contributions to collaborative grants so that they can explain them to the tenured faculty in their departments at the time of their tenure review. In addition, faculty, staff, and students can collaborate every day on committees, in classrooms, in offices, with community partners, with foundations and agencies, and yet feel that this is invisible work in comparison to the collaborative "authorship" of high profile and highly funded research—research that tends to reward highly cited individual "stars."

---

15 References are to the College of Medicine's Appointments, Promotion and Tenure document, dated September 9, 2012; and the Department of Design's Appointments, Promotion and Tenure document, approved March 18, 2016, both at https://oaa.osu.edu/governance.html.

The answer to these challenges is not to support the continued emergence of cliques of one. At the same time, however, it is important to be aware that depending on one's role in the university (and in other organizations), the word "collaboration" will be heard and interpreted differently. It is important for each, individual to be open and curious about what collaboration means to those around them, and especially when creating working partnerships, to spend time talking about those perceptions and acknowledging the "conceptual incoherence" that they can bring.[16] This time is difficult to report or make visible in the reward and recognition systems of most universities—a challenge that we in higher education might do well to collaboratively address. As economist Tim Harford recently posted, "the basic principle in any incentive scheme is this: can you measure everything that matters. If you can't, then high-powered financial incentives will simply produce short-sightedness, narrow-mindedness, or outright fraud. If a job is complex, multifaceted, and involves subtle trade-offs, the best approach is to hire good people, pay them the going rate, and tell them to do the job to the best of their ability."[17]

As an administrator, I have learned that incentives and measurements are important to documenting progress and reporting our stories, and they can also help ensure equity and fairness for the good people who are working to the best of their ability. And of course, grading student work is itself a high structured and measured incentive system. At the same time, we do struggle to measure everything that matters and to adequately reward those in our community who engage every day in the trade-offs of complex and multifaceted work—including the trade-offs between owning their individual efforts and supporting the collaborative work of the whole, especially when that work makes individual effort invisible and seemingly unvalued. By encouraging a wide and diverse range of contributors to tell their stories

---

16 I am grateful to Norah Zuniga-Shaw, professor of dance at Ohio State, for alerting me to the importance of curiosity in collaboration during a question and answer session following her Inaugural Lecture on April 26, 2017.

17 Cited in Mike Taylor's blog post, "Every Attempt to Manage Academia Makes It Worse." https://svpow.com/2017/03/17/every-attempt-to-manage-academia-makes-it-worse/.

and reflect on the value of collaboration, this project goes a long way toward articulating the importance of understanding and documenting the trade-offs involved. It also demonstrates what I view as one of the most exciting and promising aspects of collaboration, and interdisciplinary collaboration, in particular: at its best, it encourages us to articulate and acknowledge our conceptual and intellectual differences even as we move toward a common goal, and thereby represents one of the best ways to foster a diverse and inclusive learning environment. This may be a romantic notion, but it is one that I think holds great promise, even for individuals trained to be cliques of one.

Susan S. Williams
The Ohio State University

Contents

Acknowledgements · v

Cover Design and Photography · · · · · · · · · · · · · · · · · · vii

Dedication · ix

Preface · xi
Our Pathway

Prologue · xv

Chapter 1 Collaboration with Creativity · 1
(or, True Confessions Skeptic of a Collaboration)
Alan R. Knight

Chapter 2 My Collaborative Life & Career · 7
Leading a Collaborative Research Team of Graduate Students and Postdoctoral Fellows
Julius P. Kreier

Chapter 3 A Collaborative Life in Plants · 64
David Lee

Chapter 4   Strength of International Collaboration in the
            Globalized World··································110
            **Facilitating InterInstitutional Research and
            Teaching Programs**
            Raul Machado Neto

Chapter 5   Lifetimes of Collaboration ·······················120
            *Sally A. Miller,
            Donald J. (Chip) Styer II*

Chapter 6   Five Decades of Science and Technology at
            The Center For Nuclear Energy in Agriculture·····139
            Tsai Siu Mui

Chapter 7   A Novel Collaborative Pathway Involving
            Academia and Industry ·························166
            Launching a University Spin-off Company
            Mark T. Muller

Chapter 8   An Unusual Partnership ························254
            Thomas M. Murnane

Chapter 9   Pathways to Intra- and Inter-Institutional
            Collaboration in Plant Biology ··················264
            Neftalí Ochoa-Alejo

Chapter 10 From Cell to Plant: Biotechnology for
            Plant Propagation ····························286
            *Enio Tiago de Oliveira
            Otto J. Crocomo*

Chapter 11 Pathways to Collaboration in Agricultural
            Research and Extension························323
            Thomas Orton

Chapter 12 Pathways to Collaboration 369
        The Illusion of Collaboration
        Amanda Perrin

Chapter 13 Collaboration and Mentorship 378
        John E Peters

Chapter 14 A Study of College and Departmental
        Interactions at a Large Land Grant University 388
        Robert M. Pfister
        Patrick R. Dugan

Chapter 15 Green Genes and Hyphens and Love—Oh My! 440
        Ellen Reardon

Chapter 16 La Evolucion de Charles B. Redington 446
        Atraves de la Collaboracion
        Charles B. Redington

Chapter 17 Reflections on Collaboration in Teaching: 480
        Brigadoon and Other Myths
        Laurie Repko

Chapter 18 Building Teams in Academia for Synergy in
        Interdisciplinary Research 498
        Donnalyn Roxey
        Andy Burnett
        Erich Grotewold

Chapter 19 Pathways to Collaboration 530
        **Reinventing My Science; One Person's
        Journey to Collaborative Research and
        Development**
        Richard Sayre

Chapter 20 Nurturing Biomedical Initiatives
            Through Collaborative Interactions: ············546
            A Personal Perspective of the Process
            Thomas Michael Seed

Chapter 21 Piracy and Its Impact Upon Creative
            Collaboration in the Independent Film Industry ····574
            Jeffrey Sharp

Chapter 22 Academic and Private Sector Collaboration Models ·578
            **Spawning Interinstitutional
            Research and Spinoff Companies**
            William R Sharp

Chapter 23 Fascinated by Plants···························658
            Judy Lyman Snow

Chapter 24 A Boy Who Loves Flowers Can't Be All Bad ········679
            Roy Stahlhut

Chapter 25 A Systems Approach to Collaboration ············696
            K.C. Ting

Chapter 26 STEAM Business Collaboration ··················715
            **STEAM Education Key to Creating an
            Innovative Workforce**
            Harvey White

            Epilogue ···729

            About the Contributors ··························731

            About the Editors································765

CHAPTER 1

Collaboration with Creativity

(or, True Confessions Skeptic of a Collaboration)

Alan R. Knight
Cornell University and American
Agriculturist Magazine Retired

Collaboration is a lot like ice cream: There's a lot more flavors of it nowadays.

And we have a lot of names for it, too: partnerships, subcontracting, delegation, teamwork, borrowing ideas, building on ideas, interdisciplinary work, mutation of ideas, digital splicing of one musician's work into that of another, and even unconscious plagiarism.

Beneath it all lays the notion that the accumulation and marshaling of talent, of intellectual capital, of human brain power, can produce results unimaginable if the task were left to an individual.

Writing these words is a therapeutic step for me. They come from a man who generally views the concept of collaboration with some disdain. A keen student of history, I am aware that "collaborators" were sometimes shot.

In my career, collaboration was special because it was as rare as the indigo bunting that bounced off my windshield one day. It was beautiful, but it was an accident.

ALAN R. KNIGHT

My very first memory of collaboration is probably not unusual: the fifth grade class assignment wherein every student is assigned to a three-person team. It was to be a group project. Each student in the group would receive the same grade. The teacher, of course, did not appoint group leaders. Groups were left to flounder and founder. I watched with horror as the oldest and biggest kid in my group blustered his way into self-appointed leadership. Days went by. Weeks. The project was going nowhere.

My reaction? Do my own thing . . . just in case. Depend on myself. And, sure enough, as deadline day neared and chaos prevailed within the group, my "ace-in-the-hole" writing ended up being adopted by the group as its group effort.

This isn't meant to be bragging (my mother would not approve). It's meant as a snapshot of hardening concrete in a kid's brain. It informs every group task I have since been involved with, every personal appraisal of group leadership and team building that was in my presence ever hatched or—more commonly—stillborn.

Add to this having had to deal with an employer whose oft-employed slogan of "team" meant "do it my way or you're off the team."

So, yes, this essay might well be titled *True Confessions of a Collaboration Skeptic*.

My experiences, added up, were enough to drive me to the solace of solitude, working solo.

As a writer—an agricultural journalist, to be more precise—I was able to do that to a very high degree. Over the course of several decades, I would spend one or two weeks every month on the road, driving the dirt roads of America to visit farmers, learn their problems, chronicle their ingenuity, photograph them in their native habitat, and go back to the editorial office of *American Agriculturist*, *Farm Journal*, or *New England Farmer* and write it all down in a way that transferred that experience and knowledge in a credible, reliable, and entertaining fashion to all the thousands of farm families that found these magazines in their mailboxes every month.

Collaboration? Not much.

At least not on the surface.

And yet . . .

Yes. If we think about collaboration in a slightly broader way—if we think about it as a reliance on others so as to get our work right—then yes. Absolutely yes.

To explain: My editor and mentor at *American Agriculturist* magazine was Gordon Conklin. His policy was that every story we wrote had to be mailed (this was before the days of e-mail) to our sources—the people we interviewed and quoted in the stories—for review. We asked them to check our observations, our conclusions, our facts, and—perhaps most surprising to a 21st-century "gotcha" journalist—to ensure they were comfortable with the quotes we had attributed to them.

I know of no other publication on the planet—except *New England Farmer*, of which I later became editor—that employed that policy.

Is that collaboration?

Not in a conventional sense.

But from the standpoint of an agricultural journalist who wanted to ensure both that he got his facts straight and that he strengthened respect for his publication in the farm community, there could have been no better form of collaboration—a rare collaboration between a revered farm publication and its readers.

Surely there were more conventional forms of collaboration within the ranks of that agricultural institution (the magazine was found in 1842), as well. There would be the occasional editorial planning meeting, discussions with page designers about preferred photos, and cataloguing of story opportunities for other writers to tap-into as they planned their travels.

But for the journalist, flying solo as he conceived his stories and built them word-by-word, this rare—perhaps unique—collaboration with farmers, agricultural researchers, and agricultural entrepreneurs was surely a key to greater accuracy, relevance, and reader loyalty.

As I carried this policy with me to the editorship of *New England Farmer* newspaper, I did what my mentor at *American Agriculturist*, Gordon Conklin, often referred to as "standing on the shoulders of those who came before us." In reflecting upon this, it gives me pause to ask, "Is this not also a form of collaboration?"

Is there not an intergenerational collaboration? Does the fact that Mr. Conklin's advice rose to the surface again ten years later make it any less a collaboration?

Perhaps I am stretching. But it does make me wonder: Where does collaboration end? Where does it begin? Is it not all around us, if we are but open to it?

Collaboration and Cornell Cooperative Extension

In the 1970s I served as a County Agricultural Agent for what was then called New York State Cooperative Extension—now Cornell Cooperative Extension. I was hired fresh out of the Army to work in Tioga County, New York, as a sort of "general practitioner".

Most county Extension Associations in New York State, contractually affiliated with Cornell University, had three program divisions for their extension work: agriculture, home economics, and 4-H. Tioga County, though one of the more rural and less affluent counties in the state, had decided to add a fourth program division: Community Resource Development.

I was hired—fresh out of the Army—to be the Program Leader for that new division.

Under this new umbrella would be the development of community-targeted educational programs focused on farmland preservation, community planning, landscape design, local government operations, alternative land uses for retired farmland, environmental education for schools, forest management, and home horticulture.

Quite a list! And how to prioritize all that?

Although no one labeled it as collaboration at the time, I can now say that a kind of "community collaboration" was the answer.

A program advisory committee was recruited from the community. It was comprised of hand-picked leaders in each of these sectors: county legislature, forestry, retail garden shop, beef cattle farming, elementary education, etc.

I was required to develop an annual plan of work that estimated a percentage of total available hours that would be dedicated to each topic. For example, the plan would project, say, 45% of my time to be dedicated to farmland preservation education programs, 15% to a local government training program, 15% to classes for rural landowners, 10% to home horticulture programs, 10% to environmental education, and 5% to professional improvement. (It might well change the next year.)

I would then detail the specific projects that would address those topics.

Here's where the collaboration came in: This plan of work was reviewed by the advisory committee and had to be approved (sometimes modified) by that committee. They owned it. It was theirs. In a sense, I was theirs.

But the very fact that they came from the audiences to be served ensured the relevance of those programs. And it gave the programs both a legitimacy and a word-of-mouth marketing arm in the community.

And, yes, I had to keep track of hours spent on each area, much like a lawyer billing his hours to certain clients.

A remarkable attribute of this system was that while it did rely heavily of a kind of community-based collaboration, it left me with the opportunity to be endlessly creative in fulfilling the mission—subject, of course, to the approval of that committee and a senior staff coordinator.

In the thirty-some years since leaving that position for "greener pastures," I have never seen anything like this remarkable system employed anywhere else.

It was, to my mind, a structure that fostered both creativity and collaboration at their best.

Lessons Learned

Leadership matters.

Once, in a fit of frustration at organizational ineptitude, I telephoned a retired Air Force general who had just authored a book on management. He was attempting to convince the business community that his achievements at impressing "zero defects" accountability on the Air

Force could be transferred to the corporate world. Finally, after fifteen minutes of phone call, he said, "You know, Mr. Knight, you can't lead from the ranks."

Since then I have come to disagree with that analysis. I think there is, indeed, a lot of mentoring, "leadership by walking around," and leading by example that can be conducted "in the ranks." But an inference of his comment lingers: Leadership at the top is crucial. If the person in charge demands obedience, conformity, and strict accountability, the chances of meaningful collaboration are few.

But if the person-in-charge dares to trust the creativity, ingenuity, and passion of his/her subordinates, and models—even casually—the involvement of others, the stage is set for the synergy born of collaboration. This is the lesson taught by Frank Wiles, my mentor and manager at Cornell Cooperative Extension of Tioga County, in Owego, New York. And he was not one to overtly teach it or write c-o-l-l-a-b-o-r-a-t-i-o-n on a chalkboard. It's just who he was.

Don't get hung up on collaboration as a thing.
Just reach out for advice, guidance, or assistance, even—or maybe even especially—outside your organization. Such interaction, often unorganized, is the real deal.

If you have people who fly fast, hard, and creatively, let them.
They'll be a lot happier and the team will benefit hugely. It's the role of the leader to be the gadfly who repeatedly connects with them and keeps them involved in the collaborating team, and perhaps teaches them how to be effective collaborators in the process.

CHAPTER 2

My Collaborative Life & Career

Leading a Collaborative Research Team of Graduate Students and Postdoctoral Fellows

Julius P. Kreier
Professor Emeritus
Department of Microbiology
The Ohio State University

Preamble

The pages penned for my contribution to Pathways to Collaboration reflects on a collaborative life and career of over 92 years. These collaborations have yielded a treasured human network including my childhood family, a loving wife, two remarkable children, mentors, talented colleagues, brilliant students and loyal friends. This journey has been invaluable in allowing me to navigate a rewarding career that has been both enjoyable and satisfying. Hopefully, these network interactions have been mutually invaluable toward the achievement of one another's career goals and achievements.

The pages ahead incorporate collaborative overviews of early family life, coming of age, higher education, professional/graduate school, stints with the Collaborative USDA and US Army/Mexican Government Foot and Mouth Disease Programs in Mexico, the

University of Illinois Fellowship Program and The Ohio State University Professorship.

The key component to success of my collaborative career has been the maintenance of a viable network of family, mentors, colleagues, students and friends and the ability to bury ones ego for the greater good of developing viable partnerships. This viable collaborative network has led to successful research programs, grantsmanship, referred journal papers, international conferences, publication of a multi-volume monograph series.

Today, looking out the window on the magnificent Port Jefferson surroundings, I continue to write and edit book series with colleagues including the current "Pathways to Collaboration" Book Series.

Introduction

I was hired as an assistant professor at the Ohio State University in the summer of 1963. I retired after 26 years as a full professor in 1989 having been a teacher first of veterinary students in the veterinary school then of undergraduate and graduate students in the college of arts and science. I conducted research, guided postdoctoral fellows and last but not least advised students in their struggles to find their way in the scientific and academic world.

I did not enter the scientific and academic world directly after I graduated from veterinary school. I worked as an animal disease control officer for the federal government for several years before enrolling in graduate school and entering the academic world.

The story that follows is largely a personal story of how my career developed. I am writing it with the hope that it will help those to find their way who may be interested in considering a life in science, in academia or in public or private research institutions.

The Early Years
My Family

Like everyone I received much from my family. The gifts were both biologic and cultural. The assortment of genes and other biological characteristics of each parent during the production of egg and sperm and the combination of these characteristics at conception endowed me with the basic attributes of my being which were then much shaped by the environment in which they were developed. This started in my mother's womb and never stopped as long as I have lived.

It should be noted that the attributes I received in this process were a random selection of the attributes present in the gene pools of my two parents. As the gene pools of my two parents were a randomly selected subset of those available in the general population the collection I received was unique and I thus started my life relying on attributes which I had not chosen. In fact one may say we all start as a result of a lottery and lotteries distribute their rewards quite unequally. It is of course possible that my parents and their parents back through time had selected their mates for characteristics they considered desirable and thus decisions they made may to some degree have determined what I got. It is just that I had no role at all in determining what I got to start out on.

In writing about conception I can't resist putting in a word about when during gestation life begins. Both the egg and sperm are alive. If either were not, conception would not occur. Life began sometime in the remote past when the first living cell was formed. It never stopped. The difficult question is when does human consciousness arrive? I believe it is usually thought to occur at or shortly after birth. In passing I should also mention that I found during my youth that my father, a Lutheran, believed in the Calvinistic theory of predestination which I consider to be in contradiction to the concept of free will. I have never been able to reconcile this belief with my belief that the environment and my choices i.e. my free will, affect how my genetic endowment is realized. I however decided quite early that belief in free will is in itself required if you want to deal effectively with the problems you encounter as you move through life. But now I feel that it's time to describe my family so that the reader can understand something of what I believe they gave me and how I dealt with what I received.

My families on both sides were immigrants to the United States from Germany. My father was born in 1885 in Altstadt near Nierenberg in what is now Bavaria. His mother was of the French Protestant stock which fled to Germany when France expelled its Protestant population. His father's family members were wealthy people who lived in Bonn. Beyond that I know little about them except that my father maintained contact with a woman he called Aunt Sherman, a member of his mother's family. Aunt Sherman entered the Sherman house as a nurse to care for Frau Sherman during her terminal illness. She later married Herr Sherman after the wife died.

I did see some of the letters my father wrote to Aunt Sherman. But as they were hand written in a most elegant antique German script I was unable to read them. I do however remember a few photographs of my father taken in his youth. The one that stands out in my memory was of an elegant young man in a tuxedo preparing to attend the Bell Arts Ball at Putsi Hofstangles house in Munich. It stands out in my mind because the man I knew had abandoned all concern for his appearance and was regularly assumed by visitors to the shop who did not know him to be the janitor. I also remember several pictures of the Sherman house on the Rhine. One showed the servants lined up in front of the house and another, taken during the First World War, was of wounded German soldiers sitting on chairs on the extensive lawn between the house and the Rhine River.

I tried later to again see the letters and photographs he had from his pre-immigration life. I found out that after his death my mother had thrown all of my father's papers in the fireplace and burned them.

My mother's family came to America well before my father. The branch of her family with which I am most familiar was the Necker branch. Necker was my mother's maiden name.

My mother said the Necker who came to America in the 1840's had been a student at the University of Heidelberg where his six older brothers were professors in the arts and sciences. The young Necker, like students to this day, became involved in political activity, his in support of the socialist movement. He came to America when the revolt was put down by Bismarck and he fled Germany to save his life.

I know very little about how he made his living in America, but he obviously survived, married, and had children. One of his descendants was my mother's father, my grandfather, Julius Necker. He studied in the Academy of Fine Arts in Philadelphia. After he graduated he joined a company that produced fine arts reproductions by the lithographic method. He continued painting thereafter as a hobby.

Grandfather Necker married a woman of a German Catholic family named VonWitkampf and they had two daughters, the, younger my mother. Grandfather Necker died just before I was born so I had no direct contact with him but he was nevertheless a considerable influence on me, in part through my mother, in part from my father's somewhat negative view of him and, in part through the extensive library he left behind which ended up in our house. He was perhaps as my father said and ineffective socialist intellectual, an atheist who became the friend of the family's Catholic priest and shared many political and religious discussions over bottles of wine with him.

Strangely my political and religious views resemble my grandfather's more than my father's despite the close relations that existed between us. The Necker family was bilingual. They maintained German as the household language while using English to interact with the general non-German society. This pattern stopped after my father married my mother and we moved into the house in which I was born. My father believed that if you came to America you should become American and speak English. My father came to America in 1909 at about 24 years of age. He came after he had completed his education. He attended an art school in Munich or possibly Nierenberg, I am not sure which. After art school he did an internship in stone carving. I am not sure of many aspects of his life in Germany as he was not much for talking and rarely spoke about his past. All I know was he came as a second-class passenger, and left the ship in New York. This information my son found out from an Internet site about Ellis Island and immigrants. From New York he went directly to Indiana where he had lined up a job as a carver. He did one day tell me he did not like the job he had lined up, disliked Indiana and quite soon got on a train to Philadelphia. How he picked Philadelphia, how he met my mother, how he chose to start the business he spent the rest of his life in, I don't know. All I do know is that sometime after his arrival in Philadelphia he started the business in which he made ornamental features for buildings such as movie houses, banks, railroad stations, churches, and etc. He got the jobs by bidding, the bids were submitted to the building contractors or the architects or whoever wanted someone capable of producing the art work required.

He was quite successful until about 1935 when the depression stopped most building. The Second World War then came and there was little building during it and when building started after the war the buildings were bare of ornamentation. I have mixed feelings about the Bauhaus movement to this day. During the depression and the war and for some time thereafter he went into the shop every day and worked alone on statues for churches and other things anyone wanted.

He never called himself an artist but rather a craftsman in the old sense used by the anonymous craftsman who built Europe's churches and palaces. He never retired and continued working almost to the day he died.

The rather abrupt drop in his income resulting from the Great Depression affected him strongly. It also shaped my view of the world. What I remember from the time is my father, in the best European bourgeois tradition, saying he was spending more than he was earning and that we would end up in the poor house if we kept spending so much money. I was just a child at the time but it created a worldview that affected my behavior for the rest of my life.

I know now that he was a careful person with his money. When he was earning a lot he paid off all his debts and saved prudently. He also sent money to his father's family when they were seriously affected by the inflation and financial collapse that occurred in Germany after the First World War. This money which he sent to Aunt Sherman, who was apparently managing the family finances, permitted them to save the family home in Bonn.

When Germany created a new currency after the complete collapse of the old system the house was sold to the Catholic Church and is now a nunnery. The family which included Aunt Sherman and two girls and a boy, who I believe were my father's siblings, lived on the proceeds of the sale. My father never discussed any of this with me and what became of them I have no idea. He never visited Germany either. I do remember that after the Second World War he received a phone call in the shop. I remember him saying no to an offer from someone in the U.S. Army of a job with the occupation.

All I know about my family's finances I learned later when as the last surviving sibling I had to manage what was left and distribute it to my younger sisters and my children as directed by my brothers and elder sisters wills. The reason their wills controlled what was left of my father's estate was because they stayed in Philadelphia. George after getting a PhD in psychology and working for about six months as an assistant professor at Temple University quit and entered my father's business. He then took over the property in the city and the business after my father died. Gertrude, my older sister, moved into the house in the country and cared for my mother and my father until they died. Gertrude who had become a teacher in the Philadelphia school system chose to live in the house in the country. She set up a trust which directed that the younger siblings in order of age administer her estate after she died until the youngest that's me would distribute the assets. When my elder brother died he left his assets to the trust my elder sister set up. The main assets in the trust were the real estate taken over by my brother and sister. It was a surprise to me that there were still assets left after we all grew up, but that didn't affect the worldview I had developed as a child from observing my father who I do believe really feared poverty.

Early Years, My Childhood

I was born on November 30, 1926 in a bedroom in our house attached to my father's shop in Philadelphia. I was the fourth and last child born to the family. The eldest a girl, Gertrude, was born and lived for her first years with my mother's family. The second, a boy named George, came about six years later. After my brother, George, my sister, Elizabeth, and I followed at short intervals of about 1 and 1/2 years each. These last births proved a strain on my mother and after I was born my mother developed postpartum depression, paranoia, and she rejected her last child. As a result my father essentially took responsibility for me. The situation did not change much with the passage of time.

I have very little memory of my life before about five years of age. I recall I spend most of my time with my father following him around when he attended the furnaces that heated the huge house we lived in and playing with or at least watching the rabbits and squirrels my father kept in the yard alongside the house and connecting to the shop at the rear of the house. I also spent time in the shop, sometimes in the evening falling asleep on a pile of burlap while watching my father modeling some figure or other he was making. This memory gives me an opening for describing one of my first thoughts of a possible career. It was a negative thought. I decided I could never make a living doing that kind of work.

There was one event in those years of which I have no memory but which had lasting consequences for my life. I was a very active child. My mother said I was a little monkey who climbed on anything. It turns out I not only climbed but I also fell. Sometime when I was between one and two years of age, I don't know exactly because no one ever told me, I climbed on a high sideboard and fell off when I reached the top. I knocked out some teeth and developed an infection in my gums. Some bacteria, probably staphylococci, entered my bloodstream and lodged in my left hip joint. An abscess developed and after some time burst, drained, and healed. I understand it was touch and go for some time with periods of high fever.

In the 20's, there were no antibiotics or chemotherapeutic agents known and doctors could only give palliative treatment. I believe my parents later refusal to let me see any doctors about my hip stem from that experience.

In my childhood the hip joint gave me little trouble. I remember not being able to sit Buddha position like the other children but I had no pain in the hip joint and could run around like the other kids my age.

In retrospect I believe I was somewhat behind in my development. I had some problems with my speech and learning, probably as a result of the high fever during the infection. I failed to learn to read at the time the school thought I should and as a result I was held back in second grade. This was a shock to my parents. I had been enrolled in the same select grade school as my three older siblings all of whom were stellar students. As a result of this I was labeled as stupid. In the subsequent years I did learn to read and actually became quite proficient.

The only thing that did not change was my family's view of my intellectual capacity. As a result I was not enrolled in the academically selective high schools which my siblings attended and I did not even think about colleges or expect to attend one.

While during my childhood I was not bothered much by my damaged left hip, when I entered adolescence that began to change. Around 12 or 13 a degenerative arthritis developed in my left hip. The amount of motion became limited and it became painful. With the loss of motion by the time I was 20 years old the left hip joint became locked in a flexed and abducted position and was quite painful. As a result of the lack of motion in the hip joint when I stood or tried to walk my spine was twisted and also became painful. The use of a 2 or 3 inch lift on my left shoe did not help much.

You might think that with the hip that caused a limp and was often painful I would've become inactive, but in fact I was quite active. My parents chose to pretend that nothing was wrong. When I complained of pain and asked for medical help I would be told that if I really wanted to I could stand straight and that I should ignore any slight discomfort. I concluded that the situation was what it was and I should make the best of it. I developed stoicism. The stoic approach to life's problems served me well throughout my life. It can be considered a gift from my parents. Its development may have been reinforced by observing my father's behavior. I observed quite early that he was strongly stoic and tolerated injury and sickness with never a complaint.

I mentioned earlier that after I was born my mother entered a postpartum depression, developed paranoia, and rejected her child. She also rejected her husband and most aspects of running the house. In 1936 my father made a decision which in retrospect I am sure was made to provide a distance from my mother. What he did was buy an abandoned farm of about 15 acres which included a very old stone house. He began to rebuild the house and turned the grounds into a garden which occupied all of his spare time for the rest of his life. He still went to the shop daily and worked his eight hours there. He also kept one of the apartments in the house in the city for my mother and supported her. We children also ended up split between the two parents and the two houses. My younger sister and I would meet after school in the house in the city but at the end of the day we went with our father to the house in the country. We also spent weekends and holidays with my father. I don't know how the decisions were made but my brother stayed with my mother in the house in the city. At this time my older sister was off at college and on her own.

It turned out that my spending most of my youth, from 12 to 20 years in the country, did affect my career choices because there I started raising animals, rabbits, chickens, ducks, geese, goats, sheep, and even once a pig.

I attended the Philadelphia school system as my father retained his official residence in Philadelphia. As our house in the country was just north of the city I ended up in a high school in North Philadelphia. My father dropped me off on the way to the shop and the house in the central city.

I never worked hard in high school, I just did what I had to pass and I did all right but it was all a bit of a bore. Despite my lack of effort in high school some of my teachers thought I had some potential and did encourage me to seek post-high school education. During my second year in high school the Philadelphia school system started a half-time agricultural program. The leader of the program visited the high school I attended where he described the program and passed out literature about the program and application forms. At the time as I mentioned earlier I was quite active raising rabbits, ducks, and other fowl and attending a pet half grown goat who presented me with a baby goat some months after I got her. At any rate as I had no idea of what I would do with my life I thought perhaps some form of agriculture might be a possibility and I signed up for the program. What I got out of the program was I learned a bit about agriculture, I got outside working on the school farm some of the time, and I got summer jobs, the best of which was working during the summer on a large dairy farm filling silos and collecting hay. I also met a fellow student who became my best friend. The negative effect of the program only appeared later when I applied for admission to Temple University, a school near our house in the city, and I discovered I needed a couple of extra high school academic courses to get in. As a result my admission was delayed a semester.

As indicated in the preceding section when I finished high school I applied for admission to Temple University in Philadelphia. Temple was and still is a community college. Most students lived at home and attended classes by commuting to and from home. Tuition was the only cost for those who lived at home like I did. I chose Temple because costs were low and I could live at home. I really had no clear idea of what I would study. The only thing I did know was that I did not want to work in an office. I chose to major in some field of biology and I was pretty sure my father would pay my tuition although I never discussed any of this with him, or anyone else, until after I was admitted.

Temple University had a student body that was made up of the children of the people who owned the local grocery stores and pharmacies and etcetera. At the time, 1946, a large proportion of the students were Jewish although the school was originally founded by a Protestant group. Today it is a city school.

The general academic level was quite high. Most of the students, unlike me, seemed to know where they were headed, medicine was a favorite. I noticed this in part because I had for a period developed an interest in medicine, particularly psychiatry, as a result of observing my mother's behavior especially her periodic descents into insanity. I couldn't help observing the prodromal signs which seemed to me to be physiological and were manifested most obviously by changes in her facial expression, her face would appear swollen and wooden. At any rate I never acted on this interest as I accepted my parent's view of my ability level.

The academic environment at Temple did stimulate me to work fairly hard and I did without plan or declaration follow the premed program. The biology courses, the organic and other chemistry courses, and the physics courses I chose were full of premed students who would do anything to get a high grade so there was a stimulating competition that I never felt in any classes before.

While I was enrolled in Temple University my sister Elizabeth, who was next up for me in age and with whom I was quite close, joined the University of Pennsylvania orchestra. She was in the cello section. While playing in this orchestra she became quite close to a young man, also in the cello section, who was a student in the

University of Pennsylvania veterinary school. When he visited us he would talk about the opportunities the veterinary field offered ranging from private practice treating animals, to federal programs in animal disease control often involving public health and zoonotic diseases. One reason I was attracted to veterinary medicine was because it is a profession that would not confine me to an office. Until I met my sister's friend I had never thought of Veterinary medicine. His talk however started me thinking about the field. I realized it would combine my interests in animals and medicine. In addition the University of Pennsylvania veterinary school was near where I lived and getting my information from a student provided me with information about costs. At the time the costs were quite reasonable as the college, despite being a part of a private school, was heavily subsidized by the state government.

During my third year at Temple University I visited the veterinary college and talked with various faculty and was given application forms and some mild encouragement to apply, which I did. Later in the year I was invited to a formal interview. I remember sitting with the admissions committee and after some time being told to wait outside. More time passed until I was asked to come back in and told I could start the following September, that was 1949. I learned about a year or so later from a faculty member who'd been on the admissions committee that my long wait in the hallway outside the admissions committee's room was the result of some members questioning whether a person with a bad limp should be a veterinarian. My informant said he convinced them that there were many areas in veterinary medicine that I would be able to contribute to using my brain even with a severe limp.

In looking over my life I have often been amazed at how large a role chance has in the paths I chose to follow. If my sister hadn't met and I should add later married that veterinary student it would never have occurred to me to apply for veterinary school. If this chance meeting hadn't occurred I have no idea what other path I may have followed.

While we are on the subject of the effect chance encounters have on our life choices I think it is time to mention a couple of other chance encounters and events that played a major role in my life.

I enrolled as I said earlier, in an agricultural program in high school. This experience made me more inclined to be influenced by my chance encounter with the veterinary profession through the veterinary student my sister met. The agricultural school experience also appeared on my application to veterinary school, a use to which I never expected it to be put. The fact that one man on the admissions committee believed that a crippled leg shouldn't be a basis for keeping me out of the veterinary school also was a chance occurrence.

There was another result of my joining the high school agricultural program that had large effect on my life, although not professionally. There I met the fellow student who became a lifelong friend and who some years later played a role in my meeting the girl who became my wife. My wife affected my life in many ways not the least by providing a stable pleasant life we shared until her recent death.

As I mentioned earlier Temple University stimulated my interest in biology and also helped me learn how to study. I went through at the same time as a flood of veterans returning home from the Second World War were entering academic life with the help of the G.I. Bill. They had a beneficial effect on the college environment. They were there to study and didn't tolerate childish nonsense by the fraternity boys and other students just out of high school. I felt comfortable with the environment they created. The experiences at Temple helped me to deal with the high academic demands I encountered at the University of Pennsylvania Veterinary School.

I often thought I could've been one of those veterans. With my somewhat late development I was 18 while still in the next to last year in high school. I was called up for the draft in 1944, but rejected because of my damaged hip. My mother said how lucky I was, as if I had been drafted, I would have been just in time for the landing in Normandy. I remember telling her I would have been glad to chance getting my head blown off in exchange for a painless hip joint.

At any rate at the end of my third year in Temple University I entered the veterinary college at the University of Pennsylvania. During that first year I worked harder than I had ever worked in my life. We were enrolled in class eight hours a day, Monday through Friday and four hours on Saturday. We had assignments to complete in addition to attending class.

I remember anatomy, histology, genetics, chemistry, and many other courses that never seemed to stop during the first three years. The second half of the third year and the fourth year were devoted largely to clinical training. I remember that the program was very strong in the basic medical sciences while the clinical aspects were rather weak. It didn't bother me because I found I really preferred the basic medical sciences to clinical work.

Between my third and fourth years I had a particular learning experience. That summer I got a position with a very successful small animal practitioner in a wealthy suburb of Philadelphia. I took it largely for the money as I was not much inclined to small animal medicine. I was a general helper. In addition to cleaning cages and feeding dogs I did whatever I was asked to do and I was able to observe all aspects of how the place was run. The veterinarian who ran the practice was very smart and extremely skilled in handling people. I will describe one case that typifies how he operated and which helped form my view of small animal medicine. The first encounter with the clients was handled by a skilled receptionist. This receptionist would meet the client and collect information about them and the animal they brought for treatment. She noted any behavior patterns and the animals name and its likes and dislikes. She of course also recorded the owner's view of the animal's condition, particularly information about why the animal was brought into the veterinary hospital. She then returned to her desk and made out a file card which she showed to the doctor and briefed him about the clients and the animal. The card and the briefing system became of great value on subsequent visits, because even if he didn't remember the clients and the patient he would be prepared by the receptionist before he met them and then would be able to astonish the clients with how well he seemed to know even fine details about the patient, such as its favorite treats and etc. In this particular case the owners were elderly people, both overweight and their dog was also overweight and was brought in as the wife was concerned because the dog just refused the kidneys cooked in cream and other delicacies she had prepared. The veterinarian was very sympathetic and told the clients they should let the dog stay with him for a week during which time he would study the situation carefully and institute treatment. He would assure the clients the dog would have a good appetite when they picked him up. After they had left, the dog was brought into the back room and I was told to put him in a cage and put a sign on the cage saying water only. The only person who checked him daily was me. When the dog was picked up there was a dramatic demonstration in which the dog was brought out of the cage and offered a bowl of food which he devoured. After a long description of how carefully he had observed the dog during its stay in the hospital, he recommended a special diet for overweight dogs that he had in stock. At the time I considered the veterinarian's actions unethical. In later years I realized his diagnosis was correct, the treatment appropriate, and if he had simply told those people they overfed their dog and they should put the dog on a diet, they would have found another veterinarian to tell them what they wanted to hear. Nevertheless, this experience made me realize that I would not have been able – and would not have wanted – to do what he did, not matter how much money it would have yielded.

There are many other experiences I had during those four eventful years in veterinary school. I can't possibly describe them all, but I will describe a few that remain in my memory because they had lasting effects on my future life.

During my first year in veterinary school I turned 21 and my ability to walk deteriorated greatly. Perhaps my father recognized how bad my walking had become and using my age as an excuse my father said to me that as an adult I should be permitted to make my own medical decisions and that he would pay the associated costs. I then contacted the student health service which made an appointment for me with their orthopedic surgeon. After he examined me I told him I would like him to do a cup arthroplasty, a procedure in which the joint is opened, the joint surfaces smoothed and a metal cup inserted in the joint. He replied that he didn't do that procedure as it had, at least in his experience, a low success rate. He recommended a simpler procedure called a subtrochanteric osteotomy in which the femur is cut below the hip joint and the leg is held in a more or less standing position by a plaster cast starting just below the armpits and going to just above the genital and anal region in the middle and normal side but to the ankle on the operated side. The procedure required being in a cast for about three months. These were the options as total hip replacement did not exist in 1950. I wasn't too happy with his recommendation and should have at least gotten some additional evaluations but I was desperate and decided that I would just go ahead and accept what he recommended. Surgery was scheduled for shortly after the end of the spring semester.

My elder sister, Gertrude, had become a teacher in the Philadelphia school system at this time and had decided to move into the house in the country, bringing my mother and brother there also, and thereby trying to patch up the split in the family. Gertrude took responsibility for me during the summer I was in the cast and confined to bed. She cared for me carefully and I thank her for what she did. My close friend Harold who always spent a lot of time at our house continued to visit. It was only much later that I found out that while I was confined to bed that he and my sister became friendly. Later when I was working in Mexico they got married. I was sawed out of the cast just before class started in the autumn quarter. I started attending classes about two weeks late. I got a room in a veterinary fraternity near the veterinary school and somehow or other got through the year. After I had recovered from the surgery I found I could walk and stand much better than before. The long rest gave the hip joint time to heal, but as the motion of the joint was still very limited I had more trouble sitting and I discovered I couldn't drive a car with a standard transmission as I couldn't operate the clutch. It may seem strange but that played a role in my becoming a professor as I will explain later.

As I mentioned earlier it was during my second year in veterinary school that I met the woman who later became my wife. As she became such a large part of my life I feel it is appropriate for me to expand a bit on the meeting. I had been dating a girl named Naomi who was some remote relative of Harold, my close friend. Naomi decided she didn't really find me that attractive and decided to pass me on to another girl named Ruth, a friend of hers. To get things started Harold arranged that the four of us would go to dinner together. Harold provided the car. It was an old model A Ford from 1930. After dinner we dropped Naomi off at her house and decided to take a ride around

Fairmount Park as it was a fine warm but slightly rainy night. It was actually weather caused by the tail end of a hurricane up from Florida. The three of us were sharing the front seat with Ruth in the middle. I guess I got a bit carried away and as a result Ruth accidentally hit the accelerator with her foot. The motor raced and the fan came off and the motor stalled. Harold told us to get out and walk around in the park while he fixed the car. It seems a bit strange that despite my behavior we hit it off that night and for the next three years when she came back to Philadelphia from Pennsylvania State University we would get together. The same arrangement persisted after I graduated from veterinary school and went to Mexico to work on a program to eradicate foot and mouth disease there. She came to visit me in Mexico in the fall of my first year there. My choice of the job in Mexico oddly enough, despite the physical separation, reinforced the relationship. To help explain how this helped bind us together I will jump ahead a bit and describe her first visit there with me.

This first visit occurred when I decided to purchase a car. To avoid the high taxes on cars purchased in Mexico I made the purchase in the United States in the town of Laredo. I arranged with Ruth for her to meet me in Mexico City where we spent several days as tourists and then flew up to Laredo where we picked up the car.

The drive back to Mexico City was an adventure. After crossing into Mexico we chose to take secondary roads to the Atlantic Coast and then head south to reach the area of Veracruz in which I was stationed. Leaving the US I had trouble finding the International Bridge I asked a group of men standing alongside the road how to get to the bridge. They didn't answer. I then asked in Spanish. They laughed and told me exactly how to get to the bridge. They just weren't going to talk to an English speaker.

I was fortunate to have bought the car during the dry season because when we got on the back roads, many of which were unpaved, it would have been impossible to use them when they were wet because of the mud. In many cases there were no bridges and where the roads crossed the streams we had to ford through the water. In one small town where we had stopped to eat, the local Catholic priest recognizing we were strangers said hello to us and when we expressed interest in archaeology invited us to his house to see his collection of pre-Columbian artifacts. It was a wonder and as good as many museum displays. I think we gave him pleasure also as he was an educated man living in a very small town and was quite isolated. I believe he was happy to have had us as visitors.

When we reached the area in which I was stationed we entered a more developed region. The town of Tampico on the northern fringe of the inspection area had a lovely small hotel where we stayed a few days. It had a restaurant that served fish caught in the gulf right near where the town was located. As we continued southward the next town we reached was Papantla a fairly large town which was the district headquarters of the foot and mouth disease eradication program. The town had a very nice market and was located near a rich archaeological site. There is a pyramid called the Tajin located in the site (Fig.1). A large proportion of the population, in that region, are Totonac Indians, who congregate on Saturday nights in the town square all dressed in their tribal costumes (Fig.2).

At the end of my second year in Mexico we had eliminated the disease and I was discharged and reassigned to a disease control program in Maryland to deal with tuberculosis and brucellosis of cattle there. When I received my discharge I invited Ruth to meet me in Mexico City and we drove back to Philadelphia together. We married shortly after we got back to Philadelphia. I came back to Philadelphia during the Christmas holidays in my second year in Mexico. It was a longer stay than I expected as I developed viral hepatitis on the way home and spent most of the visit in the University of Pennsylvania Hospital. Other than a brief episode of vivax malaria hepatitis was the only serious disease I encountered in the two years I was in Mexico. Ruth visited me in the hospital but a visit in the hospital was not what I had been looking forward to.

In a way my career choices did play a role in my marriage. Ruth it turned out, liked animals and that gave us common ground. Ruth also was interested in archaeology so my working in Mexico in an area rich in pre-Columbian ruins provided us with another rich area of common interest.

Now I will turn to events that occurred near the end of my time in veterinary school, events which directly shaped my future. A professor who taught biochemistry to the veterinary students approached me and asked me if I would be interested in going into graduate school. I replied no because as I explained I had been in school all my life and felt the need to get out of school and start working. This occurred before I had thought much beyond getting my veterinary degree and working as a veterinarian.

I had been following the progress of the US Mexican program for the eradication of foot and mouth disease, but my hope for getting into that program looked dim as in my senior year it appeared that the program had been successful and was in the process of being shut down.

I had applied for several positions with rural veterinary practitioners but had been rejected because they felt I couldn't handle the rigors of a large animal practice. A good friend of mine in the class who intended to set up a small animal practice asked me if I would join him in that effort. We discussed it, did some investigation, but my heart was not in it as I didn't really want to run a business or work as a small animal practitioner. During this period, when I was studying for the Pennsylvania State veterinary license examination and trying to decide on what aspect of the veterinary field I would pursue a notice came to my attention that there was an outbreak of foot and mouth disease in an area of Veracruz, Mexico which had been considered cleared of the disease and that the US government was again setting up a unit to deal with the new outbreak. I immediately contacted the local USDA office, obtained a job application form, and applied for a position with the group.

There were great differences in the hiring policies of the USDA and how you are enrolled in the U.S. Army. They are relevant to this story because if the USDA had given me a physical examination as did the U.S. Army when I was called up in 1944 I would never have gone to Mexico and my entire career would have been different. The USDA didn't even ask me if I had any physical problems and I didn't volunteer any information either. There was another interesting aspect of the government's hiring policy. We were to be sent to a Spanish-speaking country yet no one asked if we spoke Spanish which in fact I didn't.

A short time after I graduated and got my license to practice veterinary medicine in Pennsylvania I received a letter from the Department of Agriculture saying that I was hired and would join the group as a veterinary disease control officer and would report to the office in Mexico City as soon as the negotiations with the Mexican government setting up the reactivated plan were completed. In the meantime, as I was being paid, I was assigned to work with a group of meat inspectors in a slaughterhouse in Philadelphia. I worked in the slaughterhouse for about two months before I was transferred to Mexico I must admit I did not much like working in the slaughterhouse but I stuck with it because I very much wanted to work on the program in Mexico. I also was aware that meat inspection was important component of the public health field which did interest me.

In the next few paragraphs I will describe a few of the things I observed during the months I worked as a meat inspector. I found for example that meat inspection included the inspection of livestock before slaughter in part to control what is called emergency slaughter of sick animals, an effort by the owner to recover some value before the animal died. I also observed that veterinary inspectors assume responsibility for the general sanitation of the entire meat handling process as well as play a role in the grading of the meat. Even I, just out of veterinary school, was surprised to learn how large a role veterinarians play in public health. The Army Veterinary Corps for example plays a major role in the Army's Health Programs. A number of veterinarians with whom I worked during this time were veterans who described to me what they had done in the military. Their activities ranged from supervising base food purchases to overseeing base sanitation and tracing the sources of outbreaks of food borne illness. I also encountered veterinarians who had worked in similar activities in the general society. The largest public health program run by veterinarians is a well-established program to control and ultimately eliminate bovine tuberculosis and brucellosis from domestic cattle. These are animal diseases readily transmitted to humans which before the program started caused much serious disease in both cattle and humans. The program for the eradication of tuberculosis and brucellosis in cattle tied in with my meat inspection experience as cattle suspected of infection by the tests used were branded and slaughtered in the federally controlled slaughterhouses. I learned more about this connection later when I worked for a year in the tuberculosis and brucellosis eradication program after the foot and mouth disease eradication program in Mexico was successfully completed. Working in these programs was a valuable component of my education and participating in actual public health programs did help me later when I started teaching students who intended to enter the fields of medicine, veterinary medicine, and public health. The next part of this chapter will deal primarily with my experiences in Mexico.

Foot and mouth disease was brought into Mexico with some latently infected Brahman bulls purchased in Argentina by a Mexican rancher who believed that cattle of Indian origin would be more suitable to the tropical climate of Mexico than cattle of European origin. Disease appeared in the susceptible Mexican cattle shortly after these bulls were introduced to Mexico. Infection spread rapidly throughout Mexico. The American and Canadian governments had eliminated the infection from their countries. The disease had never occurred in Mexico and Central America and the undeveloped jungles of southern Panama served as a barrier to the disease entering North America from South America. The disease in Mexico was considered likely to spread to the US through the highly porous Mexican-American border. As foot and mouth disease is highly contagious and spreads rapidly by direct contact or by contact with farmer's shoes or other contaminated items the method of control used in the USA and Canada and most of Europe is slaughter and burial of infected and contact animals. Vaccination is sometimes used to control the rapid spread of the disease, but as there are several antigenic strains of virus and the duration of immunity from vaccination is only about six months the vaccine is only used to slow the spread of the infection. Slaughter of infected herds and direct contact animals is then used after vaccination is stopped to deal with any outbreaks that then occur.

Slaughter and burial of infected and contact animals is a harsh method for the control of disease. Many people have questioned its use to control foot and mouth disease especially as fatality from the disease is usually only five or at most 10% and as foot and mouth disease does not affect humans. Control of diseases of farm animals particularly ones that are not transmissible to humans is justified on an economic base. The cost of living with the disease is compared to the cost of eradicating it and eradication is used when eradication, a single effort for isolated countries like those of North America, is calculated to be less costly than living with the disease. Living with foot and mouth disease is quite costly, as immunity is short-lived, vaccines are not very effective and must be made for each strain of the virus, and spread is rapid among the not immune animals. Infected animals can't walk well or eat easily, milk animals stop producing milk and range animals lose weight and may die if they lose their hooves and are unable to feed because of a sore mouth and inability to walk around to reach their food. The costs are perpetual if the choice is made to live with the disease. Eradication on the other hand is a single expense and continues only for a finite time.

At this time I will describe the organization of the foot and mouth disease eradication program on which I worked. It is necessary to understand the organization of the program to understand how it affected my career development. The title of the program was the cooperative program for the eradication of foot and mouth disease in Mexico. In passing I might mention that among the US personnel the term cooperative was often considered a bit of a joke, but we did cooperate enough to successfully eliminate foot and mouth disease from Mexico.

The region where I worked for about two years was in the north central part of Veracruz State. It extended roughly from north of the city of Veracruz to the South of Tampico. It was bounded on the east by the Atlantic Ocean and on the west by the foothills of the mountains that rise abruptly to the Mexican central plateau. It covered roughly an area surrounding the unexpected outbreak of foot and mouth disease on a ranch near the town of Gutierrez, Samora. The outbreak was in the middle of a region that was considered large enough to cover any infections that might spread from the infection which had occurred. The area which surrounded the unexpected infection was divided into districts to which veterinarians were assigned. Each of these districts had a town where the veterinarians stayed. These districts were subdivided into sectors to each of which a pair of cowboys were assigned (Fig.3). In each section there were also towns selected as bases where the Cowboys stayed. The Cowboys traveled over their sectors on horseback following a route map showing where ranches with cattle were present. The map included a timetable showing the time and day they were expected to be inspecting each location. The town of Papantla was near the middle of the zone put under inspection. It was chosen as the headquarters where the overall supervisors worked and it had a radio system connecting the headquarters to each of the vehicles used by the pairs of district veterinarians.

Practically all of the positions in the program were staffed by two people, one Mexican and one a citizen of the United States. There were some exceptions to this role. One exception was a laboratory in Mexico City run by an employee of the US Department of Agriculture who supervised the use of serological test to determine if foot and mouth virus was present in samples collected by the field veterinarians. The antigenic strain of the virus was also determined by this laboratory. A second exception was a bilingual aide assigned to each American field veterinarian. He was called an inspector A. He was usually a person who had experience supervising Cowboys. His main duty was to supervise the Cowboys who did the day to day inspection of the cattle and to give the American veterinarians aid and advice when requested. The third exception was a financial officer who paid the expenses encountered in the operation such as the wages of local help to clean and disinfect areas were disease occurred as well as incidental expenses for supplies obtained locally. He was an American who was bilingual and had experience as a paymaster.

When not otherwise occupied the pairs of district veterinarians moved around their districts using the maps of the Cowboys' routes. They would spot check the cowboys at random to assure that all of the cattle in the district were looked at by the Cowboys at the scheduled times.

As noted earlier each of the vehicles driven by the district veterinarians had a two-way radio to connect them to the head office. If the Cowboys saw any sick animals, that is, one's dripping excess saliva or limping badly, they were instructed to notify the district veterinarians or the main office by any means possible. If the main office was called they would radio the district veterinarians. After the Cowboys notified the appropriate authorities they returned to the ranch to await the arrival of the district veterinarians. If the district veterinarians, after examining the animals (Fig.4), considered that the animals may have had foot and mouth disease they would notify the head office, collect tissue and fluid samples from the lesions (Fig.5) and in collaboration with the veterinarians in the headquarters arrange to get the samples to the Mexico City laboratory. If the samples proved to be positive the process of eradication would be started (Fig .6).

In a peculiar way the relationship between the pairs of veterinarians was in some ways similar to a marriage. We both were told what our duties were but neither of us could give orders to the other. We were instructed to actually plan our day's activities by joint agreement. Most of the Mexican veterinarians were not local to the area in which we worked. In many towns to which we were assigned the Mexicans were almost as foreign as we Americans were. We were forced to be together in these small towns as we only had a single government vehicle assigned to us. In the small towns there was not much to do. We would eat together and usually rented rooms fairly close together also. We would usually meet each other for breakfast in some local restaurant and while eating agree on what we were to do that day.

As I mentioned earlier, that after my first hip surgery I was unable to drive a car with a standard shift. The vehicles we were assigned were Second World War type jeeps or four-wheel drive trucks all with standard transmissions. I was unable to drive these vehicles. What made it possible for me to carry out my duties was a result of the way the agreement between the US and Mexican governments was written. Neither of us the Mexican or the American veterinarian were permitted to do our work alone. We were required to travel together at all times while working on the program. While I never discussed my inability to drive the vehicles we were assigned I am sure my Mexican partners figured it out quite quickly and did all the driving. None of them ever complained to me or in any way mentioned their awareness that I couldn't drive. None of them ever said anything to my supervisors either. They just seemed to love to drive and I think were just very kind and considerate people. I of course did all of the other things that were required and I was the one to hop out of the truck and open and close the gates when we entered the ranches or went from pasture to pasture while supervising our Cowboys and examining the cattle. I also was the one working the winch to pull us out of mud holes in the rainy season and of course I examined the mouths and feet of the cattle when necessary. I also rode horses when we had to go to ranches where the roads were inadequate for the truck to pass. In the mountains some of the rides were spectacular and I really enjoyed them. And speaking of enjoyment I want again to say how much I enjoyed working with the Mexican personnel and how much I appreciated their consideration and help to me.

Thoughts about Academia

In the following section I will describe a few experiences that provoked thoughts in me that played a role in my developing desire to enter the academic world. They are randomly remembered from my time of employment by the Federal Government first briefly as a meat inspector in Philadelphia, then as a livestock disease control officer working to eradicate foot and mouth disease from Mexico and later in Maryland on the tuberculosis and brucellosis control program.

I will start off with a few words about my early political views. They will help you to understand some aspects of my behavior. If you wonder where these views came from remember my mother's father mentioned earlier. As a young man I believed strongly that democratic socialism was the most humane form of government and I also believed that people who worked in the civil service were there in part because they felt that their work in that capacity would help bring about a better society. My experiences in the civil service brought about some modifications in my views on the subject, modifications that could perhaps be best considered to be maturation of my thoughts. What I learned from my experiences during that period was that civil servants were people with the same goals, hopes, fears, and insecurities at work in them as in all other people. I began to realize that very few of them even thought about democratic socialism or any other ideology.

From my experience as a meat inspector I realized that some very necessary jobs had to be done even though to me at least, they were quite unpleasant. In fact I worked as a meat inspector for a short time only and only because I wanted to work on another type of job and I had to wait for that job to open up. The people running the branch of the civil service that employed me wanted me to do some type of work as I was being paid.

During the short period that I worked as a meat inspector I met many people who are making a career in that field. On those rare occasions when they talked about their employment they would say that it was a steady, secure, job with reasonable benefits, reasonable pay, and with a decent pension plan and medical insurance. I never heard anyone talk about socialist ideals or other abstract concepts and that certainly caused me to think critically about many aspects of my own beliefs.

When I did finally get to the job in Mexico my views of the civil service and people in it continued to develop.

I was rather surprised to find out that almost all of the veterinarians in the program in Mexico in which I worked were graduates of the veterinary schools at Texas A and M and Auburn Alabama. I don't know how that happened. I was moreover the only graduate of the veterinary school at the University of Pennsylvania in the group. I became friends with quite a few of these people but I always felt a bit like the odd man out as there was a cliquishness based on shared Southern culture which played a role in many decisions made by them and particularly by the man in the central office. For example it seemed to me that the veterinarians who played cards and drank with him were usually assigned to the nicer districts and ones near to the headquarters town. And here also I noticed as I became acquainted with the people in the group that ideology seemed to not play any role in their decision to join the civil service. What they talked about was their careers, their pay scales, security of employment and etc. They were in general good people and they did their job fairly well, idealistic thoughts just didn't seem to be important to them. This seems strange to me as the concepts given to them by the Southern culture they shared obviously did affect their behavior just as I realized my culture affected my behavior.

I will jump ahead here to extend this discussion of views held by people in the civil service to my later observations on why I decided to join the academic world. In academia I thought that idealistic thoughts played a larger role in career choices than I observed in actual practice. The concept that the business world should be applied to universities was strong particularly among the administrative personnel. Idealistic views of the importance of teaching and increasing knowledge by research played a lesser role in the lives of faculty members than I had anticipated. I should note that I felt this more strongly at Ohio State University than at the University of Illinois.

I do wish to add that none of what I have said here should be taken as a condemnation of the people in the two types of organizations in which I worked. It should rather be interpreted as my gaining a better view of reality. I worked to try to act by my ideals, it was just that learning how people and institutions function made me more able to function better myself. To survive you must learn to adjust and not give up.

An event that occurred in my second year in Mexico gave me additional information on the nature of civil servants. Early in my second year, several months after what turned out to be the last infection had occurred, and I may add in which I led the eradication team, I was told by the supervisor of the program that there was to be a reduction in the staff and that I would be sent back to US and offered a position there. I accepted that and started to make arrangements for leaving Mexico. Several days later I received another call from my supervisor telling me I could continue for the second year of the program. I was not told why there was a change but that I should consider myself lucky to be kept on as he knew I wanted to stay. I replied that yes I would like to continue but as I had already made arrangements to return to the US I would therefore only stay if I received a promotion of one grade in the civil service ranking. He then gave me a spiel that I should not make any conditions but consider myself lucky and take the offer. I replied that if I got no promotion I would not stay. I was then told he would have to contact the central office in Washington and he could not say what the outcome would be. I then hung up. Within not more than 5 min. he called me back and said it was all approved, I would get the promotion and could stay in Mexico.

I have no proof of what I will say next but I am sure that there was no way he could have gotten that type of approval from the central office in Washington that fast, so I believe he already had been told to keep me on and wanted to brag that he had saved money for the government. I had never heard from anyone else that there was to be a staff reduction at that time. I knew I was the odd man out in a group of Southerners and I suspect that he had a friend he wanted to bring aboard and someone would need to go in order to make that happen. Someone in Washington told him they would not be prepared to transfer out a satisfactory employee and spend money to bring in a new recruit and that he should forget the whole thing. So I stayed in Mexico for a second year, but my view of the morals of some civil servants fell quite a bit.

There was another experience during my stay in Mexico that lowered my respect for civil service employees while at the same time helped me to understand the workings of the civil service. I had read a short novel called: *Dead Souls* by the Russian author Gogol sometime earlier. I didn't really understand the novel entirely at the time I read it but the events that I observed while working as a civil servant in Mexico gave me a basis for understanding it better. Bear with me as I explain how that occurred. Sometime during my first year, when the program was pretty much fully operational a new man appeared on the staff. He was a veterinarian, the only one other than me who was a graduate of the veterinary school at the University of Pennsylvania. He was assigned to the program by someone in the Washington office. He was introduced as a relief man, which meant that he was never given a regular assignment in any district, but was temporarily assigned to fill in for anyone on vacation, or ill, or where temporary help was needed. As a result he had the opportunity to observe all aspects of the program. He was treated with some deference by the local supervisor of the program and his staff. Rumors circulated that he was really an investigator who was sent to report to Washington about the field program.

He and I became fairly friendly and we would meet for dinner whenever he was posted to a district near where I was stationed. When the program closed he stayed with the veterinary disease control division of the Department of Agriculture. I met him some years later when he came to give a seminar at the school of veterinary medicine at the Ohio State University. At that time he told me he had been working with US programs in various countries.

I never knew if the rumors that he was an investigator were true. I never had any reason to believe he was anything but the relief man he was introduced as. He could of course have been both.

The Gogol novella centered on the activities of a man who appeared in a town in rural Russia. He went in a rich carriage to the various landed estates there asking about the status of the serfs on the estates. He was particularly interested in the serfs who had recently died and offered to purchase the death certificates of those dead.

The officials of the town, who were all civil servants, appointed by the central government and my colleagues were very much concerned about this man who acted much like an official. They thought he could be an investigator sent to investigate them. In their meetings to discuss him and his actions they couldn't decide if he should be arrested or whether he would be the one who came to arrest them. It turned out he was not an official but a confidence man. His scam depended on a quirk in a program designed to subsidize the owners of the landed estates. Under this program the landowners were given a subsidy each year for each serf on their estates. The flaw in the program was that the census of the serfs only occurred every 10 years so that if a serf died during the 10 years before the census and the landholder did not send in the death certificate they continued to collect the subsidy until the next census revealed the death. The landowners, who were always short of cash, were glad to sign a paper saying they had sold the dead serfs and given the death certificates to the buyer for immediate cash. The holder of the bill of sale would then file the necessary papers in the capital and collect the subsidy until the next census.

What struck me when I observed the behavior of my supervisor and his aides in dealing with the new man in our group was the similarity of their behavior to that of the civil servants in the Gogol novel. The rumors about the man described in the novel by Gogol were also quite similar to those about the new man who joined our group in Mexico.

It is true that some aspects of the workings of the Russian civil service described in the novel were quite different from those of the program I worked in, but the responses of people in the head office to the problem of how to deal with the new man and the nature of the rumors that spread in both cases were very similar.

When I had read the novel I had had no experience working in any civil service position and I really had no basis for judging the story, thus I thought the story pure fiction. What I observed while working as an employee of an American bureaucracy brought to my attention the similarities between what I observed in my job and what was described in the novel. I began to feel that the workings of the present day American bureaucracy and that of the Russian one in the 19th century were not all that different. I came to believe that Gogol's story was not pure fiction.

I may not have had a very favorable view of some aspects of human behavior observed in my job and described in the novel but the dawning belief I had that people in the same fields are quite similar in their responses to similar events and that human behavior has not changed much with the passage of time was strongly reinforced.

And Now to Another Story

The Eastern shore region of Maryland was somewhat Southern at the time. In 1956, it had two county agents in each county, a black one to work with the black farmers and the white one to work with the white farmers. When I was first there I went out with these men to meet the farmers, to explain the programs and sign up those farmers who were not already in the program. When it was lunch time on days I worked with the black county agent we had a problem. He couldn't go into the white restaurants, so we went into the black restaurants. It created a bit of a stir until they got used to seeing me there.

This brings up the opportunity to describe two experiences I had with local people, one in Mexico and one in Maryland. They illustrate how relations with the local people affect your ability to carry out your job—In my case as an animal disease control official.

I will start with the experience in Maryland. I went out one day to determine the status of a particular farmer's cattle. I got lost and decided to ask someone for directions to the farm. I saw a black man working in a field by the side of the road. I pulled to the side of the road and called to him and proceeded to ask directions. He pulled off his hat and held it by his chest and said no sir I don't know sir where that man lives. He then looked up and recognized who I was. He put his hat back on, adopted a different accent, and proceeded to give me exact directions to the farm in question.

The experience in Mexico was potentially more serious but it tells the same story about the role of personal relations in determining one's ability to carry out one's job. At the time I was assigned to a small town called Misantla as my base of operation. Misantla was off the main road and had only one road leading into it. I had used my own car to go to a larger town which had a very nice French style restaurant. It was quite late when I returned. I had almost reached the town when I saw a barrier blocking the road. I stopped and was immediately surrounded by a group of armed men. I rolled down my window when the leader of the group tapped on the glass. He looked in, recognized me, I didn't recognize him, and said oh it's you Dr. Kreier don't worry there is no problem for you. He then signaled to one of the men to remove the barrier, wished me good night and waved me through. I don't know who they were looking for, but whoever he was he certainly would not have received such a pleasant greeting.

To conclude this section describing the role of random thoughts and experiences on my career choices I will tell one more story. While I was stationed in Maryland some new rules were formulated which modified the role of the publicly employed veterinarians in the tuberculosis and brucellosis control program. These new rules were designed to bring the private veterinary practitioners into the control program. It took me some time to realize how these rules would affect the program and my role in it.

I will start this section with a bit of background about the program I joined in Maryland. After I transferred to Maryland to join the tuberculosis and brucellosis control program I spent time getting acquainted with the two counties to which I was assigned. I visited the farmers who had cattle to determine their status in the program. Largely in this area they were dairy cattle. When the animals had already been tested I explained the program and its goals to the farmers before I left. If the animals had not been tested within the previous year, I made appointments to test the animals and spent some time explaining the nature and goals of the program and the consequences of positive tests.

Most of the animals I encountered which had not been tested were on the poorer farms with just a few animals and in many cases they were let loose in the pasture most of the time. At the same time I began to get papers from the central office that cattle on various farms that had tested positive for tuberculosis or brucellosis and that I was to go to the designated farms to inform the farmers of these results.

As I continued to work on the program and to study the new rules I began to understand that the new rules were largely responsible for the obvious failure to test the small herds and for my receiving the notices of infected animals in herds I had not tested myself. The failure to have the small herds tested was a direct result of how the local practitioners were paid to test cattle in the program. They were paid a relatively small sum for each herd when they signed up for the program but they were also paid a fee for each individual animal tested. Animals in large well managed herds could be tested rapidly and easily and returns for these tests were quite good. The returns for testing small herds were poor. The herd stop fee was small and testing of a few often semi-wild animals took time and did not yield much money.

When I began to act on the notices of infected animals in herds I had not signed up or tested I got some real surprises. Very often the farmer would not seem to know that his animals had even been tested. When I showed them the paper with their signature on it, stating that they had agreed to have their animals tested for tuberculosis and brucellosis by their regular veterinarians on a specific date they would say oh yes they remembered that their veterinarian had been there on the date noted and that he told them they had to have their animals tested, but he said not to worry about it and he would take care of the whole thing. At that point I had to spend a fair amount of time explaining to the farmers the purpose of the program, how it worked, and what the consequences of positive tests were. I then had to mark the reactor animals with a cold brand showing a T or B. I then explained to them that the branded animal was to be turned over promptly to a dealer who would take it to a federally inspected slaughterhouse where a final decision would be made as to the deposition of the carcass. There was a federal compensation paid for the condemned animals. I however don't remember the details of how it was worked out, but I do remember that I had to determine that also.

I will note here that as the veterinarian was paid only a small fee for signing up the farmer in the program, but a much better one for testing the cattle based on the number of animals tested. Thus the veterinarian had little incentive to spend time testing small herds or explaining the goals of the program and the consequences of positive tests. Under the rules that brought the private practitioner into the program the practitioner also did not have to deal with the notification of the farmers of the results of the test. They were thus spared the unpleasant task of dealing with the upset farmer who owned the condemned animals. That was left to the civil servant also.

The program to eliminate brucellosis was, at the time, fairly new. Most of the animals that tested positive were actually infected. In addition most of the farmers had experience of losing calves as result of abortion caused by *Brucella abortis* or at least of seeing the disease in nearby herds. They therefore took these results fairly well. The program to control tuberculosis in cattle on the other hand was an old well-established program already at the time I started working on it. As result the actual incidence of infection was quite low. Despite this there was a low but consistent incidence of positive tests. When the results came back from the inspection at the slaughterhouse they usually reported no visible lesions. To explain these results to the farmer was a part of the unpleasant job reserved for the publicly employed veterinarians. It was not easy. To start off the discussion it must be said that there is no diagnostic test that does not have some false positive and false negative results. When the disease incidence is high it is easy to accept the small numbers of false positive tests and they are not even discussed in many cases. When the incidence of infection is very low and almost all of the reactors are false positives it becomes a real problem and examinations are required. As bovine tuberculosis still exists at a very low level if animals are not tested regularly the disease could spread thus testing must continue. This concept is difficult for the farmers to accept. Scientists are actively looking for better tests than the tuberculin test for tuberculosis but so far have not found one. Some of the false positive tests are not really false in one sense. Chicken tuberculosis for example does not cause disease in cattle or healthy humans but it does cause sensitization to the test for bovine tuberculosis. The human strain of tuberculosis does not cause disease in cattle but does sensitize them to the test. These facts provide good reasons to tell humans not to spit in cattle barns and for keeping chickens confined but not everyone wants to hear that. I should add that bovine tuberculosis causes a severe disease in humans.

But I have gotten off the track again, this chapter is supposed to explain how and why I ended up in academia. In a sense all that I have been describing has played a role in my decision to leave the civil service. For example I resented having the public actions belittled and bringing in the private sector even though the private sector only creamed off the profitable components. The time-consuming activity of explaining the nature of the program, why it was necessary and the consequences of testing were also poorly done or not even done at all by the private practitioners mainly because they couldn't make much money doing them. The practitioners also rejected the unpleasant duties, such as notifying the farmer of positive tests leaving that necessary but not profitable and disagreeable action to the publicly employed veterinarian.

When the program in Mexico ended because it was successful I was offered several positions in the United States. I chose a position as a field veterinarian in Maryland in the Tuberculosis Brucellosis Control Program.

I chose this course of action as it was the easiest course to follow and would provide me with an income while I decided what to do. In addition to uncertainties about my career choices I had decided to propose marriage to my longtime friend, Ruth, and I was not sure what her reply would be. If it were yes I felt she should have a role in choosing a joint future for us. She in fact did say yes and shortly thereafter we moved to Maryland. The year we spent in Maryland was when we actually made the final decision to look for a job in academia. As I noted previously there were many factors which caused me to undertake making the change and they were drawn from a hodgepodge of experiences and conditions in my work. Overwhelmingly however two things finally determined the decision to leave the civil service and to join academia. They were my problem with my left hip bringing about a desire to enter a field and my desire to enter a field with lower physical demands and with a greater intellectual component. I will discuss this matter more fully in the next section.

Factors Influencing My Decision to Become an Academic

I realized at the time that my left hip was again beginning to degenerate. It wasn't yet so bad that I had trouble carrying out my duties but I thought I should start looking for less physically demanding job well before I had a serious problem. My problem with not being able to drive the fleet car kept the issue alive. I explained to my supervisor my problem and he said I could drive my own car with an automatic shift and turn in a mileage record for when I used it in my work. But at that time there were no laws defining special consideration for people with physical problems and the financial office in Washington repeatedly sent me letters questioning why I was not using a fleet car. I would show them to my supervisor and he would say he would deal with it and he always did but it was nevertheless disturbing to me.

As I was almost 30, I thought I should not delay in starting my search for an academic job. I started to seriously search for a less physically demanding and more intellectually challenging work sometime after I had been in Maryland about six months. I had by then become fairly familiar with the area for which I was responsible. I had started bleeding cattle to obtain blood samples to be sent to the laboratory and tested for brucellosis. I had also started doing tuberculin tests. This work was quite routine and required little thought. Once I became proficient at bleeding the cattle and skilled at doing the tuberculin test

I began to doubt that I would wish to do these tests for the rest of my life.

These kinds of thoughts were suppressed in Mexico as the program there had been an exciting new world to me. Every day there were new experiences. Rural Mexico and the Mexican people were very different from anything I, a middleclass American from the northern city of Philadelphia, had ever experienced. The goals of the program also excited me and every day yielded new exciting experiences. There were some negative factors, I for example did not really like the bureaucratic organization and the somewhat arbitrary decisions by my supervisors even though I recognized that the type of program we were engaged in required the almost military organization used if we were to achieve our goal of eradication of the disease.

The domination of the group by Southerners also made me somewhat uncomfortable. This bothered some of the Mexican personnel also who commented to me about the race views of some of the Southerners in the program. My inability to drive the fleet vehicles was also always a worry to me even though the unspoken understanding of my Mexican partners prevented it from being a real problem it still caused me to worry. In the final analysis the excitement of being in Mexico, working in a foreign country in a difficult situation, and doing demanding work, kept me from boredom and left me with little time for thoughts about the future. After I left Mexico and started working in Maryland much of the excitement was gone and thoughts of a less physically demanding and more intellectually stimulating work came to the fore.

I discussed the matter with Ruth who had said yes and was now my wife. She was sympathetic and said she would like to move to a university town and undertake a study program leading to a career also.

As I already had a degree in veterinary medicine and some experience in the profession I decided to limit my search to an academic position in a veterinary college. With the aid of my wife who had a degree in English we composed a letter and *Curriculum vitae* to be sent to the 18 veterinary schools than in existence in the USA. The college of veterinary medicine at the University of Illinois was the only one to reply to my letter with an offer. The position I was offered was as a research associate and included the opportunity to work for a graduate degree. I was to be paid roughly what I was earning as a civil servant. The position was in the Department of Physiology and the funding came from a research grant from the U.S. Army to a professor in that department. The funding was for several years and the research was to determine if radiation, as a means of preservation of meat and flour, caused toxicity in the irradiated product.

I accepted the position offered and resigned from the civil service. My wife and I packed our things and we started our drive to Champaign-Urbana in central Illinois.

In passing I will mention that Ruth was pregnant at that time, an event which occurred shortly after our marriage despite her earlier insistence that she wanted to wait to have children until she'd gotten her career started. The event like most of my previous experiences was not planned. I was not upset at the time nor was I upset when a second pregnancy followed shortly after the first birth. It wasn't planned either. Looking back I am happy it all happened as it did for I now know you need to be young and strong to raise children. Now in my old age, I am glad I have two young families to which I am connected. Having children was another unplanned event which like most of the other unplanned events affecting my life was good.

When we arrived in Urbana, Illinois, we rented an apartment and spent a few days settling in. Then I went to the school of veterinary medicine to meet the people with whom I would work and study with. The professor who held the grant introduced me to two other veterinarians who were hired as I was to carry out the project. He then briefly described the nature of the project. In the main part of the project the experimental animals were to be beagle dogs. I was told I would work on the part of the project using the dogs. There was also to be a section of the project using rats but I was not involved in that section. The project I was involved in would start with 24 puppies and would continue for three years. The dogs were to be divided into two groups, one fed a diet containing irradiated beef and flour the other an identical diet but with beef and flour that had not been irradiated. I was not involved in the preparation of the diets nor was I told which dogs were in which group. I was told I would be responsible for monitoring the blood of the dogs. This included total red cell and white cell counts, percent volume of cells in the blood, differential counts of the white cells and the determination of the percent of immature red cells in the blood. The latter determinations were made by microscopic examination of thin blood films stained by the Giemsa technique. Sometime later I undertook a valuation of bone marrow obtained by needle puncture of bone in the hip.

I don't know why I was chosen for the hematologic evaluation of the dogs as I had no more training in that field than what I had received as a student in veterinary school. Perhaps my experience handling animals and bleeding them during my year in Maryland and my time in Mexico played role in that decision.

I don't remember clearly, but I think I'd bled all of the dogs monthly starting on the day the 24 little wriggling puppies arrived and just after we put ear tags in to identify them. I chose to bleed the dogs from the jugular vein which involved my first teaching experience, teaching a veterinary student how to hold the dogs while I bleed them.

It was a busy time as I had to learn all of the techniques I would use and establish the record-keeping system to keep the data I would collect so that I could prepare regular reports of my observations. I also enrolled in the Masters Degree program of the college and helped my wife to get us settled in. She needed some help as the unplanned pregnancy was advancing rapidly.

We started to look for a place to live. The apartment we had rented was very small and we didn't feel it would be adequate when the child arrived.

One of the younger faculty members in the school told me they had a small house near the college that they wanted to sell as they wanted to move to a larger house. It was a small one-story house in a group of houses built just after the Second World War to house returning soldiers. It was built on a concrete slab. Central heating was by a gas furnace in the small room in central part of the house. Heat was blown into the living room and to heat the bedrooms, you had, it turned out, to keep the doors open. The house it turned out, as we discovered that first winter, was poorly insulated. When winter came it came furiously with a strong wind from the Northwest which explained why all the trees leaned eastward. Urbana-Champaign had hot muggy summers and very cold windy winters. It was great for corn and soybeans as the central region of Illinois had some of the best soil in the world. For people like myself, on the other hand, it had a marvelous University.

The classes I took in my master's program were mostly in the colleges of arts and sciences. One of the best courses I ever took was one in virology offered by Salvador Luria, the only Nobel Prize winner I ever had the pleasure of meeting. When I much later was a faculty member at the Ohio State University it often surprised me when the young virologists we interviewed for jobs would talk about the exciting new concepts they just discovered. I remembered that Dr. Luria had covered most of these concepts in his beginning virology course, many years earlier.

I often had thought I would want to enter the field of infectious diseases as that is what I worked on previously. However as the only clear offer I received from an academic institution was not in that field I didn't feel strong enough to continue looking although Dr. Luria's course did stir some thoughts about what I would do when I finished my Masters Degree in Physiology.

When both my Masters program and the study of toxicity of irradiated foods was very near completion I started looking for a place where I could study infectious diseases and virology. A faculty member in the Department of Pathology and Hygiene told me that the University of Wisconsin had a strong program on infectious diseases. He had some information about that program as his brother was a professor of virology at University of Wisconsin. I wrote to the people at the University of Wisconsin and was told I could join them when I had completed my Masters program. As an aside I will note that the irradiated foods were not toxic in any way for the dog and that I had become fairly comfortable working as a hematologist.

I did learn something more than just hematology while working on the job. I had developed a relationship with two senior faculty members, one a pathologist and one a parasitologist, while seeking help in identification of the leukocytes by their morphology. Knowledge of their morphology is necessary for doing the differential counts on the blood films and later on thin films of the bone marrow. The parasitologist was very self-confident and would make rapid decisions about the cell type. The pathologist on the other hand would study the cell in question carefully and then explain at some length why he thought the cell fit the criteria to warrant its placement in a particular category. He would then discuss reasons why he could be wrong in his classification. At times he would recommend listing the cell if not identifiable. At first all this discussion of what was what confused me and I was impressed by the rapid and certain approach of the other man. As my experience increased I finally concluded that the uncertainty of the pathologist fit what I saw as opposed to the certainty of the other man. This was particularly the case with the cells in the bone marrow which were rapidly changing their morphology as they developed from stem cells to highly differentiated cell types.

As time passed, and my confidence increased, I became somewhat unhappy with the professor with whom I worked and who was also my academic advisor. He was rather dull and had little imagination. He was quite suited for a long-term feeding study, collecting data carefully and regularly. He didn't seem to want more than that.

Sometime after I had received an offer from Wisconsin and before I had formally accepted it the chairman of the pathology and hygiene department walked into my office and said in a cheery voice I hear you are not too happy with your advisor and are going to leave us and go to Wisconsin to study virology. We have a virologist in our department and if you want to you can join our department. I replied let me discuss it with my wife and I'll tell you tomorrow what we decide. We had settled into life in Champaign-Urbana, our little girl was in daycare and my wife was enrolled in the Masters of social work program and had a job at the University teaching their football players to read and write. In short we decided to change departments and stay in Illinois.

We have now arrived at the next-to-last stage of my search for an intellectual career. I may add the search included getting a PhD because with rare exceptions you don't get anywhere in academia without one.

The decision to stay in Illinois after I got my Masters degree turned out to be a good one but it didn't get off to a good start. After I moved to the new department I was introduced to the man who was to be my advisor. He had gotten a grant to study and hopefully produce a vaccine for prevention of shipping fever of cattle. This disease is assumed to be a viral disease that causes a serious sickness in cattle shipped from ranches and farms to feed lots were they are to be fattened before slaughter. It also develops in other cattle following long and stressful travel for any reason. I never got any real grasp of the project during the less than a year that I worked with him. I however started taking courses for my PhD program and also going to farms with him to administer vaccines. He however kept the vaccine production in his own hands and told me very little about what was actually being done. One day he called me into his office and said he had taken a position at the University of Colorado and was leaving Illinois almost immediately. I soon found myself without an advisor and helping a junior faculty member trying ineffectively to keep the research project going. I was kept on as a research associate but spent most of my time taking courses required for the PhD program and wondering what would happen next. In several of the courses I took I became friendly with a somewhat older man, also a veterinarian, who was a professor in the veterinary college at the University of Florida. He said he was taking a leave of absence from his job to get a PhD. We became laboratory partners in a biochemistry course and in general got along quite well. At the end of the year he went back to Florida and I assumed I would never see him again. Sometime during the following summer he came into my office and announced he had completed his PhD program and had been hired as a full professor in the college of veterinary medicine at Illinois with full authorization to advise graduate students. He then said to me he was bringing several large grants to Illinois and would need help in carrying them out and that as we had gotten along pretty well as fellow graduate students he would like me to join him and would serve as my advisor. He then told me that one of his projects was a study of *Vibrio fetus* and the other of *Anaplasma marginali*, a parasite of the blood of cattle. It is tick-borne and semitropical in occurrence. Even though it all seemed a bit strange I decided then and there to go for it. I had spent a lot of time learning hematology so I said I would like to work on the research project concerning the blood parasite *Anaplasma marginali*.

As time passed I learned a bit about how he was brought to Illinois. It is an interesting story that tells a lot about how universities actually work. It isn't always just like they say in the literature you get when you apply for a degree program or a job at a University. I do believe it is a story that belongs in a book for young people considering an academic career. The key to understanding it is realizing that the people running the college will bend the rules as much as possible to recruit people they want to implement their efforts to develop their programs and bring in research grants and projects to enhance their units reputation.

A short time before he showed up here to get a PhD we had gotten a new Dean of the veterinary college. He was an ambitious man who I believe was recruited to improve the scientific level at the veterinary school. This man knew of Dr. Rustic's achievements and his record of getting grants to finance his projects. The University of Illinois had a rule that all faculty must have a PhD. Apparently the University of Florida at Gainesville had no such rule.

Dr. Ristic was a Serbian national who had spent the bulk of the time during the war in a German prison camp. He and several other Serbian men escaped the camp as the Western Allies approached the area. They were being marched to a new camp when allied planes spotted the lines of marching men and strafed them thinking they were German troops. During the strafing everyone scattered and jumped into the scrub along the side of the road. When the planes left Ristic and several other Serbian man found they were huddled together in the ditch along with a German soldier who had been their guard. Ristic who spoke fluent German, persuaded the guard to unload his rifle and pretend he was escorting the prisoners back to the camp but actually they walked toward the Allied lines. The next morning they encountered a column of Canadian troops. The German guard surrendered and Ristic, who also spoke English, spoke to the officer in charge of the Canadian troops. The officer decided that here was what they needed, a multilingual translator and recruited him into his unit. He spent the remaining months of the war with the Canadians and was rewarded with a stipend after he was discharged.

After the war Ristic decided to stay in Germany at least long enough to get a professional degree. He applied and got admitted to a dental school but didn't like it in part because the practical work was on preserved heads of people who had been killed during the war. He then transferred to a veterinary college. After he completed his study, he emigrated to the United States where he got a job at the University of Florida veterinary college. We met as I mentioned earlier when he came to Illinois to obtain a PhD.

My years with him were exciting and stimulating and strangely for a graduate student in a demanding graduate program pleasant. I learned a great deal from him not just science but to the day I retired I treated my graduate students largely as he treated me. He was constantly optimistic and cheerful and constantly spilling out new ideas and discussing projects. We were all encouraged to talk with him about our projects and we discussed all of the projects going on in the laboratory with him almost as equals. One interesting aspect of his leadership was his ability to pick up students who for some reason were in trouble, invite them to his laboratory, and get them back on track. I guess I was one of them. I continued a relationship with him until his death.

I personally am not always optimistic and during my years with him I learned to at least partly overcome my periods of depression or to hide them from my students.

During my period as a doctoral student and actually for the rest of my academic career I expanded my work with blood parasites. I started projects on *Babesia* and later on its close relative *Plasmodium*, the parasite causing malaria. As my projects were largely on tropical diseases of animals including man I attracted many students from tropical countries including Africa, South America and India. I was funded by the Army malaria project and on programs concerning Trypanosomes and Leishmamia.

The information gained during my years learning hematology in the physiology department became a major component of my research on infectious diseases. This was another example of chance events turning out well.

I will now explain how I got to Ohio State University and how I ended up in a microbiology department in the college of arts and sciences

After I completed my PhD program with Dr. Ristic I continued to work in his laboratory and was told I could continue with him as a post-doctoral fellow. It was a tempting prospect but I wanted to get a regular academic position and start teaching and developing a laboratory on my own. I saw an advertisement in a Journal saying there was a position in the Ohio State University Department of microbiology for a veterinarian with a PhD who would teach veterinary students in the veterinary college but be actually employed in the department of Microbiology in the college of arts and sciences. It was an unusual arrangement and it was unique to the Ohio State University. I later found out that a similar arrangement existed with the medical and dental schools. I sent my vitae to the department of microbiology with a letter expressing my interest in the job. Some time passed and I received no answer until one day a professor from the Ohio State Department of microbiology came to my office, introduced himself, and said, he was visiting his son, who was a professor of zoology at Illinois and had decided to look me up while visiting his son. He inquired if I was still interested in a job at the Ohio State University. I replied yes and we talked for some time. He then asked if he could use my phone to call his department chairman. He made the call and I heard him ask if the chairman still had my vitae and application. Some time passed, he then hung up and turned to me and asked if I had another copy of my vitae. I gave it to him and he said he would call me later to set up an interview for the job.

A few days later he called and we selected a date and time for the interview. My wife and I both went to the interview. We were introduced to a member of the veterinary school faculty who turned out to know my wife from social connections in Philadelphia. I never mentioned it earlier but my wife's family were members of the Jewish community in Philadelphia and I met her through my best friend Harold who also belonged to that community. The children of that community with whom I associated were largely students who went to schools I attended and I became attached to them as we seemed compatible. We were mostly unaffiliated to the religions of our parents and were trying to become intellectuals as many young people do. In reality these connections didn't directly shape my career choices but my desire to enter an intellectual environment did push me to strive to work in a university.

But I am off the track again. The bulk of people I met during the interview were faculty of the department of microbiology in the college of arts and sciences. They were not veterinarians they were however members of the department that actually was to employ me and set my pay levels and determined my promotions although I was to be stationed in the veterinary college and teach microbiology and immunology to veterinary students.

I learned during the interview that the person who had had the job for which I was interviewing felt strongly that a second person should be hired to join him in the teaching of the veterinary students. He was the one who had placed the ad. When the department didn't cooperate in this he took a job at another institution and resigned. The faculty then realized they would have no one to teach the veterinary students in the coming autumn semester. Dr. Stahley who was the man who visited my office in Illinois took it upon himself to take steps to resolve the problem. He did this because the chairman, who was near retirement, just didn't seem to be able to act on the matter.

I learned later that the college of arts and sciences was in some turmoil at the time and was trying to decide whether the microbiology department should go to the medical school or whether they should create a division of biological sciences to include microbiology and several departments including zoology, botany, biochemistry, and entomology which at the time were in the college of agriculture

It took several years for these issues to be resolved. When I was offered and accepted the position I had no idea of how the reorganization would affect my career. In fact it never occurred to me that I should even worry about the matter.

It was late spring when I accepted the position. I was pressured to come to Ohio as soon as possible so that I should be able to prepare for my teaching and receive help in getting started. I arrived in Columbus in early summer. I was shown the very nice office and laboratory and classrooms in the veterinary college where I was to work. As the veterinary college was on the west side of the campus and the microbiology department in the central campus there was quite a distance between the two units. I was told to get ready to teach in the fall. When I tried to obtain course outlines from the faculty of my department no one seemed to know anything. My chairman was in India for the summer and the whole department seemed fairly inactive. I found out where my predecessor was working and then called him and asked if he could provide me with course outlines for the courses he had taught. He told me he had no course outlines and could not help me at all. He appeared quite angry with the department and didn't want to help me or anyone else hired to replace him. I continued to search for information about what I was to teach and finally encountered a young man, a veterinarian who was a graduate student with my predecessor and who had been teaching assistant for the courses my predecessor had taught. He gave me copies of the course outlines and course descriptions. They provided me with what I needed to prepare myself for the courses I would teach beginning in the fall. He was a mature young man who had almost finished his degree program having only some research needed to complete his PhD thesis. My predecessor continued as his advisor and the student chose to remain at the Ohio State University. I told him he could continue to work in what had become my laboratory and offered him help with whatever administrative problems he, as a result of having an absent advisor encountered. He remained in my laboratory for about a year until he completed his PhD. He was always pleasant and helpful when I requested information about the courses I taught. Interestingly I never again spoke to his advisor, my predecessor, nor was I ever asked by his advisor to serve on committees to guide or evaluate his research.

These first years were very demanding. I had to prepare my lectures and develop laboratories associated with each course. I wrote grant applications, started my own research programs, and recruited several graduate students to work with me. When I obtained grant money my wife joined me doing the literature research for my projects and helping me to write grant applications, research reports, and papers for publication. She continued doing this until she started work at the Ohio State University for a Masters Degree in Educational Psychology.

When she completed the degree she went to work in the public school system as a school psychologist evaluating students about any problems they had and placing them in special programs available to them for help.

My work in the veterinary college proceeded quite well. I obtained research funds, attracted graduate students and developed the courses I taught in veterinary microbiology and immunology. The only problem arose from my providing service to one academic unit, the veterinary college, while being employed in another, the microbiology department of the college of arts and sciences. If I needed help with anything and asked my chairman he would tell me to speak to the Dean of the veterinary college who would tell me to speak to the microbiology chairman. It wasn't a serious problem as I had grant money to support my graduate students and research and a teaching assistant to help in running the laboratories attached to the courses I taught. Everything went well. I was happy with my job and I just didn't ask for much from either group.

The first hint that there might be a problem came several years later when I heard that the medical school was setting up a Department of medical microbiology. I did nothing about it but did anticipate that it was possible that the veterinary college would soon do the same. At the time I was still an assistant professor and had not yet been granted tenure, an action that usually occurs when one is promoted to associate professor. The evaluation leading to promotion and the granting of tenure occurs at the end of your probation, which period usually lasts about five years. If the faculty committee evaluating you does not approve your promotion you are notified that within about one year that your employment at the University will end. I bring this up because my status was a major factor in the decision I soon had to make.

The Dean of the veterinary college was quite a decent man but his chief assistant, who was the chairman of the veterinary pathology department was not much liked by the bulk of the veterinary faculty in part because he used his relationship with the Dean to build up his department and himself at the expense of the other departments and faculty. The Dean did control his excesses in that respect but as he was an energetic and intelligent man the Dean depended on him extensively and thus did not want to lose his services. When the veterinary college Dean retired the president of the University chose the assistant Dean to replace him. The bulk of the veterinary faculty did not want him to be Dean and wrote a letter opposing his appointment and calling for an outside search for the old Dean's replacement. Most of the veterinary faculty signed the letter and I was asked to sign it also, which I did. The university president appointed the man Dean ignoring the faculty's advice and even gave the man a copy of the letter. After he was appointed the new Dean called for a college wide meeting in which he showed his copy of the letter given to him by the president, but otherwise nothing much happened right away. One thing however did occur soon thereafter. He came to my office and said he wished to create a veterinary microbiology department and asked me to help him but not discuss the matter with anyone. He said I would be head of his team, which is a nonexistent academic title. He also said he would take care of me which I doubted. I replied I couldn't do that as I was employed by the microbiology department and they would consider such actions to be a betrayal. He then abruptly walked out of my office. I was perplexed for a few moments and then decided to call my chairman, tell him what had occurred and ask for his advice. He was after all, the man who would play a major role in my promotion and tenure. After listening to me, my chairman, replied by asking a question. He asked what I wanted to do. I replied that I didn't really trust the Dean of the veterinary college and as I was happy with how things were going I thought it would be best to stay with the department of which I was a member. He then said he had to ask the rest of the faculty of the department and get their opinions. He added that he would let me know the results the next day. When he called back he said the faculty was agreeable and that as there was an empty office and laboratory available I could move in at my convenience. As this all occurred during the summer break I was free to move as I was not teaching courses and just working with my graduate students doing research. I asked the man who was taking care of my research animals, largely rats and chickens at the time, if he could help me move. The next day he brought his pickup truck and we transferred all the equipment belonging to the microbiology department and my research materials to the microbiology building. This was the last move shaping my career I made and I remained in the department of microbiology until I retired in 1989. In one sense this is a possible point to end the story of how my academic career developed. With the passage of time I became a professor, I taught students, ran a seminar program, did research, published papers describing my research, published books on my subjects of interest in parasitic protozoa, and organized several international conferences on blood inhabiting parasites. Despite this being a possible end of this paper I will nevertheless now tell a few stories to give the reader a feeling about some personal aspects of my life in academia.

In general my life in academia was good although the stories I will now tell often describe things not so good because I want to present reality and not create an unreal picture. After all life is not all perfect and to be happy and survive you must take some aspects of life as they come. My experience as a professor was in the medical sciences. A university hires you and tells you about your responsibility to teach students, set up a laboratory and use the laboratory to train students, however they provide limited monetary resources. The professor is expected to apply for external grant funds to support research, a percentage of which they take to cover what they call administrative costs. The constant search for grants to fund your research and support your graduate students was for me the most unpleasant part of being a professor. I enjoyed teaching undergraduate students and working with graduate students who in my case did most of the actual laboratory work under my guidance. I met with my graduate students weekly in a formal way requiring each one to present a complete report each week of what they had done on their projects. The group then discussed each report. I of course would also work with the student when I felt it necessary or they required help. Each student would work with me to develop their project. What they would do was of course shaped by the nature of the grants I received. If one didn't do what you had proposed to the granting agency you had real problems. An unexpected type of teaching that I became aware of as I worked with my graduate students arose as I began evaluating their research reports, and later the drafts of their theses. I found I had to become an English teacher. I had to teach English writing skills and how to prepare coherent reports written in logical form. No one entering the academic world, even those hoping to work in science should not underestimate the importance of being able to speak and write in a clear and logical way. I later found I had to use my skills in expository writing not just to help my graduate students but also in preparing papers written by many of the people who contributed chapters to the books I published and papers from conferences I organized. I was constantly surprised to find that many established scientists sent me drafts of papers that needed extensive editing before they could be published.

I will now discuss a subject, the nature of which affected my career strongly and will in some form surely continue to affect people working in science in the future. I undertook studies of medical science at a time when the study of disease processes consisted of attempts to unravel the gross histologic changes, and the nature of the immunological processes developing as the disease progressed. These studies would attempt to explore the nature of the damage and how the damage was brought about. We all know that invading organisms may secrete toxins that destroy tissue, but I worked on the assumption that much of the damage occurring during infections is caused by the immune system itself. My thoughts can be thought of in terms of war and collateral damage. When the immune system is activated it revs up the complement system and antibody production and phagocytosis. These actions destroy parasites but also do damage to body cells particularly body cells to which are attached parasite components. They may also affect tissues existing in proximity to invading parasites. Just as in war the battlefield is devastated, and must be cleaned up and the area rebuilt. Often damage cannot be repaired leaving the host body devastated or even dead.

The nature of the damage caused by the cells involved in the processes of defense and the products produced by the invading organisms, all of which must be dealt with by the body's defenses was a central part of my research. I also studied products of the invading organism as they were important in the development of diagnostic tests and vaccines. In addition study of methods to identify organisms and the use of these characteristics in classification was important to me as I recognized that you have to know what you're working on

All of this type of work was done using gross morphologic characteristics, serological tests, histopathology, and organic chemistry as tools in the research. Animals were infected and the course of the disease produced was studied to define the course of the infection and recovery. The organisms causing the diseases with which I worked were identified using classic criteria. There are problems with these classic criteria but, in general, the systems of study which I used worked and were what was then available. But I have gotten a bit off the track again. It wasn't the nature of what I was trying to do that caused trouble for me but rather how I tried to do it. A whole new technology for examining biological processes was in the process of being developed. I didn't feel that the techniques I was using and the type of work I was doing was no longer of use and I continued working as I had been working. I will explain this further in the next few paragraphs. At the time I was a graduate student at Illinois a whole new set of procedures for the study of biological systems was being developed in the microbiology and biochemistry departments there. These studies became the basis of what is now called molecular biology and molecular genetics. I was close friends with a graduate student working with Solomon Spiegelman. I remember him telling me how RNA copies of DNA left the cell nucleus, entered the cytoplasm, and bound to mitochondrial RNA and then programmed protein production. This work opened a window to understanding how genetic information in the nucleus was able to program what the cell did. This item is only a small sample of the many studies being done there that led to new techniques for study of biological systems which would later sweep through the biological research field.

The research in the veterinary school where I was working on my PhD was concerned with more immediate problems tied to prevention, treatment, and cure of diseases. It used the older more conventional techniques. By the time I was a full professor and nearing retirement age the new molecular biology and genetics had swept through the field of biological research and if you had not adopted those techniques you had trouble getting research funds from granting agencies.

In my own laboratory I was involved in the study of malaria vaccines. I was supported by the Army malaria project and worked using a rodent malaria infecting rats. In one of my projects I worked on immunity to the blood stages of the parasite using a preparation of the blood stage parasites as the vaccine. This crude vaccine contained a complex of all of the components of the blood stage parasites. This vaccine like all the other similar vaccines produced in other laboratories from other malaria species gave a low level of protection to infection. At this time the molecular biologists entered the field. The rationale for funding them was that with their techniques they could produce large volumes of antigen of great purity. These vaccines were produced by yeasts or *E. coli* in which the genes for certain components of the parasite were introduced. This was an important development as the various human malarias essentially grew only in humans and certain apes although culture of the blood phases of *Plasmodium falciperum* had been developed. The molecular biology techniques for producing antigens were very valuable. There were however errors in the basic justification for using the procedure to develop malaria vaccines. The belief that the poor quality of the immunity to malaria vaccines had resulted from the mixture of parasite components in the vaccines was the argument being used by the molecularly oriented people who argued that they could improve the vaccine by providing pure preparations of the appropriate components of the parasite, i.e. those which stimulated immunity and not those that inhibited it. The reality was that the same molecules were responsible for both of the actions. In passing, I should note it has also been shown that in many cases pure preparations of single molecular types do not produce as good immunity as mixtures as it is easier for the parasite to develop resistance to a pure preparation of a singular molecular type then to a mixture of types. In reality of course the immune response must overcome the inhibition of the immune response to be able to protect the host. As the molecules which protect the parasite are the ones that must be overcome to generate immunity you can't separate the immune generating molecules from those inhibiting immunity as they are the same molecule. It was also true that the young molecular biologists were not always knowledgeable about biology in general and in the particular case of malaria vaccines most of them did not accept the fairly well-established concept that if you don't get good immunity from infection you won't get it from a vaccine either.

Molecular biology and molecular genetics has begun to produce some remarkable results but it is simply a new tool and can only be used effectively by people who also know biology in general and where the new molecular biology can produce data that can fit in with the existing body of biological knowledge. Some of the young molecular biology people were a bit arrogant and pushed their activities while failing to appreciate the importance of understanding the nature of the larger biological systems.

I was getting a bit old and didn't really feel like learning a whole lot of new technology. I must here add that I avoided the whole problem by retiring when the university offered faculty members a five-year increase in the number of years used for calculating their retirement payments. I believe the administrators expected to save money by replacing the older faculty with younger ones starting out at lower pay scales and that they would not lose any valuable experienced people by doing it. I must say I remember listening to our newly hired faculty proposing what to them were new ideas that some of the older faculty remembered having tried and decided they were not good. Knowledge of the past stemming from experience does have some value.

I have tried to follow the careers of some of my graduate students. I tried to provide them with a broad knowledge of biology and even passed to them some veterinary knowledge. Most of my PhD students did get good jobs in universities, government laboratories, or pharmaceutical companies. Some of them were able to add new techniques to their repertory and I tell myself that they were able to use these techniques effectively because they had a good grounding in biology.

Retirement

Friends of mine in the department of microbiology knowing my penchant to work with my hands chipped in and bought me a wood turner's lath as a retirement gift. It was a good gift for me and after I retired I started making bowls, lamps, and various types of furniture. A bit later

I started to do small sculptures. I don't think it was an accident that I started this by making animals, goats, rabbits, squirrels, and other wild and domestic animals. My pets and my veterinary training helped me in this activity. Later I started making human figures also (Figures 8 and 9). These were most often female figures (Figures10 and11). I always thought that in humans and also in many other species, think of the elephant seal for example, the female is by far the better looking one.

As my retirement continues, I have increased my activities in woodworking and sculpture as above described. These activities give me pleasure, fill my time and keep me in motion. This is vital as sitting inactive is not only unpleasant, but I believe is physically damaging. There is one activity however which played a large role in my life as a scientist and academician which I continue in my retirement. This activity is speculation about patterns which exist in the world of ours. It is so much a part of me that I am unable to stop it. I can't stop it probably because it gives me much pleasure. For me, at least, the search for patterns helps me to handle the vast amounts of data that accumulate as a result of scientific studies by many people of diverse aspects of our world.

I feel that persistence of this type of thought in my head and the importance this type of thinking had on my career justified my providing a short discussion of it in in this final section of this chapter.

I believe that a variety of universal patterns exist in biologic systems and that at least in the systems we refer to animals the pain and pleasure principle is almost universal. We all repeat doing things that yield pleasure and we avoid doing things that cause pain. I believe that this type of system developed quite early in evolution. I have watched motile bacteria and protozoa in a wet preparation on a microscope slide trying to escape when a noxious chemical is introduced on one side of the slide. If on the other hand, if the chemical that could serve as a food is introduced the organisms move toward it. This behavior with much variation is the basis of the senses of taste and smell and our reaction to pain and pleasure.

There is another pattern in nature that I have found to be very interesting, one which is very significant in biology but exists to some extent in chemistry and physics also. My thoughts about this pattern

I can trace back to a course in virology I took as a graduate student. It was given by Salvador Luria then a professor at the University of Illinois. He said that there two types of building blocks making up all of the structures in nature. One of these types is the common brick which can be assembled in almost any way and in which the information for the assembly is a plan produced by the assembler while the other type of particle was one in which the information for assembly is programmed into the particle. This latter type of block makes up the structure of most of the universe. Think about the subatomic particles of so much interest in contemporary physics. It appears they all have attributes that determine how, and with which other particles they can combine. In fact the possibilities seem to be quite limited at least in their ability to produce atoms. There are only about eighty eight atoms possible. These as seen by Dimitri Mendeleev, the Russian scientist, who developed the Periodic Table, also carry much information which determines how they can interact with each other and what can be built by those unions.

The union of atoms produces structures we call molecules and these molecules make up ourselves and the world around us. There is a vast amount of information contained in each molecule just as there is in each atom. This information which exists in each molecule determines with which molecules the molecule can combine and with and how the binding may occur and how one molecule can affect other molecules. Think for example of enzymes. They are capable of modifying other molecules in specific ways. One of the most interesting attributes of molecules is their ability to assemble other molecules that carry information required for assembly of complex cells, which can then rebuild themselves and thus maintain themselves and even reproduce themselves. DNA molecules for example carry information for their own duplication, as well as information for the production of molecules that spontaneously organize themselves into cellular structures that are organized at the simplest level that manifests properties that we call life. I believe that some of our DNA also carries the information that controls when individual genes produce their products and for how long they continue to produce them which provides vital information shaping the cellular structure.

And now I will say a few words about how the ideas I have just discussed affect evolution and, in particular, natural selection. As a student many years ago, I was taught that the variations that occurred in biological systems resulted from errors in duplication of the information-bearing molecules in cells that is the genes. Most of these changes were considered to have no effect or to be lethal, but some brought about new forms that were better adapted to the environment or permitted the organism to enter new environments or survive in a changed environment. As a result of what I was taught, I always thought that the possibilities of change were unlimited and that chance selection provided the survivors in the selecting environment.

With my growing awareness of the magnitude of information programmed in the molecules of which we are assembled I have begun to think that chance selection is very much limited by the limits imposed on the pools of variance available for selection by chance. These limitations are the result of the vast amounts of information built into each particle and determines which newly assembled molecules are available to participate in the selection process and even determines if such a molecule could exist in the first place. We must consider the limitations imposed on natural selection by the limitations imposed by information programmed into all of the components available for selection. All I can say now about the process is that if other planets are similar to ours, and are made of the same molecules and atoms, there must be quite a few similarities between their biological systems and those here.

Scientists can only find how the existing systems work. They can then sometimes use the information they obtain to manipulate how it occurs. At best however they can only do what occurs naturally and tweak the system to some degree. If genes did not move around with the aid of viruses in nature than scientists would not be able to do it in the laboratory.

If we ever completely understand how all the biological systems work we would still not know why they work, or what would be the purpose of their working, and whether there exists any moral significance to it at all. Morality is a human creation or as the Jewish Bible says humans ate the apple of knowledge of good and evil. It is an interesting result that they were expelled from the Garden of Eden as a result of their eating the Apple and trying to create moral systems. At any rate science cannot tell us why we were here only how it works. The creation of moral systems is the job of theologians.

In final summary I want to emphasize the large role played chance plays in what you do but you still have some control as a result of your decisions on how to handle what chance offers you. You can even to some degree shape what chance offers by what you do. You must have some plans and goals. You must place yourself where you will encounter appropriate chances. If you want an academic life you have to enter institutions where chances in that field are likely to occur. In other words you have to be active and be there and be capable of making decisions about how to handle the chances that arise, but now I think I have said enough. I have described how my collaborative career and to a lesser degree how my life has developed. I believe that the important message for someone just starting out in the difficult task of leaving childhood and entering adulthood is to try to make the best use of your assets and then to try to enjoy what you do and be as happy and as positive as you can.

Good luck I wish you success in your search for a good carrier and happy life.

CHAPTER 3

A Collaborative Life in Plants

David Lee
Emeritus Professor of Biology Florida
International University
Emeritus Director The Kampong of the National
Tropical Botanical Garden Coconut Grove

Many people, activities and institutions, particularly while growing up, strongly influenced my development as a plant biologist and university professor. At different stages of my career I have reflected on those influences, but now I have now finished my formal work as a scientist and professor and especially welcome the opportunity to reflect on my life. Writing this chapter is an opportunity to do just that, contemplating with more than the usual focus and discipline, easy to skip in the normal day to day activities, even in retirement. Writing it also gives me another opportunity to honor those individuals who helped me along the way, and adds to my feelings of humility and gratitude.

Childhood

I was born and grew up on the Columbia Plateau of Washington State. My mother and father, John and Mary Lee, moved to the small town of Ephrata, which was the seat of Grant County, recently married and starting a new life together. My mother's family was originally from Seattle, but moved frequently in the state following the work of my grandfather as a civil engineer. She came from English and German background, from ancestors who lived in Pennsylvania in the early 19th century. My father's family moved to the town of Chelan, from Michigan and Illinois, in 1920. I was told that we came from the Lees of Virginia, but genealogical research by a distant relative indicates that our ancestor, William Lee, arrived in New York around 1675. A look at my family tree shows the good and bad sides typical of a family; a family name is Webster (my middle name) after Noah Webster, another family name is Hawkins (my dad's middle name) after the notorious pirate. My father's family moved to the town of Chelan, from Michigan and Illinois, in 1920. My grandfather practiced dentistry and was unsuccessful in starting an orchard.

Both families moved to Grand Coulee to find work associated with the dam construction in 1933, and my mom and dad met there. My father came to know Jim O'Sullivan, who was an early booster of the dam and associated irrigation project (for which Ephrata became the headquarters). Dad ran a small luncheonette near the movie theater in Grand Coulee, and he noticed that people could find the money to escape to the fantasy of movies, even in the depths of the great depression. So they moved to Ephrata, purchased and renovated the local movie house, the "Kam" renamed the "Capital", and started the "sagebrush circuit", showing movies in grange halls in the small dry land farming communities in the area. The business prospered, and my parents eventually owned and ran a chain of some twenty theaters and drive inns in that part of the state, the Columbia Basin Theaters.

My bithplace was Wenatchee, the largest nearby city, in December of 1942; there was no hospital in Ephrata until three years later (and my father was instrumental in its establishment).

I grew up in this little town, in a small house, later enlarged, on the edge of town, Ephrata was an isolated but progressive place in the middle of the sagebrush steppe (or cold desert) of the Columbia Plateau. It served outlying agricultural activity and consisted of retail business, support of the Great Northern Railway (including a row of grain elevators), county government employees, and the skilled professionals who designed the Columbia Basin Project, one of the largest irrigation projects in American history. Ephrata was known for its excellent school system, and the town was like an oasis in a harsh treeless landscape. As a child, I had a bicycle and the means to travel anywhere in town, as well as into the dry washes (alive with salamanders and frogs in the spring time) in the countryside. During the summer months, my friends and I would spend entire days together away from our homes and families. The landscape, with the Grand Coulee just north of town, was a powerful presence: blue cloudless summer skies, hot days and cold nights, dark basalt canyon walls with flecks of lime green and orange lichens, and mineral-rich lakes on the canyon floors. As a child, I did not have any real mentors leading me towards a career in biology, but was strongly influenced by my personal experiences in nature with my friends.

There were some strong themes in my childhood, associated with the institutions that were in the town and prepared children for adulthood. These institutions were the schools and the churches, and organizations for children and youth: cub and boy scouts, girl scouts, and Future Farmers of America.

I was the middle child, with an older brother and younger sister. There were fights among us kids, but we got along pretty well and stay in contact with each other today. It was a stable family situation. My mother took care of the home and family, and also helped my dad with financial aspects of his business. My father worked hard to make his businesses successful and that made him a little remote from us. He also performed a lot of volunteering in the community. He was the first president of the hospital association and a leader of the Lions Club campaign to raise funds for the first local hospital. He was active in the Lions, serving as chapter president when they built the first park and swimming pool. My mother and father also were active in the concert association, which brought performing artists to Ephrata, with concerts in the Lee Theater. Eventually, my dad served on the city council, and then served as mayor. Neither of my parents completed college, my mother went to a business school for a few months, and my father attended the University of Washington for two years before his money ran out. At 21, he was running a small mercantile and dry cleaning business, with two stores. By 23, after the beginning of the Depression, he was bankrupt. Despite his business background, he was a lifelong Roosevelt Democrat. My parents often joked that their votes cancelled each other. Education was important in the family, and each of the three kids graduated from college.

I attended the public schools in Ephrata, first Parkway Elementary, just a half block from our house (and I was frequently observed still polishing off the remains of my breakfast while walking into my classroom!). Then I attended junior and senior high school at the north end of the town. Early in the third grade, our teacher, Miss Storm, took the children to the town library. We were allowed to check out a single book. Mine was about a Dutch child who stuck his finger in the dike and held back the flood waters to save his town. It sounds pretty stale now, but it was a revelation, that a book could open up a new world to me. From that time on, I read voraciously. In the fourth grade, with crowded schools, my classroom was the Parkway School Library. I remember reading Raymond Ditmars *Snakes of the World*, and *Reptiles of the World*, which I discovered on the library shelves. By the end of the fourth grade I read books at an adult level. I read widely, but particularly enjoyed mystery novels for kids and science fiction. A notable aspect of my childhood, even fairly unusual in our town, was the absence of television in our household, until my senior year of high school. TV came to Spokane around 1950 and could be picked up in Ephrata with a high antenna, but my father refused to own a set for many years; TV was the single biggest threat to his movie business. However, in those days we had two movie houses owned by my dad, the Marjo (short for Mary and Johnny) and the premier Lee Theater, with two changes of double bills per week plus the Saturday afternoon kids' matinee—so I saw 4-5 movies every week.

I was not a great student, and was even a pest in junior high school. When I began to take studies more seriously, in high school, I did not excel. In my graduating class, and I am still friends with many of my classmates, I was a "B" student; some of my friends were quite bright and later attended some prestigious universities, including MIT, Yale, The Air Force Academy, and Cal Tech. I took the normal pre-college curriculum of Biology, Chemistry, Physics, a language (French), pre-college English, and pre-calculus mathematics. I had some notable teachers during that time. Mr. Bob McIntee was a well-trained and excellent chemistry instructor, and very enthusiastic about science. Mr. Bob Atkinson, who was also my basketball coach, taught world affairs and very carefully included a unit on Marxism (unusual during those times of McCarthyism). I had excellent English language instruction. My senior instructor, Miss Gerhardstein, was a literature Ph.D. candidate at the University of Washington. My writing was good enough for me to win the writing award for my class during graduation, but that was partly the result of the awards being spread around. Otherwise, Larry Reeker who finished Yale in three years and became a respected expert in artificial intelligence, would have one all of the awards.

An important activity for kids growing up in Ephrata (as in all towns in our region) was sports. I had some older neighbors who had excelled in high school sports, whom I idolized. My brother, three years older than I, was active in football, basketball and track, and I followed his footsteps in those sports. I was a bit over-weight in junior high school, and didn't begin to have much success until the 9th grade, when I grew several inches. At 6' 2 1/2" and 185 pounds, I was the tallest of the athletes at Ephrata High School—the Ephrata Tigers. I played end on offense and defense in football, center on the basketball team, and ran hurdles, 220 yard dash, and even competed in high jump for the track team. I played those sports for three years, and lettered my junior and senior years—was the captain on the football and basketball teams. I was very serious about sports, and from that participation I learned much about effort, focus, patience, endurance, and teamwork. These were qualities that later became important in graduate school and my career in scientific research. During that career I saw many colleagues, who I gauged as much brighter than I, fall by the wayside for lack of those qualities.

As all small towns in the region, Ephrata was a religious town, with far more churches than taverns, and lots of protestant denominations. The one family with Jewish cultural roots, the Agronoffs, eventually became Episcopalians. My family was not particularly religious, and we did not belong to any denomination when I was a young child. However, we shared a backyard boundary with a young

Lutheran Minister, Ray Pfleuger ("Pastor Ray"), and he frequently was invited for dinner. He established a congregation, and the church was constructed in our neighborhood, so our family became Lutherans (of the more progressive ALC variety). I was baptized in this church when I was about 10 years old, and was confirmed in the church at 13. I had many deep questions about death and the immensity of the universe (which was easy to imagine from the star-filled skies above our town), and got a little comfort from Christian devotion....for a while.

I had many experiences in nature, both near the town and further afield, growing up. As a child, I was active in the Scouts. In Boy Scouts, we had a great troop leader, who organized camping trips on the Columbia Plateau and in the Cascades. I have vivid memories of the places we visited. However, a new troop leader took over, insisted on treating us like little soldiers, and I quickly left. During the summers, many from my town went to the Lake Wenatchee YMCA Camp, deep in the Cascades and along the shore of Lake Wenatchee. I first was a camper for many years, and then helped out in the kitchen and as an assistant counselor as a young adolescent. My experiences at the camp, hiking and studying nature, deeply affected me. The YMCA movement had a religious/ethical program installed at these camps that combined Christianity and the native American reverence for nature. The programs involved accepting a challenge of behaving nobly and receiving a bandana (in colors denoting different stages) in a sacred ceremony. It had a profound effect on me, much more than learning the tenants of Lutheranism. My father was a very busy man, but he did take my older brother Jack and me on fishing trips, as up the Sanpoil River, and on a long trip up the Alaskan Highway to Fairbanks. We drove up on an old Dodge truck with a heavy canvas cover on the bed and side stakes—and three bunk beds. We came back with a booth of movie projection equipment he'd bought from the Air Force on auction. We stopped to sit in hot springs and fished for lake trout and grayling. I grew up a lot during that trip. We also took some family vacations, as to the Oregon coast and Glacier and Mt. Rainier National Parks, which exposed me to the beauty of those sublime landscapes.

I was part of a close group of friends, first as a child and then as an adolescent during the high school years. We talked about all sorts of topics, including the existence of evil, free will, time in the universe, utopias, and on. As we began to drive (a few owned old cars) we went on back packing trips into the High Cascades Mountains, to the west. Often, we'd hike up over a mountain pass to a high lake on Friday evenings, using carbide miners' lamps to light the way, and then return on Sunday afternoon. Occasionally the trips were a bit longer. The scenery was majestic, and inspired our conversations about the nature of the universe.

I worked summers in an aluminum fabricating business my father had started, manufacturing and installing commercial and storm windows and doors. I learned how to use many tools, including welding aluminum. This experience was invaluable in giving me some manual skills that were important to me later on in scientific research.

College Years

I graduated from Ephrata High School in spring of 1961. All of my friends were bent on attending college, and so was I. I had written a letter to the Chairperson of the Botany Department at Washington State University, asking questions about carnivorous plants. He had sent a long typewritten letter in reply, very impressive to me—and it was natural for me to be interested in attending Washington State. However, I had attended a senior open house weekend, and all of the students were drunk. It didn't seem like the place for me. In my junior year, I had been selected as a delegate to attend Boys State, which was held on the campus of Pacific Lutheran University, just south of Tacoma. I was leaning towards studying biology, and PLU had a good reputation in the sciences, so I decided to attend there. It was a good place for me, with small classes and a couple of inspiring teachers.

My freshman year I took Zoology I and II, taught by a parasitologist, Prof. Keith Strunk. This rigorous course (and I found the parasite life cycles fascinating) was the portal for the selection of pre-med students, and Prof. Strunk was their mentor. I received a high "A" and was invited to an interview with this iconic figure. When I told him that I was thinking about studying plants and certainly not medicine, a look of incredulity and disgust took over his face and the interview was cut short. I had excellent chemical background from high school and was invited to take an experimental general course, with Dr. William Giddings, a recent Harvard Ph.D., in which I spent much of my time devising experiments; it was a great entry into science and the scientific method. Most impressive among the biologists was Jens Knudsen, who was a zoologist with a love for nature and teaching, and a research program in marine invertebrates. The summer of my sophomore year, I attended a field course taught by Dr. Knudsen and his colleague Dr. Harold Leraas, a very kind elderly man, at Holden Village, high in the Cascades off of Lake Chelan. Holden Village was an old mining town converted into a Lutheran retreat site, on the edge of the Glacier Peak Wilderness and accessed by road from a remote landing on the lake. We had lectures, but spent much of our time hiking and camping in the high cascades, learning the plants and ecology as we travelled.

PLU was a liberal arts institution, and I benefited much from a variety of courses: British Empirical Philosophy with Curtis Huber and George Arbaugh, Asian History by Walter Schnackenberg, and American literature by Martin Hillger, among others. I retain an interest in these subjects to this day.

I did not return to school the fall of 1963. I was having some emotional problems; I was quite immature really, and decided to give myself some time for work and travel. This was also a time of religious yearning, not met by any experiences in Christianity, and I was reading theology: Bergson, Teilhard de Chardin, The Varieties of Religious Experience, and more. I found a job at the Weyerhaeuser Paper Mill in Longview, along the Columbia River and downstream from Portland. I found a room in a boarding house and hitch-hiked to my job at the mill. It was shift work, and I could make pretty good money during holidays with overtime. I saved most of my earnings, preparing for a trip to the South Pacific, mainly New Zealand. I wanted to visit places with great natural beauty, so this trip was definitely more attractive to me than studying in Europe, as several of my college friends did. I quit the mill in January, and boarded the S.S. Oronsay in Vancouver for an 18-day voyage to Auckland. We had layovers in San Francisco, Long

Beach, Honolulu, and Suva (Fiji Islands). Several of us took advantage of these stops to visit areas away from the port. Arriving in Auckland, New Zealand, I soon got on the road, hitch-hiking up and down the North Island, down the South Island, even to Stewart Island. I saw much of the great scenic beauty of this island nation, and also studied botany and zoology for one term at Victoria University of Wellington. I left in July, flying to the Fiji Islands and Society Islands, then Hawaii, on my way back to the U.S. In Fiji, I travelled up to a hill station on the largest island, Vita Levu, and ascended the highest peak, looking for the famous *Degeneria* tree (thought to be the most primitive angiosperm at the time). I didn't find it, but travelled through a magical cloud forest to the summit and enjoyed a Kava ceremony with some elders in a nearby village. After my return, a young British couple who were volunteering as foresters, invited me for tea. They said to me, "you can do what we're doing." They made a great impression on me, and I decided to become a botanist and study plants in different parts of the world, helping people along the way. I wasn't sure how one did this, but knew I had to study plants in earnest.

I had many opportunities to travel in mountain wilderness areas as a college student, both in New Zealand and in Washington State, and experiences during some of those sojourns were transformative. In July of 1962, I hiked up the Surprise Creek Trail in the Alpine Lakes Wilderness Area, and then joined the Pacific Crest trail to switch back up onto the ridge above Trap Lake. Just north of the trail on the ridge crest was a boggy area with low mounds of sphagnum moss amidst the subalpine setting and wildflowers. Time stopped, the vegetation began to glow with its own light, Glacier Peak beckoned to the north, and I was transformed. In April of 1964, I hitchhiked to the end of the road on the west coast of the South Island. Then I followed trails set up by surveyors (a highway now traverses the area) towards the road terminus to the south). It was late in the day. There were several trails and I got lost. Then it began to rain. And I became ecstatic; time stopped and the setting became luminous. Eventually, I found my way to the terminus and stayed the night in an abandoned house, and the memory of that experience stays with me now, just over a half a century later. These powerful experiences added to my motivation to study plants and do research in nature, a big part of the mix of motivations that led me to become a professional botanist.

So, I returned to study at PLU, finishing my science requirements and took the plant courses that were offered. I wanted to do a research project, and the physiology professor, Earl Gerheim, suggested that I start a project studying evolution by comparing the proteins of plants using immunological techniques, techniques he knew something about. I had been struck by the beauty of members of the heather family (Ericaceae) in my studies in the Cascades the previous year, and then saw other taxa in the family in the high mountains of New Zealand. I read about the geography of this widespread family and decided that I would study the evolution in this family using immunology of plant proteins. My approach was pretty crude, even by the standards at that time, but I worked entirely on my own (well, I got some help in injecting and bleeding rabbits!), conducted experiments and wrote up a report. I was given a key to the science building, so that I could use the equipment at any time of the day. In doing this research, I learned that it was conducted in a few other places, mainly in Europe, but notably in the laboratory of Prof. David Fairbrothers at Rutgers University, in New Jersey. I wrote to him, describing what I had been doing and asking some questions about methods. He quickly replied, answering the questions and suggesting that I look into the possibility of continuing this research as a graduate assistant in his laboratory.

Graduate Studies At Rutgers University

In January of 1966, David Fairbrothers met me at the plane in a driving snow storm in Newark, and took me home to spend my first days with him. Then I quickly settled in graduate student housing and started my graduate studies as his student. I was a teaching assistant in biology during my first semester, but was supported as a research assistant for most of my five years at Rutgers. I began to continue research on the seed proteins of members of the Ericaceae, but found it impossible to extract proteins from their tiny seeds, and I abandoned that project after eight months of hard work. I took advanced courses in immunology and biochemistry, plus plant systematics from David Fairbrothers.

I became friends with several very human and supportive professors, whether I had a course from them or not. Jim Gunckel instructed me in anatomy and microtechnique. Carl Price instructed in Physiology and Plant Biochemistry, Barbara Palser (who was a member of my graduate committee) in plant morphology and embryology, Charlotte Avers in cytogenetics and Ovid Shifriss (also a committee member) in the evolution of domesticated plants. I liked all of these courses, particularly because the instructors were active in research and expressed their enthusiasm in the material. I didn't take courses in ecology, but was surrounded by a very strong graduate ecology program. I knew Murray Buell, Jim Quinn, Paul Pearson, and hung out with a number of ecology graduate students. I attended the excellent ecology seminar series every week, and learned quite a bit about ecology through this exposure. Richard Forman, today acclaimed for his work in establishing landscape ecology as a legitimate field of study, arrived my second year of studies. I took bryology and lichenology from him, which involved a long field trip to West Virginia, and I helped with some of his field research on Mount Washington, in New Hampshire. A decade later we renewed our friendship when we both pursued our research interests in Montpellier, France.

Although the coursework was useful, I learned most from talking (and arguing) with my fellow graduate students, quite a diverse crew. Some new friends from my graduate immunology course took me under their wings to teach me something about urban life, classical music, and Jewish culture (of which I was totally ignorant). Much of our conversations were in labs and corridors rather late at night, In Nelson Laboratories. I met and became friends with Rod Sharp at this time. I also became friends with the Lutheran Chaplain and his wife, Warren and Joan Strickler, organizing a tutoring program for disadvantaged kids and attending organ and choral concerts of sacred music. It was a very interesting and stimulating period for me as a graduate student. Although my research involved local collecting and lots of laboratory work, I was able to take some time to travel to the tropics (Puerto Rico and Venezuela) and walked in tropical rainforests. These experiments helped sustain my interest in studying plants, counterbalancing the grind of long hours of laboratory research. My period of graduate studies was a time of great social upheaval in the United States, catalyzed by protests over the war in Indochina and civil rights issues in the U.S. Race issues had not been important to me while growing up, because I hardly knew any black students, other than a couple of athletes from the nearby town of Moses Lake during my high school years.

My graduate study years were important in my emotional maturation, and also in developing some social confidence in meeting and working with a variety of people, from diverse cultural backgrounds. I became aware of the gay and lesbian community, and my tolerance of different people and lifestyles was greatly expanded. I was active in the Graduate Student Association, playing in their basketball league, attending the weekly receptions (free beer) and editing the Graduate Student Guide.

I switched my research from the phylogeny of the Ericaceae to a masters project on hybridization and introgression in cat-tails (*Typha*), which expanded more broadly in the monocots, and to the study of the inheritance of isoenzymes for my Ph.D. In addition to the immunological techniques, I acquired other techniques of protein identification and purification, particularly polyacrylamide gel electrophoresis (PAGE as we now know it) and isoelectric focusing. I expanded my research to include the inheritance of seed proteins in castor beans, using varieties provided by Prof. Shifriss. The use of electrophoresis and the study of multiple forms of enzymes were very recent developments in biology, and our lab was on the forefront of this research. My dissertation committee consisted of David Fairbrothers, Barbara Palser, Oved Shifriss, and Nicolas Palczyuk (an immunologist).

My advisor, David Fairbrothers, was an excellent mentor. He was an accomplished scientist, a leader in the University, and led an active research program with several graduate students, undergraduates, and occasionally a senior faculty member visiting on sabbatical leave. Despite his busy schedule, he met regularly with us, and was available for personal advice when it was really needed. When I was finishing my dissertation, the University shut down over protests against the invasion of Cambodia. There was such turmoil that the completion of my Ph.D. seemed meaningless. When I talked to David about this he related to me an event in an all-university faculty meeting just held about the shutdown. A young faculty member stood up and declared to all present that he was fed up with the attitude of the administration and the stance of the University, and declared that he was resigning. Another even younger faculty member near him also declared that he, too, would resign. Later on, David learned that the first speaker had been denied tenure and was leaving anyway, but not the second speaker! The story was shared to encourage me to keep a balance and a vision for the longer run about things. He had suffered grave danger and privation during his service in Europe during World War II, particularly during the Battle of the Bulge. He didn't share any battle stories with us, and I only began hearing about his experiences during the last eight years, but those experiences gave him perspective and patience.

I received my Ph.D. in June of 1970, with my parents in attendance. I continued research that summer and then drove my old black '57 Chevy station wagon full of all of my possessions (mostly books and records) to Columbus, Ohio, to begin a post-doctoral fellowship at The Ohio State University.

The Ohio State University

My arrival in Columbus in September of 1970 coincided with a time of change at Ohio State. A College of Biological Sciences had been established, and the traditional departments as Botany and Zoology were being pushed to re-establish under more interdisciplinary lines within the College. Although I had received my graduate degrees in Botany, I had received an offer of an Ohio State University Post-doctoral Fellowship, to work under the supervision of Don Dougall, who was an Associate Dean in the newly formed College of Biological Sciences. Within days of my arrival I helped the lab move into a brand new life sciences building, devoted to research in cell biology and microbiology. My academic home was actually the Department of Microbiology. Don did research in plant tissue culture, looking at the biochemical clues to cell and tissue differentiation in the wild carrot system. He wanted someone with some background in protein chemistry to help him identify enzymes, particularly glutamine synthetase (which he believed existed in two different forms that responded to the growth regulator treatment that led to the formation of embryos). Rod Sharp, who collaborated with Don and shared a laboratory, had mentioned me and my training (my "tool kit"), and he was instrumental in my selection.

In biological research there has always been a little tension between "questions"—and hypothesis testing—and "techniques" (the tool kit part). The danger of focusing on the techniques was that I'd lose touch with the scientific reasons for conducting the research, and I was, at that time, a little critical of focusing on techniques. Yet, I was the beneficiary of practical learning of all sorts that boosted my scientific research, including carpentry and metal work. I didn't think about it too much at the time, but it was clear that the techniques I'd mastered gave me the post-doctoral opportunity I accepted, and not any basic research results I'd achieved.

My fellowship lasted one year, and Don moved on as Director of the Alton Jones Cell Science Center in Lake Placid, New York. I continued doing research a second year, and obtained support from various academic units, even the Institute of Polar Studies. I did research on the wild carrot system, looking at differences in isoenzymes, and helping Don with his glutamine synthetase research, but I did not enjoy the research and found the long hours in a windowless building to be oppressive. I could not envision myself spending the rest of my life doing such work. I did get involved in many side projects that were rewarding, such as creating multi-media programs for teaching basic biology, and I had a wide circle of friends. One of my childhood friends, Larry Reeker (the artificial intelligence guy) was a faculty member in the Computer Science Department. Through Larry, I made friends with several grad students and young faculty members. Tom Defanti, who later became an acknowledged expert for his work on internet-2 and virtual reality environments, shared an apartment during my second year. I also spent a lot of time with Rod Sharp, as well as Todd Stuessy. My time in Ohio helped me do some additional research beyond my dissertation, and provided the time to write manuscripts that led to the three articles that originated from my Ph.D. research. Ohio State was a very open and welcoming environment for me, and I developed friendships with people from many different academic backgrounds, which influenced my work and life later in my career.

To me, biology was a discipline particularly oriented towards visual information, and I felt that the visual aspects were particularly attractive to students, and supported better learning outcomes. Personally, that meant incorporating photography into my professional botanical interests, and I had begun taking pictures of plants as early as 1963. At Ohio State, I discovered the Teaching Resources Laboratory, which had the expertise and instrumentation to produce multi-media (movies, images, music, faculty voices—all on three screens) presentations for educational purposes. I created three such productions at Ohio State, in Microbiology, Polar Studies and Botany. The most impactful was the botany presentation "God Bless the Grass," which was used at the beginning and end of the new introductory botany course until the early 1990s. I presented at the annual Missouri Botanical Garden Fall Symposium in 1971, and I organized a multimedia symposium and workshop at the AIBS meetings in Minneapolis in 1972. Later on, I added presentations in my teaching at Florida International University, and this experience influenced my publication of visually-oriented books on plant color (*Nature's Palette*, Chicago, 2007) and leaves (Nature's Fabric, Chicago, 2017)

The most important event during my stay at Ohio State was meeting and ultimately marrying Carol Rotsinger. Carol was an art student, recently returned from a long trip to Europe and Asia and finishing her degree in Art Education. We met through mutual acquaintances in the Computer Science Department. We met and talked one evening in late March of 1972 at Bob Jones' house, and that brought us together; we married the following August in a remnant hardwood forest, The Gahanna Woods, on the edge of Columbus. I write this chapter after 45 years of marriage.

From the beginning, Carol and I shared a formless spiritual yearning, not Christian or denominational in any sense. For Carol it was supported by her experiences from travelling in the east, for me by my experiences in nature. We became interested in the teachings of G.I. Gurdjieff, who had come to the west to help people have an experience of the Self. We heard about these teachings from two childhood friends,

Allan Lindh and Curtis Amo. We began a correspondence with a leader based in Warwick, NY, where Curtis and his wife Laile had moved to participate in an intentional community, The Chardavogne Barn, under the leadership of Dr. Willem Nyland, a student of Gurdjieff's.

The University of Malaya

As a graduate student, I had corresponded with Benjamin Stone who was an American plant systematist working at the University of Malaya, in Kuala Lumpur. Ben was quite a remarkable man and was the world's expert on the classification and evolution of the Pandanaceae, a family of ecological and economic importance in Asia. I had needed seeds of members of this family for my immunological work, and he had helped me. He had also wondered if I might be interested in a faculty position in experimental taxonomy at the University of Malaya. This idea stayed with me and I begin to pursue this possibility as a post-doc. In 1972 I received an offer of a lectureship and tentatively accepted it. There was a long process of visa application that took time, and I was anxious about the reality of this actually happening as the wait stretched into months. I was attracted by the possibility of studying plants in the rainforests of tropical Asia, and also by the cultural and spiritual traditions of the east. The position at the University of Malaya was not only a work opportunity for me, but also a life for a newly married couple. We arrived in Kuala Lumpur in February of 1973.

When I went to the campus to begin my work I found a mixed faculty of European/ American expatriates, along with the Chinese, Malay and Indian Malaysian faculty. The Chinese were shocked and a little dismayed to see me, David Lee, of European descent; they were certain that a Lee would be Chinese-American. The Malays were quite pleased. It was a good faculty, the students were bright and hard-working and, at that time, represented the cultural diversity of the country. My teaching load was quite modest; I had a nice laboratory, and a young Chinese-Malaysian woman assigned to me as a laboratory assistant. We lived in university-subsidized housing a short distance from campus. My knowledge of the natural history of Malaysia was primarily derived from reading Alfred Russel Wallace's *The Malay Archipelago*, but I learned quickly from my colleagues and frequent field trips.

It was an interesting time in Malaysia. It was a new country, having split from Singapore a few years earlier. There were also racial tensions, primarily between Chinese and Malays, that had led to riots four years earlier. In the aftermath, there were sincere efforts of reaching out, particularly manifested during the cultural celebrations of the separate communities. We saw the seeds of Islamic fundamentalism taking root, particularly in the more rural east coast states, but the Islam of Malaysia in the 1970s was tolerant. There was a strong British influence in local institutions, befitting its colonial past. I understood the phrase "red-tape" (bureaucratic inefficiency) when I visited government offices and saw the shelves over-loaded with bundles paper.....all bound in pink or red fabric tape. I joined the Hash-House Harriers, an old running association. We met at regular intervals to follow a paper trace (with numerous false leads, and there's another phrase rooted in British tradition) through secondary forest, oil and rubber plantations, and scrub (belukar) eventually returning to our starting point, where a truck full of iced beer was awaiting. We inherited a dog, Pooch, who was an institution on the "Hash." Pooch was with us until shortly before we left Malaysia.

The shock of being in such a new place, foreign and yet quite westernized, far from family and friends, was hard on our new marriage, but we weathered the storm and had a really wonderful four years in Malaysia, with occasional trips to India, Indonesia (Java, Bali and Sumatra) and Thailand. Carol found enjoyable work in teaching printmaking to fine arts students at the Mara Institute of Technology (the MIT of Malaysia!). My mentors in learning about the biodiversity in Malaysian rainforests were Benjamin Stone (for plant diversity), Brian Lowry (phytochemical diversity) and Peter Ashton (of the University of Aberdeen and a frequent visitor, plant diversity and ecology). With frequent trips to rainforests in the mountains east of KL, I gradually became more familiar with the diversity and more comfortable in exploring the forests. Each year, faculty and the 20 or so B.S. Honors students would organize a research trip to a rainforest area to teach learn botany and ecology, and collect plants. These were also a valuable mechanism for me to learn about plants and natural history, by listening carefully to my colleague's discussions with students, as Engkik Soepadmo on plant diversity and Ratnasabapathy ("Ratna") on limnology.

Although I had been selected for the post because of my research expertise in cutting-edge techniques to address plant systematic problems, I became more and more interested in the general phenomena that I saw in the forest: (1) the physiognomy of understory plants adapted to very low light conditions; (2) the presence of iridescent blue plants in the understory; (3) the production of brilliant red young leaves; (4) the frequent presence of red undersurfaces of understory plants, (5) the presence of lectins in seeds of legumes, and much more. Gradually my interests turned from systematic botany (although I published a couple of systematic papers from work there) and moved in the direction of plant functional ecology. That meant learning more ecology (my experience at Rutgers among ecologists gave me a good start), and learning new techniques. Basically, my experiences in Malaysian rainforests gave me the research questions that I pursued for the rest of my scientific career.

After a year of living in KL, Carol and I decided to move to a rural valley south of the city, Ulu Langat. A couple of faculty friends lived there, and we learned about an empty schoolmaster's house (the "rumah guru besar") in Kampong Sungei Serai (the village of the lemon grass stream). I pursued its rental within the bureaucracy of the Ministry of Education and eventually persuaded them to rent the small house to us. We occupied it for about 6 months before the electricity was turned on. It was a great move. There was secondary rainforest behind our house and the protected forest of a drinking water catchment within walking distance. At the head of the valley there was an old British hydroelectric project that provided walking trails up to the points of water intake and into the hill forests and the highest mountain, Gunong Nuang, with moss forest at its summit. Near the head of the valley there were a couple of villages of orang asli, or aboriginal people. These were the Temoin, and they became important sources of information, as well as guides for more extensive trips into the forest. I set a goal of learning all of the walks to places of scenic beauty and of natural historic value in the valley, and our dog Pooch was an invaluable companion on those trips.

We became involved in various affairs in KL and the university. Carol's work in the arts led to contacts with local artists. I became a board member of the Malayan Nature Society, which is now the *Malaysian* Nature Society and the most important nature conservation and education organization in the country. I went on, and eventually led, nature walks in different areas near the city. Ben, who became a great friend and mentor, was in the process of establishing a new botanical garden, Rimba Ilmu, on the edge of the University of Malaya campus. I helped, particularly with the symposium held at its dedication. I was able to invite David and Marge Fairbrothers, and David gave a plenary address at the symposium; they had a wonderful visit.

At the beginning of my stay, I enrolled in an intensive Malay course offered by the same instructors who trained Peace Corps volunteers. There was a large contingent of volunteers, several became friends. Jack Putz, now a Professor at the University of Florida, was a volunteer working at the Forest Research Institute, and became a friend. My skill in Malay was adequate for me to travel comfortably in rural areas throughout Malaysia and Indonesia (it had been the market language for the region) to meet and greet local people and ask them about the plants they collected and used. We also learned phrases in Mandarin (spoken by the educated Malaysian Chinese) and Tamil (most of the local Indian residents had originated from South India); this helped us to function socially, although the students and educated older population spoke excellent British style English.

During our sojourn in Malaysia, the magnitude of the pressures of development and the environmental problems became clear to me, and my personal response was to help develop programs in environmental education. I wrote the first book on environmental problems in the region, *The Sinking Ark* (published by Heineman Books in 1980), and I wrote articles for general publications, as business magazines, etc. University-bound Malaysian students sat for a British style comprehensive exam, the scores for which determined whether they could gain entrance into a local university. Traditionally, the exam had included questions and tested on materials more appropriate for a British student than a Malaysian one (the exam was for the *Cambridge* Higher School Certificate). My colleague and neighbor, Norman Williams, and I wrote the first biology exam review to fully use Malaysian examples and thereby influenced the direction of curriculum development. I also received a grant from the Ford Foundation to produce filmstrips and slide sets on various topics to put more local examples in the science curriculum. On days away from the university in Ulu Langat, I began to explore the valley for specially attractive village settings (and the villages were settled by Malays from different parts of Indonesia, with different cuisines and arthitectures), attractive forest and streams, waterfalls, and routes towards Gunong Nuang. I had made contact with R.E. Holttum, a great British botanist who had worked in Malaysia, and I collected thelypterid ferns from various locations for which he was producing a taxonomic monograph. The results of my travels in the valley was the production of the first hiking guide written in Malaysia, and published in the Malaysian Naturalist in 1976: *Trips and Tracks in Ulu Langat*.

There was a rhythm of life in Malaysia that was initially frustrating to us, but eventually was very attractive. Things needed for research arrived with much delay, just like the visas that had frustrated our arrival. However, once those obstacles were accepted I was quite amazed by my productivity in completing projects and publishing research. My first letter in *Nature* was published in 1975 from research on an iridescent plant (and a second Nature letter was co-authored in 1977). We were blessed with some good friends, and I remain grateful for the friendship and knowledge of Ben Stone. Carol and I were also fascinated by the different sacred traditions in Malaysia, especially the Hindu and Buddhist ceremonies and the Sufi teachers, and they reinforced the sacredness of the nature I was privileged to study.

Ben Stone and David Fairbrothers shared a trait that eventually influenced me. I never heard either Ben or David speak badly of another person, no bad-mouthing or speaking behind the back. If they thought ill of someone, they remained silent. That silence, then, would speak volumes.

A number of eminent scientists visited us in Ulu Langat. Paul Richards, the author of the iconic *Tropical Rain forest*, was one. I had read this classic as a college student, and actually went up to Seattle to hear him lecture at the Forestry School of the University of Washington. I was gratified to see my work on understory plants covered and cited in his 2nd edition of 1996. Egbert Leigh also visited, as did Max von Balgooy, the Dutch plant anatomist. Francis Hallé, known for his work on tree architecture and the canopy research platform, *Le Radeau des Cimes*, stayed with us in Ulu Langat, and we became good friends.

My initial contract was for three years, and I asked for, and received, a one year extension. One important purpose of the expatriate faculty was to identify talented local students, train them, and help them obtain graduate training overseas—all so they could return and take over our jobs. In my last visit to Malaysia in 2005, to study the physiological function of blue iridescence in understory plants, I visited my old university (now the University Malaya) to meet an old student as the Dean of the Faculty of Science, and another as the Chair of the Institute of Biological Sciences. Former graduate students whom I knew had senior research positions at the Forest Research Institute of Malaysia, where I later did research on shade responses of tree seedlings with NSF support.

Thus, we made plans to leave at the beginning of September of 1976, and began a long odyssey back to the United States.

All told, I have lived and worked in tropical environments for some seven years, including living in Malaysia, the dozen or so 1-2 month trips for research throughout the tropics, along with two years of living in India. Our return to the U.S. took about eight months, all of this travel by someone who had lived in an isolated and rural town in eastern Washington State, and did not leave the northwest until that trip to the South Pacific at the age of 21 years. Well, that first trip certainly was a stimulus, and as a child I read voraciously about other parts of the world, devouring every issue of National Geographic. I also collected stamps, and enjoyed learning about the countries from where the stamps came, so that I could understand the importance of the images on the stamps. I mention this here, because the experiences were an inspiration for later research and writing. An important part of these travels has been meeting with scientists and visiting educational institutions, almost always giving seminars. I also became interested in the use of plants by local people, always visiting farms and local markets and learning of various products raised and collected by them. These observations (including color transparency photographs) were important for later teaching in introductory and economic botany, as well as tropical botany and ecology.

On our return voyage, we spent ten weeks in India, starting in the south and residing in the high foothills of the Himalayas, in Himachel Pradesh, for one month. We also spent some time in Delhi and in Rajasthan. We left India in early December on a Syrian Arab Airlines flight to Damascus (the cheapest ticket) and spent 10 days in Syria, before flying on to Greece. We expected to spend some time in Athens and then move along the southern coast of Europe. However, we did not anticipate the winter coldness in the Mediterranean region, so we decided to stay some time on Crete, in the middle of the Mediterranean—but it was quite chilly there, as well. From Crete we flew back to Athens, and then decided to travel across North Africa. We flew to Cairo and visited for a week before travelling south to Luxor, and then on to Aswan. We visited this venerable city during the street riots of 1977, the last to precede the revolution of 2011. We travelled south to avoid the winter temperatures, and Luxor was about right in January, with warm days to ride bikes to the Valley of Kings, and chilly evenings with star-filled skies. We travelled across North Africa through Tunisia and Algeria, with a longer stay in Fez, Morocco. We then ferried across the Straits of Gibralter to Spain, then France and Switzerland, to England, and then home on April 20, 1977. While in France, we visited Francis Hallé, and in the United Kingdom I visited Eric Holltum at Kew and gave a seminar there, and we travelled north to stay with Peter and Mary Ashton in Aberdeen.

We found the U.S. a different country from the one we left, more at peace and more tolerant. We had decided to accept an invitation by Francis Hallé to work and teach in his Tropical Botany Laboratory at the University of Montpellier II. In the interim, I practiced my high school and college French, and we travelled around the country for almost five months. We did this with care, as Carol was pregnant with our son Sylvan, but we had been gone well over four years and had family, relatives and friends with whom to renew ties. We also visited some local groups involved in Gurdjieff work as we continued those studies.

The University of Montpellier

I had been appointed a Maître de Conférence Associé (Visiting Professor) at the Institute Botanique, Université Montpellier II, for a year with a possible extension for a second year. My duties would be to assist Francis with the running of a post-graduate diploma program in tropical botany that attracted students from all over the world. This meant giving lectures in tropical botany, including illustrated talks on tropical plant families. We arrived in Montpellier on 24 September. Carol was now over 7 months pregnant, but our settling in was smoothed by the support of Francis and Odile Hallé and their four interesting and loving children. With their help, we bought an old Simca automobile (a baignoule!) and rented an apartment at the Chateau de la Mogère, just to the south of the city. It was a beautiful 18th century country estate (** in the Michelin Guide), once owned by the great French paleobotanist Gaston Saporta in the 19th century and with a formal garden. We actually lived in one of the outbuildings of the farm, a massive two story structure with ~2' thick stone walls (which made the place super cold during the winter). Francis quickly learned how bad my French was, so we both enrolled in intensive courses, Carol for survival and me to support more professional lecturing and interactions. I'm reminded of the extent of my learning from a visit to the rustic countryside outside of Montpellier where a local farmer asked if I were from Belgium; I later learned that the French found Belgian French to be crude and unacceptable! After I finished the French course, Francis told me that I could teach graduate and senior undergraduate students, but that the first and second year students would laugh at me. So, I limited myself to that group of students.

My old friends Richard and Barbara Forman from Rutgers days took their children to Montpellier for a year where Richard worked with Michel Godron of the CNRS Ecology Laboratory to write the first book on landscape ecology, thereby establishing a new field of investigation in ecology. They were particularly supportive after the birth of Sylvan on November 9th, as were Francis and Odile.

In late January 1977 Francis and I flew with the diploma students, and some other scientists, including Patrick Blanc, to Cayenne, French Guyana, for a month of tropical rainforest field research. During that time, we stayed at locations adjacent to, or within, tropical rainforest. A highlight was a flight to Saül, where we made a three day trip to Mt. Galbao, high enough to support montane forest. This was my first experience of forest of the Amazon region, and having Francis and other botanists well-acquainted with the vegetation enabled me to learn a lot of botany and take lots of photographs. I was also able to make observations on the physiognomy of plants, compared to my experience in Southeast Asia.

After our return from French Guyana, I was busy lecturing and helping students work on their short graduate theses. I became quite interested in the history of science, botany in particular, in this old university city. French professors took 2-3 hour afternoon breaks for lunch and a snooze. Since I usually rode a bike from La Mogère to the University, it was inconvenient for me to commute during lunch. So I'd have a quick lunch with the diploma students, and then explored the city and libraries for a couple of hours, looking for documentation of the importance of Montpellier (as locating the old homes—"hotels"—of Pierre Magnol, and other luminaries) and visiting libraries, particularly that of the University Medical School. Since the science of botany rose out of medicine in 15th century Europe, the Medical School library, adjacent to the institute and botanical garden, and near the cathedral, was a rich source of old botanical books and illuminated manuscripts. Montpellier had been an important center for the study of medicine and natural philosophy since the 12th century. Many great figures in botanical history (the Bauhin brothers, Clusius, Magnol, Rondelet, and others) had studied there as medical students. I photographed hundreds of illustrations from old botanical works and learned about them. At that time, I could request an old illuminated parchment manuscript of Hippocrates or Galen, have it brought to me, and could photograph it as I wished. I photographed hundreds of illustrations from these works and learned about them. This documentation assisted me in injecting history into my lectures on botany and biology in the next 30 years of university teaching.

I didn't do very much research in Montpellier. I did establish a collaboration with Charles Hébant for electron microscopic research, which we published in 1984, and wrote several manuscripts from late Malaysian research that were published in 1980 and after. However, it was a stimulating year for thinking and talking about tropical botany, with Francis, and many eminent figures in tropical botany. I first met Barry Tomlinson in Francis' lab, and proof-read the galleys for *Tropical Trees and Forests. An Architectural Analysis*, one of the seminal works in tropical botany in the past half-century.

By early June, the university term ended, and students and faculty dispersed. Francis and family went to their summer cottage on the Île de Groix, off the coast of Brittany. We visited them for a time, but mainly relaxed in Montpellier, staying in their vacant home. I made many bicycle trips to small villages with old Roman monuments and Romanesque churches. After a brief rest on the Mediterranean coast, we returned to The United States 22 September, 1978.

Warwick, New York

We moved to Warwick, New York, to join the Chardavogne Barn community to more intensively involve ourselves with the Work, as outlined by G.I. Gurdjieff. We had corresponded with a member of the community and had read extensively, and I had also written my old friend Curtis Amo. Curtis and Laile were there for us when we arrived, and we rented the house they left to move into another home they had purchased. Activities at the Barn included group meetings, service/work days, and movement classes. There were special days, as Gurdjieff's birthday, when many students came from New York City to the "wilds" of upstate Orange County. Warwick was a township, and included a fair amount of countryside (fields and forests) as well as several villages. We lived in an early 19th century farmhouse in the village of Amity. Shortly after our arrival, Carol became pregnant, and our daughter Katherine was born in July of 1979.

There was the question of making a living in this new place, and we were naively optimistic. I had decided to write articles for magazines and produce educational materials as a major supplement to our income. I also prepared a proposal for a trade book about tropical plants, and met some editors in New York City. There was some interest by Viking Press, but their market analysis discouraged any further discussion. Thus, I pursued a number of jobs, involving skilled manual labor, to make a living. Members of the "Barn" ran businesses (often cooperatively and with the intention of making that labor an extension of the Work). In Warwick Village there was a bookstore, craft gallery, and auto repair shop, all run by members of the Barn. The people at the Barn came from very diverse backgrounds, but generally were highly educated and with interests in the creative arts; we made several friendships. We helped in the community day care program, and I was a volunteer teacher in the community school, which taught children from kindergarten to grade six. So, I performed the following work: landscaping, carpentry and home building (my principal occupation), apple picking, and piano re-building and regulation. I looked around for some part-time teaching. I was hired to teach biology to nurses at Orange County Community College in Middletown for a semester. Then I was hired to teach general biology and environmental science courses at a new private community college campus run by Upsala College, in Sussex, New Jersey. Upsala was a Lutheran liberal arts college, much like Pacific Lutheran where I had studied as an undergraduate, and this new campus was hoped to breathe some life into a college that was shut down a few years later. Also, through the support of Iaian Prance, who was then the Vice-President for Research at the New York botanical Garden, I became an Honorary Research Associate, to help me keep my academic life alive.

We continued the spiritual work at the Barn, but it was clear that no one was truly knowledgeable of the teachings of Gurdjieff, as his student and the founder of the Barn, Dr. Nyland, had passed away two years earlier. On the 26th of August, 1979, just a few weeks after the birth of our daughter, the Lee family drove an hour north to South Fallsburg, on the edge of the Catskills, to meet the Indian meditation teacher, Swami Muktananda. We had seen posters about his visit in

Warwick. My first meeting with Baba, as we called him, changed my life. I began to meditate regularly, and had deep experiences of the truth that exists within each of us. It was revolutionary. Other members of the Barn were also visiting the Sri Muktananda Ashram, and having similar experiences. Eventually, we gradually pulled away from many of the activities of the Barn, and took on the discipline of meditation and the ancillary activities of chanting (to still the mind) and the study of various teachings in the Hindu spiritual tradition, such as the Upanishads and the Bhagavad Gita.

At about the same time we first encountered Baba Muktananda, Barry Tomlinson, an eminent Harvard Professor of tropical botany (who was a friend of Francis and a co-author of the book *Tropical Trees and Forests: An Architectural Analysis* and who I had met in Montpellier), told me about a job at a new university in Miami: Florida International University. These were the days before the internet, and it was difficult for me to learn about this place, other than it was a state university which had begun to instruct students in 1972. At any rate, with little expectation (and I had been applying to other schools, with little interest—mostly no response at all), I sent in an application. Sometime later, I received a response and, eventually, an invitation to come for an interview. Then I was offered a position. We accepted. I needed a job badly to properly support my family, and it seemed that I would be able to pursue the research interests that had been ignited in Malaysia in this strange place on the edge of the tropics. Thus, we continued our life in Warwick, with friends from the Barn, teaching, building houses, and visiting the Ashram—until it was time to move.

It is useful to review what I had learned in that I would take with me to this new life and professional position in Miami, at the age of thirty-eight years. I had developed a "spiritual" curiosity and yearning, deeply informed by experiences in nature and in eastern philosophy. I had accumulated a strong classical background in botany with familiarity of the physiology and biochemistry of plants (at FIU I would teach Plant Physiology and Tropical Botany, and help out in General Biology). I had a rich practical experience of the tropics, particularly the Asian tropics but with some field work in the new world tropics, as well. I had learned much by observing traditional cultures and their uses of plants (I would later use this in the courses of Introductory Botany and Economic Botany). I had moved my research from experimental systematics into functional ecology, although I still had much to learn about new techniques being developed to study the function of plants. I had also matured as a person, and that was a slow process. Coming from a good family, with the support of my parents, made a good start. I had learned about persistence and hard work through sports, and was fortunate to have some really good teachers in high school. I was aided by the support of mentors, as David Fairbrothers and other Rutgers faculty, by Benjamin Stone and Francis Halle. Mostly, I learned through my marriage to Carol and acknowledging the responsibility I had for nurturing the development of our two children. Although I had accepted the offer of a position at the Assistant Professor level, my experience was far beyond that.

I had been a member of one professional society throughout that time, and even today: the Botanical Society of America. David Fairbrothers strongly recommended such a commitment, and I joined in 1966—now 47 years! I also learned an invaluable lesson from an old neighbor and family friend, Paul Hamilton, from a hospital bed as he was dying of cancer. Paul had risen from running a hamburger restaurant in my home town of Ephrata to become the Secretary of the Department of Ecology for the State of Washington. He shared with me the secret of his success: work hard to make the institution a more effective and successful, but never take credit for any of the fruits of your labors—leaving that to your superiors, as they will take care of you, encourage and support you in your career.

Miami And Florida International University

We arrived, moved into a temporary home, and I arrived for work at a new university. I found Florida International University (FIU) a new, highly immature in good and bad ways, and very idealistic place. It had opened eight years previously with about 6000 students, the largest initial enrollment of any university in U.S. history, and was at about 11,000 students in 1980. The statistics were a bit misleading, because the number was a head count, and did not reveal that 80 % of the students were older and with jobs, and part-time enrollment. They were a lot of fun to teach; they were mostly older (mean student age of ~28) and serious about their studies. FIU was in the process of becoming a more main-stream university, with a four-year program (in 1980 it was taking community college transfers and had a few graduate programs in education and business) and a breadth of graduate programs. It had two campuses. The south, and principal, campus where I taught was on the site of an old municipal airport, and a smaller campus was located in the northeastern corner of the county, on Biscayne Bay—the site of a botched trade exposition. As a young university, there was an urgent need for faculty involvement in institution building. It was important for the university, students, and the ultimate success of faculty and faculty scholarship. There was also a need for institutional involvement in the community. Despite its glitz, Miami has always been a poor city, seen in low family income and the percentage of school-age children eligible for free meals. FIU as a public low-cost university was a needed addition, to the few private institutions, particularly the University of Miami.

The Department of Biological Sciences had an interesting mix of faculty members. Many had unusual records, with international experience similar to my own, and were mostly relatively early in their careers. However, not much research was happening, and there were no real opportunities for graduate study. The department was located in an interesting setting, on the edge of a very cosmopolitan and Latin city and surrounded by tropical marine and terrestrial ecosystems. So, the opportunities to study tropical plants were excellent. Furthermore, Miami was well-connected to countries throughout the neotropics, and there were lots of opportunities for research there, supported by the university's strongest academic program, The Latin and Caribbean Center (LACC).

In Miami, I renewed my friendship with Rod Sharp. He arranged my giving an invited talk at a national food science meeting (on exotic tropical fruits and vegetables), and enlisted me as a horticultural consultant in providing plant materials for the newly formed DNA Plant Technology, Inc. (DNAP).

My efforts at FIU were well divided into teaching, service, and scholarship. In retrospect, I believe that my most inspiring college and graduate school mentors led the way in showing that it wasn't just about research (and certainly the most efficient way to success and salary increases was to minimize teaching and service and focus on the success of research—visibility and outside funding). The two individuals who were the most influential were Jens Knudsen at PLU and David Fairbrothers at Rutgers. In my previous academic position at the University of Malaya, I had little impact on the institution, partly because I was an expat; my efforts went into research and teaching.

Teaching. I was hired to teach two courses that had been regularly taught by my single predecessor and were part of the regular curriculum: plant physiology and tropical botany. Plant Physiology was taught with laboratory, and most of the biology majors took it. It fulfilled the graduation requirement for (1) a plant course; (2) a physiology course; and (3) a lab. I quickly developed the reputation of being organized, fair and interesting (I was able to integrate my extensive experience into the course). This was also true for Tropical Botany, a course taken as an elective by biology majors and Environmental Studies majors. That course included lecture and laboratory, and the latter was primarily visiting local plant communities and learning about plants: their functional ecology, development, systematic relationships, and uses. In 1988, we hired a plant physiologist, Steve Oberbauer, and I stopped teaching that course. I had taught other courses, as plant morphology and economic botany, to later drop them as we hired faculty in those specialties. I taught a portion of the general biology course, for a special program for gifted high school students. In 1984, FIU was granted the ability to establish four year programs, and I began to teach in the general biology course for our own freshmen students. As the lower division program expanded, a need to add our offerings in first year non-major science courses was partly fulfilled by my offering of a non-major introductory botany course. I developed a style of teaching that was most effective for upper division students, but over time (particularly in the last 10 years of my work) I became more frustrated by my ability to reach the first-year general biology students; as the university grew, those students became more traditional, i.e. 18-19 years in age, fewer with jobs and supported by their parents. Our teaching loads were somewhat intermediate between a teaching college and a high level research university. It was more of a challenge to do research, but definitely doable.

The aftermath of hurricane Andrew in 1992 was a traumatic time for Miami and our family. Our home was seriously damaged during the storm, and it took four months of repairs before we could move back into our home. I was particularly struck by the damage to our urban landscapes and how emotionally affected we were by it. It was difficult to drive around with familiar tree landmarks lost. I contemplated the impact of these changes and came up with an idea for a totally new and inter-disciplinary course: "The Meaning of the Garden". The course was offered by the Liberal Studies Program, and I received students with all sorts of interests. The course met once a week, on Friday, and began with about two hours of physical work on various garden projects, including weeding and planting. The students then washed up, had a cold drink, and we re-assembled for a lecture/discussion section. The topics often were delivered by outside experts in landscape architecture, ethnobotany, horticultural therapy, art history, poetry, and more. I found that the physical work by the students together created friendships and broke down barriers that inhibited free discussion. I assigned writing projects, including an autobiographical essay on "my first garden experience" and a Haiku. The greatest student effort went into a project, and I worked with each student on defining what that project would be and how the student was connected to it. At our final class meeting, we created a reception like environment with excellent snacks (some of which were products of their projects) and the students gave presentations on their projects to everyone present. This is the only course I'd taught where several students told me that it had changed their lives. However, even today I occasionally run into former students who mentioned that my lectures on plants had made them interested in the environment or in gardening. In our non-major botany course, each laboratory section produced and maintained a garden plot on campus, and students could consume its products at the end of the spring term (gardening is a winter activity in Miami).

I reached out beyond the university by giving talks and making friends with groups interested in plants. I made a particular effort to connect to the large nursery and landscape nursery, mainly centered in the Redlands, an agricultural area south of Miami. I gave talks at their meetings and was able to obtain a book fund from them that added plant titles to our library collections. Early in my teaching career, I was involved in the training of science teachers in botany (many of them had learned human physiology and kinesiology, and were coaches) during the summer. This also helped to enhance my nine month salary a bit. I also took up carpentry jobs during summers for several years.

Service. On one hand, tenure-earning faculty members like me were not encouraged to take on too much service, but circumstances in the department demanded it. My first service assignment was as head of the Curriculum Committee. In that I also was a member of the College Committee. It was interesting to me to see how new courses were developed and approved, and then became part of the course descriptions of the State University System, and assigned a course number. Issues came up for courses of an interdisciplinary nature that required consultation with cognate departments. In time, I also served as member of the Faculty Senate.

When I arrived at FIU, there was no advanced degree program in the department. The amount of research improved steadily after my arrival (not just because of me, as a majority of the faculty was motivated to pursue research). We could produce M.S. students through a master's program run by the School of Technology, in "Environmental and Urban Systems". Then, we established a cooperative program with Florida Atlantic University. This was a sister member of the State University System, slightly older than us, and some 60 miles north, in Boca Raton. They had an M.S. program and allowed us to produce master's theses through them. This was onerous; theses were defended in Boca Raton, and also demeaning because our faculty was more energetic and research-minded than theirs. I became chair of our small graduate committee, and created and guided our proposal for an M.S. degree through the university. By 1984 we had received approval for our own independent M.S. degree. We had serious problems with a disruptive and abusive senior faculty member, which blew up over the treatment of a graduate student. I had to take care of this issue, which resulted in protection of the student and the transfer of the professor to the north campus, and he soon retired. Some of the elements of the M.S. program, as the core beginning course, Introduction to Biological Research, also became an important feature of our Ph.D. program. The size of our M.S. program, and the growing quality of students (as well as the need for graduate teaching assistants to serve our expanding undergraduate population) led to our development of a Ph.D. program. At first, it was to be a cooperative program between us, FAU and the University of Central Florida (UCF) in Orlando. However, a very strong external review mandated by the Board of Regents gave us the opportunity to push through an independent Ph.D. program in 1989; I also served on the Graduate Committee at that time.

I had been interested in environmental issues since my days as a graduate student, increased by what I learned in living and travelling overseas, and by my brief teaching position at Upsala College. FIU had offered B.A. and B.S. degrees in Environmental Studies since opening in 1972. Ironically, it was one of the oldest such programs in the country in one of its youngest universities. Its director and cheerleader was Jack Parker, and he was aided by the Environmental Council, a group of individuals with environmental interests in various departments, as Philosophy, Economics, Political Science and International Relations. I became a member and enjoyed the interactions with those people.

In addition to dealing with program issues, the Council had also supported the maintenance of the Environmental Preserve, since its establishment in 1978. I became particularly concerned with the Preserve, along with Jack, and had to defend/protect it from development on numerous occasions. I became good friends with Charlie Hennington, the Grounds Superintendent, from the beginning of my work at FIU. Charlie understood the value of the university landscape for teaching, and was always looking for opportunities to plant unusual natives and interesting tropical plants. I was asked by the Campus Architect to serve as the chairperson of a new committee, the Landscape Advisory Committee, which advised on the master planning process and on landscape plans for new building projects. That committee then became the first Environmental Committee, later banished by a vice-president, and then re-established. I had to stick my neck out on many an occasion to uphold environmental values on campus, and received a University Service Award in 1991 for my environmental work. In the late 1990s the Preserve was threatened again, and I organized a charrette for the proper development of the area, the first such design activity on campus involving faculty, staff, students and outside professionals. The results of that chrarette are still being used to guide development of that part of the campus.

I was asked by the Dean of the College of Arts and Sciences to lead a review of the Environmental studies program around 1993. The committee recommended that the program become a free-standing department, and the Dean concurred. In 1995, I became the first Chairperson of the new department, helping it to add faculty and eventually finding a physical home for it. I am reminded of the ground-breaking work David Fairbrothers was doing at that time, in preserving natural areas in New Jersey, and helping with the establishment of the Pinelands National Preserve. My service was tiny compared to that. I also remember that David was supportive of athletics, being a good personal friend of the football coach. I also became active in athletics, being appointed to the Athletic Council and serving for some time. Later, I became a vocal critic of the campaign to start a football team, and was a faculty leader in trying to reign in some abuses of the administration with regard to sports.

I also served as Chairperson of the Department of Biological Sciences for a year, not long before my retirement. That term was cut short when I took up another service responsibility as Director of the Kampong, of the National Tropical Botanical Garden, mainly based in Hawaii but with a garden in Miami, the historically important Kampong--the old home of the great plant explorer David Fairchild. I pushed for a close relationship with FIU, to give the garden more of an academic/scientific mission. As I write this, those plans are being realized.

I feel some satisfaction in serving a university that is so vital to the well-being of this area, with its problems and opportunities. Now, FIU is a university approaching 50,000 students, with professional schools of Law and Architecture, a full Engineering College and a new Medical School (which I helped as chairperson by serving on organizing committees).

Research.

After leaving Malaysia until arriving in Miami I was not able to engage in research. I did write up the rest of the papers from my four years in Malaysia, and they were published during my first year at FIU. I had a lot of motivation to get that research going, but there were obstacles. It was months before my lab was made available to me, and there was no startup funds for my position. Furthermore, it was clear to me that I would have to do the research myself; there was not a graduate program and students available. That became the case for most of my research in Miami, although some excellent students came through my lab towards the end. My mechanical skills were helpful as I renovated my laboratory by building my own furniture, and renovated an old spectrophotometer to make optical measurements of leaves. I received my first outside funding at FIU from the Whitehall Foundation in 1984. My research agenda was to study the functional ecology of tropical rainforest plants. I soon discovered that the tropical forests of south Florida were seasonally too dry for my research. I travelled to Costa Rica my first year at FIU and found ideal conditions at the La Selva Research Station, run by OTS. Later, I also visited the station at Barro Colorado Island, run by the Smithsonian Institution. These sites had good infrastructure, and it was possible to quickly learn about plants of interest to me, and the stations were a short flight from Miami. I wanted to document the light environments of these forests, to help me in my study of the adaptations of the plants, and I was able to purchase a new Li-Cor spectroradiometer through the support of FIU's Division of Sponsored Research.

An underlying theme in my research was beauty; I was attracted to phenomena and structures that were esthetically beautiful and emotionally attractive to me. Two phenomena I returned to again and again were the subject of blue iridescence (structural color) in tropical plants and the function of anthocyanic coloration in leaves. I collected leaf samples of iridescent plants from La Selva and analyzed them in Miami, and I found iridescent fruits from exotic trees in Miami to study. For studying anthocyanic leaves, I initially chose the production of anthocyanins during the development of leaves of mango and cacao. I also got interested in the leaf surfaces of understory plants, particularly the lens functions of convexly curved epidermal cells. The papers from this research began to appear in 1985.

When I first arrived at FIU, I was the only person in the department who studied plants. I made friends with scientists at Fairchild Tropical Botanic Garden, particularly Jack Fisher, but there was not much research collaboration. However, with the expansion of the department, and the university's recognition that tropical plants were a natural for research development, we added colleagues. The first was Jennifer Richards, a plant development specialist. Then we hired a plant physiologist, Steve Oberbauer, who was a physiological ecologist and was primarily studying in tropical rainforests at that time. We hired an ecologist, Suzanne Koptur, who worked on the interactions between insects and plants. Then we hired a plant biochemist, Kelsey Downum. These were colleagues and friends with whom I published papers. We hired several other plant specialists and formed a strong area of botanical research within the department. My approach in this was not to push to aggressively and selfishly for plant people, but partly to encourage candidates to apply for positions that were generally very broadly described. Kelsey's hiring was the result of plans to hire a biochemist. Probably, I promoted the hiring of more plant faculty through my own example.

My research on tropical rainforest light climates stimulated me to find means to duplicate the differences in the spectral quality between extreme shade and light flecks (with the spectral quality of sunlight). I was interested in the plasticity of plants, as well as the advantages of plants producing different kinds of leaves at different life history stages, what we call heteroblasty. In 1983, I developed a spray paint that could be applied to any transparent medium, as commercial greenhouse plastic, that would produce the spectral quality of rainforest shade. That could be contrasted with a normal black spray to distinguish between the two light signals of quantity and quality. I published those methods in 1985 and used them on several research projects. However, applying the spray was pretty cumbersome, requiring multiple light coats of spray paint. I eventually figured out that one pigment most crucial for altering spectral quality was purchased by companies that manufactured commercial energy films, i.e. the plastic films applied to automobile windows and windows of commercial buildings to reduce energy costs. Then I settled on a couple of film products from 3M and got them to supply me rolls of film for building walk-in shadehouses.

Back to Tropical Asia.

Our meditation teacher, Swami Muktananda, died in 1982, and he announced a brother and sister as his successors, and eventually that became the sister, Swami Chidvilasananda. We were able to visit them in the summers a bit in South Fallsburg, near our former home, but were attracted to the idea of living in the home ashram in India. Gurudev Siddha Peeth is a large ashram in the small village of Ganeshpuri, northeast of Mumbai. I applied for an Indo-American Fellowship, which would provide funds for travel and subsistence in India for a year. I received the fellowship, and made connections with two educational institutions, one with K.R. Patel at Bhavan's College in Mumbai, and with Kailash Paliwal at Madurai Kamaraj University, a new and very progressive research university in South India. We would be able to live in the ashram, and it had a small school for our children, and I would be able to conduct research in nearby forest and at an experimental farm run by a family that was connected to the ashram. Then I could occasionally travel to Mumbai, and less frequently but for a longer time, visit Kailash Paliwal in Madurai. We arrived in September of 1984 and departed at the end of July, 1985. I set up a forest plot for assessment of tree phenology and light measurements, an hour's walk north of the ashram and at the foot of a sacred mountain. I constructed shadehouses at the ASPEE farm, near the ashram, and studied the developmental plasticity of three vines. Those vines responded well to the treatments and resulted in a paper in the Journal of Tropical Ecology, as did the results of my forest measurements. It was an excellent year for my research, and also for our family staying in the ashram.

We travelled to Ganeshpuri for another year's stay in 1988-89. This was a year of sabbatical leave (one year at half salary). My service work in the ashram included frequent travel to collect sacred and medicinal plants to add to its gardens. So, I travelled to the northeast (Kalimpong), the south (Cochin and Madurai), and the west (southwest, Uttarkhand) looking for plants. I also received some funds from the American Philosophical Society to travel to Malaysia to establish some collaborators for research that would require submission to NSF for funding. During my trip to Malaysia, I formed a collaboration with the Seed Technology Laboratory at the Forest Research Institute of Malaysia (FRIM). I hadn't done much with them other than visit occasionally when I worked at the University of Malaya, but some former UM graduate students were on staff there, and S.K. Yap as head of the seed lab became my grant collaborator. Later on Marzalina Mansor took over. This was a logical connection, because I proposed to study the effects of light on the development of seedlings of tropical rainforest trees. We had a good year in India, in the ashram, but Carol had come down with the symptoms of what came to be called chronic fatigue and immune deficiency syndrome (CFIDS), and it took many years after our visit for the symptoms to largely disappear. We returned to Miami in early August of 1989.

We obtained funding from NSF to start the research at FRIM, in Malaysia, and I began to visit Malaysia most summers for approximately a month, starting in 1991 and lasting through 1998. This was a successful project, resulting in some solid publications. Its success was due, in part, to the skill of our research technician, Haris Mohamed., who was adept at constructions and electronics (such as installing and running the dataloggers and sensors). Its success led to the establishment of another NSF-funded project with Kailash Paliwal in Madurai; this project was not successful, but I continued to travel to India until 2000. In all of these research trips there were opportunities to visit natural areas of great interest and beauty, partly through visiting scientific colleagues and offering seminars. These tropical trips were typically 2-4 weeks, limited by me need to be home and help my wife recover her health, and help care for our children.

In 1999, I had the opportunity to join Francis Hallé on a canopy raft research expedition to a tropical rainforest site in Gabon. That was particularly valuable to me because it provided the opportunity to experience the third major tropical rainforest region and compare it to Central America and Asia. I have truly been blessed to be able to visit such beautiful places and study such remarkable plants. Kelsey Downum and I, with Francis, tested his hypothesis that secondary and biological active compounds will be more numerous and at higher concentrations in the leaves of target species in the forest canopy than in individuals in the understory. We completed that research and published the results in the Journal of Tropical Ecology

My last research trip to tropical Asia was in 2005, with support of a National Geographic Society travel grant. The primary purpose of this trip was to test a hypothesis on the function of blue leaf iridescent in these deep shade plants. This was a two month trip that included a short visit to Chiang Mai and a 10 day trip to Xishuangbanna and Lijiang, in southwest China. From this trip I discovered a novel mechanism of structural color production involving silica nanoparticles in an understory plant.

Red Leaves and Autumn Color.

From my initial interest in the function of anthocyanins in red developing leaves, and also in the undersurface of shade plants, I still continue a little research . The classical explanation had been protection against UV, but I showed that not to be the case for mango and cacao. However, the discovery of photoinhibition in photosynthesis suggested that these pigments could be photoprotective by reducing photoinhibition. Kevin Gould, then at the University of Auckland, proposed that he work with me on this problem during a sabbatical leave, in 1993. We published a short article in Nature in 1995 that generated some interest—but not to the level I'd hoped. It came to me that the phenomenon that could be studied and would create some interest in anthocyanin function in leaves is the autumn coloration in temperate deciduous forests, particularly in New England. I approached Missy Holbrook, now a professor at Harvard, about working on this problem. I received a Bullard Fellowship from Harvard to work at the Harvard Forest on autumn color. My initial stay was late summer through early winter in 1998, and I returned for a second stay in 2004. Our hypothesis was physiological, that anthocyanins are produced during senescence (producing the red color) to provide photoprotection against the destructive activity of light-activated reactive oxygen species, thereby reducing the amount of nitrogen resorbed by the plant for the next growing season. At the same time another group proposed a co-evolutionary hypothesis: that the color could warn potential herbivores and reduce the load of insect (aphid, in their case) eggs that could attack the tree the following year. We published a cover article in *Plant Physiology* with evidence in support of photoprotection, and also a data-rich general paper about color change in these forests. These ideas got a lot of exposure, including an article in the *New York Times* and other papers. The controversy over these two hypotheses continues today. Kevin and I also organized a symposium on "anthocyanin function in leaves" at the 2001 Botanical Society of America meetings in Albuquerque, and those papers were published as an issue ("Anthocyanins and Leaves: the function of anthocyanins") of *Advances in Botanical Research* in 2002

The Everglades. I began to work actively in the Everglades around 1996. I became part of a team of workers conducting a project mandated by the legal settlement between the National Park Service and various federal and state agencies. My role was to assess plant (as they say, "macrophyte") responses to dosages of phosphorus. I soon discovered a link between the responses of these plants to phosphorus, and the responses of my rainforest plants to shade: developmental plasticity. My final research project, in collaboration with Jenny Richards and still underway, is a study in the environmental plasticity of a common sedge, the spike rush.

Research in Perspective.

There are a number of themes that my research interests followed over the decades. First, I became interested in studying plants. I remember in high school that I took a vocational aptitude test. There were dozens of questions about likes and dislikes, and then you were matched up with a vocation or profession, based on those answers. An answer that came up: botanist. It seemed rather unlikely to me at that time, and I didn't really know how a botanist made a living. My interests in botany solidified in college, particularly after my trip to the South Pacific. None of my mentors in high school or college pointed me towards plants in particular. Certainly, my experiences in nature, surrounded by plants, influenced my choice, and my sacred personal experiences as well. As I moved into botanical research, my work was almost entirely laboratory- based, although I did collect plant specimens in nature. I struggled with the dichotomy between my working environment and my love for the natural world, and the resolution of this conflict was our moving to tropical Asia, where exploring for plants and studying them in natural environments became an important part of my research. From then on, studying plants in tropical forests required occasional travel to very beautiful places, and the plants themselves were of great beauty. Even the subjects that I studied were esthetically beautiful, iridescent colors in fruits and leaves, and red-purple leaves in development and senescence. I was certainly drawn to that.

I was also drawn to research projects that were beautiful and interesting, and not in any way because of their material importance, or value for human health. The closest I came to an application of economic value was in my study of blue leaves. In some species, the structural basis for iridescence was a periodic layering of the cellulose microfibrils in the cell wall, to produce the layers that were responsible for constructive interference in the blue wavelengths. Thus, controlling the layering of the cellulose could produce iridescence......artificially. I wrote a popular article on blue leaves for American Scientist in the 1990s. Afterwards, I received an email message from a scientist working at the National Institute of Standards and Technology (NIST), who mentioned to me that "mother nature has beaten us to the punch." I deduced that he was a paper technologist working on producing iridescence patterns that could make it very difficult to counterfeit paper for currency. I never heard anything more about that, and don't think that the technology was actually applied in that way. My graduate friend, Rod Sharp, worked in an area of high commercial potential, as

I did for a bit in Ohio. It was interesting basic research, and it also had potential applications. Having such a research agenda, interesting and with some potential applications, would've been beneficial in several ways. It would be possible to produce results that could directly benefit society, it could be interesting, and it might be easier to get financial support. However, it didn't work out that way for me.

I also chose research topics so that I could learn more about an area of knowledge. I started out studying plant systematic and evolution. Then I moved to the functional ecology of rainforest plants. I also began to do research on the responses of those plants to light, more in the area of photobiology, including the documentation of light climates and the effects on plants. I studied phytochemistry (made easy by my strong graduate background in plant biochemistry) and researched plant pigments and their function in leaves. Finally, I began to study the functional ecology of plants of the Everglades, particularly their response to light and water depth. This research was partly motivated by our shared concern for the future of this important ecosystem, but allowed me to transfer some knowledge and interests in the developmental ecology of rainforest plants to this new environment. These different projects allowed me to learn new things, not only in the experiments and observations, but also in the extensive literature research that is required to move into any new subject.

Studying plants in relatively undisturbed ecosystems in the tropics helped me become aware, fairly early in my career, of their fragility in the face of the increasing human population and growing impacts on these systems due to our exploitation of cheap energy resources. Much of my career, I have lived with an almost daily sense of grieving over the accelerating loss of nature, beautiful and sacred. That knowledge motivated my teaching, always including exposure to environmental issues in my botany courses, and solutions to those problems. This awareness was a strong motivation for me to write for a more broad public audience. This started in Malaysia with *The Sinking Ark*, along with articles in magazines. This continued in the United States. My last two books *Nature's Palette* and *Wayside Trees of Tropical Florida* both "preach" a bit about the intrinsic value of nature and the importance of conservation. My present book, about leaves, will have a similar message.

That environmental stewardship was taught to me by Jens Knudsen and David Fairbrothers. David had a great love for the natural areas of his native state of New Jersey. His later work on natural area preservation was an inspiration to me and, I am sure, to many other students. My writing has been influenced by their examples.

I never considered myself to be a brilliant person. I probably was better at mathematics than I thought. However, as a teenager I took math courses with some friends who did higher math at Cal Tech, Yale, and the Air Force Academy; I suffered in comparison with them. My high school friend, Jim Arnold, later commiserated with me that he was discouraged about taking higher math in college because of the same high school experience. He ended up as a philosophy major when he really wanted to pursue electrical engineering to fulfill his passion for radio communication. He later studied Indian philosophy and music, living in India for many years. There he began to work for the State Department, and gradually moved back into his love for radio communications, helping to set up communications networks for the distribution of foods in drought stricken regions, finally working for FAO. I certainly could've benefited from a stronger math background. My strengths in graduate school and as a working scientist were a strong work ethic (past summer work and sports), persistence and endurance, and an ability to focus on subjects or work for long periods of time. Those traits contributed to my relative success as an adult scientist. Although I've made a bit of a name for myself, as for work on iridescence in plants and in autumn leaf color, none of my research led to any "paradigm shifts." I was one of many people "mopping up after Darwin", as a colleague Doug Schemske once remarked.

I spent most of my career at a growing public university in a rather poor large city, to which the university contributed greatly. Considerable demands were made for teaching and serving to establish new programs. In such a setting, with no graduate student tradition, research productivity was bound to suffer. I learned to function without students, especially in comparison with more research-productive faculty who came along later. I published an average of about two articles per year (peer reviewed research publications or book chapters) during my career, my first paper published in 1969. By today's standards at FIU, and at larger more established universities, this is not a strong record. Yet, I enjoyed doing the research, it helped inform my teaching and my service, and a place like FIU probably was the best career choice for me. If I had been hired at a larger university with greater demands on the levels of external funding and in publishing in high impact journals, I might have been much less happy. At FIU, I also had greater opportunities to meet interesting colleagues with a range of interests, from science, history, philosophy, art and music. I learned much from those friendships.

I did not have a lot of graduate students during my career at FIU, six M.S. students and five Ph.D. students. I tried to treat them well, being available whenever I was needed but also trying to empower them to develop and test their own ideas. I was definitely influenced by the mentorship of David Fairbrothers as an example. I encouraged them to publish their results as quickly as possible, and generally did not co-author articles with them unless I was substantially involved in the research. In all cases, I spent substantial time helping each student to develop skills in science writing: concise and direct.

Winding Down

I write this short autobiography moving towards the age of 71, over three years past my retirement now. I completely stopped teaching, but visit the university a couple of times a week. I attend most of the departmental seminars, and other lectures as well. I am completing a couple of research projects, and writing papers with collaborators on research already completed: perhaps another four articles to finish my research career. I travel quite a bit, primarily to see family and friends, and plan make some longer trips now that my wife recently retired from her work at the USDA Agricultural Research Service—tropical Asia beckons. I am writing a book about leaves, intended for a general audience, to be published by the University of Chicago Press. This book is the culmination of decades of research on leaves, just as the successful book on plant color, *Nature's Palette* (Chicago, 2007), was. It is enjoyable to pull ideas together from history, philosophy and biology to weave a coherent story; I'm thinking the title might be "Nature's

Fabric". Partly based on my work at The Kampong, I am compiling an anthology of David Fairchild's writings, with commentaries. There may be another book or two, depending upon how I last. I'm enjoying gardening more, and spending time with our two children and grandson. We are thinking seriously about moving out of this large city to a smaller place, probably in the West. However, we are not in a hurry to move.

I've received two awards that recognize the achievements of this career, not a prolific one in a scientific sense. I received the Botanical Society of America's Bessey Award for contributions in education, in 2005, and I received The FIU Alumni Association Golden Torch Award as outstanding University Professor in 2007.

I've greatly appreciated the invitation by Rod Sharp to write this autobiographical chapter about my collaborative career, and I look forward to seeing what others have written. I have seen Rod's story, and also that of Julius Kreier, a person I remember affectionately from my days at Ohio State. I remember Julius once telling me: "You know, a disease is nothing but an ecological problem." Thinking about that, every disease manifests in an environmental context. Writing this chapter has evoked in me a deep sense of gratitude for the life I've lived (with a few regrets), blessed by family and friends, influenced by some important mentors, and privileged to immerse myself in the sacred nature of the world's diverse ecosystems. Contemplating this long life of pursuit of truth in nature and in my own life, I am reminded of what Albert Einstein wrote about his pursuit of truth:

I have never imputed to Nature a purpose or a goal, or anything that could be understood as anthropomorphic. What I see in Nature is a magnificent structure that can be comprehended only very imperfectly, and that must fill the thinking person with a feeling of humility.

UPPER LEFT: David at age seven, Blue Lake, WA, with sister Mary Ann and Mother Mary.

LOWER LEFT: David with mentor, David Fairbrothers, at dedication of Rimba Ilmu, Malaysia, in 1974.

RIGHT: David and Carol, in Salida Colorado, August 2016.

CHAPTER 4

Strength of International Collaboration in the Globalized World

Facilitating InterInstitutional Research and Teaching Programs

Raul Machado Neto
Provost for International Cooperation
Cofounder of the OSU/Rutgers/USP Tripartite Institute
University of Sao Paulo

I was born in 1949 in Piracicaba, in the State of São Paulo, Brazil, son of sweet and kind Helena Moreira Cesar Machado and Raul MS in Animal Science (1974–1977) at Escola Superior de Agricultura Luiz de Queiroz, the College of Machado Filho. My father was a traditional MD in our town and greatly influenced me with his attitude and scientific mind. In 1974 I married with the wise and generous Maria Luiza Barros Cavalcanti Machado and we have two admirable children, Carolina and José Eduardo. Carolina married special Rodrigo and now we have three wonderful grandchildren, Helena, João and Pedro. I am who I am today because of my family.

About Education:
BS in Agricultural Science (1970-1973) and Agriculture of Universidade de São Paulo, USP/ESALQ, Piracicaba, São Paulo, Brazil; PhD in Animal Physiology (1976-1980), University of Illinois at Urbana Campaign, USA. 1980; Postdoctoral Fellow at Agricultural and Food Research Council-AFRC, Institute for Animal Health, England, (1989-1990).

About Career:
Assistant Professor of Universidade de São Paulo/Escola Superior de Agricultura Luiz de Queiroz, USP/ESALQ USP/ESALQ (1974-1980); Doctor Assistant Professor (1980-1985); Associate Professor (1985); Full Professor (1997); Visiting Professor at University of Bristol and Unilever Research Center, England, 1982; Member of the Postgraduate Committee – Animal Science, ESALQ/USP, 1984-1989; Coordinator of Inter-American Bank of Development Program (IBD) for ESALQ/USP equipments, 1987-1989; Member of the University's Board Meeting, ESALQ/USP, 1989-2007; Head of the Zoology Department, ESALQ/USP, 1991-1996; Coordinator of the Electron Microscopy Research Support Nucleus (NAP/MEPA) of ESALQ/USP, 1991-1994; Member of the Coordination Committee for Specialized Institutes of USP, 1991-1994; President of Research Committee, ESALQ/USP, 1991-2007; Coordinator of CNPq Scholarships (PIBIC) for USP Undergraduate Research Students, 1995-2005; President of USP Undergraduate Research Program, 1995-2005; Assistant of Pro-Rectory of Research, USP, 1998-2005; Associate Provost for Research, 1995-2005; Coordinator of the USP Research Fund Committee, 1996-2005; Vice Dean of USP College of Agriculture – ESALQ, 2003-2007; President of USP Call Technology Academic Committee, 2005-2006; Visiting Distinguished Professor at Rutgers, 2007. Current Assistant of Pro-Rectory of USP Graduate College, Assistant of Research Pro-Rectory and Vice-President for USP International Relation Board.

About Honors and Professional Service:
Undergraduate Research Scholarship, FAPESP, 1972-1974; Research Scholarship from Coordination of Brazilian Postgraduate Programs (CAPES), USA, 1976-1980; Research Scholarship from British Council, England, 1983; Honored by the Undergraduate Students of College of Agriculture ESALQ/USP, 1985 and 1987; Research Fellow of CNPq, 1985-present; best paper presented at National Conference of Animal Science (XXIV SBZ), nominated to receive two prizes, from EMBRAPA and AGROCERES, 1987; elected by the undergraduate students for one of 10 best teachers of ESALQ, 1994; Scientific Merit Medal of State of São Paulo Governor, 2001; Reviewer for the Coordination of Brazilian Postgraduate Programs (CAPES), 1997-present; Reviewer for the Brazilian National Research Council (CNPq), 1988-present; Reviewer for the São Paulo State Research Foundation (FAPESP), 1988-present; Reviewer for the Government's Education Ministry's (MEC), 1996-present; Associate Coordinator of Executive Committee for the State of São Paulo Higher Education Project, 2005-2007; Member of National Committee for Undergraduate Research Program (CNPq), 2007-present; Coordinator and founder of the Tripartite PhD – International Graduate Program in Molecular Cell Biology–Plant Science, USP/OSU/Rutgers; Co-Coordinator for the Project FIPSE/CAPES, USP/UFRGS and Rutgers/OHIO State University, 2007-2010; currently coordinator of the agreement between USP-The Ohio State University; currently coordinator of the agreement between USP-Rutgers University, Member Special FAPESP Committee to evaluate grants, Member Special CNPq Committee to evaluate grants

About Undergraduate Research (Iniciação Científica/Science Initiation in Brazil) during my college days:
I began my research activity in 1971 as an undergraduate research student developing projects in the area of plant nematodes with Prof. Luiz Gonzaga E. Lordello. From 1972 to 1973, our project was supported by FAPESP, for which I qualified for a scholarship. During the

same period I developed research activities in the biochemistry area at CENA under the supervision of Prof. Otto Jesu Crocomo, a special adviser from whom I learned a lot. Another important contribution to my early days in science was Professor Henrique Vianna de Amorim, a man whose scientific entrepreneurship spirit I also admire.

In 1972 I met William Rod Sharp, a talented young professor from The Ohio State University, USA, who came to work with Prof. Crocomo. I was one of his monitors in the course "Application of Nuclear Energy in Plant Tissue Culture", an international course in the new area of tissue culture. The course was coordinated by Prof. Linda Caldas and Rod Sharp and supported by CNEN (National Nuclear Energy Commission) and The Organization of American States (OAS). Rod was a very special person and became my generous friend, my partner and my professor since then, for 40 years now.

About USP Undergraduate Research Program Under My Responsibility:

As the first President of USP Undergraduate Research Committee, my contributions included: organizing the USP symposium initiative and mobilizing and aggregating all our colleges in an event called SIICUSP. It became USP's most important undergraduate academic event with nearly five thousand presentations. Considering advisers and coauthors, this would involve more than twenty thousand USP participants. The result was an organized system of scholarship distribution/selection, and the creation of an identity for this activity at USP.

The internationalization of this activity started when Rod Sharp visited my office at ESALQ/USP and asked about two books, on my desk containing the abstract summaries for the undergraduate students participating in the USP Undergraduate Research Program (Science Initiation). I explained that the books contained the student research abstracts resulting from the undergraduate student's research projects to be presented in the forthcoming Undergraduate Research Symposium (SIICUSP). He was very impressed, and with his entrepreneurial and visionary spirit, asked if I could talk with his colleagues at Rutgers University about this initiative during my next visit. I accepted, suggesting this would be an opportunity to develop an exchange program of undergraduate research scholars from USP and Rutgers. We agreed and that is how we broadened the USP event expanded to a global event. Initially the event was called SICUSP, but it evolved to become SIICUSP in 2000, with an additional "I" in the acronym representing the internationalization of the event – Simpósio Internacional de Iniciacao Científica da USP (International Symposium of Undergraduate Research of USP.) Rutgers and OSU undergraduate scholars participate in SIICUSP during November and USP undergraduate research scholars participate in the Rutgers and OSU Undergraduate Research Scholar Symposia during May. OSU and Rutgers have both been successful in establishing five million dollar endowments in support of their symposia. The recent inclusion of other universities has resulted in further expansion of the initiative.

About the Electron Microscopy Nucleus at ESALQ:

In 1987 I was designated by the USP Rector Prof. José Goldenberg the coordinator of USP Inter-American Development Bank (IDB) for ESALQ-equipment financing. This grant was very important to the acquisition of state-of-the-art equipment for the USP research facilities, allowing us to perform world-class research. This initiative and the efforts of Prof. Goldenberg to upgrade the USP infrastructure significantly contributed to USP's reputation for global academic research and teaching. After two years of reviewing departmental requests for equipment purchases at ESALQ under my coordination, I proposed to all departments to abdicate the remaining individual grant requests to buy an electron microscope and create a center to serve the entire academic community. After personally communicating with and a long process of convincing each of the department heads, the remaining funds for two years of projects became available to buy the electron microscopy. The Rector, driven by higher academic spirit granted approval for two equipment purchases instead of one, and we acquired transmission and scanning electron microscopy equipment.

This center is called NAP/MEPA, Nucleo de Apoio a Pesquisa em Microscopia Eletronica Aplicada a Agricultura – (Research Nucleus on Electron Microscopy Applied to Agriculture Research). Prof. Elliot Watanabe Kitajima, whom we hired, after a complex negotiation, from the University of Brasília, played a fundamental role in the organization and functioning of the Center. Under his coordination, the center dramatically enhanced research analytical capacity, becoming one of the most active centers in this area in the country. I have to highlight the relevant support of Prof. João Lúcio de Azevedo, dean of ESALQ at the time.

About the Tripartite PhD Program on Plant Molecular and Cell Biology:

In 1996, Rod Sharp and I, as Director Rutgers University Experimental Station and USP Associate Provost for Research, respectively, decided to involve our two institutions in biotechnology, a very hot topic at the time. We decided to organize a workshop of large dimensions at ESALQ in the area, along with other institutions of the US and Europe. The two-week event took place in December 1997. We dedicated an exhibit hall to accommodate booths and poster for the display of laboratories research information of both institutions. In an additional section with representatives of all participating institutions, we did a reflection about the future of academic relations. The event was a great success and this initiative continues today with the addition of our The Ohio State University partner. Since the first event, the workshop has been conducted on a biannual basis alternating between institutions: 1º Workshop – 1997 USP/ESALQ; 2º Workshop – 2001 Rutgers; 3º Workshop – 2003 USP/ESALQ; 4º Workshop – 2004 Ohio State University; 5º Workshop – 2007 Rutgers; 6º Workshop – 2009 USP, 7º Workshop – 2012 The Ohio State University – 8th Workshop 2014 Rutgers and 9th Workshop 2016 USP/ESALQ.

In 2004, we organized a brainstorming conference to explore additional synergies between the institutions beyond workshops and undergraduate research scholar exchanges. To accommodate research faculty and administrator leadership schedules, of the three universities we met at the VIP American Airlines lounge at Newark International Airport (a creative idea arranged by Rod). It was the first time I had to go through airport security checkpoint to attend a meeting. After a long lunch discussion, I proposed that we do something quite different: create a tripartite graduate program, making use of the competence already shared in research initiatives by the three institutions. Thus, Rod and I began a long endeavor, still a work in progress, to create a unique joint PhD program.

The three research institutions formally agreed during September 2004 to develop a tripartite Ph.D. Graduate Program, initially in Plant Biology and Plant Biotechnology. During the 2007 Tripartite Workshop, the institutions reported plans for execution of the Ph.D. Graduate program, which is expected to expand in the future to encompass additional disciplines. The program is designed to provide adjunct faculty status appointments for faculty members in their respective graduate programs and the joint mentoring of graduate students. The mobility of students and faculties is an important program characteristic, creating a real and complete international academic environment. The program provides graduate students the opportunity to conduct research at USP, Rutgers and The Ohio State University. Participating graduate students have the opportunity to qualify for a Ph.D. degree from two or three of the partner institutions. Students enrolled in the program are expected to demonstrate language proficiency in both English and Portuguese. Faculties in tie humanities and linguistics departments of the three institutions have been engaged in the preparation of new language and culture courses, resulting in yet another academic collaboration. The program comprises national and international course modules, embracing the campuses of USP, Rutgers and OSU. Students are required to take basic courses at their home institution during the first year of the program. Only students who complete the national module are allowed to enroll in the international module.

The remarkable synergism and commitment of faculty and administrative leadership from these three institutions allowed the accommodation of undergraduate research scholars. In 2006 Rutgers, Ohio State, USP and UFRGS received grant awards from CAPES and FIPSE for a four-year exchange of undergraduate research scholars in plant biology and microbiology for one semester of academic studies, an internship and cultural immersion. The program is expected to provide a pipeline into the Tripartite Graduate Program.

Related to the "tripartite" initiative, Rod and I are pleased to acknowledge the great effort and competent support of the following professors from the three institutions: Helaine Carrer, Marcio Castro Filho, Ricardo Azevedo, Michael Lawton, Eric Lam, Gerben Zylstra, Jerry Kukor, Bob Tabita, Erich Grotewold, Andrea Dosself and Pat Osmer.

Today, the Brazilian end of the program is coordinated by the dedicated and enthusiastic Helaine Carrer, a key person who has worked with us from the beginning. The program has been approved by CAPES, Brazil's federal agency that regulates graduate programs, as the first in the country with an international characteristic. Because the program is a reference point of the national academic scenario, I have been regularly invited by CAPES president, Prof. Jorge Guimarães to attend meetings to discuss the program with other research institutions. Prof. Guimarães has enthusiastically supported the initiative and highlights the tripartite proposal as a template for new initiatives at other institutions. We are currently working on some specific and final adjustments required by the US. The program has enrolled seven students that are finishing the national module and starting the international module.

The magnitude of the collaboration between these three institutions is due to the academic excellence, institutional respect, and commitment by the respective administrations and faculties. The qualifications of these institutions and the shared expertise of their researchers was the motivation to do something more. This international synergism allowed the creation of an outstanding program of human resource training at the PhD level in a truly international academic environment. Looking at the future, the USP global collaborative degree granting approach provides an opportunity to integrate the recent Massive Open Online Courses (MOOCs) initiative.

About Other Areas of Internationalization:
As vice-dean of ESALQ, working with dean Parra, my competent friend of many years, I had great support in implementing several initiatives that contribute to the consolidation of the internationalizationat ESALQ. Contributions from these international collaborations include establishment of the first double degrees in ESALQ, with the French Agriculture College, ParisTech, and with group FESIA, headquartered in Toulouse. Prof. Maria Lucia Carneiro, with her dedicated competence, has been instrumental in coordinating this initiative with French institutions. I also had the opportunity to take part in the process of establishing Wageningen University representation in the ESALQ, the first initiative of its kind in our campus.

As a result of our collaborative relationships with Rutgers University and Ohio State University, we have been able to enhance our partnership to include chemistry, mathematics and humanities. In the area of bioenergy and biomass research, we are working to organize an Inter-American consortium including Rutgers University, The Ohio State University, Michigan State University, the University of Wisconsin and the University of Georgia, that will deal with mega-research projects for alternative energy.

With the recent increased visibility of USP resulting from increased improvement of our academic indices, we have been sought after by a large number of qualified institutions. In 2012, working with Prof. Marco Antonio Zago, USP provost for Research, we established, among several others, two very special new strategic partnerships with the University of Toronto and Princeton University. We have two main areas of mutual interest with Toronto, medical science and study of cities, and with Princeton, global health and anthropology. The process of establishing the partnership, was very enriching, resulting in friendships with the two presidents, David Naylor, from the University of Toronto and Shirley M. Tilghman, from Princeton University. It is worth noting that these two universities have very few international agreements. At Princeton, the partnership with USP is the only formal existing international agreement.

As professor of animal physiology, in my research activity, I have had several outstanding students, but three of them were very special,

Rosana Bessi, Patricia Pauleti and Débora Moretti, not just as advisees, they become my partners and colleagues who shared with me the responsibilities in achieving the goals of my lab. The students are thanked for their intellect and continuous stimulation which is so important to the academy's teaching and research endeavors.

Finally, I have been privileged during life trajectory, to meet and share experiences with very special people of almost fifty years, Paulo Botelho, Osny Bacchi, wistful Raul d'Arce, Parra and Rod Sharp, all of them related to agriculture research and teaching.

At USP, we continue to pursue "consolidation of a world class international academic environment, where excellence prevails over borders".

CHAPTER 5

Lifetimes of Collaboration

Sally A. Miller,
Professor Vegetable Pathology, Diagnostics and International Development, ORADC, The Ohio State University and

Donald J. (Chip) Styer II
Resource Planning Analyst, ORADC,
The Ohio State University

Taken broadly, the term collaboration encompasses many of the activities of daily life. Working together to develop or create something new applies to building a family as much as to creating a product or process. Many people, especially those of us from large families, learned at an early age that cooperating with siblings was usually more effective in achieving a desired outcome than going it alone. Children are taught from early grades in school to work in teams to complete assignments; and from these experiences students emerge in different roles, from the natural leaders, to the deep thinkers, to the task-oriented worker bees, to those who really don't have much interest in the subject and would rather be somewhere else. With few exceptions, particularly in science, being part of the workforce means developing and maintaining collaborations, preferably with clearly defined goals and responsibilities. Working in a silo is no longer feasible for most scientific disciplines, particularly the biological sciences. The challenge is in overcoming the barriers to cooperation and communication, and learning to value the contributions of others with different personality types, work styles and expertise within and outside one's own discipline. This is not always easy for scientists, many of whom are introverts and draw energy from within themselves – for deep introverts, working closely with others may be very difficult. Extroverts, who draw their energy from others, may lose patience with those around them whose personalities don't easily mesh with their own. Despite these and many other challenges, true collaborations are common and necessary in science and in life.

It has been at least a few generations in our and numerous other cultures since all of the major family decisions were made by one person – usually a man – from where to live and work to how to handle the family finances. In successful families, these decisions are made in a collaborative process within the family unit, whatever that may be. We met in 1972 as undergraduates at The Ohio State University, and our first major decision as a couple was to find educational opportunities and, later-on jobs that would allow us to live in the same city. As undergraduates, we studied in similar disciplines and collaborated informally on our Honors thesis projects under Professor Rod Sharp's guidance. Our coursework focused on plant science and microbiology, and we made the decision, with Rod's encouragement and after much discussion, to apply to graduate school in plant pathology, a field that combines these two disciplines that we both found so interesting. We were accepted into and eventually earned Ph.D. degrees in this field at the University of Wisconsin-Madison (UW-M). We chose to join DNA Plant Technology Corporation (DNAP) in Cinnaminson, NJ, at Rod's invitation in 1982, where we remained until moving back to Ohio in 1991. Miller accepted an assistant professorship at OSU in the Department of Plant Pathology at the Ohio Agricultural Research and Development Center (OARDC) in Wooster, and Styer joined the OARDC as a data management specialist after several years of working in information technology (IT) in Wooster.

The UW-M Department of Plant Pathology was highly ranked within the discipline, and in the 1970s included two members of the

National Academy of Sciences, Professors Luis Sequeira and Arthur Kelman. The atmosphere was vibrant and collegial, with many leading-edge research labs, active Extension programs, and a graduate student cohort of 50, including for the first time a substantial number of women. Miller's advisor, Professor Doug Maxwell, was just transitioning his lab away from fungal physiology and into work on *Phytophthora* diseases of field crops when she arrived in 1976. Her research focused on "host" and "non-host" interactions of alfalfa with *Phytophthora megasperma* formae speciales from alfalfa and soybean, respectively. These formae speciales have now been elevated to species and renamed *P. medicaginis* and *P. sojae*. She spent countless hours at the light microscope, microtome and transmission electron microscope examining the process of colonization or attempted colonization of alfalfa seedlings by these pathogens (*Can. J. Bot.* 62:109-116). She also documented specific physiological changes associated with these interactions at the cellular level (*Can. J. Bot.* 62:117- 128). Miller and Professor Maxwell collaborated with Dr. Leen Davidse, a visiting scientist from Wageningen University, to identify the comparative biochemical changes occurring in alfalfa challenged with *P. medicaginis* and *P. sojae*, and focused on analysis of phytoalexin production, using an alfalfa tissue culture system (*Phytopathology* 74:345-348). Styer joined the lab of Dr. Rick Durbin, one of several USDA Agricultural Research Service (ARS) scientists embedded in the Plant Pathology Department. Dr. Durbin worked in the area of microbial toxin characterization and mode of action, and Styer chose a project on *Pseudomonas syringae* pv. *tagetis*, a pathogen of marigold, sunflower, ragweed and other plants (*Plant Dis*ease 64:101-2; 66:71; 66:601; *HortSci* 16:768-9). This pathogen produced tagetitoxin, a toxin that caused a striking apical chlorosis of infected plants. During his graduate program Styer collaborated with a team from the labs of Dr. John Helgeson and Dr. Durbin to develop a simple, rapid process to isolate protoplasts from unsterilized leaves (*Plant Science Letters* 18:151-154).

While our opportunities for scientific collaboration were somewhat limited in undergraduate and graduate school, our educational and social experiences helped to prepare us for our first positions in the private sector where collaboration skills are critically important, whether in service aspects or product development. Styer initially worked in plant tissue culture, developing bioreactor systems for development of somatic embryos in tomato, carrot, coffee and other crops. With the advent of personal computers and data management software in the mid-1980s, he moved into data analytics, then in its infancy. He designed and installed a data acquisition system from Hewlett Packard that captured and analyzed the raw digital data from lab instruments, in this case primarily gas chromatographs. This automation increased the number of samples that could be analyzed by ten-fold, and flipped the analytical lab from a cost center to a revenue source. Styer recognized that data analytics would become a foundation of the digital world, and left DNAP in 1990 to pursue consulting in this burgeoning new field.

After consulting with numerous companies large and small, and a stint in computer sales, Styer joined OSU in 1999 to utilize data analytics tools to make sense of reams of financial, operational and human resource data in OARDC. In a time of almost continuous budget cuts from state and federal sources, it became clear that universities had to be able to document their impact to stakeholders. It became necessary to collect faculty activity information in a digital format, and in a consistent, organized way from multiple departments and other entities. Only four months after purchasing the Accountability, Information and Communication System (ACIS) application from Washington State University, and after making some OSU-specific customizations, OARDC and our College (Food, Agricultural and Environmental Sciences; CFAES), launched our version of the application, the Unified Reporting System (URS) in January 2001. Many of the faculty members, especially from departments that had not taken annual reporting seriously in the past, did not like the new system, to say the least. Styer worked with the diverse faculty and departments in CFAES to gain acceptance and adoption of this system. Over the next several years many design and infrastructure upgrades were made to improve performance and address user requirements. Styer then analyzed the data submitted by the faculty and presented it in a form that was usable by the administration. For the first time in the College, a centralized data source that documented the depth and breadth of faculty activities and their impacts was available. One of the biggest advantages of the URS was that administrators could efficiently mine the data on faculty research and impacts, without the direct involvement of the faculty member or the department chair. While CFAES was using the URS, the OSU Medical School started an independent development project of a similar reporting system, called OSU:Pro, geared towards the needs of the medical faculty. OSU:Pro had many advantages over the URS, including direct links to other internal OSU databases that streamlined some data entry. However, the new and improved user interface caused headaches for many faculty members as they were required to switch reporting systems when the university adopted OSU:Pro university-wide in 2009. The one component that OSU:Pro was missing was a module to track activities of CFAES Extension faculty and staff. The CFAES team had built an Extension module for the URS, so Styer collaborated with the OSU:Pro development team to duplicate this module in OSU:Pro. Eventually most faculty members became proficient at using OSU:Pro, only to see it replaced by the Thomson Reuters "Research In View" application a couple of years later. Research in View unfortunately was also short-lived, and a new system is currently being launched. Styer continues to assist OARDC and CFAES in reaching acceptable middle ground between the data needs of administration and reporting burdens on the faculty.

Miller was privileged to work with Rod Sharp, beginning in 1983, to start a spin-off company that would focus on developing and marketing diagnostic tools for plant diseases and other uses. The technology for producing monoclonal antibodies had only recently been introduced into the mainstream, and made rapid detection of relatively complex microorganisms like fungi and bacteria feasible. Until then, use of serological tests in plant-based agriculture had been almost exclusively limited to virus detection. Rod chose to start with products to detect fungal pathogens of turfgrass, focusing on the golf course industry. The idea was to tie fungicide use to accurate diagnostics, removing the guesswork for the golf course superintendent and at the same time eliminating incorrect or unnecessary applications of these pesticides. Rod secured the funding and pulled together a technical team that included Dr. Dave Grothaus, an OSU grad and microbiologist, Dr. Frank Petersen, an expert in monoclonal antibody/hybridoma development, and Dr. Jim Rittenburg, who was very clever with the platform side of serological diagnostics. Miller's role was on the plant pathogen side, and she participated in many stages of product development, from marketing to applications testing, quality control and tech sheet preparation. This was Miller's first real opportunity to work in diverse teams composed of individuals who did not always share the same vision but in the end came up with some truly exciting products. The company was called Agri-Diagnostics Associates (ADA), and during its time it was at the cutting edge of plant disease diagnostics. ADA developed the forerunner of today's rather ubiquitous Lateral Flow Device (LFD).

The product, called "Reveal", was a "flow-through" assay that for the first time allowed pathogen diagnostics in the field in a short time (less than 10 minutes). The test could be done in a golf course superintendent's office or even out on the course. ADA soon also branched out into other pathogens and crops, and in collaboration with Ciba-Geigy (now Syngenta Crop Protection) developed the "Alert" product line that included both the flow-through technology and lab-based 96-well enzyme-linked immunoassay (ELISA) formats. Ciba-Geigy commissioned these assays to promote the proper use of its fungicides against *Phytophthora* on soybean and other crops, *Septoria* diseases (now *Parastagonospora nodorum* and *Septoria tritici*) of wheat, and *Mycosphaerella fijiensis* (black Sigatoka) of banana. Although ADA did not continue after the mid-1990s, the monoclonal antibody against *Phytophthora* that ADA developed was incorporated by others into a lateral flow device to screen woody plants imported into the UK for *Phytophthora ramorum*. This destructive oomycete causes sudden death of oaks and other trees and woody ornamental plants, and cannot be treated effectively with fungicides; therefore exclusion is the most important preventative measure. In the UK, the *Phytophthtora* LFD test was carried out at import inspection stations, and positive-testing samples were sent to specialized labs for confirmation. This proved to be highly effective in preventing the pathogen from entering the UK.

None of ADA's diagnostic products could have been developed and marketed without the close collaboration of scientists with different disciplinary expertise (serology/immunology, biochemistry, pathology/microbiology), marketing and sales specialists to move the products to the public, and researchers outside ADA who evaluated the products and helped develop applications. Since in-field diagnostics were very new to plant pathology in the 1980s, beginning in 1988 Miller conducted a National Workshop on Rapid Diagnostic Assays for Plant Pathogens during the annual meeting of the American Phytopathological Society (APS). Its purpose was to acquaint professional plant pathologists and other scientists with modern techniques for pathogen detection and disease diagnosis. She met hundreds of plant pathologists during the 10 years that these workshops were conducted, providing untold networking opportunities that contributed not only to product development but also to her entire career. Developing applications for the diagnostic tests also allowed Miller to travel widely in the US and internationally. She met and worked with excellent plant pathologists like Professors John Menge and Jim MacDonald at the University of California, Pete Timmer at the University of Florida, Bruce Clarke at Rutgers University, Fritz Schmitthenner and Mike Ellis at OSU, and Alex Csinos at the University of Georgia. In Europe, she worked with Ciba-Geigy scientists Drs. Ludwig Mittermeier and Wilhelm Dercks. Their enthusiasm for this technology was infectious – they were all excited about the chance to apply these diagnostics to real-life problems in agriculture. The lessons in collaboration and networking that Miller learned in the early days of ADA were never forgotten and were the basis for numerous collaborative programs later in her career.

Miller began working at OSU on July 1, 1991 as an Assistant Professor of Plant Pathology, with responsibilities split between Extension, research and teaching, and focused on vegetable crops. This position specifically required translational research on the management of bacterial and other diseases of vegetable crops. As she had never worked with bacterial phytopathogens, or with vegetables, the learning curve was initially very steep. However, the skills in collaboration and networking that she learned in the private sector were put to good use as she developed her research program. Her first significant federally funded project was developed and conducted in collaboration with Professors Skip Nault and Casey Hoy, both in the Entomology Department. The project was focused on the management of aster yellows in lettuce, a disease caused by a phytoplasma that was vectored by leafhoppers, and serious problem in the Ohio vegetable industry. The preliminary data that led to this successful federal grant application was generated with funding from an OSU Interdisciplinary Seed Grant. This grant program was designed to encourage interdisciplinary collaboration and required faculty participation from at least two OSU Colleges – at the time the Department of Entomology was in the College of Biological Sciences. Later on in 1996, OARDC developed an internal grant program called SEEDS: The OARDC Research Enhancement Competitive Grants program, which continues to this day. The goal of the SEEDS program is to promote scientific progress and innovation in CFAES, and to encourage collaboration with the private sector and additional stakeholders. It includes seven competitions, and is currently funded at $1.2 million annually. Many of these programs allow OSU CFAES faculty to develop concepts and projects to the point that they can be competitive for federal and other grants. One of the programs within SEEDS is a Team Science award, which promotes the formation of new teams from diverse areas of agricultural science. OSU-OARDC is unique among state-supported universities in offering a grant program of this kind. Since its inception, SEEDS invested $25.3 million, helping CFAES faculty to develop successful proposals for extramural funding of more than $136.4 million, a remarkable return on investment of $5.39.

Miller continued to develop and apply plant disease diagnostic tools at OSU as part of a sustainable, integrated approach to vegetable disease management. Without the backup of a lab dedicated to monoclonal antibody discovery within OSU-OARDC, she found it impractical to continue to do research on monoclonal antibodies against plant pathogens. However, through external collaborations it was possible to develop serologically based assays for critical diagnostic applications. For example, a collaboration with Drs. Doug Luster and Reid Frederick of USDA ARS, Dr. Jill Czarnecki of the Naval Medical Research Center and Professors Anne Dorrance and Mike Boehm of

The OSU Department of Plant Pathology resulted in the development of an immunofluorescence assay to detect airborne spores of the soybean rust pathogen, *Phakopsora pachyrhizi* (*Plant Dis*. 92:1387-1393). This disease has caused severe economic damage since its introduction into Brazil, and it continues to be monitored in the US to predict its potential entry into the soybean belt. Monoclonal antibodies were also developed (*Appl. Env. Microbiol*. 78:3890-3895) and have been licensed to a diagnostics company for field tests.

By the early 1990s, polymerase chain reaction (PCR) assay technology was being adopted quite rapidly in plant pathology, and proved to be an excellent tool for diagnostics. The ability to generate genome sequence data took much of the guesswork out of assay development. PCR primers could be generated easily based at first on a number of tricks used to identify unique sequences, and later on sequencing targets within the genome. Mega-databases such as GenBank could be used with BLAST software to compare sequence data among many more organisms than could be screened physically. While the Miller Lab continues to use serological assays in laboratory and field diagnostics, PCR has become the go-to technology for detection and classification of many plant-associated microorganisms. The lab receives more than 300 vegetable samples annually, and PCR has become routine for diagnosis of many diseases, reducing turnaround time to a few days in many instances. Newer forms of nucleic acid amplification, including isothermal amplification, show great promise for rapid identification of phytopathogens in the laboratory and field. The Miller lab collaborated with Professors Anne Alvarez and Dan Jenkins, and graduate student Jarred Yasuhara-Bell at the University of Hawaii to develop and test tissue and seed applications for their Smart-Dart loop-mediated amplification (LAMP) assay for detection of the pathogen *Clavibacter michiganensis* subsp. *michiganensis* (Cmm). This LAMP assay was proven to be comparable to endpoint and quantitative PCR assays in diagnosis of tissue samples with symptoms, and more specific than a commercial LFD assay (*Can. J. Plant Pathology* 37:260-266). The lab also collaborated with Agdia, Inc. to develop an application of their AmplifyRP® XRT Cmm recombinase polymerase isothermal amplification assay to detect this pathogen in water samples. These and other collaborative projects in plant disease diagnostics with public and private sector entities were developed through Miller's intensive networks of potential collaborators and serve to validate new technology and promote its adoption in crop productions systems.

Some of the most pervasive and challenging bacterial pathogens of vegetables crops are *Xanthomonas* species. Like other diseases caused by bacterial pathogens, there are no highly effective means of controlling them in susceptible varieties once the disease becomes established. The treatment of choice is currently to apply a copper-based product multiple times throughout the growing season. Unfortunately, rapid evolution of phytobacteria towards insensitivity to copper rapidly diminishes the utility of this approach, and overuse of copper also causes environmental problems. Therefore, management efforts are focused on disease resistance and prevention. The Miller lab has worked hard to develop or adapt intermediate, integrated measures that when taken as a whole will reduce the negative impact of bacterial diseases of vegetables, including clean seed protocols, biological control, and use of systemic resistance inducers and cultural practices. For the tomato bacterial spot caused by *Xanthomonas* spp. Miller's first Ph.D. student, Fikrettin Sahin, characterized hundreds of strains of *Xanthomonas* and helped establish the Miller lab in the field of phytobacteriology (*Plant Disease* 80:773-778; *Plant Disease* 81: 1443-1446). More than a decade later, another Miller lab student, Xing Ma, identified *X. gardneri* as the causal agent of a serious outbreak of bacterial spot in processing tomatoes in northwest Ohio (*Plant Disease* 95:1584). The Miller lab collaborated with tomato breeders (OSU Professor David Francis, University of Florida Professor Jay Scott) and UF bacteriologist Professor Jeff Jones to incorporate resistance to *Xanthomonas* spp tomato breeding lines. The magnitude of the tomato bacterial spot problem in tomato production areas characterized by high rainfall and high relative humidity during the growing season, including most of the US east of the Mississippi River, called for a large team of researchers and a multi-institutional, multi-disciplinary approach. Led by UF Professor Gary Vallad, a team of researchers from UF, OSU, the University of California Berkeley, Cornell University and the private sector was formed to put forward and integrated research proposal to the USDA

NIFA Specialty Crops Research Initiative (SCRI) program. The SCRI program is part of the U.S. Farm Bill, and meant to provide funding for research on fruits, vegetables and other specialty crops with the expectation of near or medium term outputs that would directly benefit these industries. The team was eventually successful, in 2014, in winning a four-year, $3.4 million project to tackle bacterial spot in tomato using a broadly-based research approach that encompassed breeding, biotechnology, seed pathology, epidemiology and management tactics such as biological control and novel small inhibitory molecules. One of the ways the Miller Lab is contributing to this effort is with the construction of green fluorescent protein (GFP)-marked and bioluminescent strains of *X. gardneri* and *X. perforans*, which are being used to understand the biology of tomato leaf and seed infection by these pathogens and the efficacy of various intervention strategies.

The crop protection industry has supplied a steady stream of fungicides to treat problems caused by fungi and oomycetes, and the Miller Lab has conducted hundreds of trials to assess the efficacy of these products and provide results and non-biased interpretations to farmers. This has required collaboration with industry representatives, extension educators, field staff and farmers. For example, several years ago some Ohio farmers came to us with a disease never previously observed in Ohio in parsley, which is widely grown on our muck soils. We identified the pathogen as *Septoria petroselini*, immediately set up on-farm trials with various fungicides, and quickly identified an appropriate treatment. This saved the farmers hundreds of thousands of dollars in crop losses in a single season. The Miller Lab maintains an active field program each year to evaluate new products and approaches, with the assistance of the staff of OARDC experiment stations in several Ohio locations. On-farm research is also a significant part of the field research program, particularly for our recent studies on management strategies for vegetables produced in protected culture. We have developed a network of producer-cooperators and worked hard to understand their needs for crop disease management as well as the approaches that are practical and most likely to be beneficial. Understanding the end users of any system or technology is critical to eventual adoption – some of our seemingly good ideas may never be practical and involving end users in research and development prevents wasted time and effort and increases greatly the chance for viable solutions that are likely to be adopted.

The Miller Lab has worked with the greenhouse vegetable industry nationally and internationally for more than a decade. One of the most important diseases of tomatoes in greenhouse systems is bacterial canker, caused by *Clavibacter michiganensis* subsp. *michiganensis* (Cmm). This pathogen is systemic, seedborne and easily transmissible via plant sap, water and contaminated surfaces. We were interested in factors affecting the colonization of tomato plants from infested seed to seedlings and older plants. Ph.D. student Xiulan Xu inserted Lux genes into the Cmm chromosome, resulting in marked strains that emit light visible with a special charge couple device (CCD) camera (*Appl. Env. Microbiol.* 76:3978-3988). Xiulan showed using real time bioluminescent imaging that high relative humidity influences endophytic colonization of tomato plants by Cmm, and that the pathogen moves relatively rapidly from the point of entry up and down the plants, also colonizing roots (*Phytopathology* 102:177-84). This work would not have been possible without the collaboration of Professor Gireesh Rajashekara, a molecular biologist in OSU's Food Animal Health Research Program (FAHRP) in Wooster, which is part of OSU's College of Veterinary Medicine. Collaboration with scientists in veterinary medicine is somewhat unusual among plant pathologists, but has proven to be highly productive at OSU, with research on the interaction of plant pathogens with noroviruses (*J. Food Protection* 78:1472-80), *Salmonella* (*J. Food Protection* 77:359-64) and other zoonotic pathogens on tomato and other types of fresh produce (more on this later in the chapter).

The Miller lab also collaborated with plant pathologists, entomologists and horticulturists from Iowa State University and Penn State University on another USDA NIFA SCRI project, led by Professor Mark Gleason of ISU. We used the bioluminescence approach to study the pathology of the interaction of *Erwinia tracheiphila* (Et) with cucurbit plants. This pathogen colonizes the xylem of cucurbit plants after transmission by striped or spotted cucumber beetles, resulting in wilting and death. This pathosystem has not been well studied and there are numerous gaps in knowledge – from basic biology to effective management. Under Professor Rajashekara's guidance, Miller's Ph.D. student Cláudio Vrisman transformed a strain of Et, which showed a preference for *Cucumis* spp. over *Cucurbita* spp., with the lux genes and used the CCD camera system to visualize the colonization in real time of melon (preferred) and squash (non-preferred) hosts with this bioluminescent strain. This worked showed that Et quickly colonized the plant, including the roots of melon plants after leaves were inoculated; this was a new finding with implications for disease management (*Phytopathology* 106:684-92). The study also showed that Et can colonize a non-preferred host without causing wilting symptoms – also a finding with implications for disease management. We are currently screening small molecule inhibitors of Et with the goal of identifying candidates for new, effective antimicrobials against this pathogen.

After several serious outbreaks of zoonotic human pathogens such as *Salmonella* and *E. coli* O157:H7 on fresh produce in the early 2000s, the Miller lab began to collaborate with Professor Jeff LeJeune, also in FAHRP, an international expert on food safety based on his work with cattle and wild? birds. We have worked on several USDA-funded grants exploring the interactions of plant and human pathogens on plants, means of reducing the risk of human pathogen contamination of plants pre-and post harvest, and approaches to optimize the delivery of food safety information to farmers. Miller's long-time Research Associate Melanie Lewis Ivey chose one of these projects for her Ph.D. research, focusing on both the information delivery (*Food Control* 26: 453-465) and co-management of plant and human pathogens in surface irrigation water (*Water Research* 47:4639-4651). During this time, Miller organized a large interdisciplinary team to compete for USDA NIFA SCRI funding to tackle microbial risks – both plant and human pathogens, in greenhouse tomato production. The resulting four-year, $2 million grant funded teams from OSU (Miller, LeJeune), USDA Agricultural Research Service Vegetable Lab, Mississippi State University, the University of Hawaii, and Louisiana State University that worked closely with cooperators in the greenhouse tomato and diagnostics industries. We developed a systems approach to co-management of plant and human pathogens by first identifying critical points within the production systems where pathogens can enter, persist and spread (*Acta Hort.* 1069:167-72), then developed integrated approaches to manage these risks, such as intensive sanitation practices (*Virology J.* 12:5; *Acta Hort.* 1069:275-80). In addition to development and application of modern diagnostics, including isothermal amplification assays, this collaboration resulted in the development of small molecule inhibitors of Cmm (*Frontiers Microbiology* 6:1127). The project also embraced social science approaches, including the Delphi expert elicitation technique (*Food Control* 78:108-15

One of the collaborative highlights of Miller's career at OSU has been her involvement in international agricultural development programs, beginning in 1994. She received a call from Dr. Tom Payne, then the Director of OSU-OARDC, asking if she would join the Integrated Pest Management Collaborative Research Support Program (IPM CRSP). Dr. Payne chaired the advisory board of the IPM CRSP, which was managed by Virginia Tech and had several US Land Grant university partners including OSU, Penn State, UC-Davis and Purdue. This large, multidisciplinary program was funded by USAID and had CRSP projects all over the world; these have since been renamed Innovation Laboratories (IL). The project in the Philippines was in need of a plant pathologist, and Miller's participation started her on a path that led her all over the world and helped her build relationships with biological and social scientists worldwide. The IPM IL is one of several funded by USAID, most of which cover commodities such as bean/cowpea, aquaculture, horticultural crops, and sorghum/millet. The IPM IL, currently in its third 10-year iteration led by Virginia Tech, focuses on integrated management of horticultural crops and encompasses pathology, entomology, weed science, horticulture, economics and gender studies. We work closely with institutions in host countries to solve technical and social problems in agriculture identified through a participatory process that includes comprehensive stakeholder input. The ILs are designed to build capacity in host countries through short- and long-term training and research support.

Miller joined the Philippines site of the IPM CRSP in 1995 to provide advice on plant pathology research. Her partners were Professors Ed Rajotte, an entomologist from Penn State University and George

Norton, an agricultural economist from Virginia Tech. We worked on this site for about 10 years, traveling to the Philippines together up to three times a year. In the Philippines, we interacted with scientists at the International Rice Research Institute (IRRI), the Philippines Rice Research Institute (PhilRice), the Asian Vegetable Research and Development Center (AVRDC), the University of the Philippines at Los Baños (UPLB) and other institutions, to develop IPM methods for diseases of vegetables grown in rotation with rice. The project involved 40 scientists, technicians and students. Among its many research accomplishments, the IPM IL project was first to characterize the effects of the root-knot nematode on onion yield and quality in the Philippines, and developed cultural and biological strategies to manage this destructive disease. Project scientists also combined host resistance and grafting technology to manage bacterial wilt disease of eggplant at the small farm level, and evaluated methods of pink root control in onion. Our UPLB collaborator Professor Aurora Baltazar developed strategies to reduce the amount of hand weeding, often done by children, in onions and other vegetables, and eventually became our site coordinator. Professor Rajotte brought pheromones from the US in his suitcase for years for research on pest monitoring, which eventually resulted in major changes in the pest management regulatory framework in the country. Dr. Sally Hamilton, then a gender specialist at VT, found that women in farm families often held the purse strings and made decisions about spending for farm inputs, including pesticides, but rarely received any training in IPM. We particularly enjoyed working with Mrs. Dulce Gozon, the leader of a large onion growers' cooperative in the northern part of the main island of Luzon. Our Philippine cooperators conducted field trials on the farms of organization members and met with them often to provide results and recommendations. There was always a good give-and-take between the farmers and researchers that influenced the direction of the research.

The Philippines project was expanded in 1998 to include Bangladesh, which Miller joined in 2000. Miller's first visit to the Philippines in 1995 profoundly influenced the way she saw the world, having never seen poverty in her previous travels to the degree she had seen in the Philippines, with so many people lacking proper housing and clean water. However, the experiences in the Philippines scarcely prepared her for what she saw in Bangladesh. A dangerously overcrowded country, it is one of the poorest in the world. Our project continues in Bangladesh today, and we have made much progress in developing IPM solutions for the benefit of smallholder vegetable farmers, including tomato and eggplant grafting to manage bacterial wilt and root knot nematode, a range of biological controls for insect pests and improved vegetable varieties. During one visit, a young farmer approached and asked us to see the small patch of land where he was growing cabbage. He proudly pointed out his new house nearby, a small but sturdy structure, which he said was built because he had made money using practices developed by the IPM IL. This is what we are striving for – to use research to solve problems that hold poor farmers back and prevent them from obtaining the basics like nutritious food, adequate shelter, clean water and education for their children.

During the second phase of the IPM IL, which began in 2004, all of the sites were regionalized and additional countries were added. We had finished our work in the Philippines and added Nepal and India (Tamil Nadu) to the project in Bangladesh. Miller also began working with sites in East and West Africa. There is much in the IPM IL to recommend it, but its management as a system of interconnected programs, rather than isolated projects, is most critical to its success. This was a requirement of the original principal investigator of the project, Dr. S. K. DeDatta, now retired. Since then well-known IPM proponents including Dr. Short Heinrichs and Dr. R. Muniappan have served as project directors and encouraged communication and technology sharing between regional programs. The second phase also ushered in cross-cutting global theme projects in areas such as insect transmitted viruses, impact assessment, gender and diagnostics. Miller became the PI of the diagnostics effort – the International Plant Diagnostic Network (IPDN). This project was predicated on the deep conviction that diagnostics are important but neglected in the developing world, and that something ought to and can be done about it. The IPDN operated in four regions and 12 countries in collaboration with the IPM CRSP regional programs. These are Guatemala, Ecuador, Honduras, Uganda, Tanzania, Kenya, Senegal, Mali, Ghana,

Nepal, India and Bangladesh. The goal was to connect pathologists and entomologists within regions to each other and to experts in and outside their regions. We have documented the needs of scientists and technicians, standardized diagnostic protocols, developed diagnostic assays and built human resource capacity through intensive regional training programs. In many if not most developing countries, scientists have neither training nor infrastructure to identify invasive pathogens. When the aggressive bacterial wilt pathogen *Xanthomonas musacearum* "jumped" from ensete in Ethiopia to banana in Uganda about a decade ago, samples were shipped to the UK for identification. The IPDN strove to remedy this situation in all of its member countries. We have trained hundreds of scientists in intensive regional programs focusing on diagnosis of diseases and pests important in their regions, utilizing technology appropriate to their infrastructure capacity. US colleagues Drs. Sue Tolin (VT), Bob Gilbertson (UC-Davis) and Carrie LaPaire Harmon (UF), have participated with regional experts including Drs. Fen Beed, Ranajit Bandyopadhyay and Lava Kumar (IITA), Marco Arevalo (Agroexpertos, Guatemala), Zachary Kinyua and Monicah Waiganjo (Kenya Agricultural Research Institute), Delphina Mamiro and M. Mwatawala (Sokoine University of Agriculture, Tanzania), Mildred Ssemakula and Jeninah Karunji (Makerere University, Uganda), and Eric Cornelius and Rodney Oswu-Darko (University of Ghana), among others, in providing these training opportunities. Interestingly, in some regions, particularly in Africa, our training programs have allowed pathologists and entomologists to network with one another, as other opportunities such as annual meetings and workshops that we take for granted are rare. The value of diagnostic networks becomes more and more clear as factors such as climate change and increased movement of people and goods across borders enhance the risk of invasive species arrival and establishment, especially as funding for applied research and development continues to decline (*Annu. Rev. Phytopathol.* 47:15-38). The IPM IL team was the 2009 recipient of the International IPM Excellence Award given by the International IPM Symposium. The Bangladesh program of the South Asia project was awarded the Ryutaro Hashimoto Asia-Pacific Forum for Environment and Development silver medal in 2008 and it was one of three finalists for the Ashoka Change Makers 24th Collaborative Competition in 2009.

The most recent phase of the IPM IL began in 2015, with programs in East Africa, South and Southeast Asia, and South America. Miller is co-PI on two projects: the Vegetable Crops and Mango IPM in Asia, led by Virginia Tech beginning in 2015, and the Vegetable Crops IPM in East Africa, led by Ohio State since 2016. Miller's work is focused on developing and incorporating disease management approaches into IPM packages for major vegetable crops, building on progress in the previous IPM IL programs in Nepal and Bangladesh, and extending the technologies to Cambodia. Similarly, emphasis in East Africa is on extending previously developed technologies and developing new approaches for disease management in vegetables in commercial fields and home gardens in Ethiopia, Kenya, and Tanzania.

While the IPM IL occupied most of Miller's time spent on international development, she also was privileged to be involved in other USAID-funded projects including the Pest and Pesticide Management Program in D'nepropetrovsk, Ukraine between 1997 and 1999. She worked with OSU colleague Professor Pat Lipps and Ukrainian scientists to upgrade laboratory facilities and develop field and laboratory research projects on wheat and tomato disease management. She was honored to be the first American woman given the title of Honorary Professor of the D'nepropetrovsk State Agricultural University to recognize the accomplishments of the project. In another collaborative program, Miller directed an "Immediate Impact Project" under the USAID Horticulture IL in Nigeria, in cooperation with Ahmadu Bello University. This 18-month project, which began in 2010, assessed plant disease and food safety issues pre- and post-harvest in Nigerian fresh market tomatoes. The study showed that both on-farm and market sources of coliform bacteria contributed to tomato contamination. Professors Lejeune and Mark Erbaugh were OSU project collaborators.

The ability to build teams is not necessarily innate in people, although some scientists seem to have a "knack" for this while others may struggle. By its very nature, graduate research often may not lend itself to team building, since during this time it is critical for students to become immersed in their own discipline, and expert in their specific research area of study. However, students can learn to be collaborative within teams in their own labs, on shared projects between labs, and by participation in organizations within their department, university or professional society. Our most influential mentor early in our careers was Dr. Rod Sharp, who led by example and assembled effective teams within DNAP and ADA. Dr. Sharp understood that cooperation was essential among team members and never succumbed to micromanagement – the killer of effective collaboration. We also appreciated the foresight of OSU CFAES Dean Bobby Moser, who encouraged multidisciplinary collaboration within the College as early as the mid-1990s through both policy and funding.

Successful teams require delegation, communication, assumption of responsibility by individual members and respect for the contributions and work styles of all team members. LEAD21 (formerly the ESCOP-ACOP Leadership Program) is a training program for Land Grant University faculty members and other personnel in or likely to be in positions of leadership. This program is designed to increase awareness of personal strengths, weaknesses, work styles, and ability to communicate, as well as group dynamics and collaboration. Miller is grateful for the opportunity to have participated in this program in 1999 as it enhanced her ability to develop and participate in collaborative teams with a deeper understanding of individual styles and contributions, as well as the dynamics of effective vs. ineffective teams. Our advice to young scientists entering their respective fields is to be open to collaboration and engage in purposeful networking within and outside one's discipline. Disciplinary excellence is the foundation for team building as individuals are sought after to contribute what they know for the greater good. For example, if a team is forming that needs an expert in bioinformatics, individuals who are known to possess that expertise will be approached to join. Each individual can be an active member of the team, based on his or her work style and ability to contribute. The corporate world has long understood the necessity of collaborative work, and academia now also values this truth and is actively breaking down the silos that prevent its realization.

CHAPTER 6

Five Decades of Science and Technology at The Center For Nuclear Energy in Agriculture

Tsai Siu Mui
Professor and Director Center For
Nuclear Energy in Agriculture
ESALQ/University of Sao Paulo

n my designation as Director of CENA-Center for Nuclear Energy in Agriculture by the Rector of USP – Prof. Antonio Zago, I began my speech with a tribute to all former directors and especially to the founder of CENA-Prof. Admar Cervellini, from the Physics Department of ESALQ/USP. In addition to this, many ESALQ–College of Agriculture Luiz de Queiroz professors participated in this foundation and collaboration with the advanced research development and the complementing scientific training of undergraduate and graduate students.

I believe that my mission as director, the fullfilment of a dream that any professor should aim at devoting to his/her institution. And in my case, I consider this fact an acknowledgment to the whole community, whom has placed on me this confidence in electing me their director. But I also consider that many of my colleagues are also ready for this mission.

My trajectory, in an area still of male predominance, did not differ from many others that have occurred within the Brazilian scientific establishment. I started at CENA indirectly because in my first year as undergraduate student I was not admitted to an internship by my professor of Geology, who confessed to me that a trainee, being a female, would be faced with problems of all kinds when dealing with field expeditions. He would accept me to support his secretarial work and correspondence resonsibiities, since I passed in the English test during the interview. This refusal was the best thing that ever happened to me. I had to learn early on about pursuing faith and perseverance and try to turn the "no" to "yes". With the diploma of a typist after five months of training at the Presidente Kennedy School, I again applied for an internship, this time with Prof. André Louis Neptune, who was Professor of Soil Fertility at the Department of Soils at ESALQ and also at CENA. After completing my master's degree at CENA, I was hired as lab assistant by the CNEN- National Commission of Nuclear Energy, a position which I occupied for years, when I became an assistant professor in Soil Microbiology, associate professor in Plant Biotechnology and full professor in Microbial Ecology.

Prof. Admar Cervellini

Prof. Otto Jesu Crocomo

My Dreams and Impressions of Cena

As we entered the XXI century and yet living with enormous challenges, some vital questions can be outlined for today's young generation, who will be facing the environmental consequences of human activities. A crucial question is whether *Homo sapiens* can successfully find a way to change from exhausting our natural capital, while fighting over what remains, to establish a sustainable society. We agree with this concern and take it as ours, as we all have to face on how to live peacefully on the income flow of services while taking effective measures to increase equity within and between groups and nations, to suppress war and other forms of violence, and to avoid public health disasters. In this unprecendentelly large and technically sophisticated new world, a great concern exists about the growing losses of biodiversity and/ or the rapid climate change especially in the Tropics which could lead to a disatrous ecological collapse and social breakdown. In addition to this factor, one can ask how overconsumption of our natural ecosystems will be able to degrade our finite resources. To counterpart these factors, one must learn the importance of science and technology to developing societies to avoid great losses with the "human predicament".

Therefore the search for alternative strategies to the interrelated dilemmas imposed by the growing ecological environmental degradation, there is a clear imposition for improvement of a cultural evolution in technological development to achieve social and economic strengths toward a faster transition to a more sustainable society. This multidisciplinary challenge especially to the agrifood sector will require scientists to move toward a powerful force for environmental quality. All efforts should be paid to developing and deploying sustainable agriculture and restoring oceanic fisheries, which will require innovation on the part of the scientists under the educational, economic and social points of view. Much more environmentally benign technological changes in material and process throughputs must be required in order to accomplish these tasks.

Throughout its history, CENA has developed the most varied projects, aiming to collaborate in solving the great problems of the country and participating effectively in the battle against hunger and in the defense of environmental patrimony. For these studies, it was necessary to create innovative techniques that are used worldwide today. In almost 50 years of its establishment, it has become one of the most prestigious specialized institute of the University of São Paulo (USP), being considered an academic centre of international excellence in the development of research programs in the agricultural and livestock areas and environment, through nuclear and innovative techniques. Its scope, the programs still apply to other fields of science, also acting in the areas of applied environmental and social sciences. The centre has 40 professors and 125 non-teaching staff, 40 post-doctoral students, two hundred graduate students (master's and doctorate) and around 150 undergraduate students. Among the professors, five of them belong to the Brazilian Academy of Sciences and three to the Paulista Academy of Sciences.

The Early Days of Cena

In 1961, professors of the chairs of Physics and Meteorology, Analytical Chemistry, Agricultural Chemistry, Chemistry and Entomology and by the then director of ESALQ, already planned to create an organ with the objective of concentrating work on isotopes (radioactive and stable) and irradiation in Agriculture.

The continuous commitment of these professors in this area of research guaranteed the creation of the Nuclear Energy Center (CENA) on September 22, 1966, by means of a state decree that made it official as an institute linked to ESALQ and USP. This Center pioneered in Latin America for the advancement on the use of radioisotopes applied to agriculture.

In 1968, CENA signed an agreement with CNEN for financial support, still in force, and began to operate in an new building, on land donated by the 14th chair of Animal Science of Non-Ruminants of ESALQ.

CENA is a research center founded on the initiative of a group of teachers at College of Agriculture Luiz de Queiroz (ESALQ),

University of Sao Paulo, in Piracicaba and led by Professor Admar Cervellini, who recognized the potential of using nuclear agricultural and environmental policies. The research followed a worldwide trend, after World War II, to establish the use of nuclear energy for peaceful purposes. In fact, the population growth rate already pointed out to the exhaustion of non-renewable sources of energy, Creating the need for alternatives. In this way, already in the decade of 50, in the ESALQ, The first works were started, in line with the most disciplines of Physics, Agricultural Chemistry and Genetics, with the Support from USP, IAEA (International Atomic Energy Agency) and CNEN (National Commission of Nuclear Energy).

Although not limited to the use and development of nuclear technologies, radiation is being widely used in its various experiences, among which many are already inserted in our daily life—some of which are very important. Although it is a science still little known to Brazilians, the peaceful use of nuclear energy brings countless benefits to the development and progress of mankind. Several achievements and developments were due to irradiation or ionizing radiation, through emmissions of gamma rays of cobalt-60 or electron beam, used for many years by CENA and IPEN – Institute of Energy and Nuclear Research. With respect to stable isotopes, CENA is the pioneer and the only institute in South America to develop research for the separation and production/synthesis of compounds enriched in the stable isotopes of light elements (sulfur, carbon, nitrogen, boron) used in several areas of science (agricultural, environmental, biomedical, animal nutrition, among others).

In Brazil, CENA has contributed and still continues to collaborate a lot for this evolution, allowing the use of irradiation as a phytosanitary treatment to become an efficient technique in the conservation of fruits and other foodstuffs, reducing natural losses caused by physiological processes, maturation and aging. As for pest risk management, it is able to eliminate or reduce microorganisms and parasites, without causing any damage to the food, making them safer to the consumer.

It was also an agreement, signed in 1971, with the IAEA, UNDP-United Nation Development Programme and CNEN-Brazilian National Commission for Nuclear Energy, which allowed the intensification of international scientific exchange, with the arrival of scientists and the Brazilian scholars abroad. In view of the importance of the work being carried out, the Agency International installed in CENA the only exclusive office in Latin America, outside the embassy area, which remained in operation until 1991. The IAEA and PNUD were instrumental in the development of CENA, both for the provision of equipment and International exchange of ideas and training of specialists, and also by broadening research lines.

We applaud the contribution of the professors from ESALQ-College of Agriculture Luiz de Queiroz, responsible for the technical-scientific training with complementary subjects in several areas and the Course of Introduction to Nuclear Energy (CIENA).

And recognize the twenty years of intense dedication from both undergraduate students and teachers. We owe this patrimony to a dedicated dreamteam of scientists – Epaminondas S. Ferraz, Enéas Salati, Henrique Bergamin Filho, Otto Jesu Crocomo, Nilson Villa Nova, Darcy Martins da Silva, André Lous Neptune, Klaus Reichardt, Akihiko Ando, Eurípedes Malavolta, Eiichi Matsui, among others, the formation of the majority of the first generation of researchers hired by CENA. These pioneering scientists have brought, above all, the innovative spirit of our Science.

The Past 50 Years of Science and Technology at Cena

If we look at the five decades of CENA, one can realize that practically everything was done with a teamwork of atomic ants, that followed the same trail of CENA's pioneers, with tenacious efforts carried out by researchers and students, whose associations stood out for their trust, freedom and dedication in the search for the new. And, in order to keep up with CENA's progress towards its 50th anniversary, new actions and indicators should be adopted with a view to institutional performance regarding the quality of scientific production and the fulfillment of goals for the training of human resources with excellence and the necessary transparency and visibility of the institution.

Desertification of Semi-Arid Regions in Brazil

Among the projects developed at CENA during the 1970s, the studies on groundwater in the Brazilian Northeast and on the hydrological cycle in the Amazonian Rivers.

A major project was carried out in the early 70's by CENA in the Brazilian Northeast region, in collaboration with the Brazilian Government, in the area of hydrology. The problem was due to the lack of adequate management, a problem that was difficult to solve, since the region's rainfall was concentrated during a short period of time and most of it was lost through evaporation and transpiration. A small portion of the precipitation gave rise to water courses, many of which were intermittent. On the occasion, the age and the mechanism of groundwater recharge of the aquifers of the Northeast were studied, through the use of stable isotopes. It has been discovered that the main cause of the concentration of salts in the waters of that region is of marine origin, brought by the atmosphere. Based on this principle, the possibilities of obtaining, through various methods were created to achieve qualitative and quantitative improvements of the groundwater, aiming at its use for irrigation in drought-prone areas.

Discovering the Amazon

In 1971, ten CENA researchers lauched an expedition to the Amazon and tributaries to collect water samples. The purpose was to understand the dynamics of the river under natural conditions for develop of specific methodologies of analysis for contributing to its preservation. The first concern was to study water in the atmosphere and assess the importance of the forest in this ecosystem, determining whether it existed because of the tropical climate, or whether it was the climate that was responsible for its existence. At that time, it was possible to determine that 50% of the Amazonian hydrological systems came from the oceans, while the other half came from the evaporation of the forest trees, demonstrating definitively, in a scientific way, the importance of the function of the vegetation. These pioneering investigations were carried out by the isotopic analysis of water vapor and precipitation.

The Fight Against Hunger

The great contribution of CENA in the fight against the food scarcety was the obtaining of new varieties of plants, in a continuous process of genetic improvement. Scientists are also working to increase productivity and improve food quality with the application of unconventional research techniques, especially nuclear techniques, when a single dose of radiation can either be used to sterilize a needle or to create a new variety of pest-resistant plant. These surveys, as well as many others, have created important varieties that are already commercialized.

The researchers also examined the life and breeding habits of various pests in Brazilian crops, trying to determine the doses of radiation necessary to sterilize them, returning them to the field and, in this way, to combat them as natural enemies.

In so many years of history, the institution can count on very successful experiences applied to agricultural and environmental issues, some very important that are even used on a commercial scale, as is the case of rice and beans.

The Atomic Beans
At the beginning of 1970, some Brazilian newspapers published the news that a "superfeijão" ("superbean"), capable of resisting diseases, pests and variations of atmospheric conditions, was being developed at CENA. The news soon spread, raised phone calls from all over the country interested in the subject and the researchers were called to Brasilia to explain what was happening.

In so many years of history, the institution counts on very successful experiences applied in agriculture, some very important that are even used on a commercial scale, as is the case of rice and beans. What actually occurred is researchers at CENA launched a project aimed at obtaining a variety resistant to the golden mosaic virus, a disease that attacks the leaves of the plant of the bean under drought cobitions, preventing normal development. With the irradiation of the seeds, a mutant tolerant to this disease was obtained, but initially showed low productivity. However, a long process of cross-breeding and selection began, in a joint effort with the Agronomic Institute of Paraná (Iapar). The result was the cultivation of high productivity and viral disease tolerant cultivar, which has been cultivated since 1992. Currently, this bean cultivat yields 1,400 kilos per hectare (kg/ha), while the common variety produces only 400 kg/ha..

"Afterwards, CENA produced a larger bean cultivar, two and a half times higher than the common one, which keeps the pods farther from the ground, which may serve those who are interested in mechanized harvesting" Tsai recalls. The precocity and the change of habit of growth of the Carioca bean results from the CENA researchers, becoming the first mutant to be released for planting in Brazil in 1986.

Cereals and legumes

Studies on grain breeding with the use of nuclear techniques began in 1966 and, along with the use of chemical mutagens, early harvest and other mutant rice strains were obtained without loss of productivity. Thus, demonstrating the utility of nuclear energy in plant breeding, early strains of soybean were obtained for use in crop rotation programs with sugarcane, maintaining the same beneficial agronomic characteristics as the original. A wheat breeding program began in 1975. The objective was to obtain smaller sized genetic lines to prevent wind tipping, resistantance to stem and leaf rust and toleranance to aluminum toxicity.

Floriculture

Radiation induction can also be used to create genetic mutations with improved characteristics and unique cultivars. A good example was the work developed with flower producers in Holambra/SP, creating two varieties of chrysanthemums ehibiting unique colors. The research obtained coloration of the petals from light pink to dark pink and white.

Fruticulture

Thanks to other research programs at CENA, a seedless orange cultivar will soon enter the consumer and inudstrial market. The fruit was obtained by the induction of mutations and will be the first variety in the country to use this methodology.

The experimental woek was initiated in 1983 with the production of approximately 8,000 plants obtained from sweet orange blossoms irradiated with a dose of 40 grays (unit of radiation dosage). These plnts formed the initial population that were used for selection. "After two cycles of choice, 29 mutant clones were selected, 24 of which had completely seedless fruits." Some of these clones are being tested on three experimental farms in the state of São Paulo, Brazil, in order to evaluate their potential for commercial launch" explains Dr. Augusto Tulmann Neto, the coordinator of this project. "To date, it can be seen that, despite the absence of seeds, mutants have maintained their sensory patterns of taste and aroma, an important advantage when using the mutation induction technique," he says.

The professor also emphasizes that hundreds of new cultivars or varieties have been released to farmers for planting and are already being consumed in dozens of countries, without risks, since the materials and mutants obtained do not become radioactive, only being modified

In their genetic material. Due to the success obtained in this project, the same methodology has been used to obtain unique cultivars with fruits of earlier maturity, plants with low or more resistance to diseases and pests. As for example, we can mention the research involving the main citrus rootstock in Brazil, with the purpose of obtaining small plants tolerant to sudden death of citrus. Additionally, another citrus project is attempting to obtain Fremont and Thomas mandarins with seedless fruits and orange mutants resistant to infection by the Huanglongbing bacterium (HLB), a disease with a high potential for orchard destruction.

Pest Control

Another important example of research being carried out in the Laboratory of Radiobiology and Environment is the sterilization of the Mediterranean fly. Known as one of the main pests of fruit growing, the radiation made the male sterile, and when crossing the female, there is no fertilization, which considerably decreases its incidence. The result is greater control of the pest and the reduction of the phytosanitary barriers of Brazilian fruit in the international market. Through the use of a radioactive apparatus, the technique is quite simple with the irradiation of the pupa, making the male to be born infertile. In addition to being cheaper and less damaging to the environment, it has been shown to be more efficient.

The research outcome interferes with the Mediteerranean fly's reproductive cycle through a radioactive process, without the use of chemicals and without generating any kind of environmental impact. Unheard of in Brazil, the method made the mosquito non-infectious, which even lays eggs, but they do not hatch the larvae. "We use a quantity of energy that does not kill the insect but rather causes genetic changes in its biological system," explains Dr. Valter Arthur, research coordinator.

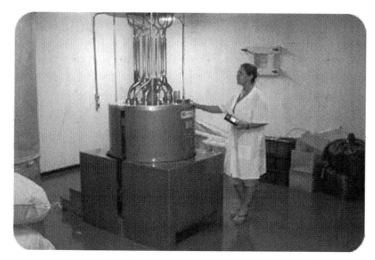

The 60-Cobalt Irradiator

The Environmental Issues: Three Decades Studying Climate Changes and Greenhouse Gases

For more than 30 years, CENA's Environmental Biogeochemistry Laboratory (LBA) has analyzed the effects of land use change and agricultural practices on soil carbon stocks and their implications for greenhouse gas emissions. The concern about global warming has led to the need to inventory these emissions at all geopolitical levels so that mitigation actions could be based on actual data. Thus, starting from this premise, the LBA team produced and published inventories of emissions from the Brazilian agricultural sector, Piracicaba municipality and several campuses of the University of São Paulo (USP). The intense scientific activity of Professor Carlos C. Cerri in this sphere of knowledge made him worthy of the Certificate of the Nobel Peace Prize awarded to the IPCC (Intergovernmental Panel of Climate Change) in 2007.

Studies of this nature have also begun in the Amazon and Cerrado of the central-west region, focusing on deforestation to give way to agriculture and extensive pastures. In collaboration with other CENA and US researchers, it has been found in several studies, and more recently in an article published in the Proceedings of the National Academy of Sciences (PNAS), that the recovery of the microbiota from pasture soils takes decades to for restoration of functional diversity in natural environments. Sustainable management systems can minimize these losses after deforestation in areas used for soybean and sugarcane crops. With the growing demand for biofuels, whether in substitution for gasoline or diesel, they has enabled the team able to inventory other commodities, such as beef, poultry and coffee. Results of these surveys have also been used in support of the argument in favor of policies for expanding the use of biofuels, demonstrating that the change in land use from low productivity pastures mainly to sugarcane, avoids further deforestation and competition for foods.

Flow Injection Analytical Automation

In 1974, researchers from the Analytical Chemistry laboratory at CENA began to develop the first experiments carried out in Brazil on flow injection analaysis. Using the materials and equipment available, often improvised and creatively adapted, after a year of research, the first work was published. The flow injection process consists of pumping chemical solutions with equipment that develops the same peripheral movement of the human intestine—called the peristaltic pump.

In the year 1978, a series of six articles was published in the international scientific literature dealing with these procedures that made the projects for simultaneous determinations simpler and more economical, allowing the exploration of new chemical reactions. Their employment improved the performance of many traditional analytical techniques, from 40 to 50 determinations per day to 40 to 400 determinations per hour. The development of this system placed five

CENA researchers in the ranking of the most productive in Brazil regarding the impact index (that is, how often they are cited in other scientific works). They are: Henrique Bergamin Filho, Elias Ayres Guidetti Zagatto, Francisco José Krug, Bonaventura Freire dos Reis and Antonio Octavio Jacintho. Currently, the team is working to achieve full system automation, that is, to have it fully computer-controlled. Over the last twenty years, flow injection analysis systems have brought numerous benefits to institutions and laboratories in various parts of the world. In Brazil, the most important applications were in the formation of new nuclei of research in analytical chemistry and in the improvement of the performance of water, plant and soil analyses. They also enabled the creation of analytical lab services and post-graduate human resources training.

Paleoenvironmental Studies on the Reconstruction of Paleoenvironmental Use Technology

The ^{14}C methodology can determine the dynamics of thousand-years vegetation and their relationships with natural environments or with the anthropic activities, using fragments of naturally buried coal in the soils and micro-fragments or phytoliths found in sediments. And give a picture of the past forest fires. From these studies the following can be determined: 1) the isotope studies of carbon in the organic matter of plants and 2) isotopic analysis of C and N and of sediment pollen lakes. Thus elucidating the great influence of the Amazonian Forest in maintaining the humidity of other regions of Brazil and the predominance of some plants on the maintenance of the Atlantic Forest during several periods of the Brazilian hydrological cycle.

Advanced Research with Isotope Enrichment

Nitrogen is one of the major mineral nutrients among all living organisms, most limiting the productivity of agricultural crops, the use of nitrogen as fertilizer has sustained global agriculture at increasing levels of productivity. However, it is what can generate the of worst effects to the ecosystems of the planet, due to its pollution risks of water and the atmosphere, besides being one of the gases that cause the greenhouse effect and promoters of acid rain. To try to solve this, the Laboratory of Stable Isotopes of the CENA/USP, from the Division of Development of Analytical and Nuclear Methods and Techniques, coordinated by Professor Paulo Cesar Ocheuze Trivelin, has been working for 40 years in the development of isotopic enrichment and the synthesis technology of labeled compounds with the nitrogen isotope ^{15}N.

The research developed in CENA has no similar identity in the country and in Latin America as these technologies involving isotopic enrichment and synthesis of labeled compounds support the advanced research on the nutrient cycling in agriculture, by providing compounds enriched with stable isotopes, following the standard required by the commercial inputs.

A Noninvasive Method to Diagnose Gastritis, Ulcer and Gastric Cancer

The Laboratory of Stable Isotopes has created an innovative work in Brazil by developing an unprecedented method for the non-evasively diagnosis of human gastritis, ulcer and gastric cancer. In this study, the patient ingests an ^{15}N-enriched compound, nonradioactive element, dissolved in orange juice or water. Afterwards, the beverage reaches the gastric mucosa and, in the presence of the bacterium is metabolized by the enzyme urease. The produced carbon dioxide diffuses into the blood vessels, being transported in the form of bicarbonate to the lungs, and released as carbon gas in the expelled air.

In the presence of bacterial urease, the proportion of carbon in the expelled air sample expresses as absolute difference the presence of *Helicobacter pylori* bacteria (the main cause of chronic gastrites and peptic ulcers) in the patient.

"The method allows for high precision results in humans by the Medical School of Ribeirão Preto, University of São Paulo," explains Dr. José Albertino Bendassolli, author of the discovery.

Introducing Omics In Microbial Ecology Focusing on The Conversion Forest-Pasture in Amazon

Soil microorganisms are sensitive to environment disturbances, and such alterations have consequences on microbial diversity and functions. Studies at the Cell and Molecular Biology Laboratory at CENA have indicated that alpha diversity of microbial communities and functional diversity decrease from undisturbed to disturbed soils, with consequences for functional redundancy in the soil ecosystem. Agriculture and pasture soils were among the most diverse and presented higher functional redundancy, which is important to maintain the ecosystem functioning after the forest conversion. On the other hand, the ecosystem equilibrium in forest is maintained based on a lower alpha diversity but higher abundance of microorganisms. Therefore, the omics metadata can indicate how land-use change alters the structure and composition of microbial communities; however, ecosystem functionality is overcome by different strategies based on the abundance and diversity of the communities.

Slash-and-burn clearing of forest typically results in an increase in soil nutrient availability. Using next generation sequencing of 16S rRNA gene and shotgun metagenomic DNA. Deforestation decreased soil organic matter content and factors linked to soil acidity and raised soil pH, base saturation and exchangeable bases. Using molecular methods, changes can be observed in community functions such as increases in DNA repair, protein processing, modification, degradation and folding functions, and these functions might reflect adaptation to changes in soil characteristics due to forest clear-cutting and burning and give support to the idea of taxonomic and functional adaptations in the soil bacterial community following deforestation. We hypothesize that these microbial adaptations may serve as a buffer to drastic changes in soil fertility after slash-and-burning deforestation in the Amazon region and that preserving the forest should be a ultimate need for the preservation of biodiversity and water reservoirs.

The Teaching Activities

The multidisciplinary nature of CENA, unique in Brazil that encompasses the training of human resources in an integrated way in analytical sciences, environmental sciences, biological sciences, geological sciences, nuclear and agronomic sciences, has been highlighted as the basis for continuous training of excellent professionals. A profile strongly delineated in scientific methodology for solving problems in the field of agricultural production and conservation of natural resources and the environment. In this sense, dissertation projects focused on the use and / or development of nuclear techniques and methods, such as the conservation of foods with gamma radiation, the genetic improvement of plants with gamma radiation for induction of mutations, the use of radioisotopes as tracers in studies of soil fertility, plant nutrition and animal nutrition, the application of radioisotopes in analytical chemistry, the use of nuclear analytical techniques based on attenuation of gamma radiation in soil physics and wood densimetry, among many another examples. Since its creation, more than 450 master's dissertations and 350 doctoral theses have been defended. Since 2004, the PPG-CENA received in the evaluations carried out by CAPES, maximum concepts of excellence for the Master's and Doctoral courses.

One of the topics that stands out as CENA envolves is the so-called spectroanalytic techniques, emphasizing the excellence of the centre and its professors in the development and applications in atomic emission spectrometry with plasma, flame atomic absorption spectrometry electrochemical atomic absorption spectrometry, molecular absorption spectrometry, plasma mass spectrometry, mass spectrometry for special isotopic analyzes (nitrogen, oxygen, hydrogen, sulfur, carbon and nitrogen isotopes, boron), in addition to gamma spectrometry, beta spectrometry, alpha spectrometry and X-ray fluorescence spectrometry. Another highlight of CENA is the training of human resources in analytical automation. CENA is the cradle of analytical automation processes employing continuous flow injection analysis, and has in its roster of accredited professors, scientists with excellent citation indexes in chemistry, particularly in analytical chemistry. In this context, the centre can be considered one of the top scientific insitutions in the country, because it offers the conditions for a intensive training in automation, which encompasses not only new analytical procedures but the development of new instruments.

CENA has promoted integrated training in ecology, biogeochemistry and ecotoxicology with a staff of renowned international experts. This team has been prolific in contributing research related to natural and altered ecosystems, with a long tradition of research in the Amazon and in the Piracicaba River Basin from São Paulo. Advanced research is possible in view of the multidisciplinary nature of the programs, since in these cases students have the opportunity to participate in the development of sampling strategies, sample collection, preparation of samples using modern techniques and determinations of the chemical species of interest.

Other areas of great activity involve biotechnology and genomics, which involve several internationally renowned experts conducting leading research in the areas of genomics and proteomics of pathogenic and plant microorganisms, molecular markers in biodegradation studies, biodiversity conservation and genetic resources; Genetic manipulation aimed at plant breeding and studies on plant development, plant micropropagation, among others.

Among the advanced outcomes, CENA has a biobank of cyanobacteria available for the benefit of the country for years to come. One of the major ecosystem services provided by the cyanobacteria is the production of new bioactive compounds since they are from diverse environments, so novel bioactive compounds can lead to new biosynthetic pathways and novel enzymes.

The Contribution of The International Atomic Energy Program (Vienna, Austria)

One of the most extraordinary experiences in my academic life was to have witnessed one of the most outstanding scientific program at CENA, funded by IAEA-International Atomic Energy Agency and UNDP-United Nation Development Program. I owe to Prof. Admar Cervellini and ESALQ's team of scientists for the opportunity to observe nearly two decades of superb scientific development provided by this IAEA Program to the students and assistants, by sending them abroad for one year fellowships for technical training at renowned universities and research institutes. At that time, we were deeply influenced by the directors sent by the IAEA, who encouraged us to evolve in a concrete and challenging way for development of advanced research programs in agriculture and environment, in general by focusing on aspects such as conservation of the Brazilian biomes and food security in the tropics. Dr. Carl Goram Lamm and Dr. Peter Vose came to CENA aiming at this special mission. In particular, Dr. Lamm who made endless friendships with the CENA's scientists along with Mrs. Diva Athié, who assisted us perfectly throughout the program. During this period, we received the visit of several world experts on soil and nuclear physics, plant biochemistry, analytical chemistry, plant and animal nutrition, soil microbiology and entomology, among others.

As one result from this program was that CENA's most recent advances have not been limited only to application of nuclear and isotope techniques as new techniques applied to plant biotechnology, cellular and molecular biology began to be used with great success in agricultural as well as environmental studies. Several new research lines were added to the Graduate Programs in Sciences (CENA) and Applied Ecology (CENA / ESALQ), both ranked as excellent by CAPES, the federal foundation for improvement of education at superior level.

The Fundamental Interaction Between University and The Agribusiness Sector

A very active modality of extension in the CENA is the development of methods of analysis to directly meet the demands of the agricultural and livestock sectors. In addition to acting in the development of methods, CENA also performs specialized analytical services, generating considerable revenue of its own. In this sense, attention should be paid to the export sector of agricultural commodities, such as sugar and meat, for the analysis necessary for the acceptance of Brazilian products abroad. For example, the issuance of certificates of non-radioactivity, required by many importing countries since the Chernobyl nuclear accident in 1986, has led to increased demand from the Brazilian export sector, culminating with almost five thousand radiometric analyzes carried out at CENA during 2013.

Some CENA research groups have been heavily involved in metrology, with emphasis on their applications in agriculture and the environment. Due to this involvement, researchers from the institute collaborated in the elaboration of the National Metrology Plan (PNM) in the area of agriculture and also in the establishment of the Brazilian Program of Metrology in Chemistry (PBMQ). The long history of metrology, which began in the 1980s, reached the highest global forum on metrology in chemistry, the CCQM (Consultative Committee on Amount of Matter). Since 2001, CENA has participated in fourteen metrological studies organized by CCQM, collaborating to establish global comparability of measurements. Another important extension action has been represented by the development of reference materials to serve the agricultural sector, aiming at providing materials adequate to the needs of Brazilian laboratories and to minimize dependence on imports from other countries. Also in the area of metrology, several training courses have been offered to disseminate the concepts of metrology and quality, serving the academic public as well as professionals from private companies and laboratories.

The international recognition of the consistent performance in research applied to agriculture and the environment, led to the creation, at CENA, of the Brazilian Satellite Centre of Trace Element Institute for UNESCO. This important centre, established in 2004 and unique in activity in Latin America, is part of a set of fifteen centres established by UNESCO in several countries, with the mission of making available technological and educational resources to disseminate knowledge and solve problems in related agriculture and environment with trace substances, aiming at improving the quality of life.

Final Remarks

From our understanding, CENA has considered Science and Technology a central core permeated by the critical analysis of knowledge based on our cultural reality and the current socioeconomic issues. From these experiences, efforts have been made to strengthen training of students based on technological innovation, competence and entrepreneurship toward a socially fair and more sustainable environment. That is why innovative technologies for application in university-company interaction have been spelled out, since they add value to knowledge produced by CENA and drive advances and independence to scientific and technological advances for our country. To this end, innovative methods of knowledge transfer and for the development of laboratories for scientific dissemination, forming educational networks that act locally or at a distance. In this way, CENA has broadened its mission of performing research, teaching and extension activities to attract young scientists to promote scientific and technological development with beneficial actions especially targeted at local and regional communities.

Acknowledgments

We would like to thank the many funding agencies which have greatly contributed to strengthening strategic areas of research and the joint actions to accompany the rapid technological advances in recent years at CENA.

Special thanks must also attributed to FAPESP, CNPq and CAPES for the granting of scholarships and human resources training and research support, as well as to FINEP, FEALQ and FUSP, IAEA, PNUD and Betty Moore Foundation, among others for national and international scientific and financial support.

Prof. Klaus Reichardt of the Soil Physics lab at CENA illustrated in sequence the CENA's evolution throughout five decades —at 25, 30 and 50 years of existence

CHAPTER 7

A Novel Collaborative Pathway Involving Academia and Industry

Launching a University Spin-off Company

Mark T. Muller
Founder and CEO TopoGEN, Inc.

An Overview.

Every scientific publication has an abstract that defines the body of the work and crystalizes the key findings. This is a good way to start. As a child, while living in the Orient, I developed an interest in science and specifically in microbiology. I questioned everything and dismantled just about anything that I could. Years later as a second year undergraduate, I finally got my chance to experience the thrill of learning, problem solving, discovery and research. Graduate school followed and by the age of 26, as a newly minted Ph.D. with a reasonably good publication record, I started Post-doctoral studies. At age 29, I joined the faculty at The Ohio State University, and in 1987 with several colleagues, we founded the Department of Molecular Genetics, the first in the country. A few years later, I started a small but profitable biotechnology company and 25 years later, I was recruited to the University of Central Florida in Orlando and retired from OSU. This is my story that is defined by influential colleagues, collaborators, mentors, family and friends. Along the way, I developed new passions in aviation, music, photography and the freedom that comes with greater financial independence. A man's life is his message to the universe; I hope mine can inspire others in some small way.

The Early Years: Coming of age and developing an interest in Science.

My father and I share the same name, Mark Twain Muller. My paternal grandparents were emigrants from Austria (Vienna) arriving in NY in or around 1910. My Grandmother (maiden name, Topper) arrived a few years after my Grandfather, I'm told. I have a number of relatives, according to my father, that were Jewish (including a great Uncle who was a rabbi). Evidently my Grandmother was a Samuel Clements fan, hence the namesake. After arriving in NY City, my Grandfather worked as a diesel mechanic and was one of the first Daimler engine experts in the US. They lived in Brooklyn, NY. The Muller family was small by early 20th century standards (from youngest to oldest, a daughter, Rita, Paul, Mark and William). My father was born in 1915 and William (Bill) Muller was born in 1911 (Bill was my favorite uncle and I got to know him well). My father graduated from Cornell in 1939 and promptly entered WWII as a signal officer. He was in the Pacific theater and worked tangentially with some famous people while stationed in Australia, including Douglas MacArthur, John D. Bulkley and L. Ron Hubbard and a number of NY Times correspondents. Years later, I met Admiral Bulkley (nickname the "Sea-Wolf") who was awarded the medal of honor for his role in getting General MacArthur out of the Philippines after the Japanese invaded and conquered these islands. My parents met in Australia during the war, fell in love and were secretly married in Australia in 1945 and then 'officially' married back stateside in 1946. Soon thereafter, my siblings arrived (Conni, the oldest, Mary, next). I was born at Walter Reed Hospital, in Washington, D.C. in 1950 when the family was stationed in Baltimore, MD.

As a career military officer in the early 50's my Father was getting his Masters Degree from Boston College as well as teaching communications and military science at MIT. I don't recall too much about living in the Boston area, other than the house we occupied seemed huge to me, with a large basement where I recall getting a fishhook under my tender skin and occasional visits from my grandparents who lived in NY City.

My father fought in the Korean conflict and when I was about 3 years of age the family relocated to small town in east Texas (Pittsburg), my Mother's hometown. I recall more about this time of my life and the tragedy that shaped me from a young age. My mother came from a large family (7 boys, 2 girls) and most lived in the little east Texas town of Pittsburg. A couple of my uncles were prominent citizens. I spent some time with my Uncle Leo and Willie, who pioneered the sweet potato industry in Texas. It was big operation and I grew accustomed to eating raw sweet potatoes for breakfast, while spending time at the warehouse. To this day, I only really eat raw sweet potatoes. I also witnessed day-to-day operation of a highly successful business venture, and the trappings of that success. I was imprinted at an early age by this experience, I believe. Life in east Texas in the early fifties was horribly marked by intolerance, bigotry and segregation, something that I could not comprehend at such an early age. The town had two main streets, one for whites and behind another for blacks. All stores had front (white only) and rear entrances (blacks) to maintain separation. In my opinion, bigotry is still pervasive in the rural areas of Texas, sadly.

The tragedy I spoke of arrived on a warm spring day in 1956, while I was playing at my Aunt's home outside of town. My Mother had left that morning early to drive to Dallas with Uncle Willie and his wife Girlie for a medical checkup (Willie was a diabetic). My Grandmother was babysitting for the day. A man walked up, while we were all sitting on the porch, and started acting strangely; almost as if he could not speak the words. What came out sent my Grandmother in a wailing, screaming, crying hysterical fit. My older sister, Conni, was crying and wailing. Mama (as everyone called my grandmother) told me in a calm voice that my Mother was in an accident. Actually, it was a head-on collision, and my Uncle Willie was killed instantly and my Mother was not likely to survive the massive head trauma. (My Aunt Girlie also had life-threatening injuries including a nearly severed foot and many broken bones.) All were on the way to the ER. In those days, cars were like huge metal ramming machines and without seat belts or airbags or any safety features we take for granted. Occupants became human projectiles driven into whatever immovable object was in the path. My Mother was thrown clear and found 100 feet from the wreckage. There were a number of fatalities in the other car, driven by a young man (that car also had a number of children). I recall Willie's funeral. I had 'shadowed' him at the Sweet Potato House and really liked him; however, I really could not understand the loss. My Uncle Frank quietly stated that Willie was sleeping as he held me over the casket to view the body. I accepted his explanation, which seemed reasonable since Willie did appear to be asleep. Mom was in the hospital and when I saw her I was horrified. I simply did not recognize my Mother who had a swollen, stitched and blood caked face. This mangled body in the bed could not possibly be my Mother, I thought in horror. She looked more like a monster and it was frightening to the core. Her injuries were very severe and included a shattered femur, massive internal injuries, head trauma and being partially scalped. Mentally Mom was not functional, but awake and aware. My Father came home on emergency leave from active duty in Korea and we started the long process of rehabilitation and recovery. Some months went by and gradually she improved and after plastic surgery, a metal thigh pin implant and much rehab, she was released but wheelchair bound. Her mental state was still not back to normal and she was not capable of being a responsible mother. About six months after the accident, my Father was stationed in Okinawa. I was five years old. There was some disagreement in the family with my Dad suggesting that he go with the kids to Japan, and leave Mom to recuperate in Pittsburg. Mother refused and we all moved to a new existence on the tropical island of Okinawa. Prior to arriving in Japan, my Father spent time explaining Japanese culture and a little bit of the language and customs as I recall. It came in handy actually when the family boarded a taxi in Naha Airbase and the driver took off leaving my Dad on the curb. Everyone was screaming for him to stop, but the poor guy spoke no English, but I piped up and said "Papa-san, Papa-san" and he instantly knew the situation. It was at this age that I realized that speaking a new language had some real rewards and I have always enjoyed learning languages. While not fluent, I have working knowledge of German, Danish, Italian and Japanese.

Since my mother was not fit to take care of us, my Dad hired two young Japanese women, Kazuko and Sudoko, as nannies. Kazuko was tasked with dealing with me and she spoke little if any English. This turned out to be a good opportunity for me to learn some Japanese. I started to learn the language at a very early age, and got reasonably proficient according to my Dad. The bad news? Well, the Japanese language is not complicated but it is somewhat different between males, females and children. Essentially, in this context the language was different in tones, construct and what I call 'harshness' of the dialect. There are also multiple levels of 'politeness' or supplication. As an adult male, visiting Japan many years later, the language I recalled was largely inappropriate in polite society. This led to some interesting and awkward scenarios (when speaking Japanese in the lab I visited, a graduate student asked if I was gay, since I used female oriented language cues). On the other hand, when dealing with Tokyo businessmen (on business matters), I never let them know that I understood the gist of what was being said in various business meetings. This gave me an edge, since I could easily peg friend from foe. When they would refer to me with term 'gaijin' which is generally considered politically incorrect (GAI meaning outsider, JIN is person), it was easy to see who was on my side.

I recall a few other snippets of early events in Okinawa. I recall sitting with my Dad at the beach while he was painting a seascape. While exploring, I stumbled across a live land mine buried in beach sand and for once refrained from trying to take it apart and study its inner workings. I promptly reported the find to my Father who turned it in to the authorities. I also recall that my Father had many Japanese friends and associates and that he was acutely interested in Oriental culture.

We spent about 2-3 years in Okinawa and Mom finally recovered. The next move took us to Ft. Huachuca, Arizona in 1959. We lived on the base, which became my new world. Ft. Huachuca is near Sierra Vista and has an elevation of almost 5000ft. While hot and dry in the summer, we sometimes had snow in the winter months, a new thrill.

There were miles of hiking trails, rattlesnakes, venomous Gila monsters, horny toads that defined a biological potpourri to be sampled and studied. My Dad had this tiny little Vespa scooter and he and I would trundle through the back roads on weekends, exploring and generally making random searches for interesting bits of culture, antiques and crafts. I'm convinced that several events at the time impacted my future proclivities. For example, the Vespa sojourns got me interested in motorcycling and I later learned that my paternal grandfather was an avid motorcyclist who owned a 1915 Indian side-car bike. As part of my Father's duty assignment, he worked on communications systems in unmanned drones and I watched a number of drone launches. I was fascinated by flying and took every opportunity to watch and learn about drones. Even at this young age, the thrill of full 3-D movement in space seemed so exciting. I acted on this fascination many years later, as described below and I believe that my aviation interest grew from watching drones fire off with the JATO (or Jet Associated Take Off) bottles. One Christmas, my parents got me a telescope. Not some small tripod window toy but a real nice 6-foot-long refractor telescope with reasonable light gathering ability and floor-based tripod. I systematically studied the heavens, but soon realized it was far more fun to view the Sierra Vista Drive-in movies about 4-6 miles down in the valley. No sound of course, but I viewed first run movies and endured the eye strain that attended the process. Evidently, astronomy had little if any allure.

There were many fond memories, including working with my Dad, an avid ham radio operator (K5LOW), who taught me basic Morse code and the phonetic alphabet. We spent time on hunting, fishing and camping trips around Cochise country with my Father and his friends and we visited Bisbee, Tombstone, large copper mines, the OK Corral and many other sites. I also recall getting in major trouble for setting off a fire alarm in the school (remember, I was curious). Basically, I was a good kid but very active with a reasonably active social life. I love to take chances and push the envelope. My life promptly changed from a very comfortable social my Dad got his next duty assignment. The family packed up and again we made a move abroad, this time to Taipei, Taiwan. The family drove from Arizona to San Diego to board a military ship called the USS Barrett. The whole family then endured a three-week voyage to Taiwan. I don't recall my Dad being with us on the drive from Arizona to California but we had a fun and exciting time driving the '57 Chevy wagon across half of the country. My Mom had a wonderful sense of humor and spent several days laughing and poking fun at each other.

The Military transport ship (USS Barrett, which was scrapped in 1973) was immense and insanely complex to my 10-year old brain. There were not so many families, and few kids my age. I recall a large number of the passengers were US or Chinese soldiers (mostly enlisted men). We had a small berth high up on the port side and porthole views of the water. My parents had close friends who had a son my age. Danny and I became fast friends and we got into considerable mischief. The ship was this enormous city with a heartbeat that was manifest as central activities including ping pong with the Chinese enlisted men, free movies, lots of food, arts and crafts each morning at 10am and so on. Still, Danny and I got bored and engaged in monkey business. My sister, Mary, gave me this plastic light bulb (a gag) that looked exactly like a real glass bulb but unbreakable. The ship had a central staircase winding up about 10-12 floors and open in the middle. I would stand on the top floor and drop the fake bulb down to Danny on the first floor. The MP's caught us and hauled us both away after closing down the staircase due to some 'idiots dropping light bulbs'. Lesson learned on this one, courtesy of my Dad's stern verbal thrashing (and confinement). On day three at sea, everyone got sick including yours truly. It was dreadful and you just had to ride it out for about 12 hours before you get your 'sea legs'. After that, it was no problem. Going across the international dateline was a both fun yet disgusting (blindfolded, hands placed into vats of spaghetti, jello, being hosed down with frigid seawater). We were 'pollywogs' and Neptune (my Dad) did the initiation-rights.

In 1961, we arrived at the Port of Keelung and moved promptly to Tianmu at the base of Grass Mountain outside of Taipei. Many American service families and expatriates lived in Tianmu which was a lovely rural setting surrounded by lush rice paddies. I was fascinated with reptiles, which were plentiful. I started a reptile club and we captured and kept a number of snakes, all fodder for my science fair projects. I asked the local army hospital if they would provide me with sterile agar plates for bacterial growth, as I was becoming more interested in culturing bacteria from my snakes. Despite repeated requests, the military technicians refused, saying it was too dangerous to let a 10-year-old play with bugs (and they refused to offer oversight). Again, an early influence was an acute interest in microbiology, although I was unable to act on this desire. So I turned back to my snake 'zoo'. Tropical Taiwan is a haven for venomous snakes. Vipers, bamboo snakes and other colorful serpents were interesting subjects of study. I was careful not to handle the real killers, for example the '100 pacer' (100 steps and death) or the Habu but many others while venomous were not capable of killing with a single bite. Fortunately, I never got bitten but I had close calls while hiking in the hills around our home.

Based on my interest in language, I tried to learn Mandarin and my Father was supportive since he spoke the language with reasonable fluency. I totally faltered in learning the language for a couple of reasons. First, I was not really immersed in the Chinese culture and did not really use what I learned along the way. Second, Mandarin is extremely difficult for English speakers, especially for a 12-year-old. I really admired my Dad's ability to communicate with the locals and in Mandarin. My Dad had many Taiwanese friends and associates. He was acutely interested in oriental antiques (such as cloisonné vases, coins, jade snuff bottles, jewelry) and rather unique among American personnel (many shunned the local indigenous people and had no interest in language or culture). I had many interesting family dinners with other Chinese families, courtesy of my Dad. We lived in a very nice home in Tianmu, with a large pond with fish, a lush garden, a walled-in yard and servants. Charlie and Su-yen (husband and wife) were Chinese expatriates who escaped through Hong Kong in the early 1950's. Charlie was the cook and Su-yen the maid. They had four sons (all boys) ranging in age from 10 to 18 years of age. Jer-Pong was my age and I had a built-in playmate who was salaried! He spoke no English, and as I said, my Mandarin was terrible, but we managed to communicate with sign-language. He was a good baseball player and kept me in training for little league (I was a catcher). Most of the language I learned from

Jer-Pong should not be repeated in polite company and I can to this day shock Chinese colleagues (and wives) with expletives. Chinese is an inflective language and otherwise rather difficult to learn. During this time, while attending Shi-Lin Middle school (part of the Taipei American School system) I discovered that I was particularly good at gymnastics; actually, any sort of activity that involved innate knowledge of the position of one's body aerial space. Several 'offshoots' of this ability made me good at peripheral activities, including pole vaulting, high jump, diving and of course tumbling. As a catcher in little league, I was enthusiastic and aggressive but not great. I loved being the center of attention however since every pitch was watched as the ball terminated in my well-oiled mitt. My enthusiasm was significantly attenuated when a tipped fastball made it somehow into the side of my facemask, leading to massive shiner. The physics of impact is a good teacher it seems. I switched my attention to soccer and enjoyed playing goalie, for the same reasons I liked playing catcher I suppose.

My time in Taiwan taught me so many things about myself, largely through trial and error. One influence, I believe positive, was the fact that all the years growing up in Asia, there was no television so very little time was devoted to this particular distraction. I developed an appreciation for listening to the radio (local US Army media). Like many in that generation, I loved rock and roll (early-mid 60's). Another defining event was being beaten up by a Chinese man while riding a bus to the American Compound in downtown Taipei. In retrospect, I believe this person was mentally ill. After ranting in broken English about atrocities in 'Red China' he turned his invective to me and began a tirade about America. This rant was terminated by a rather painful pummeling and I was unable to defend or protect myself against this attack (he was a full-grown man in serious anger-mode and I was an 80 pound 11-year old). The bus driver pulled him off me, thankfully. No major injury but I was terrified.

My friend from the USS Barrett (Danny Robbins) lived in Hsin-Shu, about a 3-4 hour drive down island. Hsin-Shu is now a suburb of Taipei, but back then it had a small Army compound with about 50-100 families, a nice pool and officers club. Danny was a rather sadistic young man and while I enjoyed catching and studying frogs, reptiles as noted, he took great pleasure in exploring such life-forms from the inside out. While cruel, it was nonetheless morbidly interesting and satisfied my enquiring mind. I really

Dan's father, Lt. Col. Robbins (aka Robbie), was with MAAG (Military American Advisory Group) and we sometimes got to accompany the him on field exercises (as observers). Robbie was a hardcore career military man; all business. At the time, I recognized that career experts were a wonderful resource to learn and I was full of questions regarding organizational details, 'what if' scenarios and just general insight. My father, being career military (but not regular army) clearly enjoyed his work and I considered that such a career path may work for me as well. Regrettably, my questions to Robbie were usually answered in a way that involved ridicule. "How could you be so ignorant" he would say with a scowl. I quickly learned three things. First, don't even think about asking questions to people with closed minds. Second, I vowed never to put another down for asking a simple question. Third, it seemed that a military career would never work for me. I would say he was a negative role model. A real negative inspiration! The rocky relationship persisted and I especially noticed how that Robbie was rather harsh with his son, Danny. I believe this is reason Danny took his own life years later at the age of 21 (Dan was their only child). The parents became bitter, and actually blamed me, rock music or whatever was convenient, never considering that high, unachievable expectations are a crippling and demoralizing attitude. I heard he left a suicide note but the contents were never revealed. I will never forget his mother throwing herself on the casket and wailing, while Robbie stood stoically by with no emotion. Actually, Danny was supposed to be in my wedding as a groomsman; my comment to his father that I hoped he and Mrs. Robbins would try to attend my wedding, was not well received. Not surprising given the circumstances. Oddly, the Robbins family and my parents remained good friends for many years; however, they never ever enquired about me or my career (but asked regularly about my sisters). Bitterness and despair terminated the life of these two individuals and they passed on.

In 1963, my father was assigned to Washington, D.C. (my birthplace) and we packed up and moved again. I started the 7th grade at

Gunston Junior High in Arlington, VA. We lived on Columbia Pike, a pretty busy road, in an apartment complex. I completed grades 7-9 at Gunston and during these three years learned a bit more about myself as I matured toward puberty. I loved music and especially The Beatles (didn't everyone?). I was a pretty quick study on the guitar, but I was cash-strapped and could not by my dream guitar (Gibson SG) and amplifier (Gibson Eagle) and my parents were no help. I was fortunate, however, and managed to secure (in 8th grade) rather lucrative paper route delivering the Washington Post to several nearby apartment buildings. I had roughly 200+ customers and garnered an income of about $150/month including tips. This doubled over Christmas (bonus tips). I learned the value of working in a business and the reward structure that comes with being clever and working hard. The Gibson/amp combination soon followed, but I got buyer's remorse, because I actually decided on a Gretsch Country Gentleman that Harrison played (gold hardware, sophisticated electronics, a visual treat). This was almost $800, an ungodly amount of money, so I stuck with the SG. In the 8th grade, I was reasonably accomplished on lead guitar, so I put together a band called "The Dimensions" which included lead guitar (me), a bass (Rob Hughes), a lead singer (Mervin Hall), a rhythm guitar (Rob McHeleny) and drummer (Gary Padgett). Our repertoire included Beatles, Stones, popular rock tunes from one-hit wonders and a lot of 3 chord progressions that everyone loved to jam and improvise over. Probably the weakest musician in the group was Rob Hughes, my best friend. He was such a popular and good looking guy (and a jock), I convinced all band members that we needed his help to get gigs (but he really did not contribute musically). We played small venues, private parties, school dances and so on and only did cover songs. We never composed our own music, however, and this clearly limited my advancement in music. Although I did not realize this limitation, I thoroughly enjoyed the popularity, notoriety and financial returns of playing semi-professionally. In the 9th grade, the band significantly improved when Lenny Aaronson moved into the Riverside Apartments (by the way, Ponce Cruse aka 'hints from Heloise' also lived in Riverside and was a close friend).I knew Lenny in Taiwan (his Father worked for Voice of America) and we quickly re-established our friendship. Len was a wonderfully gifted bass player (and as good as I was on guitar, perhaps a shade better). I invited Len to substitute for Rob and I came to realize just how important a bass player is in a small group! So Len came on board. Something else I learned about myself from this experience was that I am very uncomfortable making decisions that hurt friends (Rob took it very hard). To this day I tend to be conciliatory and I place collegiality as a valued virtue. The bass defines the 'pocket' that glues everything together rhythmically. Most people (including me) may not realize just how critical a good bass player is to the overall connection in the group. The band prospered and improved with Len holding it all together at the low end. We made decent money and invested in better equipment including matching outfits ("Beatle boots" and equipment upgrades) which made for a more professional package.

A major influence on me at the time was my track coach in 9th grade. James Van Dyke played college basketball who was a spitting image of the 'Marlboro Man'. I was also on the gymnastics team specializing in tumbling, trampoline, horse and horizontal bar; however, rings were not possible due to my poor upper body strength. I excelled in track and field (like my Uncle Bill and to a lesser extent my own Dad). There was no pole vault in Junior High school, which I was reasonably good at, so I focused on high jump. At the time, I recall being about 5'5" and setting the school record in 9th grade by clearing 5'9". I performed best with a crowd, probably because I could muster a rush of adrenaline and focus my effort. Mr. Van Dyke really encouraged me and often gave me a ride home after practice, since he lived in the next apartment complex. I looked up to him (as did many) and he was consistently positive and well disciplined. He was also a tough taskmaster and would take this huge paddle to guys who stepped out of line. I recall that he told my Mother that I was cocky and arrogant, but he viewed that as a positive attribute. I am not sure my Mom liked or agreed with this assessment. In summary, these years in Washington DC area were primarily dedicated to music, sports and socializing, all of which are linked closely to mating behavior. Academic pursuit was pretty low down on the priority spectrum, however, I made excellent grades and was not challenged in any classes. I suppose there was no room in my life at the time, although I still enjoyed reading science fiction and learning about scientific developments of the time. My Father was very active with early computer technology at the Pentagon and I recall seeing the CRT displays in his office. This was another source of fascination since the project involved AI (artificial intelligence) and my Dad was way ahead of his time because of his job at the Pentagon. My Father told me that the very early AI programs were tested in a variety of ways. One question that was asked was "are you happy with your job?" and the program responded with "who wants to know?". Basic AI routines understood well the chain of command!

In 1966, my Father made a decision that impacted the family directly. For his career advancement, he agreed to a tour in Vietnam and left us for a year. He informed me of my new role as 'man of the house'. With his tour in the Vietnam conflict, my Father would be on track for General Officer (he as a Colonel at the time). Father never spoke much about his experience in Vietnam, but based on his biography, he was General Westmoreland's Chief of Communications. As such he had a high security clearance and was not allowed to fly in helicopters or aircraft with less than 4 engines. In any case, the year he was away came and went quickly. A new duty assignment followed his return to the US and we once again moved. This time we relocated to Hampton Roads, Virginia (Ft. Monroe). I spent the first semester of the 10th grade at Kecoughtan High School, named after the Algonquin Indians who settled at Hampton Roads in the early 1600s'. I spent only one semester at Kecoughtan High, but many years later I collaborated with a fellow faculty member at OSU who was in my class. We did not know each other at the time (she was a cheer leader and I was a transient nobody). Still it was a surprising coincidence and my colleague showed me the yearbook and my 10th grade picture, which I had never seen.

The military brass gave new orders to my Father for another year in Vietnam, ostensibly to be promoted to General. I am not sure of the details, but within a few months of moving to Hampton, my Father retired from the Army as a full Colonel, after almost 30 years of service. I recall getting into a fistht with the son of a Master Sargent at Fort Monroe, but I cannot recall why. I took a beating that required 4 stiches in my face and my Father got a 'juvenile delinquent' report over the incident. He always joked that this JD report prompted his retirement; at least I think he was kidding.

We moved to Austin, Texas where my Father took a staff position at the University of Texas in electrical engineering and worked on computer aided instruction (CAI). A Google search reveals a number of publications from my Father and his team at UT Austin on CAI and they attracted considerable federal grant support for the project. I was intensely interested in the project and learned much from working with faculty on the project and in particular interacting with my Father who took me to the CAI lab on weekends. This influenced my thinking about a future in science. I liked the problem solving environment, I enjoyed interacting with highly intelligent researchers and perhaps most importantly, I saw people intellectually engaged in an academic environment that was not 'work' or a job. I realized that if you love what you do, the reward is simply showing up (Woody Allen claims that 95% of life is simply 'showing up' anyway). This was the first and single most influential event in my young life. I saw a viable future path and was intrigued.

In high school in Austin, I re-established myself in music and got into a local rock group. Being a bit older and more experienced, I was highly selective about getting the best mix of talent and we were reasonably good, but not great. We played a lot of gigs, usually fraternity parties, local dance and high school events around Austin and most weekends were taken up with this activity. I tried out for sports (track) but realized that there were many more athletes at the high school level who were much better and competition was fierce. I was simply not big and strong enough to compete and win medals, so I quit the team. For example, my best pole vault was about 11'10" feet and while other team mates were easily clearing 12' on the first vault. Contributing to my exit from track was an ankle injury stemming from an aborted vault where I came down in the foam feet first and twisted my foot (you are supposed to land on your back in the netted foam). I chipped a bone in my ankle and was out for the season. I still recall the intense pain of the injury and I have an oversized left ankle to this day.

Inspirational events, both positive and negative, during my Austin high school days are noteworthy. In the latter category, I witnessed a bad outcome of a University spin-off company gone terribly wrong. My Father got involved with 4-5 other U.T. engineering faculty on a failed business venture. The business was a printing company located in San Antonio and had some links to CAI and publishing somehow (details unknown to me). All partners put up cash to buy the company and my Dad worked long hours each weekend to grow the business. In retrospect, I believe that the company 'cooked the books' to make the business appear highly profitable. On top of this misinformation, the partners trusted a manager and former equity partner to oversee the business. Long story short, the business was mismanaged and to make matters worse, the partners were pointing fingers at each other and no one was accountable. There was no conductor with an equity stake who could take the time to run the company on-site full time. The company was mismanaged by the administrative staff (former owners) and within 6-12 months the company went under. All of the faculty partners filed bankruptcy and did not have to re-pay loans (although they had ruined credit ratings). My Father refused on principle and repaid the bank his share on the equity in monthly installments over many years. Lessons learned from this experience were manifold. First, it is important to control the business if possible. Limit the number of chiefs and keep it small initially. Second, never put your own money on the line. Use OPM models (other people's money) or grant funds and bring expertise and scientific acumen to the table. Third, control the equity and use that equity as leverage to motivate (and control) the stakeholders. Fourth, recognize that a start-up must evolve and the business model originally proposed can be re-directed as opportunities arise. Fifth, risk taking must be carefully managed and when money is 'on the table' be highly suspicious of input that can lead to misdirection. Finally, I realized why people don't like to start businesses. This was a painful and highly destructive experience that my Father had to suffer through over a number of years. He was a highly honorable person who repaid every penny to the bank, when all other partners bailed out with bankruptcy filings.

I made mention of the positive influences during this period of my life. I was strongly inspired by my Father, who set an amazing example of honesty, integrity and honor. There were others along the way, including parents of my high school friends, who were successful entrepreneurs. My best friend, Joe Bond who lived across the street, moved to Austin my senior year. Joe's Father worked at IBM and was a very impressive guy who influenced my thinking about business. Mr. Bond started a splinter company with links to IBM that was highly successful. I still recall his advice fondly. "When you start a business as a young man, and you lose the shirt off your back, all you lose is your shirt." This is sage advice. As you age and responsibilities increase (kids, family, debt, etc.) the risk to benefit ratios change considerably. Seize the opportunity when all you have is the shirt. In fact, I discussed some ideas for business start-ups with my Father, while in High School; however, he vigorously discouraged me and stressed that I should get an education first and foremost. In high school, I also worked at a Department Store called 'Gulf Mart' in Austin (in the sports department). The manager, whose name I do not recall, made a compelling statement with such conviction that I still recall it verbatim. "Go to school, and stay in school as long as possible". I'm thankful that I followed this advice. While I did not act on Mr. Bond's edict, I took a somewhat derivative route by combining my academic pathway with an entrepreneurial one, as described below.

Choices of undergraduate and graduate education.

Academically, I was mostly an A student with B level performance in areas of low interest. I did well on testing platforms but was never really challenged and other activities held my attention. During my senior year, I made the rational decision to focus on studies and become engaged in curricular and extra- curricular activity. I started to look into different colleges and universities and my Dad encouraged me to apply to his alma mater (Cornell). However, I was reasonably sure that I would not get into an Ivy League program (grades) despite doing well on the SAT exam.

Choice of a University was molded by a number of internal and external factors. I was very concerned about getting drafted and slotted into the Vietnam conflict as a foot grunt enlisted man in a rifle company. This was a major issue driven by positive survival above all else. So, if I'm going in, I wanted to be an officer. In addition, I was leaning toward engineering (specifically electrical). I decided on Texas A&M which is a 2+ hour drive from Austin because it had ROTC and a strong engineering major. I also considered a major in microbiology because I was also interested in quantitative biology, derived from my numerous science fair projects. To sort this out and make an informed decision, I decided to attend summer school at A&M prior to starting my freshman year. In this way, I could sample some courses (and my performance), while learning more detail opportunities available in graduate or professional school. I quickly realized that the math and calculus (differential equations) was not my strength. Although I could do well in such courses, it did not come easy. A decision to major in microbiology was made at the end of my summer term; however, my next step (graduate or professional school) was far off and I was not focused on this point. Unfortunately, I was not able to get good counseling at the time, so I was in limbo anyway. I finished out my freshman year in the A&M Corps of Cadets as "Fish Muller" in Medical Company E-1. In this first year I met many interesting and lifelong friends. My parents were very proud of my academic performance, as I made the Dean's list and managed to survive the Corps (hazing, crap-out sessions, white rats, the Fighting Texas Aggie Bonfire, etc.). The Bonfire, which preceded the fall classic 'Turkey Day" football game with Texas University (aka University of Texas at Austin), was a great experience and I saw a fantastic entrepreneurial opportunity, which I will describe later. In sum, there were no real academic influences worth noting in my freshman year; however, being in the ROTC, I learned military discipline and organization. The Corps imposes its collective will on its members, which includes attributes like the value of hard work, discipline, honor and respect. Such attributes are important to a 19-year old kid like me and despite the hardships, it was extremely important in my maturation.

In the summer of 1970, I moved back to Austin to live at home. I got a job as an orderly at a local hospital (Brackenridge). That summer I fell in love and met my future wife, Annette, who was enrolled as a nursing student, taking courses at U.T. and performing clinical duties. I had to work hard to win her over, since she was involved with a rival suitor in Vietnam. Lucky for me, I won out and we have been together for almost 44 years. She has been a huge and ongoing inspiration with skill sets that complement some huge voids associated with my character. She is a genius with people excellent social skills and is also extremely positive and optimistic in all matters. Thus, she is well liked by any who meet her. Sadly, I am just the opposite, so we make a good team. In some situations, I may not feel like interacting socially, she will come to my aid and act as the interface.

In the Fall of 1970, I started back at A&M, now as a "Piss-head" in the Corps (2nd year). Things got more interesting academically when I took my first genetics course and started the chemistry series. I especially like genetics and got to know one of the instructors, Dr. Clint McGill, an assistant professor in the Genetics Department. His wife, Jane, was also on faculty, but I'm not sure if she was tenure track. Jane taught in the Department of Biochemistry as I recall. Clint worked on *Aspergillus nidulans* and I approached him to inquire about undergraduate research. I asked if there might be someone to work with on a project, but unfortunately, his lab was full. He directed me to Dr. Gerard A. O'Donovan (Gerry) who was in the Department of Biochemistry and looking for students. Jerry was a fiery Irishman who could really spin a yarn. His stories were legendary and he was one of the most entertaining individuals I've ever met. He was a former Soccer player (he claimed) and actually taught the A&M punter how to kick field goals. Jerry claimed he could nail the uprights at 40 yards. It made for great story telling, but I have my doubts about the veracity of his claims. Gerry's lab worked on bacterial pyrimidine metabolism and he and Jan Neuhard (University of Copenhagen) published a very nice J. Bacteriology review on the subject in 1970, and I read and re-read this review so many times I practically knew it by rote. That semester I read James D. Watson's book entitled the "Molecular Biology of the Gene" and I was hooked. For the first time, life was not a mystery but founded in solid chemical principles and I was ecstatic. I read his book at least three times and had many discussions with Gerry, Clint and other lab members. In the spring semester, I started auditing graduate courses in biochemistry and genetics, in addition to my other courses. This was not necessarily a good thing since I devoted too much time to the lab and faltered on organic chemistry (making my first B- in a science course). I started thinking about a future in academic science at the time and received encouragement from the McGill's and Gerry O'Donovan (along with some of his post-docs). I finished my sophomore year and was excited about the future. I was fascinated by molecular biology and microbial genetics. I struggled with the primary literature so most of my reading centered on textbook sources and reviews. I developed strong expertise in nucleotide metabolism, at least at a theoretical level and even at that early time of my career, I saw the potential for applications in cancer (at the time, 5 Fluorouracil was just starting clinical use). In retrospect, it was unfortunate that I did not start working in the lab on a specific project; however, my duties in the Corps, a heavy course load and evening audits of graduate courses left no time to get going in the lab.

Due to my poor performance in Organic chemistry, I decided to take my last chemistry course over the summer term (Quantitative Analysis) at U.T. in Austin. This would free up some time in the normal academic year for other activities related to undergraduate research. I spent time hanging around the UT campus, well spring of liberal anti-war sentiment at the time and interacted with my Dad whose office was near the chemistry labs. I did not take a job that summer and focused on reading and my studies. The Quant instructor was a chemistry graduate student and we had many lively discussions about science. I did well in the class and enjoyed a carefree time spent with two things I loved most, academics and my soon to be wife. Things were definitely looking up, except for a major issue that loomed before anybody of draft age: Vietnam. My UT summer experience made re-consider my stance on the war, which as a Fighten' Texas Aggie, had been rather hawkish. I began to realize the futility of the war and how irrational it was to most young Americans who would fight, die or be injured. I met several "SDS" advocates (Students for a Democratic Society) and they made persuasive arguments against the Vietnam conflict. These guys were serious archradicals and I recognized this as well. On the otherhand I recognized flawed logic being perpetrated on the public and when events affect you personally, you will think long and hard. The prospect of having my education derailed by the draft hung over me like an ugly black cloud. I could never openly discuss this with my Dad, a retired and decorated career man who served this country in WWII, Korea and Vietnam. Some things are best kept to oneself. My mother, in contrast, clearly did not want her only son going off to war, but she kept quiet about such matters.

Starting back at A&M in the fall, as a 3rd year student, I declared my major officially as microbiology and began to think about getting into a research project in earnest. I did not sign the ROTC 'contract' to enlist as an officer, but instead continued through the program as a "D&C" or Drills and Ceremony cadet. I began working with Jerry O'Donovan's group and learning microbial genetics with a focus on *Pseudomonas aeroginosa*. I always liked working with Pseudomonads, simply because they always smelled nice (sort of grape like). To this day, I can tell *P. aeroginosa* spoilage a mile away using my nose as a diagnostic tool.

Late in the semester, I recall that President Nixon established what I call a 'quantitative metric' on the draft lottery. The lottery system, based on birthdates, established a priority list based on random drawings of the date. For example, if your date of birth was June 12th, and that date was assigned a lottery number (say 1), all men born on this date were inducted first. Clearly, the lower the number the more likely you would be called up. The process was not necessarily random and there were differences between draft boards. For this reason, I stayed in ROTC since my number was 127, which is well within striking distance for Vietnam! In 1971, it was decreed (I think by Nixon) that all draft boards would cutoff at 125. This meant that I would not likely be inducted; thus, in December of 1971, I dropped my student deferment and became 1A because I was surely not going to be drafted. In January of 1972, I then would be '2nd priority' meaning that I would not be drafted unless everyone from 1 to 356 got drafted first. I was safe! At the end of my junior semester, I dropped out of the Corps of Cadets, handed in the uniform, grew my hair and a beard and led the liberal life of a 'non-reg' (slang for an aggie outside the Corps). This opened up more opportunities for spending time in the lab.

In early 1972, I met several individuals who influenced me significantly. Dr. O'Donovan continued to be a jovial figurehead and a source for great entertainment, but offered little research direction (his initials were prominently displayed on all lab items as "G.O.D.") He was typically 'hands-off' with graduate student and post-docs, so I decided to work more closely with lab members. Gerry O'Donovan had two lab groups, one in genetics and one in biochemistry but most of my time was spent in the genetics group (with Clint and Jane McGill and a graduate students, John Womack, Cassandra or Cassie Smith). These individuals provided research training microbial genetics and worked with me on the project, which involved analysis of pyrimidine metabolism (specifically salvage pathways) in *P. aeroginosa*. During this time, I met a Danish couple, who were visiting post-docs from Jan Neuhard's lab at the University of Copenhagen (Soren and Marianne Norby). Soren (actually the 'o' has a slash making his name sound like "Siren" to English speakers) was an MD researcher while his wife a Ph.D. Marianne was rather cold and distant with classic Scandinavian features. She was probably the most beautiful female I had ever seen, with large exotic and intense blue-green eyes and a lithe, athletic physique. She made an impact on all around her, yet was largely unaware of the affectations of natural feminine beauty. Too bad her personality did not match her looks. She barely acknowledged me and was fiercely arrogant. Her arrogance was not a result of her looks but rather derived from an intellectual haughtiness borne from a keen analytical mind and acute intelligence. It was intimidating and I stayed well away. Soren was just the opposite, however. Soren looked like Steve McQueen and many people made note of this while he was living in the U.S. His persona was engaging and he was extremely articulate, speaking essentially unaccented English. On occasion, he would recite poetry or launch into a Shakespearean sonnet with a proper British accent of course. Everyone liked him and he was very helpful to me. Soren was more of a classical geneticist working with Drosophila (fruit flies) as a model system to probe nucleotide metabolism in a tractable eukaryotic system. He was also well read and broad based in his frame of reference. For example, he had an interest in comparative linguistics and when I expressed an interest in learning languages, he worked with me to learn some Danish phrases. Being exposed to such interesting and intelligent young scientists (both were post-docs) convinced me that academic science was an ideal pathway for me. I continued to struggle with the lab chief (aka "G.O.D.") largely because he did not provide any reasonable direction or objectives, but was more intent in 'holding an audience' with any who would listen. Soren and Marianna also complained about Gerry O'Donovan. Evidently, Gerry had made wide sweeping claims about the availability of resources and equipment in order to lure them into the lab. They were most unhappy about the mis-direction. For my own work, I decided to focus on a key enzyme, ATCase (aspartate transcarbamylase) a key early step in pyrimidine synthesis. I obtained a diploid strain to over-produce the enzyme for biochemical studies.

Another influential person I met during that semester was Rodney Kellems, then a Ph.D. student at the University of British Columbia in Vancouver. Rodney worked with Tony Warren at UBC (Dept. of Microbiology) and was collaborating with Gerry on the Pseudomonas project. Rodney was also outgoing and extremely knowledgeable. By outgoing I mean, in your face, up close and non-stop, but I liked that. We worked closely together and despite his short visit (1 month) I learned so much about the biological system (Pseudomonas). He strongly encouraged me to consider UBC for graduate school, which was sage advice.

At some point, early in the Spring of 1971, I asked G.O.D. if there was any chance to go to Jan's lab and work over the summer at the Enzyme Division at the University of Copenhagen B in Denmark. As usual Gerry was very positive and encouraging saying that he had Nato Funding for this exact purpose. He said he would arrange my visit to Denmark on the Nato Fellowship. All I had to do was purchase a ticket and upon arrival, contact Soren (no email back then, so communication was slow). In summary, I trusted that all the arrangements would be made, based on reassurance from my boss.

I was thrilled to be working abroad and excited about the prospect of learning Danish and becoming culturally immersed in everyday life in Copenhagen. I arrived in early June with a backpack and a gut string classical guitar that was my 'road guitar'. I was given the lab number to call on arrival. Much to my total surprise and dismay, no one knew that I was coming. Gerry had totally misled me on the whole affair! Gerry clearly screwed everything up and a number of people (me included) were upset. Soren and Marianne were very kind and I could tell felt sorry for my plight. There were some perplexed and probably angry phone calls from Jan's lab (Gerry's collaborator) and I don't know the details; however, somehow things got settled and I was provided a dorm room in "Nordisk Collegium" near the campus (after a temporary residence in an vacant apartment of one of the lab staff). Soren and Marianne were managing the Collegium facility, probably like dorm supervisors, in exchange for a nice spacious apartment (they were in the process of buying home in a place called Birkerod (slash o), a suburb in Copenhagen. This was a nice fit for me and I was grateful to have my own place that was rent free.

That summer, I worked closely with Soren and Jan (and Elsebeth, Jan's Technician). Some of the highlights were as follows. Learning to speak Danish (at a "Folk University") made little sense for a couple of reasons. First, only about 6 million people worldwide speak Danish and second, nearly all Danes speak English. I enjoyed mastering the language AND going to bars and using my language skills. Most were quite surprised! Other notable events included learning to get to know the lab staff who became close personal friends, including Just Justesen who later visited me in the US. While practicing Danish, I asked Jan (the lab chief) a question which I frequently employed in my evening exploits in local Copenhagen bars. The direct translation is "are you happily married?" I found this phrase useful for obvious reasons but Soren also pointed out that the Danish word for marriage (gift) also means 'poison'. Thus, when you ask "Er du lykklelig gift?" you are also asking if you are happily poisoned. Those Danes have a real sense of humor! This humor was lost on Jan. He was outraged that I would ask such a question, even in jest. I later learned he was having an affair with his technician (Elsebet) who he later married (following the divorce from his attorney wife, which must have been interesting). Clearly, I hit a nerve. Lesson learned: laboratory romance is an ongoing phenomenon in Danish academic settings.

My unannounced arrival in Copenhagen landed G.O.D. in serious hot water with his colleagues and collaborators. I think it was the first time he really got caught in this fantasy world of storytelling that he created. Gerry turned his vindictiveness toward me and I was caught between the two warring factions. This was my introduction to University politics on an international level. I recognized that truth was on my side and Gerry clearly knew he was culpable; still I had to stand my ground yet not totally alienate my boss in the US. The Danes were impressed with me and I accomplished a lot that summer, but I was not able to get published, unfortunately. The training and real world experience was priceless and despite the backlash due to irresponsible behaviors, I do not regret the experience.

One experience that I will always cherish was an invitation to visit Soren and Marianne in Jutland at their summer home on the sea. I borrowed a small motorbike from Just Justesen, strapped on a backpack and took the ferry from Sjaelland (the island where Copenhagen is located) to Jutland (a peninsula that connects to Germany). This involved many hours of driving 50km/hr on side roads and shoulders across the whole country of Denmark. I got by easily with my newly acquired language skills as long as I was in Sjaelland; however, Jutland was a totally different experience. I could not understand the Jutland accent. They seem to swallow whole sentences and spit back some strange guttural explosion of words that sounded like they were gargling fish. They, on the other hand, had no problem understanding me and often commented "you are from the city". I slept in youth hostels for the most part. Just Justesen had given me the address for a farm his family owned in Jutland and told me I could sleep in the barn (the place was abandoned) so I spent one sort of spooky night in the countryside with no one for miles around.

I arrived at Soren's summer home and slept on the couch in their small bungalow. Soren and I played Frisbee, rode bikes through the countryside and fished. He had a small rowboat and a gill net and we would go out and get our day's catch for dinner. One time, I got terribly seasick due to the large rollers, so I was reluctant to go back. Soren had a great sense of humor, usually play on word humor, so I spent a lot of time laughing. (Example: while pointing out cows, he asked which were females and quipped… it should be utterly obvious.). Marianne was quiet and aloof for the most part; however, she spent the entire week topless (and recall she was a perfect 10). Soren suggested

I wear blinders; more cow humor, I guess. We had a visitor, Elsebeth Lund, from Aarhus University. She was a post-doc who spent several nights. I also found Elsebeth to be cold and distant, like Marianne. I figured out that this must a Danish trait shared with female scientists, and accepted it for face value. Soren told me that Elsebeth was a bit of a home wrecker and was known to sleep with senior faculty; more intralab romance drama. The Danes are pretty tolerant and tend to be open minded about these things. I returned to Copenhagen and completed my work in the lab and packed up for home. The week or so before leaving Gerry O'Donovan paid a visit. In the end, he made good on his promise to provide the Nato Fellowship support and I was reimbursed for most of my expenses over the summer, so things turned out well indeed.

I recall returning to Austin and seeing my fiancée (Annette) who had since graduated and was a practicing R.N. making very good money. She had her own apartment in North Austin, a nice new car and was very happy to see me. This was one of the happiest times in my life, being young, in love and experiencing a new beginning. The future looked very good indeed and I was thoroughly invigorated.

I started my senior year with all batteries charged up. I saw my pathway as an academic scientist. I next needed to find a graduate program. My positive experience with Rodney (from UBC) influenced my decision and I applied to UBC Department of Microbiology in Vancouver, British Columbia. I got very strong letters of recommendation from Gerry, Rodney, Soren and Jan Neuhard (I learned later) and was accepted with full support into the program on a "Ph.D. Direct" path, which meant that I would bypass the Masters degree. The Ph.D. direct path was contingent upon passing a rather rigorous general and written exam and required a perfect 4.0 performance in all graduate courses. I graduated with honors from Texas A&M in early May of 1973.

I would like to digress a bit from my academic history and discuss a business venture that I started as a junior at A&M. I learned from this experience that creating a business is exciting and that a for-profit outcome is unbelievably seductive. I seriously considered getting out of science and honing my business skills as an entrepreneur and risk taker; however, my Dad talked me out of it (and I am glad he did). I started a photography business that filled a needed niche and was totally a cash activity. I have always like photography and with my Dad, we built a home darkroom in Austin that was set up for B&W processing. I convinced my Dad that we should invest in professional grade equipment (high end enlargers, contact printer, high capacity drum dryer, print washers and of course a panoply of medium and large format cameras). It was done right and had reasonably high throughput. It took very little to convince him to invest. He collected antique cameras and was a total camera-phile, so it was an easy sell. As an aside, my Father's antique camera collection was donated to the University of Texas and is still on display in Austin (the "Mark T. Muller Camera Collection"). There are hundreds of cameras dating back to the 1860's along with daguerreotypes, tintypes, ambrotypes, carte de vis, and Civil War images in wonderfully carved union cases. I recall him saying that the world's oldest known photograph is in the collection, but I have not verified this.

In the fall of 1971, 72, during construction of the Texas Aggie Bonfire, I recognized that many in the Corps of Cadets would pay for 8x10 B&W pictures of their company activities, peers and themselves working building and organizing bonfire activities. Nobody was providing this service and since I was now an upperclassman, I had easy access to all bonfire activities. I bulk loaded 35mm film and made 40 frame cassettes, carefully labeled and cross-referenced with detailed record keeping. I used a state of art Nikon 35 (with multiple lenses) to capture thousands of images of individuals, groups of working aggies, whole companies and of course the bonfire itself. These images were all contact printed and I handed them out to the company sergeants in each dorm in the quadrangle and the orders rolled in. I charged $1 for an 8x10" print (only 1 size was offered) which was very fair and provided me a tidy profit margin. That first year, I cleared more than $5000 in two weeks of work. This was a huge sum of money back then and I put it to good use (saving for the future, paying back my Dad, buying a rather pricey ring for Annette). The next year was a repeat, but I engaged a sales force and paid them to help peddle the images and for darkroom help, I hired one of my best friends (Bill Gillespie, aka 'Skyboy' since he lived his life in a weed infused fog for most of his undergraduate years at A&M). Bill was no dummy and got an engineering degree from A&M and is an oil executive! I recall charging a bit more per picture that year, and reaping an even larger amount of money. It was easy money, it was my hobby and it was great fun. These funds were put in a savings account. During my Senior year, I also did several commercial photography jobs including shooting portraits and weddings. I hated wedding photography since it was high stress and sometimes the personalities were difficult. There was very little profit in weddings in any case, so this was a low priority activity.

After graduation, I started flying lessons. I have always been fascinated with flight and aviation and signed up for the ground school at Bergstrom Air Force Base (in Austin) and enlisted a flight instructor (CFI or certified flight instructor) named Wendell Fuqua to train me in a Piper 140 (a low wing trainer). It was hot that summer (as always in Austin) and the thermals (turbulence) were brutal but I enjoyed the flying nonetheless. Since my Dad was retired military, and technically I was still a dependent, I was allowed to use the Air Force Base facilities for all of my training. I passed the medical and an easy FAA written exam and did my solo. I needed some cross country time to complete the program (along with night flying); however, I simply ran out of time. I was to be married in late July followed by our honeymoon in Vancouver (to find a place to live for graduate school). In Vancouver, I met several faculty including Tony Warren, Bob Miller, Jack Campbell, Barry McBride, Julia Levy to name a few. All were extremely nice and acutely intelligent. They were genuinely interested in me as a first year Ph.D. student who might be interested in joining their respective research programs. I returned to Austin and in August (1973), packed up a U-haul trailer with my new wife and we drove our Dodge van from Texas to B.C. to begin graduate school. The cross-country trip gave me time to think and reflect about my life and the future. I was awash with enthusiasm for the future.

My choice for graduate school was strongly influenced by the people I worked with as an undergraduate; however, I was careful to validate that choice. My 'due diligence' involved looking carefully at the UBC research base and curriculum. I evaluated funding potential (stipend support) but never considered how much I would be making as a Ph.D. student. It was important to have some sort of ongoing support, but actual amount seemed irrelevant at the time. Part of the reasoning was that my wife could work as an R.N. and would make very good money, so I was less concerned about such matters. UBC is an exceptionally strong Canadian university. The Department of Microbiology was also a strong academic program, perhaps even the best in Canada. UBC is a currently a premier center for biomedical research in Canada. I have no regrets on this choice.

Choosing a Research Lab: Graduate School

I started graduate school at UBC in September of '73. The UBC Ph.D. program is loosely patterned after the British graduate education paradigm (hence the name 'British' Columbia). In a nutshell, the program is characterized by minimal course requirement and the overarching view that the Ph.D. is a research terminal degree and students should start working on projects with little or no coursework after that first year. To allow nascent Ph.D. students to make informed decisions about laboratory choice, the first year also involved 10 week rotations in at least three different areas within the broad field of Microbiology. I did four rotations in a phage/microbial genetics lab (Bob Miller), in a bacterial physiology group (Barry McBride), an immunology lab (Julia Levy) and a molecular virology lab (Jim Hudson). I learned so much from this experience and developed a broad appreciation for model system science, available research techniques and hypothesis driven science. Most of the courses were seminar style courses where the students presented papers to groups of faculty who posed questions and probed the student's basic understanding of the primary literature. I recall my graduate class, where Bob Miller assigned 7 papers for the next class period (the class had 8 students). We were told to be prepared to present all 7 papers in the next meeting and students will be selected at random to present one of the papers. This was pretty intense and the pace was maintained throughout the semester. I also took a course on "Nucleic Acids" that was taught by Gordon Tenor and Michael Smith.

Michael Smith was a very influential scientist in Canada and I would like to discuss his influence in my own career. Many years after graduate school (1991-92), I did a sabbatical in Mike's lab in the Department of Biochemistry at UBC. Like me, Mike was a morning person, and I loved coming into the lab and having coffee with him early in the day. The next year, 1993, Mike won the Nobel Prize in Chemistry for his work on oligo directed site mutagenesis. That year was an unusual Nobel year because two 'technique-Nobel prizes were awarded (Kerry Mullis, shared the prize for PCR). Mike gave me the following sage advice to those who aspire to win the Nobel Prize. Wear Birkenstock sandals and sleep naked. Mike's sense of humor was legendary. I also met Mike in the late 70's when he gave a seminar at McArdle Laboratory for Cancer Research (University of Wisconsin, where I was a Post-doctoral Fellow with Dr. Gerry Mueller). Mike had done a sabbatical in Switzerland (to learn molecular cloning which was just taking off) and was invited to Madison to give a seminar. He told the audience that when he returned to UBC, the Dean asked him to give a seminar on his accomplishments in the area of recombinant DNA. Mike then proceeded to report on his sabbatical 'progress'. His project was to craft recombinant DNA strategies to turn cow manure into chocolate (he was in a Swiss lab after all) and he was delighted to report that he made great advances on the project. A major advance had been made in fact. They had already successfully used recombinant DNA to get the color just right and now were diligently working on taste, texture and aroma!

My graduate school research rotations were challenging and intellectually rewarding. In each lab, my curiosity and creativity was stimulated and my scientific maturity advanced. I was fascinated with viruses and their simplistic life-plan yet complex pirating of the host biochemistry. Molecular virology became my passion and I enjoyed the trappings of the field; specifically, working with animal cell cultures, molecular aspects of DNA and RNA, analysis of novel viral proteins and thinking about the work from a molecular perspective. The decision to join Dr. Hudson's group was made. I liked Jim because of he was very soft spoken and had an easygoing personality. On the other hand, Jim's easy going character meant less direction on the research, which presented a problem at first. Fortunately, however, there were several good people in the lab that helped offset the problem. Also, I tend to be a self-starter and independence came natural. One of my class mates, Vikram Misra, was a very positive influence on my life. Vikram was a strapping 6' tall guy from Jodhpur, India, who oozed charisma and we became fast friends. We shared a house for a while in 1974 with Vikram and his wife, Lyn, living downstairs and my wife and I upstairs. At the end of the rotation year, Vikram also elected to join the Hudson lab, which was fantastic. Vikram worked on transcriptional control in lytic MCMV (murine cytomegalovirus or MCV, mouse cytomegalovirus as the Hudson lab called it) while I worked on the impact of the host cell cycle on viral replication. We were a good collaborative team and complemented each other. This worked out to be a synergy that led to a productive outcome. I established a nice project looking at the delay in replication of MCMV in G1 arrested cells and using this as a possible model for herpesvirus latency. It was an exciting project and my advisor, Jim Hudson had little if any role in deciding my research direction. Jim was better at organizing data and writing up papers but otherwise was a pretty loose lab chief. I learned the importance of self-reliance and independence in the lab. My Ph.D. committee included Hudson (chair), Gordon Tenor (Biochemistry), Bob Miller (a T-phage expert), Gerry Weeks (Microbiology) and Ray Reeves (from the Zoology Department and a chromatin expert). When my thesis was completed, an external committee member from the University of Calgary was added. All were very good scientifically and brought their unique expertise to the committee. Ray Reeves was instrumental in providing advice for a post-doctoral position a few years later. I got very little input from Jim on post-doc positions as I recall; however, he was very supportive in my decision.

My next hurdle was the qualifying exam (or general exam), a three-day written portion and a 2-3 hour oral exam on general knowledge related to your research area. Late in year 2 of my graduate studies, both Vikram and I took the general exam to officially enter the Ph.D. track. I worked every day at a cubicle in the library, designing the future project and establishing a frame of reference in the literature. I did this over a 1-month period prior to the exam. Vikram went first (about a week before me). Both of us did well on the written and the project-based oral loomed before us. Much to my surprise and dismay, Vikram did not pass; however, he was given an opportunity to retake the oral portion. Since he was a more seasoned graduate student and scientifically more mature, I felt my chances on the oral portion were remote at best. This forced me to work doubly hard at the preparation stage. I passed with surprising ease and got glowing recommendations and positive comments from all of the committee members. I learned something about myself in the process, specifically that I can rise to an occasion given enough motivational time. Vikram eventually took the oral again and passed. We both set out working on our respective projects in earnest and in year 3 we made significant progress. I eventually published 8 papers from my Ph.D. thesis (not counting the thesis itself). Some of these were collaborative manuscripts. One paper that was very nicely done and was a chapter in my thesis was the demonstration that MCMV did not encode its own viral thymidine kinase (TK). In science, it is very difficult to prove a negative; however, I engineered a foolproof approach using a TK minus HSV-1 mutant from Saul Kit (I recall having to drive down to the Univ. of Washington, in Seattle, to avoid a customs hangup). TK is an import 'achilles heel' in herpes virus since drugs like Valtrex and acyclovir target the viral enzyme selectively. However, it was important to determine whether the MCMV genome encoded this enzyme, which I showed using a halogenated pyrimidine analog (IUdR). IUdr (and related BUdR) both strongly inhibit HSV-1 replication and the TK mutant was an important control to show that in our hands, these mutants were wholly resistant to the drug. MCMV behaved exactly as the TK minus mutant, being resistant; therefore, the virus must not encode for TK. This paper was accepted immediately and without revision and is well cited.

I went through some personal problems after our first son was born that nearly de-railed my marriage and career. My wife Annette suffered post-partum depression for some months and I felt the marriage was doomed. I eventually suggested a trial separation (which in my mind meant divorce). Contributing to this was my desire to be free to do what I wanted, a terribly self-serving attitude driven by hormones and a narcissistic attitude. She moved to Austin with my first born (Soren, named for Soren Norby now on faculty at the University of Copenhagen, Department of Genetics). Coincidentally, my Ph.D. advisor went on sabbatical for a year and I was largely unaccountable for any research progress since no committee meetings were held. The day of reckoning came after his return and the committee really unloaded on me for lack of productivity. After much discussion, Annette and I decided to give our marriage another try and after a 6-month separation we were re-united. Both of us adjusted our attitudes with Annette becoming fiercely independent and less 'clingy' and me settling down and nosing into the grindstone while being an attentive father and husband. I am so glad that we both gave the marriage a second try.

I worked exceptionally long hours in the final year of my thesis. I developed, in collaboration with Vikram, computer software to analyze RNA expression complexity based on "R_0T Curves" and regression analyses. I loved working with DNA/DNA and DNA/RNA hybridization kinetics and the data analyses that followed. I designed and implemented machine based programs to analyze the data (on an HP 'desktop') and we recruited a software consultant to run the mainframe analysis of complex regression analysis.

Nearing completion of my Ph.D. research, I began a quest for a good post-doctoral lab in the U.S. I had the opportunity to attend a symposium in early 1977 and heard a fascinating seminar by Gerald C. Mueller, M.D., Ph.D. from The McArdle Laboratory for Cancer Research at the University of Wisconsin. He gave a wonderful talk on eukaryotic DNA replication. I was advised by several people that one should do a post-doc in an area that is distinctly different from one's thesis topic. The idea was to be employable and enhance one's resume to fit different teaching needs in the job market. This is very good advice in point of fact as I had job offers in both areas of expertise (in my case, virology and cancer). I made a formal application to Dr. Mueller's lab and was quickly accepted into The McArdle Laboratory for Cancer Research to begin post-doctoral studies in the fall of '77; I was 26 years old. I found out later that Dr. Mueller had made several phone calls about me and spoke with my committee members, including Ray Reeves. The thesis defense went well; however, there were a couple of committee members who were quite formal about the writing style. Gerry Weeks, a recent addition to the committee strongly objected to my 'loose' writing style, which others did not seem to mind (for example referring to protein 'cognates' as two different DNA binding proteins that bind the same DNA sequence). I made the edits of course, all the while grumbling under my breath. Gordon Tenor made a rather humorous comment I thought (which was valid). I commented in the presentation and thesis about virus yields being a 'log' apart. I knew it was jargon, but he asked me if I meant 'presto logs'? More corrections but it was an easy fix. Recall that this was in the days before word processors. I wrote my thesis out longhand and because my penmanship was terrible, I had my wife recopy it into beautiful script and then the Division secretary (aka Rosie) typed it up. I will forever be in debt to my wife for this herculean effort and of course Rosie. I finished up my Ph.D. about a year before Vikram, which worked out very well since he and I had collaborated on a few papers. Vikram stayed in the Hudson lab to oversee and complete these manuscripts and perform the necessary changes that reviewers always impose (in some cases, adding experimental data). This was a great synergy and we both benefited. I will always be indebted to Vikram for following up on the publications and seeing that I was represented. He is a very good friend. Vikram completed his Ph.D. and went to Roger Hand's lab in Montreal. Vikram is currently Chair of the Department of Microbiology at the University of Saskatchewan in Saskatoon, Canada. He has had a distinguished career and has remained with his wife Lyn.

Post-Doctoral Studies.

After completing the editorial changes, getting papers submitted, attending an international meeting in Calgary (and presenting) and saying our goodbyes, we packed up our household goods in a U-haul and set out across the country for the mid-west. Fortunately, I was able to sell the small sailboat-trailer combination that I had acquired two years before when my wife was employed as an R.N. working at VGH (Vancouver General Hospital). We were flat broke and this small sum allowed us to defray the cost of moving back to the States. The sailboat had a small cabin and we did a number of very fun trips around English Bay (avoiding the cargo ships was daunting), up Howe Sound and to the Gulf Islands while living in B.C. Vikram and his wife Lyn also had a sloop and there is more safety in numbers, so we ventured far and wide on our explorations of the Gulf Islands.

Driving over the mountains pulling a trailer with an aging van led to some problems that had to be corrected enroute (radiator issues). We did an overnight stay in Wall, South Dakota since we saw signs hundreds of miles away drawing us in! We got up early the next morning and enjoyed a 57 cent breakfast, one of big attracts at Wall Drug Store. Along the way, we paid a visit to my Aunt Rita in Minnesota and spent time with my paternal grandmother. My grandmother looked like a plump version of a little muffin, with wiry white hair pointed in all directions looking much like a version Einstein in drag. She was in fact a little old Jewish lady in her nineties in a nursing home who looked at me and recognized me as her son (my Father). My name was always 'Markie' so when she called me 'Mark', it was clear. Granny spoke with a heavy German (Austrian actually) accent and when I spoke to her in German she became visibly upset because I butchered the language so badly; ok… English only! Granny lived to be 100 but was in her own world the last years of life. My Father said that he believed that she was older than her stated age, because she kept her actual birth year a secret (there were no records from Vienna in any case). It was good to see her one last time, even if she was in a fog.

After a long trip (40 hours of windshield time) we arrived in Madison, unpacked our belongings in the storage basement of our apartment (we did not move in) and then got in the van and drove to Austin to visit my folks. More drive time with a 2-year old (Soren) and a van without air conditioning! Good training for purgatory. I tried to keep everyone's spirits up but we were miserable moving into hot weather in August. We finally got to Austin and spent some needed vacation wrapped in the cloak of luxury that was my parent's very nice home in an upscale suburb of Austin called Northwest Hills. The baby was whisked away by my Mother and Annette and I were free to reconnect socially with old friends, classmates and others. We spent a very pleasant time for about 2 weeks. We were back on the road to Madison to start my post-doc in G.C. Mueller's lab at McArdle in Madison. This was in September of 1977.

I started working in the lab on a project trying to understand the role of cytosolic support factors in DNA replication using permeabilized cells. We devised a clever strategy to analyze events in vitro. DNA replication origins do not initiate in permeabilized cells; thus, we were looking only at completing already initiated DNA chains (pre-existing *in vivo* 'extension'). To discriminate, we used BrDU (bromodeoxyuridine) to tag the replication chains in the intact cell, then we isolated and prepared the permeabilized cells and 'completed' the chains of DNA synthesis. Here is the cool part: BrDU substituted DNA is highly sensitive to long wave UV irradiation and becomes fragmented. The 'new' DNA that was made in permeable cells was released and we analyzed this part without complications of the bound DNA from intact cells. I was the first one in the lab to run 'submarine' agarose gels for this analysis. Back then, DNA cloning was in its infancy and gel separations were the hot new ticket in technology (of course routine these days). We published a very nice paper on this work (after two years of post-doctoral research). I came to realize that my mentor was only interested in publishing very high profile papers and he was not inclined to allow post-docs to put out anything less. While this is laudable, it can get out of hand since post-docs need publications to get jobs and if they don't strike gold on a project, they get nothing. Hard work and long hours in the lab are no assurance; it is necessary but not sufficient. I was in a big group with many post-docs and all were competing for that next big Science, Cell or Nature paper. Welcome to the world of high profile, high impact research, I told myself. For the first time, it became obvious that working extra hard to gain an edge was not going to work (it was necessary but not sufficient). After my second post-doctoral year, I informed Dr. Mueller that I had sufficient data to publish another paper (or two even); however, he resisted. I considered changing labs and going into Janet Mertz's group. Janet had done some exceptionally nice work on *X. laevis* microinjection with John Gurdon (Nobel Laureate). When Dr. Mueller got wind of this, he changed his demeanor and was a bit more encouraging since he did not want me leaving the group (in retrospect, I should have left). I discussed matters with Bill Sugden, a younger faculty member at McArdle (working with EBV and a rising star from Harvard). Bill saw my point of view and felt that Dr. Mueller was acting a bit irresponsibly, but to keep the peace, he suggested staying in the lab. I stayed on but my ambition was blunted by the experience and I came to grips with the prospect of only getting a single publication from my post-doc experience.

During my time at McArdle, I got more experience and maturity from a vast number of individuals, many of whom I am still in close contact to this day. Probably the most influential was Howard Temin who won the Nobel Prize (shared with David Baltimore) for discovery of reverse transcriptase in retroviruses. Dr. Temin was very well known of course and respected. He worked at the bench (seven days a week). He would come to the lab early and examine the cell cultures using an inverted phase microscope, looking at various retroviral mutants and cytopathology. He had an intense demeanor and was highly focused. Several years later, I invited him to Ohio State and he gave a high profile seminar which was one of the best attended talks ever given. During this visit, he was interviewed on Radio and TV program. Dr. Temin also oversaw the tumor virology training grant with many talented trainees. We got along well and I respected him. He died of lung cancer at a relatively early age after I left McArdle.

One of brightest people at McArdle (beside Dr. Mueller who was a true genius) was Bill Sudgen. Bill and Gerry Mueller did not get along well for some reason (probably due to age related divergent opinions about how to conduct research). Bill was the most creative and amazing intellect I have ever known. We got along well and he was receptive, kind and giving of his time; he read my proposals, gave insight on experiments and was spot-on with his advice. Bill is still active in science but at a greatly slowed pace it seems. Many years later (mid 90's) he was called in as a consultant on a Venture with Senmed Medical, VC firm out of Cincinnati, Ohio. There were other influences at McArdle. Richard Burgess, a mid-career associate professor, was arrogant but an excellent biochemist with wonderful insight on protein structure and function (he had worked extensively with E. coli RNA polymerase and sigma factor). There were a couple of graduate students that I respected. One was Jeronimo Blanco, from Barcelona, working on a Ph.D.

(in the Mueller lab). Jeronimo worked 12-16 hr days on technology to analyze protein-DNA binding in HeLa cells. He did crazy experiments, like hooking up Sucrose gradients to electrophoresis systems to resolve chromatin structures. This was also messy business as you can imagine, with sticky sugar solutions all over the bench (and lab). I became close personal friends with Jeronimo and his wife Jeannie (an American) and after leaving McArdle he took a faculty position in Spain. I visited him once back in the 1990's and was impressed with the quality of life and his academic environment. I overlapped briefly with a graduate student (Dan Schoenberg) who received his Ph.D. working with Dr. Mueller. Dan and I had many discussions over Dr. Mueller's resistance to publish good science (not great science but nonetheless solid). I met Dan years later when he joined the Medical Biochemistry Department at OSU (mid 1990s) and established a successful RNA processing program. Dan was a bright guy who produced a quality Ph.D. thesis that really never saw the light of day, publication-wise, thanks to Dr. Mueller's lust for great papers at the expense of the careers of his PhD and Post-doctoral fellows. I also met and became close to a husband and wife team from Japan. Both were M.D./Ph.D. researchers that I collaborated with for some years on topoisomerase projects. Ken and Kimiko Tsutsui were both on faculty in the medical school at Okayama University (well south of Tokyo) and I worked with them in Japan (summer of '83) and they both worked in my lab on projects. Ken was pathologically quiet, unless he was lubricated with his favorite beverage (single malt scotch). Ken is unusual for a Japanese guy because he speaks essentially unaccented English, that is on rare occasions when he actually speaks. Ken's father was the Dean at Okayama Medical school and his mother spoke fluent Esperanto (I never met anyone who learned the 'universal' language). I liked Ken immensely. He was very intelligent and had unique insight on all scientific matters. His reticence probably did not help him career-wise. For both Ken and Kim, science was their life. They never had kids and were totally dedicated to research. Ken was also an accomplished jazz pianist and had a special room in their home for his 1885 Steinway (dissembled in New York City, and re-assembled in Okayama). His music room was accessible through a trap door from the first-floor master closet. Go figure! Both Ken and Kim were major influences in my life and are good friends to this day. My last visit was in 2010 where we made a sojourn over to Naoshima Island (the art island) which was an amazing experience.

I would like to make few brief comments about Japanese academic science and my peer group operating that environment. It seems that Japan acquired the German (or European) structure for academic hierarchical organization. Most likely this comes from WWII. While this system functions reasonably well in Germany, it is not ideal for a homogeneous society like Japan. Essentially there is one full professor who runs a large research enterprise (equivalent to a small Department in the US) while there are several underling associates and assistant professors. The full professorship is loosely based on seniority and political capital and this person (usually a male) totally dominates all resource allocation in the group. This imposes strict funding penalties on young investigators who don't tow the line. If the lab chief is brilliant, creative, well balanced and a good manager, the system can work, but I believe this is generally not the case. Advancement based solely on age is really not a good practice because not everybody gets 'old and wise' (some just get old). Some senior investigators are intellectually tired, moribund or scientifically out of touch. To put such individuals into a power position controlling younger researchers can effectively stifle a generation of researchers. I spent many hours bemoaning this problem and being critical of the system when Ken, Kim and I were young assistants. We all recognized the major defects; however, nothing could be done. The Japanese have an expression. "If the nail sticks up above the board, it must be hammered flat." For Ken and Kim, they were in a somewhat oppressive lab environment (lab chief was a guy name Professor T. Oda) and held hostage. The basic problem is that young investigators tend to be more productive and creative than their senior colleagues. They must pay homage to an individual who has no skin in the game, only the power to control others. This is stifling in science and there is an acute need for sweeping reform. Such reforms can only spring from senior faculty who control policy. Of course, that would mean imposing changes that work against their own self interests. Once in power, the full professor has paid his dues so change is unlikely. Those discussions long ago with Ken and Kim, bemoaning the Japanese system, are long forgotten. They also paid their dues. Adding to the problem is the mandatory retirement at age 65. Usually, the lab chief is not appointed until late in the career (mid-late 50's I recall). Thus, there is little time to change the system, even if the senior faculty were so motivated.

Kim Tustsui was very successful and managed to advance to full professor status. I think that she is one of the very few full professors in Japan that is a woman and at the time of her official promotion, I think she was one of the first. Like Ken, she paid her dues, enduring long clinical duties as a psychiatrist at distal hospitals. She published with Ken for the most part. Kim's CV was probably very similar to Ken's record of publication and they both are full professors and share a large lab with associate and assistant professors under foot. The Japanese hierarchy of academic science will carry on it seems.

My First Academic Position

Sometime in late 1979 (Fall), I started on the job circuit looking for a tenure track assistant professor. I had a good project (analysis of nucleosome assembly factors in cancer cells) and a reasonable overall publication record (despite only one paper as a post-doc in two years of work). Fortunately for me, there were plenty of viable positions for someone with a molecular virology background, an area where I was well established. Reading through each issue of Science magazine, I looked for ads for assistant professors in either virology or molecular biology. I interviewed at a number of state universities (and one in Canada) and got multiple offers. I only considered tenure track appointments. My selection was based on academic environment, research infrastructure, collegiality, teaching demands and lab start up package. Salary was not a serious consideration. Ohio State University offered me an attractive package; however, the salary was the lowest of all of my offers (my 9-month salary was $21,000 starting in September of 1980). I really enjoyed my visit and seminar in the Department of Microbiology. Everyone was enthusiastic and sincerely interested in my research. I recall a lively meeting with the Dean (Pat Dugan) and the Chair (Bob Pfister) and being impressed with both. The Dean informed me that they were quite impressed with my credentials and he wanted to 'sweeten' the offer with some additional attractions. Dugan informed me that being on faculty, I could get OSU season football tickets! I thanked him and said it was very nice to offer me tickets; to which he said that I would have the 'privilege of buying tickets' and they would not be gratis. I am not a football fan, so this whole concept was lost on me. My wife however, loves college football and was thrilled to get tickets. I also recall meeting Julius Kreier, who was on the search committee (composed of John Reeve, Neil Baker and Julius). I liked Julius immediately and after joining the faculty at OSU, we became close personal friends. Julius is well known in the malaria field. He has a Willie Nelson phenotype and a limp that imposed a bird-like dynamic to his gait; however, he was still quite agile and nimble. Julius was very bright and had a reputation for being a bit quirky but I really liked this about him. I recall seeing a 'rodent zoo' in his -20 freezer, courtesy of Dave, a graduate student working on rat malaria (*P. berghei*). After euthanizing adult rats, Dave had frozen the animals in doll furniture sitting in various poses around a tiny round table. Some of the rats were smoking tiny cigars while others appeared to be holding small playing cards. All were frozen in place, waiting for necropsy. While strange, it was very entertaining! I suppose that some students get bored after long hours in the lab!

1980-1986: Getting Tenure at OSU.

One of the great things about OSU Microbiology was that I had a teaching free year to establish my research program. I was replacing another assistant professor who was denied tenure due to low research productivity. This outgoing faculty member was very bitter of course and I was able to avoid him most of the first year when we overlapped. He felt he got a raw deal from senior colleagues. Evidently he was partially appointed by the Cancer Center in the OSU Medical School (with very attractive start up package and minimal teaching loads); thus, when he did not deliver on publications, he got denied tenure. This person left science and completed law school and is now a highly successful patent attorney in Washington, D.C. I worked with him many years later when he prosecuted a patent I developed on gene delivery; small world it seems!

I worked extremely long hours in the lab, in addition to writing NIH grants, papers, dealing with graduate students and teaching. My service work was minimal and the Chairman shielded me from committee assignments. In those early years, I arrived at the lab around 8am, worked until 6pm, went home to dinner and returned by 7-8pm and worked until 11pm. I did this 6-days a week leaving Sundays to spend time with my family and new baby (my second son, Branden). I built the lab up with some highly capable people, including my first graduate student (Douglas Trask) who received his Ph.D. in 1986 and then went to medical school and a successful career as a physician-scientist. After I secured my first NIH grant (a cancer grant on topoisomerase, an important anticancer target protein), I opened up a second project area on Herpes Immediate Early gene regulation and was fortunate to get another concurrent RO1 grant. With multiple RO1 grants, I expanded the lab with post-docs and technicians; however, I was having problems attracting Ph.D. students from the Microbiology Department. I joined another graduate program, the MCDB or Molecular Cellular Developmental Biology program. This interdisciplinary program was more focused on eukaryotic models and was an excellent fit for my research interests. I was actively involved in the MCDB program, from an administrative standpoint (running the seminar program, committees, etc.). A couple of senior faculty were administering the program, including Phil Perlman, Tom Byers and George Marzluf, all very good scientists whom I respected. The only problem with the program was the lack of training grant support; however, this was remedied eventually. In addition to the MCDB group, I was invited to join the OSU Comprehensive Cancer Center, which grew into a very large and active program as an NCI designated cancer center. In the early 80's, the Cancer Center was rather loosely knit and not well organized. The OSU-CCC did however provide some support for my start-up activities and provided access to clinicians interested in basic science (but there were very few of these opportunities).

In the early 1980's biotechnology startups were ubiquitous and the investor community was ablaze with activity. Fueling the process was the enormous perceived potential for recombinant DNA in general (and gene cloning in particular) for improving the human condition. Early patents by Boyer and Cohen showed that restriction and ligation of DNA could create new DNA 'chimerias'. Thus, molecular (not reproductive) cloning was big news and investors were salivating. The very early startups like Genentech in the mid 1970's, established the biotechnology industry. With cloning and overexpression approaches, Genentech had its first FDA approved product (human insulin) in the early 1980s. Everyone recognized the potential in human medicine, veterinary medicine and agriculture. For the first time in history, biology was transformed into a predictable and quantitative hard science. Model system science was all the rage and a historic reset of phage systems biology (dating back to the 40's) was being re-established in more complex systems, such as yeast, human cells in culture, plants, worms, and flies to name a few. The driver for all this work was the lowly bacterium, E. coli, and its engineered plasmid (an extrachromosomal element which served as a vector for cloning). In addition, phage and cosmid based gene library technology was well established (a gene library is similar to a conventional library but instead of a collection of books, it has a diverse collection of gene fragments). As the field advanced, major revolutionary technologies punctuated the meteoric rise of biotech. These included the development of transgenic technologies in mice, the polymerase chain reaction (PCR), site directed mutagenesis, DNA sequencing, over-expression systems (in diverse model organisms), plant transformation with agrobacteria, gene and expression libraries and ultimately the human genome project. All of the above were made possible by the basic research on restriction enzymes followed by rational extension by Berg, Mertz, Cohen, Boyer, Axel and many others. As noted above, I knew a number of these folks. Janet Mertz working in Paul Berg's lab made the first recombinant DNAs. Michael Smith at UBC (my instructor in a Nucleic Acids) later developed oligo directed site-specific mutagenesis in the 80's and was awarded a Nobel Prize for this effort. My sabbatical with Mike

(1991-92) was the year before he won the Nobel Prize. This was indeed an exciting time.

As a young faculty member at OSU in the early 80's, I was not directly involved in biotechnology business activities. I was building a research program and trying to get tenure; however, I did get an occasional glimpse of the business end of science. I recall giving a presentation to Isaac and David Blech, out of NYC, two shakers and movers in startup funding (organized by Rod Sharp who founded DNA Plant Technology, another successful startup). The business of biotechnology involves commercializing exciting new ideas and products, attracting investors and creating spin-off companies. Everything about the process was appealing. In addition, my experience with teaching undergraduates gave me an ability to convey complex scientific ideas to business professionals and investors who were very bright people but lacked scientific backgrounds. It is important to reach such people effectively and carefully titrate the amount of information to be concise yet simplistic.

I came up for promotion and tenure in 1985. I was well funded and had published well-cited papers. While it seemed highly likely that I would be promoted, I needed backup plans; therefore, I put my C.V. out for consideration at other institutions (confidentially). I interviewed at several different places and received offers. I delayed my decision on accepting any offers until after the promotion and tenure review, which came back positive. One of the offers (U.C. Davis) was attractive. The research infrastructure was excellent and the academic environment was very rich with many excellent colleagues. I was tempted. I was a little unhappy about not having access to graduate students in my home department at OSU (Microbiology). Relocating my lab was going to disrupt my research program and I would lose at least one year of being productive; this was a huge negative and seriously eroded my enthusiasm. In the end, I stayed at OSU. This was the right decision.

The Creation of a New Department of Molecular Genetics.

About this time, the Department was undergoing some leadership changes. John Reeve, who had the lab next to mine, became the

Department Chair, replacing Bob Pfister. I respected John and we got along well, so I was very encouraged about the new leadership. The future of the Department was in good hands and a new beginning was taking place.

In early 1987, Phil Perlman, the Chair of the Department of Genetics, asked if I might be interested in joining a new program. Phil asked me to help him create a Department of Molecular Genetics, the first in the country. The idea of creating something new was intoxicating and Phil was enormously enthusiastic. He could really excite a crowd and he was extremely careful about who should join this new program. The new Molecular Genetics Department would focus on eukaryotic models. It was immediately obvious that my research 'fit' in this academic program would be ideal. Moreover, I should be able to attract students from a pool of Ph.D. applicants with interests similar to my own. There was another aspect of the new program that I found attractive. I would be able to select my colleagues. Usually, the reverse is true (they select you).

Switching academic departments is risky business and can alienate your colleagues. There is considerable territorialism in academic units since each department is competing for a fix sum of the available budget. When a well-funded faculty member leaves, that department is diminished in its grant portfolio and teaching support. I met with the Micro Chair and explained my reasons for leaving Microbiology. He understood my rationale (I was a poor fit in a prokaryotic based research unit) and seemed supportive; however, other faculty were not as sanguine. I told the Department that I would try to help with teaching duties until a replacement could be found for my main course (Virology) and that I would be happy to retain a courtesy appointment if they were agreeable (they were not). In the end, I decided that a clean break was the best exit strategy. Fortunately, people tend to forget, and over time things got back to normal. I never regretted joining the new department and I relished in the creative process.

Starting a Company: 1990

In the late 1980s I noticed that some faculty were very active in consulting and outside entrepreneurial activity. One faculty member in the Biochemistry Department was quite active in this arena and my 'hallway' discussions with him were very stimulating. My work with topoisomerases was really getting traction and after publishing papers showing that these proteins were high value drug targets in cancer, I started getting calls from different pharmaceutical companies to come and give seminars or consult. Indeed, I was traveling quite frequently and the compensation was a very nice perk. I liked the idea of outside consulting and recognized the potential for a profitable startup company, solely based on the kind of consultation I was providing. My thinking followed along these lines:

1. There is a demand for my expertise, technology transfer and reagents in the field of anticancer drug discovery.
2. I was spending a fair amount of my time visiting various companies and consulting in the area.
3. Why not develop a Research Diagnostic company to meet the demand as a way to reach many other academic and industry labs in the U.S. and abroad?

While this was a great concept for a small startup business, there were serious rate limiting steps to consider (along with some risks). I am not risk averse by nature, so I decided to figure out a pathway through the maize. It might sound trivial now, but to learn as much as possible about start-ups, I enrolled in an evening course at a local community college on "how to start a business". This gave me a basic foundation within a short time and I found it useful to know the nuts and bolts of running a generic business. I also did a fair amount of reading on the subject of gorilla or bootstrap marketing and advertising. These resources were not sophisticated but helped me with the basics. A major influence in my life at the time was my Uncle (William Muller), my Dad's older brother, a Ph.D. in Chemical Engineering who had started several successful companies and was well-versed in the IP arena.

There are many reasons why people do not start companies but emotional and psychological risk factors are clearly high on the list. On top of the emotional issues, there were serious legal concerns. For example, at the time the State of Ohio had antiquated laws making it illegal to own more that 5% equity in a company, as a state employee. This was an old law to keep politicians honest (or so I was told). Clearly, risk factor number one was jail time! This puts an overriding damper on matters! Here are less weighty concerns that I had to consider (in no particular order).

1. Seed Funding.

No matter how small the start-up or venture, you need cash. I could not approach venture capitalists or investors for a number of reasons (lack of time, no networking, a poorly defined business model and no business plan, among others). So my idea was to start an escrow account (with a new LLC) to put my consulting funds. These funds were signed over to escrow over a period of about 1 year. It was not a fortune but it was sufficient to defray some basic costs (incorporating, paying attorneys, CPA, etc.).

2. IP and OSU Conflicts.

As a University faculty member, everything I do in science, related to my research, is owned as IP by OSU. Things can be murky here, but OSU could claim ownership (or worse) terminate my employment due to conflict of interest issues. On the other hand, there was no formal policy in place, so they might be open to some creative solutions. While I was nervous about this potential complication, I figured there must be a rational strategy to make it all work. This involved a dual pronged approach: First, implicate everyone above me in the chain of command (full disclosure) and get them on board; second, file a complete invention disclosure to the University officials. First, I met with Dean Jensen (Biological Sciences Dean) who was largely asleep during the meeting; however, Associate Dean Gary Floyd was fully engaged. I explained what I planned to do, specifically, create a company spin-off based on my research and use my own lab facilities to do so. Gary Floyd was a capable administrator with a good head. I was surprised when he said (without hesitation!) "go for it". This was 1989 and no faculty (to my knowledge anyway) were bootstrapping startups. There was no playbook on how to proceed, so the Associate Dean decided to give it a shot. One other reason he was supportive was my prior disclosure of the technology to the Patents and Licensing Committee at OSU (*viz*, technology that founded the company concept). In 1988, I disclosed the technology and the concept for a company to the Committee, loosely composed of faculty members from chemistry, engineering, physics and biochemistry. The IP disclosure was reasonably well detailed and I argued strongly that OSU should file at least provisional patents on these ideas. The Physics guy said bluntly "everyone knows there is no real money in biology". Interesting perspective! Thank you very much. I got a formal letter from Ed Jennings (OSU President) releasing all disclosed IP back to me, with no strings. Such "no strings'" releases are a thing of the past because, these days, the University 'release' actually has a 10% (or similar) option that benefits the institution. This is really absurd in my opinion for one reason. The faculty member has to pay for the IP and commercialization and take on all risk. For the University to then turn around and make claim on successful commercialization seems outrageous because they gave up their first refusal rights (sort of like the "cake and eat it" concept). My current employer, the University of Central Florida has adopted this policy. Perhaps a class action litigation process will be required to stop this institutional behavior (which stifles the entrepreneurial spirit).

The letter was very nice and while at first I was upset, I later realized this was a great outcome; very nice indeed. Since all technological aspects of the company start up were released back to me, I could approach the Dean of Biological Sciences and legitimately ask for approval without any conflicts. I still have the letter of release from Jennings. The IP associated with the company was to be considered 'background IP'. I used the concept of background IP to negotiate a new faculty position at the University of Central Florida in Orlando (College of Medicine, my current employer). This shields me from Licensing and Patent "tech transfer" predators who are suspicious of faculty who create new University spin-offs. I simply do not understand why any University should look suspiciously at faculty who start companies; however, the current 'compliance' climate in U.S. science is largely all stick and no carrot. Major state universities are risk averse as a result.

3. Bricks and Mortar.

At the time (1990) OSU did not have a wet lab incubator; at least not as a formal, functional facility (although there were some unofficial pockets here and there around the campus). I was in no position to create production, shipping or business facilities for the company I had in mind. I approached Gary Floyd (now the Dean of the College of Biological Sciences), and bluntly asked if I could use my lab as 'seed space' to ramp up the business. I explained that there were no conflicts (*vis a vis* IP or commitment) and assured him that any sales activity (shipping of products for example and a business office for billing and tracking purposes) would take place off site. (I created a separate business office in rented space and all shipping billing and accounting activity took place at this facility.) I still needed a production facility. Since the kits and reagents which I planned to market as "research diagnostics" were in my research area (topoisomerase biochemistry) I explained a bootstrap model for production of products. In a nutshell, I told him that the Company (TopoGEN, Inc.) would defray all costs associated with materials for both inventory AND my research. For example, a typical enzyme preparation would yield one million units, which the company would defray in toto. Half of the preparation would then go into inventory (500K units) and the other half would go to my research (which would help me get future grants and maintain my research). In this way, I created a win-win situation for OSU and for TopoGEN. I did not think he would approve but he did so enthusiastically. I was thrilled and he was excited to see a new growth enterprise and was keen to see how things worked. Nobody was thinking about such entrepreneurial ventures at the time. I had crafted an innovative strategy that got people's attention. All the negotiation took place over a period of about 3 months and the next phase was ready to begin: Putting together a technology transfer company that would market a number of molecular biology kits and reagents.

4. Products and Inventory.

Having reasonable experience with designing undergraduate laboratories for teaching purposes, gave me reasonable insight into design and implementation of 'kitable' technology. I recall having a meeting the Arthur Kornberg, a distinguished Nobel Laureate (discovered DNA polymerase) who was giving a seminar at OSU. I mentioned in passing the startup concept and he wanted to know more about my idea. We spent most of the hour in my office discussing entrepreneurial inroads in science. He must have been impressed because he made note of our discussion in his seminar later that day. He explained that providing products to promote science was innovative and honorable and he commended me for my efforts.

I spent about 6 months, never on University time but in the evening and weekends, designing the products we would sell. Recall that I was consulting with many different companies on how to do these sorts of assays and utilize the enzymes for drug discovery, so I knew there was a demand and based on the published literature, which was showing exponential increases in topoisomerase related papers, I had a very good idea of what would sell. All commercial products were based on some aspect of topoisomerase biochemistry and/or molecular biology. Many of these same products are sold even today, and I have opened up other niche markets. Basically, I put together kits for drug discovery using DNA based assays, such as relaxation of plasmid, cleavage assays of DNA targets with high affinity topoisomerase binding or recognition elements, decatenation assays and so on. None of the kits were sold with enzyme, so I created a suite of enzyme products that has grown over the years.

We also made and sold DNA substrates, antibodies to key topo enzymes and what I call "support" products (reagents to replenish kits). In addition, we started to collect and market as many different topo active drugs as possible and we became a repository for these compounds for researchers. Note that any investigator could approach our chemical suppliers and get drugs or other companies and get DNA for that matter; however, the catch was that we certified the drugs, DNA and related reagents as being pre-tested and guaranteed to work for the topo research in question. This certification was akin to a 'technology lead' or trade secret. Recall that we really had not patent protection, so we relied on trade secrets and careful marketing to get sales and repeat sales of our products. Moreover, the margins are huge on these products (we can produce $100K worth of enzyme for less than $2500, including tech time). Any time an end user was not happy with a product, we simply replaced it gratis and gave the the customer receives even more than they ordered. This yields many satisfied and repeat customers. Often we find that the end users can be unsophisticated, sloppy or just inexperienced; however, they rarely admit fault. By simply replacing the product for free, they will eventually realize that they themselves are often at fault. Clearly this is a niche market and some of the 'market forces' that drive retail simply do not apply. Another advantage to a 'niche' business is technical support. Other companies can purchase bulk quantities of our enzymes (topoisomerase, Gyrases etc.) and sell them at highly competitive prices. The problem is when the end user has technical issues with the product. The warehouse concept of reagent sales, cannot offer detailed support to clients. The company, started by experts in the field, can offer very strong technical support. When dealing with technology transfer, this is a very important advantage.

A Successful University Spin-off.

TopoGEN was officially incorporated in 1991. I was President and CEO and the major stockholder. I relied on my accumulated consulting funds to launch TopoGEN, Inc. These funds were used to defray the set up costs, including attorney's fees, miscellaneous filling fees, paying for a very creative and excellent CPA (Thomas W. Brandkamp and Associates). The key to creating a good income streaming enterprise is to minimize overhead. Don't create infrastructure unless unavoidable. Use all available resources, but do so with full disclosure and implicate everyone by being totally honest and above board. That said, I tend to use the 'thin end of the wedge model' whereby I start small and expand. This means that I adhere to a policy of "asking for forgiveness rather than for permission". I structure things so that I can always apologize for any miscommunication or mis-steps and immediately back away. Mea culpa. This is risky, but I like and manage risk well.

I needed technical help with the company and that meant man (or woman) power. I asked my Ph.D. students if they would like to earn extra funds by helping the Company on weekends. I paid the students for their time on an attractive hourly rate and I never demanded their participation. It was voluntary and there was no requirement for students to perform Company duties. I also made sure that their research activities would not suffer by monitoring their project progress. In most cases, Company duties overlapped with research directives. For example, at one time I had three Ph.D. student working on various topoisomerase problems in cancer. There was an ongoing demand for resources (plasmids, kDNA, enzymes, antisera, etc.) and as noted above, the preparation of these key reagents was paid for by TopoGEN and the students had access to Company products gratis. These reagents were pre-tested and well controlled and materially contributed to students' progress toward their Ph.D. This lead to publications and made me more competitive for future funding.

One other safeguard I built into the Company/OSU relationship. I told the business office at TopoGEN to never process purchase orders from OSU researchers. Sales back to OSU were absolutely forbidden. I was to be told who wanted our products if such orders were sent. I then contacted that faculty member and explained that we could not sell them any TopoGEN product; however, I informed these faculty that they could have any product free of charge. The only thing I asked for in return was a nice letter (or email) stipulating that all products were supplied by TopoGEN without charge (or that the Company had donated the products). In all cases these faculty were very grateful and also acknowledged how important TopoGEN was in the success of their research. I have a stack of such letters of gratitude from numerous colleagues in the OSU College of Medicine. I call this good, cheap insurance, when someone comes sniffing around thinking that I was exploiting my position as a University faculty member by doing business back with OSU and profiteering on the backs of colleagues who don't have tenure. It paid off in fact. Some years later, a colleague of mine started a company with family members, however his company was a middleman type of day to day business that sold plasticware and disposables (tips, pipettes, tubes, racks, etc). He was essentially a warehouse that advertised these things that he obtained from a variety of vendors. His company (run by his wife and adult children) would mark up and distribute the products. This was a sales operation of a very different type. The problem was that he was selling back to OSU faculty labs and making a profit. People in his own department were buying these items, and he was in a position to purchase these products using his own NIH grant funds, clearly a conflict of interest. The local newspaper got wind of his operation and a reporter called the faculty member, ostensibly to interview him on his "exciting new research findings". The interview quickly turned ugly when the reporter wanted statements regarding his company dealings with OSU. In other words, a trap was set and sprung on the poor guy and they even got a photographer to document with guilty looking photographs. It was major embarrassment to OSU and the faculty member, who was reprimanded and forced to dissociate from all business relationships and the company. I was also contacted by the same reporter, who asked to 'interview' me about my latest research findings. He showed up in my office with a photographer. We spoke briefly about my science and the topic turned to TopoGEN and he asked how it is that a faculty member could be profiteering off OSU colleagues. He had done his homework and knew about TopoGEN. He requested a full explanation of my relationship with OSU and the Company. I explained that my company was a business, separated from OSU and that the University had released all IP back to me to develop as I see fit. I further explained that TopoGEN was a manufacturing enterprise that made products for science and our customers were worldwide. Leaning forward on my desk he asked pointedly to see records of sales to OSU faculty. I informed him that TopoGEN conducted no business with OSU investigators. I further explained to the reporter that any researcher wishing to purchase TopoGEN products would be denied; however, all Company products were provided free of charge to any OSU lab. As proof, I pulled out the stack of emails and letters from OSU Cancer Researchers expressing their gratitude for the Company largesse. The reporter spent a few minutes thumbing through the support letters in silence. He then stood up, told the photographer that pictures were not necessary and that there was 'no story here'. He did not thank me or shake my hand on leaving. I never saw anything in the local newspaper and there was no follow-up. Nonetheless, the whole experience left me shaken. After all, the State of Ohio had not yet repealed the law stipulating limited equity ownership for state employees; thus, I was still vulnerable. That law has since been changed, thankfully.

The OSU Edison Foundation: A New Research Park and Incubator.

Word got around fast that I had created a successful for-profit company. TopoGEN was in the black and a strong income streaming enterprise. Eventually, OSU administrators were asking questions about faculty entrepreneurism. Why were there so few spin-offs or start-up companies emanating from OSU faculty? What was missing? First and foremost, it was recognized that ownership in a corporation was a 4th degree felony in the State of Ohio. As noted, this law has since been repealed. Another problem was the lack of incubator wet lab space near the campus. I was asked by the VP of Research, to sit on a blue-ribbon committee to create from scratch a new research park and spin-off incubator. The committee operated under the aegis of the VP for Research. It took many months of meetings to flesh out the details but the general idea was as follows. The University purchased (or was gifted?) the old Simmons mattress factory on Kinnear Road (near campus). The building was at more than 100,000 square feet and over several years was renovated into a first rate facility. We organized the space for wet labs, central equipment, engineering, chemistry, bioscience labs and so on. In addition, we built infrastructure for secretarial support, reception staff, mailroom and janitorial services. Labs were well organized and reasonably priced at subsidized rates. There was a business board of professional and local business leaders (including some faculty from the Fisher Business College at OSU). Client companies were given modules of space of 600 square feet and each company had to be reviewed by the board of directors. Criteria were established to ensure that growth-oriented, high technology would populate the incubator.

TopoGEN, Inc. was quickly approved as a tenant in the new incubator. The facilities were very nice. We incorporated our shipping, production and business office in the space and I gained access to free consulting input on business activity and new ventures that I was working on with colleagues. Twice each year, I made presentations to the Edison Business Board and garnered input and suggestions for new products and business opportunities.

One new joint venture was started by myself and two other individuals. The spin off attracted a prominent Venture capital firm and we managed to secure some SBIR funding to develop the company. TopoGEN sponsored the grant and paid for a business plan development class to create a full-blown plan. There were some "teething" problems as the company founders and I attempted to figure out equity splits for the new entity. The situation was acute because there was money (in the form of equity) on the table and each founder had his own disparate vision for what was fair. For my part, I had assumed all along that equal partitioning was appropriate. Imagine my surprise when I was informed by the two other partners that I would actually get less than 10% of the equity. There are no ground rules for this situation. One of the partners was completely implacable and insisted that he would be diminished if I got more than this arbitrary percentage. When the Venture firm saw this behavior on behalf of one partner, they immediately declined future funding. No VC investor wants to inherit litigious partners. Several years later, the company did get going somewhat and was acquired by another company (and I received equity through that acquisition). The other founders migrated into the new company. Roughly 4-5 years later, that parent company went under and there was no return on equity. I learned a few powerful and valuable lessons. First, don't work with greedy people who value their efforts above others. Instead, work with well-well-adjusted people who understand that if the business is successful, there will be plenty for everyone. Do write an MOU (memorandum of understanding) that spells out all details of the relationship before there is a funding event. Make sure everyone signs off and has a chance to edit the document; get signatures and keep copies. Be sure everyone is comfortable with full disclosure to University officials, if appropriate. Maintain open lines of communication and engage everyone in the discussion process. Whenever possible, use the OPM model (other people's money) as seed funds to add early value to the company. OPM can be in the form of NIH-SBIR funds, angel investors, venture input or any other sources (crowd funding through the internet is a new and attractive model). Be creative and tap all available resources.

TopoGEN, Inc. was my first company, as noted, and for many years it has provided me a pool of funds to support activities that I was passionate about. This company is still going today and revenues are stable. Over the years, I have made improvements that keep abreast of the internet and e-commerce marketplace. I designed and implemented the first generation Website for the company (www.topogen.com) in 1998. In the early 2000's e-commerce was put in place with on-line ordering and feedback. Our distributor network is now worldwide. We have more than 20 distributors around the globe including in Asia (three in Japan, two in Korea, one in China), South America, Israel, Europe, Mexico, Singapore and Scandinavia. The Company has its own IT staff, a business office (and MBA who direct all business and sales) a technical staff, a business board and a SAB (Scientific Advisory Board) that I currently chair. TopoGEN owns and occupies a 3600 square foot building in Daytona Beach. This facility houses a business office, production lab, cell culture facility, QC clean room facility, business office, conference rooms and wet lab capability. The income stream is based from three sources: product sales, grants and contract research (and related subcontracts for drug testing). In addition, the Company has recently acquired new IP assignments to promote growth. Since TopoGEN is able to sponsor NIH research grants, such as "R" grants (R01, R21, R43) we can partner with other researchers and form alliances with these investigators to develop new technology, new business ideas and products for funding.

Many may consider that TopoGEN, which was founded on a niche R&D market, may be self-limited and not a strong growth model as a business. Moreover, the company was founded based on 'technology leads' and trade secrets rather than an IP portfolio. Despite such criticism, the Company continues to be profitable. I have met a few University administrators over the years who don't understand (nor support) my business approach. I shake off negativity and keep pushing. As the Chinese proverb says, 'the tiger does not lose sleep over the opinions of sheep'. A positive attitude is critical especially in the face of hard economic times. Due to the recent downturn in the economy, where the US Congress has been cutting the NIH budget, sales activity dipped by 10-20%; however, screening contracts continued, most likely because our big pharma customers cut their R&D staff and outsourced. It also worth noting that a 'trade secret' based company is, in some ways, superior to a fully IP driven enterprise for a couple key reasons. First, trade secret-based companies do not experience the 'patent time-line'; thus, it is possible to keep things going for an infinite time. In the situation with TopoGEN, we have been profitable for >20 years (i.e., long past a patent lifespan). A trade-secret based operation is more efficient and less costly because of ongoing expenses associated with IP filings (government fees, attorney fees, etc.). An IP portfolio can get costly, especially when you consider that not every patent is a winner. Finally, the TopoGEN model is a rapid or at least expedited pathway to profitability, where income is rapidly generated early on since it is based on sales of a product that can be made in large quantities with enormous margins. Also noteworthy is that once a startup is profitable, the company can still acquire technology and conventional IP.

I have been involved in a number of other startups, some of which are still incubating. These are all cancer based enterprises in various stages of development. My business model, which is a bootstrapping approach to growth of a startup, is applicable in all cases.

A Passion for Aviation (1996-present).

I started flight training in 1973 and my aviation interests were on hold due to many other obligations (family, expenses, career, business, consulting, etc.). Once established as senior faculty member and having a critical mass of researchers in my lab, I decided to get back to flying. My goal was to regain currency and get my private pilot's credentials, obtain an instrument rating (for IFR, 'instrument flight rules' flights) and acquire a suitable airplane to meet my business needs. Airplanes are strongly mission specific, but I had in mind the type of flying that would help the Company and provide a traveling machine for personal use.

<u>Getting my Private Pilot's License</u>. There are a couple pathways that have evolved, under FAA oversight, that can be used to obtain the Private (Visual or VFR) rating. The Private Pilots certificate is a VFR only rating, which allows the pilot to fly an aircraft when visibility is good (typically >3-5 miles). This rating prohibits flying in zero or low visibility and in clouds. The VFR rating is pretty limited, but still a necessary first step. This rating can be obtained by training with a certified flight instructor (or CFI) within a flight school program or as a standalone individual with or without a school affiliation. Also, there are higher education based training programs (OSU has a flight school) that are called "141 Programs", which are more structured with formal curricula, integrated ground school and 'stage checks' by other check pilots to ensure that students are being properly trained. The 141 programs are rigorous and, as a result, more expensive. As an educator, I opted for the 141 approach and OSU has a very respectable aviation training program and a dedicated airport (Don Scott Field, KOSU).

As a consummate 'morning person', I decided to do my training at least 3 times/week at 6:30am. This had several advantages. Mornings are almost always calm and cool. Low turbulence, minimal winds and comfortable temperatures would allow me to focus on technique (stick/rudder, landing etc.) in a consistent external environment. Also, the OSU airport is located just north of my home in Upper Arlington and I could drive over in a 10-12 min, complete the flights, debrief and get to my lab by 9am (and still be at my office well before most other faculty show up). I also signed up for ground school that met two days/week in the evenings at the OSU airport. In addition, the 141 program involves pre and post flight discussions with a formal syllabus, which I found immensely helpful. As an OSU Faculty member, I also received a hefty discount on wet rental of the aircraft and instructor flight fees. Any faculty member who has an interest in flight training should take advantage of the 141 Aviation Program.

My flight training progressed well and the other areas (airwork, groundschool, radio communications, ATC interface and numerous stage checks, part of the 141 program) progressed smoothly. My biggest hurdle was landing. Maneuvering the airplane accurately within a few feet of the ground is a challenge. You need to control your airspeed within a few mph window, you must maintain a proper landing configuration/attitude and most critically, manipulate the controls to land straight ahead without 'side loading' the landing gear. Part of the landing process is a something called the 'flare', where the nose is gently raised to bleed off airspeed and allow the airplane to 'settle' on the runway and stop flying. In zero wind or with a direct headwind, it's relatively easy to get; however, throw in a slight cross wind component and the devils come out. My biggest obstacle was getting the airplane alignment straight with my tracking over the runway, especially in cross winds. If you touch down while 'cocked' left or right of your forward vector, the resulting side loading can blow out tires, damage the gear, or worse (dip a wing, strike the prop, etc.). Also, landing an airplane involves the basic physics of energy management. On my second or third stage check during my training, the chief pilot (a fellow faculty member in the Aviation Department) did something to solve my problem of keeping the airplane straight on landing. He took a 3 foot piece of blue painter's tape and placed it on the cowl directly in front of the left (pilot) seat. This provided a good reference point to 'feel' the airplane going in a straight line for landing. After a few perfect touch and goes, he moved the tape to the middle of the cowl (between the seats). This gave me the correct sight picture and solved the problem quickly and effectively. The tape came off after a few more landings. Ah, the value of a great instructor!

My first solo flight, staying in the pattern doing touch and go landings, was watched by my instructor and wife standing by nervously on the ramp. It all went well. I started going to the practice area solo and working on flight standards necessary to pass the checkride with an FAA designated examiner. I made a perfect score on the FAA written and was nearly ready. One last thing was required. I had to plan and execute a long cross country flight of at least 250 nautical miles and two different airports. I chose to fly from Columbus to Toledo to Muncie

Indiana and back to OSU airport. I selected a nice summer day for the flight. It all went well until the last leg from Muncie to Columbus. While in Muncie, I had a chicken salad sandwich, which I believe was tainted with Staph. Staphylococcus produces a toxin and in minute amounts makes one violently ill. The organism need not actually be present, only the toxin. This type of food poisoning is characterized by a sudden onset (within one hour). About an hour and a half after departure, it hit me. I was at 3500 feet when the vomiting started. These trainers have no autopilot, so I panicked because I would not be able to control the airplane if I got the dry heaves. In addition, I was not talking to ATC, so no one could offer assistance. I vomited into my (hastily emptied) nylon flight bag. Going into a sort of survival mode, I knew that altitude was my friend, so I trimmed the airplane into a climb and just tried to keep the wings level while being sick. Thankfully, at about 6000 feet, the vomiting stopped (I was empty) and I began to improve. I leveled back to a VFR altitude (5500) and eventually landed safely back at OSU. I quickly cleaned out the airplane as best I could, throwing my flight bag and its contents in the trash. I left the doors open on the ramp to help air things out but the stench in the airplane was overpowering. I really felt sorry for the next student/instructor who flew that airplane (they took it immediately after I landed). About two weeks later, I passed the VFR check ride with flying colors. The process requires a minimum of 40 flight hour (dual plus solo combined) and it took me about 50 hours (average is 60 hours). I was finally "free to move about the country" as the commercial for Southwest Airlines proclaims!

    I totally embraced my new found flying skills. I purchased my first airplane, a very nice Cessna 182Q model. A four-place single engine that could cruise at 140 mph; however, it haul a huge load (I called it my suburban of the sky). It was not terribly fast by aviation standards but very stable and a good platform for IFR training. The instrument rating (or IFR Rating) is required to fully utilize the airplane for business travel. Many people think that IFR simply means flying by instruments in clouds; however, it is that plus much more. It's certifies the pilot to use the instrument/ATC system world-wide. In addition, flight standards are more rigorous because ATC may issue an altitude restriction (or compass heading) and the pilot must comply within tight parameters. For example, altitudes must be held +/- 100 and climbs or descents are expected to be 500 fpm (feet per minute) unless otherwise stipulated by ATC. Deviation from these parameters will get you in trouble with the FAA.

After getting the instrument rating (far more difficult than the VFR rating), I used the airplane frequently (going to meetings, visiting clients, giving seminars and so on). Commercial flying on jets became less frequent, as I developed my instrument flying skills. At the time, most of my flying was up and down the eastern seaboard and only rarely involved long east to west trips. This is important because weather patterns move west to east and long flights across the country are likely to involve fronts, storms and low visibility. In contrast, north/south travels were less weather dependent. Note that propeller aircraft typically fly less than 18000 feet (and I usually fly <12500 since above this altitude, supplemental oxygen is required). Commercial flights are in the flight levels above FL180 and usually from FL300-400 (30-40 thousand feet). In other words, my airplane is firmly embedded in the weather while jets are usually above the weather. I have learned to become an amateur meteorologist as a result of my IFR training. I watch cloud shapes, temperature due point spreads, visibility and (importantly) I pay close attention to visible moisture (clouds) and ambient temperature at altitude. All airplanes have an accurate external temperature probe so if the temperature hovers near freezing or below and you are in clouds, ice will form. If the airplane ices up, it can stop flying. I have no de-ice ability and am forbidden from flying into "known icing" conditions.

TopoGEN continued to thrive and by getting reliable staff, I could delegate routine operations and my time was spent running my research program, attending meetings and doing the things that I enjoyed. The airplane allowed me to travel with little or no advanced planning and my passion for aviation and the financial freedom to explore other avenues of creative enjoyment started in the mid-late 1990s. I did two things that greatly improved my life. First, I purchased a 2nd home in a 'Fly-in' community in Daytona Beach (Spruce Creek, the 'premier' fly in community). Spruce Creek is an amazing place and I started meeting and interacting with some famous folks (John Travolta had a home in Spruce Creek as well as some NASCAR drivers, like Mark Martin and Mike Skinner). I made many good friends and keep in contact to this day with these folks. The second thing I did was to purchase a place north of Columbus called the "Pond Farm". I would like to digress a bit off topic to discuss a very special country experience living in Amish country.

A Molecular Biologist Living with the Amish?

I purchased a rural property with outbuildings for the specific purpose of performing animal work for TopoGEN product development. At the time, there were rather few outsourcing entities for antibody production and I wanted to add topoisomerase antibodies to our inventory. A working farm with outbuildings and animal 'infrastructure' fit the bill perfectly.

The Pond Farm was a historical property of about 130+ acres of rolling farm land with a small lake and a wonderful original Victorian style farmhouse built in 1870. There were numerous outbuildings (large barns) and a modern pole barn that I converted into a makeshift lab for animal work. I never owned such a large property with a lake (full of large mouth bass), hiking trails, large pastures of cleared land, an old growth forest and nobody around except the Amish (on all sides) who I came to admire and respect. These people were an inspiration to me and I think the feeling was mutual. My father-in-law had a great expression. "To have good neighbors, you have to be a great neighbor." I went out of my way to get to know these fine people, and to learn their customs, culture and language (we were called "English"). The Pond Farm was only one hour north of the outer belt of the Columbus metroplex! Amazing indeed!

Just a bit of Ohio history first. The Pond Farm is well known in Morrow County. We were only the 2nd owners since 1820 (give or take a few years). The property sits on the north edge of the Greenville Treaty Line, which bisected the state of Ohio east to west. In the mid to late 1700s, Tecumseh and the 100 tribes were provided reservation land that was north of this line and there were numerous native settlements on our land. This was set aside land ordained for the Indians and all went well until about 1795 when the newly formed Continental Congress went into the red. A major problem was that our fledging government could not support the large (and aging) veteran population who fought in the revolution. To stem the tide of red ink, the US Congress decided to give land to surviving veterans, as payment for their services. Abel Pond and his first wife were bequeathed one section of land (640 acres) just on the north side of the Greenville Line. Of course, the native Indians were dealt a bad hand on this deal since the US gave their land away. I am not sure about all the details that followed but I'm sure it was not a healthy situation. The Government handed the deeds to the veterans and simply stipulated to the recipients, we are rooting for you! Abel Pond took over the land in the early 1800's and it was deeded officially sometime around 1820, probably after the Indians were pushed out.

I found the family burial plot within the original 640 acres of land but it is no longer part of my property. On inspecting the small cemetery, I located his grave marker and his first and second wife buried at 90 degrees on each side. Talking to the Pond heirs, I learned his first wife died in childbirth and he remarried and outlived the second wife. The children and other assorted relatives (grandchildren) are all interred in the small cemetery that was not being maintained. My son, Branden, and several friends and my wife and I did what we could to clear and clean the cemetery; however, it was too much. I later found out that the US government is obligated to maintain any cemetery containing the remains of US veterans and I was able to coax Morrow County to come in with a crew and perform a first rate restoration. There was an enormous sense of accomplishment that came with this activity and I was very pleased with the outcome.

Andrew Miller, my closest neighbor, was a rotund, loquacious Amish gentleman with a wife and 8 children (two girls and six boys). He was a small man with a quick wit and a toothy smile in serious need of cosmetic dental work. Like most of the other Amish, he was bearded (married) and wore glasses. I got to know Andy and his sons rather well and developed a close relationship with their families in the neighborhood. Andy and Clara, at last count, had 58 grand kids and probably others have been added my last visit in 2004. Clara knew all the names and birthdays by heart (not so for Andy however). She commented to my wife Annette once that it was her great disappointment in life that she had only eight offspring! This is not unusual, since there was another Amish family down the road with 18 kids. Two baseball teams! (One set of twins if memory serves.)

Andy was an amazing businessman who ran a canvas tarp making operation (covers for semi-trailers, boats, buggies, porch surrounds and the like). The Amish can use any technology that existed in 1880 (my interpretation of their lifestyle). His workshop had an old time central pulley system drive belt to power all of the sewing machines for these industrial tarps. They cannot own or use any vehicle that has an inflatable tire for example. They are not connected to the grid and do not use electricity (solar or other) although they use batteries, lanterns, liquid propane source for light and in some rare cases they operate small internal combustion engines (use of modern conveniences is mandated by the church elders and can vary somewhat). The rules of the Church district (Ordnung) must be observed by all members and not only includes modern technology prohibitions, but also on dress (no zippers) and social behaviors. The Amish travel by horse and buggy and do not own phones (neither cell nor landline), hot water heaters, central heat or power tools of any sort. I once looked at an Amish home under construction and noticed that the bathtub had only one water line (cold) as the feed. Ohio has cold winters! They bathe once a week (Saturday) and on Friday, the aroma is a mix of horse musk, body odor and chicken crap. They go to school until the eighth grade (age 14) in one-room schools and do not learn English until they are about 10 years old. They own guns and hunt and fish and live off the land as much as possible. They have no refrigeration. They do have access to and utilize modern medicine, however. They also rely on old fashion type of medical intervention (chiropractors, healers, and natural products, etc.). A typical community will involve 50-100 families, all in the same church group, who pay into a sort of self-insurance program for health care. The church elders make the rules as a collective regarding all matters, as I noted above. There is no formal Church building; rather, they hold services at various homes in their community every two weeks. The location of the services is easy to spot because there is a special horse drawn wagon (painted dull grey) that holds all the pews. In addition, there will be 50 or more horse and buggy outfits tied up outside.

The Amish eschew legal pathways and avoid the court system whenever possible. As far as I can tell, they practice a kind of submissive or "leave it be" mental perspective as the religion places high value on "Demut" or humility and "Gelassenheit" (calmness, placidity). Individualism is generally frowned up in the culture and self-promotion is taboo. This explains much about the Amish. They will not engage in lawsuits, file criminal charges, challenge any party legally or use or game the legal system at any level. In one rather famous case, a drunk driver ran into a group of Amish kids from one single family who were walking home from school. Tragically, all five children were killed and the driver skipped the scene. When apprehended, the parents did not even want to press charges; of course, the law intervenes here and justice was swiftly meted out. There was no litigation of course. The community gathered around the family and there was collective grieving, but life went on.

I got to know one of Andy's sons rather well. Wayne was 28 years old and, like his Father, of small stature but a powerful upper body frame. He and his wife had 6 kids and lived down the road about half a mile west of us. Both Wayne and his wife were wonderful people with soft European features and clear, fair complexions. Wayne had brown eyes and his wife had blue-green eyes and blond hair. I hired Wayne to help me build a porch on the old farmhouse. I was very happy with the result and spent many blissful hours on that porch watching horse and buggy traffic travel to and fro over, up and down the Greenville Treaty line. Like all Amish males, he was a good carpenter and was very good with his hands. They had a farm and raised their own crops and their kids were like little dolls, so incredibly cute and shy. The kids loved me to the bone because I always brought treats and ice cream in summer, which was enjoyed by all. Lacking refrigeration, an ice cream bar to an Amish 6-year-old is like heaven. I spoke German to the kids and they would always giggle and squirm about. Wayne told me that my "German" was the same language as in their bible and only used in religious services. The Amish German was also somewhat hybridized with English (or Dutch?). For example, "What is your name?" would be "Wie heissen sie?" in hoch deutsch (formal tone) but the Amish would say "Was ist du namen?". Clearly the latter is very close to English and would be considered "Pennsylvanian Dutch". As far as I could tell, the Amish are tri-lingual (English, Hoch Deutsch, and Pennsylvania Dutch) with most family language around the dinner table utilizing Pennsylvania Dutch.

On more than one occasion, I had to get up in the middle of the night to drive one of the kids to the Amish "Doctor" in the next county or to the hospital in Mt. Gilead nearby. In addition, I installed a land line phone in my workshop and gave Andy and sons a key for them to use the telephone for their business. (Wayne worked in the tarp shop.) The Amish are totally honest in all matters and the family kept meticulous records of all long-distance calls and reimbursed me each month to the penny. I tried to refuse such paltry payments but Andy insisted, so each month I might get a personal check for "three dollars and fourteen cents". They don't own credit cards or get mortgages and never work on business credit lines.

To the Amish, I was viewed as an outsider of course, but also they considered me to be a strange duck, even for an "English". I had motorcycles, nice cars, a collection of tractors, mowers, implements and tools and generally was a serious technocrat; someone who relishes in the use of modern technology. I was accepted and well liked and the Amish were very concerned about watching my home at all times since I only came on weekends. Andy's presence at all times, using the telephone for example, also helped ease my mind about security. Burglaries and break-ins are a fact of life, sadly, even in these very rural areas (we were burglarized twice).

In about 2001, I purchased an antique airplane (an Aeronca Chief) that was a conventional gear (tailwheel), two seater single engine aircraft. It was a beautifully restored fabric covered airframe (ceconite). The restoration was done by two airline pilots who were brothers living in a small rural town near Pittsburgh. The Chief had no electrical system (I had to 'hand prop' to start the darn thing), a 65 hp Continental engine and it cruised at 85 mph. This is a very light ship and I had to get a special rating for the tailwheel, which was NOT easy (it took about 10 hours of instruction). But once you learn to fly a taildragger, your flying skills improve enormously since you learn fine rudder control. Landing the Chief was like wrestling a pissed off alligator with the tail whipping about while rolling out. And you never stop flying the aircraft until you come to a dead stop. The problem here is that a conventional gear aircraft has its center of gravity further aft (compared to a nosewheel airplane) and on roll out you have to literally dance on the rudder pedals (ie making constant adjustments ever so slight) to keep the thing from swapping ends. The Chief is also 'short coupled' meaning that the tailwheel is relatively close to the mains which makes it directionally highly unstable and susceptible to ground looping. I ground looped the Chief twice: Once while learning to transition into the tailwheel while attempting a 'wheel landing' (as opposed to a 3-point touchdown). This cost the insurance company about $6000 in wing repair. Another time I ground looped on purpose to keep from hitting a tree, after losing control on a very gusty cross wind landing that did no damage.

I wanted to keep the Chief at the farm property and I decided to build a turf runway on high ground (east-west orientation) on the extreme north side of the property. I had to bring in fill dirt to make a 2200-foot landing strip and clear trees on one end for an open approach through the very thick forest. The project took a total of three years to get a manicured turf runway, build a 50x50 foot hangar, and put up a 18 foot tall deck as the "control tower". The raised 12 x 12 deck was on high ground and a provided gorgeous view of the entire farm and the whole valley below. Most of the project was paid for by the hardwood I harvested from 3 acres of cherry, oak, and ash trees that were cleared on the east side of the runway. I kept my Chief at the Pond Farm Airport and had many happy days of buzzing the countryside, going for nice Sunday morning breakfasts, and landing at different country grass strips owned by a few Morrow County residents. On a few occasions in the winter, I flew out of a snow covered field and landed back in the snow which was risky but fun. I almost hit three deer that were eating grass on the runway at sunset. Evidently, deer have no predators in the sky so they generally don't look up. They are very hard to spot in the waning hours of daylight and a quick go-round saved me from destroying the Chief along with Bambi and her friends. Learning to fly out of a short, unimproved strip taught me to be a better pilot as well. I learned energy management and how to really nail the approach speeds and to 'hang on the prop' for tight landings in the Cessna 182. I enjoyed runway maintenance (mowing) and had the proper equipment to get a finished cut on the runway. The runway looked like a golf green after a few years and I was very proud of the result. I held numerous fly-ins with fellow pilots and EAA members (Experimental Aviation Association) in the area.

During construction of the runway, I asked Wayne and Vern (Andy's sons) to help me clear trees. I offered an attractive hourly wage for their services which was money well spent because I was deathly afraid of dropping multi-ton trees and having a bad outcome. Wayne and Vern assured me that they had the necessary expertise and experience and saw no problem with the job. One fine Saturday morning, I was wiring up the new hangar with fluorescent lights while the Amish boys were felling trees when Vern ran up and breathlessly explained that I needed to come quick as Wayne was hurt 'real bad'. One look at Vern's face told the horrible tale of what was to come. The tree had suffered a lightning strike at some point and as a result had twisted unpredictably in the felling process. It released from the stump and came directly into Wayne, who was handcuffed by the heft of the chainsaw. He dived away and the tree came down squarely on his foot, crushing the ankle bone. His foot was horribly mangled but held in place by the leather boot. Wayne was clearly in agony and I carried him out of the forest on my shoulders, with the help of a neighbor who spelled me off on the long trek back to the farmhouse. My wife, an RN, informed me that this was a serious injury and Wayne must not remove his boot. We iced the injury and took him to the E. R. in Mt. Gilead (20 miles away). I later found out that Wayne was life-flighted back to Columbus for Orthopedic surgeries (multiple) to repair his ankle. My heart was broken over this incident. Wayne had 6 kids to feed, crops to harvest and manual work to support his family. He was now crippled and I was at least partially at fault.

The recovery process was slow and the Amish families in the Church group went into a rotation of sorts to support his family. They harvested and plowed his fields, managed the livestock and horses, did his work in shifts at Andy's tarp facility and delivered dinner and lunch everyday so his wife (with kids in tow) could be at the hospital during the lengthy recovery. My wife and I visited him as well and did what we could to provide for his family and help out on weekends when we were in the country. We gave the kids wrapped Christmas gifts and I spent time with the kids, bringing goodies and toys whenever I stopped by. Wayne was back home within few weeks, on crutches of course. About two months after the incident, I was paid a visit by Andy and the church elders. They very politely asked me how I was going to pay for brother Wayne's medical expenses which were approaching $30,000 and would continue to accrue. I explained to them that Wayne was working on my land and thus was in the 'English world' when the accident occurred. The way we handle such matters, I explained, was through my homeowner's insurance. I further informed them that I was not going to simply write a check for the medical bills because I have insurance that I pay to protect me from such catastrophic events. They collectively glared at me, spoke to each other in the native dialect (which was incomprehensible) and shook my hand and left. Before leaving, I told them that I would investigate how to handle the medical bills with my agent. Andy simply shrugged and bid me a very polite farewell. I figured that my good, working relationship with the Amish was finished and that I would forever be despised. The insurance company contacted me with a claim number and said that the injured party needs to simply submit up to $5000 in medical expenses and they would reimburse, no questions asked. It's a formal process I explained to Andy, so please follow through. Moreover, they informed me that it would be possible, even very likely, to get the whole bill settled if they would go to an attorney and arrange for a settlement. Not only did the Amish not go to the legal system, but they even refused to file a claim number for the $5K. The incident was never mentioned again and there were no vindictive directed my way. It was as if nothing ever happened. Wayne eventually recovered but will walk with a serious limp for the rest of his life. He remains a good friend to this day and I occasionally visit and check on him and his family.

I miss the pond farm enormously. I will never own such a unique property, I realize, nor will I have such interesting and diverse neighbors and friends. In 2003-4 I was recruited to join a new medical school in Orlando (see below) and the while the value of real estate was strong in Central Ohio (2003), I sold the property by dividing it into multiple large parcels. I sold the house and 10 acres, the remaining crop and pasture land (120 give or take), but kept the lake plus 5 acres for myself. I later sold the lake to another family in the area, so I am fully divested of the Pond Farm and I did well financially. The timing of the sale could not have been better, since property values dipped terribly in the crash of 2008. I have no regrets. The Pond Farm also contributed to TopoGEN because I used the facilities to raise New Zealand White rabbits for antibody production. As noted above, these antibodies were sold as inventory and I relied on the Amish to maintain my rabbit population. How many molecular biologists have hired Amish technicians I wonder?

2003—Life After OSU

I contacted a former OSU colleague who had been recruited to join the University of Central Florida, in Orlando, to direct a biomedical sciences program. Pappachan Kolattukudy was recruited to OSU in the mid-1980s to oversee and grow a new "Biotechnology Center". I met Pappachan (or PK as everyone calls him) in 1986 soon after he was appointed as the new Biotech Center Director at OSU. PK was a dynamic and powerful intellectual force who was responsible for many (>75) Ph.D. level hires into the Center and across the campus over the years. He has a reputation for being hard to work with but that is because of high standards he imposes on everyone in his orbit. I got along well with PK; however, the Department Chair (Phil Perlman) did not. Phil and PK were at odds and eventually, joint hires between Biotechnology and Molecular Genetics completely ceased. This was regrettable and hurt both programs. Due to the blood-letting, I did not interact with PK or the Biotechnology Center faculty (another regrettable outcome). Later on, as the OSU medical school started recruiting more powerful leaders, PK was marginalized I suspect because of his leadership style and strong personality. Eventually, the Biotechnology Center was splintered and I believe PK gained control of a new "Neurobiology" group affiliated with the OSU College of Medicine. This arrangement did not work out and PK was back on the job circuit, eventually landing as the Dean and Director of the Biomedical Sciences as the University of Central Florida in 2003 and later as Chair of a large undergraduate program in Molecular Biology and Microbiology (in other words, he wore multiple hats). He was a savvy negotiator and received a very lucrative start up package that included a large number of faculty hires.

In 2003, I was getting concerned about the future of the OSU College of Biological Sciences because we were a small College led by a weak Dean and it seemed likely that we would be merged with a larger, more powerful College (Math and Physical Sciences). I had nearly 25 years of service and was feeling like I was in a rut. My R01 had just been funded and I thought it was a good time to look around a bit. I interviewed at some places for a chair position, but my heart just was not in it. In fact, I hated the idea of becoming an administrator. I had a home in Daytona Beach (Spruce Creek) an hour's drive north of UCF (in Northeast Orlando), so I contacted PK to see if there would be any interest in joining the faculty in the Department of Molecular Biology and Microbiology. In the fall of 2003, I gave a seminar at UCF and began the process of negotiating to join as a senior faculty member. On my second visit, I met deans, VP, provost and of course John Hitt, the UCF President. President Hitt was especially enthusiastic about my entrepreneurial activities and strongly encouraged me to come to UCF and bring TopoGEN in tow. He assured me that accommodations would be made to bring the company into the academic fold with the UCF Research Park facility. I negotiated a decent start up package and salary. I identified acceptable lab space and facilities and all was going according to plan. This was not going to be a lateral move.

Suddenly things stopped moving forward, for reasons I cannot explain. The communications with PK simply stopped coming and I assumed that they (UCF) got cold feet or perhaps had found a better candidate. I still did not have a letter of offer. At the time I was on the Scientific Advisory Board for a company called "Genomics USA" or GUSA, an academic startup company from the University of Arizona (a microarray fabrication company using new IP for producing the arrays). At one of the board meetings, I suggested that GUSA should investigate Central Florida as a place to base their operations because the State was interested in subsidizing Biotech companies who come to the sunshine state and the availability of a skilled labor force at UCF. Plus, commercial real estate was widely available (and affordable). Within a few weeks, I contacted the Economic Development Board (EDB) in Daytona and asked if they would be willing to consider GUSA as a tenant in the new "ATC" (Advanced Tech Center) near Beachside. Their enthusiasm was palpable. We arranged a dog and pony show with GUSA and various business leaders, bankers and investors in Daytona and Central Florida area. The day before the meeting, the EDB director told me that he had invited 'several prominent UCF staff' to attend the meeting. This was a bit surprising, since I could not see the relevance of including UCF people in a venture so far from campus in Orlando. The meeting was well-attended and I acted as the master of ceremonies for the board presentations. Much to my surprise, the VP of Research from UCF was in attendance as was PK. The meeting was well received with many questions and general enthusiasm. After the meeting, PK apologized profusely about not getting back to me and vowed that things would move ahead. The very next day I had a letter of offer in hand, clearly laying out all I had asked for and then some. Lady luck smiled on me that day! I went back to Columbus but kept the job offer a secret for several months, while I was actively investigating all legal matters (regarding the Company and any IP or other conflicts). I began to feel bad about keeping things from my Department since my absence would create a vacuum in teaching. Moreover, I felt advanced notice was appropriate in this case and it just seemed the right thing to do. I regret that decision. In situations like these, where one is leaving the university, it is a good idea to play your cards close.

I informed the chair that I had an offer about one year before my planned move to UCF. The chair was a close personal friend (Lee Johnson, also a fellow pilot) and is as respectable and forthright as they come. Lee did not want to see me leave the Department and approached the Dean of Biological Sciences for a counter offer. Essentially, the Dean said no way could the College match such a strong offer. Moreover, the Dean informed my chair that if I stayed on at OSU that following academic year, I would be strapped with a heavy teaching assignment in general biology the next Fall. Thus, by trying to be a good citizen and help, our Dean came after me with impunity. I don't know what I did to deserve this response. The Dean seemed to want me out. I had just been awarded a 5 year R01 the previous year, so this decision could not be due to 'dead wood' status of a senior faculty member. The next thing that happened was the Dean called for a detailed audit or some kind of accounting of all my lab expenditures over the years that might have come from Departmental funds. I suppose there was some coordinated digging up of "debts now due" to the College and I was to held accountable. Basically, the College was trying to rape the NIH grant for funds that I ostensibly owed for past support. The College claimed I owed something like $85K in miscellaneous supply and equipment expenses. Like many research active faculty, I occasionally would be in between grants, and the Department had a liberal policy of interim support. The College now wanted payback for all accumulated expenses (I was never informed of such a payback policy). Lee informed me by official email that the funds would have to come from operating expenses of my current R01 grant prior to transferring any funds to my new position in Florida. I had to inform these good folks that I could not simply transfer funds from the grant, other than the indirect costs which were allowable payments to OSU. The grant was set up to do a body of work and NIH would take a very dim view of diversion of funds in this manner. The Dean was most upset. Finally, Lee suggested that I pay with some release time in the coming year to help offset. This would net the Department about 1/3 of the red ink which in retrospect seemed fair; however, there were clearly some lingering hurt feelings. I appreciate Lee's handling of the situation and all turned out well, thanks to his skillful and creative problem solving. In contrast, the Dean was a bumbling idiot, in my opinion. She got greedy and saw an opportunity to pillage the grant and in the process penalize me for finding a better deal. This was but one example of the Dean screwing things up and creating grief. A few years later she was fired and the College of Biological Sciences no longer exists, thanks to her 'leadership'. I was not the only senior faculty member the Dean ran off. One of the most productive colleagues in our Department, with a recently awarded program project grant, left the College and joined the OSU Medical School. The Dean was wholly responsible for this as well (it happened soon after my departure from OSU).

In spite of the bad turn of events, my final year at OSU was nonetheless a happy one. The Departmental staff did a superb job of making up a commemorative picture book and throwing a very nice retirement party. They really took the high road on this and I will be forever in debt to Lee Johnson and Jessica Siegman for a fabulous and well organized send off. Many of my friends, colleagues and past students were in attendance. It was punctuated by a number of moving and in some cases humorous speeches.

I did not move TopoGEN to Florida right away and this turned out to be a very wise decision. Back at UCF, the Dean (PK) asked if I would consider moving the company into University lab space, presumably to garner some PR about Biotechnology company startups in Central Florida. I immediately saw compliance problems by moving a for-profit enterprise into UCF designated space. The legality of this arrangement was a serious concern for me, but not others at UCF. I thanked PK and respectfully declined his offer. I thought to myself "there is no way on earth that I am going to link TopoGEN with UCF lab space". To do so would invite serious trouble (destroy the Company for instance if there was a falling out with UCF administrators). In retrospect, it is my view that Universities may view a faculty start-up company as a resource to garner new funding (as grants or contracts) that will result in a flow of indirect costs back to University budgets. This 'cash-cow' indirect funding model is short sighted and misses the more important contribution of general economic development. Moreover, it is very naïve, if not patently spurious, to think that a company would simply give up the indirect costs to the University, unless of course, the University holds the IP (which is sometimes the case) and the company and University are co-funding the project (through STTR NIH programs). In my case, TopoGEN is able to sponsor research funded by NIH; thus, the indirect costs legitimately belong to the company.

Given the situation, I took my time and built suitable R&D facilities for TopoGEN in Florida, which was still housed in the Edison Incubator on Kinnear road, west of campus. It took a couple of years to identify and create space for TopoGEN in Central Florida, but I should tell you of a clever solution to the problem (described next).

Combining Aviation Resources and TopoGEN

The solution to my dilemma of building a respectable R&D production and shipping lab for the company came to me soon after I purchased a commercial airplane hangar in Spruce Creek Fly-in where we lived. Aviation was an essential element of my business model and it made sense to utilize corporate resources to create a modern lab facility.

I was the proud owner of a new airplane called a Columbia 300. I purchased this high-performance fiberglass state of art aircraft in 2002 from the factory in Bend, Oregon. This was a different breed of airplane and exceptionally fast and efficient. Because it is fiberglass, it had to be kept out of the hot Florida sun; thus, the need for a hangar. As an aside, I had never purchased a factory new airplane before, especially one like this. The Columbia is totally amazing. While the Cessna 182 had a cruise speed of 130-140 mph, the Columbia clocked in at 225 mph (roughly 3-4 miles/min). I have seen ground speeds in excess of 300 mph (with a good tailwind at altitude). The airplane was not only fast but it was quiet, tight and had jet like performance with high wing loading and a side stick (not a yoke like the Cessna). Moreover, the avionics were fantastic, with moving maps, autopilot, altitude pre-select, fuel computer, pressurized doors and, as the advertisement stated, "the interior is one well fed cow". Because it is fast, I paid a bit extra and got 'speed brakes' which are spoilers to help manage energy and scrubbing off speed. Near the ground, the Columbia has the performance profile of a light jet, which also have spoilers to slow down. Because of speed brakes, ATC would slot me in with the faster jet traffic in busy airspace like Dallas, Chicago, Orlando, etc. Not only is the Columbia fast, but it has amazing endurance (i.e. it carries a lot of gas). Fuel is safety and as my IFR instructor was fond of saying "the only time you have too much gas is when you are on fire". I once flew from Central Colorado (200 miles west of Denver) to Orlando, Florida non-stop (>1600 statute miles). Of course that is a fair amount of sitting still in one place (8+ hours). The winds were neutral on that flight by the way, so I did not get much of a push.

The commercial hangar is 60 x 70 feet and big enough for 4 aircraft the size of the Columbia. I had an architect draw up a design for a two story lab facility in the rear of the hangar. The lab is almost 1500 square feet and hosts a production lab for biochemistry, a cell culture lab, a business office, two conference rooms, desks for staff and a shipping facility. Even with the build out, there is plenty of room in the hangar for my Columbia and another smaller aircraft that leases space (at one time, I also had a helicopter in the hangar as well). Once the hangar build-out was completed and equipment purchased and up and running, only then did I move TopoGEN to Florida. The Company is fully independent from the University and will forever stay that way. As noted, TopoGEN can sponsor NIH funded research in the same way that UCF, OSU, MIT or any University for that matter. I suppose this makes the company a competitor to the University and that can create consternation between the Company and the University, especially when the academic side is predatory about harvesting indirect costs from the Federal government.

Moving on to Florida

In the summer of 2004, I vacated my lab in Room 224 of the Biological Sciences Building at 484 W. 12th Ave and the moving vans packed it all up for UCF lab space. I was very careful to play it by the book with inventory tracking and reporting of all equipment items. I informed my post-docs, technician and Ph.D. students several months back about the move to Florida. I extolled the quality of life in the Sunshine State. I explained that the dreary, overcast Columbus winters are a thing of the past. No more snow, no more shoveling snow, you can sit on the beach in mid-winter! Hooray! Everybody get on board. Some of my staff came with me enthusiastically. I flew several folks down in the Columbia to let them see for themselves. Everything went great and the lab staff moved in July 2004 to set up shop and start buying the equipment. Now the bad news: For the first time in 50 years, Orlando got hit by a hurricane the very next month (August). In fact, Central Florida got nailed directly or indirectly by four named hurricanes in August 2004. When a place like Orlando has no major wind or hurricane for over 50 years, the trees get very big and mature. They also fall on stuff, like cars, houses and even people. A large oak tree landed on my post-doc's car (obliterated). He approached me and basically said "I was safe in Ohio"! Of course I felt bad but I don't control weather.

Before the first hurricane (Charlie) hit us, I flew the Columbia to Texas, to get it out of harm's way. In some Central Florida airports, hangar doors were blown in by the strong winds and airplanes were damaged or destroyed. The day after the hurricane moved out, I flew into Sanford Airport (South of Daytona) to fuel up. On the ramp, I always tie down with the lines provided; however, in this case the tie down rope had a metal chunk of airplane attached. Asking line service what happened they reported that the airplane was blown off its moorings by Charlie and was gone. Gone where I asked? Dunno he said. They later found the aircraft (a Piper Cherokee) in a retention pond several miles away. Little airplanes start flying at 40-50 mph, thus 100+ mph winds are at 'cruise speed' and the rest is pure physics.

I set my lab up and got new equipment in and functioning. I settled in and re-established my research program. My first year was without teaching, which was wonderful; however, the first year after the move was spent tooling up the new lab and I was not very productive. Research productivity is very difficult even when things working perfectly. With a relocation of lab space, the process is dealt a death blow.

Operating an Established Biotechnology Company in a New Academic Environment Requires Pioneering Spirit: Some Recent History.

From 2004-2007, I worked as a full professor in the Biomedical Sciences Center in the Department of Molecular Biology and Microbiology. I was teaching graduate and undergraduate courses, running my research group and generally doing the same things I did while at OSU. PK, as Dean and Center Director clearly had his favorite faculty who were largely untenured and therefore easily controlled. I was left alone for the most part, although the administration's philosophy for senior faculty like myself was unambiguous. I was given a very nice start up but after that, there was no support of any kind (no annual equipment upgrades, service contracts, peripheral support for research, etc.). To make matters worse, our program had no speaker program for prominent scientists to come and give seminars. Consequently, I began to feel scientifically malnourished. This culture was very different than OSU and unfortunately there was little that could be done about it. As far as I could tell, all senior faculty got the same deal, except for the Director (PK) who had his hands in the startup kitty and was free to support his own needs. I began to sense that senior faculty were either a threat or a competitor, so I stayed well away and did my own deal.

From the moment I arrived, PK was making plans to create a new 5 story research building, fully flush with state of art equipment. Also, based on a lucrative start up package negotiated with the VP of Research, PK was to fill about >30 faculty lines in the new building. I was hands-on involved with the building planning and design from the start (as part of a faculty committee). Soon, it was revealed by PK that he was making plans to build a new Medical School (2005) and he was pushing hard to get the administration and the State of Florida onboard. I have to give him credit; it was a wonderful vision. PK is a builder and I have always been impressed by his vigor, insight and ability to motivate people above him to join his cause. He worked tirelessly on this and went through open heart surgery in the middle of the action! This slowed but did not stop the progression.

By way of political background, it is sad to note that Florida is not an 'education' state and University budgets reflect a highly conservative (now tea party) legislature. The aging population represented by retirees from places like NY, NJ, Michigan, Ohio (the Northeastern demographic) explains our current political climate. These fixed incomers do not want taxes and do not wish to support education of any sort. They already educated their own kids, so they will not pay a penny more! I could make the same argument that my kids are already grown, so why pay taxes for schools? I personally support education because I don't want to live in a country populated by uneducated citizens.

There was much resistance at the Florida State level to add another medical school. John Hitt, the UCF President, desperately needed to prime the pump somehow. A company called Tavistock stepped up to the plate and donated 50 acres of prime Lake Nona land (southeast of Orlando and about 20 miles South of the UCF main campus) along with something like $10M. The idea was that Joe Lewis (CEO of Tavistock and a very wealthy guy from the UK) wanted to develop the Lake Nona area of Orlando. The plan was to create a 'medical city' just five miles east of the International Airport (MCO). The Medical City would have it all eventually (MD Anderson, Mayo, a State Medical School, Children's Hospital, a new VA, Dental School, and a large number of primary care facilities for specific diseases). The Florida Legislature could not say no and the process began in 2006. To his credit, President Hitt attracted substantial donor funds to the fledgling concept.

In 2007, largely as a result of leadership by PK and the President (and many others) the new UCF College of Medicine (or COM) was created. A COM Dean was identified after a short search and the arduous process of creating something from nothing was started. The first class (which was in 2009) was most critically secure LCME (Liaison Committee on Medical Education) approval to operate. The ranks of administrators expanded quickly but little effort went into organizing conventional departmental structures at first. Most of the early College of Medicine (COM) hires were in medical education, which is sensible. Additionally, the COM did not want a tenure track system, but instead placed any and all recruited faculty on contracts and consequently, these positions had no job security. No active researcher will be attracted to this sort of academic structure. On the other hand, all researchers (new and pre-existing) were recruited in the newly formed "Burnett School of Biomedical Sciences" (BSBS) as tenured or tenure track.

In order to 'migrate' the tenured or tenure track BSBS research faculty into the new UCF medical school, some changes were in order. Because the new COM was recruiting contract faculty, tenure and tenure track faculty had to be given some kind of arrangement or grandfathered in as tenure track lines. Main campus UCF faculty work under a collective bargaining agreement involving the union; however, medical school faculty in Florida are not unionized. The pre-existing faculty had to be moved 'out of unit'. To address this, an MOU (memorandum of understanding) was designed to protect tenure and operational features of the Department, including budgets and future tenure track positions yet to be filled. This MOU was an operating document between the COM Dean and the research faculty and signed off by administrators (VP for Research, the Center Director and Chair) and was only in effect for a few years. Soon after UCF hired a new provost, the MOU was dissolved. My colleagues were concerned about this naturally (since our tenure was no longer protected and we were no longer represented by the union). Soon thereafter, PK was relieved of all leadership duties the COM Dean put an interim director of the BSBS research program. The COM Dean is a highly capable individual with regard to PR and schmoozing with potential donors or making grandiose plans to play to the local press. I give her credit for this insight, and our program is moving forward with excellent momentum, even in the post-sequester, shrinking NIH budget environment.

After the new interim director came onboard, COM became aware of the fact that I had an established and profitable Company operating independently from UCF. I had previously disclosed this of course, but eventually it was a topic of discussion. Adding to complexity of the situation was my lapse in NIH funding (never a good thing). The COM administrators decided that entrepreneurial faculty must be scrubbed robustly for conflict of interest issues. To be fair, this came from new federal guidelines on compliance and is the closest thing to Mr. Orwell's 1984 that I have ever experienced. I was hauled up in front of COM attorneys and miscellaneous 'deanlets' and forced to explain all details of dealings with my Company. It was like a firing squad tribunal and I felt victimized. When I explained to them that the Company had nothing to do with UCF (and never would have a relationship), and that no IP was involved, they changed the accusation. They then said I must be guilty of other crimes against humanity such as "conflict of commitment" because how could I run the Company and be a productive faculty member? Furthermore, one individual claimed he heard some 'rumors' about me, and that unnamed parties had come forward stating that I was using UCF resources and had been for many years. Why someone would fabricate such a yarn is unclear but petty jealousy is a safe bet or possibly it was an incorrect assumption stemming from the early UCF invitation to move the Company to my lab. In a fledgling academic environment like UCF, some of my colleagues, I believe, are insecure. I never noticed this at OSU; however, this place is still young and in a growth mode. The administration appeared to be questioning my integrity, saying in effect that TopoGEN did not exist and it was all made up somehow. The only way to deal with such hostile accusatory behavior is with the truth. I invited any who might be interested to visit the lab (located in Daytona Beach). One individual demanded to see photo-evidence instead. So I sent them pictures of the lab with staff members in various states of official activity. In the end, I think I won them over but it was highly stressful. If I was bringing in a few million dollars of NIH grant money, I believe there would have been no real issue with compliance, but this is pure speculation. A well-known quote on funding goes like this: "if you have sufficient grant funding, you do what you want, if not, you do what you're told". The indirect cost recovery model from Federal dollars can be a pernicious metric to live by.

Sadly, the Orwellian compliance situation in medical schools can be used to punish faculty who don't bring in large grants (by aggressively cracking down on conflict of interest approvals and using intimidation tactics on senior faculty). These compliance laws are designed to make sure that clinicians engaged in drug trials are not being bribed by a drug company (with free trips, meals, cushy consulting deals, etc). I witnessed this sort of thing at OSU with physicians engaged in clinical trials. An easy way to deal with this is through full disclosure and mitigation if required. My situation is very different but still falls under that purview it seems. Moreover, administrators were afraid to sign off on a document that mitigates perceived conflicts because they fear for their own skin. Basic risk aversion behavior, I suppose. I could go on, but in closing, I do not understand why these administrators cannot adopt a more positive and broad perspective on things. Active and vigorous faculty do many different things to contribute to the general mission of the University. Besides research, teaching and service, some of us are passionate about economic development. After all, academia should be a contributor to the economy and not just a consumer. As the new UCF provost once said about the faculty "no conflict….no interest". At least someone really gets it. The administration must recognize that any time a faculty member is successful, be it in outreach, economic impact or entrepreneurial activity, the university also wins.

Things are getting better. The new UCF College of Medicine is growing and we are recruiting competent and experienced academic leaders who should understand the real and manifold missions of the medical school and university. I saw this progression and evolution in the OSU School of Medicine when really gifted and bright leadership was recruited in the Cancer Center in late 1990s. The program ramped up considerably and became a state and national treasure trove of talented folks. These 'growing pains' are a natural process with a new academic program, and I am eternally optimistic about he future of the medical school and the entire 'medical city concept' that is actively growing at Lake Nona in SE Orlando.

The current status of the operation is impressive (after only 5-6 years). The COM has been granted LCME approval and has graduated its first medical class. UCF itself has nearly 60,000 students with 177 bachelor's and master's degree programs, >30 doctoral program and an annual operating budget of $1.4 billion. Total research funding stands at $129 million with endowments of >$125 million. My specific program, the Burnett School for Biomedical Sciences directs three undergraduate degree programs (Biomedical Sciences, Biotechnology, and Medical Laboratory Sciences) and has a Ph.D. program. Our program has 41 faculty that teach in COM, undergraduate, graduate programs, and do basic and translational research. COM has a new 200,000 sq.

ft. research facility located at Lake Nona (20 min from Campus) and I now have a new lab in this very well equipped space

My Current Life in the New UCF College of Medicine.

The UCF COM is unusual because it contains multiple undergraduate. There are few other similar programs in the country. My teaching involves a high enrollment UG course on "Introduction to Biotechnology" (several hundred per term) and graduate courses. As COM matures, I believe that the UG program will revert back to main campus and live in the College of Sciences. Despite some recent compliance issues, I am very happy with the situation I find myself. I run a funded lab still (although one never has enough research support).

I spend a crazy inordinate amount of time slaving away writing grants. With our government deficits, sequestration and a hawk-like congress bent on defense spending in various parts of the world, NIH budgets shrink by default. Our Department of Defense consumes resources faster than a sailor on a weekend furlough.

In addition to tight budgets, NIH Review procedures have changed and not for the better, I would argue. In the past, NIH panels would write full reviews on the science being proposed and generally I received useful insight from the 'pink sheet' reviews. Reviewers had to spend time reading and thinking about the research being proposed, including reading over the PI's past publications that form the foundation of the proposal. Thanks to new NIH leadership, along with a high profile panel of selected top researchers, the review process has been reduced to bullet points and a summary paragraph of discussion. Metrics are applied for several broad categories with the "Approach" being the most critical. This creates a situation where reviewers can cheat in a sense. They can simply decide to not spend time on the proposal and because of the truncated nature of the review, a few simple negative bullet points, and the proposal is doomed. Fortunately, there are others on the panel who review the grant, so there are some safeguards. Why reviewers would shirk their responsibilities may be related to job demands and over-commitment issues. I have also found a few NIH program officials are really lousy at what they do and misrepresent events, either intentionally or due to incompetence. I do not believe this to be a widespread problem at NIH but I have noticed it with NCI, since I usually deal with this particular institute.

Our government has its priorities in a constant state of irrational dithering. Ideologically driven members of Congress are a serious problem. I love airplanes and aviation and I support this activity but there are limits. According to what I've read, a single F-35 fighter jet rings in around a $250 million and as far as I can tell, they still don't work. In 2014 the Department of Defense (DOD) proposes to spend over $8B for this single aircraft. This is about 1/3 of the whole NIH budget. I believe that the DOD has invested well over $120B on this program; roughly more than 4 times our national research budget for all diseases (cancer, cardio, aids and infectious diseases). Can this be justified?

My life is comfortable and I am blessed with a great support network in my family, friends and social environment. I rarely fly commercial airlines when moving about the country. We have a lovely home in Central Colorado, on the Arkansas River, where I can mow the grass and then catch speckled brown trout off my boat ramp. My wife Annette cannot tolerate the summer in Florida, so around May 15, I fly her out to our Colorado home until sometime in the Fall. I own a second hangar at a regional airport very near our home in Buena Vista, CO where I keep my Columbia over the summer months (in the Winter, she is in Florida). I can easily beat the airlines from Orlando to Central Colorado, even though Jets are 2-3 times faster than my Columbia. This is because I can fly directly to my home in the mountains from Florida, whereas commercial flights land in Denver and I have to drive for 3 more hours to get home.

I like my UCF colleagues here and everyone seems to get along for the most part; although, I don't like the petty jealousy that I noted above. My compliance problems with the medical school have been resolved to a large extent. TopoGEN continues to thrive, even in a hardscrabble funding environment. Eventually, I will sell TopoGEN when I retire, which will be in the next 4-5 years most likely. I have recently taken on a new Ph.D. student who will likely be my last. I continued to feel great excitement about science but really about this Ph.D. project. Just allow me a moment to digress on my recent work.

I do cancer research and I am interested in epigenetic programming in somatic cells. Specifically, when a single Cytosine residue get methylated (at CpG sites), it tends to silence the expression of an underlying gene. Such C residue modifications are stable and inherited in daughter cells, largely due to a highly active DNA methylase that operates coordinately with DNA synthesis. Gene silencing in cancer is important because scientists have observed that tumors often have genes that are silenced inappropriately and conversely, other genes have CpG methylation reprogrammed. How and why epigenetic cues are altered with aging is not well understood. A fair amount is known about the DNA methylase that places a methyl-group on cytosine, but far less is known about how the methylations can be revised (removed or reset). In collaboration with a very bright and innovative group in Naples, Italy and independently in my own group, we have published a number of papers showing that when genomic DNA is damaged (both strands are broken) then repaired by a process of homologous recombination, the epigenome can be reprogrammed. Reprogramming takes place over a short (<500bp) segment downstream or 3' of the break. We designed clever GFP (green fluorescent protein) reporters to make this important discovery. The GFP reporter gene has a unique cut site that introduces a single double-strand DNA break in the coding sequence of the GFP cassette. The cell dutifully repairs this break by recombination and the cells turn bright green as GFP is produced in tractable amounts. Sorting the cells based on GFP expression reveals that some cells express high levels of GFP and other cells express very low levels. These expression differences are due to epigenetic reprogramming that attends DNA repair. We got a very interesting result recently. We used "live imaging" confocal microscopy to view the cells as they turn green and divide. We saw a single cell turn bright green (making GFP product) and after cell division, one daughter cell was exceptionally bright and the other was very dim. It is nice to see visual proof ('film at 10!') that our model is correct, although we still have more experiments to fully validate the findings. While a picture is worth a 1000 words (so say the Chinese) a video must be worth at least 10^6 words. Modern technology continues to be a wonder source of inspiration.

Reflecting on the People Influencing My Career Pathway.

I respect myself. This is not arrogance. I am, without any doubt, an overachiever. I really don't deserve anything that I achieved based on some sort of superior intellect. I did it by sheer hard work and perseverance and passion for my objectives and this is the key. My Post-doc advisor had a great expression that aptly applies to the ivory tower of niche knowledge we build in academia. "We learn more and more about less and less" he would say. To put it another way, I know a lot about very little.

Influential people can be positive or negative. In this mini-biography, I choose to focus mostly on the positive influences but recognize that I also learn from negative role models. I appreciate the negative people who stood in my way, since they forced me to find creative pathways and solutions. I learn something from each person I meet. I also learn from students and some may be surprised by this, but everyone can be some sort of influence, be it minor or major. A separate section listing family, mentor, student, friend and colleague influences is woven into the fabric of my story. Writing a separate section would difficult without getting maudlin and sounding like an acknowledgement in a Ph.D. thesis preface. For this reason, I will not re-list the influential people in my life. I am a sum of the individual parts that impacted my thinking and decision making over the years.

Along the lines of David Letterman, here is my top ten list of behavioral guidelines, regarding what I have learned from my life long journey of education.

1. Place a high value on collegiality and civil behavior. Treat everyone with respect. This might sound like an obvious platitude, but I place high value on this. I tried to bully people and it does not work. If you are in a leadership or mentor's role, your challenge is to get people to work hard and do their

job without creating acrimony. This is harder than you might think.
2. Disclose your activities and implicate everyone above you in the chain of command. This is a self-preservation tactic but make sure you have hard evidence (letters, emails, etc.). It can backfire when moving from one university to another, so beware.
3. Don't be risk averse. Life is about taking chances. If you never step out of your safe zone, you are not alive.
4. Related to risk taking, given the option, I tend to ask for forgiveness, rather than asking for permission. Be careful with this one as well… it can bite back.
5. Show enthusiasm for what you do. People may disagree with what you say but with sufficient passion, people will listen.
6. Try hard to communicate at the other person's level, on all matters. As a scientist, I often discuss complex matters with business-oriented audiences and investors. Being able to crystalize complexity into a concise and basic framework is not that hard, with practice. Be responsive to audience response, body language and group behaviors. Adjust accordingly and make eye contact to engage and be inclusive.
7. Be careful who you associate in an academic environment, both as colleagues and collaborators. Since some dogs have fleas, you need to alert. Usually, your colleagues choose you (when you apply of a tenured job for example). Starting a company, selecting collaborators, creating a new academic department are those rare occasions. Who you select to join the lab (Ph.D. students, post-docs and technicians) also qualifies.
8. Research is definitely a niche market that favors those who are creative. New model systems, novel technology with collaborators well outside your field will help. I put together an NIH collaborative Project with an acarologist (an specialty field of entomology that focuses on ticks and mites). We had lunch together and it lead to a tick gene cloning and expression project (that was very well funded). My theory is that "niche" science tends to breed rather tightly focused bands of new

information. When two diverse niche projects can find common ground, it defines an overlap of knowledge that is highly creative and novel. In my case, I really enjoy talking to colleagues in diverse fields for this very reason. At OSU, I was a 'graduate school representative' on Ph.D. theses (oral defense) in areas like psychology, pharmacology, English literature, and history (there were others as well). This was great fun and a wonderful chance to learn.

9. Take advantage of sabbatical opportunities whenever possible. DO NOT do a 'stay at home' sabbatical, since this does not serve any purpose other than encourage vacation minded faculty to shirk responsibility (my opinion only). Leave your home base and go to a different lab to re-tool. Learn a new model system, gain new technology insight and work hard to implement the true purpose of the sabbatical. It should all be focused on making you more competitive in research.

10. Finally, avoid negativity in all matters. It is draining and toxic. Stay positive and don't screw people over. It will come back because the world is round! On a related note, use criticism of your work as a source of strength and do not let it erode you (see next section). Non illegitimi carborundum (don't let the bastards wear you down, in Latin; however, the actual phrase should read: Noli nothis permittere te terere). You get the picture either way.

It's a Wrap.

In science, you must develop a thick skin against failure. Papers that get rejected, grants not renewed, faltered career plans, lack of jobs, tenure denial, and oppressive, demanding administrators will affect your equanimity. This is why senior faculty become jaded dead wood hulks in my opinion. One of my favorite artists is a folk singer named John Prine. I know and sing many of his songs and am a huge fan. His lyrics really hit home, but there is one song (and line in the chorus) that

I love. Through a mutual friend in Scotland (a radio personality who interviews country singers) I obtained a signed card from Mr. Prine that is my personal treasure. I asked Mr. Prine to write the line out in his own hand and sign and date it (see underscored lines below). The song is called "That's the way".

> "That's the way that the world goes round
> You're up one day and then you're down
> <u>It's a half an inch of water and you think you're gonna drown.</u>
> <u>That's the way that the world goes round</u>".

In particular, this speaks to so much of what I do as an academic scientist and to the idea that one must be resilient. Failure is in the eye of the beholder and actual definition of failure is either giving up or not reaching beyond your grasp. Be bold and committed with passion. Use negative outcomes (failed grants or rejected papers) to build your resolve and adopt the attitude the "I'm going to do this and nobody can stop my momentum…. I will prove them wrong". J. Craig Ventner (founded TIGR, his own institute and one of the first to sequence the human genome) told this great story. Some years back, he submitted an NIH grant proposing a new sequencing technology that was soundly and repeatedly rejected by the NIH Study Section. He kept the names of the panel members and the harsh negative reviews as a reminder to build his resolve. Many years later, after sequencing the human genome and establishing his private institute (JCVI), he cross-referenced the names of individuals who consistently torpedoed his proposals. Guess what? These same individuals had adopted his technology and were using the same process they had previously rejected. He was not angry, on the contrary, he embraced this seemingly ironic outcome as validation of his ideas. His 'half an inch of water' was the panel of close minded NIH reviewers who could not appreciate novelty that comes with revolutionary science. Clearly, he did NOT drown.

Completed October 3, 2016

CHAPTER 8

An Unusual Partnership

Thomas M. Murnane
Principal ARC Business Advisors

Inspiration

My story begins in the late '60's as an undergraduate student at Ohio State, majoring in Accounting (mostly because I'd heard of that field and some of my friends were doing the same). Like all undergraduate Business Administration majors, I was required to take introductory courses in Management, Marketing, Finance and Business Law, not that I really knew what any of them entailed. Nonetheless, I dutifully enrolled in Marketing 650 in the Autumn of 1968 and showed up for my first class with Professor Alton Doody, not realizing that my life would never be the same from the first moment Dr. Doody walked into that classroom. To say that he exuded charm and personal charisma would be a massive understatement. He was impeccably dressed in a double-breasted suit, white shirt, silk foulard tie and perfectly polished shoes. As he began to speak, a hush rolled through the hundred or so mere mortals in attendance that day. He regaled us with stories about his ongoing consulting work with a number of the largest and most successful companies of that period, including the mighty Sears, Roebuck and Co., which he portrayed as "capital intensive, professionally managed and vertically integrated"; and practicing the art of marketing without peer to achieve previously unforeseen levels of profitable growth. Well, at that point, I was simply mesmerized. Following that first class, I marched right down to the College Office and changed my major to Marketing, making a mental note to myself that this thing called "consulting" sounded pretty interesting, as well.

As the weeks of the term progressed, my total awe of Dr. Doody and the fields of Marketing and Consulting multiplied logarithmically. From what I could observe, he never wore the same suit, tie, shoes or watch twice during the term. One day when I arrived a little early for class, I saw him pull into the parking garage across from Hagerty Hall in his Rolls Royce. In addition, the stories of his consulting exploits continued to get better and better. He spoke of retiring to his private island to think deeply about marketing, write academic treatises and prepare consulting reports.

And then one day, the coup de grace – he related the story of the genesis of his consulting firm, Management Horizons, which he and two other Ohio State professors and an executive from National Cash Register Company had agreed to start by throwing checks into the middle of a bar table one evening after indulging in a few cocktails. Focused on research-based marketing and business strategy development for retailers and consumer products companies, the firm had already established an enviable reputation as the premiere consulting enterprise in that space, its name becoming a synonymous with retailing excellence. Over time, and in addition to the founders, several other Marketing and Finance Professors from Ohio State signed on to consult and do research under the Management Horizons umbrella, forever linking these two prestigious institutions. And so, in addition to my new passion for Marketing, I filed away for future reference my desire to eventually become a consultant and maybe someday even ascend to the altar of the mighty Management Horizons.

An Inauspicious Start
Flash forward a couple of years (1980 to be exact), and I was approaching graduation with my BSBA degree, a major in Marketing and lofty aspirations for a job with some high-flying marketing juggernaut, or

possibly even a strategy apprentice position with a consultancy not dissimilar from the famed Management Horizons.

Well, as luck would have it, my dreams clashed with the unfortunate reality of a poor economy and an even poorer job market. After a few unsuccessful interviews on campus with corporate recruiters that seemed more like they were fulfilling their company's commitment to be there than actually trying to hire newly-minted graduates, I attended graduation, still full of hope, but without a job.

For the next couple of months, I filled out applications, pounded the pavement and sat for interviews, but still no luck. At this point, with the financial (gas) gauge nearing empty, and my dreams of a marketing or strategy job dashed, I finally secured a position as a "management trainee" with one of the big banks in Columbus, Ohio – hardly the marketing juggernaut I had dreamed about, but a job (and an income!).

The next five years or so represented a rather unremarkable stretch in my budding career, as I rotated through department after department at the bank (commercial loans, automated banking, auditing – you get the idea), all the while telling anyone who would listen that my goal was to get to the Marketing Department. Finally, in year six, I got the call that I was being transferred to Marketing, and would work in New Product Development. I reported for duty with great anticipation, only to quickly discern that, like most financial institutions in that era, marketing was a misnomer for what was nothing more than advertising and special promotions (giveaways).

At that point, I realized that there was nothing more in banking that would take me to the elusive marketing/strategy pinnacle I aspired to.

Time to move on, but where? To do what? It struck me then that advancing my education with an MBA would likely be the best route to my career goal, so I applied for and was awarded a fellowship to pursue an MBA at Ohio State.

Rejuvenation

I resigned from the bank, and dove into my coursework, anxious to get back to an environment where open dialogue about innovative marketing and business strategy was welcomed and even encouraged. I dutifully worked my way through the required courses, and selected electives that would further my understanding in my chosen fields, even finding and enrolling in a course devoted to the nascent discipline of consulting. During my time in the program, I also had the opportunity to meet several additional professors who were actively engaged in consulting work, two or three of whom had actually done work with the renowned Management Horizons. I dwelt on every word of their consulting exploits, hoping someday to have stories of my own to convey; but, more importantly, to learn and grow from them in support of my own career aspirations.

Then, as graduation time approached, my thoughts returned to the possibilities that the job market might present to me, and I could barely contain my excitement and enthusiasm. I hadn't even had so much as an interview, but I was sure I'd find something that would jump-start my career in my intended field (whatever exactly that was – marketing, strategy, and consulting were all over-lapping possibilities).

My Big Break

During my time in the MBA program, one of my Marketing professors, who had an affiliation with Management Horizons, took note of my passion for marketing and strategy and my related interest in the field of consulting. Unbeknownst to me, he approached the leadership at Management Horizons, suggesting that they interview me for an entry level position there upon graduation.

Well, I can't even begin to communicate my sheer surprise and delight when I received a call one afternoon from the Chairman of Management Horizons asking if I would be interested in interviewing for a position there. Of course, I agreed, subsequently accepting a job as an analyst in the Retail Strategy Consulting practice.

And so, with MBA sheepskin in hand, I was finally on my way to becoming a consultant in the purest of commercial disciplines, business strategy. I dove into the role with my usual level of enthusiasm, and was rewarded handsomely for my efforts. I had the opportunity to work on strategy development engagements for some of the largest and most well-known retail and consumer products companies in the world. I traveled across the country and around the world, engaging with senior management teams to tackle their most challenging strategic issues. I had the opportunity to work with and learn from some of the top business strategists in the world. In the process, I moved up the corporate ladder very quickly, becoming a full-fledged strategy consultant after about three years.

Then in 1984, Management Horizons' Chairman and CEO/President approached me and four other mid-senior executives about making an investment in the company and taking a minority ownership position. The company was on solid footing financially and business was good; but, maybe more importantly, I was having the time of my life. Given that fact pattern, making an investment and becoming an owner seemed like a "no-brainer", and so I proudly accepted the offer. Talk about sitting on top of the world – I was a full-fledged strategy consultant, working on the highest-level business issues with senior executives of top-tier clients around the globe and an owner of the premier retail and consumer products consultancy in the world. Life was good!

What Just Happened Here?

Then, in 1985, my whole world changed again. Probably because Management Horizons played bigger than its actual size (our entire staff numbered under 100 people, yet we had a globally recognized name and brand in the retail and consumer products sectors), we attracted attention from a number of suitors who coveted the reputation and greater access to retail and consumer products companies that owning Management Horizons would bring them.

Our two most senior executives/shareholders, who owned controlling interest and were both getting up in years, had been looking for a way to monetize their ownership, while securing the long-term future of the company. Selling to a much larger firm, who would allow us to maintain some degree of autonomy and continue doing what we were doing, seemed like the perfect solution. Many of the suitors who were pursuing us most intently were members of the so-called "Big-8" accounting firms, as they sought opportunities to diversify beyond their slow-growth accounting businesses into the relatively new, high-growth field of consulting. Our majority owners finally settled on one of the suitors, Price Waterhouse, and bought a financially attractive proposal to our full partnership for consideration. I guess I should have been more grateful, because the proposal promised to substantially reward all of us financially, while allowing us to continue doing what we had been doing and loved so much. But I was apoplectic! We were at the very pinnacle of the greatest and purest of business professions – strategy consulting for the world's best companies—and we owned the company. Why would we want to sell our beloved enterprise and affiliate with a bunch of "bean counters?" What benefits could possibly accrue to us, the vaunted strategy consultants, from these green eye-shade wearing, compliance-oriented, numbers crunchers.

Supported by a couple of the other, younger owners, I fought back hard against the deal, but to no avail – we simply didn't have the votes to block it. Later in 1985, the transaction was completed, the money changed hands and we were now the Management Horizons Division of Price Waterhouse. While my bank account had grown significantly, I wasn't a happy camper.

As the dust of the transaction settled and business returned to some semblance of order, I was still indignant. They may have taken the pride I felt in owning a part of Management Horizons away from me, but they couldn't force me to align and cooperate with a bunch of lowly accountants. I resolved to keep my head down, continue with my high-level strategy consulting work and ignore to the extent possible any overtures from Price Waterhouse to work together in any way, shape or form. I was reasonably successful in doing so over the next three years or so; but in 1988, Price Waterhouse made me a Partner in the Firm anyway. It was a wonderful gesture, meant to recognize my success as a strategy consultant; but it most certainly couldn't have been based on any visible cooperation with the larger Firm on my part, because there wasn't any. I was still just as smug (and retrospectively, immature) about the preeminence of strategy consulting, compared to the lowly role of the rank and file Price Waterhouse accountants.

The next couple of years proved to be uneventful, as I continued along with my strategy consulting work out of Management Horizons headquarters office in Columbus, Ohio and in virtual isolation from Price Waterhouse.

A Change of Venue

Then, in 1990, I got the call from Price Waterhouse, asking me to relocate to Southern California to jump-start the Firm's Retail Consulting practice on the West Coast. The realty was that they were asking me to leave to cozy cocoon of the Management Horizons headquarters, where I could work, coalesce and commiserate with my own kind, and take up residence in a far-away office, teeming with bean-counters. Worse yet, I didn't even know anyone there (not that I necessarily even wanted to at that point).

After some considerable deliberation and soul-searching, I reluctantly decided to accept the transfer – reluctant not because of the move to beautiful, sunny Southern California, but because of a sinking feeling that I would be forced into some measure of cooperation, or possibly even collaboration, with (God forbid!) accountants.

It was decided that I would begin the assignment by traveling back and forth from Columbus to Los Angeles each week, while my wife (Kandy) dealt with selling our house in Columbus, buying one in Southern California and preparing our family of five for the move West. This meant lots of flight time and weekly stays in a Los Angeles hotel for me, and extremely busy days for Kandy, tending to our children alone and organizing our relocation. It promised to be a stressful time for all of us to be sure.

As I prepared to start my weekly treks to Los Angeles, I was surprised to receive a call from Dan Lyle, the Los Angeles-based, Managing Partner for the Firm's Retail Practice on the West Coast. He called to introduce himself; offer any assistance he could provide either professionally or personally as I/we got acclimated to working in the Price Waterhouse Los Angeles Office and living in Southern California; and, maybe most appreciated, invite me to dinner at his home during my first week in Los Angeles. I must admit to being a bit taken aback by his gracious welcome and offers of assistance. He seemed like a really nice guy; but then I caught myself with the reminder that, at the end of the day, he was still an accountant. Dan and his wife, Myra, turned out to be wonderful hosts (they subsequently invited Kandy and me to dinner on her first house-hunting trip) and a huge help to us in the transition. And so, a budding personal friendship was taking hold.

An Unusual Partnership

As I began work in the Los Angeles Price Waterhouse Office, still a nomad, I found myself spending more and more time with Dan, whose office was about three doors down the hall from mine. We frequently had lunch together or just engaged in water-cooler conversations, with him asking me questions about my practice, the type of work I did and the kinds of problems I could help clients solve; and me discussing with him the client targets I had identified in the West Region and how best to approach meeting them.

And then one day, Dan surprised me by saying that he thought I might be able to help one of his clients, a major department store chain, headquartered in Los Angeles. He indicated that they were facing some significant strategic challenges that I might be able to help them solve. Now don't get me wrong – this was never about Dan and me actually working together; it was simply him bringing me in to work with one of his clients. A nice gesture to be sure, but certainly not collaboration – after all, Dan was an accountant and I was a strategy consultant. I went along with Dan, met with the client and ended up doing a fair amount of consulting work for them, all the while keeping Dan apprised of what I was doing, but at arms-length in terms of the actual work.

I was very appreciative of Dan's introduction to the client, but no more convinced than ever that an accountant and a strategy consultant could create value for a client by working together. By then it happened again. Dan invited me in to meet another of his clients, a major athletic footwear manufacturer; and, once again, I consulted with them on some strategy issues, keeping Dan informed, but at bay in terms of the actual work. And then it happened again with a toy manufacturer client of Dan's. I could see a pattern of cooperation developing here, but nothing approaching collaboration.

Now I was starting to feel a little guilty. Dan had been so gracious in inviting me in to work with his clients; yet, so far, I hadn't reciprocated. And yet I was facing a dilemma—while Dan had invited me in to meet his clients out of need, all of my clients already had auditors on retainer. How would I justify bringing him along? As I pondered this question, an opportunity presented itself. My strategy work with one of my clients, the Consumer Products Division of a major movie studio, involved some capital allocation planning, which was not really a specialty of mine or my team of strategy consultants. So here was my opening to introduce Dan. He would have a look at the work we'd done, and provide me with some guidance on the appropriateness of the model we were using and the accuracy of our work.

Well, once I turned Dan loose, his value to us and the client immediately became apparent, not only through his insights and suggestions related specifically to the capital allocations, but also in the broader and very penetrating questions he raised about the assumptions we had made in the development of the strategy and the risks the strategy would bring to bear for the client, all gleaned from information he picked up in reviewing the capital allocation plans. His questions caused us to go back and make some significant revisions to the strategy we had developed for the client, making it a much more relevant and enduring plan. In addition, the client was thrilled with Dan's input, because it had made the case for the strategy stronger and reduced the risks inherent in its implementation.

Through this dialogue with Dan, it also became clear to me that he was, in fact, far more than just an accountant. His years of experience in dealing with senior managements of large companies on major accounting issues had turned him into an astute businessman, very capable of opining effectively on strategy issues/options; while his natural skepticism as an auditor made him a great foil for discussions about the risks inherent in any strategy – all of which added great value to our strategy consulting work.

We went on to do considerably more strategy work for that client, and with their blessing (even insistence), Dan became an integral part of our strategy team there. So, it worked once, but could we repeat this success with other of my strategy clients. I wasn't sure, but I was convinced it would be a mistake not to try. So, I took Dan to another client, and then another – always with the same result.

In addition, now when Dan took me to one of his clients, I no longer held him at bay while I did the important strategy work; rather I engaged him in the work, much like I had done with my clients, and achieved better results for his clients as well.

As Dan and I collaborated more and more on my clients and his own, word of our unusual partnership went viral in the Firm and we became poster boys (eventually even legends) in the Firm for the kind of cooperation and collaboration they were seeking in order to grow and develop the practice at a faster pace and better serve clients. Dan and I have now been retired from the Firm (it's now called PricewaterhouseCoopers) for 14 years, but you still occasionally hear reference made to the unusual partnership formed many years ago, between the accountant and the strategy consultant, and the great work that was done for our clients as a result.

In Retrospect

As I reflect upon this brief history of my career in the consulting profession, I'm disappointed in myself for my immaturity and shortsightedness for not seeing the value in collaboration sooner; for missing the potential for the whole to be greater than the sum of the parts when people of different disciplines put their egos aside and work together for the common good. I often wonder what heights I could have scaled had I come to this recognition 20, 10 or even 5 years earlier. At the same time, I'm so very grateful that Dan came along when he did, and that, together, we learned the value of true collaboration – just in time.

CHAPTER 9

Pathways to Intra- and Inter-Institutional Collaboration in Plant Biology

Neftalí Ochoa-Alejo
Professor Unidad Irapuato, Centro de Investigación y de Estudios Avanzados del Instituto Politécnico Nacional

Summary

Plant biotechnology has been a very interesting and important area in the last decades because of its impact in agriculture. Plant biotechnology applications involve micropropagation of different plant species, generation of virus-free important crop species, production of hybrid plants, creation of isogenic, homozygous or pure lines, biosynthesis of secondary metabolites, conservation and preservation of plant genetic resources, and plant genetic engineering as a modern crop improvement alternative. It is easy to perceive that plant biotechnology requires the complementation and collaboration of experts in recombinant DNA technologies and plant cell, tissue and organ culture to render different biotechnological products. Plant biotechnology groups or institutions devoted to this research area are very scarce in Latin-American countries mainly due to the lack of specialized human resources, the inexistence of appropriate infrastructure and very often the absence of financial support for scientific activities. A long-term program for preparing specialized human resources and for building the necessary infrastructure to carryout research on plant biotechnology has been adopted by some developing countries as a strategy to overcome the lack of highly specialized human resources. Examples of this kind of efforts and some alternatives of collaboration are described in this chapter as important actions to succeed in biotechnological research projects in Latin-American institutions.

Early years at the Faculty of Medicine (UNAM)

I started my research activities as research assistant in 1972 at the Unidad de Biología Experimental (Unit of Experimental Biology), Facultad de Medicina (Faculty of Medicine), Universidad Nacional Autónoma de México (UNAM) (National Autonomous University of Mexico), working on the isolation, purification and characterization of hemisphaericin, a cysteine-protease from *Bromelia hemisphaerica* (Ochoa-Alejo et al., 1987). This was among my early plant biotechnology research projects as a laboratory technician with Dr. Félix Córdoba Alva, my former mentor, who at the time, served as head of an immunochemistry group. And sporadic collaboration was established with Dr. Barbarin Arreguin, researcher at the Instituto de Química (Chemistry Institute), UNAM.

Early years at CIB

In 1975 Dr. Córdoba Alva invitd me to participate as a young researcher in the proposed creation of the Centro de Investigaciones Biológicas (CIB) (Biological Research Center) at La Paz, Baja California Sur, Mexico, an isolated arid region, This research center started from ground zero and evolved into a center promoting scientific and technological development in a very isolated and arid region of the Baja California Peninsula under the Consejo Nacional de Ciencia y Tecnología (Conacyt) (National Council of Science and Technology) and the Government of Baja California Sur. .The challenge that faced Dr. Córdoba Alva was that some of the prominent scientists participating in the elaboration of CIB were not willing to relocate to La Paz. The solution was to contract B. Sci. and M. Sci. professionals to the scientific staff of the incipient Marine Biology and Plant Biology groups. High school students were enrolled and trained to assist in research projects since no universities or similar institutions existed in Baja California Sur at that time. A house was rented and adapted to establish the laboratory facilities, a maintenance workshop, whereas the administrative offices were in a secondary house. Projects focused on the study of economic plant species, plant products or biological problems faced by plants in the arid zones [examples: lectins from cacti, drought resistance mechanisms in cacti, salt tolerance mechanisms in mangroves, sex determination in the dioecious plant jojoba (*Simmondsia chinensis*)], and some early work on plant tissue culture. My research at CIB extended to three years without collaboration with other groups because of the inexistence of neighboring research institutions in Baja California Sur. A plan was implemented to address the human resources issue and by sending young researchers abroad for advanced degrees.

My Master and Ph. D. programs at the University of São Paulo

After my research appointment at CIB, I chose the University of Sao Paulo, ESALQ Campus in Brazil to continue my academic preparation since I considered the institution to have high academic reputation in the plant sciences and agricultural challenges like those in Mexico. I started my master degree program (Soil and Mineral Nutrition of Plants) at the Escola Superior de Agricultura "Luiz de Queiróz", Universidade de São Paulo (USP) (University of São Paulo), Piracicaba, São Paulo, Brazil, under the mentorship of Prof. Dr. Otto Jesu Crocomo, head of the Seção de Bioquímica de Plantas (Plant Biochemistry Section) of the Centro de Energia Nuclear na Agricultura (CENA) (Center of Nuclear Energy for Agriculture), USP. My thesis research was about the effect of different nitrogen sources (NO_3^-, NH_4^+ and urea) on the growth and carbohydrates and nitrogenous chemistry in sugarcane (Ochoa-Alejo and Crocomo, 1981; Ochoa-Alejo and Crocomo, 1982), a crop of fundamental importance the bioethanol industry in Brazil. During my Ph. D. program at the Institute of Chemistry, University of São Paulo, Prof. Crocomo was also my advisor while I pursued research on the mechanism of action of the herbicide ametryn in non-chlorophyllaceous sugarcane cell cultures (Ochoa-Alejo and Crocomo, 1987; Ochoa-Alejo and Crocomo, 1988). In both theses, Enio Thiago Oliveira was invaluable as a technician since he assisted me with the required chemical analyses and tissue culture work; this was a new way of assistance because until that time the CENA technicians were highly specialized and only carried out specific and limited activities. Enio earned a Ph.D. and became a scientist and he was incorporated to the Centro de Biotecnología Agricola (CEBTEC) years later.

Back to CIB

After completion of the M. Sci. and Ph. D. programs, I returned in 1983 to CIB, which was now occupied three adapted houses a new research building was constructed on 217 hectares of land donated by the Baja California Sur government. My research was focused on problems inherent to arid zones with high salinity soils. We decided to commit my laboratory to the isolation and characterization of NaCl-resistant variant cells from the glycophyte sweet potato (*Ipomoea batatas* L. Poir), and a comparative study on the salt tolerance mechanisms in *Ipomoea pes-caprae* Roth (known as railroad vine), a pantropical, perennial vine that grows on coastal beaches (shorelines) and dunes throughout the tropical and subtropical areas of the world (Devall, 1990), and the salt-sensitive species *I. batatas*. Two B. Sci. students carried out these researches: Rafael Salgado-Garciglia (Salgado-Garciglia et al., 1985), and Francisco López-Gutiérrez (Ochoa-Alejo and López-Gutierrez, 1987). In 1983, I received an invitation by Dr. Alejandro Blanco Labra to join Cinvestav-Irapuato Unit and I moved to this institution in 1984.

Research activities at Cinvestav-Irapuato Unit

My activities at the Centro de Investigación y de Estudios Avanzados del Instituto Politécnico Nacional (IPN)-Unidad Irapuato (Center for Research and Advanced Studies of the National Polytechnic Institute-Irapuato Unit) (Cinvestav-Irapuato Unit) (Fig. 1) began in April of 1984, three years after its founding as an action of a decentralization research program of Cinvestav, institution founded in Mexico City in 1961 devoted to carry out advanced research in the areas of mathematics, physics, biochemistry, chemistry and physiology with the goal of educating graduate students in all those areas. This was another challenging endeavor since Irapuato Unit was created in 1981 in the agricultural important zone (Bajío Guanajuatense) with the aim of promoting high quality research and a graduate program on Plant Biology. Like the case of CIB, research activities at Irapuato Unit were initiated in a rented house with five or six rustic laboratories, a modest library, a seminar room, and a maintenance workshop. However, unlike CIB, Ph. D. and some M. Sci. researchers from different foreign institutions constituted the scientific staff. A graduate program on Plant Biology was inaugurated with a few students.

Collaborative work in Latin-American institutions is of fundamental importance to successful research programs because very often there are limitations regarding equipment, reagents, laboratory materials and expertise. or skills. Collaborative research programs were established with the Cinvestav-Irapuato Unit to develop protocols for *in vitro* plant regeneration and genetic transformation of certain plant species; for example, *Physalis ixocarpa* Brot, a member of the Solanaceae family, which also includes other agronomic important crops such as *Solanum copernicium* (tomato), chili pepper (*Capsicum* spp.), *Solanum tuberosum* (potato), *Solanum melongena* (eggplant) and *Nicotiana tabacum* (tobacco). *Physalis ixocarpa* is known as tomatillo or Mexican husk tomato and is native to Mexico; the fruits are of commercial value for elaboration of green sauces and Mexican dishes since pre-columbian times. This is a gametophytic self-incompatible species (an obligated allogamous species) and, therefore, the populations exhibit great genetic variability. Like any horticultural crop, Mexican husk tomato is affected by different diseases and pests, which reduce the yield (Valverde et al., 1993, Crespo-Herrera et al., 2012). Biotechnological tools have potential value for the genetic improvement of *Physalis ixocarpa* for generation of resistant plants to different biotic and abiotic factors. One of the first steps in establishment of a research effort was to develop an efficient *in vitro* plant regeneration protocol for use in genetic manipulation. Rafael Ramírez-Malagón, a M. Sci. student of the Plant Biotechnology Graduate Program at Cinvestav-Irapuato Unit, developed a regeneration protocol by culturing tissues from aseptic seedlings on media with different concentrations and combinations of auxins and cytokinins (Ramírez-Malagón and Ochoa-Alejo, 1991). Hypocotyl explants cultured on MS medium (Murashige and Skoog, 1962) supplemented with 1-5 mM naphthaleneacetic acid (NAA) + 12.5-25 mM benzyladenine (BA) produced shoots, which subsequently formed roots on MS medium with 1mM NAA + 1 mM BA. A modified protocol based on these results was subsequently used by Nacyra Assad-García, a B. Sci. student, for *Agrobacterium*-mediated genetic transformation experiments in an intra-departmental collaborative work with Dr. Luis Herrera-Estrella and June Simpson of the Departamento de Ingeniería Genética (Genetic Engineering Department, Cinvestav-Irapuato Unit). This collaboration rendered the establishment of a genetic transformation system that can be used for *Physalis ixocarpa* improvement programs or basic research (Assad-García et al., 1992). Plant tissue techniques have also been applied to *Physalis ixocarpa* to generate isogenic, homozygous or pure lines in this allogamous species through *in vitro* anther culture by Rocío Escobar Guzmán, a Bolivian M. Sci. student, at Cinvestav-Irapuato Unit, which should be otherwise impossible to be produced by traditional breeding techniques (Escobar-Guzman et al., 2009). This research was conducted at the Genetic Engineering Department in collaboration with Dr. Octavio Martínez de la Vega, an expert in biostatistics and bioinformatics.

A comparative study of volatile compounds and fatty acids of plants and *in vitro* cultures of parsley (*Petroselinum crispum*) was carried out in collaboration with Dr. Mercedes G. López-Pérez of the Departamento de Biotecnología y Bioquímica (Biotechnology and Biochemistry Department), Cinvestav-Irapuato Unit, by combining her expertise in volatile compounds characterization by GC-Mass spectrometry and my knowledge in tissue culture systems. Irma Romelia Sánchez-Mendoza, a M. Sci. student, was co-directed by us in this work. In general, differences in volatile compounds were observed: parsley plants produced more monoterpenes, whereas callus and cell suspension cultures showed accumulation of aldehydes (López et al., 1999); higher contents in palmitic and stearic acids were recorded in plants than in callus and cell suspension cultures.

Chili peppers are important items for a diverse kinds of typical dishes in different countries, and also the source of pharmaceutical active compounds such as capsaicinoids, pigments (anthocyanins and carotenoids) and vitamins (A, B and C). Biotechnology is seen as a fundamental area for modern genetic improvement of *Capsicum* species (Ochoa-Alejo and Ramírez-Malagón 2001). In our group, protocols for different *in vitro* systems have been established for plant regeneration, cell suspensions, callus cultures and anther culture (Ochoa-Alejo and Ireta-Moreno 1990; Ochoa-Alejo and García-Bautista 1990; Salgado-Garciglia and Ochoa-Alejo 1990; Ochoa-Alejo and Salgado-Garciglia 1992; Valera-Montero and Ochoa-Alejo 1992; Ochoa-Alejo and Gómez-Peralta 1993; Santos-Díaz and Ochoa-Alejo 1994; Ramírez-Malagón and Ochoa-Alejo 1996; Núñez-Palenius and Ochoa-Alejo 2005; Ochoa-Alejo 2006; Ochoa-Alejo 2012). A research program was conducted by the Ph. D. student Victor M. Martínez-Juárez with cell cultures of chili pepper (*C. annuum*; Jalapeño type) revealed the formation of 5,5'-dicapsaicin as a product of the catabolism of exogenous applied capsaicin (Martínez-Juárez et al., 2004). This project was a collaboration between colleagues of the Departamento de Biotecnología y Bioingeniería (Biotechnology and Bioengineering

Department) (Drs. Graciano Calva-Calva and Fernando J. Esparza-García), Departamento de Química (Chemistry Department) (Dr. Armando Ariza-Castolo) from Cinvestav-México City, Centro de Investigación en Biotecnología, Universidad Autónoma del Estado de Morelos (Biotechnology Center, Autonomous University of Morelos State) (Dr. Maria Luisa Villarreal-Ortega), and the Genetic Engineering Department at Cinvestav-Irapuato Unit (Drs. Edmundo Lozoya-Gloria and Neftalí Ochoa-Alejo).

As a part of another collaboration, my student Yolanda Margarita Camacho-Villasana, enrolled in the Ph. D. Plant Biotechnology Program of the Cinvestav-Irapuato Unit, established a method for RNA isolation from tissues of water-stressed chili pepper plants at the University of California at Riverside, USA in a collaboration with Drs. Elizabeth A. Bray and Linda Walling within a bi-national project through the UC-MEXUS program (Camacho-Villasana et al., 2002). Yolanda Margarita also participated in another collaborative work with Dr. Juan Francisco Jiménez Bremont, researcher of the Instituto Potosino de Investigación Científica y Tecnológica (Potosino Institute of Scientific and Technological Research), in which a comparison of sequences of ornithine decarboxylases (involved in polyamine biosynthesis) from different plant species (including *Capsicum annuum* L.) was reported (Jiménez-Bremont et al., 2004).

Geminivirus infection is very common in chili peppers. *Pepper huasteco virus* (PHV) is a geminivirus that is transmitted by whiteflies and is one of the most important viral pathogens for chili peppers (Garzón-Tiznado et al., 1993; Torres-Pacheco et al., 1996). In a multi-institutional collaborative study between researchers from the Instituto Tecnológico de Celaya (Technological Institute of Celaya) (Drs. Ramón Guevara-González, Claudia Ivonne Muñoz-Sánchez and Lorenzo Guevara-Olvera), from the Instituto Nacional de Investigaciones Forestales, Agrícolas y Pecuarias, Campo Experimental Bajío) (National Institute of Forestry, Agriculture and Livestock Research, Bajío Experimental Station) (Drs. Irineo Torres-Pacheco and Mario González-Chavira) and from Cinvestav-Irapuato Unit (Drs. Rafael F. Rivera-Bustamante) *in vitro* propagation of *Capsicum chinense* BG-3821 accession with resistance to PHV was carried out by Elizabeth

Pérez-Mora (M. Sci. student) in my laboratory to get virus-free plants. Infection of cloned PHV-resistant chili pepper plants proceeded by microparticle bombardment with PHV DNAs and the responses of infected and noninfected plants were analyzed by differential display by José Luis Anaya-López to investigate differences in gene expression as an approach to gain information on the resistance mechanisms to viral infection (Anaya-López et al., 2005). Some differentially expressed genes (45) were detected and two of them showing similarity with a bacterial methyl transferase gene (*CbiL*) and with an *NADP-malic enzyme* gene, respectively, were further characterized.

Using a *Pepper huasteco yellow veins virus* (PHYVV; formerly PHV)-derived vector generated by the group of Dr. Rafael F. Rivera-Bustamante (Genetic Engineering Department, Cinvestav-Irapuato Unit), María del Rosario Abraham-Juárez, a Ph. D. student of the Plant Biotechnology graduate program, investigated the function of genes *Comt* (encoding a caffeic acid *O*-methyltransferase), p*Amt* (a putative aminotransferase) and *Kas* (a b–keto-acyl-[acyl-carrier-protein] synthase) in the biosynthesis of capsaicinoids in chili pepper fruits through the virus-induced gene silencing approach. Chili pepper plants were infected by particle bombardment using PHYVV constructs with partial sequences of each of these genes under the control of the capside protein gene promoter. Analysis of transcripts of each gene in placenta tissues of fruits from infected plants revealed a statistically significant reduction and also a significant decrease in capsaicinoid content in comparison with the control non-infected plants indicating that indeed these genes participate in the biosynthetic capsaicinoid pathway (Abraham-Juárez et al., 2008). Dr. Mercedes G. López-Pérez, a researcher of the Biotechnology and Biochemistry Department, Cinvestav-Irapuato Unit, collaborated in the separation and quantitation of capsaicinoids in chili pepper fruits.

Efficient genetic transformation protocols are necessary for genetic engineering of important crops. A chili pepper genetic transformation system using *Agrobacterium tumefaciens* was established in my group but the efficiency was very low (0.1%), which precludes its utilization for genetic engineering projects. This genetic transformation recalcitrancy problem is mainly due to the fault of an efficient *in vitro* plant regeneration protocol. In collaboration with Professor Shanker Lal Kothari from the Department of Botany, University of Rajasthan, Jaipur, India, we revised the chili pepper tissue culture and transgenesis status, and this recalcitrancy problem was emphasized and discussed in terms of the limitation for the application of genetic engineering to *Capsicum* species (Kothari et al., 2010).

Recently, genomic, transcriptomic, proteomic and metabolomic studies are strategic approaches applied to several important crops for different purposes or goals. Collaborative projects of genomics and transcriptomics of chili pepper have been established at Cinvestav-Irapuato; for example, a project on the genomics of the Mexican chili pepper was financially supported by the Ministry of Agriculture of Mexico (Secretaría de Agricultura, Ganadería, Desarrollo Rural, Pesca y Alimentación; SAGARPA), and also a transcriptomics project for the identification and isolation of genes expressed during the chili pepper fruit development was financed by a partnership between the Consejo Nacional de Ciencia y Tecnología (Conacyt) (National Council of Science and Technology, Mexico) and the Guanajuato State government. These two projects were carried out with the participation of Dr. Rafael F. Rivera-Bustamante (virologist), Edmundo Lozoya-Glória (plant molecular biologist), Octavio Martínez de la Vega (statistician and bioinformatics expert), Dr. Ana María Bailey (phytopathologist) and myself (plant biochemist, plant tissue culturist), all researchers of the Genetic Engineering Department staff at Cinvestav-Irapuato-Unit involved in studies having *Capsicum* species as model systems. As a result, cDNA libraries (ESTs) were generated from entire chili pepper fruits at different developmental stages, from different tissues (pericarp, roots, stem, leaves and flowers) and also subtractive libraries between anthocyanin or carotenoid producing pericarps and green pericarp to enrich transcripts from genes involved in anthocyanin or carotenoid biosynthesis, or between pungent and non-pungent chili pepper fruits to enrich transcripts from genes of the pungent compounds (capsaicinoids) biosynthetic pathway were established. A total of 29,778 sequences were obtained from fruits at different developmental or ripening stages, and a total of 23,337 sequences were generated from roots (6,490), stem (7,178), leaves (5,189) and flowers

(4,480), respectively. This information served as a starting point to carry out further collaborative studies on the biochemistry and molecular biology of anthocyanins biosynthesis in chili pepper fruits (Aza-González et al., 2013). In a further collaborative project at the Genetic Engineering Department and the Laboratorio Nacional de Genómica para la Biodiversidad (Langebio) (National Laboratory of Genomics for Biodiversity) at Cinvestav-Irapuato a chili pepper database was generated from the transcriptome generated by the Ph. D. student Elsa Góngora-Castillo (Góngora-Castillo et al., 2012).

A study on the dynamics of chili pepper fruit transcriptome at different developmental stages using next-generation sequencing technology was reported in a collaborative research (Martínez-López et al., 2014). In this case we complemented the expertise in bioinformatics of Dr. Octavio Martínez de la Vega (Langebio) and my own experience in plant biochemistry to act as advisors of Luis Alberto Martínez-López, a M. Sci. student. In this work, 15,550,468 Illumina MiSeq reads were generated and assembled into 34,066 genes from the transcriptome of 'Tampiqueño 74' chili pepper fruits (*C. annuum*; Serrano type) (Fig. 3). RNA-seq analysis of this transcriptome gave global information on the changes in gene expression of biological processes and metabolic pathways. Expression of genes involved in carotenoid biosynthesis was analyzed by RNA-seq and was further validated by qRT-PCR as an example of the utility of this transcriptomic data.

In a series of very fruitful collaborations with my graduate student Dr. Rafael Ramírez-Malagón at the Instituto de Ciencias Agrícolas, Universidad de Guanajuato (Institute of Agricultural Sciences, University of Guanajuato), we complemented our different interests and expertise to develop several *in vitro* protocols for different plant species; for example, the generation of micropropagation systems for the ornamental species fraser photinia (*Photinia* X *fraseri*) (Ramírez-Malagón et al., 1997) and *Spathiphyllium floribundum* L. (Ramírez-Malagón et al., 2001), or the establishment of tissue culture conditions for the propagation of threatened species of *Mammillaria* (Cactaceae) (Ramírez-Malagón et al., 2007), and *Agave* species (Ramírez-Malagón et al., 2008). Moreover, an *in vitro* protocol for potyvirus free-garlic plant generation was developed for the Aguilares S.P.R. Company with a financial support shared with Fundación Guanajuato Produce (Ramírez-Malagón et al., 2006). More recently, we reported a vegetative propagation method for mesquite (*Prosopis laevigata*), a highly drought tolerant species (Ramírez-Malagón et al., 2014). Additionally, together with my graduated Ph. D. students Dr. María del Socorro Santos-Díaz incorporated to the Universidad Autónoma de San Luis Potosí (Autonomous University of San Luis Potosí) and Dr. Eugenio Pérez-Molphe-Balch at the Universidad Autónoma de Aguascalientes (Autonomous University of Aguascalientes), we published a plant tissue culture book (Pérez-Molphe-Balch et al., 1999), a chapter on the "Current status and strategies for conservation of Mexican threatened cacti" (Santos-Díaz et al., 2010) and a review article on "Tissue culture of ornamental cacti" (Pérez-Molphe-Balch et al., 2015).

Collaborative academic activities with members of CICY

CICY is the abbreviation of Centro de Investigación Científica de Yucatán (Center of Scientific Research of Yucatán) located at the Yucatán Peninsula in the southeastern region of Mexico. CICY was founded in 1979 as a project of scientific and technological research decentralization by the Consejo Nacional de Ciencia y Tecnología (Conacyt; Mexico) (National Council of Science and Technology) with the aim of promoting the development of science to attend and solve problems in that region. I met Dr. Victor Manuel Loyola-Vargas, one of the most distinguished members of the CICY staff, in 1983 at the meeting of the Mexican Association for Plant Tissue Culture held in México City, but our collaboration activities began some years later through a shared plant tissue culture course for graduate students and also by my participation as external member in a series of tuition committees of students of the CICY graduate program that continue until the present days. I have also participated on committees of students under the supervision of Dr. Teresa Hernández-Sotomayor and Dr. Felipe Vázquez-Flota, and as co-advisor, together with Dr. Nancy Santana-Buzzy, of the Ph. D. student Raúl Enrique Valle Gough who carried out his experimental work entitled "Expression analysis of

WOX genes during the somatic embryogenesis of Habanero chili pepper (*Capsicum chinense* Jascq.)" under our tuition (Valle-Gough et al., 2015).

One important aspect of collaboration with Dr. Loyola-Vargas has been the edition of books as a means of diffusion of plant biotechnology protocols. Together, we prepared the third edition of the book entitled *"Plant cell culture protocols"* (Loyola-Vargas and Ochoa-Alejo, 2012), and more recently the book *"Somatic embryogenesis: Fundamental aspects and applications"* (Loyola-Vargas and Ochoa-Alejo, 2016), published by Humana Press, and Springer, respectively. In these cases, we received the collaboration of experts from institutions around the world.

Concluding remarks

Collaborative partnerships in Latin-American research institutions are of essential importance to complement human resources expertise, infrastructure and also to facilitate the consecution of financial support for plant biotechnology projects. Personally, I myself have received benefits from collaborations with colleagues working at different academic units of my institution or from other national or international institutions. Advances in science are easier, faster and successful when we combine and complement different academic backgrounds and expertise to achieve common goals or objectives. I have been fortunate with the opportunity for sharing graduate students with colleagues that mentor them to successfully develop their research dissertations or projects or, in the opposite way, to help students of my colleagues by participating on their graduate committees contributing ideas or solving experimental problems. In some situations, the infrastructure of my laboratory has been important to carry out complementary experimental work of graduate students of our Plant Biotechnology Program or, vice versa, my students have taken advantages of these facilities and the complementary expertise of my colleagues. Moreover, working as a group, we have successfully garnered financial funds (grants) to support important plant biotechnology projects of scientific relevance or of high impact, which would not have been otherwise possible.

References

Abraham-Juárez, M. S., Rocha-Granados, M. C., López, M. G., Rivera-Bustamante, R. F., & Ochoa-Alejo, N. (2008). Virus-induced silencing of *Comt*, p*Amt* and *Kas* genes results in a reduction of capsaicinoid accumulation in chili pepper fruits. *Planta, 227,* 681-695.

Anaya-López, J. L., Pérez-Mora, E., Torres-Pacheco, I., Muñoz-Sánchez, C. I., Guevara-Olvera, L., González-Chavira, M., Ochoa-Alejo, N., Rivera-Bustamante, R. F., & Guevara-González, R. G. (2005). Inducible gene expression by *Pepper huasteco virus* in *Capsicum chinense* plants with resistance to geminivirus infections. *Canadian Journal of Plant Pathology, 27,* 276:282.

Aza-González, C., Herrera-Isidrón, L., Núñez-Palenius, H. G., Martínez de la Vega, O., & Ochoa-Alejo, N. (2013). Anthocyanin accumulation and expression analysis on biosynthesis-related genes during chili pepper fruit development. *Biologia Plantarum, 57,* 49-55.

Camacho-Villasana, Y. M., Ochoa-Alejo, N., Walling, L., & Bray, E. A. (2002). An improved method for isolating RNA from dehydrated and nondehydrated chili pepper (*Capsicum annuum* L.) plant tissues. *Plant Molecular Biology Reporter, 20,* 407-414.

Crespo-Herrera, L. A., Rodríguez-Leyva, E., Ortega-Arenas, L. D., & Solís-Aguilar, J. F. (2012). Spatial distribution of *Bactericera cockerelli* (Sulc) (Hemiptera: Triozidae) on green tomato (*Physalis ixocarpa* Brot.). *Agrociencia 46,* 289-298.

Devall, M. S. (1992). The biological flora of coastal dunes and wetlands. 2. *Ipomoea pes-caprae* (L.) Roth. *Journal of Coastal Research, 8,* 442-446.

Escobar-Guzmán, R. E., & Ochoa-Alejo, N. (2009). *In vitro* formation and plant regeneration from anther culture of different cultivars of

Mexican husk tomato (*Physalis ixocarpa* Brot.). *Plant Cell, Tissue and Organ Culture, 96*, 181-189.

Garzón-Tiznado, J. A., Torres-Pacheco, I., Ascencio-Ibañez, J. T., Herrera-Estrella, L., & Rivera-Bustamante, R. F. (1993). Inoculation of peppers with infectious clones of a new geminivirus by a biolistic procedure. *Phythopathology, 53*, 514-521.

Góngora-Castillo, E., Fajardo-Jaime, R., Fernández-Cortés, A., Jofre-Garfias, A. E., Lozoya-Glória, E., Martínez, O., Ochoa-Alejo, N., & Rivera-Bustamante, R. F. (2012). The *Capsicum* transcriptome DB: a "hot" tool for genomic research. *Bioinformation, 8*, 43-47.

Jiménez-Bremont, J. F., Camacho-Villasana, Y. M., Cabrera-Ponce, J. L., Barba de la Rosa, A. P., & Ochoa-Alejo, N. (2004). Sequence comparison of plant ornithine decarboxylases reveals high homology and lack of introns. *Biologia Plantarum, 48*, 193-198.

López, M. G., Sánchez-Mendoza, I. R., & Ochoa-Alejo, N. (1999). Comparative study of volatile components and fatty acids of plants and *in vitro* cultures of parsley (*Petroselinum crispum* (Mill) Nym ex Hill). *Journal of Agricultural and Food Chemistry, 47*, 3292-3296.

Loyola-Vargas, V. M., & Ochoa-Alejo, N. (2012). *Plant cell culture protocols*. Third edition. Humana Press, New York. 430 p.

Loyola-Vargas, V. M., & Ochoa-Alejo, N. (2016). *Somatic embryogenesis: Fundamental aspects and applications*. Springer, Switzerland. 506 p.

Martínez-Juárez, V. M., Ochoa-Alejo, N., Ariza-Castolo, A., Ortega-López, J., Lozoya-Glória, E., Esparza, F., Villarreal, M. L., & Calva-Calva, G. (2004). Specific synthesis of 5,5'-dicapsaicin by a NaCl-extracted cell wall protein fraction from cell suspension cultures of chilli pepper (*Capsicum annuum* var. *annuum*) (Chile jalapeño chigol). *Journal of Agricultural and Food Chemistry, 52*, 972-979.

Martínez-López, L. A., Ochoa-Alejo, N., & Martínez, O. (2014). Dynamics of the chili pepper transcriptome during fruit development. *BMC Genomics, 15*, 143.

Núñez-Palenius, H. G., & Ochoa-Alejo, N. (2005). Effect of phenylalanine and phenylpropanoids on the accumulation of capsaicinoids and lignin in cell cultures of chili pepper (*Capsicum annuum* L.). *In Vitro Cellular and Developmental Biology-Plant, 41*, 801-805.

Ochoa-Alejo, N. (2006). Capsaicin accumulation in *Capsicum* spp. suspension cultures. In V. M. Loyola-Vargas and F. Vázquez-Flota (Eds.), *Plant cell culture protocols*. Second edition. Humana Press, Totowa, NJ, USA. Pp. 327-334.

Ochoa-Alejo, N. (2012). Anther culture of chili pepper (*Capsicum* spp.). In V. M. Loyola-Vargas and N. Ochoa-Alej (Eds.), *Plant cell culture protocols*. Third edition. Humana Press, New York. Pp. 227-231.

Ochoa-Alejo, N., Agundis, C., & Cordoba, F. (1987). Isolation and partial characterization of *Bromelia hemisphaerica* protease by affinity chromatography. *Preparative Biochemistry, 17*, 337-347.

Ochoa-Alejo, N., & Crocomo, O. J. (1981). Biochemical and physiological aspects of sugarcane (*Saccharum* spp.). II. Effect of NO_3-N, NH_4-N and urea-N on carbohydrate level and growth of cv. NA56-79. *Energia Nuclear na Agricultura, 3*, 137-151.

Ochoa-Alejo, N., & Crocomo, O. J. (1982). Biochemical and physiological aspects of sugarcane (*Saccharum* spp.). III. Influence of nitrate, ammonium and urea on the metabolism of nitrogen compounds in cv. NA56-79. *Energia Nuclear na Agricultura, 4*, 3-20.

Ochoa-Alejo, N., & Crocomo, O. J. (1987). Influence of ametryn on chromatin activity and on RNA synthesis in a non-chlorophyllaceous sugarcane cell suspension. *Journal of Plant Physiology, 126*, 355-363.

Ochoa-Alejo, N., & Crocomo, O. J. (1988). Inhibition of growth and interference with ^{14}C-leucine uptake and incorporation into protein in non-chlorophyllaceous sugarcane cells by ametryn. *Turrialba, 38*, 59-63.

Ochoa-Alejo, N., & García-Bautista, M. A. R. (1990). Morphogenetic responses *in vitro* of hypocotyl tissues of chili pepper (*Capsicum annuum* L.) to growth regulators. *Turrialba, 40*, 311-318.

Ochoa-Alejo, N., & Gómez-Peralta, J. E. (1993). Activity of enzymes involved in capsaicin biosynthesis in callus tissue of chili pepper (*Capsicum annuum* L.) *Journal of Plant Physiology, 141*, 147-152.

Ochoa-Alejo, N., & Ireta-Moreno, L. (1990). Cultivar differences in shoot-forming capacity of hypocotyl tissues of chilli pepper (*Capsicum annuum* L.) cultured *in vitro*. *Scientia Horticulturae, 42*, 21-28.

Ochoa-Alejo, N., López-Gutiérrez, F. (1987). Effect of light and NaCl salinity on the growth of callus cultures of *Ipomoea pescaprae* (L) Brown and *Ipomoea batatas* (L) Lam. *Annals of Botany, 59*, 495-497.

Ochoa-Alejo, N., & Ramírez-Malagón, R. (2001). *In vitro* chili pepper biotechnology. *In Vitro Cellular and Developmental Biology-Plant, 37*, 701-729.

Ochoa-Alejo, N., & Salgado-Garciglia, R. (1992). Phenylalanine ammonia-lyase activity and capsaicin-precursor compounds in *p*-fluorophenylalanine-resistant and –sensitive variant cells of chili pepper (*Capsicum annuum*). *Physiologia Plantarum, 85*, 173-179.

Pérez-Molphe-Balch, E. M., Ramírez-Malagón, R., Núñez-Palenius, H. G., & Ochoa-Alejo, N. (1999). *Introducción al cultivo de tejidos vegetales*. Universidad Autónoma de Aguascalientes, Aguascalientes, México. 179 p.

Pérez-Molphe-Balch, E., Santos-Díaz, M. S., Ramírez-Malagón, R., & Ochoa-Alejo, N. (2015). Tissue culture of ornamental cacti. *Scientia Agricola, 72*, 540-561.

Ramírez-Malagón, R., Aguilar-Ramírez, I., Borodanenko, A., Pérez-Moreno, L., Barrera-Guerra, J. L., Núñez-Palenius, H. G., & Ochoa-Alejo, N. (2007). *In vitro* propagation of ten threatened species of *Mammillaria* (Cactaceae). *In Vitro Cellular and Developmental Biology-Plant, 43*, 660-665.

Ramírez-Malagón, R., Borodanenko, A., Barrera-Guerra, J. L., & Ochoa-Alejo, N. (1997). Micropropagation for fraser photinia (*Photinia X fraseri*). *Plant Cell, Tissue and Organ Culture, 48*, 219-222.

Ramírez-Malagón, R., Borodanenko, A., Barrera-Guerra, J. L., & Ochoa-Alejo, N. (2001). Shoot number and shoot size as affected by growth regulators in *in vitro* cultures of *Spathiphyllium floribundum* L. *Scientia Horticulturae, 89*, 227-236.

Ramírez-Malagón, R., Borodanenko, A., Pérez-Moreno, L., Salas-Araize, M. D., Núñez-Palenius, H. G., & Ochoa-Alejo, N. (2008). *In vitro* propagation of three *Agave* species used for liquor distillation and three for landscape. *Plant Cell, Tissue and Organ Culture, 94*, 201-207.

Ramírez-Malagón, R., Delgado-Bernal, E., Borodanenko, A., Pérez-Moreno, L., Barrera-Guerra, J. L., Núñez-Palenius, H. G., Ochoa-Alejo, N. (2014). Air layering and tiny-air layering techniques for mesquite [*Prosopis laevigata* (H.B. ex Willd.) Johnst. M.C.] tree propagation. *Arid Land Research and Management, 28*, 118-128.

Ramírez-Malagón, R., & Ochoa-Alejo, N. (1991). Adventitious shoot formation and plant regeneration from tissues of tomatillo (*Physalis ixocarpa* Brot.). *Plant Cell, Tissue and Organ Culture, 25*, 185-188.

Ramírez-Malagón, R., & Ochoa-Alejo, N. (1996). An improved and reliable chili pepper (*Capsicum annuum* L.) plant regeneration method. *Plant Cell Reports, 16*, 226-231.

Ramírez-Malagón, R., Pérez-Moreno, L., Borodanenko, A., Salinas-González, G. J., & Ochoa-Alejo, N. (2006). Differential organ infection studies, potyvirus elimination, and field performance of virus-free garlic plants produced by tissue culture. *Plant Cell, Tissue and Organ Culture, 86*, 103-110.

Salgado-Garciglia, R., López-Gutiérrez, F., & Ochoa-Alejo, N. (1985). NaCl-resistant variant cells isolated from sweet potato cell suspensions. *Plant Cell, Tissue and Organ Culture, 5*, 3-12.

Salgado-Garciclia, R., & Ochoa-Alejo, N. (1990). Increased capsaicin content in PFP-resistant cells of chili pepper (*Capsicum annuum* L.). *Plant Cell Reports, 8*, 617-620.

Santos-Díaz, M. S., Pérez-Molphe, E., Ramírez-Malgón, R., Núñez-Palenius, H. G., and Ochoa-Alejo, N. (2010). Mexican threatened cacti: Current status and strategies for their conservation. In G. H. Tepper (Ed.), *Species diversity and extinction*. Nova Science Publishers, Inc., New York. Pp. 1-59.

Santos-Díaz, M. S., & Ochoa-Alejo, N. (1994). PEG-tolerant cell clones of chili pepper (*Capsicum annuum* L.): growth, osmotic potentials and solute accumulation. *Plant Cell, Tissue and Organ Culture, 37*, 1-8.

Valera-Montero, L. L., & Ochoa-Alejo, N. (1992). A novel approach for chili pepper (*Capsicum annuum* L.) plant regeneration: shoot induction in rooted hypocotyls. *Plant Science, 84*, 215-219.

Valle-Gough, R. E., Avilés-Viñas, S. A., López-Erosa, S., Canto-Flick, A., Gómez-Uc, E., Sáenz-Carbonell, L. A., Ochoa-Alejo, N., & Santana-Buzzy, N. (2015). Polyamines and *WOX* genes in the recalcitrance to plant conversion of somatic embryos of Habanero pepper (*Capsicum chinense* Jacq.). *African Journal of Biotechnology, 14*, 569-581.

Valverde, R. A., Can, F., & Rush, M. C. (1993). Yellow mottle of tomatillo (*Physalis ixocarpa*) caused by *Physalis mottle virus*. Plant Pathol. 42: 657-660.

Figure 1. Partial external views of Cinvestav-Irapuato Unit installations.

TOP: Fruits of Mexican husk tomato (Physalis ixocarpa Brot.).
BOTTOM: Fruits of chili pepper 'Tampiqueño 74' (Capsicum annuum, Serrano type).

Contact Information:

Departamento de Ingeniería Genética, and Departamento de Biotecnología y Bioquímica, Centro de Investigación y de Estudios Avanzados del Instituto Politécnico Nacional, Unidad Irapuato, Km 9.6 libramiento norte carretera Irapuato-León, 36821-Irapuato, Gto., México. E-mail: nochoa@ira.cinvestav.mx; Phone: (+52) 462 623 9654.

CHAPTER 10

From Cell to Plant: Biotechnology for Plant Propagation

Enio Tiago de Oliveira
Research Biologist

Otto J. Crocomo
CEBTEC Founder and Emeritus Director
Emertitus Professor ESALQ University of Sao Paulo

Introduction

The pages ahead chronicle the collaborative careers of Drs. Enio Tiago de Oliveira and Otto J. Crocomo. The two scientists celebrate a collaborative partnership spanning over forty-years. Dr. Oliveria, was originally employed at the Center for Nuclear Energy in Agriculture (CENA) /ESALQ/University of São Paulo, Plant Biochemistry Sector, enrolled in the graduate program and earned a Ph.D. in Plant Biology under the mentorship of Professor Crocomo at ESALQ. Enio was an invaluable colleague during Professor Crocomo founding of CEBTEC—The Center for Agricultural Biotechnology—located at the "Luiz de Queiroz" School of Agriculture (ESALQ), campus of the University of São Paulo in Piracicaba -SP.

The Center has been dedicated to Extension Services to the Community conducting Research and Development (R & D) in the field of Biotechnology of Plants and Microorganisms for the Brazilian Agribusiness Sector, in close harmony with the university, government institutions and the private sector. Research and product development studies are carried out through agreements with official Brazilian and private institutions, as well as foreign entities. Biotechnology research and development programs are conducted in plant biology among others, include research on *in vitro* production of disease-free seedlings of strawberry, banana, sugarcane, eucalyptus clones and citrus plants free of the "tristeza" virus through micrografting, and eucalyptus clones. Dr. Enio activities include the *Xyllela* Genome Project financed by FAPESP.

Enio's Collaborative Efforts

In almost 40 years of university activities, I have always experienced the spirit of collaboration both in my scientific training and in the development of technical-scientific projects that required and still require my collaboration. In fact, my father Jones was one of the first to be responsible for my future academic training.

I am a native of the city of Taiobeiras, located in the north of the state of Minas Gerais, Brazil, one of the corridors used by the northeastern retreatants heading towards the State of São Paulo during the 20th century. In my childhood, in late 1960s, I witnessed this northeastern exodus. It seemed that São Paulo would be the Promised Land for almost the entire northeastern population of Brazil.

In August 1970, at the age of 11, with my father, mother Olivia and 9 siblings, I arrived in Piracicaba, State of São Paulo. Then my struggle for survival began. I was a seller of flowers, toys and gas balloons, and shined shoes in public squares. The Brazilian legislation prohibits child labor, but my father obtained the necessary authorization from the juvenile court. My father's encouragement and vision of the future was *sine qua non*.

This allowed me to continue attending school at night while working at restaurants and gas stations during the daytime. My father was always present for me during the course during my intellectual formation. Throughout this period, I received several other incentives for my studies. I will never forget the important collaborative input received from the lawyer Nelson Rodrigues Martinez.

My high school education was completed at the Alcides Guidetti Zagatto State School, located at that time, on the outskirts of Piracicaba. I have many memories of that School and I am proud of having collaborated, as a student, in its foundation. At that time, I built many friendships that I have cherished to this day, such as my Portuguese and English Language teacher, Vilma Carolina dos Santos, not to mention my beloved friend and teacher Plinio Montagner.

With the encouragement of my family, I enrolled in a Technical Course in Chemistry at the Industrial College "Dom Bosco". I continued working during the day, also serving in the Army. In the beginning, it was very difficult. I was introduced to chemistry by Carlos Roberto Furlan and then to the world of atoms: an indivisible and invisible particle in naked eyes, the atom combining with other atoms to form molecules and, thus, forming the matter we see and feel! The atoms themselves formed by a nucleus around which electrons gravitate, imitating the solar system! I was astonished. In mathematics classes, with logarithms and trigonometry, I did not understand anything, while my classmates won Math Olympiads. I almost gave up the course if it were not for the invaluable collaborative tutorials from my physics professor Carlos Gregório, who guided me on the right way to study and, consequently, to understand the difficult subjects presented to me in classes. I followed his recommendations. He was right. With effort and dedication, I succeeded in overcoming my own difficulties in Chemistry, Mathematics, Physics and Biology. Good teachers, those who really want to teach, are always right.

In 1977, the doors of science began to open-up for me. The Plant Biochemistry Sector of the Center for Nuclear Energy in Agriculture (CENA), headed by Professor Otto Jesu Crocomo, that here I will call Dr. Otto, announced a position for a traineeship with a scientific research grant. Three students would be selected and, after three months, only one would be selected for the position. I was selected and began to be guided by Dr. Otto.

At this point, I met my father, not biological, of course, but my scientific father, friend and guide to the scientific life. Dr. Otto sent me to follow and help a student of Mexican origin in his master's thesis and later during his doctorate, Neftali Ochoa Alejo. Now he is a research scientist at the Instituto Politécnico Nacional, Irapuato, Mexico. I assisted and learned a lot with Neftali: to cultivate sugarcane cells *in vitro*, to control cellular morphogenetic and organogenetic processes, to regenerate plants tolerant to high doses of herbicides, etc. In the laboratory, I also learned techniques for the evaluation of biochemical substances in plant tissues.

At that time, I was toward the end of adolescence and developing my personality I would like to emphasize the mentorship under supervision of Dr. Otto and Neftali, which influenced my maturation as a person and student of plant biology and biochemistry, was important for my later entry into the world of plant biotechnology. My intellectual development occurred while participating in the discussions of scientific issues between Dr. Otto and Neftali. Much of my scientific development is also due to the lectures and lab work of Prof. William R. Sharp during his frequent visits to CENA at the beginning of CEBTEC.

Over many years working with Dr. Otto, I was involved in dozens of scientific projects, and participated in the training of dozens of undergraduate students and their graduate courses. The students today have been successful with research and faculty appointments. I would like to highlight Helaine Carrer, currently at CEBTEC / ESALQ, who I collaborated from the beginning of her undergraduate program with Dr. Otto. Now she is Full Professor at "Luiz de Queiroz" School of Agriculture (ESALQ / USP) and my immediate superior. Her scientific activity is recognized nationally and internationally. With Helaine, I have been currently involved as collaborative researcher on several international research projects including the genome sequencing of *Xilella fastidiosa*: a megaproject conducted by several Brazilian Universities and Research Institutes. This was the first completed sequenced genome made in Brazil, winning several honors.

In 1981, I collaborated with Dr. Otto during discussions with the creation of the Center for Agricultural Biotechnology (CEBTEC) and in the development of technical-scientific projects with official entities and private companies. I participated in the design of the new CEBTEC building, from the launching of its foundation stone (on January 6, 1986) until its construction and its inauguration on October 28, 1988. Simultaneously and under the influence of Dr. Otto, I took the Course of Biology at the Methodist University of Piracicaba (UNIMEP), at night and worked during the day. In 1985, under the direction of Dr. Otto, my position was transferred from CENA to ESALQ. Even though not being part of the ESALQ's teaching program, due to the encouragement and influence of Dr. Otto, I joined the first group of the Master's Degree Graduate Program in Plant Physiology and Biochemistry at ESALQ / USP, under his guidance. My dissertation thesis was approved with distinction and praise. Later I received my Doctorate degree in the same program under the guidance of Prof. Luiz Antonio Gallo. Currently, I continue to work at CEBTEC. Dr. Otto's has completed his final retirement and a sector of the Department of Biological Sciences of ESALQ has been named in his honor.

An important moment in this long trajectory, which I think it was very fast, happened. In 1984 when I married Joan of Arc (the name translates her strength). I have lived with her for 28 years, until her death in January 2013. From that marriage, we had two children: Tiago, now 24 years old, is a commercial airplane pilot, and Marcele, a doctor with specialization in Otorhinolaryngology, now 30 years old. Remembering the closeness of our family, I would like to mention my brothers who with me and our parents left the poor northeast Brazilian and, after a long journey, settled in this safe harbor that is Piracicaba. They are: Nailda, Alaide, Eliene, Dinarte, Ana Maria, Neuda, Wildes and Weldner. I still collaborate with all of them, and I receive encouragement and collaboration from them.

Collaborative Works

2.1. Early Experiences
My earliest recollections of collaborative work refer to the Debates of Chemistry, when I was a high school student at the "O Piracicabano" in Piracicaba, from 1950 to 1952. I was then 18 years old. I participated

in three intercollegiate debates and one intra-collegiate debate all as a team leader. It was three days of laboratory testing and public discussion of the results. My teams won all the debates. The teams were always formed of 6 participants, under the general coordination of Professor Demosthenes Santos Corrêa, who proposed practical questions that could be solved in the laboratory. It was one of my best experiences working as a group. All the participants collaborated effectively.

It was these experiences involving collaboration between individuals that guided my life as a student of agronomy at the "Luiz de Queiroz" College of Agriculture (ESALQ), University of São Paulo (USP), Piracicaba, and later in my academic life in that College and in other institutions in Brazil and abroad. Still as a student of Agronomy, I developed several research works in collaboration with my colleague Ary A. Salibe. The results of presented to the Agronomy Students' Congresses held at ESALQ and other Brazilian Universities (1954, 1955 and 1956). These congresses were among the activities of the Center for Agronomic Debates, of which I was one of the directors, and had the collaboration of my colleagues. Here I met the one person who would become one of my best friends in both academic life or in private life: André Louis Neptune, of Haitian origin, from the Department of Soils of ESALQ. We both collaborated in several research programs related to the metabolism of chemical nutrients in plants. Our families were very close. He and his wife Nair were godparents of my marriage to Diva and the godparents of one of our children, Adolfo Egídio.

I was interested in the chemical reactions and in particular, in the cellular biochemical reactions occurring in animal, plants and microorganisms. I was also interested in the cells themselves, how they are formed, how they multiply, how they communicate with each other, how they differentiate into specialized tissues. The complexity and beauty of nature fascinated me. I quote myself: "biochemical reactions occur only because cells exist; at the same time, biochemical reactions are responsible for the existence of the cells!" (Crocomo, 2014, vol. 1, p.126). Wonderful nature!

This complexity revealed an intense activity of mutual collaboration in the organization of beings. Even more so: in a chemical solution, the substances that make it up contribute their properties to the property of the whole, while preserving their own individuality! So also in human work teams: while preserving their own individualities, each member contributes his knowledge and ideas to the development of a project or program of whatever the nature, of which he participates.

2.2. Academy Collaborationa

After graduation (1956) and before being employment by ESALQ/USP, I was an Assistant Professor at the School of Dentistry of Piracicaba (1959-1960), teaching Biochemistry in close collaboration with the Professor of Physiology, Bem-Hur Carvalhaes de Paiva, in the same Department. Our classes were mutually supportive. It was a very productive time. One of our students, Antonio Carlos Neder, was interested in the content of Biochemistry classes, collaborating in our didactic activities, and later became an excellent professor of Pharmacology. He always reiterates "the biochemistry and collaborative environment" in our existing activities at that time, were essential for his introduction of biochemical pharmacology into the curriculum of the Faculties of Dentistry in Brazil." He became Director of The Faculty of Dentistry as part of the University of Campinas (UNICAMP) in Piracicaba.

During the years 1958/59, at the invitation of Professor E. Malavolta, I prepared for the contest of "Free Professorship" of Organic Chemistry and Biological Chemistry at ESALQ which required intensive four-day exams. During my preparation, I had the collaboration of the Professors Euripedes Malavolta and José Dal Pozzo Arzolla. The examinations took place in September 1959. In April 1960 I was hired by ESALQ, as Assistant Professor under Professor Malavolta, with whom I collaborated in several of his research projects on fertilization and mineral nutrition of coffee.

October 1961 to December 1962 I served as Professor of Chemistry and Biochemistry at the Faculty of Agronomy of Zulia, Maracaibo, Venezuela. The collaboration with the Director, Professor Gonzales Mateus, was essential to the development of several projects. In addition to teaching, I installed a Radioisotope Laboratory, preparing the university environment for the incorporation of future radioactive isotope projects in the solution of agricultural problems. During my professorship, I was very impressed by the dedication of two students: J. J. Villasmil and Tibério Perozo Yory. Not only did they take an interest in the content of my classes, but collaborated in the delivery of practical classes. Tibério collaborated in the installation of my experiments on maize fertilization on one of the farms owned by his father. The faculty considered him not to be a good student at the time, but through collaboration with our team, he became a scholar and later an excellent professional, which gave me great satisfaction! Villasmil became professor and later its director.

Upon returning to ESALQ, late 1962, I started several projects, one of which was funded by FAPESP (Foundation for Research Support of the State of São Paulo). On this occasion, and later, Luiz Carlos Basso, Celso Rossi and Oswaldo Galvão Brasil, my students, collaborated with me on various projects during their undergraduate program. I served as their mentor for their master's and doctoral programs. In 1966, the three collaborated with me in the installation of the Plant Biochemistry Sector of the newly created Center for Nuclear Energy in Agriculture (CENA), now belonging to ESALQ.

From 1964 to 1965, as a postdoctoral fellow at the University of California, Davis *campus*, the collaboration of C.C. Delwiche was essential for me to develop research on microorganism metabolism. I deepened my passion for biochemistry in the theoretical and laboratory classes of professors Eric C. Conn and P. K. Stumpf whose collaboration was invaluable to my professional training. In the academy, teachers, like them, are totally committed to the transmission of knowledge for the scientific development of their students!

During mid-1967, I was with some of my students in the biochemistry laboratory located in the basement of the Chemistry Building of the "Luiz de Queiroz" College of Agriculture (ESALQ), University of Sao Paulo. The ESALQ Dean and Director Euripedes Malavolta entered the laboratory and invited us to transport our research equipment and materials to the new, recently built building the Nuclear Energy Center in Agriculture – CENA, An institute of the Brazilian Nuclear Energy Commission.

CENA was created in 1966 on the ESALQ campus. The building, to which we relocated was constructed with funds from the Brazilian Nuclear Energy Commission and Malavolta research projects. We occupied four laboratories, as well as rooms for researchers and students' offices. These were exciting moments for me and my three undergraduate students who accompanied me: Celso Rossi, Luiz Carlos Basso and Oswaldo Galvão Brazil. A new situation: the beginning of a long journey through the world of plant cell biology, seeking to understand the biochemical pathways that allow their existence and, at the same time, they exist because the cell exists as a wonder of nature!

This moment of excitement for the new opportunity was a consequence of my paths through scientific life during prior years. It had all started much earlier with my interest in chemistry in high school (1950/1952), my preparation (self-taught) in plant biochemistry for the achievement of the title of Livre-Docente prior to appointment to the ESALQ faculty (1958/1959), the theoretical and practical courses in plant biochemistry at the Davis campus, University of California, in 1964/1965 (see Crocomo, 2014). Despite my personal efforts, I have done nothing alone. I have always had excellent collaborators, whether they were my teachers, colleagues or my undergraduate and graduate students. And even more: after returning to Brazil, coming back from California in 1965, Malavolta invited me to lead the Plant Biochemical Graduate Program for the Mineral Nutrition of Plants at ESALQ during 1966 to 1989. In the 1980s I collaborated with Eduardo Ferraz, Professor of Plant Physiology, in the creation of the Graduate Program in Plant Physiology and Biochemistry.

The move to the new facilities at CENA provided advanced laboratories for my colleagues to employ radioisotopes for understanding the intricate metabolic pathways that occurring within plant cells. In fact, my experience with the use of radioisotopes began in the experimental section of my "Free Teaching" thesis: "Metabolism of urea-14C in coffee", in 1959. At ESALQ the experiments were conducted in the laboratories of the Zimotechical Institute and the analyses of the radioactivity of the molecules, detected by paper chromatography, were carried out in the "Isotope Laboratory" of the then Chair of Physics and Meteorology, Admar Cervellini. He was passionate about the use of stable radioactive isotopes to solve agricultural problems for which he founded a dedicated laboratory in mid 1950s. It was he who, with the collaboration of Euripides Malavolta (Mineral Plant Nutrition) pioneered the proposal for creation of CENA supported by Friedrich Gustav Brieger (Genetics). Many ESALQ professors, with Cervellini's coordination, effectively collaborated to realize this Institute of Study, Research and Extension of University of the University of São Paulo, in Piracicaba.

The research programs in the Plant Biochemistry Sector were funded through collaboration of the National Nuclear Energy Commission (CNEN), the United Nations Development Program (UNDP), the Atomic Energy Institute (AEI, Vienna, Austria), Foundation for Research Support of the State of São Paulo, National Research Council (CNPq), Project Financier (FINEP) and many other official institutions. This research programs conducted in my laboratories were in collaboration with Enio Tiago de Oliveira and countless numbers of my undergraduate and graduate students, among them Helaine Carrer, José Barbosa Cabral, Joaquim Albenísio da Silveira, Luiz Antono Gallo, Fernando Broetto, Celso Rossi, Luiz Carlos Basso, Oswaldo Galvão Brasil, Leonardo Carneiro Alvez, Maro Ran-Ir Sondahl, Jaime Cury and many others (see Crocomo, 2014).

William R. Sharp of The Ohio State University, USA, in his first scientific visit to the Sector in 1971, joined me to introduce in CENA, and the scientific community to the techniques of plant cell and tissue culture in agriculture. It was my dream: to manipulate the plant cell using *in vitro* techniques during the process of obtaining healthy plants. During the period in which I was in charge of the Plant Biochemistry Sector from 1967-1988, numerous teaching and research activities were carried out with Sharp's *sine qua non* collaboration. This partnership continued with the creation of the Center for Agricultural Biotechnology-CEBTEC at ESALQ and continues to this day (see Crocomo, 2014 and Oliveira & Crocomo's Chapter in this Book Series entitled, "Pathways to Collaboration").

From October 1968 to February 1969, as Fellow Researcher of The British Council at London University College on Gower Street in London, UK, I developed research on the enzymes of the nitrogen metabolism in plants, collaborating with Professor L. Fowden. Returning to ESALQ, I developed, with the collaboration of Luiz Carlos Basso, Celso Rossi and Oswaldo Brasil, research on potassium nutrition in plants, which led to the detection of the enzyme N-carbamylputrescine decarboxylase which acts in the pathway to formation of putrescine in potassium-deficient plants.

From 1968 to 1969 I was Professor of Biochemistry at the University of the State of São Paulo (UNESP), Botucatu *campus*. Basso, Rossi and Brasil were hired as my Assistants, collaborating in the practical classes of Biochemistry.

After I left UNESP, Celso Rossi and Oswaldo Brasil remained on the Botucatu *campus*. Later they became Full Professors of Biochemistry at the Faculty of Agronomy. Luiz Carlos Basso was hired by me and became professor of biochemistry at ESALQ. All three are now retired. Basso continues at ESALQ developing projects for the enzymatic control of alcoholic fermentation, of great importance in the Brazilian economy, collaborating with private alcohol-sugar industries.

From 1966 to 1988 I was responsible for the Plant Biochemistry Sector at CENA and at the same time Professor of Biochemistry, Head and/or Deputy-Chief of the Chemistry Department of ESALQ. This period was very productive both scientifically and administratively, with the collaboration of colleagues, students and the staff for the development of many projects. From 1961 to 1994 I participated in 69 congresses and scientific meetings in Brazil and 69 abroad, presenting and discussing scientific projects, all carried out in collaboration with professionals from my laboratories at ESALQ and/or from other Brazilian or foreign Institutions. At that time I organized the Agricultural Biotechnology Seminars (SEBIAGRI) at CEBTEC/ESALQ from 1985 to 1994, with the collaboration of many ESALQ colleagues and professionals from private companies.

During the year of 1976 I was Visiting Professor at the Department of Botany in the University of Durham, in Durham, North England, UK, developing research on pea reserve proteins in collaboration with Prof. Donald Boulter, Head of Department, and Prof. Eric Derbyshire. Upon my return to Brazil I hired Derbyshire to collaborate with my research in plant biochemistry at CENA, in close collaboration with

Maria Tereza Vitral de Carvalho, my Assistant, who later became his wife.

From 1973 to 1978, at the invitation of Admar Cervellini, Director of CENA, I participated in the Program for Improvement of Proteins of Legume Seeds sponsored by the Food Agriculture Organizativo (FAO, Italy), The International Atomic Energy Agency (IAEA, Austria) and the German Federal Government. During my five-year involvement with the International Program, the Meetings, of which I participated were held in Ibadan, Nigeria, Africa (1973); Hahnenklee, Germany (1975); Baden, Vienna, Austria (1977) and Munich, Germany (1978). It provided an important opportunity to expand opportunities for international collaborative research work.

As part of that International Program a research project was developed under my Coordination at CENA to improve the content and quality of storage proteins in seed of beans (*Phaseolu vulgaris*), using mutagenic treatments, in collaboration with Augusto Tulmann Neto, from CENA, and Donald Boulter, from University of Durham, England. Gerald Lee-Sheng Tsheng, under my guidance, developed his doctoral thesis using bean seeds of a mutant of the variety Carioca, obtained by Tulmann during the development of the Project. His Thesis was defended in the Department of Biochemistry of the Institute of Chemistry/USP, São Paulo *campus*. During my twenty-three years, I had an excellent teaching and research collaborative experience in plant biochemistry with the colleagues in the department. Many students from sister campuses took classes in our department and, at the same time, developed their doctoral theses in my laboratories with committee members from other campuses and defended their thesis at the *campus* of USP in São Paulo.

During all my professional activities, I have lived the real meaning of mutual collaboration. Often after or before these scientific meetings, and even when I participated in other congresses in various countries, I visited and exchanged scientific experiences with researchers in Universities and Research Laboratories of private companies.

In June 1971, something significant happened in my professional life. I received in my labs the then young William Rod Sharp of The Ohio State University, Columbus, Ohio, USA. With him we began the research on the behavior of cells and tissues of plants grown *in vitro* at CENA/ESALQ. The pioneer introduction of these techniques in Brazil, by both of us, greatly contributed to the advent and expansion of Plant Biotechnology in the 1980s in my country. As a result, of this intense and extensive collaboration, which has lasted now 45 years (1971-present), many projects were developed, generating many scientific publications, and the training of dozens of professionals in this area (see Crocomo, 2014 and Sharp's Chapter in this Book Series). A highlight was the realization of my desire: the creation, in 1981, of the Center for Agricultural Biotechnology at ESALQ (CEBTEC).

In December 1981, I organized at ESALQ the "International Symposium on Biotechnology for Genetic Engineering", with the collaboration of Flavio C. A. Tavares, of the Genetics Department at ESALQ and Decio Sodrezeieski, of the State Government of São Paulo. The collaboration of Paulo Fernando Cidade de Araújo and Joaquim José de Camargo Engler, Directors of FEALQ, was essential for the accomplishment of this scientific event that brought together scientists from several countries. In October 1988, with the collaboration of William Rod Sharp and Murilo Melo. Again, many scientists from various countries contributed their knowledge to the brilliance of this Scientific Meeting. On that occasion, the new CEBTEC building was inaugurated, designed by Justo Moretti Filho, Professor of Agricultural Engineering at ESALQ and my former teacher: an example of invaluable collaboration!

Many professionals have contributed and others still contribute to CEBTEC's continuous progress, among them Helaine Carrer, who is responsible for the molecular biology and genomics projects (see Carrer, 2014) and Enio Tiago de Oliveira, my student and collaborator since 1977. After my official retirement, I continued R&D at CEBTEC and Enio continued to be, as he was, my *sine qua non*-partner in my research projects with public and private companies until my final retirement!

In 2012, by determination of the ESALQ Congregation, the CEBTEC building was named after me. In it, the Meeting Room is named after William R. Sharp, as a symbol of his continued collaboration in my adventures in the scientific world. Details of my life, how I developed scientifically and got involved in projects with the collaboration of many people, and on the creation of CEBTEC, are chronicled in CROCOMO, 2014 (vol. 1, pages 95-189 and 681-687).

Besides those students aforementioned and those to be mentioned (see item II), I had the pleasure of collaborating with many others in their undergraduate and graduate courses while offering motivation and encouragement for their Master and Doctor Theses. I would like to mention some of my graduate students: Maro Ran-Ir Sondahl, Jaime A. Cury, Luiz Antonio Gallo, Irenice Maria Santos Vieira, Maria Aparecida Schiavuzzo, Marina Yuke Muraiama, Roberval de Cassia Ribeiro, Sandra Aparecida Tabai, Carlos Eduardo Corssato, Geraldo E. Cuzzuol, João Chadad Junior, Daniela Marques Argollo, Fatima Odahara Kajiki, Antonio Barioni Gusman, Isaac Stringueta Machado, João Suzuki, Marcilio de Almeida, Sidival Lourenço. This last one was my first student in the Master's Course of ESALQ, in 1966. I personally collaborated with him in the development of his laboratory experiments. For the interpretation of the data of his Master's Thesis, it was essential the collaboration of Isaias Nogueira, Professor of Mathematics at ESALQ. He was my teacher in my undergraduate course.

Group socialization has always been important in my private and professional life. In 2001 a group of ESALQ's retired professors led by Prof. Zilmar Ziller Marcos created the Retired ESALQ Professors Association (ADAE). I was President of that Association for 4 years (2009-2013) and President-in-Office for 2 years (2013-2015). The activities of this Association demonstrated the importance of collaboration among its members, their families and friends, who socialize frequently in a mutual, emotional environment. The headquarters of the Association are located at ESALQ, a metaphor of the same university environment in which its members worked!

II. Agricultural Biotechnology Collaboration

Agricultural biotechnology is usually defined as an application of plant molecular biology by manipulating the plant cells, tissues and organs for creation of genetically modified cells, to improve agricultural productivity and consumer benefits, e.g., appearance, flavor, nutrition, shelf life, etc. And other important aspect of agricultural biotechnology relates to crop propagation and/or breeding, such as (1) efficient year around propagation; (2) reducing time for release of new varieties; (3) control the reversion to juvenility in forest species; (4) control pests without causing environmental pollution; (5) regenerate of adult transgenic plants after DNA insertion into cells or organelles; (6) transfer genetic characters between incompatible plant species; (7) selection of somaclones resistant to adverse conditions;(8) identification of the molecular mechanisms governing the processes of plant cell morphogenesis, and (9) how to control molecular mechanisms to obtain better agricultural performance.

Many of these issues were addressed through a research and development (R&D) collaboration with the public and private sectors at the laboratories of the now named "Laboratory of Agricultural Biotechnology – CEBTEC", *campus* Luiz de Queiroz, University of São Paulo, Piracicaba/SP, Brazil. Techniques of plant cells and tissue culture *in vitro*, as part of a biotechnological process to propagate plants of economic interest, were applied. These techniques, also referred to as axenic, or sterile culture, are generally used for the aseptic culture of cells, tissues, organs, and their components under defined physical and chemical conditions *in vitro* and are important tools in both basic and applied studies as well as in commercial application (Crocomo, 1989; Sharp, 1991; Gamborg, 2002; Thorpe, 2007).

Early years
One of the first observations in the history of plant cell and tissue culture techniques was the observation of callus formation on wound-healing plants by H.D. du Monceau, in 1756 (Thorpe, 2007). Before that, a well-known major milestone in cell biology was the Hooke discovery. On November 23rd, 1664, the Council of the Royal Society of London, England, authorized the printing of the text presented by Robert Hooke before this Council. The title is "Micrographia: or Some of Physiological Descriptions of Minute Bodies Made by Magnifying Glasses with Observations and Inquires Thereupon". On March 20,

1665, the scientific world learned that within the cork cuts, observed by Hooke under the microscope, were holes distributed as in a honeycomb, which he called "cell".

Since then, microscopic studies led to the independent and almost simultaneous development of the cell theory in 1838 by Schleiden and in 1839 by Schwann. This theory holds that the cell is "the unit of structure and function in an organism and therefore capable of autonomy." This idea was tested by several researchers, but the work of the pathologist Vöchting in 1878 (Thorpe. 2007) on callus formation and on the limits to the divisibility of plant segments was perhaps the most important. He showed that the upper part of a stem segment always produced buds, and the lower end callus or roots. His phrase *"Omnia cellula ex cellula"*: every cell has its origin in another preexisting cell, made him very well known.

In 1902, relying upon his experiments on the culture of isolated photosynthetic cell and other differentiated cells, Haberlandt laid the theoretical basis for plant cell and tissue culture techniques. From his experimental observations, Haberlandt predicted that "one could successfully cultivate artificial embryos from vegetative cells". He established the ability of a plant cell to perform all the functions of development, which is a characteristic of zygote, i.e., the ability to develop into a complete plant. The concept of totipotency of plant cells was then established. Furthermore, he indicated that the technique of cultivating isolated plant cells in nutrient solution allows for the investigation of important problems from a new experimental approach. Due to his pioneering work on these techniques, Haberlandt is justifiably recognized as the father of plant tissue culture.

The use of meristematic cells of tomato root tips by White, 1934 was crucial for the successful use of undefined media for *in vitro* culture. Later, the use of fully defined culture media for cultivating meristem cells, permitted the development of virus-free plantlets, also allowing for comprehensive studies of plant physiology (Street, 1969).

It is interesting to observe that until the 1930s, *in vitro* culture media formulations were empirical. In the search for chemical principles to control the morphogenetic process *in vitro*, various nutritional ingredients, such as vegetable extracts, fruit pulp, potato, coconut milk, salmon sperm and others were used. In 1934, White isolated indole acetic acid (IAA), an auxin, and proved its efficiency as responsible for the growth of plant cells *in vitro*. Moreover, in 1935, Miller (Miller et al.,1955) observed that IAA acted synergistically with kinetin, a phytohormone of the cytokinin group, analogous to cytokinesis in cell division. A major contribution was made by Gautheret, 1934 was able to demonstrate what is considered the first plant tissue cultures from cambial tissue of *Acer pseudoplatanus* (Thorpe, 2007).

Positive experimental results were obtained when an exogenous balance of auxin and kinetin in the culture media influenced the morphogenetic fate of tobacco callus by Skoog & Miller, 1957. These authors also showed that rooting was favored in presence of high level of auxin to kinetin, the reverse promoting shoot formation. Intermediate levels led to the proliferation of callus or wound parenchyma tobacco tissue.

In that context, Morel 1960, while working with orchids, obtained the first virus-free plants of *Cymbidium* from pseudobulbs buds. This technique allowed Wimber,1962 to obtain the first commercial micropropagated virus-free clones of *Cymbidium*. In that same year, Murashige and Skoog (1962) established a synthetic culture media: the salt formulation most widely used to present days. In 1965, Earle & Torrey introduced the first concepts of induction, competence, and determination of morphogenetic processes in plants.

2. Technological Achievements

Advances in refinements of the *in vitro* techniques to cultivate plant cells & tissues, achieved in the second part of the twentieth century and beginning of this century, made them an important tool in basic studies such as cytology, nutrition (mineral and organic), metabolism, embryogenesis, pathology, morphogenesis and applied studies, namely secondary products formation, as well as in commercial application. *In vitro* techniques are used to recover genetically modified plants as well as pathogen-free plantlets leading to plant propagation, which is the objective of agricultural biotechnology.

Within these objectives, another area widely studied in the decades of 1970/1980 was the exploration of genetic variations caused by cell culture and *in vitro* plant regeneration. Among these works those by Carlson et al., 1972 on somatic hybrids in tobacco and Evans & Sharp, 1983 obtaining commercial varieties of tomato from somaclones should be highlighted.

As it was mentioned in the Introduction (item 1.2) in 1971 as a Fellow of the Fulbright–Hays Award Fellowship, William Rod Sharp, from the Ohio State University/USA, joinedthe Plant Biochemistry Sector at the Center for Nuclear Energy in Agriculture (CENA/ University of São Paulo), in Piracicaba. We introduced these techniques in a systematic way, *which launched the beginnings of plant biotechnology in Brazil: the application of these in vitro techniques in agriculture* (for an overview of the collaborative work between Crocomo and Sharp see: W. R. Sharp's Chapter in this Book Series).

As was also mentioned in the Introduction (item 1.2) in 1981 the interest of the private sector in the production of plants with desirable agronomic characteristics led, by the initiative of Otto J. Crocomo and Flavio Tavares, to the creation of the Center for Agricultural Biotechnology at ESALQ, by the Foundation for Agricultural Studies Luiz de Queiroz (FEALQ) under the approval of ESALQ Administration.

As a result, of this pioneering, research work developed by the staff and students from ESALQ/USP and other Brazilian and South and North American Universities and Research Institutes trained in these techniques at the CENA and CEBTEC premises, and thus began their implementation. Several years of intense collaboration occurred between CENA and CEBTEC staffs with students and trainees in laboratory and greenhouse trials: from the cells and tissues of plants to the acclimatization of the plantlets obtained *in vitro* and, in some cases, to filed. Various plant species were the objects of research: sugarcane, citrus, banana, strawberry sesame, tomato, peanuts, beans, pineapple, coffee, peas, eucalyptus, pine, ornamental plants, medicinal plants and many others.

Among many research scientific works developed by our team during the 1970, 1980, 1990 and 2000 decades, as part of collaborative projects with Brazilian and foreign institutions, and with the private sector, was the tissue culture of sugarcane *(Sacharum* spp). Somaclonal variation was induced in callus tissue of this species to select tolerance to the herbicide ametrin, in a research work by Neftali Ochoa Alejo, at that time scientific researcher at the Centro de Investigaciones Biológicas de Baja California Sur, La Paz, BCS, México (Ochoa-Alejo & Crocomo 1987; 1988 and Ochoa-Alejo's Chapter in this Book Series). A close collaboration allowed the scientific staff of the PLANALSUCAR Research Institute to train in our laboratories in the *in vitro* techniques to obtain sugarcane variant cells, in the 1980s.

The viability of embryos derived from interspecific crosses of beans was a collaborative research project in collaboration with IPA, an agricultural research institute in Pernambuco in the Brazilian Northeast. Embryos were rescued and cultured *in vitro* from crosses involving *Phaseolus vulgaris, Phaseous acutifolius* and *Phaseous lunatus,* developed by Jose Barbosa Cabral, from IPA, resulted in regeneration of hybrid bean fertile adult plants (Crocomo, 1986; Cabral & Crocomo, 1989). One major research work developed by CEBTEC during the 1980 decade was the *in vitro* clone production of *Eucaliptus* in collaboration with the Brazilian private company Duratex (Gonçalves et al., 1986).

Carica papaya in vitro morphogenesis developed by Helaine Carrer (Carrer & Crocomo, 1987) and the in *vitro* control of morphogenesis of endemic bromeliads from southeastern Brazil developed by Leonardo Alves Carneiro, from the University of the State of Rio de Janeiro, Brazil (Carneiro et al., 1998) are two examples of collaborative research work: the use of plant tissue culture techniques as auxiliary to plant propagation. Also, during the process of banana micropropagation (*Musa* sp.) for commercial purposes, as described below (Agricultural Biotechnology Section), research was conducted on the nitrogen nutrition of banana vitroplants by Humberto Zaidan, in collaboration with Fernando Broeto, from Faculty of Agronomy of UNESP, Botucatu, SP (Zaidan et al., 1999). Fernando Broetto was Crocomo's graduate student for his Master Degree at CENA/ESALQ. He developed part of his Master Thesis in the laboratories of Prof. Ulrich Zeitz, in a collaborative scientific work with the University of Tubingen, Germany.

To conduct research and development projects (R & D), CEBTEC established collaborative relationships with public sectors. The Brazilian public funding agencies:

FAPESP (São Paulo Research Foundation) (CNPq (National Council of Research); FINEP (Financier of Studies and Projects); CAPES (Coordination for Improvement of Higher Education Personnel, of the Brazilian Ministry of Education); EMBRAPA (Brazilian Agricultural Research Corporation, of the Brazilian Ministry of Agriculture); CNEN (National Nuclear Energy Commission) and CENA.

Among the foreign public funding agencies were: the British Council; the OAS (Organization of American States); Fulbright Commission; the UNDP (United Nations Development Programme); the IAEA (International Atomic Energy Agency, Vienna, Austria); the French Government; the DADD (Germany Government); the Scientific Commission of the European Communities; the USA Government *I* Blue Ribbon Project; the CAF (Corporacion Andina de Fomento, Venezuela); and the NIHERST (National Institute of Higher Education, Trinidad & Tobago.

Examples of CEBTEC's collaborative works with private companies are shown below.

3. Agricultural Biotechnology

In our view, agricultural biotechnology is a plant production process during which, at any given time, *in vitro* techniques are used. The result of the process can be virus-free plants, clones, somaclones or individual plants (e.g. flowers) which may be, if it is the case, subjected to suitable methods of plant breeding, selected and transferred to producers and then eventually to the final consumer, as follows: Cells, tissues, organs → *in vitro* cultures (for micropropagation, somaclones, genetic modified, etc.) → *in vitro* plantlets →greenhouse acclimatization and screening → field selection using suitable methods of plant breeding (if necessary) → producer → final consumer

From its beginning in 1981, CEBTEC focused on developing research (R&D) on species important from a scientific point of view as well as being of commercial interest in the agricultural and food industry marketplace. When it comes to agricultural interest, it basically refers to important aspects of the cultures as, for instance, plant health. The micropropagation, in turn, has its foundation in the mass production and the virus elimination of clonal species which are vegetatively propagated, functioning as an excellent process of eradication of pathogens that cause various diseases. Thus, before starting the work with certain species, one must question (1) why micro propagate such species; (2) does the species require an acclimatization process; (3) does the species require clonal cleaning

That protocol has been used in collaboration with the private sector to propagate several plant species of economic interest. Summarized results of the use by CEBTEC of biotechnological processes to propagate sugarcane, citrus, banana, strawberry and *Aloe vera* are presented below.

Sugarcane

Regarding to the economic aspects, the sugarcane can be classified as a multiple utility culture. These cultures may be employed in *natura* for animal feed or for the manufacturing of sugar and alcohol. Brazil occupies the position of world's largest producer of sugarcane, followed respectively by India, China, Thailand and Pakistan (FAO, 2013). In a survey by CONAB (Brazilian Supply Company), it is estimated that in the 2016/2017 harvest the total of Brazilian production of sugarcane will be 690.98 million tons, sugar production will be 37,509,900 tons and ethanol production will be 30.3 billion liters.

Sugarcane culture is affected by various pests and diseases. Among the diseases caused by fungus are coal cane (*Ustilago scitaminea*), brown rust (*Puccinia melanocephala*), leaf rust (*Puccinia kuehnii*), pineapple disease (*Ceratocystis paradoxa*), red rot (*Colletotrichum falcatum*), head blight (*Fusarium moniliforme*), eyespot (*Bipolaris sacchari*) and yellow stain (*Mycovellosiella koepkey*) all causing damage to the leaves or the stem region.

Among the diseases caused by bacteria are the leaf scald (*Xanthomonas albilineans*), red streak (*Pseudomonas rubrilineans*) and rickets-of-ratoon

(*Leifsonia xyli* subsp. Xyli). Virus diseases also found in the culture of sugarcane are mosaic (SCMV–Sugarcane Mosaic Virus) and yellowing (ScYLV–Sugarcane Yellow Leaf Virus).

In the 1980s, the National Alcohol Program (PROÁLCOOL) had been established in Brazil. The Institute of Sugar and Alcohol (IAA) proposed that CEBTEC develop tissue culture protocols to be applied as part of its breeding program and protocol for *in vitro* propagation of sugarcane.

Given its economic importance and plant susceptibility, the culture of sugarcane requires continuous attention for it to be maintained and for its productivity to be enhanced. In this scenario, biotechnological approaches are of great importance primarily through transgenesis and micropropagation using apical meristems (with a maximum size of 0.1 mm). In the latter, the micro plants obtained are free of disease-causing pathogens. Once certified, they are submitted to the mass multiplication process, yielding healthy clones.

At our laboratories, protocols to obtain sugarcane callus and subsequent protocols for the regeneration of sugarcane plantlets from callus were established. These protocols allowed the development of somaclonal variants, somatic hybrids from protoplast fusion and development of the technique of micropropagation (Figure 1).

Other techniques can be used, such as biolistics (particle bombardment) and/or using *Agrobacterium* as an intermediate stage in the transfer of genetic material among plant cells, to produce genetically modified sugarcane plantlets. Then these could be micropropagated producing millions of identical sugarcane plants. (Research works by Helaine Carrer at CEBTEC, see Carrer, 2014).

Citrus

Worldwide, the annual production of all citrus species is around 100 million tons in an area around 7 million hectares, surpassing other tropical fruits such as banana, apple, mango, pear, peach and papaya (IAC, 2005). According to FAO, 2013, Brazil ranks as the world's largest producer of orange, followed respectively by the United States, China, India, Mexico and Spain. Orange juice is the most widely consumed fruit-derived drink in the world, with the US being its world's largest consumer (38% of total).

In Brazil, the state of São Paulo and the Southwest region of the state of Minas Gerais are the main producers of orange. It is estimated that in 2015/2016 the production was about 300 million orange boxes of 48 kg each (FUNDECITRUS, personal communication).

Citrus is infected by various diseases caused by fungi: scab (three species of fungus: *Sphaceloma fawceti*, *S. fawceti* var scabiosa and *S. australis*), gummosis (*P. parasitica* and *P. citrophthora*), melanosis (*Phomopsis citri*), rubelose (*Corticium salmonicolor*) and black spot (*Guignardia citricarpa*). Among the diseases caused by bacteria are: citrus canker (*Xhantomonas axonopodis* pv citri.), variegated yellowing or chlorosis (CVC–Xylella Xilella) and greening or huanglongbing (HLB–*Liberibacter Candidatus asiaticus* and *Candidatus Liberibacter americanus*).

Special attention should be given to virus diseases. When infected by viruses there is a reduction of citrus immunity, when it becomes weakened and susceptible to various other diseases. Among the viruses that attack citrus, some are highly aggressive: tristeza, exocortis, xiloporose.

The most effective way to eliminate these viruses is to obtain plants from the apical meristem (meristem culture). It is noteworthy that the cleaning efficiency is inversely proportional to the size of the isolated meristematic tissue. The meristem must not exceed 0.1 mm and one of the best ways to get citrus microplants from meristems is the use of the micrografting technique.

At our laboratories, the meristem of a selected adult citrus plant was isolated and micrografting on a rootstock. In the late 1980s, Ary A. Salibe, a virologist based at the Faculty of Agronomy – Botucatu/State of São Paulo, of the University of the State of São Paulo (UNESP), joined our staff to develop a citrus micrografting project funded by Citrovita, a private Company belonging to the Votorantim Group. This collaborative work aimed to obtain virus-free orange plants, mainly the tristeza virus. More than 10,000 micrografts from the "pear" variety were produced at CEBTEC and 2,500 were preselected. From these completed tristeza virus-free citrus plants were selected, and certified. These were named "Super Laranjeira" (super "pear" orange) which were grown in a greenhouse under a protected system at Botucatu, producing hundreds of orange matrices which were submitted to controlled conventional graft, yielding thousands of plants which are mantained in Citrovita fields in the city of Itapetininga, State of São Paulo These selected plants are characterized as a doubling of productivity as compared to the common "pear" orange (Salibe et al., 1993) (Figure 2).

Banana

Banana is another important crop with which we developed several collaborative works in partnership with final banana producers. Banana is the second most consumed fruit in the world, with 11.4 kg / person / year, second only to orange with 12.2 kg / person / year. The American continent is the largest consumer, with 15.2 kg / person / year, especially South America, with 20 kg / person / year and Central America, with 13.9 kg / person / year (FAO, 2013). India ranks as the world's largest producer of banana, while Brazil is in fourth position. According to the data released in May 2016 by IBGE (Brazilian Institute of Geography and Statistics), the Northeast and Southeast regions lead the Brazilian production of bananas, with 2,239,261 and 2,252,954 tons respectively.

Among the existing varieties of banana, the best known and consumed in Brazil are plantain ("banana-nanica" and "banana-da-terra"), banana-silver ("banana-prata") and banana gold ("banana-ouro").

The diseases of banana crops that are worth mentioning are: leaf spots (compromise photosynthesis), vascular wilted (interfere with the absorption and transport of water and nutrients), nematodes and viruses (prevent the distribution of the products of photosynthesis to other parts of the plant). Foliar diseases caused by fungus are: Black Sigatoka (*Mycosphaerella fijiensis*), Yellow Sigatoka (*Mycosphaerella musicola*), Spot Cordana (*Cordana musae*), Spot Cladosporium (*Cladosporium musae*), Spot Deightoniella (*Deightoniela torulosa*) and Spot Chloridium (*Chloridium musae*).

Vascular disease can be caused by fungi such as Panama disease (*Fusarium oxysporum* fsp. Foc) and bacteria such as Soft Rot (*Erwinia carotovora* subsp. *Carotovora*) and Moko banana (*Ralstonia solanacearum*).

Nemantode infections damage the water absorption and nutrients distribution inside banana plant are: *Radophulus*, *Pratylenchus*, *Helicotylenchus* and *Meloydogine* genera. Among the viruses: Banana Tree Streaks (BSV) and the mosaic virus of cucurbits (CMV). The transmission of these viruses usually occurs through contaminated cuttings as well as by insect vectors such as mealybugs and aphid insects.

Micropropagation protocols developed in our laboratories have been generally used. The mass cloning banana begins with the selection of a matrice in the field, from which young rhizome-bearing buds of approximately 20 cm in diameter and coated pseudostem sheaths 50 cm long are collected. These shoots are disinfected by removing the outer sheath and immersing the material into sodium hypochlorite solution. This procedure is repeated successively and apexes of approximately 5 cm are eventually obtained. Subsequently, in a laminar flow chamber, the apexes undergo the last thinning and disinfestation. In this step, the apical bud has about 1 cm in size. Inoculation into culture medium plus cytokinin follows. The shoots are transferred to culture medium lacking cytokinin to promote elongation and rooting. When ready, banana plantlets are transferred from *in vitro* conditions to *ex vitro* conditions in trays and acclimatized in a greenhouse with controlled temperature and humidity. Pests and disease-free banana plants are transferred to producers and then eventually the fruits produced for the market. (Figure 3).

Strawberry

The cultivated strawberry is an herbaceous plant of small size, of which there are known 11 species distributed in 4 ploidy groups: diploid, tetraploid, hexaploid and octaploids. The currently cultivated clones are interspecific hybrids, originally obtained from the species *Fragaria chiloensis* and *Fragaria virgiana*. The hybrids were crossed among themselves, creating many clones. It should be noted that *F. chiloensis* had its origin in the South American continent (Chilean coast) and *F. virginiana*, in USA. Both were cultivated by the indigenous people and during the early colonization of the continent. These two species were taken to Europe, where they were crossed and their hybrids brought back to America after World War II.

The productivity of the strawberry is closely related to the seedling phytosanitary aspects. In 1972, Betti (Betti, 1991) observed that healthy seedlings of the cultivar IAC-2712, showed increased production up to 100% compared to the production obtained with ordinary seedlings of the same cultivar. Carvalho & Costa 1961 showed that varieties traditionally grown in the state of São Paulo were carrying at least the mottle virus and probably others whose symptoms were not noticeable. Moreover, Aerts, 1972 studying strawberry crops in several countries listed 54 viruses and 8 mycoplasmas that caused loss in strawberry production.

The vegetative propagation system using exclusively stolons contributes to the transmission of pests and diseases, especially viruses. Four of the viruses should be highlighted: speckles of strawberry (strawberry mottle virus–SMOV), the ribs track (strawberry vein banding virus–SVBV), marginal chlorosis of strawberry (strawberry mild yellow edge virus–SMYEV) and virus crimp the strawberry (strawberry crinkle virus –SCV). These viral diseases can reduce plant productivity by more than 50%, mainly when several of them are present. In this case, the plant turns to being susceptible to other bacterial and fungal diseases such as angular leaf spot (*Xanthomonas fragariae*), anthracnose (*Colletotrichum gloeosporioides, C. fragariae* and *C. acutatum*), micosferela spot (*Mycosphaerella fragariae*), Diplocarpon spot (*Diplocarpon earliana*), dendrofoma spot (*Dendrophoma obscurans*), Verticillium wilt (*Verticillium dahliae*), root rot (*Rhizoctonia spp., Fusarium sp., Sclerotium rolfsii, Phytophthora spp.*), Phytophthora rot (*Phytophthora spp.*) and several others.

The diseases aforementioned, especially the viral diseases transmitted by specific aphids, claim an urgent need for healthy seedlings on a large scale. This situation led CEBTEC to develop micropropagation protocols to produce healthy strawberry plantlets from isolated meristem size around 0.1 mm (Crocomo et al., 1998).

In the mid-1980 CEBTEC produced thousands of virus and diseases-free *in vitro* strawberry cloned plantlets which were released for field multiplication by producers. However, the cost of each seedling was around 10 times higher than the market could afford. In order to reduce costs, a new protocol was developed in a collaborative project involving CEBTEC and the private company "Brasil Venture Capital". Virus-free strawberries matrice plantlets obtained through micropropagation in its premises were conventionally multiplied at "Serra do Japi", yielding thousands of plants ready for supply to the fruit producers. The chosen mountainous region located in the southeastern of the State of São Paulo, has altitude of 1000 meters and mild temperatures, which greatly limit the presence of strawberry aphid virus vectors. Currently, over 30 years later, it is very gratifying to know that in Brazil the strawberry plants are still produced in this way (Figure 4).

Aloe vera

Numerous biological properties have been studied and assigned to *Aloe vera* (L.) Burm f. plant species particularly concerning its foliar pulp gel including activities such as antiviral, antibacterial, antifungal, laxative, anti-inflammatory, radiation protection, treatment for burns, stimulating the immune system, acceleration for healing wounds, treatment of edema, adjuvant in the treatment of arthritis, gastrointestinal disorders, ulcers, diabetes, and even some forms of cancer (Reynolds & Dweck, 1999). Molreove, *Aloe vera* is also used for the preparation of cosmetic products.

The medicinal principles of *Aloe* genus so far identified are attributed to phenolic and polysaccharide compounds. Among the various phenolic compounds, are aloíns (barbaloin and isobarbaloín), aloe-emodin, aloenin, aloesin, aloeresin and isoaloeresin (Okamura et al., 1996; Park et al., 1998). Among the polysaccharides are polymers consisting primarily of mannose with β $(1 \rightarrow 4)$ links.

Commercial and industrial production of *Aloe vera* has increased dramatically as a result of scientific studies published in recent years. Industrial raw material has been obtained primarily from North American field plantations in the States of Texas and Florida in USA and countries such as Mexico, Costa Rica, Venezuela and Australia. This raw material is processed, industrialized and exported to various parts of the world.

One of the main steps in the mass production chain of *Aloe vera* refers to the production of seedlings, most of the time conventionally produced through vegetative reproduction of tillers.

However, when it is intended to introduce a new *Aloe* plantation, the farmer needs a large quantity of standardized and certified healthy and uniform size seedlings, allowing for production planning. Also, perhaps because it is a new, emerging market, and economically highly promising, most *Aloe* production chain processes are patented. Research, especially related to farming systems to obtain seedlings, cultivation and mineral nutrition is greatly needed.

CEBTEC developed physiological and nutritional research along with the use of plant tissue culture techniques as a major initial step for the propagation of *Aloe vera*. In this context research was developed to produce large scale apex disinfested clonal *aloe* microplants. That was followed by acclimatization *ex vitro* of the plantlets under controlled physical conditions in a greenhouse. During this stage, the developing plants were monitored physiologically (height, size and number of tillers per plant) and nutritionally (nitrogen levels) (Oliveira et al., 2009) (Figure 5).

III. Final Remarks

Since we are born, we continuously need the collaboration of others, we grow, we develop physically and intellectually and we undertake our own lives. If it had not been for the encouragement and collaboration of our chemistry teachers in the days of the high school and the chemistry, biology and biochemistry professors in the days of the University none of us would have had our university lives of studies and research in plant biochemistry and biotechnology. The mutual collaboration was always present in our activities and to close we quote Crocomo, 2014a: "We all need one another. We are not juxtaposed individuals, each one living their own lives oblivious to what happens to their surroundings. As in all areas of the universe of human knowledge, in the world of biological sciences in which I live, an idea can arise in a single mind, but the realization of it requires many other minds to reason and observe with critical and keen eyes the results of the experiments: there needs to be many other hands to manipulate the test tubes and culture flasks, and many other feet to support the bodies that stand by the laboratory counters or walk between the lines, as if they were backstreets, and to separate and identify creeping or slender plants in the agricultural fields with the desirable agronomic characteristics." These words are a metaphor for the collaboration that must exist also among researchers that use *in vitro* techniques in the process of plant propagation.

IV. References

Aerts, J., 1972. Survey of viruses and micoplasmas in strawberry. Netherlands Journal of Plant Pathology, Meerle, Belgium, 80: 215-27.

Betti, J. A., 1991. Obtenção de material vegetal testado livre de vírus. In: Biotechnology for Plant Propagation. O.J. Crocomo, W. R. Sharp, M. Melo (Eds.). CEBTEC/FEALQ, Piracicaba, Brasil, p. 145-170.

Cabral, J. B., O. J. Crocomo, 1989. Interspecific hybridization of *P. vulgaris x P. acutifolius* and *P, lunatus* using *in vitro* techniques. Turrialba, Costa Rica, v. 39, (2) 243-246.

Carlson, P. S., Smith, H. H., R. D. Dearing, R. D., 1972. Parasexual interspecific plant hybridization. Proceedings of the National Academy of Sciences, U.S.A., 69, 2292–2294.

Carneiro, L. A., M.S.D. Candido, R.F.C. Araújo, M.H.P. Fonseca, O.J. Crocomo, E. Mansur, 1998. Clonal propragation of *Cryptanthus Sinuosus* L.B.Smith, an endemic Bromeliaceae species from Rio de Janeiro, Brazil. Plant Tissue Culture and Biotechnology, Israel, v. 4 (3-4):152-158

Carrer, H., 2014. Genomics and Molecular Biology at CEBTEC. In: Reflections & Connections – Personal Journeys through the

Life Sciences. O. J. Crocomo, J. P. Kreier, W. R. sharp (Eds.). ScienceTechPublishers LLC, NY, USA, p.71-81

Carrer, H., O. J. Crocomo, 1987. Control of morphogenesis in papaya (Carica papaya). Symposium Florizel 87, Plant Micropropagation in Horticultural industries- Belgium 0-0.

Carvalho. A. M. B.; Costa, A. S., 1961. Ocorrência do vírus do mosqueado do morangueiro no Estado de São Paulo. Bragantia, Campinas, 20 (19): 563-78.

CONAB, 2016. Available in:

http://www.conab.gov.br/conteudos.php?a=1253&t=&Pagina_objcmsconteudos=1#A_objcmsconteudos. Access in: June 21.

Crocomo, O. J., 1989. Biotecnological approaches for the control of plant morphogenesis and their applications in agriculture. GENOME, Canada, v. 31 p. 1034-1041.

Crocomo, O. J., 2014. Merging Chemistry, Cell Biology & the Understanding of Life. In: Reflections & Connections – Personal Journeys through the Life Sciences. O. J. Crocomo, J. P. Kreier, W. R. Sharp (Eds.) ScienceTechPublishers LLC, NY, USA, v. 1, p. 95-189.

Crocomo, O. J., 2014a. For Those Who Made a Difference in My Scientific Life. In: Reflections & Connections – Personal Journeys through the Life Sciences. O. J. Crocomo, J. P. Kreier, W. R. Sharp (Eds.). ScienceTechPublishers LLC, NY, USA, v. 1, p.681-687.

Crocomo, O.J., V.S. Scheffer, C. E. Corsato, V. L. M. Romani, E. T. Oliveira, L. A. Gallo, 1998. Physiological processes in strawberry vitroplants during the pre-field adaptation phase. In: Abstract of the IX International Congress of Plant Tissue and Cell Culutre, Tel Aviv, Israel, 0-0

Earle, E. D.; Torrey, J. G., 1965. Colony formation by isolated convolvulus cells plated on defined media. Plant Physiology, 40 (3), 520-528.

Evans, D. A. & W.R. Sharp, 1983. Single gene mutations in tomato plants regenerate from tissue culture. Science 221: 949-951.

FAO, 2016. Available in:

http://faostat3.fao.org/browse/rankings/countries_by_commodity/E. Access in: June 21.

Gamborg, O.L., 2002. Plant Tissue Culture.Biotechnology.Milestones. In vitro Cell. Dev. Biol-Plant 38:84-92 doi:10.1079/IVP2001281

Gautheret, R. J., 1934. Culture du tissus cambial. C. R. Hebd. Seances Acad. Sc., 198, 2195–2196.

Gonçalves, A.N., O.J. Crocomo, C.V. Almeida, J.P. Unterpertinger & R.A. Chaves, 1986. Reversion to juvenility of *Eucalyptus*. In: Summaries. International Congress of Plant Tissue and Cell Culture, Minneapolis, USA, p. 110.

IBGE, 2016. Available in: http://www.sidra.ibge.gov.br/bda/tabela/listabl.asp?c=1618&z=t&o=26. Access in: July 05.

Miller, C., F. Skoog, M. H. Von Saltza, F.M. Strong, 1955. Kinetin, a cell division factor from desoxyribonucleic acid. Journal of the American Chemical Society, 77, 1392

Morel, G., 1960. Producing virus-free cymbidium. American Orchid Society Bulletin, 29, p. 495–497.

Murashige, T., & F. Skoog, 1962. A revised medium for rapid growth and bioassays with tobacco tissue cultures. Physiologia Plantrum, 15, 473–497.

Ochoa-Alejo, N. & O. J. Crocomo, 1987. Influence of ametryn on chromatin activity and on RNA synthesis in a non-chlorophyllaceous sugarcane cell suspension. Journal of Plant Physiology 126: 355-363.

Ochoa-Alejo & O. J. Crocomo, 1988. Inhibition of growth and interference with ^{14}C-leucine uptake and incorporation into protein in non-chlorophyllaceous sugarcane cells by ametryn. Turrialba, Costa Rica, 38: 59-63.

Okamura, N.; Asai, M.; Hine, N.; Yagi, A., 1996. High-performance liquid chromatographic determination of phenolic compounds in *Aloe* species. Journal of Chromatography A, Amsterdam, v. 746, p. 225-231.

Oliveira, E. T., L.A. Gallo, O.J. Crocomo, T.B. Farinha, 2009. Large-scale micropropagation of *Aloe vera*. HortScience, 44: 1675-1678.

Park, M. K., J.H. Park, N.Y. Kim, Y.G. Shin, Y.S. Choi, J.G. Lee, K.H. Kim, S.K. Lee, 1998. Analysis of 13 Phenolic Compounds in *Aloe* species by High Performance Liquid Chromatography. Phytochemical Analysis, Sussex, v. 9, p. 186-191.

Reynolds, T. & A. C. Dweck, 1999. Aloe vera leaf gel: a review update. Journal of Ethnopharmacology, Lausanne, v. 68, p. 3-37.

Salibe, A. A., O. J. Crocomo, A. Tubelis, L. A. Gallo, E. T. Oliveira, 1993. A new program for citrus budwood improvement In São Paulo, Brazil. Proceedings of the 12th Conference of the International Organization of Citrus Virologists, India, p. 392-396.

Sharp, W. R., 1991. Introduction: New horizons in the plant improvement. In: Biotechnology for Plant Propagation. O. J. Crocomo, W. R. Sharp, M. Melo (Eds.). CEBTEC/FEALQ, Piracicaba, Brasil, p. xvii-xxxiii.

Skoog, F., & C. O. Miller, 1957. Chemical regulation of growth and organ formation in plant tissue cultures *in vitro*. Symposium of the Society of Experimental Biology, 11, p. 118–131.

Street, H. E., 1969. Growth in organized and unorganized systems. In F. C. Steward (Ed.), Plant Physiology 5B, p. 3–224. Academic Press, N.Y.

Thorpe, T. A., 2007. History of Plant Cell Culture. Molecular Biotechnology 37 (2):169-80

Zaidan, H. A., F. Broetto, E.T. Oliveira, L. A. Gallo, O. J. Crocomo, 1999. Influence of potassium nutrition and the nitrate/ammonium ratio on the putrescine and spermidine contents in banana vitroplants. Journal of Plant Nutrition, 22 (7), p. 1123-1140.

White, P. R., 1934. Potentially unlimited growth of excised tomato root tips in a liquid medium. Plant Physiology, 9, p.585–600.

Wimber, D. E., 1962. Clonal multiplication of Cymbidiums through tissue culture of the shoot meristem. American Orchid Society Bulletin 32, p.105-107.

Acknowledgements: We thank the CENA and CEBTEC/ESALQ colleague collaborators who for their invaluable participation in the research programs. And special thanks to Carla Maisa Lovadino Crocomo and Maria Paula Lovadino Crocomo for their superb editorial contributions to preparing the text in English.

Photos

Figure 1. Sugarcane micropropagation. A. *In vitro* sugarcane leaves calli. B. Sugarcane tissue regeneration from calli. C. Developing sugarcane plantlets. D. Individual *ex vitro* sugarcane plantlets at CEBTEC greenhouse premises ready to go to producers.

Figure 2. Citrus. A. First "superorange" obtained from micrografting (Salibe at left and Crocomo at right). B. Developed "superorange" at CEBTEC greenhouse. C. "Supeorange" plants at Citrovita greenhouse premises (Crocomo at left, Salibe at right). D. Tristeza virus-free "Superorange" at Citrovita citrus field (Itapetininga, State of São Paulo south). From left to right: Salibe, Oliveira & Crocomo.

Figure 3. Banana. A. Banana matrices selected in the field: young rhizome-bearing buds. B. Apical bud (1 cm size) from disinfected banana apex in culture. C. Banana plantlets (*ex vitro*) ready to be acclimatized. D. Banana plants in the greenhouse ready to go to producers.

Figure 4. Strawberry. A. Isolation of strawberry meristem (0.1 mm size). B. Development of plantlets, from meristem (extreme left side). C. Development of individual strawberry plantlets. D. Multiplication of developed & acclimatized strawberry plants in the field (see text); Crocomo is on the extreme left side and Oliveira is on the extreme right side.

Figure 5. *Aloe vera*. A. Acclimatization of obtained *in vitro* plantlets at CEBTEC greenhouse premises. B. Developed *Aloe vera* plants ready to go to producers.

CHAPTER 11

Pathways to Collaboration in Agricultural Research and Extension

Thomas Orton
Professor Department of Plant Biology,
SEBS, Rutgers Cooperative Extension
Rutgers University

The individual and the team; there is a time and need for both. The knowledge of when and where a team will be more effective and efficient than the individual comes with experience and wisdom. Humans around the world are strikingly similar in their basic makeup and values. It comes as a shock, however, to the child who realizes that not everyone necessarily sees the same things the same way. We gradually learn that diversity is not only inevitable, but presents opportunities for the building of successful teams. Even more unsettling is the difficulty in predicting how humans will react or respond to different situations, and constant reminders in news media about intolerance of diversity. The truly successful individual is fascinated and inspired by diversity, not threatened by it. The minor differences in nature and nurture that exist are the catalyst to both social evolution and strife. The subtle differences that pervade human societies are the raw materials for innovation and changes that improve the quality and quantity of life here on Earth. Diversity makes life more interesting and challenging.

How is the desire to collaborate born? Parents usually instill the values of cooperation and teamwork in children only indirectly, through sharing of limited resources within the family. Few parents tell their children: "You will grow up to be an effective member of a team". More likely, parents will inspire their children to excel as individuals, relegating the value of collaboration to a more obscure or secondary status. We learn to "get along" with our siblings and family cohorts, and may be rewarded for participating in roles of more active assistance, but rarely mature to functioning adulthood with a full appreciation of the need for teamwork, or how we will participate in teams.

For example, the family of Joseph and Katherine Jackson of Gary, Indiana exhibited a wealth of musical talent through both nature and nurture. The entrepreneurial patriarch Joe Jackson had the vision to meld male siblings into an instrumental/dance/voice group "The Jackson Five" during the mid-1960s. The group caught on, and rose to prominence in the popular music arena through the mid-1970s. The group dynamic that featured the collective talents of the brothers was the essence of the success of the venture. Ultimately, however, one individual, Michael Jackson, was viewed by consumers as the most compelling talent, and elevated to singular superstar status. The Jackson family went on to produce female acts as well, most notably Janet Jackson who had a string of hits in the 1980s and 1990s. None of this would have been possible without the vision of Joe Jackson and the collective abilities of "The Jackson Five". Joe was able to vision the value in fomenting a collaboration, but driven by commercial and financial rewards.

This leads to the next dilemma: The prevailing reward system within our workplace networks. In my experiences with six diverse enterprises over a period of 50 years, none were successful in the development of an effective method to reward individual vs. collective accomplishments and performance. Most organizations simply ignored activities within the context of collaborations except to the extent they could be quantified and evaluated individually. One organization did acknowledge the existence of teams and that a measure of overall performance was attributable to the collective accomplishments of these teams. But the method used to account for contributions to collaborative teams was trivial, simply requesting a numerical accounting of the percentage of overall effort contributed by team constituents. I served on many evaluation committees that considered these contributions to collaborations, but witnessed very few that were taken very seriously. Any individual that was perceived to be more of a team player than an individual performer was discounted in the evaluation process. Lip service was often accorded to the value of collaboration and teamwork, but the reward system was never adequately designed and/or implemented to support this notion. A spate of "Team Awards" was developed that included modest monetary stipends, but these benefits paled in comparison to those heaped onto individuals feted as mavericks, pioneers, and superstars.

The elements of a successful collaboration:

- A clear vision of the new product, service, or process being targeted
- A team comprised of elements that contribute complementary skill and knowledge sets to the project
- Shared understanding and appreciation of this vision and the process to achieve project goals and objectives
- A collegial and respectful attitude among team members
- A clear leadership hierarchy that is flexible and accountable
- Dedication of the team and leadership to the vision and process to reach project goals and objectives
- Effective, timely, and respectful communication among team members
- Equitably shared rewards during and after the project window

The Vision of the U.S. Cooperative Extension Service

I was born into a world that was already highly organized into geopolitical and societal subunits. There were countries, states, municipalities, schools, companies, churches, and everyone was linked to a network of these organizations in a unique way. In my case, Detroit, Michigan and a traditional U.S. middle class family. As I matured, I came to appreciate the reasons for and challenges associated with these organizational units. They are all comprised of humans, and exhibit the typical characteristics of humans; suffice it to say "not perfect".

I also came to appreciate the history of specific organizations and how the priorities and needs shifted over time. As society changes, organizations that reflect societies also change, and sometimes become irrelevant. One excellent example is the Cooperative Extension Service organization of the U.S. Like the rest of the world in the 17th and early 18th centuries, the United States was overwhelmingly agrarian and rural. Successful societies depend on stable food systems, and the U.S. was blessed with seemingly unlimited land and water on which to promulgate agriculture. Hunger and starvation were rampant, however, since agriculture was vulnerable to climate, pests, and diseases, and the food security systems of communities was exceedingly fragile.

The Birth of the U.S. Cooperative Extension Service

The organization of agriculture into defined units, and the associated birth of the extension concept are well described by Jones and Garforth (2013). By the mid-18th century, technology was beginning to impact the lives of citizens in the area of mass transportation. Potential applications of mechanization to agriculture were obvious, but it was also apparent to political leaders at the time that work was necessary to reduce these concepts to practice and to foster the adoption of technology onto America's farms.

The Morrill Acts of 1862, 1890, and 1994 deeded federal lands to each constituent state with the stipulation that the funds derived from sale of these lands be used to establish and support a college with the purpose of developing and applying technologies for enhanced agricultural efficiency and profitability. This was a unique and innovative approach to the challenge of developing and adapting technology for agriculture. Most other nations have established a centralized system of agricultural research and technology transfer that usually grew to become as bureaucratic and unresponsive as the rest of the government. The individual state Land Grant Colleges and Agricultural Experiment Stations focused generally on their own specific needs. They were expected to compete for resources not only within the state, but also with each other at the national level. This competitive element served to minimize ineffective bureaucracies and promote the development and deployment of new ideas.

The Land Grant University system provided for the development of new technologies for agriculture and for the training of practitioners who would be integrating new technologies on individual farms, but it became apparent that factors were missing from a winning formula. The Hatch Act was passed in 1884 aimed at providing funding to states for the establishment of Agricultural Experiment Stations for the development of new technologies, processes, and machines for agriculture. To realize the full benefits of new technologies, a system of continuing education was needed to identify, test, and integrate these new elements from the AESs into functioning agriculture. Thus, the Smith-Lever Act of 1914 established the individual states' Cooperative Extension Service organizations, to fulfill the need for continuing education, on-farm demonstrations, and administration of government agricultural programming.

My Life Experiences

During my college years, I spent summers working for a construction company; 3 summers then an entire year after I graduated with a B.S. degree in Biology. My official title was "Layout Engineer", or "Field Engineer", the person charged with interpreting the plans ("blueprints") and determining where everything had to be located. This entailed the establishment of a 3-dimensional grid of control planes to ensure that all the structural, cosmetic, electrical, and mechanical elements came together as the architect intended. Constructing a building from a theoretical plan provided me with an excellent example of the power of collaboration and teamwork. The architect and owner/producer are charged with the inspiration and general concept, reduced to a set of diagrams that depict the finished product and its elements. A contractor is secured to devise the most effective and efficient sequence of events to convert the plan into reality. Then a diverse group of craftspeople are engaged to convert the conceptual drawings into a tangible piece of iron, concrete, and composite materials.

The process is not static; rather it is iterative. In this respect, it emulates life, also an iterative endeavor. Every day presented new challenges of the best way to apply the talents and creative abilities of the team to transform the growing object into something that resembled the conceptual visions of the owner and architect, more and more each passing day. Challenges emerged constantly that often, necessitated complex, multi-disciplinary negotiations to meet and resolve. Sometimes, the original plan had to be altered or radically changed to accommodate new evidence about the vision or process to get it done.

Pouring a concrete floor slab is an expensive prospect. Once it is poured, the slab is difficult or nearly impossible to change. The team of layout engineers must work closely together with carpenters, formers, electricians, reinforcing steel fabricators, plumbers and steam-fitters, structural iron workers, materials engineers, and concrete finishers to ensure that the slab is in the correct place, consists of the specified materials, and incorporates the intended electrical and mechanical elements. Time is a complicating factor, since concrete sets into an intractable state very quickly. On a large, multi-dimensional construction job, an effective team is absolutely essential to getting this job done.

Early Successes of the U.S. Cooperative Extension Service

Collaboration is a ubiquitous element of Cooperative Extension organizations throughout the U.S. Each state Cooperative Extension Service is comprised of a team of scientists, engineers, and technical experts arrayed in teams to serve a myriad of specific economic sectors.

I will describe one of these sectors (vegetable production) later in this chapter. Additionally, state Extension Organizations and focus teams also collaborate across state lines. Competition and collaboration are both important elements in keeping the organizations effective and responsive.

No two states are alike in the way the Land Grant Universities, Agricultural Experiment Stations, and Cooperative Extension Services are organized, supported, and interconnected. In some states, the AES and CES components are kept totally separate from the general university; all land grant universities have grown and expanded their scope to become much broader than agriculture. Over time, agriculture has also expanded to become much more diverse and diffused than it was perceived in the mid-19th century. In most states, CES is intermingled both organizationally and functionally within the Land Grant University and AES. In a few states, however, CES and/or AES are organizationally separate from the Land Grant Institution. This diversity of organization has ultimately served to strengthen the system and foster teamwork within and among states.

The establishment of the Land Grant University system also portended the rise of higher education in the U.S. In the mid-19th century, few high school graduates continued their studies. Most colleges were private, and many were associated with religious organizations. The sectarian "public" university system provided new opportunities for training in technological occupations at a very reasonable cost. The resulting competition of private and public institutions for students and financial support has made the U.S. higher education system the best in the world.

The results achieved by the collective Morrill, Hatch, and Smith-Lever Acts have been nothing short of breathtaking. The U.S. was a backward nation full of small subsistence farmers in 1950. The railroads were being built to connect the Atlantic and Pacific coasts, and oil and coal had been discovered in numerous locations throughout North America. As one Land Grant College after another was established and went into operation, the impacts of science and technology on the efficiency and productivity of agriculture began to accumulate. These colleges also trained students in mechanical sciences, engineering, and arts that were applied in the development of factories, ships, cars, airplanes, and military hardware. As a nation, the U.S. grew stronger, and youth began to leave farms to live in cities and work in the growing manufacturing sector.

By the early 20th century, about 50% of the population of the U.S. was still connected directly to agriculture. Most of the food consumed by families was grown within a few miles of the home on a small farm. Flour came from local grist mills, still powered mostly by rivers and streams. Fresh fruits and vegetables were available for only a short time during the late summer and early fall. Only about 2% of the U.S. population had a college degree (Anon 2017).

The impacts of the Land Grant/Experiment Station/Cooperative Extension legislation and resulting collaborative organizations were taking hold during the early 20th century. Most importantly, powered machinery and the horse-less tractor made it possible for an individual farmer to dramatically increase the acreage cultivated. One farmer could now feed 100 instead of only 10, allowing more youth to depart for the city. AES and CES organizations were charged with the development of new mechanization applications for planting, cultivation (weed management), harvesting, and processing. Also, the new field of genetics and plant breeding was beginning to show promise, and the AES and CES system led the way to the incorporation of new varieties of corn, wheat, oats, sorghum, cotton, soybeans, fruits, and vegetables. More and more of the harvest of perishable fruits and vegetables was processed into canned and frozen products that could be consumed during the "off-season".

By 1950, the potential of new chemicals to control weeds, insect pests, and disease pathogens was apparent. The AES/CES system was once again instrumental in the verification of product efficacy and the forging of a regulatory framework for chemicals to be used for the balanced benefits of farmers, farm labor, consumers, and the environment. Though the benefits of agricultural chemicals to farmers have been relatively easy to establish, achieving a balance with worker and consumer safety and long-term environmental sustainability has proven to be a much greater challenge.

This huge experiment in human and institutional collaboration has reaped incredible benefits in terms of human health and longevity. Hunger and starvation are virtually eradicated from the U.S. since there is such an abundance of affordable, nutritious food. Since 1930, the average proportion of the disposable income of Americans used to purchase food has dropped from 24.2 to 9.7%. The proportion of food costs prepared in the home has decreased from 87.3 to 55.3%, while the proportion of food costs attributable to food consumed outside of the home has increased from 12.7 to 43.7% (Table 1).

Success of the AES/CES concept is also apparent from the historical transition of research and development activities. In the 19th and early 20th centuries, it was viewed as a public imperative to support research and development into agricultural applications of new technologies that would benefit the populace. By the end of the 20th century, the majority of these programs, in mechanization, agricultural chemicals, food processing, preservation, and packaging, and plant and animal breeding and seed production had been assumed by the private sector and were vibrant facets of the U.S. economy. In 2015, 32.5% of Americans have a college degree (from 2% in 1900).

Everyone is born with innate abilities that are stimulated, stifled, or ignored, during the course of human development. Some of us have great intellectual powers, and others must work harder to glean out limited cognitive potential. A few are gifted athletes, and with the proper nurturing can develop into elite, professional players in an individual or team sport. But most of us are born with slower reaction times and limited eye-hand coordination, and will struggle to keep up with a slow-pitch baseball league. In the real world, progress is made in solving complex problems facing human cultures through teamwork. No one individual possesses all the knowledge and skills necessary to solve these daunting problems, like health and nutrition, understanding and utilizing Earth's resources, space exploration, etc.

Table 1. United States Proportion of Disposable Income Spent on Food 1930–Present

Year	$billion disp income	% in house	% out of house	% total
1930	74.9	21.09	3.07	24.17
1935	59.8	20.23	3.01	23.24
1940	77.7	17.37	3.09	20.46
1945	156.3	15.08	3.65	18.73
1950	215.0	16.59	3.53	20.12
1955	291.7	14.70	3.36	18.06
1960	376.5	13.67	3.34	17.01
1965	513.2	11.38	3.30	14.69
1970	761.5	9.92	3.47	13.39
1975	1219.3	9.63	3.77	13.39
1980	2018.0	8.96	4.22	13.18
1985	3098.5	7.55	4.15	11.70
1990	4311.8	7.29	4.06	11.35
1995	5532.6	6.50	4.14	10.63
2000	7400.5	5.83	3.94	9.77
2005	9400.8	5.68	4.06	9.74
2010	11237.9	5.52	4.02	9.54
2014	12913.9	5.48	4.26	9.74

Source: Calculated by the Economic Research Service, USDA, from various data sets from the U.S. Census Bureau and the Bureau of Labor Statistics.

My College Days

I was born a loner. I enjoy being alone with my thoughts. The most comfortable day for me is one without commitments involving other people or groups, where I can pore over research materials and data uninterrupted. Over the years, I have tried to cultivate my sense of humanity, and push myself to live with a better balance of self and others, to develop a better appreciation of the context of the work that I do. After nearly 40 years working in academia and private research and development, I am still challenged daily with my own personal preferences. Often, I must force myself to do what is necessary to achieve balance. I've known, and do still know, many who have the opposite challenge. They enjoy the team environment more than being alone, and must also push themselves to be more balanced. To be a better person.

The following are a few examples of the collaborative programs I have been involved with during my professional career. I will strive to address how the programs came about, how the teams were formed, special problems that were encountered along the way, and notable outcomes. Further, I will expand on lessons that I learned from each episode about the value of teamwork, and how I could alter my own behavior and attitudes to enhance outcomes and impacts.

While I was an undergraduate student, I took a few courses in the emerging field of information technology. This consisted primarily of the computer programming of large mainframe machines to carry out repetitive computational tasks. This was revolutionary in the 1960s and 1970s, of course. An application of information technology that was envisioned within the field of biology was "numerical taxonomy". This application posited that taxonomy/systematics was driven by predictable phenotypic differences among groups of related individuals that could be used to impute phylogeny. The most closely related groups evolutionarily will most resemble each other phenotypically. If this hypothesis is valid, information technology could be invoked to measure a large number of subtle phenotypic attributes, and to submit the data to analysis to calculate coefficients of relatedness or parsimony.

I worked with systematics experts to explore the application of information technology in the classification of organisms. This entailed the identification of a set of unknown taxonomic groups with the expert systematists, a set of phenotypic parameters that could be readily measured, and the development of an adapted computer program to forge the mountains of raw data into a phylogenetic tree. The team included mainly biologists and information scientists, with me as the hub of the wheel, communicating with both sets of experts. Ultimately, phylogenies were developed for a set of plants ( ) and insects (Hymenoptera; bumblebees). In both cases, the taxonomic experts discounted the resulting phylogenies because they disagreed with prevailing dogma; totally missing the point. Over the past 50 years, the rapidly advancing field of molecular biology has revolutionized the fields of taxonomy and systematics. Cumulative and quantitative/qualitative changes in genomic DNA sequences are now the prevailing criteria instead of subjective phenotypic characteristics. "Numerical Taxonomy" is merely a footnote in history.

My graduate studies at Michigan State University started out as a simple cytogenetic study of interspecific hybrids in the genus *Hordeum* (barley and relatives) with Drs. William Tai and John Grafius. It was the mid-1970s, and plant cell and tissue culture technologies were advancing rapidly. The range of species that could be cultured and regenerated into whole plants was expanding substantially. New discoveries in the culture and regeneration of plants from protoplasts, fused protoplasts, and cultured microspores were appearing constantly. An established expert in the field, Dr. Peter S. Carlson, was recruited by MSU and charged in part with contributing to this expansion of the cutting edge in plant cell and tissue culture.

The cytogenetic and agronomic study of *Hordeum* interspecific hybrids was discussed with Peter with respect to a possible cell and tissue culture component to the research. A collaborative project was born among the three faculty members, with me as the designated academic work horse. In addition to the originally planned research, in the area of classical cytogenetics, I ventured into the culture and regeneration of *Hordeum* species and interspecific hybrids as well. My research shifted to the use of cytogenetics as a tool to measure genetic changes that occurred during the cell/tissue culture phase. I maintained the dialogue among the constituent faculty experts, who remained as members on my thesis committee. The research ultimately demonstrated that both subtle and genomic changes were evident in both cultures and regenerates. By culturing an interspecific hybrid *H. vulgare* (cultivated barley) x *H. jubatum*, it was possible to recover haploid *H. vulgare*, possibly with translocated or substituted chromosome segments from *H. jubatum*, a new discovery. The intersection provided by classical breeding and genetics (Grafius) with classical cytogenetics (Tai) and cell/tissue culture (Carlson) was essential to achieve this result.

The U.S. Cooperative Extension Service Adapts to a Changing World

During the mid to late-20th century, the farmer lost relative shares of overall revenues from sales of food products to consumers (Table 2). Over this period, the relative proportion to the farm gate dropped from 72.2 to 63.8% relative to indexed grocery prices. Since 1990, however, the farm gate has increased dramatically to 116% of the grocery sector, due in part to the decline of this industry. Over this same period, the proportion of indexed revenues attributable to the food service sector has soared from 124.0 to 384.2%, due mostly to the rapid increase of disposable income. The AES/CES system has worked mostly with farmers to increase productivity, initially resulting in reduced indexed profitability. Currently, AES/CES is working with farmers and food processors to develop more value-added products that will shift dollars back to the farmer.

Table 2. United States Food Shares to Wholesalers and Retailers Indexed to Grocery Sector

Year	Restaurant prices[1]	Retail store prices	Manufacturers' and shippers' prices[2]
1939	124.0	100	72.2
1948	127.2	100	81.4
1958	134.6	100	71.6
1968	161.7	100	69.2
1978	164.4	100	67.9
1988	188.0	100	63.8
1998	248.6	100	76.0
2008	333.1	100	101.0
2014	384.2	100	115.8

[1] The ratio of restaurant prices to the gross margin of grocery store food sales.

[2] The ratio of manufacturers' selling prices to grocery store retail prices

Source: Calculated by the Economic Research Service, USDA, from various data sets U.S. Census Bureau and the

During the first phase of implementation, the U.S. land grant university AES/CES system focused almost entirely on what we now call food security. Until the 1960s, agricultural research and extension were focused almost exclusively on reducing farmer risks and increasing profitability through higher net per acre yields. The overall outcome of this over-arching program has been wildly successful. In the mid-19th century, farmers were vulnerable to adverse weather, weeds, pests, diseases, and barriers to marketing. 100 years later, new varieties and production methods have been developed to allow for productivity and even profitability under adverse environmental conditions. Weeds, pests, and diseases are mostly controlled by selective chemical agents developed and sold by private sector companies, the availability of which is controlled by the U.S. government (USDA and EPA). Harvesting, packaging, and distribution systems have been well developed, and the U.S. government provides marketing support through the USDA (AMS).

By the 1960s, these advances along with cheap energy and a proliferation of farm machinery resulted in huge commodity food surpluses. The U.S. government negotiated massive trade deals to sell off these surpluses to underperforming economies such as China and the USSR. Unfortunately, these indirect subsidies didn't last very long. Political discord mostly scuttled these agreements during the 1980s, and the surpluses returned. Farm profitability plummeted. When corn, soybeans, and wheat are not profitable, farmers migrate to other alternatives such as horticultural crops. Higher volumes lead to reduced unit prices (Anon 2017).

Also during the 1960s and 1970s, an abundance of cheap labor and energy resulted in the gradual dismantling of the U.S. manufacturing economy. One by one, manufacturing jobs left the U.S. for Latin America and Asia. As this was occurring, U.S. scientists and engineers were forging new advances in electronics and biology. The service sector expanded to support the growing middle class. Eventually (though painfully) the manufacturing jobs migrated into these new sectors, and employment has remained relatively stable, though commensurate with overall economic health.

The AES/CES system responded with new ideas and projects for differentiated products that set them apart from commodities. This overall strategy is challenging because the number of product concepts is infinite, but the market size is finite. The higher overall volume commanded by a new product, the more it resembles a commodity. In general, farmers have embraced the new paradigm of specialized, vertically integrated, targeted agriculture. In many cases, farmers were the original sources of new ideas, demonstrating the potential power of the connected AES/CES model (Auburn and Baker 1992). This is reflected in the recent trend of increasing share of total proceeds going to farmers (Table 2). While wholesale prices declined relative to retail until the late 1980s, there has been a marked rebound since that time, due in part to market differentiation and the appearance of new value-added products.

While it is true that the U.S. is still blessed with an abundance of land, excellent soils, high quality water, and a plethora of beneficial climates, there are many other locations on Earth that are equally well endowed with enviable natural resources. The average annual per capita income of U.S. citizens is #2 in the world behind Switzerland ($37,253.40), and the proportion of income used to buy food is the lowest in the world (6.42%; Table 3). Why has the U.S. prospered over the past 200+ years while other nations have not fared as well, and some have languished altogether? The story of the success of the U.S. is a confluence of several factors, the main one being an abundance of cheap, nutritious food. Other factors include a rich base of natural resources, a diverse and talented labor force, and a government that seeks to foster, not to control the economy (Anon 2017).

Yet another force in the recipe for economic success has been the U.S. system of higher education, particularly the public universities. Objective assessments of the standing of higher education institutions consistently place the U.S. at the top (see for example http://www.4icu.org/top-universities-world/2017), with over 70% of the top universities. Consequently, the world sends its students to the U.S. for the most effective, advanced training in areas such as science, engineering, information management, and business administration. Most of these students return to their native countries and not only apply what they have learned, but they also maintain the networks of people that were established during the times of their studies in the U.S. Cumulatively, the resulting influence of the U.S. higher education system on activities elsewhere in the world is enormous.

Table 3. Comparison of Disposable Income and Proportion of Income Spent on Food Among Selected Countries

Country	% food	% EtOH Tob	Disp Income	$ on food
USA	6.42	2.00	37253.4	2391.8
United Kingdom	8.22	3.93	26975.6	2217.2
Switzerland	8.74	3.61	43061.3	3762.6
Canada	9.12	3.32	23763.9	2168.4
Australia	9.81	3.43	29709.3	2914.8
Austria	9.90	3.37	23443.3	2322.0
Qatar	11.73	0.25	12917.9	1515.9
Norway	12.27	4.08	28836.1	3538.2
Belgium	12.87	4.23	19675.2	2532.1
Bahrain	12.95	0.37	11409.1	1477.3
South Korea	13.03	2.15	12584.4	1639.9
France	13.22	3.51	20022.5	2646.7
United Arab Emirates	13.77	0.20	22944.6	3158.6
Japan	14.15	2.55	18588.6	2630.9
Brazil	15.51	2.20	5256.5	815.3
Poland	16.50	7.37	7195.9	1187.6
Colombia	17.43	2.93	3731.0	650.4
Uruguay	18.21	1.20	11163.1	2033.1
Bulgaria	18.37	6.89	4425.2	812.9
Venezuela	19.59	3.71	842.8	165.1
Costa Rica	19.94	0.94	7542.7	1503.7
Malaysia	20.63	1.79	5436.5	1121.5
Turkey	21.54	5.10	6688.2	1440.4
Tunisia	22.33	3.22	2877.8	642.5
Mexico	23.13	2.56	6143.5	1420.7
Iran	24.22	0.41	2232.5	540.7
China	24.96	3.47	3005.1	750.0
Saudi Arabia	24.97	0.62	7826.9	1954.1
Russia	28.02	9.20	4707.8	1319.0
India	30.47	2.32	1033.3	314.8
Indonesia	32.89	5.22	1912.8	629.1
Ukraine	38.06	8.09	1347.1	512.7
Pakistan	40.91	0.97	1118.6	457.6
Philippines	41.89	1.17	2134.1	894.0
Cameroon	45.55	2.10	934.3	425.6
Nigeria	56.41	1.33	2006.3	1131.8

Sources: Euromonitor.com and USDA/EMS

The U.S. AES/CES system has been and continues to be influenced greatly by the forces of change. During the 19th and early

20th centuries, there was a great emphasis on farm mechanization. Gradually, starting in the late 19th century, more attention was paid to the development and integration of new genetic inputs into the agricultural production picture. The most notable overall advance was the successful development of hybrid populations to capitalize on the phenomenon of heterosis. Consequently, average yields of grain corn have increased 5-fold since the early 20th century (http://passel.unl.edu/pages/informationmodule.php?idinformationmodule=1075412493&topicorder=10&maxto=12). As the commercial potential of new varieties was demonstrated, products were absorbed by the growing seed industry. Currently, the AES/CES system still engages in the development of new varieties of small acreage specialty crops, but activities in larger acreage crops are mostly aimed at local performance trials of new varieties developed in the private sector. These trials are most effective when AES/CES works together with local farmers in a team to demonstrate variety performance in a truly applied context.

During the 1980s and 1990s, technological advances in cell and molecular biology led to the possibility of GMO crop varieties. The AES/CES system participated in the development and testing of GMO varieties, and also in the forging of a government regulatory framework that addresses this new concept (see web pages from CES in Colorado, Florida, Wisconsin, Ohio, Vermont, and others). The integration of GMO varieties and technologies into the agricultural industry has been much slower than originally anticipated due to sociological factors. Consumers are resistant to the concept of transgenic crop and animal species until it can be proven that long-term environmental and health risks are nil.

AES/CES system was also quick to embrace the applications of agricultural chemicals for farming. Before the mid-20th century, U.S. agriculture was comprised of relatively small units that were diverse and a working cooperative effort of crop and animal operations. The animal operations provided nutrients in the form of composted wastes. Farms were diverse and crop rotations were essential to minimize the effects of antagonistic weeds, arthropod pests, animal pests, and diseases.

The chemical industry thrived in the 1950-1980 timeframe when their products pervaded in a broad spectrum of consumer products. In agriculture, weed, pest, and disease management strategies moved from tolerance and economic thresholds to mass eradication. The allure of eradication proved to be far too seductive to farmers who were eager to dispatch the long lists of chronic risks faced by their businesses. The AES/CES system listened to the growers, who needed product efficacy trialing and pesticide applicator training. By the 1990s, most extension agents and specialists had become experts in the direct and indirect effects of pesticides. They were regarded by the new organic farming industry as unwitting puppets of the chemical companies.

Each agricultural subsector has specific needs that recur across a broad geographical range. Simultaneously, each geographical area also has specific problems to address. The AES/CES system has responded to this challenge well with a state-based grid structure. The organization of the human elements that address the specific and general challenges faced by agricultural subsectors in geographical areas is very loose, especially across state lines. Within states, the structure of a unit working with a specific subsector, for example vegetables, can be well defined or diffused. In larger states like Texas or California, the challenges tend to be much less monolithic than in smaller states. The organization is usually comprised of a group of specialists, professors, and agents that work on a common subsector (e.g. vegetables). These groups may or may not be mandated by the overarching institutional administrative structure, and are often difficult to find from the "outside". AES/CES subsector groups usually interact or participate with the business commodity advocacy group that supports constituent farmers in the state.

The 50-state AES/CES matrix that is focused on the vegetable subsector of the agricultural economy is summarized in Table 4. For each state, the primary land grant university is listed; this is the location of most of the specialists and professors that focus on applied agricultural problems. Local CES agents are dispersed in each state either by county or district, and they also address the needs of specific agricultural subsectors. Since the activities of local CES agents are impossible to quantify and qualify, these FTEs are not included in the matrix. Also, difficult to characterize, are the many ways that all of these individuals, and organizations work together to solve problems of regional and national significance. There are also interactions on another dimension, for example the food retailing or processing subsectors of agriculture. This matrix is but one example of how the U.S. AES/CES system works to support and further the interests of the American agricultural economy. The extent of coverage and the breadth of expertise that moves from the universities to farmers and from farmers to universities is unprecedented.

The AES/CES system to support the U.S. vegetable industry evolved over the past 100 years to meet the needs that were communicated to the individual land grant universities from farmers, processors, retailers, and farm service providers. Each state or region consists of a network of commodity and industry organizations that have also coalesced over time to advocate for the common policy and technical support needs of all members. These associations keep a periscope on their respective industries, and when needs rise to the level of action, they issue formal communications (and exert informal pressure) to local governments and to AES/CES to make policy changes or move to provide needed technical support. In some states, the local Farm Bureau affiliate also serves this purpose.

AES/CES communicates regularly to practitioners in the vegetable industry through these local organizations. Table 5 lists examples of vegetable commodity organizations that serve the needs of specific states or regions, but the list is not exhaustive. There are many layers of associations that advocate for the needs of any given farmer, processor, retailer, etc. For example, in New Jersey, many or most vegetable growers are affiliated with the Vegetable Growers' Association of New Jersey. They may also be affiliated with the New Jersey Food Processors' Association and/or one of many other associations connected with other (agronomic, ornamental/nursery, greenhouse) industries they are involved with, since farmers typically operate diversified businesses, and also engage in crop rotation practices.

I am one of the 8 FTE reported for the state of New Jersey. The projects I am relating in this chapter are typical of those that all the AES/CES participants would be engaging in to support the needs of their respective industries. The system is flexible and responsive, and information flows effectively in both directions: from farmer to land grant university and vice versa. The system changes over time as the industry and technology change. This example of a highly successful collaboration is rife with breakdowns in communication and unfulfilled expectations, but any attempts to integrate changes will be mostly futile. The organization is loose, ad hoc, and decentralized. It exists because everybody wants it to exist, not because some higher authority has mandated it to exist.

Table 4. AES/CES Support of the Vegetable Subsector of the U.S. Agricultural Economy

State	Primary Land Grant University	Acres Vegetables*	Approx #FTE	Extension/Outreach and Industry Resources & Groups
Alabama	Auburn University	6,700	4	Alabama Cooperative Extension Service (ACES) Extension Vegetable IPM Project, ACES crop guides, Alabama Fruit & Vegetable Growers' Association
Alaska	University of Alaska Fairbanks	600	3	UAFCE Master Gardener web page includes vegetable resource links; Alaska Farmers' Market Association
Arizona	University of Arizona	111,200	5	UACE "Vegetable Gardening Resources" web page; Yuma Fresh Vegetable Association
Arkansas	University of Arkansas	2,500	5	UACE "Commercial Vegetables" web page
California	University of California CE	720,200	21	UCCE Vegetable Research & Information Center web page (including extensive links to resources); Commodity Marketing and Advisory Boards, Western Growers' Assoc.
Colorado	Colorado State University	12,350	4	CSUCE "Co-Horts" blog web page; printed resources for onion and potato growers; Colorado Fruit and Vegetable Association
Connecticut	University of Connecticut	3,900	2	UCCE Vegetable IPM Program, Newsletter, website
Delaware	University of Delaware	6,100	2	DE Vegetable and Small Fruits Program
Florida	University of Florida/IFAS	163,800	14	Southeastern U.S. Vegetable Production Guide, Florida Vegetable Production Guide, Florida Fruit & Vegetable Association
Georgia	University of Georgia	96,500	13	UGACE Vegetable Web Page, Georgia Fruit and Vegetable Growers' Association
Hawaii	University of Hawaii	5,500	7	UHCE "Commercial Agriculture" web site links to resources; Hawaii Organic Farming Association
Idaho	University of Idaho	8,000	7	UICE "Small Acreage" web page; Idaho-Oregon Fruit and Vegetable Association; Idaho Potato Growers' Association

Illinois	University of Illinois	21,600	4	ILCE "Common Vegetable Problems" and "Harvesting Vegetables" web pages; Illinois Vegetable Growers Assoc.
Indiana	Purdue University	15,400	10	Purdue CE Hort Extension Vegetable & Melon Web Page; Indiana Vegetable Growers' Association
Iowa	Iowa State University	3,120	5	ISUCE "Sustainable Vegetable Production" web page; Iowa Fruit and Vegetable Growers' Association
Kansas	Kansas State University	3,400	3	KSUCE Commercial Fruits and Vegetables Web Page; Kansas Vegetable Growers' Association
Kentucky	University of Kentucky	4,550	5	UKCE IPM scouting; Kentucky Vegetable Growers' Association
Louisiana	Louisiana State University	12,000	6	LSUCE Vegetables Resources Web Page; LA Commercial Vegetable Production Recommendations
Maine	University of Maine	1,500	3	Demonstrations at Highmoor Farm; Maine Vegetables and Small Fruits Association
Maryland	University of Maryland	8,940	4	Maryland Vegetables UMdCE website; Maryland Vegetable Growers Association
Massachusetts	University of Massachusetts	3,400	6	UM Vegetable Group, Newsletter; New England Vegetable Production Guide
Michigan	Michigan State University	51,200	7	MSUCE Vegetable Web Page; MSU Vegetable Extension Production Team; Michigan Vegetable Council; Great Lakes Vegetable Working Group
Minnesota	University of Minnesota	64,000	7	UMCE "Commercial Fruit and Vegetable Production" web page; Minnesota Fruit and Vegetable Growers' Association
Mississippi	Mississippi State University	2,000	5	MSU web pages for specific vegetables; Mississippi Fruit and Vegetable Growers Association
Missouri	University of Missouri	2,700	2	UMCE Vegetable web page; Missouri Vegetable Growers Association
Montana	Montana State University	5,260	2	Montana Organic Association
Nebraska	University of Nebraska	25,000	3	UNCE "CropWatch" GAPs for Fruit and Vegetable Production; Nebraska Fruit and Vegetable Association
Nevada	University of Nevada, Reno	4,200	1	UNCE Horticulture web subdirectory
New Hampshire	University of New Hampshire	1,400	0	None apparent
New Jersey	Rutgers University	23,800	8	Vegetable Growers Association of New Jersey; Rutgers Vegetable Working Group & website, Mid-Atlantic Vegetable Production Guide
New Mexico	New Mexico State University	13,500	4	NMSU Chile Pepper Institute; New Mexico Farmers' Marketing Association
New York	Cornell University	99,300	14	Vegetable Crops Work Team & website; New York State Vegetable Growers' Association
North Carolina	North Carolina State University	32,100	11	NC Vegetable Growers Association
North Dakota	North Dakota State University	35,000	1	NDSUCE Potato Production web page
Ohio	Ohio State University	31,700	7	"VegNet" web page from OSUCE Vegetable Crops Team; Ohio Vegetable and Potato Growers' Association
Oklahoma	Oklahoma State University	5,500	2	Oklahoma Fruit and Vegetable Association
Oregon	Oregon State University	30,100	10	OSUCE "Small Farms" and "Oregon Vegetables" web pages; Idaho-Oregon Fruit and Vegetable Association
Pennsylvania	Pennsylvania State University	30,230	14	PA Vegetable & Small Fruit Guide, PA Vegetable Growers Association, Horticulture Team
Rhode Island	University of Rhode Island	700	1	URI Extension Outreach Center, demonstrations
South Carolina	Clemson University	15,800	7	Coastal Research & Extension Center, demonstrations
South Dakota	South Dakota State University	340	1	South Dakota Specialty Producers' Association
Tennessee	University of Tennessee	12,150	4	Tennessee Vegetable Growers' Association

Texas	Texas A&M University	63,400	14	"Aggie Horticulture" Vegetable Resources Web Page; Texas Vegetable Association
Utah	Utah State University	1,400	3	USUCE "Production Horticulture - Commercial Vegetables" web page; Diversified Agriculture Consortium web page; Utah Fruit and Vegetable Association
Vermont	University of Vermont	900	3	Vermont Vegetable and Berry Association
Virginia	Virginia Tech & Poly University	8,750	7	VA Community, Local, and Regional Food Systems Group
Washington	Washington State University	54,600	12	Home of Pacific Northwest Vegetable Extension Group and web site; Mt. Vernon Vegetable Research and Extension Center web site; WSU Potato Research Group web page; Pacific Northwest Vegetable Association
West Virginia	West Virginia University	350	1	Focused on Master Gardener and Small Farms programs
Wisconsin	University of Wisconsin	8,400	6	UWCE "Vegetable and Fruit Crop Storage" web page; Farmers' Market web pages; Wisconsin Potato and Vegetable Growers Association
Wyoming	University of Wyoming	140	1	Wyoming Farmers' Market Association

ᵃ 2015 commercial vegetables + potatoes unless noted otherwise below
All crop acreage estimates from: http://usda.mannlib.cornell.edu/usda/current/VegeSumm/VegeSumm-02-04-2016.pdf with exceptions below
Average total income per acre U.S. $6,320.50
Alaska acreage: From https://www.nass.usda.gov/Quick_Stats/Ag_Overview/stateOverview.php?state=ALASKA 540 potatoes + 60 misc vegetables
Hawaii acreage: From https://www.nass.usda.gov/Statistics_by_State/Hawaii/Publications/Vegetables/2016/20160818vegrv.pdf
Iowa acreage: From https://www.nass.usda.gov/Quick_Stats/Ag_Overview/stateOverview.php?state=IOWA
Kansas acreage: From https://www.nass.usda.gov/Quick_Stats/Ag_Overview/stateOverview.php?state=kansas
Kentucky acreage: From https://www.nass.usda.gov/Quick_Stats/Ag_Overview/stateOverview.php?state=KENTUCKY
Louisiana acreage: From https://www.agcensus.usda.gov/Publications/2012/Full_Report/Volume_1,_Chapter_1_State_Level/Louisiana/st22_1_038_038.pdf (2012)
Montana acreage: From https://www.nass.usda.gov/Quick_Stats/Ag_Overview/stateOverview.php?state=MONTANA (predominantly potatoes)
Minnesota acreage: From https://www.nass.usda.gov/Quick_Stats/Ag_Overview/stateOverview.php?state=minnesota
Nebraska acreage: From http://usda.mannlib.cornell.edu/usda/current/VegeSumm/VegeSumm-02-04-2016.pdf (predominantly potatoes, 20,000 acres)
North Dakota acreage: From https://www.nass.usda.gov/Quick_Stats/Ag_Overview/stateOverview.php?state=north%20dakota all attributable to potatoes
South Dakota acreage: From https://www.nass.usda.gov/Quick_Stats/Ag_Overview/stateOverview.php?state=south%20dakota
West Virginia acreage: From https://www.nass.usda.gov/Quick_Stats/Ag_Overview/stateOverview.php?state=west%20virginia
Wyoming acreage: From https://www.nass.usda.gov/Quick_Stats/Ag_Overview/stateOverview.php?state=WYOMING

My Career Path 1978—1995

From MSU, I moved to the University of California, Davis as an Assistant Professor in 1978 to start a new program in the breeding and genetics of cool season vegetables. I envisioned a progressive approach that melded traditional and novel cell and molecular strategies to understand the inheritance of agriculturally important crop characteristics and to develop new, valuable cultivars. The university setting is an ideal place to build multi-disciplinary teams, but teamwork is often discouraged by the prevailing reward system, especially for an Assistant Professor charged with attaining academic tenure within 6 years of joining the institution. The reward system at UCD in the late 1970s was heavily weighted toward individual vs. team performance. Nonetheless, I forged partnerships with growers, Extension Specialists and Agents, and other faculty members that complemented my range of expertise.

During this period, I gained an appreciation for marker-assisted breeding methods. The molecular biology of genomic polymorphisms was very crude during this period. The most effective genetic and breeding tool that had been reduced to practice was isozyme electrophoresis. I collaborated with Dr. Charles Rick and others who were pioneering the use of this technology, and ultimately became proficient in the application in *Apium* (celery) and *Brassica*. My laboratory group, was able to forge new knowledge in the reproductive biology of these crop species, and use isozymes as surrogate markers to accelerate the breeding process. A 2-volume monograph series was co-edited with Dr. Stephen Tanksley "Isozymes in Plant Genetics and Breeding" (1984) that summarized the state of the art of this field and the power of marker-assisted plant breeding. These humble beginnings led to a revolution in plant breeding; virtually all comprehensive commercial plant breeding programs currently feature marker-assistance (e.g. QTLs) and genomics elements.

The isolation, restriction, and visualization of DNA sequence content in the 1970s and 1980s was expensive, laborious, time-consuming, wrought with technical challenges, and crude. The most powerful method at the time was Southern blotting, an early strategy that incorporated the immobilization of substrate DNA on filter paper, hybridization with radiolabeled probe DNA or RNA, and visualization with autoradiography. I worked with a postdoctoral scientist at Stanford University, Dr. Jeffrey Palmer, along with colleagues at UCD (Dr. Daniel Cohen) to study the inheritance of maternally-inherited traits in Brassica parental and hybrid species. This collaboration led to the unexpected discovery of mitochondrial plasmids that were replicated and distributed to daughter organelles independently of the main genome. This was an early demonstration of the plasticity of plant organelle (mitochondrial and plastid) inheritance mechanisms.

My graduate studies in the 1970s focused on applications of cell and tissue culture in agriculture, but I was always attracted to the field of plant breeding. While at UC Davis, I collaborated on the development and release of a breeding line of celery that carried a new gene for resistance to *Fusarium oxysporum* f. sp. *apii* race 2, the biggest problem facing celery growers in North America. Later, at DNAP (see below), I worked closely with growers and other scientists to develop a new variety of celery that featured longer petioles, resulting in increased yields of "celery sticks" in the line of packaged value-added perishables. A patent was obtained on this invention.

While at UCD, I established a funded program relationship with a new biotechnology company Agrigenetics. The vision of Agrigenetics was to build a balanced organization consisting of cutting-edge plant and molecular biology, classical plant breeding, and the commercial planting seed industry. A limited R&D partnership was established by the founders, David Padwa and Samuel Dryden, the source of funding for university and government institutional researchers. In addition to the acquisition of several successful seed companies, Agrigenetics also established two distinct internal R&D organizations, the Advanced Genetics Laboratory (Madison, WI) and the Applied Genetics Laboratory (Boulder, CO).

I was offered a position at the AGL in Boulder and made the personal and professional decision to accept it in 1982. My challenge was to build a team of talented cell and molecular biologists positioned to capitalize on near-term opportunities in vegetable crop improvement.

The AGL Director Dr. Robert Lawrence with managers (including myself) spent the initial phase of establishment (design and construction of the facility; recruitment of the teams) also establishing a close working relationship with one of the constituent seed companies (Sun Seeds). The traditional Sun Seeds plant breeders were mostly skeptical of the value of the partnership, but I was convinced that we would be able to contribute powerful new tools to the arsenal. The skepticism was born from suspicions about perceived value placed on traditional vs. novel technologies by Agrigenetics leaders. Through careful nurturing of the relationships, and an atmosphere of mutual respect, we were able to deliver on the applications, in somaclonal variation, microspore culture, and micropropagation. The AGL and Sun Seeds collaboration was well on its way to pioneering new horizons in vegetable breeding when the parent company, Agrigenetics, came apart at the seams financially. The AGL was closed and consolidated in 1985 with the Madison, WI group, and eventually all the assets were sold to a Cleveland, OH petroleum company.

After failed attempts to start a new venture "Heartland Technologies" in Boulder, CO based in applications of biotechnology in canola, I joined DNA Plant Technology Corporation in 1986 as Director of the Western R&D Station in Watsonville, CA. The company founders Drs. W. Rod Sharp and David Evans entrusted me with the establishment and staffing of the station that was charged with developing and adapting new cell and molecular technologies in vegetable crop improvement.

One of DNAP's key business targets was in the area of value-added perishable fruit, vegetable products, and biotechnology was viewed as an important catalyst for bridging consumers with better flavor and nutrition. Eventually, I also assumed the role as coordinator of raw material acquisition for the operational team that produced and marketed a line of consumer products. Later, the enterprise was reorganized into a semi-autonomous and self-supporting organization owned by DNAP and E.I.DuPont named "FreshWorld". I remained with DNAP, and continued to support FreshWorld in the quality assurance of existing products and the development of new ones. The teamwork that was necessary in making these diverse entities mesh together was extremely challenging, especially on the scale we were operating. New protocols had to be devised for virtually all facets of the business, from seed production of finished varieties (in Asia) to geographically diverse year-round growing schedules (Mexico to Oregon and Florida to New Jersey), and especially quality assurance of the value-added components of new products. Not surprisingly, meeting these challenges necessitated the constant formation and tweaking of technical support teams. An appreciation was gained for the "big picture" of new product development, manufacturing processes, packaging and distribution, and assurance of consistent quality. Building a business and brand around perishable commodities is exceedingly challenging, and redundancy, repetition, and attention to detail are all essential to achieve success.

DNAP also encountered financial difficulties, and was forced to undergo divestiture and downsizing during the early-mid 1990s. I left during one of the waves of downsizing in 1994, and spent a year trying to catch on as an independent consultant (AgriSynergies, Inc.). This was a very interesting and enriching experience, and I did forge several ongoing partnerships with companies that sought my expertise in applications of biotechnology in plant improvement. Working independently was very stressful for me, and the difficulty in managing cash flow for the new company was a constant source of strife. I spent more than half of my time reminding clients it was time (or more often past time) for them to pay me. In retrospect, this enterprise could have been a lucrative career path for me, but other opportunities interceded.

The U.S. Cooperative Extension System Must Adapt To More Changes

Wisdom tells us there are no simple solutions to the world's problems. The promise of chemistry to eradicate pests has proven to be overly simplified. Many or most of the chemicals that are released into the environment to eradicate one or a few pests have many other secondary, tertiary, and other indirect effects that are often not desirable. One example of an unintended consequence is pesticide (and herbicide, fungicide) resistance. Organisms are not static or monolithic. All these extant organisms have followed a pathway of evolution on Earth to exist in the currently flora and fauna. And have the ability, to respond to adverse environmental challenges to survive and reproduce, including exposure to agents of extermination. Resistance to pesticides has been observed often enough that new general strategies to alternate modes of action have been developed to discourage the appearance of genetic resistance. These new resistance avoidance strategies were developed by AES/CES in cooperation with the agricultural chemical industry.

Some studies have shown that tillage and synthetic fertilizers destroy the soil ecosystem (Galvez et al. 2001), promote erosion, promote moisture loss (Crowell 2012), and increase the volumetric release of CO_2 and NO_2 (Schonbeck 2015). The soil ecosystem is essential to the future health of Earth since it is the cornerstone of the recycling of elements on the planet. An alternative is the practice of conservation tillage where the agroecosystem soil is retained in a relatively undisturbed state during the production of consecutive cycles of crops and fallow periods. Conservation tillage is not compatible with the mainstream agricultural strategy of tillage and synthetic chemical supplements.

The AES/CES system has been slow to embrace the backlash to the oversimplified pest eradication and chemical fertilizer crop strategy. Part of the reason for the slow response resides in the attitudes of the industry being served. Farmers realize that the use of pesticides is coming under fire, but most continue to cling to pesticides. The agents who purchase their crops are mandating an absence of superficial blemishes or damage, nearly impossible to achieve without pesticides. Pesticides are legal to use and are accepted by most mainstream food companies. Following 2-3 generations of pesticide dependence, many farmers perceive that the absence of chemical fertilizers and pesticides constitutes a step backward in time.

Perhaps most importantly, AES/CES is under financial strain, like all units within the public universities. Individuals are being challenged more and more to garner outside resources to support their own activities and the administrative costs of the unit. The primary "product" of AES/CES is information, and many state AES/CES organizations have been selling information for dollars for a long time. Agriculture and the chemical industry has continued to support AES/CES, the latter with the impartial efficacy trials of new products. This makes it difficult, of course, for practitioners to engage in alternative or sustainable agriculture. In most states, agriculture is changing rapidly, and shrinking in many cases. Since agriculture is the traditional target of AES/CES, the organizations are re-inventing themselves to serve new sectors outside of agriculture.

In a speech delivered to the National Association of County Agents in 2008, John Ikerd said: "All agricultural productivity and economic value comes from either land or people from nature or society." If the productivity of nature and society are depleted, there will be no source of productivity or profitability. Unfortunately, the economy provides strong incentives for investments that benefit individuals but provides no incentives for investments that benefit society in general or those of future generations. All economic value is individualistic; it accrues only to individuals, not societies. Thus, economic value must at least be expected to accrue during the lifetime of the individual decision maker. Interest rates are a reflection on the economic value of time. At an interest rate of seven-percent, for example, for a dollar, requires a wait of ten years to get its worth which is valued at only fifty-cents today. That's why corporations operate have five-to-seven-year planning horizons. Anything beyond that has very little economic value." (Ikerd 2008).

Later in the same speech: "Questions concerning the sustainability of agriculture continue to grow because more people are coming to understand that an agriculture driven solely by the economic bottom line is not sustainable. The future of humanity depends on farmers being willing and able to balance their legitimate individual economic needs with their social and ethical responsibilities for the well-being of others, both of current and future generations. Such restraint of narrow self-interests isn't some radical, new-age way of thinking; it's as old as the history of human civilization. People have always understood that we humans are not purely self-seeking physical beings; we are social and spiritual beings as well. We need the sense of belonging that comes from caring for others. We need the sense of ethical and moral rightness that comes from caring for the earth. The ancient philosophers understood that happiness requires a sense of rightness in our relationships with each other and with the earth. Sustainable agriculture only requires a return to our historical sense of human happiness."

In 1850, four years was a very long time. Things didn't change much during that four year time period. In 2017, four years is an eternity. Everything changes drastically, yet our institutions are still grounded in a much slower pace of change.

Become Part of the U.S. Cooperative Extension Organization 1995-Present

I was contacted in mid-1994 about an open position at Rutgers University as Chair of the Department of Extension Specialists, a key leadership role in the New Jersey Agricultural Experiment Station. It took about six months to develop the opportunity, and to disengage from the AgriSynergies consulting business, but I ultimately decided this was the best career path for me at that time. This department was by far the most diverse within the School unit and probably within the university. Represented areas of academic expertise spanned from the social sciences to economics, soil science, animal science, plant science, agronomy and horticulture, entomology, plant pathology, forestry, environmental science, nutrition and food science, marine sciences, meteorology, and ecology.

I viewed my job as the pursuit of any and all leadership efforts, on my part that allow the constituent faculty members to become more productive. This included the navigation of institutional red tape and hurdles, finding financial and other resources to support faculty programs, and especially to build multi-disciplinary teams. Parenthetically, others (including direct supervisors) viewed my purview more as a transactional manager who kept faculty in line. Since academic faculty members are usually protected by tenure, and compensation mechanisms are mostly intractable, I disagreed with this approach. Better, I thought, to build organizational morale and comradery, and squeeze more outputs out of the sizable investment into payroll, especially since over 95% of the total budget was tied up in personnel direct and indirect costs.

I met with each of the approximate 40 faculty members within the first year of appointment, and generally met with everyone again at least every other year on a formal basis; more frequently than that on an informal basis. Getting to know and respect the programs of individuals is the first step to gain their willingness to submit to suggestions pertaining to change and new challenges. Next, I added a dimension to the regular department meetings where the individual faculty members gave "mini-presentations", 5 minutes each, to the department. These mini-presentations were a very effective and non-threatening way to bring such a diverse department together. 15-20 years later, I still hear from faculty members that they valued these experiences, and replicated them in the units they became leaders of.

In 2002, I left the department chair position and assumed a temporary post as the County Agricultural Agent for Essex and Passaic Counties in northern New Jersey. This was to accommodate a changing personal situation (spouse changing job location to New York City) and to address the chronic absence of an Agricultural Agent in these counties. I quickly learned that the County Agent role is probably the most challenging within the land grant university system. Serving as the representative of the state public research university to all prospective clientele is daunting and, at times, overwhelming. Both Essex and Passaic Counties are largely urban, and traditional agriculture has waned substantially since the early 20th century. New constituencies, such as nurseries, small roadside farms, Christmas tree farms, community/urban gardens, etc. appeared and prospered as dairies and truck farms disappeared. The County Agent is expected to be all things to all citizens, and expected to serve on many historic and functional county and regional policy boards and standing governmental committees. A typical day includes several site visits to constituents who are experiencing difficulties that may be resolved by university intellectual resources, serving as representative on committees and boards, conducting applied research (necessary for promotion and tenure at the university), and participating on university and departmental committees and other obligations. Serving two counties simultaneously is obviously even more challenging. The assignment is a huge challenge that is also very rewarding, especially when constituents' problems were resolved. I would have continued to serve and improve in this role, but a personal situation again intervened; my spouse relocating jobs from New York to Delaware.

In 2004, I relocated to Salem County in southern New Jersey, equidistant between the bridge to Delaware and the Rutgers Agricultural Research and Extension Center near Bridgeton, NJ, where I asked to be housed. My supervisors generously consented, though it left Passaic and Essex Counties without an Agricultural Agent for a period of time. However, I was not provided with any resources at all to re-start a program of research and extension; no budget, no staff, no space, no equipment. Only a paycheck and an office with an old desktop computer.

The new post started formally on January 1, 2005. I consulted with the County Agent network to gain a sense of what was needed, and how it fit with my training and capabilities. I also joined the staff of the Rutgers Food Innovation Center in Bridgeton, NJ as a Faculty Associate. During my time at DNAP working with raw material procurement and packaging of perishable commodities into value-added products, I gained an appreciation and some know-how in this area of economic opportunity. I was a good fit for RFIC since they needed insights about how to interact with the complexities of the university, School of Environmental and Biological Sciences, and the New Jersey Agricultural Experiment Station. I needed more ideas and a prospective team to move forward with to try to define the future of New Jersey agriculture: Highly profitable specialty, value-added food, phytopharmaceutical, and aesthetic products.

One project I assumed leadership of was the "Commercial Vegetable Production Recommendations", a compendium of science-based information to help farmers to make decisions in their operations and businesses. The product was originally in hard copy book form, and updated annually. The need for frequent updates was driven by the constant changes in regulation of agricultural chemicals, especially pesticides.

The CVPR book had its origins in the late 1950s when extension faculty and staff surmised the utility in summarizing and disseminating all the recommendations they were communicating to individual operators. A single source of the information reduced the need to repeat the same recommendations over and over. At first, the recommendations were comprised mostly of variety trial results and production practice field experiment results. Gradually, the publication changed to become the definitive local source of current information on farming practices subject to government regulations. The publication was and is used frequently in legal cases as the authority for acceptable practices pertaining to vegetable agriculture.

As individual states' CES organizations were challenged with the need for greater efficiency, the benefits of inter-state cooperation became more apparent in the 1970s and beyond. The CVPR publication is an excellent example of this trend. Over time, NJ joined together with PA, DE, MD, VA, and later WV to co-produce the annual revisions of CVPR. The collective expertise of the CES organizations of the six constituent states was invested into each production. Each state designed a custom cover, and reaped financial benefits from the sales of hard copies of the publication to farmers.

The revolution of information management technology overtook CVPR starting in about 2010. Since then, the information was posted on the internet in addition to the production of hard copies. Over time, the number of hard copies has greatly diminished while the dissemination of information by virtual means has blossomed. Progressive farmers receive up-to-date information on their smart phones and make decisions on the fly. But old timers still prefer the hard copy, on which they scribble copious notes on the adaptation of information for their purposes (and phone numbers, of course). Through all these changes, the intra- and inter-state association of CES faculty and staff has remained strong, even as production agriculture continues to lose technical FTE support.

Working with an old partner from DNAP, Dr. William Romig (a plant physiologist specializing in postharvest processes and disorders), we developed a new packaged asparagus spear product for a southern New Jersey asparagus grower (Sheppard Farms) that could be stored for up to three weeks under refrigeration and was microwavable for ease of preparation. Bill, Sheppard Farms, and I worked with RFIC to obtain funding from the USDA Rural Development Program to develop the product and underlying processes further. The product caught on, and is still marketed in "Trader Joe's" and "Whole Foods" stores in the northeastern U.S.

One potential area of need articulated by County Agents when I started working in southern New Jersey was tantamount to the re-establishment of the "Jersey Tomato" product concept. New Jersey has always enjoyed an excellent reputation for high quality fruits and vegetables, including sweet corn, peaches, blueberries, and especially tomatoes. Rutgers was constantly bombarded with laments about the demise of fresh tomatoes in New Jersey, due in part to the adoption of new varieties bred for ability to withstand the rigors of packaging and distribution, not necessarily for consumer quality and flavor perception. New Jersey's tomato industry shrank from over 25,000 to less than 3,000 acres from the 1950s to 2015. Most of the fresh tomatoes consumed in New Jersey were produced elsewhere (usually Florida or Mexico) and shipped as immature green fruits.

The Future of the U.S. Cooperative Extension Organization

There are a plethora of initiatives and suggestions aimed at the improvement of the AES/CES system. The system is huge, bureaucratic, and very expensive to maintain. There is no question that the system has struggled to keep up with changes in the industry, due to the differences between the public university and private business sectors. Most public universities make commitments of FTE to programmatic areas on a career basis, using academic tenure as part of the overall compensation package. These careers can often last for over 40 years, and changes inevitably occur that render certain skill sets obsolete. While it is possible to teach old dogs new tricks, old dogs are usually old dogs. As technology accelerates, this issue will become more intractable. Many academic institutions are making changes that are designed to instill more responsiveness to change and accountability to support resources. Academic tenure in AES/CES is on the decline.

In 2008, the U.S. congress mandated a new unit within USDA as part of the Farm Bill, the National Institute of Food and Agriculture (NIFA; Anon 2016). The charge of NIFA was and is as follows:

To collaborate with leading scientists, policymakers, experts, and educators in organizations throughout the world to find innovative solutions to the most pressing local and global problems. Scientific progress, made through discovery and application with emphasis on these areas:

- Advance the competitiveness of American agriculture;
- Bolster the U.S. economy;
- Enhance the safety of the nation's food supply;
- Improve the nutrition and well-being of American citizens;
- Sustain natural resources and the environment;
- Build energy independence;

Later, NIFA refined its approach to the upgrading of the U.S. agricultural economy with the following new paradigms (Anon 2014a):

- Translate science for practical application;
- Identify emerging research questions, find answers and encourage application of science and technology to improve agricultural, economic, and social conditions;
- Prepare people to break the cycle of poverty, encourage healthful lifestyles, and prepare youth for responsible adulthood;
- Provide rapid response regarding disasters and emergencies;
- Connect people to information and assistance available online through eXtension.org;

The main overarching issue that NIFA will grapple with, especially with regard to horticultural crops, is the growing demand of consumers for ornamental, food, and pharmaceutical crops that are produced using "sustainable" methods. The adaptation and regulation of the "organic" designation is outside of the scope of this chapter, but the steadily increasing demand for organic products is one facet of the overall national (and international) trend. Consumers are willing to pay more for agricultural products that they believe were produced using socially and environmentally responsible methods (Olson and Lyson 1998, Lyson 2004; Ikerd 2008). This includes local production to reduce the need for energy-intensive long-distance transport, t and also to support the local economy. "Socially and environmentally responsible" also includes the use of genetic variability as a pest management system, and avoidance of GMO varieties. Some organic producers even shun F_1 hybrid populations, though this distinction is generally quite arbitrary.

The impetus of organic and sustainable agriculture is perceived by many agricultural practitioners as lacking a scientific foundation (Batie and Swinton 1994). These new concepts are viewed with suspicion that there is a political agenda at work to gain more power over agriculture under the auspices of alleged environmental peril. Much of the support cited by organic and "sustainable" advocates has historically, been anecdotal, not scientific. AES/CES needs to engage in more and more credible on-farm demonstrations of the implementation of organic and/or sustainable technology to accelerate its adoption (Kranz et al. 2010). More and more, farmers will need to become entrepreneurs to adapt to the new agricultural order that will be progressively more consumer-driven (Muhammad et al. 2009; Zamudio et al. 2016). Despite the stereotype of the hopelessly entrenched farmer, studies have shown that necessity does breed a willingness to change (Goldberger and Buttel 2001)

Agriculture has traditionally been a life style that has transcended generations. Children grow up on farms and learn the trade from an early age. By the time, they are ready to take on adult responsibilities, they are already well trained and oriented to life and cash flow on the farm. Farming, however, has not been a historically lucrative career, and especially given the required labor input for success. Many sons and daughters of farms left the countryside for the cities during the 20th century to seek a more risk-free and better compensated alternatives. The trend seems to be slowing, as more and more young people are deciding that the independence and entrepreneurial opportunities of agriculture are more attractive than sitting in a cubicle and shuffling papers. One aspect of this trend is the growing tendency for women to pursue careers in agriculture (Barbercheck et al., 2009; Kiernan et al. 2012)

Once again, the U.S. federal government responded with a program to support this growing movement, termed "sustainable agriculture" by most. Ikerd (2008) does an excellent job summarizing the factors that evolved within U.S. agriculture and ultimately led to the formation of USDA/SARE. He also advocated a new direction in the mid-1990s that would have steered the AES/CES system more in the direction of a sustainable agriculture agenda, but the system resisted the proposal at the time. Despite the resistance, and a general undertow of agricultural conservatism, organic farming is making impressive inroads in the U.S. corn belt (Lockeretz et al. 1981).

The U.S. government approach to fomenting change is to shift tax dollars into an area of concern. Starting in 1988, $3.8 million was allocated to the infant SARE program administered by USDA (Anon 2014a). By 2008, this allocation had grown to $19 million, the majority, of which is disseminated to AES/CES in the form of competitive grants for the development of new technologies that fit this paradigm. Feenstra et al. (2016) produced an excellent overall treatise on the need for and development of support programs for sustainable agriculture. Factors identified for successful team building to integrate new organic farming concepts into traditional agriculture: The first five factors include shared values, balance in technical competence, institutional capacity for research, team capacity for problem solving and institutional resistance. The research team also identified three other factors that evoked confusion and divergence during the project, and include the ambiguity of power and control of knowledge, the proposed experimental plan and terms of team engagement (Barbercheck et al. 2012)

One ongoing problem with AES/CES is poor public awareness of the system and its benefits. There is probably more awareness of cooperative extension from the 1960s TV program "Green Acres" and the Hank Kimble County Agent character than all the marketing and promotional materials that AES/CES has produced over the past 60 years. And, of course, that perception was not very flattering. A recent study among a broad spectrum of Ohio residents revealed that only 20% were even aware of the existence of CES (Loibl et al. 2010).

There is a huge opportunity for the integration of information management technologies into agriculture. The most well developed example of this is in dairy, where many computer software packages have been developed to maximize the yield and quality of milk from herds (Rutherford 2000). Another example is the use of bioinformatics to manage weed populations, reducing dependency on herbicides (Colbach and Mãziãre 2013).

Another area where AES/CES has embraced change is in the identification and implementation of new "value-added" agricultural product or production concepts, particularly ethnic and specialty crop varieties. Newly patriated immigrants are clearly willing to pay premium prices for agricultural products that fit their ethnic culinary requirements (Govindasamy et al. 2010). Crop species that impart specific culinary and health benefits, such as the chile peppers, are associated with a growing cohort of enthusiasts that are also willing to pay more for products that are novel and put forth culinary or health benefits (Sammis et al. 2009).

I have been involved with one specific example of this trend. A group of Rutgers County Agricultural Agents and Specialists came together starting in the 1990s to address this perception and the possible opportunity it could present. The "Rediscovering the Jersey Tomato" project was born, and focused first on the re-introduction of a variety originally released in 1968, 'Ramapo'. NJAES Associate Director and Professor Jack Rabin played a key role in establishing the project, and getting new seeds of this variety produced in Israel. The variety was offered again to home gardeners in 2007 due to Jack's persistent efforts. From there on, it was more of a team effort. I maintained the inbred parent populations and arranged for ongoing seed increases of 'Ramapo' in Costa Rica, while Jack and Cindy Rovins (of the Rutgers NJAES Communications Department) addressed the packaging and distribution of seeds, and financial matters.

"Rediscovering the Jersey Tomato" really struck a chord with a broad swath of U.S. residents. These were primarily home gardeners who had one thing in common: they all had outstanding culinary experiences with fresh tomatoes brandished into their memories. What happened to the incredible flavor of summer tomatoes in America? Not only were the tomatoes of winter being harvested and shipped as green fruits, most of the summer products offered in supermarket chains were as well. The tomatoes sold at roadside stands were mostly of varieties adapted more for the gassed-green system. It was clear that a huge latent demand exists for ripe-red tomato fruits bursting with flavor.

Cindy championed the expansion of the "Rediscovering the Jersey Tomato" offerings to include two other high-flavor varieties from the mid-20th century: 'KC-146' and 'Moreton'. The former was a Campbell Soup flavor standard from the 1950s, and the latter was developed in the mid-Atlantic U.S. region, including testing in New Jersey. Jack learned that Campbell Soup had retained the original parent populations that were used in the development of another important variety, 'Rutgers'. He proceeded to acquire seeds and transplants of these parents, and our colleagues at Campbell Soup proposed that they be used to develop a new version of this variety. This prospect was compelling because the original 'Rutgers' had lost it's identity. No "foundation" population was retained and perpetuated by Rutgers University, and commercially available seed lots from different seed companies all perform differently; mostly at an unacceptable level.

Cindy, Peter Nitzsche (Agricultural Agent in Morris County and Rutgers faculty member), and I started this project, the development of a new version of 'Rutgers', in 2011. Traditional breeding methods were used, like the original strategy, that was published in a 1934 paper by Rutgers Professor Lyman Schermerhorn. We followed the same protocol in general, but added new criteria for the targeted finished variety, including smaller, more determinate growth habit, earlier maturation, higher yield, resistance to contemporary diseases, and, especially, high flavor and high consumer preference.

By summer 2014, it was evident that some of the selections substantially exceeded the parents and the hybrid between them with regard to yield, fruit quality, and fruit flavor. In fact, the flavor rivaled that of the high-flavor standards we had used in variety trials. But the controls were all F_1 hybrid varieties, while the new selected breeding lines were "open-pollinated" (OP), like the original 'Rutgers'. In fact, virtually all contemporary tomato varieties are F_1 hybrids; while traditional "heirloom" varieties like 'Brandywine', 'Mortgage Lifter', 'JTD',

'Globe', 'Marvel', 'Pritchard', 'Mister Stripy', and 'Box Car Willie' are OPs. F_1 hybrid tomato varieties are generally regarded as higher-yielding, more resilient, and more disease-resistant than OP varieties, but this paradigm is not absolute.

A larger team was formed in 2015 to test the panel of selections in the field and consumer tastings, and to nominate one to be named the new 'Rutgers'. This team consisted of the original core plus an additional group of Rutgers County Agents, independent county-based Master Gardener organizations, a group of the original (and subsequently retired) Campbell Soup colleagues and mid/small commercial growers engaged in direct marketing. A competitive Partnership Grant was obtained from the USDA/NESARE (Sustainable Agriculture Research and Education) program to plan and execute a statewide system of field trials, ultimately numbering seven that spanned the length of New Jersey. Additionally, seven public tomato tasting events were conducted in venues all over the state, such as county fairs, extension twilight grower meetings, farm-based open events, and one in a community college cafeteria.

After all the field performance data and taste-test results were analyzed and summarized, a meeting of the composite team was held in early November 2015 to decide on a path forward. The outcome was that one of the candidate breeding lines was deemed to stand out from the others, especially in regard to flavor and consumer preference, and this population was nominated to be named the 'New Rutgers'. This was later changed to 'Rutgers 250' in consideration of the 250th anniversary of Rutgers University, celebrated from 2015-2016.

The next step was to produce seeds of 'Rutgers 250' and get it into the hands of home gardeners and small commercial growers in New Jersey and the mid-Atlantic U.S. Using very primitive methods and mechanical aids, and working within the confines of the breeding program, about 2.0 pounds of seeds of the new variety were produced. These seeds were also processed and cleaned within Rutgers University, then sent to operatives within the planting seed industry for packaging. For various reasons, it was necessary to package many of the seed lots by hand, using available and generous staff from the Rutgers Plant Diagnostic Laboratory. Both commercial packages (for transplant nurseries) and small consumer packages were distributed. The product was promoted by the 'Rutgers 250' support team, led by Anna Molinsky, of the New Jersey Agricultural Experiment Station. Everything sold out for 2016 by March 1. As this is written, reports of the excellent performance of this new variety across the U.S. are filtering in, and it appears that the project has been a great success. But it would not have been possible if not for the willingness of people in different roles working together in concert.

In another example: Currently, I am involved with a very challenging collaborative effort aimed at the development of new "exotic" pepper (*Capsicum* sp.) based products in the food and food-pharma industries. Another Rutgers University faculty member (Dr. Albert Ayeni) and myself started the program in late 2009 with the acquisition of a unique cache of *Capsicum* germplasm that exhibited characteristics we deemed to be of high commercial potential. From the start, we struggled with resources, and progress was slow. From 2010-2013, we selected the populations from the original germplasm cache that had the highest potential. Since then, an active breeding component supported by very advanced physiological screening techniques has been added. Another faculty member (Dr. James Simon) joined the team, and the program was funded by the New Jersey Agricultural Experiment Station with hopes that new releases would be forthcoming. Examples of new pepper-based products include smooth red and tangerine jalapeno and poblano types that have high overall flavor impact (sugar/acid/volatiles) but moderate pungency (capsaicins); high-yielding habernero types that have high levels of beneficial carotenoid pigments; and new plant architectures that reduce growing and harvesting costs of all varieties.

The rigors of meeting other obligations, difficulties in maintaining regular communications, inadequate resources, and physical distances among program participants have all been challenges to this collaboration. The project has lacked a strong leadership component, and a consistent vision has been difficult to establish. The difficulties encountered are instructive of the challenges faced in the forging of an effective and successful collaboration. Many of the basic tenets of a successful collaboration have been strained, a factor that is very common in the establishment and shepherding of projects. Humans are human, not machines. Everybody has strengths and weaknesses, and it is impossible to meld people into something perfect.

First and foremost, the vision for the exotic pepper project is very broad and obtuse. "Specialty peppers that impart added value to consumers" is not specific enough to enable leadership to build a collaboration that is accountable. The vision has been driven mostly by opportunity, not uncommon in the world of academia where the realm of possibilities is endless. Each new discovery is also a new product opportunity. Over time, the vision evolved from yellow bird eye to mild jalapeno and finally to habernero pepper fruits with interesting shapes, colors, and nutritional attributes. It wasn't clear to team members exactly what the vision, goals, objectives have been at all times, although there is a general level of excitement for all the nascent products that have been imagined.

Secondly, the team has lacked effective leadership. Ultimately, the three faculty members working on the project have taken on leadership roles at different times and in different ways. One has mostly been charged with the vision, another with the garnering and management of financial resources, and the third collaborator overseeing much of the process and technology. Still, we enjoy working together, and despite meetings to try to resolve the path forward and a better leadership structure, we continue with the same dysfunction.

Finally, rewards are not shared equitably. This is also a common problem in academia, where some faculty members are more adept at garnering resources and delegating work responsibilities than others. On the exotic pepper team, there are two faculty investigators who contribute ideas, skills, and field work and a third faculty member who is the resource getter and user, and contributes specific information to the project (fruit nutritional composition). At times, this has led to friction as all components of the team strive to keep up, but resources (financial and human) are not distributed equitably across the project.

Despite these imbalances that would not be tolerated in the private sector, we muddle forward and are making generally good progress. The progress isn't always easy to quantify and qualify because the elements of success are mutable. The team is successful because we recognize and appreciate the factors that weaken the effort, but still have a strong desire for the project to be successful. We respect and believe in each other, and have a fundamentally unshakable foundation of team success, even if we don't always agree on where the project is going.

For example: Working with an old partner from DNAP, Dr. William Romig (a plant physiologist specializing in postharvest processes and disorders), we developed a new packaged asparagus spear product for a southern New Jersey asparagus grower (Sheppard Farms) that could be stored for up to three weeks under refrigeration and was microwavable for ease of preparation. Bill, Sheppard Farms, and I worked with RFIC to obtain funding from the USDA Rural Development Program to develop the product and underlying processes further. The product caught on, and is still marketed in "Trader Joe's" and "Whole Foods" stores in the northeastern U.S.

Postscript

Hollywood produces many stories about the power of individuals to make a difference in an increasingly complex and interdependent world. The individual is indeed the fundamental driving force in our world. It is increasingly more difficult for an individual to forge impacts that affect the longevity and quality of life that we all ultimately strive for. The world our ancestors lived in has poetic appeal, but people also died young of malnutrition and horrible diseases. Science and collaborating organizations have made incredible improvements to the human existence over the past 200 years. It is incumbent on our leaders to foster policies and programs that encourage individual excellence but also the collaboration of excellence to continue this tradition of life enhancement.

Even a born loner can participate effectively in a world where collaboration is essential to make progress on health and quality of life. It all starts with mutual respect and an appreciation for the strength that an organization derives from diversity.

Literature Cited

Anonymous, 2014a. Extension: Past, Present, and Future. Archived at: https://nifa.usda.gov/extension

Anonymous, 2014b. History of SARE. Archived at: http://www.sare.org/About-SARE/Historical-Timeline.

Anonymous, 2016. NIFA Factsheet. Archived at: https://nifa.usda.gov/resource/nifa-factsheet.

Anonymous, 2017. The U.S. Economy: A Brief History. In: Outline of the U.S. Economy, Chapter 3, U.S. Department of State, archived at: https://usa.usembassy.de/etexts/oecon/chap3.htm

Auburn, J. S. and Baker, B. P. 1992. Re-Integrating Agricultural Research. American Journal of Alternative Agriculture 7(3):105-110.

Barbercheck, M., Brasier, M. J., Kiernan, N. E., Sachs, C., Trauger, A., Findeis, J., Stone, A., Moist, L. S. 2009. Meeting the Extension Needs of Women Farmers: A Perspective from Pennsylvania. J. Extension 47(3).

Barbercheck, M., Kiernan, N. E., Hulting, A. G., Duiker, S., and Hyde, J. 2012. Meeting the multi-requirements in organic agriculture research: Successes, challenges and recommendations for multifunctional, multidisciplinary, participatory projects. Renewable Agric. And Food Sys. 27.2:93-106.

Batie, S. B., and Swinton, S. M. 1994. Institutional issues and strategies for sustainable agriculture: View from within the land-grant university. Amer. J. Alt. Agric. 9(1-2):23-27

Colbach, N. and Māziāre, D. 2013. Using a sensitivity analysis of a weed dynamics model to develop sustainable cropping systems. I. Annual interactions between crop management techniques and biophysical field state variables. J. Agric. Sci. 151(2):229-245

Crowell, L. 2012. No-till Farming Critical for Preventing Loss of Soil Moisture During Drought Conditions. USDA/NRCS Fact Sheet archived at: https://www.nrcs.usda.gov/wps/portal/nrcs/detail/ia/home/?cid=nrcs142p2_011847

Feenstra, G., Ingels, C., Campbell, D. Chaney, D., George, M. R., and Bradford, E. 2016. What is sustainable agriculture? UC Sustainable Agriculture Research and Education Program, archived at: www.asi.ucdavis.edu/programs/sarep

Galvez, L., Douds, D., Wagoner, P. 2001. Tillage and farming system affect AM fungus populations, mycorrhizal formation, and nutrient uptake by winter wheat in a high-P soil. Amer. J. Alt. Agric. 16(4): 152-160.

Goldberger, J R and Buttel, F H. J. 2001. Sustainable agriculture research and the land-grant system: a replication. J. Sustainable Agric. 18.2-3.: 91-104.

Govindasamy, R., VanVranken, R., Sciarappa, W., Puduri, V. S., Pappas, K., Simon, J. E., Mangan, F., Lamberts, M., and McAvoy, G. 2010. Ethnic Crop Opportunities for Growers on the East Coast: A Demand Assessment. J. Extension 48(6)

Ikerd, John, 2008. "The Agricultural Extension System and the New American Farmer: The Opportunities Have Never Been Greater", Prepared for presentation at the 2008 National Association of County Agriculture Agents Conference, Greensboro, NC, July 17, 2008, archived at: http://web.missouri.edu/~ikerdj/papers/Greensboro%20--%20Extension%20New%20American%20Farmer.htm

Jones, G. E., and Garforth, C. 2013. The history, development, and future of agricultural extension. In: *Improving Agricultural Extension: A Reference Manual*, Food and Agriculture Organization, Natural

Resource Management and Environment Department. Archived at: http://www.fao.org/docrep/w5830e/w5830e03.htm

Kiernan, N. E. Barbercheck, M., Brasier, K. J., Sachs, C., and Terman, A. R. 2012. Women Farmers: Pulling Up Their Own Educational Boot Straps with Extension. J. Extension 50(5).

Kranz, N. K., Piercy, F., Donaldson, J., Westbrook, J., and Richard, R. 2010. Farmer, agent, and specialist perspectives on preferences for learning among today's farmers. J. Extension 48(3).

Lockeretz, W., G. Shearer, and D.H. Kohl . 1981. Organic farming in the corn belt. Science 211:540–547.

Loibl, C., Diekmann, F., and Batte, M. T. 2010. Does the general public know the Extension Service? A survey of Ohio residents. J. Extension 48(2).

Lyson, T. A. 2004. *Civic Agriculture: Reconnecting Farm, Food, and Community.* Tufts Publ. 160 pp.

Muhammad, S., Isikhuemhen, O. S., and Basarir, A. 2009. Promoting alternative enterprises: Assessing farmers' needs in research, education, and extension. J. Extension 47(6)

Olson, R. K. and Lyson, T. A. 1998. Under the Blade: The Conversion of Agricultural Landscapes. Westview Press, 488 pp.

Rutherford, J. D. Jr. 2000. Comparing dairy herd management software. Penn State Cooperative Extension Farm Management Report, archived at: http://cdp.wisc.edu/pdf/DHMrpt.pdf.

Sammis, T. W., Shukla, M. K., Mexal, J. G., Bosland, P. W., and Daugherty, L. A. 2009. Improving the chile industry of New Mexico through industry, Agriculture Experiment Station, and

Cooperative Extension Service Collaboration: A case study. J. Extension 47(1)

Schonbeck, M. 2015. What is "Organic No-till," and Is It Practical? eXtension 07.15.2015 archived at: http://articles.extension.org/pages/18526/what-is-organic-no-till-and-is-it-practical

Zamudio, J., Mars, M. M., and Torres, R. M. 2016. Learning among southern Arizona small-scale farmers and ranchers. J. Extension 54(2)

CHAPTER 12

Pathways to Collaboration

The Illusion of Collaboration

Amanda Perrin
Organizational Development and
Talent Management Consultant

Collaboration is a powerful word. There is something about it that automatically conjures up the vision of hand-holding down a path towards a brightness on a horizon: a common objective. You're surrounded by swirling pastel colors and soothing tones in a meter and a melody that bring hopefulness and confidence. Your steps align with those around you, as you confidently stride towards the light, the successful outcome. Rivalries, politics and cultural differences magically fall away and teams join hands to work selflessly towards a common goal.

If the above description sounds more like a fairy tale than actual projects you have worked on, then congratulations, you live in the real world. In reality pathways to collaboration are latticed with difficulty, littered with buried boards and rusty nails of pride, tradition, ego, competition, culture, fear and other symptoms of misalignment. The very term "collaboration" is part of the problem. When a team invokes a mantra of "working together" it cloaks the group in a noble mantle that can be a smokescreen for dysfunction. "Collaboration" evokes images of millennials lounging in a coffee shop, effortlessly aligning on innovative strategies to Change the World. Pervasive as this image is, it is very far from the truth that mature companies face when confronted with the need to collaborate and innovate. Collaborating within a living mature organism has a higher degree of difficulty than a scrappy young startup venture. People in mature companies frequently walk into the room with albatrosses of biases that simply must be addressed if they ever hope to achieve a truly collaborative effort. And unfortunately, having a collective goal is not enough. Collaboration, to be successful, must start with alignment.

    I learned firsthand about the Illusion of Collaboration during my years at The New York Stock Exchange. The atmospheric conditions at NYSE Euronext created an optical illusion of collaboration. The catchphrase "working collaboratively" served as a compass for action, but without real alignment to a well-defined strategy, the direction the company was headed in was doomed.

    The New York Stock Exchange is synonymous with American capitalism. Watch any financial news report and odds are at some point in the program they will show the iconic façade of the NYSE, or perhaps a shot of the busy trading floor. Ask the average American investor where US equities trade, and the majority will reflexively answer "The NYSE". While a powerful symbol, the reality is that in 2016 the New York Stock exchange is largely just that; a symbol. Once a powerful monopoly that literally controlled the exchange of capital in the United States, over time this monopoly position eroded. Due to the powerful forces of regulation and technology, the NYSE now represents a fraction of US equity trading volume each day.

    As the core business of trading stocks eroded, so did the financial position of the company. This rapid and obvious evaporation of the core business inspired management to do the only thing they could do to save the organization: Innovate to rebuild profitability. This furious attempt at reinvention brought on a fierce and frenzied period of collaboration in a race against the close to save not only the company, but an American institution. As a witness to this period of hyper collaboration, I had a front row seat to the good, the bad and the ugly of what happens when a mature company collaborates in the face of extinction.

It is important to understand the history of the New York Stock Exchange in order to examine the challenges it faced building a collaborative, integrated company. The NYSE was founded not long after the Revolution in 1792 when a group of 24 stockbrokers signed The Buttonwood agreement, named for a buttonwood tree that stood on Wall Street. For nearly two hundred years, the Exchange was a member owned monopoly. All US equities were required to be traded on the floor of the NYSE by a "specialist", a designated market maker for a given stock responsible for posting active markets. As a monopoly, these specialists set their prices and set their own margins, known as "bid/ask spread", which was essentially a toll that every investor had to pay to buy or sell stock. It was, in short, a license to print money that heavily favored the profitability of the specialist over the interests of investors.

In the early 1970's the Nasdaq came along, a new electronic-only trading platform that relied on computers rather than a trading floor to buy and sell stock. The competition and efficiency of a transparent, electronic market was welcome by investors and the monopoly in US stock trading became a duopoly. While this new competition did lower costs for investors, the NYSE retained many rules designed to protect its own profitability. Over time investors grew increasingly frustrated with the NYSE over unfair rules and high transaction costs to the point where in 2005 the SEC passed "Reg NMS", which created a "best execution" requirement for all US equity trading. Reg NMS was designed to increase competition by creating a level playing field where stock quotes had to be posted simultaneously on every exchange and trading platform. The rule was designed to break the NYSE/Nasdaq duopoly, and it was wildly successful.

2005 was also the dawn of the electronic trading revolution, where computers replaced humans in high speed transactions that both increased transaction speeds and radically reduced trading costs. With new technology and new regulation, dozens of new low-cost exchanges were launched. Instead of competing only against NASDAQ, the NYSE now had to compete against many low cost electronic platforms. All the rules designed to protect their market share were eliminated. And as the competition slashed fees, the NYSE was faced with plummeting market share on its remaining business. It was against this dire backdrop that the organization started to rapidly change and reinvent itself to compete.

In 2006, the New York Stock Exchange merged with an electronic trading exchange based in Chicago called Archipelago Holdings, creating NYSE Group, a publicly traded company. In 2007, NYSE Group bought TransactTools Inc., a messaging infrastructure software solution company. In 2007, NYSE Group also merged with Euronext, a European stock exchange, which operated exchanges in Paris, Lisbon, Brussels, Amsterdam, and a derivatives exchange, in London, creating the world's largest global exchange group: NYSE Euronext. In 2008, NYSE Euronext acquired the CME's gold and silver futures exchange, giving the company an entry point to the U.S. Futures industry. In 2008 they also acquired Wombat, a market-leading data management solutions company, further supporting their ambitions in the commercial technology space. In 2009, they acquired NYFIX, a provider of electronic trading services. Under this new organization, emerged three distinct and vastly different business lines: Derivatives, Cash and Listings, and Technologies. It should come as no surprise that in 2009, under new leadership, within this setting of plummeting market share and the erosion of NYSE's core business, in this loosely stitched together patchwork of companies, geographies and products, came the BIG push for innovation and collaboration.

To say this was an intense period is an understatement. Most companies can collaborate at a measured pace; NYSE Euronext did not have that luxury. When the merger with Euronext was announced, an air horn had been blown and teams charged forward, in different directions. The company was manic about ushering in change because the future of the organization depended on its ability to innovate. Very few of these changes were slowly staged. New leaders were transitioned in, and with them came promising new initiatives. The company started to frantically diversify and pursue costly business activities such as re-vamping the trading floor, converging technology platforms and infrastructure, and building state of the art data centers in New Jersey and Basildon, London, without adequately considering how customers would respond.

Furthermore, many of these projects were heralded as "game-changers" and carried the promise of creating new markets and solving NYSE's problems in its existing markets. As a matter of fact, any one of these initiatives, if successful, could have been a game-changer, but they weren't successful enough in time.

If the old NYSE was blissfully unaware of the possibility of extinction, the new NYSE was not. NYSE Euronext c-suite did not suffer from complacency, they were very aware of the dangers of failing and were determined in their pursuit to innovate. As such, there was an impulse to rush to collaborate. And though they set out to build a collaborative organization, they neglected to fully appreciate that the framework and environment was not conducive for it: 5 different cultures, 5 different geographies, 5 different regulatory environments, a strikingly new commercial business line, cults of personality supporting different leaders, some managers passionate about leading a Renaissance while others were just as passionate about preserving tradition, virtual teams, groupthink, social distance, teams that were geographically and culturally dispersed, silos and business lines each fighting for resources and recognition. The challenges to collaborate were escalating, all the while the message from the top was the same: Hurry up, get together, there's no time to disagree. We need to innovate!

There was a resounding chorus from senior leaders saying that the company was facing it's most exciting and challenging time yet. Dramatic tension was mounting and there was a feverishness about the possibility that with the many mergers and acquisitions, the company was assembling an arsenal of resources to enhance their global position. Mistakenly, many efforts were stamped "collaborative" because they were captained by cross-cultural and multi-disciplined teams. Some businesses had "co-heads" giving the impression of a coalition, when in actuality they were just two rivals jockeying for better position. Culturally, the definition of collaboration meant different things to different people. The flurry of business activities deemed collaborative made people feel purposeful and virtuous, but this brand of false collaboration was very misleading. Employees were operating in an environment without real alignment and cloaking business initiatives in "team-work" and "cooperation" was steering them to believe their efforts were adding real value.

As the competitive market intensified, NYSE Euronext tried to adapt using disruptive measures by expanding globally and undertaking a myriad of acquisitions that changed its technology, strategy and infrastructure. The company was fragmented and the business strategy driving these changes was exhaustive and misunderstood. To offset this the CEO put in a concerted effort to increase communication and transparency around business activities, developing a bi-annual leadership forum with 100 of the top leaders in the organization, and broadcasting a monthly newsletter that gave staff a clear rundown of what was happening globally. This however, was not enough to get the entire global team pulling in the same direction or focused on the same desired outcome. After two years, the gap between expectation and reward was widening to the point that leadership hit pause to examine the resistance to progress. The top brass at NYSE Euronext had grown tired of cutting through the jungle with a butter knife. Gaining alignment among the senior leaders of the company was finally made a top priority.

In 2009 NYSE Euronext developed a program to produce alignment among leaders and clarify what must be done to succeed, using people, process, resources, inputs and enablers. It actively drew participants from all countries and across all functions. This was an opportunity for them to learn from one another, bridge teams and strengthen relationships. It gave people time and space to step away from their immediate business issues to come face-to-face with the hard facts: the company had been frantically trying to collaborate and innovate without proper alignment, in multiple environments with competing and incompatible agendas. Through this program and a willingness on the part of leaders to commit to change, cooperation among senior leaders was achieved, and the program was productive and successful in unearthing the sad truth that few leaders felt connected to the global corporate strategy, and fewer could even articulate it themselves. Though the company was neither advancing nor falling back, it was abundantly clear that they needed to change the factors impeding progress.

Once this realization had been made, the view was that if alignment was formed at the top, to a strategy that could be realized, and if the people at the top made a commitment to cascade that strategy and connect teams to a unified purpose, the company might be able to salvage a future. Management styles started to adapt to a multicultural environment, communication style and discourse began to shift in a more sensitive way, a well-articulated strategy, was developed and great effort was made to cascade that strategy through all levels of the company. Small communities of dialogue were set so that leaders could tap into internal wellsprings for feedback on business activities, mentoring circles were formed where leaders met with employees from different divisions to understand business challenges better. The strategy team held roundtable discussions where staff could engage in discourse about where the company was going and why. Client and Employee surveys were conducted to take the pulse of the environment, and dashboards were drafted and managed to keep a transparent record of objectives and progress.

Even rewards and recognition programs were implemented to acknowledge and celebrate collaborative achievements. These programs encouraged employees to find value in unexpected places and rewarded individuals that partnered effectively and drove the bottom line. A corporate-wide engagement campaign called "It Happens Here" fortified team spirit and engagement by featuring standout performances of teams. The Human Resources and Marketing Departments teamed up to carry out the campaign to publicize accomplishments, put them in writing, award them, spread the word across the company, and arrange for featured teams to present their results to NYSE Euronext senior management. Photos of teams were placed along the buildings serpentine corridors. Spaces that hadn't been used before were being colored by familiar faces of employees demonstrating partnership and collaboration. "It Happens Here" showcased what the company valued, celebrated victories publicly through various physical and electronic mediums and personalized the work that employees were doing.

Furthermore, a "Global Recognition Award Program" was instituted and it consisted of two tiers: Recognition Awards and Thank You Notes. The Recognition Awards celebrated the outstanding achievement of an employee who had gone above and beyond his or her usual responsibilities with regards to Innovating with Purpose, Collaborating Productively, Engaging Clients, Thinking Broadly, or making a Valiant Effort. The Thank You Notes were sent electronically and allowed for employees to formally thank, record and show appreciation for an employee's contribution.

In addition to the engagement campaign and the rewards program, the company prioritized the development of top talent and individuals that had been identified as "high-potential". Top talent and emerging talent was selected from each country and from various divisions. The program was one of the most meaningful acts of recognition in that it illustrated that the organization was invested in supporting and improving teams, and showed that the company cared about building careers as well as the business. Developing leaders, encouraging their professional development, and presenting them with advancement opportunities were just some of the ways NYSE Euronext was augmenting employee recognition and reward.

Through this period of collaboration and change, trust had formed between business functions, between leaders and staff, and employee satisfaction ratings were at their peak. The problem was that many of these developments came too late: the hull had broken off the ship well before these progressive measures had been realized. Before long, the stock price had begun to plummet and NYSE Euronext was bought by ICE Intercontinental Exchange at $33.12 per share, a quarter of what it was worth at its peak.

If this testimony is a lesson in anything, it is this: Do not get doe-eyed about collaboration. Collaborating within a living mature company is very difficult and the path to collaboration will not be paved, guarded or well lit. Should the pathway to collaboration appear to be facile, be wary of the mirage. Here are four rules to avoiding the illusion of collaboration:

1. Collaboration, to have value, must have a specific purpose, strategy, commitment from key parties and alignment.
2. Don't rush to collaborate before you have alignment. Without alignment collaboration is a wasted effort. Alignment should

be anchored to a strategy that is formed jointly and it should have commitment from key parties. You will not be successful if you try to collaborate in a vacuum.
3. Desperation and urgency are the enemies of collaboration. Collaboration is a capability that takes time to develop; you can't rush through it and it is very hard to do under duress. It takes time to foster common understandings and group synergies. A hurried attempt to collaborate will result in mistakes, frustration and burnout.
4. Collaboration is the art of compromising around ideas and the degree of difficulty goes up with cultural and geographic differences. And sometimes no matter how much work you put in to cooperate, the environment may work against you.

Success is not a forgone conclusion with collaboration but it is essential, especially for mature companies faced with changing markets, clients and technology. If you are blind to the illusion of collaboration, you will be seduced by it. If you go into it eyes wide open, you will guard yourself against the illusion and your odds of success will dramatically increase.

CHAPTER 13

Collaboration and Mentorship

John E Peters
Emeritus Professor Department of Biology
McHenry County College

As I review my career in science I recognize that much of my personal success was a result of collaboration and superior mentorship. I will share some of my own experiences with collaboration to show how I benefited from working so closely with a variety of students and professionals.

Undergraduate Education

Like many new college students, I entered Otterbein College with a vague idea of what career I wanted to pursue. I thought that I might like to be a high school biology teacher. I had received a significant scholarship from the theater department with an emphasis on technical theater (set design and lighting), so I tried to double major in biology and theater. I was successful with this during my freshman year, but began to struggle in my sophomore year. Near the end of my second year, the four faculty members of the Biology Department met with each biology major to review their academic plan. At this meeting, one of them asked me where I had been hiding. She said she was impressed with my performance in class, but knew little about me before this meeting. As a result of this meeting, I was offered a work study position as a laboratory assistant. I was now entering my first collaboration. Although a significant part of this job was cleaning glassware, I also learned to prepare reagents and media and to have all supplies ready for laboratory classes. I was entrusted with keys so I had access to the department laboratories in the evening and on weekends. I was able to demonstrate that I was a responsible laboratory assistant. Later in my academic career as an educator, I was able to offer students the same opportunity in our college biology department. As students left our campus to continue their education, I recommended that they approach faculty at their new school to assist in their laboratory and demonstrate their skills and work ethic. At the end of my junior year at Otterbein College, I was offered the opportunity to do a senior research project. I could choose the topic I wanted to study and would be able to purchase up to $2000 of supplies to support the project. At the start of my senior year, I presented my proposal to a faculty committee for approval. Faculty members were available for consultation and the laboratory resources were opened for my use. The college library supported access to journal articles for my literature review and helped me submit requests for photocopies and reprints. Although this project could not be correctly described as "research", it was a great opportunity for my learning. I wanted to study the chromosomes of a specific strain of fruit flies. This required writing letters to a laboratory that was using the flies and having them mail me flies for my research. I studied the change of chromosome shape stimulated by an insect hormone. Through the year-long project I learned advanced microscopy skills including microphotography and micromanipulation using an instrument with glass needles that worked under the objective of the microscope. I also learned photography skills including film development and printing. The project prepared me for research that I would perform upon my entry into graduate school the following year.

Graduate school – Master's Degree

During my freshman year of undergraduate school, I was offered a full scholarship from the Air Force Reserve Officer Training (ROTC) program at Otterbein College. Accepting this, I incurred a 4-year commitment to enter the Air Force upon graduation. I requested a delay to pursue my Master's degree prior to active duty. Even though the Vietnam War was still ongoing, I was granted the delay and was accepted in Dr. Rod Sharp's laboratory at The Ohio State University. Rod immediately made me aware of the collaborative nature of our relationship as advisor/student when he asked me to call him by his first name since we were now colleagues. The laboratory worked as a team with all members aware of each other's research and assisting each other in literature reviews and experimental techniques and procedures. Rod encouraged me to invite prior professors including some of my undergraduate school professors to review our research and critique our work and to become co-authors on published papers. It was a way of showing respect for their mentorship and payback for the developmental role they played in my education.

As I finished my Master's degree in 1973, Rod invited me to join in a collaboration that he had developed with Otto Crocomo at the Center for Nuclear Energy in Agriculture (CENA) in Piracicaba, Brazil. I will leave it to Rod to tell the story of this important and productive collaboration. For me, it was an opportunity to be a part of research project that was well-supported with technicians and laboratory facilities. The research was some of the initial study of using plant tissue culture to develop superior varieties of the bean, *Phaseolus vulgaris*, a food staple in Brazil. Rod and I were primarily engaged in experimental design, initiating cultures and data analysis. Because we had significant technician assistance, we were able to initiate over 3000 plant cultures and analyze data during the four months that we were there. This resulted in multiple papers over the next few years detailing our findings. The collaboration between Rod, The Ohio State University, and Brazil, has continued and grown over 45 years.

The Air Force Years

I entered the Air Force as an officer in 1973 following completion of my Master's degree. Initially, I was assigned to a position working with radar. Early in my AF career, I began pursuing opportunities in other career fields that would better utilize my education. I was successful in cross-training to the clinical laboratory field and completed an internship to become certified as a medical technologist. As the officer-in-charge of various hospital laboratories, I worked closely with health care professionals to provide further studies and data reviews for presentation of case studies and publish papers about our findings. Early in my career, the Air Force Base veterinarian asked if I could culture a newly discovered bacterium that was causing premature death in puppies and kittens. Most media required to grow bacteria could be commercially acquired or the constituents of the media could be purchased for preparation in the laboratory. The required medium was not commercially available and one constituent, horse blood, was not available either. When I explained this problem to the veterinarian, he told me that this was not a problem since as the base veterinarian, he provided care for horses in the base stables and we could obtain blood there. I learned how phlebotomy was performed on a horse. I made the medium and we were diagnosing cases of this bacterial infection in humans and animals within a week. As one of the first military hospitals to grow this bacterium species, I was able to present findings and methodology to other military hospitals at the annual meeting of military clinical laboratory scientists.

In 1982 I was invited to become a Biology Department faculty member at The United States Air Force Academy in Colorado Springs, Colorado. In my previous academic environments as a student, I had been the recipient of collaboration initiated by faculty and my new teaching position permitted me to return the favor to cadets at the Academy. Much like my undergraduate experience, I sponsored two students doing senior research projects. Both of their projects were presented at the annual meetings of the Southwestern and Rocky Mountain Division of the American Association for the Advancement of Science. One of the papers was recognized as the outstanding presentation by a student at the conference. The projects introduced the students to the laboratory, experimental design and organization to complete a project and present findings. Both of the cadets became career Air Force officers as medical doctors. One of my favorite anecdotes from this experience demonstrates the practical knowledge gained doing senior research. Both of these cadets were extremely bright and carried high grade point averages throughout their undergraduate experience. The Air Force Academy requires all graduates to complete a core education in calculus, physics, and engineering. One day in the lab, I asked them to dilute a 25% solution to a 15% solution. They both told me that they had no idea how to do this. The undergraduate research problem helped transform them from "book" smart to "practical application" smart. As a part of this collaboration with cadets, I was also recognized with an Air Force Research and Development award.

The Air Force recognized the importance of advanced education for officers and sponsored individuals to pursue graduate education while on active duty. I applied for sponsorship to obtain my Ph.D. and was selected for this program in 1987. The sponsorship permitted me to pursue a Ph.D. at an institution of my choice. I was given a three-year period to obtain my degree with no chance of extension. I would have to return to an operational assignment at the end of the three-year period. I received my normal salary, a book allowance, and all tuition and fees paid by the Air Force. I chose a school and program to attend and was invited to interview for admission into their graduate program. During the interview, the director of the program that interested me said that he could not permit a student to complete a Ph.D. in only three years. I believed that I could complete in this time since I already had a Master's degree and would be a full-time student with no teaching responsibilities. He argued that it would take me a year to learn the instrumentation in the lab. I replied that I was familiar with most of the instrumentation, since I used it in the clinical laboratory that I had managed and had repaired most of the analyzers. I appreciated his honesty that he would not grant a Ph.D. for three years of work and inquired elsewhere.

I called my Master's degree advisor, Rod Sharp, to ask for an introduction to the Microbiology Department at The Ohio State University. Rod called Dr. Robert Pfister, a former colleague at Ohio State who remembered me. Dr. Pfister believed that he had the perfect fit for me with Dr. Darrell Galloway's lab. Darrell was about my age and a military officer in the Navy Reserve. We approached our collaboration as a contract where my effort and accomplishments could result in a Ph.D. within the three-year timeframe. Within a year and a half, I discovered a new enzyme that enhanced the ability of certain bacteria to invade human tissue (flesh-eating bacteria) and we had published our findings in a leading scientific journal. Darrell was invited to write a monograph about our research for a scientific journal and he obtained a $250,000 grant to continue the research. At the end of the three-year period, I received my Ph.D. and returned to the Air Force to direct the largest clinical microbiology laboratory in the Air Force. This collaboration was the result of a combination of superior mentorship by Darrell, my strong work ethic, and combined intellectual skills working together.

In August 1994, I became the director of the Microbiology Branch of Wilford Hall Medical Center (WHMC) at Lackland Air Force Base. San Antonio, Texas. This was the largest hospital in the Air Force with approximately 1000 beds. Air Force members and dependents were transferred to this hospital from bases from all over the world. It was also a primary reference lab for specimens from other Air Force bases. We had 25 laboratory technologists and performed many of the most sophisticated procedures in clinical microbiology including bacteriology, parasitology, virology and mycology. Most of the technologists had more clinical microbiology experience than I did and were some of the best in the country. I respected their knowledge and empowered them to make efficient decisions in workload management. Due to high workload, restrained budgets and restricted manpower allotments, efficiency and cost-effectiveness was paramount to our success.

During this time, I was invited to become a member of inspection teams for the College of American Pathologists. This was a national laboratory certification agency which validated the performance of medical laboratories around the country. I inspected a laboratory directed by Dr. James Musser, a leading investigator of pathogenic streptococcal infections, including flesh-eating strep. Within a few months of inspecting his lab, we had an outbreak of strep infections on Lackland Air Force base. A newly enlisted Air Force trainee died due to the flesh-eating strep during his 7-week basic training. He lived in a barracks building housing 800 other trainees. We immediately did throat cultures on all trainees living in the building and isolated numerous positive strep throat cultures. I contacted Dr. Musser to see if he could do DNA studies on the positive cultures to see any were the same isolate that had killed the trainee. He agreed to do the testing and we found between 10-15 isolates which were identical. The positive individuals did not even report a sore throat, but all were treated with antibiotics and the outbreak was contained. This incident led to interesting epidemiological study collaboration between our lab and Dr. Musser's lab.

We decided to perform throat cultures on over 10,000 basic trainees during a four-month period. A throat culture was obtained during the trainee's second day of basic training and then a second culture was obtained on the same trainee during their last day of training for a total of over 20,000 cultures. All positive strep throat cultures obtained from the trainee clinic were also kept. Only trainees with positive throat cultures isolated from a clinic visit were treated with antibiotics. Trainees with positive isolates from the start and finish of training were not treated with antibiotics or notified of positive cultures. We found that the incidence of positive strep throat cultures at the start of training was the same for male and female trainees at the start of training at approximately 2.0%. At the end of training, incidence in males increased to 4.3%, but female incidence only increased to 2.9%. We then determined that the increase in males was probably due to sharing sinks and commodes to avoid having to clean them for daily inspection. We also found that many individuals who had positive cultures when they on the second day of training were still positive at the end of training with no apparent problem. When a trainee had a positive culture obtained as a result of a visit to the clinic, there was a significant chance that the other trainees who slept in the same barracks would also visit the clinic with sore throat symptoms and positive cultures.

The study yielded at total of 675 strep isolates which were all saved for further analysis. Dr. Musser inquired about the possibility of doing further studies on the isolates. He had a graduate student who wanted to perform DNA studies on the isolates to find if there were certain strains of the bacteria that were more virulent than others. Two DNA types were identified that accounted for 70% of all positive cultures isolated in the clinic. These isolates appeared to have an enhanced ability to disseminate and cause disease in the trainee population. There were multiple other isolates carried by trainees that did not appear to cause disease. In this collaboration, we had the ability to conduct a controlled population study and obtain isolates that could be analyzed by sophisticated DNA analysis at another lab.

College Teaching – A Second Career

In 1994 I retired from the Air Force and began a second 20-year career as a community college faculty member teaching microbiology and introductory biology for biology and health career majors. Very early in my undergraduate education, I realized that I had a goal of teaching. Initially, I thought this would be at the high school level, but before I graduated from college, I knew my preference was to teach at the college level. Although my Air Force career delayed my entry into college teaching, my experience as an Air Force Academy faculty member reinforced my goal. I believe that mentorship and collaboration are strongly linked. As a student, my professors offered me opportunities to work for them, and with them, for my personal benefit and to benefit their program or research. Until the biology faculty at Otterbein College reached out to me, I was floundering in my undergraduate education.

I accepted a full-time faculty position at McHenry County College, a community college in north east Illinois. Many of the students that I had in my introductory biology course were 30 to 40-year-old women who had been unsuccessful or uninterested in pursuing a college degree following high school. They had raised children to a point where they could begin to pursue a degree in nursing or some other area of allied health. Most were extremely apprehensive due to their earlier lack of success in education. I assured them that we would work together and they would have their degree within a few years. My experience as a graduate included a full Air Force scholarship, working part-time for spending money, and living in a dormitory with no family responsibilities. My students were often using student loans to attend college and working to support a family. In the very first class meeting, I emphasized the collaborative nature of their education. Our college had mandatory "office hours" where I would publish my availability for their assistance. They had a responsibility to immediately communicate personal conflicts with me so we could make accommodations. Surprisingly, I never felt that students abused this arrangement. I also told my class that they could stop me at any time during instruction and ask me why the information that I was passing was important to them. My "real world" education in the clinical laboratory, enabled me to relate case studies that I had seen and that I thought that they would also be meaningful. The digital age has confirmed the usefulness of this approach as several of my former students have provided me feedback of cases that they have experienced that they remembered from my class.

My college offered independent study projects for student credit. Students could perform research or study a topic in more detail under the direction of a faculty member. This program received a boost with the STEM (Science, Technology, Engineering, and Mathematics) initiatives. Now, all students were invited to participate in faculty-directed research and present their work at regional community college science fairs. Like my senior research project, this provided these students with experiences in experimental design, self-discipline in completing a project in a defined time, and tremendous self-esteem. My personal gratification with combining collaboration with mentorship came to fruition when I was a patient in our local hospital for minor back surgery. In my single overnight stay, I had seven former students providing for my care. I had complete confidence in their capability, skills, and knowledge.

Conclusion

Collaboration implies a symbiotic relationship where participants all benefit by working together, but I view myself as more of a "recipient" of successful collaboration than an "initiator" or "provider" of it. As a student, I believe I gained the most from the experience. My professors gave me opportunity, financing, and knowledge. I only had to give a willingness and effort to learn. As an educator, I think I was able to give a little bit of this back. Many of my collaborations were symbiotic where we each brought talents and financing to our mutual benefit. Perhaps the only limitation to successful collaboration is the vision to recognize the opportunities where all collaborators gain. As a retired senior, I look back on my experiences with collaboration with great appreciation and gratitude.

CHAPTER 14

A Study of College and Departmental Interactions at a Large Land Grant University

Robert M. Pfister
Patrick R. Dugan
Emeritus Professors Department of Microbiology
The Ohio State University

Introduction

The evolution of cooperative ventures has long been an important aspect of the human species. One factor that has separated humans from other animals is the ability to cooperate to solve problems.

History shows, perhaps with the exception of a few such as Einstein, that many of man's significant achievements have required cooperative efforts among selected groups. The advances in medicine, space research and energy are just a few examples. This chapter encompasses several important aspects of cooperative work at The Ohio State University within the present authors' experience. Understanding of the role of administration in the process and the agreement among faculty and administrators to carry out the research to a productive finish. The second important factor is that administrators within the college understand the difficulties of their particular job in providing a comfortable and productive environment. The reader should be aware that the Ohio State University is a very large comprehensive University involving education and research and involving baccalaureate, graduate, masters, PhD, postdoctoral education and research. There is also involvement with extension services and continuing education. A number of examples of the types of problems that may be encountered within any complicated program are cited.

As an example of a major successful cooperation, we can examine the question of what was involved in putting a man on the moon. The National Aeronautics and Space Administration (NASA) was given a mission to accomplish this feat by the President of the United States. It required the cooperation of many different industries plus engineers and scientists from all over the world. The overall guiding principle here was that there was total committed support from the federal government at the top level. This opens a door and a question which must be examined at any university or other cooperating or cooperative institutions or organizations.

An individual faculty member can start a research program, request financial support, recruit graduate students, and work on a cooperative program in their own small organization. In a very real sense, the faculty member who has the program represents the president and government, and the graduate students, and working technicians represent the committed employees or hired staff of the organization. This can be controlled completely by the senior researcher at the top. We are saying that this represents a mechanism similar to what the Congress and/or the US. President would do. If a given aspect of the research wasn't needed, congress simply wouldn't fund it. This is no different than telling your organization in the laboratory that they cannot have a new "spectrophotometer" or essential hardware.

The chapter examines many of the questions that would require answers before any large cooperative venture can be accomplished. We cite examples of the difficulties in a free market, free university approach to solving a problem.

The following chapter will show that a cooperative venture at the university level may be more difficult than imagined because of the freedom of activity and speech inherent in the university. These difficulties should not discourage any attempts at cooperative ventures among universities, but we point out that certain factors must be seriously considered in order to obtain positive cooperative result.

A Recent Cooperative Venture at The Ohio State University.

The title of a new program at OSU is "Discovery Themes". More than 60 new researchers have been hired. The following comments are quoted from an article in the Columbus Dispatch on Sunday, June 5, 2016, from an article by Mary Megan Edwards, titled "OSU Jumps On Big Ideas Research".

The article discusses the Ohio State University's involvement in establishing a huge research hiring campaign which will involve many to be hired in various fields including biomedical, material science and anthropology. At this point, the university is only about one third of the way through the planned "Discovery Themes" hiring. There are searches for 81 more positions that will add up to about 19 million dollars in annual salary and benefits which will be paid with the discovery themes funding as well as individual department budgets.

There are other universities announcing similar programs. All universities proclaim the benefits of interdisciplinary work and that scientists from different fields combining their expertise will tackle complex problems. While this clearly understands that cooperative ventures are an important way to achieve success in penetrating "new" fields of science, the article also points out the many difficulties that will be required to be solved. The final paragraph in the article states "Technical solutions alone don't solve these problems, solutions have to involve humans—understanding how they behave and interact." It may seem to some that universities may be placing a wedge between sectors (faculty) within the university that teach and do research and those hired to do only research.

Evaluation of Collaborative Scientific Programs at a Large Land Grant University

This chapter will attempt to explain our thoughts regarding the administration, education and application at the Ohio State University.

It turns out, because the Ohio State University is both a land-grant college which became a very large university, there are many respective sub-topics to be considered. Included is an "Addendum" description of how land-grant colleges came into existence. We suspect that most faculty and some administrators do not realize the benefits, constraints and requirements that were established under the Land-Grant designation.

We carefully explain our approach here because the administration of such a large land-grant university is very different than the administration of a small private college or University. In this chapter a former Dean will explain his position with regard to occurrences that happened within the college and a former chairman will describe in detail the activity that is required to operate and administer a large academic, science department as compared for example, to a language or art department. The word science is important here because a department that requires different laboratory facilities, and analytical equipment along with technical and functional use of the laboratories, is different than that observed in a department that is less scientific (technological) in origin.

Governance of a large scientific organization in an educational institution requires that their administrators also simultaneously maintain their high level of academic instructional and research duties in addition to their administrative responsibilities. We emphasize that this is difficult to accomplish in an academic scientific research setting.

To properly administer an academic science department or college and simultaneously run an active research program is counterintuitive. It is necessary for the chairperson to represent the faculty to the administration and required that the faculty understand that the administration does control certain aspects of faculty life. In essence a chairman walks a tight line between faculty who expect he or she to represent their interests and the central administration who expects the department chairman to represent the interests of the University as well as to maintain an active research reputation.

This document presents explanation of some time consuming and unanticipated situations (circumstances) that, in retrospect, one may expect to be involved in when accepting an academic chair or dean position. The reader will see, in general, the decision to accept the position of leadership of a department, is generally made in ignorance of what is required for that position.

This section will go through, in some detail, events which could in no way have been anticipated prior to accepting the position. We feel the explanation of these activities will be helpful to anyone who thinks they may want to accept an administrative position at any academic institution. There always will be a few individuals who are so scientifically well-known that they can bring with them an entourage of assistants to carry out their research. Unless you have that kind of support, to do that alone is a very onerous task.

As noted in a subsequent section on the explanation of the land-grant college, the assumption is that the university or college will provide a good education in both the liberal arts and sciences as well as topics devoted to "land- grant" activities such as farming, engineering, etc. Difficulties arise in a huge institution because people are hired to operate in one type of educational arena and may not recognize or appreciate what the function of the land-grant college really is.

The Land Grant Institution

The enclosed addendum is an explanation of just how land-grant institutions came into being and what is expected of them. The comparison, in this case, of The Ohio State University as a land-grant institution with institutions in either other countries or other venues in the United States, is important. We do not know the historical background of most other institutions or the complex legislation required to form them. This is true with regard, to institutions in the United States as well as Institutions around the world. It is important to recognize what may happen to an institution based upon the requirements set by the government or governing body including those from private institutions and their missions. It is clear that to make such comparisons is not a simple task. We speak now from very personal experiences and can state that when the job of administration was offered, nowhere was there any explanation of what the total amount and involvement of complexities would be. We feel that to make comparisons among various universities is desirable but that it is also recommended that the other organizations understand the involvement and complexities of their working environment, with an understanding that any organization will have internal competition with other departments or colleges relative to politics within their particular university and perhaps even politics outside their university. These are all present prevailing human conflicts.

The College (Biological Sciences) was formed by transferring and consolidating various components from established academic departments from various colleges throughout the university, i.e. Agriculture, Arts and Sciences, Dentistry, Engineering, Medicine, Nursing, Optometry, and Veterinary Medicine. The purpose was to infuse the fundamental and application approaches to science. Simultaneously, similar approaches were undertaken to form a College of Mathematical and Physical Sciences and other colleges.

Comparison among Administrative Functions and Maintenance of an Active Scientific Research Program

At a major teaching and research institution such as the Ohio State University, it is expected that both teaching and original research opportunities will be provided to its students at the various academic levels: undergraduate, graduate and post-doctoral. Such institutions, therefore, require a faculty (capability) in fundamental instructional techniques as well as expertise with modern experimental research methods, techniques and procedures, in addition to available laboratory facilities that include modern research and analytical equipment. It is understood that in the scientific, engineering and other technical disciplines both the technical instructional capacity as well as the laboratory capabilities are significantly more involved and costly than is the case with many non-technical disciplines.

Research can be defined simply as "seeking solutions or answers to questions for which there are presently no known solutions or answers", hence the need for libraries, laboratories and access to the Internet. For the various technical fields, appropriate laboratories are required in addition to classrooms and support for the maintenance of appropriate analytical equipment. For example, an appropriate laboratory for investigations in many environmental, engineering, and medical problems require availability of relatively large outdoor scale field facilities; whereas in the fields of chemistry, entomology, geology, microbiology, molecular biology, physics, etc. require well-equipped indoor laboratories and some sub- disciplines may require both indoor laboratories and outdoor field laboratories.

At, The Ohio State University, the top administrative academic position is the president who has separate vice presidents (VP) for administration and a provost who is a VP for academic affairs. The administrative VP has several assistants who have a variety of administrative offices. The Provost has several Deans who each have individual colleges e.g. arts and sciences, engineering, medicine, dentistry, business, etc. Academic departments within each college have departmental chairpersons responsible for their respective academic topics and their faculty within their aegis. It is relatively common to have faculty with joint appointments in more than one department or college. However, administrative decisions and complex arrangements affecting individual faculty members (e.g. salary, shared teaching assignments, etc.) usually reside with the chairperson of the academic faculty member's primary department.

Ranking of active faculty positions include: instructor, assistant professor, associate professor, and professor. Upon retirement, the title emeritus may be attached to the rank held at the time of retirement. Any administrative title held in addition to a faculty title is normally removed upon retirement.

Recruitment of faculty and administrative staff at the department level is generally conducted by the appropriate department in that college usually with the aid and recommendation of faculty search committees in those departments or college offices. Any recommendation to hire is then forwarded to the Provost and employment is at the university administrative level. In the case of teaching assistants (GTA's) and graduate research assistants (GRAs) assigned to appropriate instructional lecture courses and specialized graduate research programs, assignments are made upon the agreement and recommendation by the faculty member responsible for a specialized course or who heads a particular specialized research project (usually the student's thesis or dissertation advisor).

The use of committees to recommend recruitment and possible appointment of new faculty as well as admission of new graduate students deserves greater emphasis and explanation.

Some observed conflicts and comparisons

We make the assumption that the hierarch of most college or universities prefer to appoint established, highly recognized science scholars, either from within or outside the University, to administer individual departments or other technical programs within the University. The following observations are offered. In the situation where the administrator/scientist is appointed to a specific term, e.g. four years, that appointee is very likely to calculate the new potential administrative time commitment, compared to the time required to maintain his or her status as an outstanding national or international research scientist with the knowledge that being out of the loop of publishable scientific research information for 2 to 4 years is a distinct scientific career retardant within the academic scientific community because the "publish or perish" criterion is utilized almost universally. That leaves the academic research scientist who devoted "too" much time to his or her administrative responsibilities during a four-year appointment with almost no other academic choice than to seek to continue further administrative positions.

A non-scientist appointed to oversee or administer a highly technical program rarely has the background necessary to comprehend or maintain the organization in high esteem. The following two examples may help clarify the above contention.

During a large group discussion concerning the potential funding of a highly technical potential research program, the topic of "scientific laws of nature" was being discussed when a non-scientist administrator interjected, "well, that is nonsense, we make the rule/laws and will just have to change those rules/laws". Perhaps he succeeded in getting apples to move from the ground back up into the tree branches but the project proposal was scuttled and not funded.

Another group at another time had spent considerable effort to bring together a committee of 10 faculty scientists from various departments and backgrounds to cooperate on a proposal to fund a program involving microbial animal diseases. One of the senior members of the committee had contacted a representative from a large British bank, who had expressed an interest in potentially funding such a project, and joined the group. The University administration had sent a non-scientific-technical administrator, who late in the discussion proceeded to actually dictate to the group and the banking representative just how and under what circumstances any funding was to be handled. The banking representative later indicated that he had never been involved with any demands like this before. The group was disbanded and any further consideration ceased. There was no consideration of how we might proceed in a cooperative manner and virtually all other discussion ceased. Aside from safety issues or serious ethical concerns, an administrator should take the cooperative position, "How can my office help". Unfortunately, in this case, the non-scientist administrator who insisted that the committee adhere to his procedures without any prior knowledge or understanding of a potential cooperative project, succeeded in alienating 10 senior faculty, including two deans and a banking representative.

There are relatively few educational institutions of the size equal to the Ohio State University. Most institutions are much smaller. For example, it is very difficult, if not impossible, to compare a school that has 3000 students with a large institution such as OSU, having 50 or 60,000 students (see Addendum).

The Department of Microbiology, which will be discussed in this document, was part of the College of Biological sciences now the College of Liberal arts. The microbiology department had or may have 3000 students per year just taking basic microbiology.

Many departments in smaller institutions may have five or six faculty while the microbiology department at OSU had 16 to 18 faculty members with all the attendant problems.

Delving into the challenges that are going to occur at a greater rate in a large department will be of interest for any perspective academic manager. It will also impinge upon any collaborative efforts and academic agreements.

We believe that many jobs that are taken, are done so in innocence with the lack of understanding of involvements and responsibilities. We hope this chapter will open the door to understanding a few of the many variables of this type of academic enterprise. I hope the reader will understand that we have enjoyed our working at the Ohio State University and enjoyed, in great detail, our jobs. We have no complaints or misgivings about the facts that surround these activities. One of the problems in the College of Biological Sciences was that faculty expected the Dean of the college to be a leader in the field of research. These are wonderful and high-level thoughts which are not so easy to carry out. The administration of the University is expecting the Dean and other administrators such as chairman to carry out and enforce the wishes of the upper level administrators. There are not enough hours in the day to carry out a research program heading up graduate students and doing research and following the dictates and requirements of the upper administration. Faculty expect leadership at the college level, and leadership at the departmental level. While it certainly was somewhat easier as a chairman to maintain some research activity, it was also nearly impossible to devote the time required to perform these duties in a satisfactory way. If the job was ignored and the faculty was let to drift on its own, then of course the chairman would just be another faculty member carrying out research. That certainly could be done and has been done by many departmental administrators. But if an administrator is going to respond to the needs of the department and its members this becomes a "very hard to satisfy" situation.

One of the difficulties in having an administrator who is in the biological sciences is that the shepherding of graduate students is nearly a full-time job. When a new student arrives, there is great discussion about what the student might do for a research program. When agreements are made, the mentor cannot simply turn loose an inexperienced student who may have just left undergraduate school and expect that student to be fully aware of all the existing difficulties in a research program. Both chapter authors have found that there must be a great deal of personal contact with young scientists to help steer them toward the completion of a research program that may be meaningful. Certainly, at the doctorate level it is required that the students carry out individual "original" research that has not been done by any other person. A department in an academic environment lives or dies on the completion of not only teaching programs but on the education of active scientists who will go into the world and carry out meaningful original work.

When you have a department that is very large, and is expected to educate many undergraduate students most of whom must take laboratory courses, there is a serious requirement for help to carry out all of the laboratory exercises that are required to educate a student in such a field.

The following sections in this chapter relate to personal experiences among the chairperson, faculty, graduate students and the public and are presented in first person singular. These few vignettes represent only a fraction of very time consuming non-predictable commitments that any administrator would not anticipate.

The Department

There are situations in some universities, particularly in Europe, where a chairman leads a department in a given direction and will find support for the research that goes on in that department. In large research oriented universities that I'm familiar with in this country, the faculty are responsible for generating their own research and getting it supported. Any institution will always say that teaching comes first, and the research mission of the department second.

I was very naïve when I accepted the position of chairman because having been a faculty member for seven years and at the rank of full professor, I should have had a better understanding of the complexities of an administrative position in an academic institution. I did not. I saw it only from the perspective of a faculty member.

I took over a department that had moved into a more modern approach to science, which was certainly in agreement with what the rest of major universities and science departments were doing. The previous department chairman worked very hard to establish the department of microbiology as a modern research oriented department. When I became head of the department, I was committed to carrying on these measures so that our department would rank higher in overall success.

The department of microbiology consisted of 18 faculty members with approximately 80 graduate students. Some students had not yet had an agreement with their mentor or even any idea what they would like to pursue for research. The departmental mission was to ensure that each graduate student would become involved in a research program and obtain an MS, PhD or both in as short a time as possible. In addition, we had the responsibility to make sure that a large number of undergraduate students successfully completed our course offerings toward their degrees.

Our department originated in a liberal arts college and was responsible for the instruction of large numbers of students interested in nursing, dentistry, medicine, and other fields.

The Complexities of Teaching and Internal Politics

I was appointed chairman of the department after the Dean's interaction with the faculty and the administration. I suspect that the election or hiring of a chairman at any major university is always a difficult task. I speak from a number of years of experience in having watched the process in action. The appointment of a department chairperson is the responsibility of the Dean and the upper administration. The process is far more complex than that. Each faculty member would like to have a say in who the next chairman will be; therefore, in general, the Dean will meet with the faculty of a given department and try to come to a consensus or at the very least let each faculty member have his or her say.

The stories or vignettes that are presented here are all based on actual occurrences during a 12-year period in the department of microbiology. These stories will be presented through the eyes of the former Chair and former Dean of the College.

Many faculty, when they join a department, generally feel somewhat isolated and try to exert influence in obtaining (hiring) colleagues that work in similar areas of their interest. This does not always work to their advantage. Most young faculty are aggressive in their opinions and research desires and will put forth a significant effort to enhance their research programs. In actuality, in major institutions, even though teaching is revered by some, many young faculty members would prefer to do research. Actually, that's not a surprise because after all a doctorate is a research degree and that's why they obtained it. It's also true that their success and promotion is heavily weighted on their research papers published.

Teaching will have a role but it's more difficult to evaluate. There have been many arguments at the time of promotional consideration among tenured faculty as to who should or should not be promoted.

Let me insert, at this point, a situation that occurred in the department. We had the opportunity to accept a faculty member from another department who was a tenured professor and interested in biophysics. The department that he had been in was changing its structure and he felt uncomfortable and was willing to move into microbiology. His approach to his job was somewhat old-fashioned, and he believed that the University should support his research without him having to attempt to get any financial support for it. I talked to him many times and encouraged him to write a grant proposal to support his research. He was well known, had published numerous papers, and considered by some to be a leader in his field. He simply refused to cooperate and attempt to get any funding. The department, of course, did not teach biophysics so he eventually was assigned to teach general biology. This was not to his liking but he had to accept the assignment. He started teaching a class that had several hundred students in it and began explaining modern biophysics. As one would expect, students just out of high school and taking a biology course did not respond well. It was said that the Dean's office had the longest line of complaining students that had ever been seen at the University. The unhappiness of a student is certainly the best way to remove a particular faculty member from the job that he's doing and of course in this case, they were successful. It was a very difficult job to fit him into any of the department's mission. He was unhappy with the department and the department was not particularly thrilled with his performance. He was a tenured professor and there was little that we could do about it.

The naïveté that I experienced as a new chairman was intensified by the desire to do a good job and to carry on the mission of the department. We handled the instruction of a large number of undergraduates who were heading into nursing, dentistry, food microbiology and other areas. The funding for this teaching came from the administration, based on the number of students (both undergraduate and graduate) in the department. A department that was handling hundreds of undergraduate and graduate students during the year would expect to get more funding for the support of their academic program.

Faculty who obtained grants from the United States National Science Foundation and other recognized organizations felt that their support of the department was based upon the acquisition of those funds. Some faculty resented the fact that the University took a percentage of those grants as overhead and expected each of the grantees to participate in a small measure of support for the given programs that the department was involved in. Over the years some faculty members who had engendered support through either national organizations or industry complain bitterly that the University was taking their money, and they deserved to spend all of it in the way they wanted. The spending of the money, excluding overhead, was not controlled by the University. The regulation of that spending generally came by the productivity of that grant research resulting information in the form of publications and perhaps even graduate degrees awarded. This was controlled by the grant holder. Some faculty would mentor graduate students in their program by totally directing their line of research which may be questionable because a doctorate is supposed to be original research generated by the individual receiving the degree. The difficult line that many graduate students have to walk is that they have to satisfy the desires and needs of a mentoring faculty member and produce results which will not only give them their degree but satisfy the needs of his or her research program. Faculty appointments at OSU could be either 9 or 12 month appointments.

With some exceptions, the faculty resented teaching assignments or any adjustment in their teaching schedule. It was the chairman's absolute requirement to support the courses that the department administered and that meant providing teaching faculty as well as graduate assistants to help run the laboratories. Occasionally a faculty member who obtained a grant and could support a graduate student did not want that student involved in teaching but rather involved in his or her research program. This could represent difficulty in funding the teaching program. A faculty member who had a successful course and engendered a large number of students wishing to take that course would also require additional graduate student teaching help. Most all courses in microbiology required laboratory experience. There was a dichotomy in an active department between faculty who considered themselves primarily researchers and faculty who were generally doing the bulk of the teaching. The chairman and the dean of the college representing all academic interests walk a very fine line between those faculty types. What usually happened was that faculty who could not get financial support ended up doing more teaching than faculty who could get grants. Their argument being that they received a large amount of money to do research and don't have the time to teach, versus the requirement of the subject matter that they are presently working on and the need to teach it. No one recognized this dichotomy of effort and interest more than both the chairman and the dean of the college. Frequently Deans of colleges have come up through the ranks, not necessarily at the institution that they are working at, but certainly through faculty ranks, perhaps up through the chairmanship and they understand full well the programs and problems involved with this type of administration.

The Old School Approach

At many institutions in the past, faculty did not have to have a PhD degree but were able to work their way into positions of lecturer, assistant, associate, and professor through job experience. That does not usually happen anymore. In most cases a doctorate is required to obtain a teaching job at a major institution. The doctorate indicates that they are capable of doing research but says nothing about their desire, interest or ability to do any teaching. The department chairperson finds himself or herself in between a faculty that may enjoy a small amount of teaching but will argue the requirement of research and the needs of the department.

We recognize that some of these problems may only occur in a type of department where laboratory instruction is part of the teaching mission. It really doesn't matter whether a faculty member lectures to 10 people or 500. He or she is going to give the same instruction regardless of the size of the class. Lecturing is not the issue. The issue is administering a number of laboratories during the day that requires expertise and supervision over graduate assistants who frequently are not totally knowledgeable. We could also say that working with graduate students in the laboratory is also teaching at a higher level.

The historic establishment of the academic ranks of lecturer or instructor, assistant professor, associate professor, and full professor and the combined evaluation of the job effort at each level, based upon academic performance of teaching, research, and student involvement has brought about a great deal of concern among the qualified faculty. The argument goes somewhat like this, "I'm teaching more students in the university than most of the faculty", or "I have a very large research program, a great deal of financial support and simply have to administer that effort", so "I can't possibly involve myself in a heavy teaching load".

The promotion of an individual from one rank to the next involved the decision of the faculty at ranks above the level of the individual being considered.

In this chapter, we will present a number of circumstances and events that took place during the time of our tenure in the College of Biological Sciences. These descriptions are based on evidence that guided the department of microbiology in the direction the faculty wanted to go. Suffice it to say in real terms, the faculty certainly wanted the department of microbiology and college to be successful. The vignettes that are presented will have occurred during approximately 15 years of departmental administration. These vignettes will be presented through the eyes of the Chairman and Dean.

Chairing a Department

One of the surprising results of having accepted the chairmanship was that it became a responsibility to assist faculty with many of their endeavors. This turned out to be very interesting and one of the most complex parts of the job. One morning in late summer, the Dean called me down to his office and said, "We have a new graduate student waiting over at the Provost's office so I suggest we go and pick her up". I asked, "Who might that be?" He said, "There's a lady, Ms. Pong from Thailand who says she's our graduate student and needs to be introduced to our departmental activities."

We met with the lady, who spoke English, and very politely questioned her about her graduate program desires and helped her plan a program. Our department always had a reputation of interacting well with minority students and students from foreign countries. She had previously corresponded with a faculty member who was no longer at the University. As a rule, the department (Graduate Committee) would accept a graduate student and then during a relatively short period of time try to get him or her placed in a particular laboratory. The normal procedure for a faculty member was to meet with a potential student and decide whether that student would fit into his or her program. It goes without saying that the faculty member has the desire, and some ability to support that student, so it becomes a very interesting, sometimes tenuous and difficult, to place a particular student in a faculty member's laboratory.

To have a faculty member accept a new student, both the student and faculty member should negotiate and agree with the program. One of the ever present difficulties that a department chairman and Dean must face is the concern that the graduate student will be supported. Each fiscal year the college was awarded a discrete number of dollars for the support of its programs. The Dean would then distribute these funds among the various departments and other units in the college. The total number of dollars included money not only for the support of the department's faculty salaries but for staff and students as well. So at the beginning of the academic fiscal year each department was allocated money for its total program. A faculty member who had been awarded a grant from a national supporting organization or from industry could opt to take on a new graduate student or technician specifically for the support of that program. A student who finds him or herself partway through the program with a faculty member who has been supporting him or with a technician that wants to join the graduate program, but having lost his grant now is in a quandary. For example, how does that student get supported to finish their program? The department accepted this graduate student and had a responsibility to see that that student had every opportunity to complete his or her degree. The department finds itself walking a very tight line as to the needs of the teaching aspects of the department and the needs of an individual student or an individual faculty member.

Unknown at the time was that the young woman from Thailand actually came from a very prominent and politically important family in that country. What her family really wanted was her to join our department and complete her graduate education. It was soon recognized that she would return to Thailand at the completion of her degree. We fondly called her "Ping-Pong". As it eventually turned out, she was a delight to have in the department and interacted well with other students and faculty. In the final analysis, we were all glad that she came and was part of our department programs.

There was a tremendous conflict of interest in our (and I'm sure in most) academic departments concerning the needs of individual faculty and their desires to be promoted, awarded tenure and carry on the research and the needs of the department, college and university. These conflicts of interest will become clear as this chapter develops.

There was a similar experience with a Korean student who had been accepted a number of years earlier, declined to come, but requested delays for his admission. He arrived on the scene unable to speak or write English but with a legitimate acceptance to our department. Eventually we learned that he had been a soldier in Korea but never learned to speak English. A friend helped him fill out the paperwork and write the letters for his admission. It turned out he worked in environmental microbiology. His first year he took remedial English and eventually completed his degree and went to a university in California on a post doctorate.

Another student from Hong Kong spoke excellent English and I was very encouraged that he had an interest in environmental microbiology. It is interesting to note that he was a trained geologist who had worked for a mining company for a number of years in California prospecting for gold. I came to learn that during the first Spring that he was in my laboratory because he came and asked the question was it possible for him to work for the mining company in the summer and earn some extra money. They had offered him a summer position because he had a very good reputation and ability in finding gold. As it turned out, this young man was a gold mine in his own right. He was extremely bright, worked very hard and quickly made himself a valuable part of our laboratory. He completed his doctoral program and took a position with the U.S. Army in Utah as an expert in working with micro particulates. He is now internationally known as one of the leaders of the field in dealing with substances that can be converted to micro particulates.

Some Complexities of Staffing a Science Department

The appointment of a new faculty member in an academic science department is not as easy as it may sound. The department has many missions to carry out including not only research components of various faculty but the establishment of the academic teaching program in order to qualify as a valid educational institution capable of graduating competent students. Faculty who are aggressively interested in pursuing their line of research sometimes feel isolated because the department needs to carry out various educational components of the science. Thus, it is not surprising that various faculty will push for a new faculty position in an area of specialization that may be related to their personal interests.

When the faculty met to discuss the needs of the department, the meeting, supervised by the department chairman, usually operated under "Robert's" rules. The decision to look for a new faculty member was guided by the availability of a position and a coalition of faculty who authorized the chairman to form a search committee. The search committee would be led by an appointed chairman. After considerable discussion, the usual procedure is that three candidates will be selected for further consideration. The logistics, invitations, and planning ends up in the department's hands. Remember that the department has a number of missions to carry out, including not only research but the teaching of specific courses for the departmental success. A few senior faculty members generally host any new candidate. This generally includes not only meeting the college officials, but giving the candidate a tour of the University and city. This procedure is probably no different than recruiting any senior official in any business. When the selection of the candidate was complete and that person had accepted the position, his family's arrival in the city became a problem for the department chairman. For example, the department chairman housed several families for as long as three weeks while they searched for appropriate living space and established themselves in Columbus Ohio. In retrospect, this generally turned out to be a thankless job. Our recommendation for any of you who find yourself in that position is to let the department accept the expense and delegate the sometimes difficult logistics involved.

The department must provide an appropriate space for the new faculty member. This has been known to step on a few faculty toes because space is a limiting factor and there are situations where sharing has to be done.

1. A Good Student May Need Some Prodding
One day late in the summer, a senior colleague approached requesting help with a problem. He had an excellent graduate student who had received his Master's degree. The student wanted to go on with his education, but did not want to continue in the same line of research. The question was "Could I possibly take him as a graduate student and help him complete a doctorate"? I interviewed the student who I found to be very interesting and devoted to education, but not wanting to leave the comfort and security of the graduate school. He was a person who always got the best grades, was well respected by his fellow students and simply needed to be guided to

a satisfactory research goal. He was very active in university functions and became the chairman of the University Wide Graduate Student Committee. He was an only child who came from a northern state and wanted to remain in this local region. He developed great skills with local people in the area who employed him to take care of their homes when they were away. He became a live-in caretaker of several very beautiful estates and was really not anxious to complete his doctorate degree.

At that time, I had grant support which required the hiring of a technician to complete the work. The research grant pertained to the translocation of mercury in the environment using microorganisms examining what effect the microbial populations of the soil had on the movement of mercury through the soil. Mercury is highly toxic and has been a concern in both aquatic and terrestrial environments. I offered this graduate student (GSX) a position as a graduate research assistant. We developed an excellent working relationship and GSX did a very good job in carrying out the research. The result of this effort was ultimately published and was presented at professional meetings. GSX worked for several years and passed his general exams for his doctorate. I asked him when he wanted to finish and get into the real world. He responded by saying he really didn't know what kind of problem he would like to develop to do his research. I looked him squarely in the eye and said, "What you've been working on with me for the past two years is a problem which is of PhD quality. Why not just write it up, and you can use it for your dissertation?" Surprisingly, he had not considered that and was encouraged with my proposition at that time. In any event, he did write his dissertation, graduated and eventually accepted a job at a hospital in Akron Ohio running a medical testing facility. He eventually moved into the academic world teaching microbiology at Bloomsburg University in Pennsylvania and became its Provost. This is an example of the kind of situation that a faculty member may get into and even though I was a bit devious with him, I think it worked out well because I believe he benefited greatly by what we had done. After his retirement, he left a large amount of money to the Ohio State University.

2. Midnight Requisitioning

This next section relates to a common problem in any social group. Anyone involved in the military certainly recognizes the phrase "midnight requisitioning". In our department this consisted of graduate students who needed laboratory equipment that they knew was located in someone else's laboratory, or at some other location in the department. They knew it was someone else's equipment but they requisitioned it for their own laboratory needs.

On more than one occasion, I was involved, as chairman, to adjudicate the distribution of property (belonging to the University), that faculty considered their own, because it had been placed in their laboratory at some time. I recognized that the research they were doing required this equipment and it was essential for the completion of their research. It was difficult to explain to another faculty member that had been relieved of his laboratory equipment sometime during the night by an unknown assailant. In some cases, it eventually became known as to who the marauder was, so there were bad feelings among various faculty members but no immediate act of retribution on the surface. It was similar to the phenomenon in baseball of knocking back a batter at the plate at which time later in the game there was retribution by the opposing side.

Frequently the department was required to replace missing equipment that was known to have been purloined into another area. This had to be done in such a way that various faculty egos were not trampled upon. I will say it was a balancing act which really had no financial winners but only a departmental (financial) loser. There's another point of view that can be considered. In the final analysis, the various faculty successfully completed their particular research and moved on even though it cost the department financially and, to a certain extent, gave ulcers to the chairman, it was still a success. Various faculty involved may have had grant money and were paying overhead so it could be suggested that the overhead was paying for these various purloined materials. There is even one situation where there had been a small room which was considered public (department) property, but very rarely used and certainly not well-known by the faculty. This particular room became an extra laboratory for one of the faculty members, unbeknownst to the department or anyone else. It is apparent that the various interactions of faculty members not only with their fellow colleagues within the department and the college can be very exhilarating.

3. Faculty Graduate Student Issues

There was another faculty problem, not considered seriously by many faculty, but was a problem produced by the faculty. A member who accepted a graduate student also accepted the responsibility to put a serious effort into making sure that student completed his or her degree. There had been a number of occasions where the original union, that is the agreement between the faculty member and the student, was not good and that either the student or faculty became disenchanted working in that laboratory. If the faculty member found he was unhappy with the particular student, there were many ways to negotiate a change. In some cases, it was not a pleasant situation for a student to come toward the end of a degree and find that the faculty member did not accept the particular research that the student had done. In my opinion, that would be atrocious and this occasionally happened. In one case I'm aware of, there was a lawsuit (not in our department, but in another science department) where a student, at the last moment before the defense of his dissertation, was told that the research was not of the quality that was required. It's difficult for me, as a longtime advisor of students, to understand how a mentor could not be aware of what was going on with the student's research. The lawsuit was brought against the University and the Department and failed because the various faculty members involved simply said the students research was not of the proper quality. The judge involved could not argue the point so the particular student lost out at a very last stage in his career. This was a tragic ending and was even more so because the student passed away shortly after that experience.

There were also occasions when the students tried to be shuffled into someone else's laboratory, or encouraged by their faculty advisor to leave and talk to another faculty member. These are all situations which one would think should not (and did not happen very often) but was a situation that required some departmental involvement. When the department accepted a graduate student, the department also accepted the responsibility to put forth its best effort to see that the student obtained the degree for which he or she was working. There's no guarantee of graduation but it certainly would be a very unhappy circumstance if students were to think that by entering the department they did not have strong support toward the completion of their degree.

4. Outside Influence

I will relate an incident which happened in our department that no particular administrator or faculty member would have considered to be of any valid concern. In my opinion what I'm going to describe came about, at least in part, by the fact that the university was trying to save money and did not wish to maintain its own janitorial staff. They contracted with outside companies to provide janitorial service. These services were to be of the highest order but were carried out by inexperienced men or women at a low education and salary level. There were many problems with this. For example, one day a senior faculty member went back to his laboratory in the evening and discovered a janitor sitting with his feet up on the desk making what appeared to be a purchase of drugs. The faculty member was very upset and did not know what to do. He later went to the department chairman to complain about that situation. There was no proof of anything so there was really nothing that could be done except to try to encourage the faculty to not leave things out for people to steal or break. The department went through a period in which any scale or balance in the department was at risk to be stolen because there was an active drug trade going on among the janitorial staff and perhaps students. But there was no proof so we could do nothing about it. Balances and scales as well as other gear was always being replaced. We could not prove it was the janitors but I think the situation increased when the University switched to outside janitorial employees. I remember asking the owner of the janitorial service, "how did he get his employees"? His answer was, "I back my truck up to a flea bag hotel throw in teargas and whatever runs into the truck is what I keep for work." So you can see why it was upsetting as I related earlier (need to explain this), that the department chairman (who worked for the University for more than 25 years) could not get a particular key but was automatically given to someone who had just been released from prison and only worked for the University for a week.

A horrible event occurred in the department during this time-period. Late one night a murder was committed in one of our laboratories. There had been a fight between two janitors over the affections of a particular woman. That fight ended up in the stabbing and eventual death of one of those janitors. I can almost guarantee anyone who took a job at the University at the highest academic level never anticipated there could be such a horrifying event. Just as an aside, it's certainly true that during that era and subsequently there has been a great change in our social events and expectations.

5. *Misdeeds by Graduate Students*

In a large department, it would be certain and to be expected to have a variety of types of students and faculty. This is normal and probably a good thing to understand. What is not understandable will be related to the next section as an event that occurred during that time of my chairmanship.

One of our young and successful graduate students had obtained her Master's degree and wanted to continue on for her doctorate. She was working in a particular laboratory that had several graduate students. However, a political difference ensued among the students and their emotions ran high over their differences. The young woman, while working on her doctorate, had accumulated a year's worth of data toward the completion of her degree. Her records were kept in her laboratory notebook but had not been duplicated. This was prior to easy access to computers and the duplication of results was not done as it is today. She had not protected her research effort by copying the results or keeping them with her at all times. It was not expected, in a community of high level students, that their personal belongings would be in jeopardy in the laboratory facility where they were working. In this particular case, quite clearly because of her different political views, her laboratory book of records disappeared and she had no results for a full year's worth of effort and experimentation. This was a very serious and extremely difficult problem. She was very suspicious as to what may have happened but the student was extremely unhappy and wanted out of that faculty member's laboratory environment. As department chairman, I was approached about this problem and not knowing really what to do I suggested to her that I would take her in my laboratory and be her advisor. Even though she was not terribly interested in working in my specialty (environmental microbiology), she did want to complete her degree and go on with her life. She accepted my offer and moved into my laboratory. I thought it was a wise decision. Many young people, who complete their doctorates, do not work during the rest of their career in the area in which they got their degree. The young woman was a very hard worker and a nice person who was very serious about getting the research done that would be required to complete her program with me. She did so and after completing a doctorate got a very good position. The end result was very satisfactory for her and for the department. Although it caused her to lose at least one or more years of her professional life in order to complete the tasks.

6. Revenge in The Academic World

The following section relates to an actual event that occurred as a result of a very unhappy faculty member. Our department maintained an animal facility which could be used by all other departments in the college. This facility housed many animals but, in general, were mostly rabbits, mice and a few other related rodents and an occasional monkey or snake. The research that was being supported was carried out primarily by immunologists who were conducting research experiments with various diseases including malaria, pneumonia, etc. The faculty member who was in charge of that facility was both a veterinarian (DVM) and a (PhD) protozoologist. His work was primarily with malaria. The department hired several staff members to assist in the maintenance of the animal facility. It was a large facility which occupied about two thirds of one of the floors of the building. One of the animal facility staff members had worked for the department for several years and was considered a good worker. If he had any problems, it was related to the fact that he could not read or write. He took instructions well and he carried out his job but he could not be relied on to adjudicate any animal cage identification changes where important information had to be placed on a particular cage. We also had an animal facility manager who supervised that facility under the direction of the veterinarian faculty member. The faculty who were carrying out experiments required very careful maintenance of the animals. When the laboratory manager decided to change jobs and leave the University, the staff member just described applied for the job. The job required record-keeping and careful understanding of what was going on in the laboratory. His request was denied and he thought he was due the right to become the manager of the animal facility. He became extremely upset over the fact that he was not selected. He chose to retaliate against his employer in the following manner.

Subsequently the facility, a nationally recognized animal facility, was inspected on a routine basis by a national animal monitoring organization. During one of these inspections, which I witnessed, the following event occurred. The inspector was going through the various rooms and cages turned to the veterinarian director and me and asked this simple question, "how often were these cages inspected"? The laboratory director responded that they were inspected several times a day. The inspector opened up a cage door reached in, and pulled out a rabbit which was as stiff as a board and in full rigor mortis. He held the up the animal by the paw and asked, "Are you sure of that statement"? Needless to say all hell broke loose over that incident and the guilty employee simply stood by in the corner of the room with a smile on his face. That particular incident was one that was not going to occur very often, but added to my understanding of the complexities of dealing with a large organization of complex individuals. It also helped further my understanding of the fact that the job that the chairman had was one that required much patience with a small amount of authority.

The animal facility had been established by the department of microbiology and was a tremendous asset and a problem for the department. We had any number of incidents one of which is related in the following section.

7. *The United States Energy Crisis*

During the late 1970s there was an energy shortage in the United States. The building in which we were housed had been designed, at an earlier time, in such a way that it required a great deal of energy to maintain a constant temperature environment. With the exception of the front of the building there were no windows at any location in the structure. During that energy shortage there were many arguments and problems related to temperature alterations in the building. The university maintenance engineers wanted to cut back on heating or air-conditioning to save energy. Most everyone was in sympathy with the problem the United States had. I think we all worked together to help reduce the amount of energy used to protect our oil reserves. This was reflected during the Christmas holiday when there was a reduction of outdoor lighting. We had a problem in our building in the Winter weather because in the front offices the windows were so cold that the typists could not type. They wanted to wear gloves during the working day. At the same time, in the animal facility and in the laboratories in the interior parts of the building it was so warm that one of our faculty members wore shorts to work. The situation was actually ridiculous. Here we had people in the front of the building freezing and faculty in interior parts of the building totally overheating as a result of poor design. With that in mind, the engineers decided that the aroma in the animal facility was a problem and had to be dealt with without using much energy. Their solution was piping the air from the animal facility down into the men's rooms of the building. Since the aromas were so terrible, why not put them down in the men's room, thank you very much (smile).

The animal facility was under negative air pressure in order that atmospheric contamination in the laboratory would not escape. During the inspection, I was referring to earlier, the inspector went to the entrance door of the facility and held up a piece of paper at a partially opened door to test the flow direction of air. The paper blew toward the outside into the corridor; however, the facility was designed to be under negative pressure and any movement of air should flow into the facility (not out) where most everything could be contained. I must admit there was much consternation over these events.

We had one other situation where a faculty member was furious with the director of the facility because he was not taking proper care of the mice. The concern was that the mice were being infected with some inherent microorganism and interfering with his immunologic research results. No one was aware of any of this and many very unhappy words transpired with the young faculty member being very abusive about the care given to the facility. He wanted to see the facility director removed. The conclusion of that accusation was settled when a letter of apology from the specific supplier of the mice, (a nationally known supply laboratory that was supplying all the animals), admitted to the fact that they were all contaminated and that supplier was to blame for the erroneous research results of various faculty members. Interestingly, there was never an apology made about the maintenance of our facility.

8. Graduate Student Placement in the Microbiology Program

We have talked about the difficulties and confusion involved in placing graduate students into various laboratories within the department. The arrangement had to be made with individual faculty members, having an agreement with the particular graduate student that may have an interest in his or her program.

However, in situations where both enrollments were growing and faculty were obtaining research grant support which supported new graduate students, it became more problematic because there might be a need for dual use of graduate students in laboratories and the teaching program. In a course that had 150 students and supported three or four different laboratory sections, it was required that a number of graduate students be hired to deal with the numbers of laboratories and students in those classes.

We had a circumstance occur when the department did not receive enough budget to carry out the teaching program. Faculty were successful in using graduate students and, where possible, supported them. There were situations where a student was supported by the department budget and still worked in the faculty member's laboratory. The program could get quite complicated from an administrative point of view. In any case, I was forced to hire some graduate students for the laboratory courses and unfortunately, we did not have enough budget to carry this out. I felt that the Dean had shortchanged the department in its allocation of money and simply assumed that he would help make up this misallocation.

As it turned out, this experience was both unhappy for that Dean and for me as well. To say that the Dean was furious with me would be an understatement. I think if I had not had tenure I would've been on the street looking for another job. However, the Dean managed to find the money and help support the department in its mission. He was very unhappy with this and as a result, my effectiveness as chairman diminished. So, I guess in the end we all lost something.

The next anecdote again relates to the animal facility and a particular worker that we had hired. The supervisor of the facility thought we should give this young man a chance. He was a hero of the Vietnam War and had been severely wounded. He turned out to be a very good worker but his appearance diminished his effectiveness. His full-length hair came down over his forehead beyond his chin and simply put, he scared most of the coeds in the building. I finally had to speak to him and make sure that he pulled his hair back so that people could see his face. He was a good worker and he came to the office and asked if he could take the control mice home when we were finished with any experiments. I spoke with the supervisor the animal facility and he said he didn't see what harm it would be if the mice were going to be destroyed anyway. We agreed to let him take these animals home. People living in the apartment near him detected strange odors coming from his apartment and they called the police. It became evident he was housing a large number of snakes of all types and varieties in his apartment. They were his pets and of course the mice he was taking home were used to feed the snakes. The Authorities confiscated the snakes. After the snakes were placed in a van, a number of the animals got loose and Jack Hanna (Columbus Zoo Director) was called to help assist in recovering these animals. Jack Hanna wisely suggested they get hold of the owner of the snakes and that he would be more appropriate to do that. This episode is written about in Jack Hanna's book "Monkeys on the Interstate". In the end, the employee was so distraught about losing his pets that he resigned and left the state of Ohio.

9. Student Cheating

During one of our introductory microbiology laboratories, a graduate student was supervising the laboratory and grading laboratory reports that were to be written by each student. During his reading he looked at one of the reports and thought "I think I just read that somewhere else", so he went back and looked at previous reports. He discovered that two of the reports were identical. He confronted the students about this matter and during that confrontation one of the students who was denying everything simply fainted, falling to the floor. The graduate student thought that was suspicious and reported the incident to the faculty in charge of the course.

Any faculty member who eventually becomes involved as an administrator, for example department chairman, certainly knows that there are going to be examples of students cheating. Normally such events involved the faculty of the course and interactions with a university committee which examined the data and prescribed any action. What I never anticipated was just how I would become involved in events at the departmental level.

The faculty member called in both students and wanted an explanation as to how this could happen. Of course, the students denied everything, and said they each had independently written a two-page document which turned out to be word and punctuation exactly the same. As an aside, I have to wonder how bright these two students were. But denial is a common way for people to try to escape consequences.

The faculty member reported this incident to the University committee which was responsible for these events. As chairman, I was aware of the incident because I spoke with faculty member. It was not long before I had a phone call from an Ohio Congressman who wanted to have a meeting with me and with the parents of one of the young men.

I met with them in my office and was assured by the Congressman that these people were the "salt of the earth" and that their son could not have committed such a heinous act. During the meeting the mother of the young man, looking very distraught, simply rocked back and forth in her chair gnashing her teeth and squeezing her hands together. I tried to explain the reason the faculty member reported this event, and at that time, I had the both documents on my desk. I explained to the woman that it was not possible for two people to independently write a two-page report word for word exactly the same. She would have none of it and the Congressman wanted me to punish the faculty member who was involved in the situation. I simply explained that this could not be done and that the faculty member was not at fault and that the two students did deserve some form of punishment. The parents and the Congressman were distraught and threatened that this would become an event which would be moved up to a higher level at the University.

I had spent several hours agonizing over this problem including the meeting with these people and felt that the matter should be finished. The students involved did receive a failing grade as a result of their cheating which was upheld by a committee at the university level.

We had another incident of cheating involving a graduate student. The events unfolded in the following manner. One of our graduate students was assigned to help teach laboratories in general biology. The general biology program was very large, and had a faculty administrator who supervised all of the laboratory sections. Most of the testing was done on computer in a lab that was housed in a separate building that dealt with teaching large numbers of students, such as those that were in general biology. The supervisor, looking at his master control, saw that one of the young women in the class was taking her midterm exam. He had just been in that laboratory and had not seen anyone at that particular computer that he recognized other than the graduate student in charge of the laboratory facility. He quickly checked and determined that the test was being taken in the name of the female undergraduate student by the graduate teaching assistant (GTA) in charge of the class. It turned out he (GTA) was taking the exam for her and she received an A grade. What came to light as a result of the investigation was that the particular graduate student (GTA) involved had a small enterprise on the side in which he made sure his female students received their A and in return he received their favor in the faculty member's laboratory at night. All hell broke loose over that situation and as a result the graduate student (GTA) was banned from the Ohio State University. Of course there are going to be examples of cheating any time you have a situation where you give exams to students.

The Entrance of New Horizons in The Department

A major event in any departmental history is the acquisition of a new faculty member. It's particularly satisfying when that faculty member represents an entirely new area of research interest. We had the opportunity to add a new faculty member who was instrumental in developing an entirely new line of research in botany. The reason he wanted to join our department was that microbiologists were using technology that was not generally used in the botanical world. Microbiologists use different types of culturing methods and were using Petri plates as well as submerged culture techniques. The new faculty member's ideas involved the genetic manipulation of plants and rapid culture in petri dishes much the way as was done in microbiology. Our new faculty joined our department and became a very important member of the faculty. He later worked both in industry and academia and ultimately became Dean at Rutgers University, and still consults at the Ohio State University. The advent of new lines of research interest in the department was an energizing boost in research goals.

We also had the opportunity to have a biophysicist join our department which brought a whole new molecular approach to what was going on in our research interests. His ideas about academic university life were old-school, since he was a senior professor and believed that his research should be supported in full by the University. He resisted any attempt at getting financial support for his efforts. On many occasions, I requested that he entertain the idea of helping to support the department in its financial needs as well as research and educational goals. He simply declined to do any of this. Eventually he was assigned to teach general biology, which he abhorred, but was required to do. The students that took beginning biology were generally only one year or so out of high school and had very little training at any advanced level. He started his lectures using ideas and equations which simply baffled these young students. It is sad to note that the longest line of complaining students the Dean's office ever had was as a result of this teaching enterprise.

These changes were major changes for our department because originally it had been principally responsible for teaching medically oriented microbiology. When new faculty arrive in the department with totally different ideas, while it is good for the departmental interests, it is not always easy for old-school faculty to adjust to the presence of a totally new type of thinking. So for a number of years we had a mix of medically oriented microbiologists, immunologists, environmental microbiologist, and molecular geneticists. When you have such diversity of faculty interests in a single group you are bound to run into difficulties with respect to concerns about faculty promotions, reallocation of space, as well as the normal difficulties in understanding any new scientific language. I'm referring to the fact that each science area has its own jargon and in my opinion, scientists are not easily adapted to reorganizing their thinking in those directions.

The reader can appreciate that the administration of a complex group became very difficult. The question is what type of management is appropriate for such a complex mix of individuals? If your management style is to be autocratic and somewhat of a dictator, then it will be fairly easy for you to manage any particular group. You simply expect whatever orders are given be followed. If you're willing to work with faculty and come up with composite relationships, it is going to make for a far better department but going to be much more difficult to manage. I think the reader should think in these terms and examine closely what type of management style is preferred and see whether it can be done appropriately.

Acceptance and Admission of Graduate Students

It is worth discussing, at some length, the mechanism by which our department accepted and admitted graduate students. We had a graduate committee normally of three senior faculty members who reviewed all applications for entrance into our graduate programs. This committee would look at the type of student that was requesting admission, as to what their grades were, and what their interests might be, and any other important academic documentation that came with the application. At times a student might have a specific area of research that they might want to do and were aware of a particular faculty member doing that type of research. Sometimes faculty members had communication with students especially at the doctoral level and could easily learn whether that particular student might be suitable for admission to his or her program. Remember that is not just the desire of the given faculty member, who wants a new student, that the admission would be granted. The student still had to be vetted by the graduate committee of the department so that academic standards could be maintained. In most cases, this did not present problems. Sometimes a faculty member's colleague in another University would recommend, personally, to the given faculty member that he should take this student into his/her doctoral program. That the student he was speaking about wanted to go to the Ohio State University, would be a good researcher, and would fit in the program. In some cases, this did present a problem because the recommended student was not academically qualified and so there was some consternation and difficulty between various faculty members on the graduate committee in getting a student into the department. In some cases, the chairman of the department was brought into it, unhappily, and at times tried to adjudicate the proceedings. In most admission cases, students would write an application to the department which sent it to the graduate committee for their evaluation. There were as many as 30 or 40 applications for entrance into the department each year with the potential availability for perhaps openings for five students. I think it is easy to understand that a faculty member who has an active research program and was using his graduate student as a technical assistant in carrying out the research program would be very unhappy to have his choice refused. What I'm saying is that the success of the research program of faculty depended on having good technical help, effective graduate students, and consequently department support and he generally did not want to lose any potential student. The result over the years was that there was no fixed time for a student to complete any educational program. Our average was about two years for a master's program and about three additional years for the doctoral degree. When a student was admitted to the department he or she could expect to be in that department for anywhere from 5 to 6 years. There was no guaranteed graduation date. The graduation of a particular student was dependent upon the research that the student accomplished and the agreement of the various faculty members (his advisory committee) that this student should receive the advanced degree. It was and is a complicated process. The completion of a doctoral program required the defense of dissertation with the committee that was chosen by the student and his faculty member advisor. Some faculty would deal with students more easily than others and this was part of how the department chairman would find him or herself involved in adjudicating relationships which certainly affected the outcome of both faculty and graduate students. It was and is important that a faculty member produce results, publish papers and move on to advance his or her academic position. It's also important that a graduate student complete his or her program and move into society to develop their career. There was always and I suspect will always be a lot of pulling and tugging within the departments that operate in that style. There are situations in other academic departments (usually non-technical departments) where it's a time constraint that can be easily dealt with, but because microbiology is a laboratory science and depends upon research results there can be no easily fixed date when a student will complete their research and get their degree. The graduate committee would write a letter of acceptance or rejection to the particular student application and each year a small group of new students would arrive to carry out their educational process.

Most of the students did not have a particular faculty member or research area in mind. They might have had general ideas about where they wanted to do their research, but not specifically with any given faculty individual. We generally tried to see that the student was placed in a faculty laboratory sometime within the first year. The sooner that placement was made, the better it was for everybody. As I had stated earlier, I did have a student who really wanted to make the University his permanent home.

Moving into a New Building

When the new building in the College of Biological Sciences was designed and built, it was during the era where energy was cheap and the design for the building was also energy inefficient. The construction and design of the building had a grievous effect on anyone who administered activities in that building. The new building was entered into with great pride and hope for the future and represented to us who moved into it as a great step forward, in the university's recognition of the importance of these fields of study.

It is with sadness that I relate to the readers that the building left much to be desired. The building committee made up of faculty in the departments in the colleges of biological science were given an amount of money that they were allowed to spend for scientific equipment in the building. There were numerous arguments over what should be purchased and where it was to be placed. There were even arguments over whether or not the floor should be covered with tile or just left concrete. In the end, the interior portion of the building was well finished and reasonably well-equipped with scientific equipment.

However, there were no windows in the building except for the north wall. For some reason (known only to the architect) the sides of the building were made with a 5-foot empty space from the third floor to the top (9). After moving into the building, it was noticed (within a short period of time) that the bricks in the upper stories of the building were actually becoming dislodged. We recall many times leaving the building and looking up toward the seventh or eighth floor to see just how far the bricks were extending out from the wall. There appeared to be an immediate danger (brick dislodgement) or some type of collapse. As a result, the University hired a team of building experts from New York who arrived and examined the problem. They made the suggestion that there had to be reinforcement of each of the floors to keep the outer wall in place. There were a series of cross steel beams at each floor (e.g. .in the empty wall space) that were placed all around the building to strengthen the basic structure. After the renovation of the inner and outer wall of the building there were several doors placed in the inner wall at floor 3 which allowed a substantial storage space between the walls. I requested permission to use that space to be able to store glass and plastic laboratory supplies. This request was denied and for a long time the space remained empty. Eventually the complaints were heard and after the janitorial experiences previously spoken about were evaluated, we were granted a key and we did use that space for storage.

Years later many of these construction flaws entered into departmental decisions and in effect became a problem for administration. It was mentioned earlier that the heating and cooling of the building (because of its design) was quickly a problem which probably could have been avoided if windows had been included to provide ventilation.

We remember gathering the faculty for a meeting with the university maintenance department so that they could explain to our faculty how to use a thermostat. There were several terse comments about the need to explain to a science faculty and to homeowners how to use the thermostat in their labs. This became especially interesting when several of the faculty members went back to their laboratories and attempted to adjust the thermostats only to discover that they were actually never even wired into the system, and in one case, a thermostat was pulled out and was totally unattached without any wiring. It's very hard to adjust temperature in a facility with fake thermostats. All of these outside influences became a factor in trying to administer the department. A great deal of time was wasted in meetings and explanations to the faculty and to students about problems that were never induced by any department member.

Unintended Consequences

It is not our intention to denigrate any of the fine work that was put into attempting to establish the new college of biological sciences. But what this section speaks to is what can happen to any organization that is established without complete understanding. The highest of motives were used to establish the college and was done at the correct time in the history of science. Biology was coming out into the forefront of science. Genetics was opening up with the expansion of understanding much more about the life processes and perhaps how life even arrived on our planet. As biologists, we were all very happy to see the college established. What none of us knew at the time was that there would be unintended consequences requiring an enormous expenditure of administrative time that detracted (subtracted) from the planned goals of the College. The departments that made up the college were cobbled together primarily from departments in liberal arts and from departments from the College of Agriculture. At the outset, there were problems with people coming from different colleges understanding the needs and requirements of members of different colleges. In some ways there was no good explanation as to why there was a department of microbiology from arts and sciences and the formation of a new department of microbiology in the medical school and the movement of the department of biochemistry from the agriculture college and a second department of biochemistry in liberal arts. There was bound to be some friction among various members of these colleges. This basic problem in structuring of the college of biological sciences was never fully understood by members of the college. It was a constant problem for anyone in the administration, the college and in the departments because there were always conflicting influences and outside factors creating problems. These are things that the administrators have to deal with and that no one who would take the job as such an administrator would have considered a problem at the time of employment. These problems were buried deep within the system and it took a long time to figure this out. There was even an attempt, many years after the formation of the college of biological sciences, to return the entire college back to agriculture. This caused a great deal of consternation among various faculty who could see no real gain in making such a move compared to some members in the agriculture college who apparently favored it. There was great deal of mistrust among faculty members from the two different sources within the college structure.

When the college was formed in the 1960s, the young aggressive faculty were demanding that the Dean should be a great academic leader and have an active research program. This was considered necessary to stimulate any progress the college might make. What was lost, in our opinion, is that in real terms the Dean of the college is the head of an undergraduate organization not a graduate school. There was even an attempt at restructuring the entire college into an organization which would be essentially run by various faculty and not departments. For example, as a young faculty member I suddenly heard the telephone in the "Department of Microbiology" office being answered as "Cell Biology" and not "Department of Microbiology". This, of course, came about in part by the problem of hiring new young faculty who did not regard themselves as microbiologists and thought that it would be more modern to call themselves cell biologists without sufficient consideration or thought as to what the influence of national connections with technical peer organizations would be.

There are many colleges and universities in this and other countries but there are few of a size equaling The Ohio State University. To compare a school that has only a total of three thousand students with a large institution such as OSU with 63,000 students is very difficult if not impossible to do. The department of microbiology in the college of biological sciences, now the College of Liberal arts, had or may have as many as three-thousand students per year taking a single course in basic microbiology. Many departments may have five or six faculty at smaller institutions while the microbiology department had an average of 18 faculty positions with all its attendant problems because as the faculty numbers increase, the problems increase exponentially. Delving into the challenges that occur at a greater rate in a large department should be interesting for any perspective academic manager.

The following paragraph concerns events and problems that any faculty member who was working cooperatively with another department in the college or perhaps in another college in any other University might have.

As an example, scenario: a graduate student from another department approaches a faculty member with a suggestion about looking into a research area in a cooperative way. This means that the faculty member who mentors that student have probably talked over a research idea for which they do not have all the expertise needed to complete. For example, a student or faculty member wishes to learn the techniques of microbial culturing via petri plates or submerged culture. These procedures are not usually taught in other departments where this type of expertise is covered and used in the department of microbiology. The student from the other department and the department member communicate and agree that they could work together. The idea that the graduate student or faculty member has may be a good one and deserves to be explored. The problem may need to be financed by either or both departments or in some cooperative way involving the faculty. Equipment and supplies will need to be available. Space has to be set aside for the faculty and students.

Work proceeds, results occur, and publications are written. The effort is considered a success and this work may now be an appropriate problem that can be extended and submitted for the completion of an advanced degree.

The above scenario has actually happened on several occasions and the following circumstances have to be considered when agreeing to participate in such a cooperative effort.

The graduate student who is doing most of the work has to form a committee to satisfy the requirements of the University. This committee is generally made up of various faculty members in or out of the department who are willing to participate. The committee reads the thesis or dissertation, edits manuscripts, and is involved directly with that student and the other advisor. In general, most departments and their faculty members can be fairly narrow minded. For example, if a person is in the economics department, it is generally expected that that faculty member will produce manuscripts which will satisfy the faculty in that department. The academic advancement of a faculty member, i.e. promotion and raises, is dependent upon satisfying the chairman and a promotion committee that the chairman may have formed to evaluate advancement of faculty or considered. Thus the publication of papers outside the area of expertise of the department may or may not be highly regarded.

In this case, a faculty member who cooperates outside the department may find that any work that is done may be ignored with respect to his or her advancement within the department. The problem with a cooperative venture is that it is difficult to find faculty to participate in a system where he or she must examine work that they are not necessarily experienced with.

A graduate student can quickly find he or she is in deep trouble during an exam within the department because all it takes is one individual on an examining committee to insist upon expertise in details in the particular department of the examiner. An example of this might be that a graduate student has worked on the conversion of energy using biologic systems and suddenly finds him or herself trying to answer complicated questions about the biochemistry of the Krebs cycle. That type of question may or may not be particularly important to the outcome of the study. It turns out no one can be all things to all people so the idea of cooperation is extremely important and many advancements in science have been made by people who have worked together, coming from different disciplines.

We have had circumstances in our department and in other departments where the work was not approved by the faculty committee that was controlling the program and this was not approved during the exam. The student could not appropriately answer a particular question to satisfy the questioner. This does not mean that student was not a more than well-qualified individual and extremely bright, it just means that student was not fully aware of the ultimate details that a questioning faculty member would require. This can be an impediment in many circumstances toward cooperative work and certainly needs to be considered by any faculty member before he or she gets involved in any cooperative project.

One of the circumstances that occurs in advanced education is that obtaining a doctoral degree forces an individual to become expert in a narrow specialty. In other words, you begin to hone down and sharpen the knowledge area—the area in which you plan to work so that you become very expert in a relatively small specialization within one of the sciences. As I have often jokingly commented, I can methylate right-handed door knobs but I don't know how to do left-handed ones. That very fact speaks positively for cooperative research efforts. That is, as we develop our expertise and go deeper into subject matter it becomes actually more necessary to collaborate in order to solve problems and to have other people involved who can assist and cooperate in a productive way.

Cooperation

There have been a number of cooperative efforts among various faculty members in different departments. However, to encourage cooperative efforts among different programs within the University or outside the University at other institutions or institutions in other countries, there needs to be a clear understanding as to the procedures, so that a student does not get caught up in a self-defeating administrative process or purpose.

Initiation of this section was prompted by an article in the Columbus Dispatch on September 21, 2015 by Ben Sutherly, who examined the question of licensing income among various Ohio institutions and compared it with Big Ten universities. The information was generated from licensing to the medical sections of the various schools and institutions and reflects a surprising difference between the various universities.

It also triggered questions about extension of collaborations beyond universities

It has always been clear that in the running of any institution, the upper level administration controls the various financial decisions that are made. We think it is an admirable and wise decision for various institutions to cooperate to their fullest extent. This certainly enhances the opportunities for advancement in a number of fields. We believe the problem arises when an actual cooperative event appears on the horizon.

It is suggested that cooperative efforts among any groups have to be initiated from the bottom up because two individuals in discussion, who are attempting to do collaborative research, agree that they need to share each other's expertise. This sharing of their abilities generates the eventual ideas and efforts. The administration of any institution has to be willing and able to agree to foster this type of cooperation. Most institutions will indicate that they have this type of policy in place but we have observed that this may or may not be true. It is essential that the various institutions have administrative agreements with open doors, where cooperators feel free and have the ability to get together to advance whatever cause they're interested in. The initiation of these cooperative efforts rarely arises from the top down but generally from the bottom up. You need to have multiple individuals or groups willing to work together with their various abilities to further the common cause. It is also equally essential that the administration at the top end has the capability and agrees to foster these types of endeavors; i.e. cooperation must be at all levels. We have all seen circumstances where individuals have made suggestions for cooperative efforts to only find that their suggestions are quickly squashed because there is no room at the upper end to make essential adjustments. We have no answer to this problem but one must exist or could be formulated. I believe that if cooperative effort is to be sustained then it must be agreed to by all parties. For example, it has been previously described herein that an administrative group with their expertise in the humanities, did not fully understand the basic question or nature of a planned cooperative technical program that required advanced biological science.

There needs to be available a mechanism to examine the value of questions being asked, and taken by people who are able to open the cooperative doors. We do not have the answers for these questions but recognize the value and essential nature of asking them.

We believe that many advances in our society have been made by groups with different expertise relying on each other to produce results. In this day and age of complexity and political differences it is not an easy matter for a single individual to generate science out of his lone laboratory. The following quote was taken from the Columbus Dispatch October 7, 2015. The article by "Ritter and Ritter" concerns the two scientists who just won the Nobel Prize for physics. Dr. Kajita in that article states "the universe where we live in is still full of unknowns "he said. "A major discovery cannot be achieved in a day or two. It takes a lot of people and a long time."

A Theoretical Scenario and Some Current Reality

As an example, a young researcher enters the laboratory or office of a scientist in a totally unrelated field. He or she has an idea which cuts across a number of techniques and principles in the field of the scientist he or she is visiting and raises a number of questions. The discussion is enthusiastically received and together they think that it would be a fine idea to examine the principles and problems raised during the discussion. As it happens, the individual is from another University perhaps a graduate student or young faculty and thinks the two people or two laboratories certainly could work together. There are many agreements that have to be reached before anything can proceed. It has to be decided where the funding is coming from to do the work, who is going to provide the space needed and how will the results be published or shared. These and other questions have to be addressed before any initiation or actual investigation or experimentation can begin.

Let us proceed ahead in time and say that research has been accomplished, efforts have been rewarded with published results. Perhaps the results have generated the possibility of income for the various institutions involved. How is this to be shared? Which organizations will get the majority of credit? There may even be further considerations.

The Sutherly article in the Columbus Dispatch raises the question of how various organizations obtain their licensing and the dollar amounts involved. Clearly these issues can only be resolved from the top down. So, we have a situation where the origin of work or the detailed planning done has been generated from the bottom while the solution to many of the problems or results are being controlled from the top. Answers to these problems certainly would have to be adjudicated before any serious agreements could be reached. Perhaps small committees from each institution could provide expertise into the particular question to help the administration in providing answers. This suggests that there may be no single solution to any of the particular problems being addressed. It may be required that the upper levels of administration will need to provide more flexible answers before cooperative efforts can be obtained. It also suggests that the meaning of cooperation amongst one group may not be the same as cooperation amongst different groups. A final recommendation may have to reached by establishing a separate research division to carry out cooperative research.

An article titled "An Education in Sloganeering "in the Wall Street Journal on October 1, 2015 by Dr. Harvey J. Graff, a professor at the Ohio State University, adds to some of the questions raised in this document. Dr. Graff refers to "increasing efforts to privatize major assets" and "creating economies and efficiencies". He goes on and states "Ohio State remains one of the most fragmented and divided large universities in the USA. It's many fine resources and talents are rarely brought together. I if anything, these problems have worsened in recent years." These very serious comments should be considered when attempting to form cooperative research ventures.

When dealing with an institution as large as The Ohio State University, it is clear to any of us who have worked there and with others who have attempted to negotiate with the University, that the institution, is like a large ocean liner that is very difficult to steer and takes a great deal of effort to redirect or stop. It will take major understanding and concessions from the administration and perhaps politicians at the state level, to provide this important backdrop of cooperation that we are referring to in this chapter.

It is also extremely important and in the purview of this chapter, to suggest that lower level administrators such as deans and chairman should also recognize these problems and be willing to help in whatever way they can.

After a lot of consideration and thinking about the matter of collaboration, we have reached important conclusions based upon our collective experience in these matters.

It should be clear that ideas need to be evaluated, experimented with, or certainly explored and will arise with people in the areas doing the active research. These questions need to be and will be evaluated at a higher level in whatever organizations are involved. So clearly the advent of interesting cooperative work starts at the bottom and works its way toward the top before of any work can be done. It is absolutely incumbent upon the higher administrative levels in any organization to agree with and certainly approve of these cooperative interactions.

The article in the Columbus Dispatch (Sutherly) and by others more than suggests that tinkering with agreements that the upper administration has made and then not followed through with will, in effect, destroy any progress toward cooperation.

There has to be some mechanism by which not only agreements are made but that have the capability of being fulfilled, regardless of who changes administrative positions. The article in the Dispatch newspaper examines the question of top administration leaving a University and disrupting further progress. As stated earlier in this chapter, we have seen this interruption even at the college or departmental level. The positioning of key individuals at choke points in the process, while perhaps necessary, is a major factor in success or failure of any cooperative venture.

The observations made in this chapter may, in part, be responsible for why there have been relatively few high-level scientists elevated to higher administrative levels.

Another interesting factor in this process relates to the fact that a number of scientists doing research believe that funding should come directly from government sources such as the National Science Foundation. Of course, some other government agencies would be well-qualified as well. However, we have seen a certain amount of snobbery where outside funds are concerned. During our tenure at the University we had a number of opportunities to bring in support from industrial sources and in some cases private sponsors. These were looked down upon by members of the departmental administration as well as college administration at times because they were not NSF or NIH grants. We also observed that patents that were obtained from work sponsored by industrial sources were not very highly thought of by a number of administrative people. They were considered to be without any value. That type of thinking can easily be seen or at least considered when looking at the newspaper articles cited above.

There were members of the administration that did not allow books which were generated by faculty to be used in the courses that the faculty taught. Advanced courses and sciences certainly do not bring in huge sums of money with regard to the few textbooks that would be sold. It was extremely frustrating not to be able to use one's own textbook in one's own course. This was a principal that came down from higher administrative levels. During the last few years of the chairman's involvement in course instruction he was assigned to teach general biology. The course that was taught had over 500 students in it with something like 12 or 15 graduate students to help run the labs. We feel that it was interesting that while one's own textbook was not allowed, the bookstore came and requested that notes taken by a note taker could be assembled during the course and then sold later on to students wishing to take that course. These are administrative decisions which certainly brought about negative thinking on the part of the faculty.

We believe, that cooperative endeavors are a must. Institutions just have to find a better way to stabilize them.

Summary and Conclusions

There are a number of conclusions that can be reached as a result of reading this chapter.

These conclusions and recommendations are the result of a great deal of discussion, evaluation, and the re-examination of past events.

It is concluded that it is extremely important for cooperative events to occur (in any field) in order for important advances to be made and it is recognized that shared expertise may be critical.

Universities in the United States are necessary places for cooperative research because of the freedoms of expression and experimentation.

A university is also one of the most difficult places to carry out cooperative research because of those freedoms extended to all members of the university. While these freedoms are wonderful, they may cause problems because all members of the university do not think alike.

Unless the university sets up a separate research entity to carry out cooperative ventures, we see the potential of the dangerous situation of having two types of faculty within a given department or any cooperative venture. The explanation for this is in detail within this chapter.

When cooperative ventures are proposed there is an important requirement for administrative stability. There have been a number of circumstances where the change in the upper administration has affected the outcome of cooperative events.

This conclusion is a foreshadowing of what we see as the future in cooperative ventures.

The rapid melding of government and industrial interests is a clear pointer toward what the future will be. We are already witnessing the movement of industry into outer space and the delivery of important products to our international space station using industrial rockets. There are numerous other examples which can be cited.

This chapter may be useful in helping a future administrator in understanding the various responsibilities of a college administrative position.

Addendum

The Land Grant System in The United States
Any comparison of the function and purpose among various higher education institutions should include information about the tremendously successful impact that the "land-grant system" had on higher education in the United States.

In 1862, Lincoln approved the United States Congressional Act. The act provided each state within the US, 30,000 acres of land for each senator and congressman that then represented their particular state according to the 1860 U.S. Census. Further, states without sufficient available land, received comparable amounts of land scrip to be sold to provide the money for investment in securities that yielded an amount greater than 5%.

The proceeds from the securities were to: "constitute a perpetual fund…maintained forever undiminished…for the endowment, support, and maintenance of at least one college, where the leading object shall be, without excluding other scientific and classical studies, and including military tactics, to teach such branches of learning as are related to agriculture and the mechanical arts, in such a manner as the legislatures of the states may respectively prescribe, in order to promote the liberal and practical education of the industrial classes in the several pursuits and professions of life"

Thus the Morrill act used federal aid to guarantee a network of state colleges for the "the advancement of scientific and industrial education" as Morrill would say later. The act ensured a strong research orientation centered on the sciences and liberal arts, with an emphasis on application and problem solving. In many respects, the award of land instead of dollars by the act was a substitute for levying taxes. It took most states 25 years after 1862 to provide direct operating levies to their land-grant colleges. The manner for use of the grant to each state resided with each individual state legislature and some states provided for more than one land-grant college.

Over the years, the mission of land-grant colleges expanded into universities and also was further expanded by the US Congressional Hatch Act in 1887 which provided additional federal funds to establish a series of agricultural experiment stations under the direction of each state's land-grant college, as well as to pass along new information, especially in the areas of soil minerals and plant growth. The outreach mission was further expanded by the federal Smith Lever Act of 1914 to include Cooperative Extension; the sending of agents into rural areas to help bring the results of agricultural research to the end users. Beyond the original land-grant, each college (or university) receives annual federal appropriations for research and extension on the condition that those funds are matched by state funds.

The land-grant program has continued to be expanded periodically in numbers: in 1967 the District of Columbia received a $7.24 million endowment. In 1972 a special education amendment granted $3 million to each of the following: American Samoa, Guam, Micronesia, Northern Marianas, and the Virgin Islands. In 1994, 29 Tribal colleges and universities became land-grant under the Elementary and Secondary Education Reauthorization Act. In 2008, 32 Tribal colleges and universities have land-grant status of which six are four-year institutions and the others are two-year degree granting colleges.

On February 12, 1855, the first chartered land-grant college was the Agricultural College of Michigan which ultimately became Michigan State University. On February 22, 1855 the second chartered land-grant college was the Farmers High School of Pennsylvania which ultimately became Pennsylvania State University.

The above two charters served as models for the 1862 Morrill act. On 9/11/ 1862 the third chartered land-grant college was Iowa State Agricultural College which became Iowa State University.

On February 16, 1863 the fourth chartered land-grant University was Kansas State University, Rutgers University, originally founded in 1766, is the oldest University to be designated as a land-grant University in 1864.

State of Ohio

The first operating levy in Ohio was passed in 1891. In 1862 Ohio had two senators and 19 congressmen. Consequently, it was entitled to 630,000 acres under the Morrill act. In 1864, Ohio passed a law that accepted the Morrill act and pledged the faith of the state "to the performance of all the conditions and provisions therein contained". In 1865 the state of Ohio passed legislation that specified that the land scrip which should not be sold for less than $.80 per acre. The script didn't sell and a year later the law was amended to allow the land to be sold "at the best price it could be obtained for the land", which eventually amounted to an average of $.54 per acre amounting to a total of $342,451. In 1871 Ohio passed its own act that called for "a college to be styled the Ohio agricultural and mechanical College in accordance with the conditions of an act of Congress passed on July 2, 1862" ... The leading object shall be, without excluding scientific and classical studies, and including military tactics, to teach such branches of learning as are related to agricultural and mechanical arts."

Two years later, in 1873 with seven faculty members and 17 students the Ohio State University opened its doors. As of the present writing, September 2015 OSU has >2500 faculty and >55000 students enrolled.

Ohio has a second land-grant University: Central State University. Central state started in 1887 as a two-year *normal and industrial department* located at Wilberforce University in Wilberforce Ohio which expanded to a four-year program in 1947. In 1951 central state separated from Wilberforce University and was renamed Central State College and in 1965 became central state university as a land-grant university.

Wilberforce University was originally formed by the conference of the Cincinnati Methodist Episcopal Church and the African Methodist Episcopal Church. In October 2006 Wilberforce University held the opening and dedication of the NASA Science Engineering Mathematics and Aerospace Academy (SEMAA) and the Aerospace Education Laboratory (APL); which are not to be confused with central state university.

Wikipedia

The following information concerning the Ohio State University was taken from Wikipedia (2015).

There are 19 men's and 20 women's varsity teams. The website for the Ohio state university is "osu.edu"

The motto of the Ohio state university is "Education for Citizenship" which was established in 1870 and is a "public Land grant, Sea grant, and Space grant institution". The current endowment is in the neighborhood of $3.1 billion. The current president is Michael V Drake. The academic staff numbers about 6254 and it has an administrative staff of 21,987 non-academic individuals. There are 57,466 students on the Columbus campus. There are 63,964 students in all campuses. Columbus has about 44,201 undergraduate students while all campuses have about 50,551 undergraduate students. The numbers of postgraduates are 13,265 at the Columbus site with 13,413 taking in all campuses.

The campus colors are scarlet and gray and the athletic departments are in NCAA Division I in the Big Ten conference.

CHAPTER 15

Green Genes and Hyphens and Love—Oh My!

Ellen Reardon
Research Professor and LOC Laboratory
Operations Coordinator
Rutgers University

What is a collaboration anyway? Is it a *quid pro quo*? Must there always be something in it for me? On the other hand, must I always be a philanthropist? What is the driving force that permits humans to voluntarily donate their ideas, their IDEAS, to others? To others who may, or may not, be receptive to those ideas. To others, who may, or may not, have the means, or the desire, to bring those ideas to fruition.

Academic collaborations occur on many levels; most are reciprocal. Consider the relationship between a professor and postdoctoral fellow, graduate student or undergraduate. A very wise academician once told me that if a student did not know more about his/her thesis project than did his advisor, that advisor had failed to do his/her job. Then consider the competitions that exist among principle investigators: a sometimes possible publish or perish syndrome. I intend to relate my interpretation of these situations through personal anecdotes.

Carl Price was a force to be reckoned with long before I came to his lab (Fig.1) A Cal Tech graduate and Harvard Ph.D. Carl designed and produced centrifuge rotors that separated the previously inseparable. His reverence for plants could probably be traced to his California upbringing and his year-round enjoyment of all things green. Carl was a professor of biochemistry, but he taught the scientific method. Not as a required course, surely, but as a means of taking one hypothesis to it's logical conclusion. Lettie Mendiola-Morganthalier[1] had just separated chloroplasts from nuclear cytoplasm when I arrived on the doorstep of a rundown, (dilapidated perhaps?), building on the campus of Rutgers University. As a physical chemist for a major corporation, I was longing to get back to biology: read: I didn't know a chloroplast from a mitochondrion, and my knowledge of DNA was limited to Watson and Crick circa 1953. I told Carl I would be his lab tech—but not for long. Dr. Price, formally, as he was then known, deposited all his graduate students into the same physical lab space, each with about one year's more experience than the next. This technician was expected to support the needs of all students, in addition to furthering her own thesis project, in her spare time. Fortunately as a woman, this was not difficult!

Shortly after my arrival at "Plant Phys", my first four jobs were to demonstrate the concordance, or not, with the work of Professor R. John Ellis of the University of Warwick, U.K. John's lab had churned out some monumental papers[2] on the ability of chloroplasts to make their own proteins. The time was very pre-sequencing, VERY! A conference on photosynthesis intervened on the lovely Greek island of Spetsai. At the coffee break, I literally bumped into a conferee and knocked his coffee cup to the ground. I bent to retrieve it and came up looking into the badge of one R. John Ellis. This unexpected meeting produced an "Oh my God", three times from my startled mouth, at having literally bumped into my hero. John's response: "you called?" Subsequently John went on to identify chaperonins which guide the assembly of Rubisco[3], probably the most abundant, and least efficient, protein in the galaxy.

---

1 Mendiola-Morgenthaler, L.R., J. –J. Morgenthaler and C.A. Price. 1976. FEBS Lett. 62: 96-100.
2 Ellis, R.J. 1974. Biochem. Soc. Trans. 2. 179-182.
3 Ellis, R.J. 1973. Comment. Plant Sci. 4. 29-38.

A fermentation seminar is one in which sometimes revolutionary ideas are exchanged across a platform of microbiological labors such as beer or wine. At the 1975 Asilomar conference[4] Paul Berg and Herb Boyer demonstrated DNA splicing and its utility. Prior to this, Avery et al. had shown that DNA was the heritable means of transferring genetic traits. Molecular biology was born. With our newfound physiologically active chloroplasts, we asked if these subcellular organelles were capable of making some of their own proteins from the DNA enclosed within their membranes. They were[5]. Would that chloroplast DNA be the same as the DNA of other organelles within the same plant host? A very productive collaboration with Takashi Akazawa's lab at Nagoya University allowed us to confirm the identity of amyloplast and chloroplast DNA within the rice plant.

That particular collaboration proved to be most enjoyable; a very long limousine brought me to the field where rice was growing and at a developmental stage called "milky", in which the white plastids could be harvested in a liquid form, as opposed to the hard rice grain. As I snipped a cluster of immature rice grains from the stalk and dropped it into a plastic bag, the limo driver bowed. I, of course, bowed back. This ritual proceeded until I had collected enough rice for the experiment!

It would be unfair not to mention a *fishing* expedition with the team of scientists led by Reinhold Herrmann and Peter Westhoff at the University of Dusseldorf. Expressed sequence tags (ESTs), or mRNAs for specific genes, could be located by hybridizing them to their complementary DNA sequence. This gave the researcher the ability to determine which genes were active at which time, and in which tissue, of an individual organism. Additionally, the Germans make very good bread.

If I have led you to believe that all collaborations are so rewarding as to lead one to stimulating conferences at Epcot Center, or other sunny locations, (we were studying photosynthesis, of course), I was

---

4 Mukherjee, S. 2016. *The Gene*. Schribner, Pub. ISBN 978-1-4767-3350-0
5 Reardon, E.M., et.al. 1978. In: *Chloroplast Development*, pp. 277-282. Elsevier-North Holland, Pub.

wrong. Colleagues can be thoughtless or even vengeful. Virtue is not always rewarded. Publishing first becomes an end unto itself.

The ethics of what to do with a literally earth-shaking discovery can be wrenching. Witness even today the millions of children blinded by lack of vitamin A when Ingo Potrykus's "golden rice"[6] is readily available. The planet-wide furor over GMOs has stalled the distribution of life-saving provisions to so many in need. How then will today's, and future scientists approach the CRISPR-cas9 system[7] which has the potential to do far more good—or evil: to cure all ills or destroy the earth as we know it? Michael Spector has outlined the logistics of Jennifer Doudna's group's monumental discovery in a very readable format[8]. I believe the Washington, D.C. conference is the beginning of a new awareness, as was Asilomar a generation of scientists ago, of how careful we must be in tip-toeing across the uses of our new scientific weapons.

As time went by and funding became uncertain for research, we took on the responsibilities of editor and associate editor and vice versa for the journals Plant Molecular Biology Reporter and Probe. Translating international attempts at scientific English into printed pages was humorous frustrating and rewarding. We often joked that the verbs could be found in volume two! It was during this interval that Carl became obcessed, yes OBCESSED, with hyphens! To quote Hope Jahren[9], of *Lab Girl* fame, "No writer in the world agonizes over words the way a scientist does". Carl corrected every submission that crossed our desks; he confronted store clerks in shops and students in poster sessions: "there is a hyphen missing there". Attributives came next with his humorous article on "one black shoe red hat wearing man". The obvious comparison is an offensive linebacker... We were so fortunate as to be mentored by Irving Louis Horowitz and Mary Curtis Horowitz during this interval whose group at *Transactions* kept our publications attractive, readable and comprehensible. And in the same font!!!

---

6 Burkhardt, PK et al. 1997.Plant J **11**: 1071-1078
7 Jinek et al., Science 337: 6096, pp. 816-821.
8 Spector, Michael, 2016. National Geographic 230. 30-55.
9 Jahren, Hope. 2016. *Lab Girl*. Alfred A. Knoff, Pub. ISBN 978-0-345-80986-5.

One of the simplest way to achieve collaboration is to find a group looking for solutions to common problems. Before we published *Nomenclature of Sequenced Plant Genes*[10] there was chaos in the realm of communication among plant scientists. The gene encoding a light harvesting protein, for example, enjoyed seventy-seven different appellations. We identified approximately 25 working groups led by authorities in their respective fields to determine an appropriate name for many of the then sequenced plant genes. The light-harvesting complex was reduced to Lhca and Lhcb.

Yes, as you suspected, this collaboration is a love story. One does not work, eat, talk, argue and cry with another for forty years without sparks being ignited. Long before we were actually a couple, many suspected the obvious. We sat together at conferences. Carl whispered in my ear. But- those whispers were NOT "sweet nothings". "Who was that person we just spoke with?" Carl claimed anomia long before Alzheimer's Disease was diagnosed. This distinguished professor is now blessed to be collaborating with a caring nursing staff who also love him. He still smiles for me. (Fig.2).

---

10 Plant Molecular Biology Reporter: Supplement to Volume 12, N0. 2. June 1994. Commission on Plant Gene Nomenclature

Ellen M. Reardon

Addendum: Shortly after the completion of this manuscript, Carl Price passed away. Many will miss him.

CHAPTER 16

La Evolucion de Charles B. Redington

Atraves de la Collaboracion

Charles B. Redington
Distinguished Professor of Humanics and
Professor of Biology Emeritus.
Springfield College

> "I don't know what your destiny will
> be, but one thing I know:
> The ones among you who will be really happy are
> those who have sought and found how to serve."
> ALBERT SCHWEITZER

Thomas Mann made a prophetic statement that "No Man is an Island." No person nor living organism stands alone from the biological point of view. In order to survive, organisms interact in ways positive and negative to themselves and those they interact with. Collaboration is a form of biological interaction. For example, some collaborations are mutualistic, others competitive, some predatory, and still others cooperative. I'd like to focus on the positive aspects of collaboration. It can be seen as working together through such things as partnerships, team work, delegation, reflection, and other means of accomplishing an endeavor. In the *"Redington Field Guides to*

Biological Interactions," we find that the common cattail, *Typha latifolia*, joins forces (collaborates) with over 100 different organisms, including birds, amphibians, reptiles, fish, mammals, insects, spiders, and humans, affecting the survival of all of these organisms and themselves. Well, as I reflect upon my life, it is quite clear to me that collaboration is what got me through life's challenges and to where I am today.

I am a WW II baby born in 1942, spending the war years as a small boy in Pittsburgh, PA, with my mother and her parents, while my father, a Merchant Mariner, was onboard two different ships sunk, one in the Atlantic and the other in the Mediterranean. After the war, we moved to Elyria, Ohio. My father was a wounded (physically and emotionally) veteran. I mention this because it was a factor in my being raised by a gregarious, yet at times, quick-tempered and violent father. This behavior affected me by my being scared, on guard, and feeling unsure of myself. He did want me to do the best I could but would confront me with the successes of other young boys in our neighborhood who were outstanding students or great athletes and tell me to be like them. I suppose in the end, this approach did have a positive effect on me because I have always had a competitive personality. I would affirm myself by thinking, "If so and so can do such and such, well then, so can I."

Overall, I made sure I had a fun and adventure-filled childhood, replete with camping, fishing, biking, shooting, playing baseball (even pitched tryouts for the Cleveland Indians), scouting, model building, stamp and coin collecting, astronomy, you name it. I did well academically in high school, attended the University of Michigan Biological Station, graduated from Baldwin-Wallace College (now University), was married, and then attended graduate school at Rutgers University where I earned my Master of Science degree from the Biology Department and Ph.D. in Plant Pathology and Physiology at the Rutgers College of Agriculture and Environmental Science (CAES). From there, my wife and I moved to East Longmeadow, MA, with our 2 1/2-year-old son Chuck and 3-week-old daughter Laurel, where I began my forty-four-year career as a Professor of Biology and Environmental Science at Springfield College, the birthplace of basketball. I wore many hats at the college including chair of the Bio/Chemistry Department, was appointed Springfield College Distinguished Professor of Humanics, and, upon retirement, was appointed Professor of Biology, Emeritus. During those forty-four years, I also worked as a state recognized senior environmental analyst with the Baystate Environmental Consultants of East Longmeadow, MA. As I reflect on all of these things and more, I realize without collaboration along the way, none of this would have been accomplished.

Today, I am retired happily in Florida with my wonderful wife Carolyn Frances and our regal Beagle Button. Here we enjoy new friends, fishing, boating, biking, tennis, pickle ball, etc., we make sure to get all the screenings and tests from the medical profession that people our age should, and enjoy visiting with our children and grandchildren.

Introduction To My Collaborative Experiences

I have decided to highlight events in my life story that were examples of collaboration that helped me on my path of life. I will try to do this in a sort of chronological order as best I can, with some events standing alone while others seem to connect or evolve one from another.

BULLYING *(a form of power or control over another)*

As a youngster, I was a tall skinny boy who fit the kid in the Charles Atlas ad who got sand kicked in his face and his girlfriend stolen. I did lift weights and was no weakling. However, events in my life in those days did very little to bolster my sense of worth. As I mentioned before, my father's antics did not help. He was not averse to using a belt or scaring the "h---" out of me. Furthermore, I was from a very athletically minded community, where competition was quite keen and at times demoralizing. There were several athletes in baseball and basketball who would bully me for reasons I do not know. They would make remarks, criticize my efforts, push me aside and brag of their greatness. Of course they were the coaches favorites. One of these coaches (a WW II veteran) used to rant and rave about any mistake I (and others) would make, totally embarrassing us in front of others (he dropped dead of a heart attack on the field one day). I was seventh man on the

Ohio State championship basketball team but rarely played. I felt like an outsider, and the coaches did little or nothing to ameliorate the situation for me. As I think back, many of those coaches were damaged goods from the war and probably suffered PTSD, a problem not yet recognized at the time. Had I had any understanding of this disorder with my father or the coaches and the fact that some of the players had lost the fathers in the war, I may have been better able to deal with circumstances. Many of them were angry and frustrated, I am sure.

I was too skinny to play football but loved baseball. One day my baseball coach pulled me aside and said he thought that rather than being stuck in right field, he would like to try me out at pitching. This was the very first vote of confidence that I had received in the sports arena and I was excited and, of course, nervous since I had never pitched competitively before. I also realized that I would become a central part of the team of some very fine athletes. I sensed that I had to do well to meet what I perceived as demanding standards. Furthermore, I knew that I would be thrown in against teams with some of the very best athletes in town. Many of these guys had snubbed me before and thought they were better than me and naturally I assumed would do all they could to beat me. Several of these opponents were footballs stars, one eventually going off to be quarterback at Ohio State University.

I decided to accept the challenge because I sensed our coach was presenting an opportunity to join a team and share success or failure in a competitive sport that I did not realize at the time would be through collaboration. I worked hard to develop my pitching skills. I had an opportunity to meet the great pitcher Bob Feller of the Cleveland Indians who gave me the following tip on control: hang a bed sheet from a backyard clothes line, cut a hole in it the size of the ball, and throw to go through that small hole. My mother gave me an old sheet which I used for that purpose. I perfected a number of pitches including a fast ball, terrific roundhouse curve, sinker, knuckleball, and excellent control. I also developed a move in which I would pick off a baserunner taking a lead off second base--a hard move for a right-handed pitcher.

I eventually became prepared and was ready for the showdown. The word spread that there was a new pitcher/gun in town and that Redington was hard to hit. There were other pitchers on other teams with more experience who thought they would have no trouble beating me. However, I must have begun to feel a part of something bigger than myself, a sort of synergy as it were, that was giving me added strength and purpose toward the team (of course this is my thinking of the situation today). When I began hearing about some of the big hitters I would come up against, my innate competitiveness took hold. I remember feeling confident for the first time in my life in an athletic situation. I felt in control, "in the zone," in today's parlance. There were three hitters that dominated our league: one was the quarterback I mentioned before, one a starter on the basketball team, and another was just a cocky kid that I was determined to shut down. I used every trick in the book to strike them out. I had a roundhouse curve ball that I would throw behind their head, thus throwing them off balance, that would then break across the plate. I had enough tricks up my sleeve so that I could mix up pitches to keep them guessing. It was so much fun seeing them stumble around in the batters box or step out of it. I gave up very few hits and in fact I held many strikeout records during my career The point of all this self-aggrandizing is that this great team experience, with a coach and teammates behind me, was the first step in which I took control of my world and thus began to feel good about myself against the competition that is a significant part life. There was no more bullying and making me feel inferior. I had found something I was very good at. We went on to the state quarterfinals and lost by one run. I pitched a one hitter and that one hit was a home run. We lost 1-0. Those years of success at baseball were more than gratifying and positive and probably had a subliminal driving effect on me in the years to come.

President of The Freshman Class at The University of Pittsburgh (1960)

When it came time during senior year to choose a college, I felt a pull towards the University of Pittsburgh because of my family history, interest in sports (particularly baseball), and academics. Pitt was an outstanding university and had Nobel prize winning researchers in the biological/medical sciences. I needed financial assistance and was awarded a five-hundred dollar scholarship, which was a great deal of money in 1960, to attend. I should also mention that my mother attended Pennsylvania College for Women(PCW), now known as Chatham College. I had a great first year at Pitt, joining the Sigma Chi fraternity, playing baseball, singing in the Pitt Men's Glee Club, and meeting some very interesting fellow students. including my roommate Joe Seiger. In the fall, I became president of the freshman class of approximately 1300 students while knowing only 15 or 20 classmates at the time! For me, this was an amazing story of accomplishment. Here I was, out on my own and away from home for the first time working together with my roommate and friends. Joe, who later had major success in real estate, was from New York City and had travelled throughout Europe with his friend Pete Bijur (he would later become CEO of Texaco) who also was a freshman at Pitt. So for starters, these two guys were so-called movers and shakers even then.

So how did feat happen, that I became freshman class president? Well, one day the announcement went out that elections would be held soon for freshman class officers, including president. To be honest, I paid little attention to this because I was a little overwhelmed and focused on getting adjusted to college life, mainly studies, fraternity rushing, football games, singing, and meeting people from throughout U.S.A. and world. One day I had just returned to my room when Joe came bursting in with Peter saying that they wanted me to be president of the freshman class. As I reflect today on their suggestion that I become class president, this was an example of how the two of them would eventually, through bold steps and collaboration, move to the top of their chosen professions. Anyways, I told them they were crazy and that hardly anyone knew me. They responded by saying they had a plan that almost guaranteed that the two of them could get me elected freshman class president. I found out later that they had friends from New York City who lived in the various dorms in our quad and had agreed to help with the election. I agreed to run, not knowing what lay in store for me. Did I have to campaign, give speeches, have a plan on how to work with the class? They just said no, everything was under control. I did see signs out and about to vote for other candidates, but none for me. Nothing really was happening leading up to the day of voting and so I continued to wondered what was happening. Joe and Peter told me again that things were under control and not to worry, even though I did feel caught up in the excitement and sense of mystery. On the day of voting, I returned my quad after breakfast to hear loudspeakers blasting from the four corners of our quad, "Vote Chuck Redington Freshman Class President." These announcements continued all throughout the day. I was probably quite embarrassed as I had had no prior idea of their plan. Joe, Peter, and their Nre York City friends had set up loudspeakers in the windows the four dorms. It was an amazing tactic that cemented the name Redington was on everyone's mind. So, guess who won the day? Yours truly! This was such a masterful undertaking involving a great example of collaboration and teamwork coupled with creative thinking. The point was that hardly anyone knew anyone at that time during our first semester. Yet it sounded as though Redington had quite a following, and thus vote for him. Joe and Peter led by example. They gave me my first taste of organizing and collaborating in the big world away from home and the positive results obtainable from such activity. I think back and realize this was how great odds could be overcome by those who work together to map out a concrete and workable plan. This became a signature examples to me of how to overcome difficulties and challenges as one moves through life. A person may not always think consciously about such experiences along the way, but some how they become part of one's DNA.

University of Michigan Biological Station and B-W College

I had to leave Pitt for financial reasons. My job at US Steel evaporated mid-summer the result of a wildcat strike, my father's income dropped after the recession of 1958 as he was working hard to start up his own company, and my mother was working as a first grade teacher at $3800.00 per year until she got certification. With a brother and two sisters still at home, things were too tight for me to continue at Pitt. I eventually made my way to Baldwin-Wallace College in Berea, Ohio. Here I lived off campus, had a part time job and started to take courses in biology. To make a long story short, with limited help from home, and after a couple part time semesters, I was able to land a residence hall counselor job that paid room, board, and some towards tuition. My years at B-W were rewarding and stimulating. Dr. Dean, professor of genetics and microbiology, and Mr. Barker (who went on to earn his Ph.D. in botany at the Univ. of Washington) took me under their wing. They eventually suggested that I attend The University of Michigan Biological Station (known affectionately as The Bug Station) during the summer of 1963. I applied and was awarded a summer scholarship from the University of Michigan. It was a glorious experience. I saw how the faculty thoroughly enjoyed teaching and leading field trips (all classes were held in outdoor settings). I had enrolled in Aquatic Vascular Plants with Dr. Edward Voss, an internationally recognized plant taxonomist and author of The Flora of Michigan, Boreal Taxonomy with Dr. E. Clover and various other courses e.g. ecology and aquatic mycology. That summer was the turning point in my academic life: I wanted to become a professor of biology and thus set my sights on going to graduate school for a Ph.D.

Upon returning to campus, I was hired to run the greenhouse and be a teaching/lab assistant to Dr. Calvin A. Smith, newly hired from Rutgers University. Dr. Smith had been a graduate student under Dr. Marion Johnson, Dean of the Graduate School and Professor of Biology. Dr. Smith suggested I apply to Rutgers which I did and was accepted as a student under Dr. Johnson. Unfortunately, a few months after my arrival, Dr. Johnson died unexpectedly. However, Drs. Gunckel and Fairtbrothers kept me on as a teaching fellow for the two years that I worked on my Master of Science degree. Dr. Gunckel had introduced me to Dr. Julian Steyermark of the Brooklyn Botanical Gardens with whom I worked on the wood anatomy and classification of *Pagamea* species from South America. I also was in charge of watering the plants in the large greenhouses at the Nelson Labs, in part because of my previous experience of doing so with the BW greenhouses. As I reflect on this phase of my career, it is obvious that there were connections and collaboration that kept me moving forward on my quest to get a Ph.D. and become a college professor.

Although I did well in the Biology/Botany Department, receiving my M.Sci. degree in 1966 (200th anniversary of Rutgers), I felt I needed to move away from classical botanical studies. I had enjoyed my work at "The Bug" station studying in the field, and along the way had met people who were doing what I called applied forms of research and teaching. For example, I attended lectures at Rutgers on research to solve the problem of brown rot of stone fruits, Chestnut Blight and others. While working on my Masters, I had learned about the Rutgers College of Agriculture and Environmental Studies(CAES) on the other side of New Brunswick next door to Douglass College. I had learned that CAES was where pure research was blended with applied outcomes such as finding a cure for a plant disease. It was at CAES that the famous "Rutgers Tomato" had been bred, the cure for peach rot was developed, and plant response to air pollution, root rot diseases and many other types of applied research were on-going. A former student in the Botany department that I knew suggested I make an appointment with Dr. Joseph L. Peterson, Professor of Plant Pathology and Mycology at CAES's Dept. of Plant Pathology. I headed over to Martin Hall and had a great meeting with Dr. Peterson who offered me a research fellowship working with him on *Fusarium* wilt diseases. Dr. Peterson changed the course of my graduate career in a way that I had hoped and for this I will be forever grateful. During those three years, Drs. Peterson, Varney, Davis, Cappellini, Clark, Price, and others molded me into the person I eventually became as a professor and leader at Springfield College and my community, namely always looking to make positive, current changes in students and the world around me. Part of my training during these years was conducted in the field (I had my own plot of land at the Rutgers farm to carry out some of my research and also had greenhouse space assigned to me) in collaboration with other departments at CAES, such as Plant Physiology and Horticulture.

I graduated in 1969 with a Ph.D. in Plant Pathology and Physiology from CAES. That spring, I was hired as Assistant Professor of Biology at Springfield College, where I enjoyed a marvelous career of 44 years that was, in great part, a result of the kind of applied research that I experienced working with agricultural scientists.

Winning Sc Raises for Faculty and Staff

My first day on the Springfield College campus in the fall of 1969 found me heading into the Quonsett Hut Field House (a donation from the US Government after WW II in appreciation of the use of the campus during the war as an officer training site) to check out the basketball court (SC is the birthplace of basketball). As I opened the door, a fast moving stocky fellow came through with a tennis racquet in hand. He, immediately introduced himself as Dr. Ed Steitz, Athletic Director. I mentioned I was a newly hired Assistant Professor of Biology and asked him if he could suggest where I could get a new tennis racquet. He said he would get me one which he later did. I also learned he was a great handball player and offered to instruct me in this "new to me" game. As time went on, a colleague and I often met at the underground handball courts to play Ed and his partners. Ed was a worldwide ambassador of basketball and inventor of the 3-point shot and member of the Basketball Hall of Fame. I had become very good friends with colleague Dr. Steitz who would later back me up in my battle as President of the Faculty Personnel Committee and President of the Faculty Senate (at that time, called The All College Representative Committee).During my early years at SC and because I am athletic, I met other colleagues in the Physical Education Division of the college. One was Diane Potter who was one of the first females to graduate from SC and later became a nationally recognized coach of women's softball. She was a tough but great person who became a dear friend over the years, and would support many of my future initiatives at SC.

I hit the ground running at SC regarding my contributions to the college through being elected to many committees and ultimately to president of the aforementioned committees. Salaries in the 1960's and early 70's were very low at small private colleges. For example, I was hired at $9000.00 as an Assistant Professor of Biology with a Ph.D. Raises were paltry at the time and the FPC was the bargaining body for salaries and fringe benefits. Diane Potter was my feisty Vice President. We decided to do some research on national salary averages at comparable division 2 and 3 colleges. Ultimately, we determined that we would need significant raises across the board to gain parity. We met with the College President and treasurer who, of course, at the time wanted little to do with discussing or compromising on our requests. I then began reporting at faculty meeting on our lack of progress. We had come up with a three-year plan of 11, 12, and 13% raises. It was at this time that with Ed Stietz, Diane, and many other faculty supporting me, I met with the president and presented an offer to negotiate or the possibility of having to bring in the National Labor Relations Board. At this meeting, Diane and I announced that we had 99 out of 100 faculty members behind us. The president offered to resign. We said," No, just try to meet some of our needs through negotiations. The very next day, the president announced to the SC community a plan to give us the largest raise to date in SC history amounting to the 11,12, and 13% over three years just as we had asked. Needless to say, it was "his" plan, of making such an offer to us. I learned then how to deal with such administrators: speak softly to them but carry a big stick, to sort of quote President T. Roosevelt. We let the administration take the credit, and we moved on. It was a great collaborative undertaking which, I feel, grew out of many interconnections with the faculty that I was able to cultivate over the years. I must admit that I did not know at the time where all this interacting in positive ways with my colleagues would come into play later. I do know that reaching out in genuine and supportive ways to others will come back in very positive ways in the accomplishing of a task.

An Environmental Consultant With Baystate Environmental Consultants, Inc.

While walking back to the biology department after my tour of the WW II era Quonset Hut Field House, I met a fellow strolling along with a small boy in tow. I introduced myself to Carlos Carranza, Ph.D. and professor of geology. We hit it off from the start, and he eventually introduced me to his colleague, James Walsh, Ph.D. and professor of physics and a civil engineer. These two introductions were, along with Dr. Steitz, the very beginning of my networking with faculty who, as it would later turn out were to play very important roles in my life, including achievements and contributions I would make at the college and community at large.

In 1969, the year I arrived at SC, The National Environmental Policy Act (NEPA) was passed by congress. It was signed into law in 1970. In 1972, my friends and colleagues Drs.Carranza and Walsh, founded Baystate Environmental Consultants (BEC), Inc. This was most likely, one of the first environmental consulting firms founded in the United States. At first, Carlos and Jim remained professors at the college while they grew the business on the side. In the beginning, their major emphasis was housing developments that involved wetlands and civil engineering requirements. At first, they hired independent consultants to help out in critical areas. But they soon realized there was a need for a more cohesive interacting team of environmentalists. This led them to pull together a full-time team of in-house experts. Carlos and Jim eventually resigned from the college. I watched the company grow into a highly regarded and successful company with over 25 employees, most with advanced degrees, that was straight out busy for nearly 40 years.

In 1985, after my return from having led an expedition to Africa, Dr. Carranza invited me to become a senior environmental analyst in wetlands delineation, mitigation, and restoration because of my credentials in ecology and knowledge of New England flora. Although they offered me a full- time position, I loved my teaching too much to leave SC. I thus became a part- time employee during the academic year and full time during summer college vacations. I did this for more than 20 years. This experience was an epiphany in my teaching career! I had gotten my Ph.D. in applied areas of science but was teaching mostly text book science with some field trips thrown in for good measure. Thus, up until the BEC position, I really did not have much of an understanding of how my subject matter could fit into the real world.

However, at BEC I was working and collaborating with professional engineers, ecologists, limnologists, and others of many backgrounds on major projects for a variety of clients. Now I was attending public hearings, making presentations to conservation commissions, meeting clients, identifying wetland plants, delineating wetlands and uplands as well as studying their ecology. On many occasions, I was a professional witness in court cases. For example, Carlos and I were instrumental in saving rare Sand Plain Grassland Communities on Martha's Vineyard in a court case that pitted us against one of the biggest law firms in Boston. We would always try to balance economics with ecology so that developers could use lands but doing so in an ecologically responsible manner. In still other instances, we worked with state and federal authorities on airport runway extensions, road widening projects, etc. I was now in a situation where my science background was being validated. I began to feel more relevant when I went into my classroom. I had the scars of the real world battles and could now bring the subject matter that I taught alive with practical applications of the subject matter at hand. I was able to show where reality in the field often diverged from information given in the textbooks, most of which were probably written by authors who had little practical experiences in the real world of their subject matter. I had developed a renewed sense of worth in that my many years of education were of considerable value in and out of the classroom and that my students were major benefactors of our student-professor collaborations.

In my teaching, I could bring the subject matter of ecology into focus in actual settings. I was known also as the "field trip professor." I would take students on weekend field trips to study an actual development, attend conservation commission meetings with them, visit consulting firms, etc. These experiences would lead to portfolios students would compile that often networked them into a job after graduation. Many of my students ended up starting their own environmental consulting firms that would often hire our graduates. One of our graduates has a world-wide environmental consulting firm. So many important collaborations occurred during this time of my career that flowed from previous experiences and undertakings that would lead to further such experiences in working together as I tried to show in this chapter. To this day, in many ways I feel I owe a large part of my success as a professor to my association with Drs. Carranza and Walsh and my colleagues at BEC.

SMITH COLLEGE ASSOCIATION (The other SC in the Pioneer Valley of Massachusetts)

Springfield College is known world-wide as the birthplace of Basketball and also to the invention of Volleyball by one of our graduates. As a result, for many years, Springfield College's main reputation centered around athletics. However, 1969, the year I was hired, saw the beginning of a modification of the SC mission to a stronger focus on the Arts and Sciences with the hiring of 22 new faculty members in a broad range of disciplines. A colleague and I were the only Ph.D.'s hired that year. It did not take long for me to recognize that the biology department's facilities were, let us say, quite lacking. I needed to bring about some serious changes. My teaching and advising areas were the plant sciences, ecology, and general biology. Having cared for the greenhouses at Rutgers Nelson Labs and its various biomes under glass, I found myself confronted with a small broken down greenhouse, perhaps 10' x 20' and with no working ventilation. Eventually, I did get some money to put it into working order for basic plant growing. However, it was clear that I needed to find a better solution to the problem since there would be no funds for building a new greenhouse facility any time in the immediate or long term.

I soon learned of the world famous Smith College 20 miles up the road from Springfield in Northampton, Mass. There, I discovered the wonderful Lyman Plant Houses and the many world biomes in different greenhouses, the connected plant classrooms, the annual spring and fall flower shows, the campus evolutionary gardens, and much more. To me, it was like striking gold. Thus began another of the important collaborations of my teaching career. This campus became my teaching station owing to my eventual meeting with Dr. John Burke, Professor of Botany, and many other Smith professors and greenhouse staff, all of whom I reached out to. I was invited to bring my students there any time. Now I had a rainforest, a desert, and many other biomes for my students to study. It also included an experimental greenhouse and plant nursery at my disposal. This relationship lasted for over forty years. Although most of the positive interaction of this association came my way from Smith College, on various occasions I wrote articles for their newsletter and brought in one of their faculty on a

STEM grant. Our college visits and use of their facility was important to Smith to justify their existence by way of their reaching out into the community to share the vast knowledge and resources that cost many dollars to maintain.

Dr. Burke further helped me to collaborate across disciplines at Smith. For example, I was connected to professors in the art department and art museum where I was able to expand on the understanding of human history through various art media depicting the migration of food plants and plant products throughout the world. Furthermore, I was introduced to the curator of the Rare Book Room at Smith. As we knew and further learned, most of the earliest books printed were about plants, made from plants, and printed with ink from plants. The holdings in this collection dated from the mid to late 15th century and later and included many books such as herbals, floras, gardening, including a page from the first printed book, The Guttenberg Bible. My students always enjoyed these trips and the availability of such resources. Although we had a small herbarium at Springfield, we were able to supplement our needs by using the Smith Herbarium as well. One day while visiting the Smith greenhouses, I noticed a very unusual display of paper objects. To my then astonishment, I learned that it was a collaboration between the horticultural department and a Smith professor of architecture, Dr. Middlebrook. He had brought his students to the greenhouses and challenged his students to find architectural inspiration from flower structure. They were then required to construct their idea from heavy paper. I saw examples of bridges, walls, windows, and more whose design and structure were suggested by the flower's natural beauty and form. I was inspired to share this idea with my students and thus subsequently met with Dr. Middlebrook who kindly helped run such a lab for my students. Our association eventually led to him working with us on a STEM grant to introduce this model to high school teachers as a new and creative teaching method and technique.

This examples of my reaching out to others to enrich my teaching and the academic lives of my students led me to work with many other community resources over the years. Through these connections, I found many ways to get the students out of the classroom and labs and into the real world in order to see relevance in their learning. As a graduate student of Dr. J.L. Peterson's at Rutgers CAES, I had been taken to Plant Pathology conferences at The U. of Massachusetts and the Connecticut Agricultural Experiment Station. Later as a professor, I was always seeking ways to give my students real world views of our science studies. These experiences back in graduate school served to promote my reaching out to Dr. Israel Zelitch, a renowned researcher in photosynthetic studies at the Ct. Ag. Expt. Station. He opened the door to my students to visit with him and other scientists who were working on the applied research being conducted there and paid for by the taxpayers of the state. By the way, it was at this station that dihybrid corn crosses were developed by Professor Jones. I continued to bring my students there for over 40 years. Other community resources that we visited included the U. Mass Stockbridge School of Agriculture, where I got help building a solar greenhouse at SC with my students doing the work, and The Department of Environmental Planning where my ecology class certified vernal pools for the State of Mass. My point in all this is that one should never put up false walls between disciplines. I realized my own limitations and knowledge and thus was not averse to reaching out to others to expand my knowledge and thereby hopefully become an even more effective and inspiring professor. It was important to me that my students could witness and experience the need to step out of a comfort zone and make seemingly unlikely connections that can inspire creative interdisciplinary ideas even at a later time.

African Expedition

Ernest Hemingway became my favorite author back in high school after having read "The Green Hills of Africa" and "The Snows of Kilimanjaro". I also read "Cry the Beloved Country" by J. Paton and was inspired to one day go to Africa. In these readings, I was swept away by the seeming excitement of the African bush, descriptions of wildlife and the Maasai, Boran, and other tribes of the Maasai Mara and Serengeti. I also read works by the expatriate Paul Bowles whose writings such as " The Sheltering Sky" and " Let it Come down" were about people, traditions, and the challenges of living in north Africa. My point is that what one may read along the road of life can become a spark to collaboration and a whole new discovery of life and meaning. In my case, such readings laid the groundwork for my African Expedition to Kenya, Tanzania, and Ruanda.

In the mid 1980's, I was fairly well established at the college and had been promoted to Full Professor. It was at this time that I began to think that I would like to lead an expedition to Africa, the first for the college and coincidently on the 100th anniversary of Springfield College. But who could I connect with that might help realize this goal? I knew what I wanted to do on this trip. I wanted to rough it, not go on a catered safari. I wanted to climb Kilimanjaro, go on photo game runs, meet tribes, visit the bush, scuba dive in the Indian Ocean reefs and perhaps encounter a whale shark, visit the mountain gorillas of Ruanda (Diane Fossi country), and more. I soon decided to contact Mass. Audubon to ask if they could recommend an African contact. They immediately suggested Mr. Don Turner, head of East African Ornithological Expeditions. I sent Mr. Turner a letter explaining who I was and what I wanted to accomplish. He wrote back (this was long before the internet) that "absolutely, we can do it all." So now I had an expedition leader who had over 25 years of experience working in east Africa who would make all the ground arrangements for our trip. With this information, I approached the college with my plan which they ultimately accepted. I then conducted interviews with the college and local newspapers where I explained my dream trip and eventually advertising a date for a public meeting at our library for those interested in exploring the possibility of going on this expedition. With recorded African drums and chants filling the room of over 60 people attended the first meeting. In the end, 25 people went on this expedition where we accomplished all the goals I had set even staying in the Kibo Lodge and having a beer by the same fireplace that Hemingway enjoyed and from where he left when he climbed Kilimanjaro that became his inspiration for "The Snows of Kilimanjaro."

Reaching out to others, borrowing ideas, and creating partnerships are most evident in this exciting time in my life as a professor. I might add that while in Tanzania, we visited a college that we then adopted at SC. We eventually sent them microscopes, science texts, and lab glassware. I contacted the air force at Westover Air Base near us and they agreed to add our gifts to their cargo on a flight to Tanzania…talk about collaboration!

For many years our African Expedition group met once a month at a local restaurant to share our ideas, adventures, set up other expeditions, and support our adopted school in Tanzania.

Brazilian Amazon and The YMCA

Springfield College has been and still is closely connected to the YMCA. In fact, in the early years of our founding, we were known as The YMCA Training College before our name change. Many local, national, and international YMCA management positions have been filled by our graduates. Since I had been a "YMCA Brat" in the 1950's, I always felt a close affinity to the YMCA mission.

In 1898, the YMCA of Brazil was founded by a graduate of Springfield College, and so the college has been revered always by them. In 1998, a contingent of directors from the YMCA of Rio de Janeiro attended a conference at SC. Manuel Aquino, was a member of that group who, it turned out, wanted to establish a YMCA branch in Santarem, Para State, Brazil. The YMCA of Brazil had just purchased 400+ acres of pristine wilderness in Alter do Chao, Para State on the Tapajos River, a tributary to the mighty Amazon. Their second goal was to establish an environmental education center on this land. They came to SC in order to get support for these projects. The first step would be to establish the YMCA branch in Santarem which is along the Amazon River followed by step 2, the development of the environmental center.

At the time, I was recognized by the college as an organizer and leader both on campus and the surrounding community. In addition to my professorship in biology and environmental science, I was a senior environmental analyst with Baystate Environmental Consultants. I did not know about this meeting but was asked later by one of our deans to contact Mr. Aquino to discuss their mission. Eventually I was invited to come to Santarem. When there, I was shown the potential sites for the YMCA building in Santarem and that of the environmental center in Alter do Chao. Manolo also had arranged for an expedition on the Amazon and Tapajos Rivers, the surrounding various biomes, and to meet with some of the river and forest Indians who might ultimately be served by the YMCA of Santarem. I had brought along a colleague and another friend, Ron Nizienkewicz, who had been on my African expedition to Kenya, Tanzania, and Ruanda. Ron had been on subsequent African expeditions as a team leader. And since I had ideas of leading expeditions and field trips into the Amazon, I wanted him to experience this part of the world in order to be a well informed and prepared team leader. Of course, our initial trip at this time was astonishing, from anacondas to the Mundurucu head hunting tribe! After this experience, I decided to help Manolo as best I could. The first thing we did was to get Springfield College behind my efforts, which was accomplished. After many meetings and trips to Brazil, and with the backing of the Rio YMCA headquarters and support from the college, the YMCA Santarem branch with Manolo as the executive director was founded.

Our next step was to establish the environmental education center in Alter do Chao a lovely little village about 23 miles southwest of Santarem at the confluence of the Amazon and Tapajos rivers. The 400+ acre property in Alter do Chao has several small lakes, a rustic camp site, a number of different biomes and was directly on the shore of the "Queen River", as the Tapajos is known. It is a blue water river with white sand beaches. What Manolo needed was a plan for the outdoor environmental field station. This is where I came in.

I had attended the University of Michigan Biological Station on Douglass Lake in Pellston, Michigan, just below the Mackinaw Straights. I quickly recalled the wonderful experiences I had here and the general organization of the field station. In addition, my experiences with other teacher training programs, as co-administrator, had allowed me the opportunity to set up temporary field stations. However, I decided to contact the UMBS with my plan and ask if they would be willing to send me an up- to- date rendition of the UMBS layout including such things as field labs, library, lecture rooms, dining facilities, etc. To my great pleasure, they complied with my request. This enabled me to design a workable field station that would fit the Alter do Chao site. Several years later, Manolo and several executives of the RioYMCA of Brazil came to Springfield College to present me with a certificate acknowledging me as a founding member of the YMCA of Santarem and another for the design of the field station. As can be surmised from this, I would have had little success without the support of others and the connections and collaborative efforts I had cultivated along the way. One may not realize at the time, how certain things may play an important role in life later down the road. How did I ever know that I would harken back over thirty-five years to my time as a 21-year-old student at the UMBS for understanding and help in this venture in the Amazon jungle?

Field Guides to Biological Interactions

During my years at Rutgers as a Teaching Fellow, I worked under the very bright and creative professor Dr. William Malcolm. At a time when we knew little of the fact that meteors might have transported fragments of life starting purines and pyrimidines of nucleic acids to earth, he made an interesting comment about life on earth being inoculated by the fungus interacting on an orange-peal left behind by space travelers. Seems he was on the right track back then. Back in 1964, biological interactions such as mutualism, competition, commensalism, ammensalism, and others, were hot topics to Dr. Malcolm and of which I knew very little at the time but soon learned a great deal from him. Several years later, I had to give a seminar on plant diseases and chose to discuss various interactions between plants and their community neighbors including bacteria, fungi, birds, bees, and others. In crafting my presentation for the seminar, I called upon the knowledge that Dr. Malcolm had imparted as a lecturer in the biology course I assisted in. I hung onto that seminar paper throughout my teaching years and used it as a springboard to many ecological discussions.

Much of my work as an environmental consultant was wetland delineation, mitigation, and restoration. I soon learned that it was extremely difficult to repair or build a wetland. I recalled from Dr. Malcolm and others that biological interactions were the glue that held ecosystems together. I began to wonder why, for example, many plants that seemed to be properly planted and cared for during wetland restoration, did not live. One day, it hit me like a bolt of lightning, that a plant does not live alone in their environment. I suddenly saw in my mind's eye, a common cattail with these invisible threads radiating out into the environment where they were connected to various groups of life forms. I decided to study more closely the cattail and eventually determined that in one way or another, it interacted with nearly 130 different organisms including birds, mammals, insects, spiders, reptiles, amphibians, fish, other plants, humans, and the ecosystem. For over two years I researched 100 wetland and water plants of New England and those east of the Mississippi River at such places as the Audubon Society, the Yale, Harvard, Smith College libraries, field observations, and discussions with various experts. When I decided to write a field guide, I contacted Dr. John Burke and staff of the Rare Book Room of Smith and asked if they could recommend an artist who could render drawings of the plants I chose to cover. They put me in touch with a wonderful artist and Smith graduate, Pam See, who painted wildflowers. She agreed to do the drawings for the book.

The *Redington Field Guides to Biological Interaction-- Plants in Wetlands* was published in 1992. A mentor of mine, Dr. Richard Evans Schultes of Harvard University, from whom I learned many things about the Amazon before I went, had often invited my students to his lectures on the Amazon. He was kind enough to write the introduction to my field guides. I was honored that he had strongly felt that this type of information was needed by those who were protecting, restoring, or otherwise impacting wetlands and lands under water. My field guide was successful with environmentalists and some colleges adopted it in ecology classes. I also felt there was a need to protect upland organisms as well. With this in mind, I decided to contact my old biology department Rutgers University where I earned my Masters degree to find someone who might undertake this kind of a field guide for animals in towns and cities. I was introduced to Dr. Joanna Berger of the Biology department who agreed to write the companion "Field Guide to Biological Interaction-Animals in Towns and Cities". For this overall undertaking, Baystate Environmental Consultants, Smith

College, Springfield College, Rutgers University, and others were part of a greater process that helped bring my idea of these field guides to fruition.

STEM (Science, Technology, Engineering, and Mathematics)/TERC (Teacher Education Research Center)

A colleague and I had worked together on a number of teacher training grants over the years. In the mid 1990's, we headed up several "TERC Hands On" two-week long field workshops at the Rensselaerville Institute in New York for high school teachers from across the country. TERC is a 50-year- old, nonprofit organization dedicated to improving teaching and learning in math, science, and technology. Our basic goal was to demonstrate how to observe the natural world for their students in terms of the "Burning Question" model included at the end of the chapter and how to set up a functioning, temporary field station in order to run this model. Our approach was to take all of the teachers on several field trips while making observations of what might provoke them to ask a "burning question/need to know question." For example, we might see a cattail marsh emerging at the far edge of a pond and ask, "Is this lake filling in? And if so, how long will it take until the lake converts to uplands?" The manner in which we would proceed was to group the teachers into small teams as described in the "model" section. In addition, we would have nightly "sponge" sessions where students would share their progress to date, give each other suggestions, and generally create a scientific community in a field station setting that teachers could model back at their respective schools.

Eventually my colleagues and I along with a professor of education at U. Mass., Amherst, collaborated on the development of a STEM program. This was carried out over a three-year period with teachers from the Springfield, MA general area. My initial role was to develop a theme for our STEM workshop around the biological sciences. I came up with a model that would demonstrate the interconnectedness of the biological sciences through evolution. In particular, I focused on several of the mechanisms of evolution, namely "variability", "adaptation", and "reproduction." I labelled it "VAR". This model brought together a team of professors from our Bio/Chem department including myself for "variability", an evolutionary biologist for "adaptation", and a geneticist for "reproduction." Over the years, I had recognized the need for breaking down walls between disciplines within the biological, chemical sciences, and the liberal arts. My modus operandi throughout my teaching career was to find areas within my subject matter that would lend themselves to team teaching. For example, I might bring into my Ecology class a history to discuss the possible significance of protecting an area known to have been occupied by Native Americans at an earlier period of time. Through this approach, I built up strong collaborative relationships with many of my college colleagues. This history of collaboration led us to invite onto our STEM project teams colleagues who could work to mesh our disciplines in very effective ways. We also brought in a chemistry professor who used her computer skills to create tests and measurements to evaluate the efficacy of our STEM program.

The STEM program was an example of modeling for science educators to develop skills, ways of thinking about science, and the need to work with others. We had nearly 100 teachers participate in our STEM program at Springfield College.

Community Service

I think I am basically a gregarious individual, one who enjoys actively participating in the community in a positive way. When I came to Springfield College, Dean Congdon laid out a basic tenet in order to enjoy a successful career at the college. This tenet included the following: 1. successful and continued academic development and performance, 2. contributions to the college, and 3. contributions to the community.

Upon moving to East Longmeadow, MA, I fell in with a fine group of friends who were very much community orientated. In those days, East Longmeadow was still a sleepy little farm town just beginning to undergo some changes because of an influx of a generation of war babies. Through the Congregational Church, I developed one of my earliest friendships in town with a popular and well connected chiropractor, Dr. Conrad Henrich. Dr. Henrich and I became major collaborators on many community programs, including helping start a scout troop, chairing the Fourth of July parade committee, starting the East Longmeadow Soccer Association (ELSA) of which I was the founding president, running fund raisers, building soccer fields, training soccer coaches and referees. Furthermore, I acted as starter at the high school swim meets, and he coached the high school girl's soccer team. He and I worked with the town recreation department, school system, and local businesses to get land set aside for building new soccer fields. Along the way, Springfield College played an important role in many of these endeavors. For example, we were able to use the college's lakeside camp site and Olympic pool for scouting activities. Furthermore, the college also allowed us to use their soccer fields for our intertown and Western MA competitions, a real highlight for the youth soccer program. Various administrators of the college worked with me on these activities to coordinate schedules and facilities, for which much thanks must be acknowledged. I must add, that SC is and has been a very community orientated institution.

SC is known not only for its liberal arts, physical therapy, and physician's assistance programs, school of human services, and many other viable programs, but also its long standing history of athletics and health studies. I feel that my career at the college endowed me with a mission of fitness, sports, and general good health, for which I am most thankful. Being blessed with a son and a daughter, both outstanding high school and college athletes, all the more connected me to sports. In 2008, a dear friend of mine and SC graduate, was inducted into the Chicopee (Mass) High School Athletic Hall of Fame. It suddenly occurred to me that East Longmeadow High School should have a hall of fame. Our high school has a proud athletic heritage, one in which my son Charles and daughter Laurel made major contributions in both soccer and basketball. Laurel, at 5 feet 12 inches (as a teenager, she refused to be listed at 6 feet-ha!), was the first female (and second athlete) to score over 1000 points at East Longmeadow High School and was All Western Mass in basketball and soccer. Their accomplishments propelled me forward with my goal of establishing the hall of fame for the community and school department.

The goal or "burning question or need to know" was 'can we found an athletic hall of fame'? What follows is the "how to know" and the "doing of the project" that led to the inauguration in 2010 of the first class of athletes into the East Longmeadow High School Athletic Hall of Fame. To accomplish this required a great deal of support and cooperation from many corners. Throughout this narrative, you will note that after forty- plus years active in the community of East Longmeadow, I was able to draw upon many friends and acquaintances for their help. The first call I made was to Pat Beene, an East Longmeadow junior high teacher and friend, who had been my daughter's first basketball coach. She thought it a great idea and asked that I call her nephew who happened to be the high school athletic director, to get his take on this. He gave his full support to the idea and mentioned he'd been hoping one would be established. Pat and I also went over names of people whom we thought might be interested in establishing the founding executive committee for the hall of fame. I then met with the founding athletic director of the Chicopee High School Athletic Hall of Fame who imparted many helpful suggestions on how to move forward on this. It was clear that I would also need to get approval from the school board and principal. I knew the principal well who set up a meeting with and introduced me to the school board. Being a known quantity in town, the board gave me a very respectful reception and hearing which resulted in their resounding approval for the hall of fame.

I was able to assemble a remarkable executive committee full of energy and support. The rest is history. We had our inaugural induction in 2010 of the top 20 athletes going back to the founding of the high school. There were over 250 guests in attendance including a U.S. congressman, state senator, letter from Sen. Ted Kennedy, and others. We created a HOF wall at the high school adorned with a beautiful metal plaque for each inductee, with their image and brief notes on their accomplishments thereon. I stepped down as founding president upon my retirement from Springfield College. The HOF and committee continues to this day with an annual induction each fall at a special dinner that attracts 250-300 guests. This program to date has touched over 4000 people, including the inductees and their families and friends who attend these ceremonies.

Student Advising at SC

Springfield College faculty are required to be academic advisors to students in their respective majors. Usually we keep advisee for their entire four years to graduation. Although students are held ultimately responsible for fulfilling their major requirements and credit hours for graduation, the advisor's role is to help the advisees to stay focused on a number of things. These include keeping up on the students' academic progress, suggesting ways of balancing their commitments to athletics, studies, extra-curricular involvement, personal health, helping and arranging internships, coaching on life and career goals after college, and a variety of other things that might come up. A good advisor will try to stay regularly in touch with their advisees throughout each semester. This advisor-advisee relationship is one of the most important and earliest collaborations freshmen students will develop. I have had many very positive interactions with my advisees. For example, through my teaching and environmental consulting, I have had a number of my advisees and students go on to start their own environmental consulting firms and then turn around and grant internships to our students, some of whom end up as permanently employed after graduation. This is collaboration of the most exciting and helpful sort.

Just before my retirement, I was asked by the college development office to go to New York City to meet with several of my former students who were very successful dentists and who were being courted for donations to Springfield College. It turns out that under these circumstances, a potential donor may recall a favorite professor or advisor as is the case in this situation. Upon meeting with one of them, he thanked me for the fact that he was a successful dentist, and flatly stated that he would not have done it without my early encouragement. He recalled a meeting with me when he felt frustrated and was not happy with his major program. He noted that I presented several other options that might fit him better. He said he recalled the weight being lifted off his shoulders and moved into another major with renewed vigor. To be honest, I had lost track of him after graduation and so did not even know he had become a dentist.

Springfield College Distinguished Professor of Humanics

One April day in 2012, I received an email from the Academic Dean and Vice President Dr. Jean Wyld, that she wanted to "chat" with me. Well, it seemed ominous enough but I set up an appointment soon thereafter, thinking 'what did I do now?' As I walked into Dr. Wyld's office, her executive assistant Cindy, whom I have known for over 40 years, was standing in doorway with a pleasant smile on her face. Dr. Wyld asked me to sit down and then asked if I would accept the 2012-13 academic year appointment as Springfield College Distinguished Professor of Humanics. This is the highest form of recognition our college can bestow on a faculty member. This appointment is to both honor the contributions of the faculty member, and to promote the values of our Humanics mission. The criteria for selection include the following: 1. being a current member of the faculty, 2. serves as faculty role model by demonstrating excellence in their teaching, professional/scholarly/creative work, and their service to the college and the community. 3. demonstrate, through their life and work, the principles of the college's Humanics philosophy and mission to educate students in spirit, mind, and body for leadership in service to humanity, and 4. has the potential to provide leadership for a Humanics program or project that will serve the best interests of Springfield College and its faculty, staff, and students.

I was dumbfounded--- I never expected this. I had been at SC for 43 years through many many changes in administration and faculty. And although I had a wonderful record, I seriously thought I'd been lost in time and that the present faculty were more in the limelight. So, after my initial shock wore off, I, of course, accepted her kind offer; they had not forgotten me. After coming down out of the clouds, I immediately had an idea for my Humanics project. I knew this project would involve collaborating with many people I had worked with over the years. In other words, the groundwork had been laid and now I had to pull it all together.

My Punta Finalizacion—The Humanics Project

From my perspective, a tree is a metaphor for the Humanics philosophy of Springfield College. I found that Humanics had taken root in over 100 countries in that these countries had sent their students to SC. This means that if one were to look at a world map, it would reveal that approximately 77% of the land surface of the world is represented by students attending or having attended SC. My idea was to create a small arboretum to represent my metaphor with a tree dedicated to each of these countries. We would label a tree with an identification tag and a country name. I was able to select approximately 50 different trees that not only grew in a certain country but that would also grow in the deciduous forested biome of New England. I selected three major morphological features of trees to expand on my tree-Humanics metaphor:1. roots, 2. trunk, and 3. crown or canopy of leaves and flowers. These features would further tie in with the 3 sides of the SC triangle of SPIRIT, MIND, and BODY.

The Roots/Spirit

Students come to an unknowing soil or campus as a seed. The seed or student germinates and takes root here and has the faith in our philosophy to grow. The SC education is the fertilizer for the youthful or seedling years. Putting down roots (getting their footing) here represents an opportunity for nurturing, where thought and feelings take shape for things to come. What is taken up in the soil is moved into the trunk or major part of the physical being. In this case, it is knowledge along with personality that moves upward.

The Trunk/Body

Here, SC tries to nurture the physical development of the person to become strong, sturdy, and independent. The body is also the vessel through which the SC education taken up by the roots during nurturing, flows. This "nutrition" supports the growth of the body which in turn will give support and life to the canopy or mind of the person. Without this strength, the mind will perish along with the body. During my undergraduate years, I had occasion to work with the Dean of Students who once remarked, "There is no place for athletics in an academic setting." I was surprised at the remark but suggested that with a weak body, a great mind might be buried with this weak body.

The Canopy/Mind

In our metaphor, there is science to support our comparison between the human mind and the "mind" of the canopy. For example, science has coined the term "plant intelligence", that is, plants have the ability to solve problems. Let me site a few examples. There is "plant neurobiology". Although the term sparks debate, we have detected action potentials in plants stems. Furthermore, we have found many of the neurotransmitters in plants such as acetylcholine, seretonin, GABA, and glutamate are found also in the animal kingdom. Also, we have found that plants "remember." Poplar tree leaves previously attacked by insects kick up their defenses faster than those not previously attacked. Plants also recognize self. As an example, sagebrush plants "sniffed" volatile organics from their wounded clones and thus became more resistant to attack by the same insect than non cloned sagebrush. So our students observe and respond to their environment, develop critical thinking skills to solve problems and sustain the animating principle of hope. As leaves fall from the tree to fertilize the soil for growth of other plants and seeds on the flowers spread near and far with their knowledge of the plant from which they came, our students move throughout the world where they plant the seeds of Humanics. Thus, as the "spirit, mind, and body" of plants take root to sustain our world biomes, so does our Humanics philosophy take root throughout the world to sustain Humanics. To me, the spirit, mind and body of the SC triangle says that without sustaining a healthy environment both of people throughout the world and the biomes we now live in, we will have no humanity.

This project involved getting the approval of the college president to work with a landscape consulting firm that was engaged in a major renovation of the campus. I also worked closely with the faculty and staff at Smith College. The Smith College campus is an arboretum. They were helpful in putting together a list of trees that were native to many of the countries on my list that would also grow here. They also shared a list of some of their nursery suppliers and worked with me on making and mounting tree labels. I had a computer science major who helped me develop and place "QR" codes tree labels that would allow smart phone users to scan the code and learn about the tree, country, and college.

On April 23, 2013, I presented my Humanics lecture and then took the audience on a short field trip to see some planted and labelled trees and to give a "QR" code demonstration. I am happy to report that to this day the project is ongoing with about 55 of the 103 countries honored by trees labelled on the campus. In the end, I counted over 25 people who contributed to this major project, all of whom were recognized in my printed program and without whom, this project would have been impossible. I must conclude by thanking Dr. Rod Sharp, editor of this book, for giving me the opportunity to reflect on my life in this manner. I think if I had known very early in life that so many collaborations would have been required to succeed, the journey might have seemed too overwhelming and too daunting a task. But if one takes each day and just opens up to one's own limits, admits them, and is willing to join in this great collaboration called life, success might just be the reward.

Collaborative Models
These are Models I often worked with in STEM and other teacher training programs.

The overall goals of these models included exposing participants to approaches for effective learning and teaching in a *lab* or *field trip setting* and to the value of utilizing *thinking*, *pairing* up into collaborative teams, and *sharing* ideas, observations, and results with others as a basis for sound scientific studies.

Need to Know/Burning Question Model

Our basic premise was to engage the participant in finding a *NEED TO KNOW THE ANSWER TO A BURNING QUESTION* arising from observations made on field trips, developing a *HOW TO KNOW* methodology to get an answer to their question, followed by applying the *HOW TO KNOW* through field data collecting and observation to obtain an answer. This approach also included setting up a temporary field station[11] with equipment, materials, and small library needed for field work. The collaborative model would start with a series of field trips with the participants.

An example:

1. Lead field trip to a pond with contiguous marsh, shrub swamp, tree swamp, and upland.
2. Ask participants to make observations and ask the leaders questions along the way.
3. Upon return to the field station, ask the students to compose a specific *NEED TO KNOW/BURNING QUESTION*.
4. Participants then would get into small teams focused on a specific *NEED TO KNOW/BURNING QUESTION* that was of interest to the participant.

---

11 Our Field Station was based upon my experiences as a student at the University of Michigan Biological Station. For these STEM and other workshops, our field station would have basic glassware, collecting jars, insect nets, various sampling nets, meters for measuring such parameters -- dissolved oxygen, temperature, conductivity, water clarity, pH, seepage-- slides, cover slips, field guides, cameras, boats, binoculars, dissecting scopes, microscopes, some chemicals, computers, printers, and other basic supplies.

5. At this point, the teams would meet, think, pair, and share ideas on how to answer their question; this is the *THE HOW TO KNOW STEP*. The program leaders would rotate around to each team to help develop effective *HOW TO KNOW* methods that might be effective and practicable with equipment and resources available at the time.
6. Teams would then *CONDUCT THE HOW TO KNOW STEP* lab/field work, recording all data in a field notebook supplied to each participant. During this period, the program leaders would rotate among the various teams available to answer questions or at times, prod questions from observations they were making.
7. Upon completion of the lab/field work, the teams would work up the data/observations for presentation at a poster session. Frequently, work on the team would be divided up into such areas as data analysis, writing of findings, poster preparing, and the oral presentation.
8. Frequently, we would have an independent evaluator who would determine the efficacy of our workshop.

Ecological Principles Model (AIDCHES)

This is a great collaborative tool for utilizing basic ecological principles to share ideas on how the ecosystem works and how human endeavors are also a function of these very mechanisms.

My observations of life as a biologist/environmental scientist have led me to organize some of the principle functioning mechanisms of ecosystems as follows:

- ADAPTATIONS
- INTERACTIONS
- DIVERSITY
- CHANGE
- HUMAN FACTOR
- ENERGY
- SYSTEMS

Although each of these has specific ecological meaning, say, for example, that the natural design of a flower has been ADAPTED to being pollinated by a specific bee, these terms can be applied to all aspects of life, including those dealing with human endeavors. I recall a comment made to me many years ago by Dr. Rod Sharp, the very editor of this book. He said, "Nature Speaks to us and tells us how to live our lives." That statement coincided with my convictions human beings are another community of organisms within ecosystems and thus are subject to the same laws of nature as any other plant, animal, or microbe.

Two Applications of this Ecosystem Model

1. The Field Trip
On any field trip in biology or ecology, these terms can be THE principle points of observation and discussion among the participants.

We can find a beaver pond and spend time examining how each "AIDCHES" are at work in the life of the beaver.

2. The Work Place As An Ecosystem
My son Charles was approached by his boss during a period of cutbacks at work and asked if he had any ideas on how to separate the "wheat from the chaff," so to speak. Chuck gave me a call and shared his predicament and asked if I had any ideas on how to deal with the situation. Wow, here was a real business problem with one of America's biggest risk management insurance companies, and I had an immediate and unique answer for him. I introduced Chuck to AIDCHES, and he said, "What the heck is that?" I then lead him through the following showing how the natural world does speak to us and tells us how all aspects of our world are controlled by AIDCHE as follows:

I said to examine each person being considered for the cutback and ask how these principles apply to the company's goals.

- Can this person easily ADAPT to situations?
- Does this person INTERACT effectively with others?
- Does this person have DIVERSE talents and/or able to deal well with diversity?
- Can this person handle CHANGE effectively?
- The HUMAN FACTOR: What kind of person is he/she and how do they affect and effect the workplace environment, treat coworkers, etc.?
- Does this person have ENERGY, such as enthusiasm for the company and being hardworking?
- Does this person see the big picture of the company and understand the SYSTEM that runs the company, its value, etc.?

This ecosystem approach was presented by Chuck to his boss who successfully applied it for the cutbacks. I eventually presented this idea on a public radio show!

CHAPTER 17

Reflections on Collaboration in Teaching:

Brigadoon and Other Myths

Laurie Repko
Olentangy Orange High School Educator

"Only connect."
—E.M. Forrester

While I was running my last batch of copies for the day, I inquisitively peered into the room adjacent to the workroom as I had done on numerous occasions. There was only one way in through a narrow door past the even narrower space in front of the copy machine. The pungent smell of cigarette smoke bloomed in my nostrils; simultaneously coaxing and repelling. Although I hadn't smoked a day in my life, glimpses of this paneled room, with its semi-drawn, yellowed curtains and tattered furniture beckoned to me. Its silence was, too, somehow like a comfortable blanket. The room had been glossed over on "the tour" I'd received weeks prior and now, as a full-fledged member of the team, I had a privilege—no, the *right* of access to this coveted place. The copier ground out its last sheet, I gathered my materials, straightened my back, and strode into the 9x15 space. The couch was as dingy as I had assumed, now in full view.

A woman in a pencil skirt and tucked blouse was sitting squarely in its center cushion, unaware of my shadow cast in from the doorway... unmoved and obviously not moving. A man was seated, back to the woman, at the only desk in the space to my immediate left. His chair was slightly pushed out to accommodate his girth and create necessary distance to read the butterflied newspaper. He peered over his glasses to see me and resumed reading. My papers billowed from my arms and my overstuffed bag weighed on my shoulder helping to lower me into the too-close-to-the-ground chair at the front of the room, a mere foot into the place, nearly in the doorway and under the only window. Not the ideal seat, but I was in! I tried to not make too much noise as neither occupant seemed to want bother, and I had a strong suspicion that was exactly what I would be. This was the teacher's lounge, after all, where faculty came to get away from the kids. In 1994, at only 24 years old, I straddled that line.

I forced myself to stay until the bell rang—sitting in silence with my colleagues, who I am sure were yet to know my name despite it being the end of September and having only a classroom's worth of staff members in the entire building. Many who, I later discovered, were 10 years or closer to retirement, and/or who had attended this same institution together as students themselves. Weeks later, I tried to strike up an academic conversation in the same lounge and actually, was asked to do my schoolwork someplace else—this was not the place for that. It took me another week or so to observe that the teachers who hung out there exhibited anti-kid, anti-progress, and quite possibly anti-social tendencies. The very same teachers about whom Ohio's Governor, John Kasich said, "If I were, not president, but if I were king of America, I would abolish all teachers' lounges, where they sit together and worry about 'woe is us.' "(Rowland). My first faculty lounge, it seemed, was doomed. I wasn't going to have the space I had hoped for—the synergy was going to have to manifest elsewhere, if at all. I worried that this was it. The ink had barely dried on my college diploma and my hope for a bustling, think-tank of a teacher's lounge was apparently shredded. Had my college professors been right about this, too? That teacher's "lounges" were bastions of stagnation and gossip? Where were the innovators? Where were the movers and shakers? Where were "the core" who kicked ass and took names? I would learn, not too late, that they were in their rooms. Working. All the time. The teacher's lounge for which I was searching was some sort of Brigadoon—a mythical place that appears only once in hundred years or so…

The other new hire was Julie from the Ashtabula area; we found each other as safe-haven immediately: we wore the same shoes to our teacher work day and figured that was reason enough to be fast friends and colleagues—some-kind of professional destiny. We weathered our first two years together on our $19, 000 salaries; Julie taught English to all 179 freshmen in the building and I was teaching all the sophomores. This was an unfortunate arrangement as our schedules provided few points of ingress. After commiserating over cheap dinners and chance meetings in the parking lot as means to developing our trust in each other, we gravitated to vertical alignment as our common professional ground—a way to see that the students' transition from her class to mine was at least purposeful, if not engaging, when it could be. We vowed to try to scaffold materials, skills and assignments; to piggy back actual lessons and reference each other's classes to our students to create continuity and environment that went beyond what was expected of us—which was to prepare them for the newly rolled-out state Proficiency tests, among other objectives, of course. Julie and I had tried to reach out to the other two ladies in the department, but we were always met with, "We already have our lessons planned; you're creating too much work." They always seemed interested in our ideas, but nothing ever gelled. Were we too young? Too inexperienced? Too wide eyed? Too well-versed in all the newest jargon? Or did some of our ideas really just suck? Likely all of the above. Having each other to lean on, while fumbling our way through our first five years of teaching, was an invaluable experience for both of us. From each other, we got support and criticism when we needed it while building unforgettable relationships with our students. From some of them, thanks to social media, we still have contact even all these years later.

Ah Ha

At the end of our second year, our principal told us the licensing laws were changing and despite being recently done with our undergraduate work, finishing graduate school was now imperative. Julie and I extended our collaboration into working on our English Master's degrees, resulting in not only that, but a valuable lesson in learning how collaborative relationships work. They thrive on one primary equation: common ground + common goals = continued growth

The common ground begins with a desire to work collaboratively and where common goals can be articulated and designed. When both of these attributes, combine, therein lies the opportunity for cultivating and maintaining an environment where the grounds and goals can be recognized, celebrated, reevaluated, and adapted as the collaborators deem necessary to keep the group moving forward.

Looking back now on 22 years of teaching in 2 districts, 5 buildings, and on various teams and initiatives, I find these memories of Julie and our formative years pressing nearer to me. As I engage with colleagues whose objectives include values realignments, policy campaigns, and process restructuring—serious overhauls for any status quo—I am drawn to my own center remembering that we are all in our given professions because of a genuine desire to make things better. *That all human beings are inherently good and try to do good with and for each other. And that all collaborative efforts, when they come from that shared center, cannot be misguided.* Miscommunicated, maybe, and that's where the work truly lies—in agreeing to figure out the best way to approach a new task with care, objectivity, and a willingness to improve—not only the matter at hand, but ourselves--for we are always our work's natural byproduct.

Julie and I lamented feeling frustrated and unsupported that no one on staff seemed to want to invest in our professional development. Didn't they recall what it felt like to get hired in the field of their dreams? Yes, we were eager; yes, we did know a great deal about the new trends, buzz words, techniques, and methods; but everyone seemed content to be stuck. Maybe "stuck" is an insulting description. Maybe it is a counter assumption—we assumed they were stuck; they assumed we were challenging their experience and expertise. Even as

I was retelling the opening narrative to this chapter, I realized how paradoxical my account feels. Admittedly, the details couldn't be closer to the truth, but the tone, the obsequious description, particularly capped by the Kasich quote, assumes so much that the scene could easily, equally as truthfully, appear to be hyperbole. As I weave through the definition and application of collaboration, I see I have more questions than answers.

Which is how, I teach. Frustrating to some of the 15-year-olds with whom I primarily collaborate, for they want me to be the "sage on the stage"; to inculcate them with the right answers, the only answers… the "truth", so they can regurgitate it on the state and college entrance tests. So many don't want to be bothered with the exploration, the questioning, the mounds of conflicting data through which to sift and evaluate, nor the fictional stories we study that veil the very truths for which they search in metaphors and imagery. They don't have time for that, they protest. I hope that it is not frustrating in my own writing here—the art of reflection is in the depth of the plumb. Recognizing that many students, not all, eschew the heuristic nature of real learning, I have, to be ever-aware of their levels of engagement in-order to meet them where they are. Many are not organically interested in a collaborative relationship with me, much as my lounge colleagues… but that doesn't mean they can't be…

Common Ground

I come from Youngstown, Ohio, a pretty scrappy town; and a pretty scrappy family, too, and it is from these beginnings where I learned the value of grit, and community. It is also where I developed a keen sense of self-doubt—I knew plenty of people whose life's work was crushed by economic, political, or geographic constraints, so winning is something to be really celebrated while humility and gratitude are expected. No one ever seemed to know when the rug was coming out from under them, so when it didn't, you sighed in relief; when it did, you called your neighbor, got things done and told them, "Thank you." Knowing that when their rug came out, you'd be there for them. Somebody always "knew a guy" who could help. In our neighborhood, bills still got paid, cars got fixed, and food got to the tables all because of community and collaboration. I saw early on, how collaboration at the community level was essential. When the phrase, "It takes a village" began to gain traction about a decade ago, I giggled at its ubiquity in my life—it was ingrained; I went into teaching so that I could facilitate, and benefit from, that "village". I've impressed its value upon my students from day one.

When I was in middle school, my father spent his spare time facilitating a youth club where he, with a fellow counselor, employed an ice-breaker activity that I stole and molded as the metaphor for my classroom philosophy. Participants are asked to sit in a circle and in random order, take turns tossing a ball of yarn to each member while stating, remembering, and repeating their names and some fact about themselves until every member has been included. At the end of the exercise, I ask kids to look at the yarn-made "web" that we have constructed and invite them to explain how it can resemble our classroom. They note how if someone forgot another's name, they gave them hints; if someone pulled too hard, it disturbed the whole structure—they extrapolate this into not doing homework, cheating on a test, being disruptive to someone's thinking or speaking during class. This first-day activity resonates throughout the year as each kid gets a piece of the yarn as a reminder. They stow them in their binders, phone cases, or use as back pack zipper pulls. We refer to the activity as needed so that if we are ever doing anything that prohibits the class' success, the web-as-symbol brings us back to our shared beliefs—that our job is to foster each other's individual growth through the symbiotic relationship of the whole. Our collaboration is both process and product of our English studies—our word choices, text choices, and project choices all mirror a respect for each other and the subject matter. As their communication teacher, my job is to create an environment where good communication can be made apparent and exemplified as it is occurring.

Having this fun, not "work"-related, starting point reminds me of my dinners and early parking lot conversations with Julie. Of course, our primary relationship was as co-workers, but seeking commonalities outside of our professional roles helped us see each other as *people first*. When the kids see each other as fellow athletes, travelers, siblings, children, musicians—or whatever personal facts they share when tossing the yarn—they see that our primary connection in the class is as *people*, not students. No one has the need to elbow anyone out, or elbow their way in, and although this might occur later-on in the year, we can always go back to our first day and remember that there is a bigger picture being painted here and that there really is no need for any elbowing for everyone will always have audience for their voice in our room—even if we disagree.

There is no doubt that this initial work is hard, though. It is much easier with a captive audience of students than with adults. I am fortunate enough now to be in a building where we are encouraged to share stories as a staff and to know each other—the building is only 9 years old and we who opened it shared the principal's vision of a tightly-knit, close-focused group. Other facilities were not so warmly directed. Many times administrators jump right to the professional business at hand, downplaying, or outright forgetting, the necessity of having all the team members see each other as human beings first. Building a collaborative community needs to have some organic basis—shared beliefs, common goals… *something* that draws on and keeps individuals working for the whole. Without some buy-in, the endeavor is bound to fail. Some colleagues have tried to poke holes in my first day strategy, thinking it juvenile and a waste of time, and although this push back has made me question it a thousand times over, I cannot imagine the year without that common experience-as-symbol. My kids return to see me, speak to my classes, become resources for current student's projects…all events reminding me that I am fulfilling my life's goal of making education an interconnected system of people who inspire and assist each other after commencement.

Willing Participants vs. Well, Not-Willing

The web activity, despite its relative success, has had some naysayers. Once a parent accused me of being a socialist radical who was using group work in our classroom as a way of making his daughter give her answers to the kids who couldn't figure it out for themselves. That the cooperative classroom was a way of pandering to the inept with the labors of the gifted…that was a long conversation. I made sure to tighten up my futures deployments of the web so that it was no longer misconstrued like that again. My collaboration with that parent went well the rest of the year when he saw that his daughter's work was not going to be marketed for others' use and that she would be challenged in my class based on her existing abilities, as those lower achieving would be as well. As I recall, I got a lovely end of year gift from the family—a token of our coming to a mutual understanding about the true function of a collaborative classroom.

Not all parents are interested in collaborating with me, but those who are have a voice and a role in our classroom. Same with the students. Willing participation is essential. It must be overtly fostered. When it doesn't happen for me and a student, I have, to have faith in our extended system—that one of my colleagues is connecting, inspiring…for even with every trick in my hat, I miss some. And on rare occasion I have, to let that go, and be just their English teacher. With 150+ students a year, it is bound to occur and addressing it might be uncomfortable, but is necessary. Recently I met with a boy's mother for scheduled conferences. He was doing very little work in class, but she insisted that she let him "fail" (he had a "C") so that his love for tennis didn't continue to outweigh his dedication to his classes. I agreed and stated I'd support her issuance of the natural consequences. Her husband, the boy's father, disagreed and asked 2 weeks later for another conference. I insisted the boy be present, for I tell the families that I would rather speak to, than about, any of them so no "he said/she said" are possible. I model this collaboration for both kids and parents so they can get to the heart of any matter—personal or academic—with full transparency. This particular conference was strained, yet revelatory; clunky yet, honest. It ended with the bell ringing and 25 students waiting at the door and me issuing the family out of the room with unresolved tension and sweat on my back.

I never heard back from the parents. But over the next month, the boy gained some lost ground in class—started turning things in, but I sensed coming to English was like bamboo under his nails. I felt like I had failed him…like I had had the opportunity to reel him in and missed it too many months ago. One day in class group work, a friend of his repeated some of the words I had used in that conference out loud to the class, letting me in on the fact that I had been made the butt of a joke. I did lose him. Or so I thought, until his final exam. The kids had to come to the testing period with a prepared essay, letter, presentation, video, etc. providing evidence for the question, "What did you learn this year?'" to share with the class. Sitting in our web-circle with the ball of yarn in hand, this 16-year -old boy, in front of his classmates, read aloud an essay where he admitted we had a conference with his parents and it was "the most uncomfortable 23 minutes of his life!" He relayed how he learned that he *did* have to be more than a tennis player as it was likely not going to pay his bills. And then, the words that I uttered in the conference, that had been hissed back to me in class: "Mrs. Repko helped me to see that the phrase, 'not everyone gets a trophy' is true. You have to work for everything you earn." He thanked me in front of everyone and I even got a hug on his way out the door. With this story, I see the value of persistence for unwilling participants.

Not everyone will have their words read back to them so directly, of course, but I gained some confidence knowing that when you persist in developing relationships, for the right reasons, even unwilling participants can come back around if you don't completely give up. Another boy in the same class told us in his final exam statement, that he heard my class "got personal" and for this he had hoped for another teacher and to his chagrin, ended up with me. With a trembling chin, he read the next words aloud, "But I was glad I had you, Mrs. Repko, when my mom was diagnosed with cancer this fall and you kept checking in with me and asking about my brothers and even talked to my football coach for me. It really meant a lot." Finding ways to make that connection outside of any professional tasks is the key to gelling a collaborative group.

When a fellow colleague prefers to not engage, the same is true. Although I see myself as a successful leader of my own classes, I struggle at times collaborating with adults. Teaching is a weird gig as I see the majority, of my colleagues as equals to me—save, obviously, the building and district administrators. I cannot ever see myself walking into someone else's classroom and saying, "Well, maybe you should do this this way…" And unfortunately, that is how early collaboration had been packaged for the teaching community. Used to hours of autonomy behind closed doors with only our youth as audience, getting the old guard, tenured teachers to value collaboration was a daunting task. The presumed top-down model under which so many were taught themselves, was the only model they knew for imparting instruction. In the collective mind, someone had to own the material and be the expert, and the rest had to sit quietly and unquestioningly gulp it down. I have been witness to this transformation, and at times been of it myself—either as the one giving instruction or the one receiving it. The hierarchical construct always seemed to dominate the relationship. "I have something to teach you. I know what I am doing. You must learn from me." Ack! I recall Julie and I, in our first years together, being asked to conduct professional development on writing across the curriculum. Here were the young birds, reminding the veterans that regardless of subject matter, they were still writing and reading teachers—us all, all together. Gulp. We were given the podium and mic and watched most drift off to their own tasks as we presented our well-intentioned principal-initiated, material. Some who were engaged were supportive and complimentary…and even sought further collaboration and assistance in teaching writing in science, art, and history. Those were fun conversations that took place in rooms into which we were invited…willing collaborators, exchanging ideas and setting goals, designing processes and products! Yes! The overspill of the session was a success, but the initial roll-out was cumbersome, and sweat-inducing… I learned so much about engagement and roles from that experience, and while still not perfect, believe that getting people to work together, regardless of the topic, is more beneficial than promoting the "I'm on my own island" corollary. I have been on collaborative teams where self-appointed leaders made decisions for us, made lessons for us, and even copies of worksheets for us…those teams never fared well. Voices were stifled, goals were dictated, and feelings were hurt. Conversely, I have been on teams where no leader emerged and little was accomplished. Going back to my Julie years I see how valuable it is to have a willing participant.

At my first school, I found Julie, of course, but also, all of those other teachers who chose to stay in their rooms. In fact, I created a collaborative, interdisciplinary unit centered on *Jurassic Park* which involved the kids working on fractals in geometry, genetics in science, and even the marching band playing the theme music for their halftime show. This was my first taste of how successful collaborating *can* be if the right people and the right purpose are aligned. After this, I found the teams I sought to work with progressed more effectively than those assembled via existing structures such as grade-level or subject level.

My greatest collaborative achievement was a humbling experience with a gifted specialist named Leslie. I had been resistant to send my kids to her pull-out program because I was confident my training as a regular classroom teacher was adequate and that I could get the kids to progress without this upper tier having pull-out experiences. Not only was I completely wrong, Leslie's youth and excitement was intimidating to me. She never gave up, though, and came to study my classroom, asked me questions about my kids and my approach to them. She watched for my strengths and weaknesses and then suggested I mentor a particularly gifted young man who was socially awkward and defiantly opposed to doing any work below his exceedingly high IQ. She knew she had me on the hook—citing my strengths, issuing me a challenge, placing me in a mentoring position, bolstering me with her expert support.

The kids went to her pull-out program, but they also stayed with me more often, than not and she and I collaborated in the classroom through both co-teaching and co-planning. She stretched my perception of how to create differentiated lessons for all ability types and how to better manage multi-ability classrooms. We laughed. We debated. We questioned. We got frustrated. We observed. We barbed…but above all, we remained open to possibility. She made me, the unwilling participant, open my eyes to not only this collaborative work, but immersed me in unchartered waters forcing me to learn how to swim with students in ways I never imagined. I created some of my most powerful, foundational, teaching units that year.

I also fostered relationships with students, parents, and colleagues, like never before. I realized that when people are in the metacognitive phase of learning, where reflection is a goal, when it is easy to see and articulate one's own growth, there is a surge of confidence and a lucidity in recognizing the reason *why* something is being done. Understanding that relevance is crucial and is an integral part of the collaborative process. It is highly valuable for participants to assess the dynamic of their roles, the attribution of success, the location of the goal—near or far—and a possible redesign of the steps needed to achieve it.

I moved from unwilling to willing. It took some effort on Leslie's part to get me to listen. She knew though, that through learning to listen, I would eventually listen to learn. This break though for me showed me that I could, and needed to, trust others to facilitate my growth. She helped open me to honing my craft. Our student also moved from unwilling to willing and our simultaneous growth anchored one of the best years I have ever had in the classroom. One other gifted student in that course loved the challenges I was pushed into creating for them, that now at 28, he still calls me his "favorite teacher". I know this because I have recently reconnected with his mom, a professor at a local college, who has invited me to speak to her class about exceptional students and how to approach them. The opportunities for collaboration are boundless if one is open to them and can embrace their potential for both the pushing and the pulling effects of learning—for everyone involved.

Shortly after those experiences with Leslie, on an interview for another building in our district, I used the phrase "symbiotic relationship" to describe my objective in teaching and it still holds true today. I want myself, fellow teachers, students, parents, administrators, and community members to work together for the benefit of each kid who steps into my classroom. I have the hope that all, of our contributions combined can culminate in a dynamic experience for the students... and our community. Each year I add another layer into this vision—spidering-out into more collaborative possibilities to make students' experiences richer than the year before.

Common Goals

Having a love for collaborating with others in my classroom, I once attempted to take on a student teacher. She was unwilling to reduce her social schedule: president of her sorority, working part time, volunteering for a charity. I cautioned her that this was going to get cumbersome and that our current 8th graders were her priority. Her lessons were often sketchy and late, but 6 weeks into the term, and against my better judgement, I allowed her to begin a lesson one day while I stepped out. 15 minutes into the 90-minute period, I reentered the room to see kids on their feet in anger, obviously divided by racial lines on opposite sides of the room, their eyes wide in frustration. She had gone off-plan and tried a spontaneous, and racially divisive, activity to introduce *To Kill a Mockingbird*. Under *my* watch. After quelling the crowd, relieving her from the room, and reassuming my role in the classroom, I launched into a more sound introductory lesson myself, all the while the sickening tightening in my stomach confirming the realization that this was failed collaboration at its finest. What had gone wrong? Well…everything. I didn't know the girl well—what did she believe in? Why did she want to teach? What were her goals, and plans for achieving them…what were her goals in life? I saw her lesson plans—they *seemed* fine, but her heart wasn't in the right place. She wasn't ready. She was a willing participant, but I was an errant partner. We needed that connection. We needed stated, shared goals. We needed to start over. But for that experience, it was too late, for I was too ignorant. It took a long time to recover from that; in truth, I still am. I never collaborate now without clear goals explicitly stated. That, being said, I have also come to recognize that clear goals may be simultaneously vague…

My current district is highly rated and nationally recognized. Our teachers are amazing individuals who are excellent at providing stimulating environments in which our kids learn. It wasn't always this way—but it was something we aspired to be. Our exponential growth results from acquiring residents from all parts of the country, and globe. In turn, the demand for excellence spurred a quest to meet it. As we grew into our current levels of population and excellence, our district created several initiatives to stretch teachers into accommodating this growth by fostering our *professional* growth. One such was a "collaboration period" for us where entire departments could meet during the day to work together. At the high school level, this was revolutionary. Our middle schools, where I spent 10 of my professional years, had had a collaboration period built in for the focus was more on the kids. Though the academics were excellent, it was a great opportunity to develop lessons across subjects, but our conversations more often went like this:

Math teacher, "Did you see Mary today? Is she alright?"

Science teacher, "She was crying in my class—I sent her to the guidance office; we had a lab."

History teacher, "Yes, her dog ran away last night. She won't be able to concentrate well."

English teacher, "I'll have her work in the hall if she needs the space. Did anyone email her parents?"

This socio-emotional collaboration was so beneficial to me. I had come a long way from that first teacher's lounge...Making kids better people is why so many go into teaching. I took these warm and fuzzy expectations to the HS with me. After my 10-year hiatus from the upper grades, I was in for some hard work. The high school teachers weren't as in to this. They wanted test results. They wanted the sophomore kids prepared for the AP classes in subsequent years. They wanted shared rubrics, worksheets, tests, and writing assignments. They simultaneously wanted autonomy. No one had given these people this kind of time to work together—none of our colleges provided classes that discussed teacher collaboration. No one knew what this wonderful gift should look like and we found ourselves in more disagreements about how to collaborate, rather than how to prepare for our teaching.

The sophomore team decided to agree to disagree. We struck out to use the time in a more personally satisfying way. Some teams, from other disciplines, too, stressed about the time together—feeling that the district as Big Brother was using this as a mechanism to check up on us. (Well, I suppose this might be possible as the administrators asked for team notes and goals, and quarterly reports! Accountability was at an all-time high and time-on-task was always in question.) Our sophomore English team, however, was prone to using the collaborative time to get to know each other, vent about our days, laugh with each other, and really, get little actual work *on book*. Hands-down, these are still some of my favorite people in the building! I still love this team as I have never left it. I owe them so much credit for my current work. And it is because we took the time to build these personal relationships. Bridget, one with whom I have had the pleasure of being paired for all 9 years now, and I got to the point where we'd meet for tea the first 10 minutes of every day, touch base about where we were, agree to email each other the latest worksheet or quiz we designed independently, and walk away completely satisfied knowing that our internal compasses about where the kids were, and where our instruction should be, lined up without much ado. We would then meet in our weekly small team collaboration to check in with everyone else, share where we were, see about pushing new material, hanging back to prepare for testing, or…ask about each other's own children.

In our whole-department team meeting, where all the grade levels got together, we got to hear how others in the English department were spending their time. Some were really-productive: taking group notes in shared, electronic documents; developing daily, synchronized lessons and assessments; moving as unified fronts. Our small team of 4 questioned for a minute if we wanted that, and then assessed we preferred, to have more autonomy. Our individual voices were more important than everyone doing the same units together, so long as the kids were getting the shared skills and content, did it matter that we all got there simultaneously? We sometimes doubted if we were doing this whole collaboration thing wrong. What was it supposed to look like? Will the administration take the time away if we don't meet the unspoken, assumed goal? What level of symbiosis was expected? Accepted? Well, as the test scores began accumulating, we saw that each team *could* have their own definition of "collaboration" fulfilled because the kids were doing GREAT! And so long as kids were growing, our administrators gave us the time, space, and tools needed to keep making our magic.

Surmounting the hump of the first half of our time as a building, the dynamism of "us" began to take root. Our "forced" collaboration was becoming intrinsic. It was something we all valued, and celebrated in our various applications. We also began to collaborate across disciplines, grade levels, and buildings. Moreover, the district curriculum department had shored, itself up, too, over the past decade and the message was clear: collaboration in all forms is valuable. More so, they were committed to protecting this time for us during the day, and allowing release time for district, or even teacher-initiated, collaborative efforts. Symbiosis *was* possible. And I swear I saw the mist clearing away and a bridge looming…

Continuous Growth

During this transformative time in Olentangy, Bridget and I decided that personally, having lunch or a cup of tea together was a valuable way to spend our time. We chose to meet in the English teacher's work room as it had a small kitchen, as well as all, of our textbook ancillary materials, several desktop computers and a printer. It was carpeted, hosted an 8-person conference table, and was, dare I say, a tad cozier than our classrooms. Our chance encounters grew to intentional ones and we determined that room a worthy environment for our sophomore meetings. Prior, we had met in someone's classroom, but we moved to the work room as we enjoyed, and still do, the neutrality and accessibility of the space—no one person is in charge there—and more importantly, even if not part of the sophomore team, all are welcome to join us for professional input, or friendly camaraderie; we enjoy the random interruptions of fellow faculty passersby coming for coffee, or conversation. This space is for everyone, even when one group is using it to work.

No one else, really, had lunch in the work room, though. It was bright, accessible from two doors opening to two hallways forming opposite sides of a square, it had all the right stuff to entice occupancy, but it took about 4 years for that to become a regular thing as teachers always have more work than time. In a district as competitive as ours, a building as new as ours, and a staff as driven as ours, taking time to sit and eat was an indulgence to which many were reluctant to succumb. Over time, though, people saw us in there and began to trickle in. Even at different class periods. For a small group of us, that space was becoming sanctuary.

Two years ago, when a group of student teachers from The Ohio State University M. Ed program came to us for their internships, that workroom itself played a significant role in our growth as a department. All master's degree candidates, these people were eager, knowledgeable and…infectious! Many faculty who had had grown accustomed to having lunch in that room were now also hosting those students and well, when we went to lunch, "the kids" came with us. The population of the room immediately doubled! So, did the volume, the use of social media, and the *ideas*! We watched Key and Peele on YouTube and talked about race relations in America and texts to connect with the times and the topic. These newbies had an advantage: they grew up in a time where playdates were scheduled. Cell phones have been in their hands since they were in high school. They brought inherent connectivity along and we asked them, "Because you 'get this', how can you *lead* when you might be the youngest, most innovative one on the team *without* offending your colleagues, asking them to revamp everything they have built, or reinventing the wheel? How can you integrate what you naturally do into what already exists?" But they *did* know. And they got to share, because we gave them ground, and they gave us air. We showed them the history, they showed us the future. Every conversation was an opportunity for everyone involved to learn something… and not even the main concept being shared, but maybe something peripheral yet vital. There were many instances of, "I overheard you at lunch yesterday saying…can you clarify/dig into/show me…?" And the best part? Conversations like that weren't started by the kids, but by the mentors.

Sometimes, I swore I was seeing all this happen through a veil of yellow smoke and dying sunlight through dingy curtains…but no, because at Orange, we edited their lesson plans—4 on 1 and the feedback was like granite. We opened-up our classrooms to all of them, regardless to whom they were assigned, and we processed what they saw, synthesized what they knew with what could be, and…blissfully watched *ourselves* grow. The kids gradually took control of our rooms and we adults found ourselves with nowhere else to go except into the work room. We were still collaboratively planning with the M. Ed students, writing plans, creating reports, and teaching some class periods. But there we ended up. For hours at a stretch some days. And so, we talked. We listened. We reflected. We evaluated. We began to create the next year's plans. We leaned, into each other with a recommitment to the profession and an affirmation to each other. We became better mentors, better teachers, and better friends…now no longer, really, merely colleagues. Heck, some of us are even now neighbors. Literally.

Our department has grown to 17 people and since opening 9 years ago, 5 have moved into the district, 3 more moved to being within attendance boundaries of our very building, and 2 more are considering the move when their families are ready. Other departments are experiencing some of this community benefit as well. We eat and drink at each other's houses. We babysit each other's children. We attend each other's weddings. We attend the funerals of other's family members. And isn't this what life is really all about? We care. We love us. And it is all because collaboration, as a goal, has brought us here. I am humbled to share our story, for I recognize I am a cog in the wheel. Any one of my colleagues could have contributed to this book—their words would have been different, their paths to this point varied, but the end message would resonate the same. We have built bridges with and for each other. Bridges that lead to very real places and result in very real things.

The workroom at Orange High School is *way* better than the one in which I began. Maybe I had some hand in that, because of my beginning. But I didn't transform it alone. And that is what matters. Next weekend Julie and I will be attending the wedding of a mutual friend and former colleague. I will be giving her a copy of this chapter and reminding her of the impact she made on me 22 years ago…and always. E.M. Forrester was right.

Rowland, Darrell. (August 19, 2015) John Kasich Jokes He Wants to Abolish Teacher Lounges, Talks Union, *Columbus Dispatch*, retrieved from http://www.dispatch.com/content/stories/local/2015/08/19/john-kasich-education-summit.html

CHAPTER 18

Building Teams in Academia for Synergy in Interdisciplinary Research

Donnalyn Roxey
Center for Applied Plant Sciences, The Ohio State University
Currently at KnowInnovation, Buffalo, NY

Andy Burnett
Founder and CEO KnowInnovation, Buffalo, NY

Erich Grotewold
Professor and Director, Center for Applied Plant Sciences, The Ohio State University
Currently in the Department of Biochemistry and Molecular Biology Michigan State University, MI

1.A. The Challenges Ahead

Rapid breakthroughs in technologies and computing power are allowing new fields to emerge, and challenges once thought impossible are becoming routine and easily available. Scientists are sending spacecraft to meteors (Skibba, 2016), actualizing autonomous vehicles (Davis, 2016) and inserting electronic sensors into human brains allowing paralyzed victims hope of recovering motor function (Cha, 2016). Three-dimensional (3D) printing has surpassed many expectations, now being able to synthesize metals, ceramics and even living tissue for transplants (Molitch-Hou, 2016). Any genome can be precisely engineered and new ones even created (Boeke et al., 2016); whether it happens or not becomes an issue of ethics, not of ability. In such a rapidly evolving research state, how can the expectation to make the necessary progress in key global challenges such as preventing and adapting to climate change, ensuring sufficient and healthy food, providing sufficient energy to feed our energy-demanding world without destroying the environment, furnishing clean water and improving human health for everyone, be realized? These are major challenges that require research integration across multiple disciplines, with tangible goals that will require much longer than the 3-5-year window characteristic of how federal agencies fund research today.

While the community continues to decide how to tackle these global problems, it is important to consider how the research enterprise and education systems that characterize Land Grant universities also continue to evolve. Education is slowly adapting to a more globalized system, for example, through Small Private Online and Massive Open Online Courses (MOOCs and SPOCs, respectively). It is uncertain, however, how universities will cope with the financial consequences of implementing these courses and who will teach them. Similarly, complex, multifactorial scientific problems require a diversity of expertise in the researchers tackling them. It is unclear yet, however, how even the simplest of actions will occur, the transfer of information. With rapid technological advances in communication systems, the ways in which people interact across the world, nation, institutions, and even the lab next door could fundamentally change within the next three to five years. Institutions must adapt to the next generation of millennial scientists entering the workforce with education systems and structures largely unchanged for most of the past century. The job market has and continues to rapidly change, making it very challenging for graduates and institutions to keep-up with the pace. Collaboration may look very different in the next twenty years;

it could live on the research fringe, or more than likely it will become commonplace. Add to these challenges a shrinking federal research funding landscape and "administrivia" (*i.e.*, the increasing demand on faculty and researchers for busywork to fulfill institutional bureaucratic needs) running rampant in our universities, and the challenges faculty face in tackling the global-scale grand challenges of our world today seems insurmountable.

Thus, a main challenge is to overcome these hurdles to truly engage the scientific community to come together to challenge existing dogmas and solve problems of global significance. Our funding agencies, universities, and research institutions must become even more nimble and adaptable to support such a volatile environment.

1.B. Team Science as Part of the Solution

There are many faculty around the world that are successfully traversing these issues and doing it with others, as part of complex research collaborations. What might be learned from these teams? Team science, as defined by the National Research Council, consists of "Scientific collaboration, *i.e.*, research conducted by more than one individual in an interdependent fashion, including research conducted by small teams and larger groups" (Cooke and Hilton, 2015, p.22). "Multidisciplinary teams could potentially bring novel perspectives and approaches to longstanding problems. In addition, scientists in other fields might not be vested in the current paradigm, so could ask the naïve questions that could lead to important new insights. More directly, in some cases a cognate problem in a related field may have already been approached or solved, so simply transferring that concept or approach to a new field could result in significant advances," (Collins, Kearney & Maddison, 2013). Engineers and biomedical researchers appear to have capitalized on the successes of teamwork, certainly more so than the life sciences. Learning must happen from these successful teams, adapting strategies contextually to our institutions, and when needed, forging new ground with our university's structure, organization, and culture; carefully, and with intent, looking at the entire research environment to find novel ways of infusing team science as part of the solution to our worlds grand challenges.

1.C. Creating and Sustaining Research Teams

The Ohio State University (OSU) led an experiment of integrating the life sciences into a trans-disciplinary framework of collaborative research through the Center for Applied Plant Sciences (CAPS). CAPS, was created as a cooperative venture by OSU's Colleges of Arts and Sciences (ASC), and Food, Agricultural, and Environmental Sciences (CFAES) to integrate and enhance the expertise, visibility and reach of the plant sciences at OSU. Institutionally, OSU has recently invested significant resources in the Discovery Themes (DTs). These research thrusts focus on Health and Wellness, Food Production and Security, and Energy and the Environment. From a CAPS perspective, plant sciences is at the very core of these initiatives (Figure 1). In fact, many of the challenges that society faces, and that OSU identified as part of the DTs, are captured in CAPS' continuum between basic research and practical solutions to challenges in four main Strategic Areas: (1) Photosynthesis and Carbon Fixation, (2) Biomass and Bioproducts, (3) Crop Improvement and Functional Foods, and (4) Plant-Microbe Interactions (Figure 1). The model that was implemented for CAPS is one that takes full advantage of team science and consists of interdisciplinary research teams composed exclusively of OSU faculty. This was based on the premise that an institution like OSU, with over 4,000 faculty members, contains the majority, of the expertise necessary to tackle major global challenges. Different from most other centers, membership to CAPS was team- and not individual-based. CAPS Scientific Teams were required to incorporate faculty members across disciplines, often resulting in teams that spanned departments, colleges and campuses. The goal was to build the kind of synergy that can integrate and expand basic biological research and translate it into solving a problem of major societal interest (*e.g.*, converting greenhouse gases into industrial feedstocks, or developing new tools to enhance plant tolerance to emerging pathogens or climate change).

2. The CAPS Experience

Over the course of the first five years, CAPS learned many valuable lessons. Unknown in the forming of CAPS was the quickly growing discipline, Science of Team Science (SciTS), and while *Collaboration & Team Science: A Field Guide, National Institutes of Health* was seminal in guiding the development of CAPS, the implementation of the recommendations was found to be incredibly dependent on a plethora of local environmental variables. Much of team science in practice is 'multidisciplinary'. The research is done within the boundaries of expertise, utilizing the individual talents of each faculty, their labs, equipment, expertise, etc., and the work is still of practical significance to one's own research goals. The CAPS model is based on a different approach—'interdisciplinary' team science, bringing faculty together at the edge of their expertise, maybe even slightly outside it, testing new ways of thinking that do not fit within one faculty lab, but elevate a group of faculty labs. A mission of CAPS is through creative problem solving, to engage a team of experts exploring strategic areas of global significance in the plant sciences. This 'creativity for a cause' involves leaders in the scientific, business and education fields, identifying what the major themes in plant sciences are, and coming up with novel, innovative ways to solve the problem. Faculty self-identify into these teams based on expertise and, most importantly their interest, creating a common goal of significance and intellectual curiosity.

Of course, this is the mission of many interdisciplinary teams and questions quickly emerged, while navigating the early stages of faculty cohesion. It does not matter whether teams form for internal emerging areas of interest, industry prospects, federal sources, or other opportunities; fostering the development of teams does not end after the team is generated or the proposal is submitted. The following sections outline what was learned from the CAPS experience in terms of what works (and what didn't) when developing successful teams, the impact of personalities on team success, the support that is required for teams to succeed, and conclude by revisiting the issue of return on investment (ROI), key to keeping institutional and federal support of teams going.

2.A. Team Generation: Process & Implementation

2.A.1 Team formation

The ultimate-goal of CAPS was to build a vibrant community from which a steady stream of innovative research teams could be drawn. The challenge was to re-engage faculty in what got them excited about their science, overcome the logistics of team development and the individualism of the faculty themselves. As anyone reading this chapter can acknowledge, these are no small issues to overcome.

CAPS Director, Erich Grotewold, became familiar, through conversations with Program Directors at the National Science Foundation (NSF), with how the agency was starting to use an Ideas Lab as a mechanism to bring together scientists from diverse backgrounds to generate novel research proposals. CAPS decided to adapt this model through what became known as the CAPS Synergy Workshops. These workshops were a mechanism to bring faculty together from different OSU colleges and disciplines to self-organize into teams. CAPS, has thus far held two Synergy Workshops in collaboration with KnowInnovation (KI). Combined, these workshops brought together ~70 faculty from five colleges and two OSU campuses to first identify major scientific challenges relevant to CAPS Strategic Areas, and then generate possible novel solution spaces. The objective, one that was largely foreign to most of the participating OSU faculty, was to form teams to tackle problems with a 10-20-year vision. A climate for innovation was created through KI's professional facilitation, provocative talks from leading industry representatives, and curious and willing faculty. KI facilitators guided faculty participants through a series of problem solving stages. The general challenge was posed and faculty aligned around different project ideas forming teams of investigators. Ideas Lab are inherently multi-disciplinary, explore new and/or unproven areas, and are considered high risk/high impact (National Science Foundation, 2014). Ideas Labs' proposals are meant to be wilder and more imaginative with a mix of people and expertise that leads to the novel and riskier output. The output is typically proposals that would not be funded under other circumstances (Skoltech, 2013).

While the primary output of each synergy workshop was a CAPS competitive Scientific Team, the purpose of the first event was to kick-off the Center, and therefore, a large number of faculty were invited with the hopes of producing multiple teams for review. The purpose of the second workshop was a more targeted audience. One of the CAPS Strategic Areas (Photosynthesis and Carbon Fixation) had not been represented in the originally selected four Scientific Teams. Thus, this second Synergy Workshop was targeted to that need, focusing on carbon and photon harvest and utilization. This clarity is warranted because, interestingly, during the review process for the second workshop, CAPS added a new variable. CAPS wanted the ambition of new teams to continually push beyond what was proposed (and accomplished) by the previous Scientific Teams; hence support was only consider for a team that ranked higher than any of the four previous ones. If none reached this point, then none should be funded. These two workshops produced 12 proposals for teams (see team evaluation for further discussion). From the first workshop, four proposals were selected for support. This represented 21 faculty from two campuses and three colleges. From the second workshop, one team was selected for support with eight faculty representing three colleges, which is proving highly successful in bridging engineering, chemistry and microbiology. Of the five teams receiving CAPS support resulting from the Synergy Workshops, three are still highly active (see rethinking ROI for further discussion). CAPS did also try alternate methods for team development. An open call was generated so that faculty could bring forth big ideas that may not have been presented at a workshop. This open call yielded two proposals, one of which was selected for funding. CAPS in total supported so far six Scientific Teams tackling large-scale global challenges.

Another product of the Synergy Workshops was that OSU faculty that never had a chance to meet face to face, even when they knew each other's research (one of the problems of a large university fractured over multiple campuses), developed interactions that created a local network of future collaborators. Even faculty reluctant to spend two days in a workshop concluded that the events were engaging and fun. The creative environment fostered by the workshops was ripe for intense small group breakouts, complemented with open discussions, group meals, and other activities meant to push the faculty to think outside their areas of immediate comfort. CAPS' is excited to continue to witness the team's success in typical ROI fashion, but more so, thrilled to see faculty collaborating on fresh research directions, subsequent new interactions amongst the team members, and creating new research and fresh insights in their respective fields. Faculty that once never worked together continues to explore grants and paths of research beyond the scope of the CAPS teams. These continuously developing interactions among faculty that would have never worked together before CAPS are probably the most long-lasting effect that CAPS will have on the research community at OSU.

There were other unexpected opportunities that also arose from these Synergy Workshops. In one case, a wild post-it note (a signature of the Ideas Lab methodology), sparked the curiosity of the CAPS leadership: 'How might you grow coffee in Ohio". The idea itself was deemed unfeasible (then and today), but the motivation for it resulted in conversations, relationship building with a local industry, and ultimately a new team forming to tackle a challenge completely outside the domain expertise of all the faculty involved (back then there was not a single faculty at OSU working on coffee). The CAPS team ended being generously funded through an industry sponsored research project. Exploring wild ideas and looking at problems from a new perspective is one goal of synergy workshops. Many thoughts may only come to light in an atmosphere in which faculty broaden their thinking, use different terminology and frameworks, and ultimately have exposure to diverse expertise and a collegial atmosphere.

2.A.2 Team evaluation

2.A.2.1 Forming the ESAB
An important component of CAPS was the External Scientific Advisory Board (ESAB). This board was comprised of highly accomplished and respected scientists who serve as directors or senior organizational

leaders at their home institutions, bringing to the table extensive experience in dealing with scientists and making them work in teams. The CAPS Director, in consultation with key OSU faculty stakeholders, selected members. The ESAB was tasked with being an independent and unbiased voice for the center, avoiding in this way the perceptional inbreeding and reluctance of organizations to have the 'outside' looking in. The ESAB had multiple functions, including assisting with the creation of the application and criteria for funding, review and ranking of team applications, center evaluation, and making recommendations to the CAPS and OSU leadership on possible directions and opportunities.

Textbox 1: Maximizing ESAB's Visits to OSU
While on campus the board also met with Ohio State organizational leadership including Deans, Chairs, and the VP for Research. The purpose of these meetings was to ensure the direction and alignment of CAPS activities. This visit culminated in a written report from the ESAB with recommendations for both the center and the organization leadership. As can be imagined, it is of paramount importance that faculty respect the collective members of the ESAB, in order to make this concept work.

2.A.2.2 Application and Team evaluation
The goal of CAPS Synergy Workshops was to develop multidisciplinary teams of faculty. To that end, an application request for support had to be generated. To minimize the time burden to the faculty, the application itself was only six pages long with no formal budget. In addition to a scientific summary, the application asked to discuss how the team met, how they would function as a team, milestones for first and second years, and what resources the team needed to get the proposed vision off the ground and prime for outside funding. A rubric was created for review that identified the scientific merit, ambition, and game-changeability of the proposal. In addition, the ESAB, was able to comment on the reach of the research beyond OSU, the State of Ohio, the nation, etc. All proposals were submitted and critically

reviewed by the board. The ESAB was tasked with identifying proposals that were not competitive, and to rank those that were. Based on the ranking and the available CAPS budget, CAPS leadership decided how many team's resources could be allocated and to which teams. The funding mechanism for teams was also different from the way many centers operate. The teams were asked to identify their needs, not in terms of dollars, but in terms of equipment pieces, personnel or services without an upper limit, but with a clear justification of how the requested resources would permit the team to take the initial steps towards their 10-20 year-long vision. Rather than providing the teams with cash, CAPS provided the needed resources, with personnel (*e.g.*, postdocs, technicians) being selected by the teams, but hired through CAPS. This prevented faculty members and teams from utilizing the funds for projects other than the one they were meant for. Initially, CAPS anticipated that teams would be generously funded for years one and two, tempering into year three with the goal of the teams becoming self-sufficient beyond that point through a combination of federal, industry and commodity group funding.

In addition to reviewing all applications for resources, the ESAB visited OSU and CAPS every 12-18 months to perform an evaluation of the Scientific Teams and the center's administration. The performance of each team was evaluated based on the yearly milestones that each of the teams presented when they formed. Each team presents to and met with members of the ESAB, in addition to preparing a full progress report. This allowed the board to determine if sufficient progress had been made, if center resources were still warranted, and helped identify directions and opportunities for the teams. The stringency of the evaluation and high demand for quality was evident in that funding for two of the initial teams was put in probationary status and then withdrawn after the first review (and a subsequent progress report from probationary status) because of their inability to meet the milestones that they had set. It is important to note that if sufficient progress was not achieved toward the team goals, financial support was taken away. While it would seem, that removal of financial support, would be equivalent to terminating the team, CAPS was pleasantly surprised to find that was not the case (as discussed in the Life of Teams section below). Remarkably, the two teams for which funding was terminated early continued to have faculty actively engaged in CAPS, by participating in many of the center-sponsored activities, including retreats and seminars. A culture of collaboration, innovation, and fun was being generated. At the time that this manuscript was being prepared, CAPS supported four Scientific Teams comprised of 22 faculty members from seven departments and three colleges.

2.B. Team Organization

2.B.1. Team Members: Personality Matters

A fundamental component of CAPS, although not the only one, was the faculty members that constituted the scientific teams. It became quickly evident, however, that the traits that academia usually selects for an individual to become a successful faculty member are often not those that are necessary to make the best team player. Faculty members are hired because of their usual narrow focus in a specific area of expertise (but great depth). They are required to meet the demands of promotion and tenure, which many times mean single principal investigator grants and lead/single author publications. Faculty members often have busy teaching schedules, while running their labs, performing numerous service activities to their departments, universities and scientific communities, advising graduate students, and need to be constantly writing grants to beat the odds of a low funding rate percentage. In short, faculty are busy and team science requires additional time. Lucille Ball's famous quote, "If you want something done, ask a busy person to do it. The more things you do, the more you can do'" may be applicable to many situations, but what if the energy sought is to explore expertise just outside one's comfort zone. This takes a level of commitment to dedicate additional time in an area that may not be a faculty's area of expertise. One consequence of this is that some faculty members simply prefer not to work in teams, even though they may occasionally collaborate with colleagues within or outside their institutions. In addition to the issues listed above, there are many personal reasons for this preference, including current career situations (pre-tenure for example), trust (personal and professional), past experiences (*e.g.*, they were successful before working alone), motivational (diluted recognition), conflict avoidance, personal emotional intelligence, and reluctance to change (Bennett, Gadlin, Levin-Finley, 2010). The success and value of the individual investigator to the institution is unquestionable, and a healthy organizational research enterprise benefits from having the right balance of successful individuals and team players.

Despite all the reasons for not embarking in team science in an academic setting, over the past five years CAPS was privileged to have about 55 faculty members from four different colleges and nine departments participate in scientific teams. Overall, CAPS observed of the faculty participating in teams that they had a wide diversity of expertise, were open to other's opinions, demonstrated mutual respect for colleagues, and a had high tolerance for ambiguity. The majority of the faculty members, participating in CAPS scientific teams were tenured, either associate or full professors. While the low representation of junior faculty resulted in a significant loss in fresh ideas and high energy to the teams, there were two main reasons for this. First, given the tenure pressures on assistant professors to obtain a grant as principal investigator and to be senior authors on papers from their research groups, it was perceived as counterproductive to their careers to involve them in research teams with an ambitious long-term goal. Second, we found that assistant professors were often busier than tenured faculty with teaching, research, writing grants and recruiting students, and therefore were less inclined to participate in a research team that would probably not yield them results within the 3-5 years critical for their tenure.

Academic institutions must not only re-evaluate promotion and tenure, but also the reward and recognition systems at all ranks for collaborative science. More clarity of how collaborative science should be evaluated is essential, which is likely to require new means to count contributions for co-principal investigators and in publications with multiple authors. With regards to assistant professors specifically, the National Academies 2014 document Convergence: Facilitating

Transdisciplinary Integration of Life Sciences, Physical Sciences, Engineering, and Beyond, recommends, "Universities can include expectations of collaboration during the hiring process and department leadership can make recommendations to young faculty regarding team-based projects in which they are participating...Tenure and promotion committees will also need guidance that enables them to fairly evaluate convergent as well as unidisciplinary research, teaching, student mentorship, and service efforts." But, once a faculty decided that working as part of a research team was an attractive idea, the challenge becomes to ensure that the team is successful. Later we discuss some of the mechanisms by which teams were supported, but the question was whether something could be done at the time of team formation to ensure that the correct personalities and interests came together. CAPS explored FourSight as one potential solution. Many personality assessments exist and this is not an endorsement of a specific product, more a validation and agreement with literature that preferences should be evaluated and discussed in the context of the team (Stokols, Hall, Taylor & Moser, 2008). FourSight is a problem-solving preference assessment tool to identify and leverage individuals thinking styles. While there are many combinatorial preferences, the four simplest creative style types are ideator, clarifier, developer, or implementer. A general theory is that it takes all different types working together to maximize the creative output of a challenge. CAPS offered the assessment during the Synergy Workshops, and despite the typical skepticism that characterizes faculty, many completed the assessment and learning their thinking skill preference. It was never the intention of CAPS to guide team formation based on the personality traits. While even today, several years later, faculty can be heard saying "I am an implementer", it is unclear how personality assessment information was used by the teams to maximize return.

2.B.2 Team Leadership
There is vast, extensive, yet seemingly contradictory literature on leadership within teams. For example, some of us expected that natural leaders would emerge in CAPS research teams, and sometimes they

did. However, on occasion a natural leader never emerged, and this was often to the detriment of the team. Sometimes the belief was that a fully democratic leadership style would work, and in one case that did. Leadership is tricky and difficult to point to a single correct solution. In an effort, to operationalize CAPS observations on team leadership, Drath's leadership outcome framework will be discussed, which takes into account the individual and collective leadership. These leadership tasks or outcomes—setting direction, creating alignment, and building commitment—are certainly corroborated by our observations. "In the DAC framework *direction* is the overall group mission and goals, *alignment* is the necessary coordination of action within the collective group, and *commitment* is the willingness of group members to put personal interests secondary to that of collective interest and benefit," (Drath et al., 2008). Conceptually, as a collection of tasks, this allowed to transcend the individual within any role. In this manner, leadership is defined more by task-based interactions, instead of the traditional behavior base.

2.B.2.a Setting Direction

Setting Direction: widespread agreement in a collective on overall goals, aims, and mission (Drath et al., 2008). Direction from CAPS perspective is twofold: direction within the teams and direction of the center. While traveling with no map can be adventurous, if you want to get to a destination, a clear direction and purpose is the most effective and efficient way forward. Setting direction within the teams was mostly handled within the team's themselves. During and immediately after the Synergy Workshops, when teams were preparing their applications, the team chose the goals and aims underlying the research mission. At the workshops, the teams self-selected the topics they wanted to work on, so inherently they should have already been intrinsically motivated through, at a minimum, personal curiosity.

Organizationally, it has become commonplace for institutions, centers, even individuals to create mission and vision statements. CAPS direction as a center was largely articulated through its Pattern of Administration (POA), a very standard and formal set of guidance written by CAPS to describe how the center would operate, its policies, responsibilities, services, etc. The POA, one of the first documents guiding the center, was written and shared with members of both colleges to review, comment, edit and authorize. The CAPS POA, mission and vision, were created in a best faith way to ensure that progress was towards a common goal. It is also important to note that there is an individual quality to direction as well. In order, for an individual to agree and commit to the direction it must align with the direction of their personal or professional goals as well as the teams.

A challenge that CAPS was faced multiple times was the turnover of leadership and differing views with alignment of CAPS within the colleges supporting the center. College administrators, just like everyone else, move, retire, and accept other positions. This can cause restructuring, aligning, visioning with new people filling those roles. In CAPS experience, it is very time consuming and laborious to defending a document each time a change in the administration occurs. CAPS also had to serve as its own chaperone between the two colleges from which it was being supported. This will be discussed further with respect to how the environment can support teams. Within CAPS, faculty became ambassadors to administration, and in this way helped set the direction of the center within the context of the colleges. This took time however, and time is too valuable for a new center, especially when undergoing the difficult task of building teams. Currently, OSU is in the process of centralizing this functionality for CAPS, what formal reporting will look like, what are standard ROIs, responsibilities, etc. Much the same way as having an ESAB allows the center Director to transcend funding decisions, this centralization will allow the Director to transcend the political landscape within the university. This will hopefully permit the center to focus on the output of its direction.

Creating Alignment: Alignment is the organization and coordination of knowledge and work in a collective (Drath et al., 2008). One aspect of alignment, the coordination of the team's research lies solely within the team. In some cases, a natural leader emerged and often focused on ensuring that the team members were coordinated in its efforts and if not what mutual alterations needed to happen to get the team back working in tandem toward their goals. CAPS teams presented at least yearly in a seminar series, produced research posters for symposiums where all team graduate students were invited to attend, reported their progress at least annually, and were strongly encouraged to meet as a collective team at least monthly (and in person whenever possible). CAPS had structures within OSU to align its business practices. CAPS also had a unique budget and purchasing structure that also aided in the continue alignment of the teams. Budgets were resource-based, and not dollar-figure based. Instead of turning over funding to the teams, money was managed (and reported on) within the central center, even purchasing happened through CAPS instead of home departments. During the ESAB review CAPS would prepare details reporting to demonstrate its continued alignment and commitment towards its direction.

Building Commitment: Commitment is the willingness of members of a collective to subsume their own interests and benefit within the collective interest and benefit (Drath et al., 2008). It is important to also state that commitment has varying context. There is commitment to fellow team members, to the research being done, and to the organization (there are probably even more). More so than the previous two leadership tasks, building commitment can, and should, be done at every level within an organization.

Textbox 2: Team Commitment.
Commitment to a team can supersede the research. When financial support for one of the CAPS Scientific Teams was discontinued, the team members continued to collaborate, write spin off grants, and in general maintain the relationships they had formed. They were committed to each other and had formed a trusting relationship that outlasted the funding of the research team.

Commitment is a cornerstone of building trust within a team, it pushes scientific progress forward on an agreeable time scale, and it grants permission through validation of every individual's importance and contributions to the team. Commitment leads to shared responsibility amongst the team players and meaningful relationships with more traditionally defined leadership roles (Center Director, Chairs, Deans, etc.). Through commitment and sharing of responsibilities, faculty are more likely to continue to dedicate time and effort towards the group's work, which leads to team retention. Commitment is built up over time.

CAPS commitment to researchers, staff, and students was a cornerstone of the center generation process and a key factor in most administrative decisions. Commitment within a scientific team of faculty working on interesting ideas is of course crucial, but CAPS' was able to successfully build commitment beyond the faculty. Staff and students all became entrenched in the mission and values of CAPS. Just as team members, demonstration of commitment reinforces collegial reciprocity, so does the demonstration of commitment from administrators [Director, Manager, or Chair, whomever the senior most leader(s) happened to be]. The commitment to the science, the research team's success, the team members, and every other member of the organization, proves to model the behaviors and forms a deeper connection between staff, students and faculty. This in turn leads to commitment infused at multiple layers in an organization from the director to the fiscal associate and everyone in between.

These three leadership outcomes were vital not only within the teams, but also the individuals, the center, and the organization. The three task outcomes of this leadership model can be independent of each other. A team could for example have commitment and direction, but no alignment, or direction and alignment with no commitment. CAPS discovered that often it seemed to go in phases. After a time-lag for teams to reach consensus on the direction, direction, alignment and commitment of the teams themselves produced, exactly what was hoped, great science. There are many practical strategies to set direction, create alignment, and build commitment within an organization. The above outlines a few of the fundamentals of the CAPS experience. CAPS strived for trust and cooperation as a cornerstone of its operations, and hopes with time and continued resource availability; this will build resiliency and sustainability for the research teams and center.

2.C. Team Support

2.C.1 Team support is supporting people
CAPS found great success in leveraging postdoc and graduate student support across faculty labs. For example, one CAPS Team shared a Postdoctoral Researcher among five of the faculty members. This senior postdoc synthesized the information coming from the different faculty labs to look for trends across the data. The postdoc led team meetings, organized and curated the data and provided guidance and expertise to graduate students. Personal discussions with the postdoc elucidated the complexities of so many bosses, but also stated the enjoyment of the experience. This postdoc successfully moved into a faculty position afterwards. Another example, a PhD student in the Translational Sciences Graduate Program, a new and unique PhD program that requires students be co-mentored selected for her advisors two faculty that previously never collaborated. Through this student's research these faculty labs are now working together on not only the student's work, but spin-off projects. The student has benefitted tremendously by having two faculty with which to ask questions, learn from, and utilize labs and resources. The bridging of faculty through scientific support personnel is one way the center has found beneficial for the team and fruitful for future collaborations between the faculty.

2.C.2 Team support is supporting the science
Deliberately creating and sustaining scientific teams, especially in an environment as complete as the university setting, has many unique challenges. CAPS recognized that bringing faculty, postdocs, students and staff together across the teams, not only within, was of the utmost importance to begin to tackle any challenge. To this end, CAPS assumed the responsibilities for a weekly seminar series. This series highlights research done at all levels conducted by graduate students, postdocs and faculty, all of who present throughout the year. CAPS broadened the series by offering a video-link to the OSU Wooster campus, and expanded the series to include guest presentations from

distinguished external speakers, technology, commercialization and team science experts, and a diversity of expertise from multiple departments such has molecular genetics, horticulture and crop sciences, plant pathology, and the art department. The goal of these seminars was, and continues to be, not only to remind researchers of the greater scientific landscape where their contributions are relevant, but also to expand their thinking and spark conversation around a diversity of topics. These seminars work in part due to the regularity allowing for positive habit forming, and of course, the pizza. CAPS also held multiple research symposiums. There now exists an annual Graduate Student symposium sponsored by the Translational Plant Sciences Graduate Program (TPS-GP). This is a time where all TPS-GP fellows present display their work for the entire CAPS faculty and general population at OSU. CAPS has opened the symposium to not only TPS-GP Fellows, but in an attempt to foster the synergy and collaborative spirit, CAPS invited all graduate students and postdocs associated with any CAPS team. CAPS also created what were called Morning Gatherings. These half-day symposiums are an opportunity to reach across campus and pull together faculty working in different areas with potentially similar research outcomes, for example Biofuels and Sustainable Energy Practices. CAPS sponsored the Summer Practical Functional Genomics Workshop, a two-week intense experience open to scientists around the world, to hear daily lectures from the leading experts, and gain practical experience running experiments in the afternoon. CAPS also co-hosted workshops and coordinates faculty delegations to the University of São Paulo, Brazil, as an important way to globalize students and postdocs while increasing the visibility and partnerships with CAPS faculty around the world.

To further the interaction time and cross fertilization of ideas, CAPS held annual center retreats. These 1-3 day retreats were held off-site, typically in a natural setting like an Ohio State Park. All team members, graduate students, postdocs, and even staff was encouraged to attend. Families were welcomed and enjoy the natural setting and family entertainment CAPS sponsors. This was a time to engage everyone involved in the center in poster presentations, team updates, director visioning, networking, etc. Each year the center had a 85-95%

attendance rate. The results have been tremendous; faculty enjoyed hearing about the other teams and research progress, students interacted and learned what others were doing, staff engaged with researchers regarding how their services impact the larger research being conducted, what other services are needed, where is the research leading. There are costs to such face-time interactions however. It is becoming increasingly difficult to justify purchasing food for weekly seminars, off-site multi-day events, are expensive and costs associated with bringing families unallowable for state institutions and on federal funding. CAPS felt so strongly about these opportunities for cross-fertilization however that it campaigns for its weekly pizza and the Director pays for families out of his own pockets.

CAPS also supported the science through administration services. This includes new facilities such as the CAPS Computational Biology Laboratory (CCBL), which was developed as a pilot collaborative research space for bioinformatics and computational biology. The CCBL remains open to anyone, most often housing graduate students and postdocs. Greenhouse staff and space were available for CAPS team use; education and outreach events were presented and are becoming more popular for the dissemination of faculty research.

Even the budget model was developed to support the team's research. The budget was meant to remain vague, listing resources and why, because CAPS recognized that there are true costs of research that are unallowable on certain funding (graduate student tuition and fees for example), but teams needed the flexibility to rapidly change course or explore a new lead. This could be demonstrated through CAPS paying the tuition and fees for one team, or providing travel funds for a team's travel to Mexico for meeting collaborators, go into the field, and actively participate in the work. CAPS has supported travel of experts needed for a team to develop a collaborative interface with local commodity experts from Brazil and/or Mexico. Recently, CAPS began exploring a software platform that would allow faculty to share information more seamlessly across campus (hubzero.org).

CAPS' has continued to find unique ways, to build interactions and support teams across both physical, intellectual and emotional distance. Each university must learn to appreciate and apply support services for the teams of faculty within their institutions based on their microclimate and plethora of university factors.

2.C.3 The environment that allows teams to succeed

Perhaps the most important environment to consider is the institution itself. The university administration plays a central role in making sure that incipient teams (either individual or as part of centers) with an important problem to solve, succeed. This includes of course financial support. Depending on the breadth of the teams and the interdisciplinary nature of the problems that they intend to solve, support can come from colleges (usually focuses on teams/centers with a narrower scope), or from the office of research. Something that needs to be appreciated is that a perceived competition between centers and departments in unavoidable. Given the limited nature of funds and faculty time, any resources that go to centers are (in theory) not going to departments, and faculty time dedicated to center/team activities is time that is not dedicated to service or teaching. While ultimately departments benefit from the enhanced research portfolio and ambition of scientific teams, it is often difficult for faculty that is not part of the teams to realize this. Thus, good communication between department chairs, and center and team leads is essential to minimize frictions.

But the university administration can contribute in another, less appreciated way as well. Centers and scientific teams build from the university faculty with the goal to address challenging problems that hopefully are part of the mission of the respective colleges and university. However, making sure that the objectives of the center are perfectly aligned with those of the colleges and institutions requires a good dialog between all the parties, a dialog that cannot happen *a posteriori*, but which need to occur regularly to ensure that paths don't diverge widely. This is particularly challenging in institutions in which there is a constant change of administrators. Any center or team with a goal beyond the typical four years of a dean or provost will suffer the consequence of new administrators coming in with a desire to leave their mark with a new initiative, which often departs from the previous. This is one of the main challenges that gets in the way for an institution to make a significant impact in strengthening a particular area through team science.

2.D Learning from the Experience

The previous sections outline many lessons learned through the team development and evaluation processes. Following are additional considerations on further improvements to the processes taking-action from experience and theory.

Workshop length and intensity—Faculty is always busy. The first reaction of most faculty to any request that involves more than an hour of time is: "I don't think that I can afford it as I am very busy". It was a struggle to request, and sometimes keep, faculty for the length of time of the workshops. Reimbursing travel expenses for faculty coming from the other OSU campus, providing plenty of food and coffee, ending at a reasonable time (no later than 5-6pm), highlighting the opportunity for new funding streams and new collaborations, all seemed to work moderately well. As an important note, once a faculty attended one workshop, they were much easier to convince to come to the next. A few faculty members even reached out asking when the next Synergy Workshop was going to take place and many others helped in recommending colleagues and providing enthusiastic support for continuing to hold these events. This is attributable to the agile and innovative spirit of the workshops.

Finding the right people for the room—Like many of the Land Grant institutions, OSU has so far struggled to develop and maintain an up-to-data database of faculty expertise and accomplishments. Resorting to Google and PubMed was tedious and very time consuming. Unfortunately, there still is no solution for the finding the richness and complexity that is human centered expertise around these workshops. How might a living national faculty expertise database be developed and how might such a massive data collection be curated, while maintaining the simplicity needed for frictionless collaboration? In what ways could our federal government agency sponsors be engaged to assume this burden for the good of national research development needs?

Keeping faculty involved—There are many facets to keeping faculty involved. Different intrinsic and extrinsic motivators motivate many people, faculty included. The next section discusses preference in more detail, but there were a few key learnings from the team generation phase. Try to isolate team building events; if faculty can escape to their labs or teaching or meetings, they will. It is best to hold the event off campus or far away enough that it is unlikely that faculty will leave. The nature of Synergy Workshops, modeled after the Idea's Lab methodology, is that once engaged in the workshop, seemingly unnoticeable, phones and laptops fade into disuse. Other suggestions are to incentivize participation with a minimum of covering travel expenses and meals (and serve great food, people love great food and always bring people together). CAPS hoped one small, yet significant, strategy might be to build capacity to facilitate smaller scale ideation events within our institution to further enhance the potential steady stream of new and interesting research ideas in which faculty could be engaged could be maximized and captured. CAPS sought out such training and were well underway, but unfortunately another frequent issue arose, staff turnover.

Fostering interactions—Talking big, cool science is not always enough to sustain a team. In CAPS experience, an offsite dinner or non-related social activity also seems to be wonderful for team building. CAPS learned that keeping activities relevant is not always what is needed or most engaged, snowball fights, roasting marshmallows, and carving pumpkins have all lead to deeper faculty and staff engagement. Allowing down-time for networking and social interactions, fiscal transparency, inviting postdocs, graduate students, and even families to events; all of this and more demonstrates a key component of fostering interactions to build teams, trust. Trust goes well beyond a 2-3-day event and must be maintained throughout the life cycle of a team. Trust, cohesion, and conflict, and the team's ability to understand and navigate these issues within the team and the center/institution is critical to the sustainability of the team. Trust must be carefully built over time and interactions.

Leading alone is hard and has many disadvantages—It may seem that sometimes having the full authority and autonomy could make decisions and implementation easier. Sometimes it does. However, leading alone is emotionally and intellectually challenging. A one senior leader model seems to be the norm when undergoing an experiment, adding additional leadership resources (potentially) based on perceived success. CAPS solution was to engage an External Advisory Board, to its great success. Not only did this Board serve as an independent and conflict free board of advisors, but they are a resource when working with organizational administration. They are of critical importance when there are few leaders to serve as a sounding board, panel, critic and champion. Their expertise added immediate credibility and kept funding, a crucial and typically politically charged decision, out of interinstitutional relationships.

3. Evaluating the Impact

3.1 The Life of Teams: Some die, some evolve
It is difficult to anticipate when tackling grand challenges what the outcomes will be.

As previously stated, some of CAPS teams are celebrating success, some are in the trenches, and some have dissolved. Pilot research may suggest that the research hypothesis of the team was not correct, or that the team requires expertise or technologies that are have not been developed or are unavailable at the institution. Will the team evolve, suffer in mediocrity, or will it die? In the CAPS experience, it depends. Teams were given autonomy over their budget and personnel; they were even evaluated based on their own self-imposed scientific milestones. There are so many reasons why a research thread sometimes dissolves, and CAPS found that many times the life of the team is dependent mostly on decisions reached by the team.

A major challenge that CAPS faced was the termination of the teams and the potential disenfranchisement of the faculty. Many centers and departments will maintain a status quo of average or unexceptional work. CAPS goal of having OSU elevated to a national and international bed of plant research would not happen with unremarkable research teams. This forced a policy of discontinuance with teams not meeting proper progress. Having the ESAB and a dynamic mechanism for forming new teams (open calls and synergy workshops allowed for faculty to re-engage in different research teams) allows the center to maintain a positive working relationship with faculty even if funding for their team was reallocated to other needs within the center (different teams or workshops). CAPS withdrew funding for two of the six Scientific Teams.

Not all teams disbanded upon lack of funding, nor do they when their initial research hypothesis was proven incorrect. One example of the former was what is endearingly referred to as a "zombie" team. A team in which center administration had thought no further work was being done, yet came to find out that not only were the investigators still collaborating, but a graduate student and postdoctoral researcher were still actively engaged in the pursuing the work. This came as a wonderful surprise and one metric for how CAPS knew it was truly making an impact. Test results found another team's inceptive hypothesis was incorrect. Instead of ending the team, the faculty met, discussed the results, what would be needed to continue to pursue this new avenue, added another faculty, and submitted a change of team leader and scope request (which was approved by the ESAB). This team's ability to rapidly change course allowed for little time to be misused and thereby funds to be wasted. This team developed intellectual property that has spun off into a new startup.

Evolution does not only happen when faced with challenges however. One of the teams was highly successful in bridging research within a specific crop. Because they were so eloquently able to bring faculty together, and due to their graduate student training expertise, they became very successful in applying for, and receiving, funding from commodity groups. This led to further increase the exposure of their work, their students and their resources. This team is now negotiating center status within a college at OSU. CAPS could not be a more enthusiastic supporter of such efforts.

3.2 Rethinking the return on investment

Return on investment (ROI) is typically and broadly understood to be the rate of return on monies invested, or the benefit resulting from an investment. Calculating this is standard operating procedure in most universities, even the National Science Foundation (NSF) must demonstrate their ROI when requesting the annual budget (NSF 2016). Typically, the usual factors include grants received (with indirect costs expenditures), number of publications (impact factor and citations), number of graduate students and postdoctoral researchers trained, intellectual property licensed, etc. (Figure 2). This is not new to the people reading this chapter, many of whom have had to calculate their net worth for promotion and tenure, start-up packages, retention packages and more. CAPS successfully launched a new PhD Graduate Program, an International Dual PhD Program, received an IUCRC planning grant, SBIR funding, industry support, faculty published, spun-off a startup company, graduate students received fellowships from private and federal sources, postdoctoral researchers moved into faculty positions. In sum, things happened as a consequence of the CAPS existence. In a short amount of time with limited funds and limited personnel, CAPS was able to provide leadership and support for substantial change. Along the way, however, CAPS felt increasingly aware of the time it took for accomplishments and the lack of understanding and appreciation for unquantifiable achievements. There was a feeling of excitement and progress, but the outcomes were taking far longer than the administration anticipated. In hindsight, this makes sense; how does one measure research productivity? The same it always has. The literature suggests, and our observations concur, that it takes time for the faculty to coalesce, form a cohesive team, understand the expertise and capabilities in their team, decide on the right research focuses, and all while maintaining their own research labs and academic priorities. However, with respect to publications at the very least, bibliometric data suggests this time can be offset in successful team's higher publication rates. Investments in experimental centers however are often a few years at a time, in CAPS case, five years, with four-year's worth of funding. With an academic structure that changes every three to five years, it is difficult to capture and value a moving target of metrics.

CAPS learned that there is a balance between a typical ROI and the intangibles that many times are overlooked or un-quantified. Communicating the intangibles in a ROI world is difficult. Every year different audiences would want reports in their way, typically filling out an excel spreadsheet with dollars spent, indirect costs recovered via grant funding expended, and a list of publications. Still others would ask for a "1-pager" summarizing a year's achievement in headline fashion so that busy people could easily digest just the high notes. Making more meaningful connections amongst our faculty, postdocs, and students continues to drive our center forward, recognizing the hard work of the individuals, teams, building the CAPS community, these things can be lost in the headlining style of documents.

CAPS decided to create its' own annual report. In this publication, CAPS highlighted the research updates and the achievements of the teams and many other initiatives of the center including specials guest seminars, faculty delegation travel, graduate student progress, facilities and operations. Together with presenting traditional ROI metrics (grants and publications), and how money was being received and spent, CAPS became a storyteller of accomplishments, detailing networking opportunities, bold ideas and workshops. The report was visually appealing with pictures of lab and field work, findings, and most importantly, the people. Over the course of a few years, CAPS starting better redefining how it thought of success (Figure 2) and would measure it. CAPS enlisted a software technician to help visualize the basic before and after networks. The center began experimenting with various software platforms and interfaces as a means of finding interesting combinations of faculty, research topics, facilities and communications. CAPS thought about better ways to introduce, reintroduce, re-engage faculty, postdocs and students. What would concrete intangibles look like, CAPS with others, is still exploring these concepts.

4. If the future could be anticipated...

Where do we go from here? In Robert Fritz's 1989 tension model, one navigates through structural tension from a current reality to achieve a desired future (Fritz, 1989).

Desired future: The year is 2031; Land Grant universities are once again pioneering large research development initiatives. Faculty are teaming beyond academic institutions, disciplines, and continents. They are solving the challenges of food, water, and energy; catapulting our species beyond the limitations of population density, climate change, mass species extinction, and civil wars. We are global citizens able to explore opportunities for monumental scientific innovations.

Current reality: Today's universities may not be on this path. How might we actualize our future when saddled with higher administration's vision misaligned with that of the faculty they serve, when resources for capturing and sharing data even amongst one institution across campuses is limiting, reporting, priorities, and investments are unclear, standard operating procedures for nonstandard practices are enforced? How can we move from our current reality towards this desired future? How might we solve problems as a dynamic system in flux instead of solving our piece of the puzzle only to watch the challenge move downstream to another discipline?

We would like to leave with a few questions we hope provoke thought, conversation and action upon:

- Does the modern research university need promotion and tenure, as it is understood now? How might it be modernized?
- How might faculty better connect with the appropriate resource at the appropriate time for inspiration, intervention?
- How might institutions and funders better support faculty working on the border of their comfort zones in ambiguous and oftentimes bleeding-edge, difficult to fund, research?
- How might scientists overcome challenges with collaborating across distance, both real and cognitive?

5. Conclusions

While the output is certainly much more than the sum of the parts, interdisciplinary team science is a challenging endeavor, and its success depends on numerous factors, some internal to the team, but also many external, including the institutional environment in which team are expected to thrive. Often organizations believe that they are ready for team science, but institutional barriers and rigid structures make the success of team science almost impossible. Our ability to implement team science as part of our research enterprise will be essential as the challenges that humanity faces become increasingly complex. While the formation of scientists becomes more and more focused, our institutions must figure out ways to remain nimble, better training and education for these future scientists, but also the creation of the environment in which they will graduate and work is of critical importance. High quality instruction in the time of plenty and easily accessible information requires teamwork as well.

6. Acknowledgements

We want to thank Peter March and Christopher Hadad, Deans of the Division of Natural and Mathematical Sciences in the OSU College of Arts and Sciences for their vision and support to CAPS over the years. We also want to thank Sarah Hake, Jim Carrington, Sophien Kamoun, Rob Last, Richard Flavell and David Stern for their extraordinary contributions to CAPS and OSU when they served as part of the CAPS External Scientific Advisory Board. We thank Joanna Gardner for her many invaluable contributions to CAPS.

7. Figures

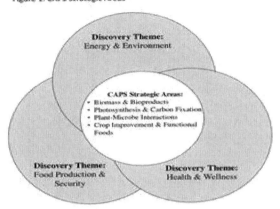

Figure 1. CAPS Strategic Areas

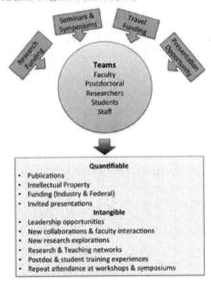

Figure 2. Quantifiable and Intangible outcomes of Team Science at the Center for Applied Plant Sciences (CAPS).

8. References

Bennett, LM, Gadlin H, Levine-Finley S. Collaboration Team Science: A Field Guide at the National Institutes of Health, Office of the Ombudsman

Boeke JD, Church G, Hessel A, Kelley NJ, Arkin A, Cai Y, Carlson R, Chakravarti A, Cornish VW, Holt L, et al. (2016). *The genome project-write*. Science, 353:126.

Cha, A.E. (2016, April 13). Ohio State's breakthrough brain chip allows paralyzed man to use hands. The Columbus Dispatch. Retrieved from: http://www.dispatch.com/content/stories/local/2016/04/13/0413-breakthrough-brain-chip.html

Collins T, Kearney M, Maddison D. (2013). The Ideas Lab Concept, Assembling the Tree of Life, and AVAToL. *PLOS Currents Tree of Life*. Edition 1. doi: 10.1371/currents.tol.0fdb85e1619f313a2a5a2ec3d7a8df9e.

Davies, A (2016 October, 25). Uber's self-driving truck makes its first delivery: 50,000 beers. Wired. Retrieved from: https://www.wired.com/2016/10/ubers-self-driving-truck-makes-first-delivery-50000-beers/

Drath WH., McCauley CD, Palus CJ and E. Van Velsor (2008) Directional, Alignment and Commitment: Toward a More Integrative Ontology of Leadership, The Leadership Quarterly 19:635-653.

Fritz, R. (1989). *Path of Least Resistance: Learning to Become the Creative Force in Your Own Life*. Ballantine Books: New York.

Hall KL1, Stokols D, Stipelman BA, Vogel AL, Feng A, Masimore B, Morgan G, Moser RP, Marcus SE, Berrigan D. (2012). Assessing the tvlue of Team Science: A study comparing center- and Investigator-Initiated grants. *American Journal of Preventive Medicine*. 2012 Feb;42(2):157-63. doi: 10.1016/j.amepre.2011.10.011.

Molitch-Hue, M. (2016, October 18). Biomaterial printing unlocks new material properties in metals, grapheme and tissues. Retrieved from: http://www.engineering.com/3DPrinting/3DPrintingArticles/ArticleID/13425/Biomaterial-Printing-Unlocks-New-Material-Properties-in-Metals-Graphene-and-Tissues.aspx

National Research Council. Enhancing the effectiveness of Team Science. Washington, DC: The National Academies Press, 2015. doi:10.17226/19007.

National Science Foundation. (2014, December 26). NSF FY 2017 Budget Request to Congress. Retrieved from: https://www.nsf.gov/about/budget/fy2017/pdf/01_fy2017.pdf

National Science Foundation (2016). Grant Proposal Guide (Chapter II.D.3). Retrieved from: https://www.nsf.gov/pubs/policydocs/pappguide/nsf15001/gpg_index.jsp

Nest, P. (2014, March 3). In Search of Lost Time. *Inside Higher Ed.* Retrieved from: https://www.insidehighered.com/advice/2014/03/03/essay-why-faculty-members-work-so-much

Sandpits and Ideas Labs (n.d.) Retrieved from http://knowinnovation.com/expertise/facilitating/

Skibba, R. (2016). OSIRIS-REx spacecraft blazes trail for asteroid miners. Nature. doi:10.1038/nature.2016.20486

Skoltech: Skolkovo Institute of Science and Technology (2013, October 16) Ideas Lab: Research with Creativity. Retrieved from: http://www.skoltech.ru/en/2013/10/ideas-lab-research-with-creativity/

Stokols D, Hall K, Taylor B, Moser R. (2008). The Science of Team Science: Overview of the Field and Introduction of the Supplement. *American Journal of Preventive Medicine.* 35: S77-S89.

CHAPTER 19

Pathways to Collaboration

Reinventing My Science; One Person's Journey to Collaborative Research and Development

Richard Sayre
Senior Research Scientist
Los Alamos National Laboratory (LANL) and
the New Mexico Consortium (NMC)

never had a set career plan when I started college. I am still impressed by those who did. I didn't think that there was much certainty to the future. As a firm believer in the opportunity of chance, the evolutionary process, and working hard, I subscribed to the concept that the best strategy for career success was to be informed as possible, celebrate that change is constant, and choose career pathways that were most interesting, challenging and fun. In short, my career objective was to constantly reinvent myself and not be constrained by a plan. It was this interest in change and discovery that eventually lead me to choose working with and managing large collaborative research programs that have been the hallmark of my scientific career for the last 15 years.

Collaborative research was certainly not the accepted pathway, however, for an early career assistant professor in 1986. It was drilled into me by my administrators and peers that I had to produce a unique body of scientific work that was distinctly of my own doing. Having a young family was certainly a motivator to fit the norm, since achieving tenure would insure financial stability. But there was another more selfish reason to master the accepted pathway to academic career success and that was I simply abhorred failure. So, my initial research efforts were not collaborative but focused on building signature research programs that grew out of my past body of work, my foundation.

It was the second year as an assistant professor at Ohio State University that I received my first NIH and DOE single investigator award grants. The focus of these programs was to characterize the topology of membrane proteins and the structure-function relationships of the photosystem II reaction center complex, respectively. Ironically, both research programs were products of my first truly collaborative research experience. While a postdoc in Lawrence Bogorad's lab, we applied for the first time the use of antibodies generated against synthetic peptides to map the folding topology of the D1, photosystem II reaction center membrane protein (Sayre et al., 1986; Andersson et al., 1987). Our strategy was to use the peptide-specific antibodies to identify predicted protein fragments generated by trypsin-digestion of right-side out and inside-out membrane topologies. Bertil Anderson's group in Lund, Sweden, had recently developed a two-phase polymer system to fractionate right-side-out from inside-out thylakoid membranes based on differences in surface charge density between the two fractions. We tried repeatedly to reproduce this partitioning system in our lab but to no avail. Fortunately, we were in a well-funded lab and so a trip was planned to do the experiments in Lund. A two-week collaboration turned into a month-long intense research project working 16 hour days non-stop. The subsequent paper that was generated on the folding topology of the D1 protein demonstrated structural homology between the D1 protein and the L-subunit of the recently crystalized bacterial photosynthetic reaction center polypeptide, adding further evidence that the quinone-type reaction centers of bacteria and eukaryotes were evolutionarily related (Ruffle and Sayre, 1998). It also started my career path towards larger and more complex collaborative research programs.

I have always felt that one of my strengths was an ability to exploit information from very disparate disciplines to generate new ideas.

Scientists all do this of course, i.e. they are constantly reinventing their research programs, but some are more creative than others. I happened to work as a postdoc with one of the masters of reinvention, Lawrence Bogorad. What could be more fun than running 4-5 different research programs simultaneously and looking for the cross-talk to emerge between the programs that would generate new ideas? Importantly, I recognized, contrary to the excepted practices of my peers, that I had to have multiple research programs going on simultaneously or I would get bored. The risk of course of this research strategy was of course becoming too shallow.

Working with students, technicians and postdocs is the pathway all academics are introduced to collaborative research. In 1988, I hired the first technician to work with me at OSU. Offiong Mkpong had grown up in Nigeria during the Biafaran Civil War. While a child and a later as a refugee, Offiong had survived on cassava as his major source of sustenance. Cassava was the major staple crop in his homeland and could be counted on providing food even in the harshest conditions. During drought, cassava would often be the only crop least consumed by herbivores. This was largely due to the fact that cassava stores potentially lethal levels of cyanogens. These cyanide producing molecules must be removed or deglcosylated and volatilized for the food to be safe to consume. This processing can take several days to complete (McMahon et al., 1995). During famine, short cuts in processing are often made, potentially resulting in poor health outcomes for the consumer. Offiong had incredible confidence in the "new" technology of plant genetic engineering to solve the cyanide problem for cassava.

Not knowing a thing about cyanide metabolism in cassava I asked Offiong to go to the library and see what he could dig up on the subject and for us to determine if there was a research pathway forward to reducing the cyanide toxicity of cassava (Mkpong et al. 1990). He came back to me with box of photocopied papers and over the next week, as we read through the papers, it became apparent that there was a pathway forward to understanding and manipulating cyanide metabolism in cassava. Unfortunately, no one was growing cassava in Ohio. So, we headed off to the local Asian market to get cassava roots. The market imported cassava roots from the Caribbean about every two weeks, so we had a constant supply. At that time, OSU was developing a center of excellence in Arabidopsis research which would eventually mature into the Arabidopsis Biological Resource Center. Given the growing investment in Arabidopsis, the lab rat of the plant world, my colleagues actively questioned my rationale for focusing on a crop plant with virtually no genetics, no transformation system, and no relevance to agriculture in the US. But what an amazing story cassava would turn out to be. Over the next 14 years, with support from USAID, the Rockefeller Foundation, and the National Starch and Chemical Company, the cyanide story in cassava turned into the foundation of one of the largest sponsored research programs ever awarded to the College of Biological Sciences. Cassava also literally changed our lives. I was soon traveling to the International Institute for Tropical Agriculture (IITA) in Nigeria and to the International Center for Tropical Agriculture (CIAT) in Colombia to see cassava first hand, and to develop long-term relationships with cassava breeders, farmers, biochemists and genetic engineers, many of whom have been among my closest friends and collaborators over the years.

Everything cassava related changed in 2004. I just had stepped down as chairman of the Department of Plant Cellular and Molecular Biology. The department had done well over the last six years and had grown to the best research funded and most productive teaching department in the College. But the push to reach that status had its consequences. Our young faculty were over-worked and so it was time for me to move on. Early in 2004, I received a phone call from Willie Gruissem at the ETH in Zurich. Willie had heard that the Bill and Melinda Gates Foundation was launching a major global development initiative, the Grand Challenge in Global Health (GCGH), and that one of the multiple focus areas of the GCGH initiative was alleviating malnutrition in developing countries. At that time, at least 1 million early childhood deaths per year could be attributed in part to malnutrition. The GCGH program proposed to address malnutrition by providing complete nutrition in a single staple crop. Cassava had to be part of that GCGH program. Cassava was the fifth largest crop consumed directly by humans and Africa, where cassava was most important in the diet, had the highest per capita rates of malnutrition in the world. Willie was pulling a team together to apply for the grant and Claude Fauquet and I were among the first persons he called to be part of his team. But, commitments can sometimes change. A week later, Willie called and said he wanted to lead a rice biofortification proposal and he was not allowed to lead two projects simultaneously. The ETH had made a major stake in the Golden Rice program under Ingo Potrykus and Ingo had just retired. Either Claude or I would have to take over the cassava proposal. Claude was hesitant, so I agreed to lead the proposal and BioCassava Plus was launched. Claude clearly had a strong network of collaborators in Africa working on cassava mosaic virus disease. The Danforth Center, where Claude was located, also had research strengths in metal (zinc) uptake, and isoprenoid (β-carotene or provitamin A) synthesis. So, together we assembled a team of 25 molecular biologists, cassava breeders, agronomists, and medical experts from 5 continents. We ended up targeting 8 traits to improve including enhanced iron, zinc, pro-vitamin A, protein, and vitamin E levels, along with reduced cyanide toxicity, enhanced shelf life and cassava mosaic virus disease resistance. Stepping down from the departmental chair position made it all possible for me to dedicate all my efforts to organize the team, draft the proposal (3 months non-stop), and successfully pull it off. In 2005, the 5 year, $12 million award was made.

The BioCassava Plus program was my first introduction to managing large-scale international research programs, particularly with a translational focus (Sayre et al., 2011). It was also my first exposure to meeting research milestones and deliverables on a regular basis. But it was also the early days of the BMGF and we were fortunate to work with a new program officer, Fil Randazzo, who did everything he could to help us become successful. By the end of the third year we had met all our target objectives for crop biofortification and introduction of traits to enhance adoption and acceptance (enhanced shelf life, reduced food cyanide levels, and virus resistance) of the new lines, with one caveat. These results were obtained with greenhouse grown plants and not in the field.

There were many lessons learned over the course (2005-2010) of phase I of the BC+ project (Sayre et al., 2011). One lesson learned was that sometimes the director needs to make final decisions that not all members agree too. One of these early decisions was the choice of where to do the first field trials. I insisted that we conduct our first field trials in Puerto Rico rather than moving immediately to Nigeria, Kenya and Uganda. GM trials in Puerto Rico were under US government regulatory control and no GMO field trial regulations were in place in Nigeria and Uganda at that time, and Kenya had reservations about doing GM cassava trials. In addition, I felt it critical that to gain acceptance of GM technology in Africa the first outdoor experiments had to be done in the US to demonstrate that "we" were willing to accept the perceived risk and not move the technology off-shore to avoid potential risk and saddle it on our international partners. This strategy was not welcomed in the BC+ management. But, field trials in Puerto Rico turned out to be a critical part of our strategy for moving into Nigeria. The Nigerian National Biosafety Committee had just been assembled and Martin Fregene, our program manager and a native of Nigeria, had gained the confidence of the committee. He soon invited the Biosafety Committee to visit the field trials in Puerto Rico. The Nigerian National Biosafety Committee came away from that visit with a very different appreciation of GM cassava. It was apparent that the GM cassava were not monster crops that were going to take over the world. In contrast to the fears and misinformation campaigns that were prevalent at the time, these new GM cassava plants could potentially address fundamental nutrition concerns and do so without a profit incentive and without the take-over of Nigerian agriculture by multi-national corporations. BC+ plants were the first GM plants approved for field trials in Nigeria.

The BC+ experience was a tremendous learning experience both scientifically and with respect to managing inter-personal interactions. I learned that the science we were doing could be secondary to the perceived safety concerns of the targeted clientele and that developing skills in personnel and crisis management were as critical to the success of the program as the foundational science. I also learned that lab science could not always be translated to the "real world", that unanticipated outcomes could torpedo the best lab technology. I also learned that tracking the products through the development pipeline was as important as developing the products. None of this was learned in a vacuum. There were many people that provided guidance and shared their personal wisdom to inform me and our team on best and standardized practices.

One of the most important management lessons learned was sharing information and knowledge and avoiding misunderstandings. More management energy was wasted on addressing misunderstandings between collaborators than any other factor. The importance of having regular and spontaneous discussions with team members cannot be overemphasized. It is necessary to insure team members are meeting expectations, to facilitate innovation, and to develop implicit trust and comradery. Managing BC+ was also the most challenging program I have ever managed. It is a common discussion in the scientific community that we are trained to do science but never taught how to manage people. Yet working with people can be the most rewarding as well as the most frustrating part of the profession.

After the first five years, BC+ was up for renewal. BC+ was moving more and more into the field trial component of the program. This critical area of product development was not my expertise. We had much more qualified experts in our team to lead phase II product development. Furthermore, Martin Fregene, our program manager was an expert in cassava field breeding and had close connections too, and was trusted by our critical African partners. It may sound trite, but I believe a good manager also knows when it's time to step down and should be sure to help pick the best successor to move the program forward.

By 2010, when the BC+ renewal was submitted, I had already moved to the Donald Danforth Plant Science Center. I left OSU in 2008, when I was made an amazing offer by Roger Beachy to become the first Director of the Enterprise-Rent-A-Car Institute for Renewable Fuels (ERAC). By 2008, my research group was exploiting our capacity to genetically transform algae to explore fundamental mechanisms in photosynthesis as well as to expand the biotechnological applications including; ameliorating heavy metal pollution in the environment, delivering antigens to orally vaccinate fish, exploring the regulation of inter-kingdom signaling by bacterial quorum sensing molecules, and others. The ERAC position, would allow us to rebalance our research portfolio which had largely moved to BC+ related work. Moving to the Danforth Center, was an amazing opportunity. There was close access to the photosynthesis group at Washington University as well as the plant biotechnology giant, Monsanto.

My first task at ERAC was to assemble a team of Danforth Center and other scientists to apply for the newly announced DOE-Energy Frontier Research Center (EFRC) Program. We would focus our efforts on advanced biofuels, particularly hydrocarbon-based biofuels produced by algae and the oil-seed crop, Camelina (Sayre, 2010). Our objectives were to enhance photosynthetic efficiency and biomass production, design biofuel feedstocks more compatible with downstream processing technologies, and produce aromatic co-products to make complete fuels from biological sources. Our team, the Center for Advanced Biofuels Systems (CABS), was chosen from colleagues whom we had identified as among the best in their field as well as persons who could work well as members of a team. I had learned in working with BC+ that there had to be an implicit trust between collaborators. A team which could be counted on to deliver results, develop novel innovate strategies to tackle problems, and collaborators who could work for the collective good would insure success. But, also engaging a select group of trusted scientific advisors and co-investigators to collectively identify and recruit the best research team was also an essential part of our success. In 2010, the CABS EFRC was awarded and research began.

But, another even larger, interdisciplinary biofuels research program was soon to emerge. As part of the American Reinvestment and Recovery Act economic recovery plan announced by the new Obama Administration, the Department of Energy targeted substantial stimulus funds to accelerate the development of algal biofuels research. In 2008, I was invited by the DOE to present a plenary talk on the future challenges facing algal biofuels development at the National Algal Biofuels Technology Roadmap Workshop. This presentation subsequently lead to an invite from Sandrasegaram Gnanakaran (Gnana) at Los Alamos National Laboratory (LANL) to present our work on enhancing photosynthetic efficiency and biomass production in algae at the Energy for the 21st Century Conference in Santa Fe (Perrine et al., 2012). Subsequently, EERE division of DOE soon (2009) announced the largest program targeted for advancing algal biofuels development since the Aquatic Species Program in 1976. There was a scramble to assemble competitive research teams with the National Labs and a few major universities leading the effort. The team that first approached me was from LANL lead by Jose Olivares. It was soon apparent that the LANL team was best-organized group among those that had approached me and that the LANL team had tremendous support development support from the lab so I joined, in the role of scientific director for the National Alliance for Advanced Biofuels and Bioproducts (NAABB). As had been done with other successful research coalitions, NAABB was out the door early recruiting the best scientific talent and bringing the team together in face-to-face planning meetings to share and develop the vision, and to integrate the programmatic effort into a coherent and well managed program. On the day that the Secretary of Energy announced the awards, I got a call at 5:00 am from Congressman Russ Carnahan, my representative and one of the Congressional Leaders for bioenergy programs. He called to inform me that the Secretary of Energy was going to announce at noon that the NAABB consortium had won a nearly $50 million DOE award matched by nearly $20 million in industrial and university funds. The award was to be managed out of the Danforth Center with Jose Olivares as the executive director. This was huge.

The three years of NAABB (2010-2013) were among the most challenging (meeting hard milestone and deliverable dates) as well as most exciting times in my professional career (Olivares et al., 2016). It was my first introduction to industrial partnerships and lead to close relationships with UOP/Honeywell, Eldorado Biofuels, Reliance Industries Limited (India), Genifuel, Pan Pacific Enterprises, and Phycal; companies that we have continued to partner with in subsequent research programs. Building professional relationships with government, academic and industrial partners is critical to building successful programs as well as an important investment for helping insure long-term federal and industrial support for renewable fuels research.

I had always been skeptical but the ability of individual scientists to impact federal research policy. But because I was in a critical political battleground state, Ohio, early in my career, I was tapped to be a member and later Chair of the Public Affairs Committee of the American Society of Plant Biologists (ASPB). The ASPB Public Affairs Committee members would annually meet with our local Congressman and Senators to promote federal support for science. I got to know the Ohio Congressional delegation well on both sides of the isle. After moving to Missouri in 2008, I had to engage a new Congressional delegation. My first meeting with Congressman Russ Carnahan was one of the most memorable. I was scheduled to meet with him for 15 minutes to promote support for basic plant sciences research, but our meeting ran on to 45 minutes. It was soon evident that Congressman Carnahan had an intense interest in renewable fuels and their potential for agricultural development in the Midwest. Each year we met our relationship grew stronger. Congressman Carnahan became a leader of the Congressional Algae Bioenergy Group and later spoke on sustainable energy policy as the lead-off speaker at the first International Algal Biomass, Biofuels and Bioproducts Conference held in St Louis. We were certainly grateful for his strong support for sustainable energy production.

The bottom line for large translational research consortia is will the products generated by the program reduce costs, be scalable, and outperform the existing technologies or provide new solutions to unaddressed problems. To guide product development and assess outcomes is the responsibility of economists. The NAABB consortium was my second exposure to life cycle (LCA) and techno-economic analysis (TEA) of integrated, cradle-to-grave research and development programs. It was evident from BC+ that economic and technical modeling of integrated systems could provide insights and identify the major bottlenecks and technological hurdles that needed to be addressed to successfully develop scalable solutions. The insights gained from LCA/TEA modeling could also assist in the visioning for follow up and future research and development programs. Perhaps, the major accomplishment of the NAABB Consortium was developing and modeling a process for moving the cost of algal biofuels from $150 a gallon gasoline equivalent (gge) to $8 gge in three years. LCA/TEA analyses also identified the primary challenges that needed to be addressed in the future to achieve economic parity with petroleum-based fuels. For algal biofuels, the major constraints were areal biomass productivity and reducing the energetic costs of harvesting algae. To achieve parity with gasoline and to enhance sustainability, LCA/TEA analyses informed us that we would have to increase biomass productivity by three-fold and reduce the energy costs of harvesting algae to less than 10% of the energy content of the algae.

Since NAABB, I have been involved in two additional algal biofuels consortia; one as a co-PI (Realization of Algae's Potential) and one as Director, Producing Algae for Co-products and Energy (PACE). Significantly, there have been marked changes in the management structure of DOE Bioenergy Technology Office programs over the last few years. There has been a substantive increase in external management directly by DOE and greater monitoring of performance metrics to assess progress towards meeting timelines, milestones and deliverables. This management transition at DOE, has led to greater time commitment to management; commitments that young scientists just beginning their careers could find challenging. For young scientists entering collaborative research and who desire to direct multi-institution and multi-partner programs it's strategically advisable to work up through the management ranks while also cultivating relationships with partners. Directors of research consortia also need to facilitate the advancement of early career scientists. This can be achieved by encouraging early career scientists to become spokespersons for the consortia, inviting them to participate in management teams and/or providing a mechanism to move into management.

The NAABB engagement lead to my final public career move (at least at this time). Early in 2011, I was approached by a university to consider an endowed research position. Since I was concerned what the impact could be on the NAABB Consortium, I contacted Jose Olivares to enquire whether he had any concerns. Jose countered by asking me if I would consider moving to LANL. I had an amazing hard money position at the Danforth Center, but what I missed mots while in St. Louis was interactions with investigators and theoreticians outside my discipline or comfort zone who could help me expand my science. Both the university and LANL provided that opportunity for further intellectual growth and development. I choose to accept the position offer at LANL for personal as well as professional reasons. At LANL there was the opportunity to help build a new bioenergy program at a very large scale. That program has now been realized by the completion of a new bioenergy research building at the New Mexico Consortium Entrada facility. Furthermore, we have been able to engage "big science" in new experimental, computational and theoretical areas (Berman et al., 2015). Without a doubt, LANL has exposed me to some of the brightest minds in the country. However, some things had to be given up with the move as well. I was required to step-down as the director of CABS EFRC center at the Danforth Center and had limited access to specialized plant cultivation systems and associate support services, although that is improving. Working in the culture of a National Lab was also a surprise. The management culture was unlike either academic or non-profit research centers. At LANL, being cognizant national security issues related to our work and the associated safe guards necessary to secure information was an entirely new experience. Having experienced three different scientific cultures over my career, however, allowed me to better appreciate the capabilities, concerns and advantages of each culture.

The forth sector of my collaborative professional development was entrepreneurial. In 2000, the State of Ohio passed legislation that allowed university faculty to have an ownership position in start-up companies they initiated. I was the first faculty member at OSU to take advantage of this provision and along with my partner started Phycotransgenics LLC. Phycotransgenics' core technology was the development of microalgal-based delivery of antigens to vaccinate fish and terrestrial farm animals (Siripornadulsil, 2006). Phycotransgenics, soon we moved into a new industrial incubator, SciTech, and hired our first personnel funded through SBIR grants. Over the next 5 years, Phycotransgenics was successful in generating substantial financial support from SBIR grants and private companies. During that time, I learned the first principles for operating in the commercial sector and developing collaborative agreements with industrial partners. We spent many weeks on the road drumming up support. But when the decision was made to support Phycotransgenics it was often quick and unburdened by excessive oversight. In contrast to academic and federal research labs where programmatic support decisions may take up to a year, in the commercial sector funding decisions and support could be decided in a matter of days, allowing the research to be quick and nimble.

I left Phycotransgenics in 2005, for personal reasons, but in 2007, was approached by a group of entrepreneurs to start the second company I was involved in, Phycal LLC. Phycal was a bioenergy corporation lead by a financially savvy group of managers and an internationally recognized board of directors. In three years Phycal grew to nearly 80 employees and was on the verge of commercial success when the US EPA relaxed requirements for advanced biofuel feedstocks at refineries and the market fell out under the company (Kumar et al., 2016). In 2014, Phycal closed its doors for good. Unlike academic research with tenure, start-ups can come and go rapidly along with financial stability.

I continue to be involved in entrepreneurial activity and find it provides valuable insights into team management and development. It has led to professional relationships that have further expanded my scientific and managerial development. As with any large collaborative group, a critical element in developing a successful commercial team is implicit trust and integrity. These personal qualities are best assessed "when the going gets rough" and are critical to the long-term success of any consortium. Those who unselfishly step up, deliver their best work, and do so with integrity are the partners you come back to time-after-time when assembling collaborative teams.

One empirically resolved model for building collaborative research and development programs:

There must be a central vision. Visioning comes from integrating information from many sources and having the insight to develop collective networks that most efficiently and with the highest probability of success address the targeted research objective. Visioning is often intuitive but is trending more towards modeling approaches to determine the bet pathways to success, particularly for large complex problems.

There must be engagement and buy-in to the vision: Creative and driven partners must not only buy into the vision but enhance it and provide critical feedback.

Focus: The vision must be focused and manageable taking into account the objectives of the program, level of funding, timing and geography.

Timing can be everything: Ideas may be unique but not for long. There is eventually someone who will come up with the same idea. So, it is critical to act fast, particularly when recruiting talent for a new collaborative program. The best talent and most motivated collaborators will be in high demand, particularly by the competition.

Environment: Promote cross-disciplinary interactions to foster creativity.

Communication: There is rarely too much communication. The lack of communication is often the major reason programs have difficulties. When going into a conversation as a manager go with the intent to listen, learn and understand, not first to reply and rebut. Go to your collaborator to hear her/his story. Manager's can be intimidating in their home environments

Transparency: A key component of building trust is sharing information and engaging talent. Do this as much as possible.

Teaming: In competitive research programs assembling your team first can be a strategic advantage.

Know your limits: Large consortia can only be assembled by a team. Be comfortable delegating responsibility and authority.

Crisis management: Having contingency plans can help address crises when they occur, and they will occur. The best practice on crisis management are transparency, to the extent possible while protecting personnel, and honesty.

Sharing success: Give credit to those due and share success. Mangers are often the first perception of the team effort, but the team generates the outputs.

There are many pathways to success: Be flexible, listen to advisors and those with experience. Just like raising children, each child has her/ his unique expectations and capabilities. There is no master formula for dealing with all collaborative programs. But there are the first principles; honesty, transparency, motivation, recognition of work by others and an ability to listen and learn. Enjoy!

References:

Andersson B, Sayre RT and Bogorad L (1987) Transbilayer organization of photosystem II proteins with special emphasis on the 32 kD Qb-binding protein. *Nobel Symposium, Membrane Proteins: Structure, Function and Assembly. Chemica Scripta*, 1987, 27B: 195-200.

Sayre RT, Andersson B and Bogorad L (1986) The topology of a membrane protein: the orientation of the 32 kD Qb-binding chloroplast thylakoid membrane protein. *Cell* 47: 601-608.

Ruffle SV and Sayre RT (1998) Functional analysis of photosystem II. In: *Molecular Biology of Chlamydomonas: Chloroplasts and Mitochondria*, Chapter 16. Pgs. 287-322; M. Goldshmidt-Clermont, S. Merchant, J.-D. Rochaix eds., Kluwer Academic Publishers.

McMahon JM, White W, and Sayre RT (1995) Cyanogenesis in Cassava (*Manihot esculenta* Crantz). *J. Exp. Bot.* 46: 731-741.

Mkpong OE, Yan H, Chism G and Sayre RT (1990) Purification, characterization and localization of linamarase in cassava. *Plant Physiol.* 93: 176-181.

Sayre RT *et al.*, (2011) Crop biofortification for Africa, the BioCassava Plus Program. *Ann. Rev. Plant Biol.* 62:251–272.

Sayre RT (2010) Microalgal biofuels; carbon capture and sequestration. *Bioscience* 60:722-727.

Perrine Z, Negi S and Sayre, RT (2012) Optimization of photosynthetic light energy utilization by microalgae. *Algal Res.* 1:134-142.

Olivares J, Unkefer CJ; Sayre RT; Magnuson JK; Anderson DB; Baxter I; Blaby IK; Brown JK; Carleton M, Cattolico RA; Dale T; Devarenne TP; C Downes CM; Dutcher SK, Fox DT; Goodenough U; Jaworski J; Holladay JE; Kramer D; Koppisch AT; Lipton MS; Marrone BL; McCormick M; Molnar I; Mott JB; Ogden KL; Panisko EL; Pellegrini M; Polle J; Richardson JW; Sabarski M; Starkenburg SR; Stormo GD; Teshima M; Twary SN; Unkefer PJ and Yuan JS (2016) Review of the algal biology program within the National Alliance for Advanced Biofuels and Bioproducts. *Algal Res.* DOI: 10.1016/j.algal.2016.06.002.

Berman G. P., Nesterov A.I., López G.V., Sayre R.T. (2015) Superradiance Transition and Nonphotochemical Quenching in Photosynthetic Complexes. *J. Phys. Chem C.* 119: 22289 – 22296.

Siripornadulsil S, Dabrowski K, Sayre RT (2006) Microalgal vaccines. In: Transgenic Microalgae as Green Factories. Emilio Fernandes, Aurora Galvan, Rosa Leon, eds. Landes Press.

Kumar A, Perrine Z, Stroff C, Postier BL, Coury DA, Sayre RT and Allnutt FCT (2016) Molecular Tools for Bioengineering Eukaryotic Microalgae. *Curr. Biotechnol.* 5:93-108.

Richard Sayre
Senior Research Scientist
Los Alamos National Laboratory
New Mexico Consortium
100 Entrada Dr.
Los Alamos, NM 87544
Phone: 505-412-6532
Email: rsayre@ newmexicoconsortium.org

CHAPTER 20

Nurturing Biomedical Initiatives Through Collaborative Interactions:

A Personal Perspective of the Process

Thomas Michael Seed
Principal, Tech Micro Services
Former Associate Chief of Research, Radiation
Effects Research Foundation Hiroshima, Japan

Introduction

> ***If***
> *"If" Such a simple, curious little word*
> *If....^{if}....$_{if..}$...**if**....if....*
> *Hardly salacious, sometimes contentious and bodacious.*
> *...but... I wonder "what" .....cedes..."if"....*
> *Still simple, but it be ....far more interesting.....*
> *TM Seed ca 2005*

'Collaborate' is by definition to work one with another; to co-operate with others in a given activity (1). This is one of pillars of human activity and societal advancements and is most certainly vital to any or all scientific endeavors.

There is an old, well-used cliché that is tossed around in casual conversations about 'advancements in science' that suggest that 'ideas are cheap, but it's the work (essential lab work devoted to the testing of those ideas) that really counts and is expensive' (from the human perspective). I'll be first to admit that in my younger days, I was guilty of expressing such sentiment, but have come to realized that the comment is, at best, only partly true and, at worst, totally fallacious. In reality, the two elements—*ideas* and *work*—go hand-in-hand and are inseparable in terms of moving science forward.

As this text is based on the premise that 'collaborations' are essential to science and its advancement, I would like to spend some time initially exploring how 'collaborative processes' factor into this 'scientific idea/laboratory work/science advancement' paradigm and, subsequently, describe some personal experiences how various collaborative initiatives have affected science outcomes.

By definition, 'scientific ideas' good, bad or indifferent are the realm of the 'individual' and not the result of 'committee'. Not many researchers would disagree with the later statement; however, the 'committee' often serves an invaluable compounding function in terms of collecting, collating and massaging ideas. In this regard, 'committee' and 'collaboration' are often synonymous and clearly critical to scientific advancements.

There is little question that with 'collaboration' and with the additional individuals that it brings, comes new expertise, new points-of-view and often synergize new ideas needed to address and to solve given scientific problems. Although intuitively obvious, for the individual scientist working alone, the estimated probability (X_1) of achieving successful outcomes to significant problems in science is restricted, but when scientists team up, the aggregate probability ($X_1+X_2+X_3+X_4$ etc.) of success by the team can be, and often is, substantially enhanced (e.g., estimated overall success rate for the problem to be solved becomes an collective function of the group rather than that of the individual).

From the 'work' side of equation, collaboration brings essential human and laboratory resources that are essential to any given scientific endeavor: no scientist can succeed 'standing alone', but can only succeed in the good company of local colleagues and the scientific community at large.

The recent brilliant astrological achievements of NASA's *'New Horizon'* space probe of the dwarf planet Pluto and Kepler Belt region of deep space provides us with an impressive example of this 'individual scientist/scientific team' paradigm (https://www.nasa.gov/mission_pages/newhorizons/main). While single individuals were responsible for creating and fostering this marvelous scientific endeavor, thousands (~4500 to be exact) of scientists and engineers formed the team that successfully carried (and still continues to carry) out the mission.

Equally impressive scientific achievements within the 'biomedical' realm of science that employed this 'individual scientist/collaborative team' paradigm could be cited as well. This includes, but certainly is not limited to the 'Human Genome Project'; a truly international, collaborative project that is considered to be the world's largest biological research project. This 'collaborative project' was conceived by individual researchers and funded by the US government some thirty years ago (ca 1984) and later, aided and abetted by several outside companies, most notably Celera Corporation (Rockville, MD USA). In aggregate, 'the human genome project' continues to pursue its primary goals, namely the determination of the precise sequence of chemical base pairs that compose DNA within the genome of humans from both physical and functional standpoints and the mapping of all genes of the human genome (https://en.wikipedia.org/wiki/Human_Genome_Project).

Early collaboration experiences

If one is taught early on of the virtues and necessities of 'collaboration' then it tends to be a part of your science and how you value it. Certainly this is true of me, as my 'lessons' were learned during graduate school within the Department of Microbiology at The Ohio State University (OSU). My mentor, Dr Julius P Kreier (a co-editor of this volume), ran a large, culturally diverse laboratory that focused on the 'pathogenesis of infectious protozoan microbes of both animals and man'. Because of the nature and design of the lab's major research activities, specific projects assigned to or chosen by students often overlapped and were complementary to one another, not only in terms of primary aims, but also in terms of experimental designs and approaches of given research.

As a result, this required students to be actively engaged with fellow lab mates and to help out whenever called upon. This interaction was clearly beneficial to all parties concerned; not only in terms of sharing of scientific concepts and technical approaches to given research problems, but also in terms of assessing data and reporting out, both orally and in writing, the overall results of given experiments. These very early collaborative experiences of mine while in the 'Kreier Lab' at OSU were vital to my academic education and, without doubt, served me well later on during my career.

Importance of collaboration in research discovery

There is no doubt that 'research collaborations' often provide the basic foundation upon which to develop and foster new research concepts. The utility of the latter is realized not only in terms of basic science, but also for applied and translational science as well. Although admittedly my experience here is limited, my involvement with several prominent national and international research efforts might serve as useful examples: these examples include, but are not limited to *i*) a national networking effort between US Department of Defense (DOD), the Armed Forces Radiobiology Research Institute (AFRRI)[12] and select pharmaceutical companies industry and *ii*) National Academies of Science (NAS), the Department of Energy (DOE), and the Radiation Effects Research Foundation (RERF)[13] relative to 'in country' Japanese collaborations.

While employed as a DOD civil servant and working at AFRRI, I was responsible for a research group charged with the responsibility to develop the basic elements of new and improved 'medical countermeasures for nuclear and radiological contingencies'. On paper at least, this effort was to positively impact the 'national medical preparedness' and in turn 'homeland defense and security' in cases of nuclear and radiological exposure contingencies. While the group was fairly large, robust and reasonably well-funded by academic standards, it was tiny

---

12 https://en.wikipedia.org/.../Armed_Forces_Radiobiology_Research_Institute
13 https://en.wikipedia.org/wiki/Radiation_Effects_Research_Foundation

when compared to pharmaceutical industry standards. In general, the group did a good job in identifying new, potentially useful medicinals, as well as performing the initial and essential preclinical efficacy and toxicological tests, but the group and the institute in general simply lacked the resources to carry out the advanced, translational R&D steps as required by the FDA in their mandatory steps for eventual drug licensing. Without FDA's full authorization for a given drug/medicinal to be used in humans, the US government and its military would not be able to make use of a given agent, regardless of how promising an agent might be: the bottom line is that the FDA dictates the rules and regs for drug use (in humans in the USA) and this of course restricts what drugs can or cannot be stockpiled (as in the case of the National Pharmaceutical Stockpile) and/or used in US citizens, military, civilian, or otherwise. However, I digress, and back to the point to be made: we were fortunate at AFRRI to be surrounded by more-than-willing corporate 'partners' within the pharmaceutical industry that shared common interests in pursuing the development of these medical countermeasures for the sake of homeland security and defense. I'd be remiss in not pointing out the obvious; namely, that marketing rights and potentials were the major drivers on the pharmaceutical industry side. Nevertheless, these partnerships invariably represented a 'win-win' situation for both collaborating parties, in that the federal government (AFRRI/DOD) and the pharmaceutical partner shared not only unique resources and expertise, but also research funding for the research toward the initial eventual goal of obtaining conditional approval (Investigative New Drug or IND approval) for emergency use and the final goal of obtaining full use authorization (Broad Licensing Approval or BLA) by the Food and Drug Administration (FDA).

Again, both large and small pharmaceutical firms were more than willing to assist us in pursuing these 'late-stages' of R&D of given medicinals as we all shared common interests in developing and marketing these 'countermeasures', thus filling a major void in the national pharmaceutical stocking pile of essential medicinals that would be used in cases of national nuclear/radiological disasters.

It might be instructive to briefly relay some of my experiences while working for NAS/DOE and the RERF relative to 'in country'

Japanese collaborations. Let me preface this by saying that 'at the institutional/administrative level, much of my work involved establishing essential research conduits between research groups in order to achieve given research objectives'. An example of this can be seen in the establishment of a major effort to document late-arising health effects associated with early-in-life and unwanted exposures to ionizing radiation. I am referring here of course to the long-term health effects associated the atomic bombing of the Japanese cities of Hiroshima and Nagasaki and that quickly brought to an end World War II. Although the radiation-associated cancers have been well documented, the myriad of other significant health problems (non-cancer health problems) caused by the atomic bomb irradiations were much less so documented. Long-term suppression of the lymphohematopoietic system in the aged, survivors seemed to be a highly plausible, long-term, adverse health outcome, with systemic linkages to a number of other medical problems that present in these surviving individuals. Following my arrival at RERF at the end of 2005 and after a review of institutional programs, it was clear to me that this potential, late-arising health effect, namely 'radiation-associated enhanced immuosenescence', needed to be pursued scientifically; however, funding was lacking for this effort and the institute's scientific 'plate' was clearly full and clearly oriented toward cancer research and not toward non-cancer related health problems. I still have a vivid recollection of my initial discussions with the senior administrators at RERF about this (being a potentially highly productive area of research at RERF) and being told .... 'Tom, we love your idea, but there's simply no additional money for this effort and we're not about to shift funds around (away from cancer studies) to cover this new initiative. However, if you want to try to secure additional funding, please feel free to do so and we'll certainly be supportive of this new work.' My first thought was 'Geez....big help guys! and thanks!' and although this was a little harsh of me to think in this manner, I did indeed success in obtaining 'institutional' permission to pursue this new line of research. ....so I was off running with the idea and spent a good part of my days tapping into my network of colleagues within various US government agencies with vested interests in radiation biology related research. My initial efforts to locate potential funding sources were pleasant enough in terms of chatting with old colleagues at NASA, DOE, DOD, DARPA, NAS, etc. but clearly unfruitful in terms of obtaining 'real' leads for additional funding. Almost invariably, folks would say '……really like your idea and, like you, I do believe that this new area would be extraordinarily useful for radiation-associated 'health risk assessments', (….then would come 'a pregnant pause'…) but, you know Tom, current funding is tight and it's not likely new funds for this effort could be found'. The conversation would end by the colleague telling me to forward 'a while-paper' detailing the new proposed work and that he/she would pass it around. The latter is a polite way to say '…it's not going to happen…'. Obviously, I was quite discouraged by all of this, but I kept on telling myself that the idea was good one and surely one of the US agencies with a vested research in radiation health effects research would have an interest in lending support for this type of work. Sure enough, a new funding possibility presented itself, namely in the form of the 'Radiation and Nuclear Countermeasures Program' within the National Institute of Allergy and Infectious Diseases (NIAID) at the NIH here in Bethesda, Maryland. My contact was one Dr Richard Hatchett who at time was acting as the Associated Director for the program.

Dr. Hatchett could see immediately the benefit to his program by teaming up with RERF. Although his program at NIAID was very basic by nature (in terms of its' funded science), it was indeed well-developed and quite functional, but it lacked a degree of relevance to human medicine as it lacked clinically-based, epidemiology-based work. By contrast, the long-standing RERF program focused on 'late health effects of prior radiation exposures in humans', so this was exactly what Hatchett's program needed. Was this a collaborative match made in heaven or what? At the time, I thought it was and over time it proved to be a highly productive scientific enterprise that carried a fairly modest 'price tag' (i.e., several million dollars per year over a span of five years). In additional to the principal funding party, NIAID/NIH and the principal recipient research organization, RERF, there were some nine additional institutions involved and scattered across Japan and the US, along with literally dozens of investigators working on their respective projects within their own facilities. Work conducted at the latter facilities was subcontracted out of the original contract to given to RERF. Five of the collaborating institutions were located in Japan (National Institutes of Science and Keo University, both in Tokyo; Chiba University in Chiba; Kyoto University in Kyoto; and Tokushima University in Tokushima), while the remaining four were located in the US (University of Arizona in Tucson, Arizona; University of Georgia in Athens, Georgia; Duke University in Durham, North Carolina; and Sloan Kettering Memorial Cancer Center in New York City, New York).

The size and complexity of the overall research group represented both significant strengths and weaknesses. In terms of 'added strength', the large number of highly qualified and motivated researchers working on the 'problem' clearly fostered a host of new ideas and problem-solving approaches, plus offered the opportunity to divide up and share the work load; however, in terms of 'added weakness', trying to keep the group focused and on track proved to be administratively problematic. Not to highlight the later, but the phrase " trying to get a large collection of scientists to work together and to agree on given approaches is like '....like trying to herd cats..."enough said...you get the point....

Nevertheless, at the 'end of day' this large, often problematic project proved to be highly productive, with essential for 'radiological health risks' assessments in humans.

The project was successful from both the clinical and basic science standpoints. The seminal elements of a predictive clinical model was developed for human health, in particular immunological health, of aged individuals exposed unwantedly to various doses of ionizing radiation early on in life. Further, direct clinical assessments were made of the immunological hardiness of the aged, atomic bomb survivors relative to their protective, vaccination responses to influenza challenge infections. Basic, radiobiological information was also successfully gathered for eventual use in 'radiological hygiene risk assessments'. This basic information related to the numbers and function of select types of blood cells (hematopoietic stem cells and immune dentric cells) that contribute to immunological competence and associated changes with age and within prior radiation exposures. What we discovered surprised us; namely, the underlying, marked functional deficits (e.g., prior radiation-dependent deficits in repair) within these vital cells, rather than the simple change in absolute numbers of these vital circulating cells.

Approaches used in cultivating and mentoring staff and organizations

As the saying goes "this topic/issue is well above my pay grade" and although I never held senior-enough positions in any of the organizations that employed me to exert fundamental changes in organizational structure or function, I did have to do at times, for one reason or another, what I like to refer to as 'reverse mentoring' of my superiors. I draw on a couple of examples in order to explain what I mean here and how sometimes it was quite successful, sometimes it was totally unsuccessful, but generally, only partially successful. A good example of one of my more successful 'reverse-mentoring' efforts lay in my employment as a civil servant within the US Department of Defense (US DoD) and as a senior researcher at the Armed Forces Radiobiological Research Institute (AFRRI). In order to better understand the situation that I'm about to describe, you need to understand that AFRRI was (as still is) a military facility first and foremost and was (and still is) commanded by the senior officer of at least the 06 rank (full colonel in the army, air force, the marines or a Captain in the navy) and with supervision over all civilian personnel regardless of position. These commanders (titled 'Directors' would rotate in and out this post on a regular basis that generally lasted ~3-4 years. Although these commanders/directors were trained generally in some aspect of the 'medical arts', their 'hands-on' experience in directing biomedical research was invariably limited, especially in terms of medically oriented radiobiological R&D. Consequently, when there was a 'change in command', the new Director invariably needed to be 'brought up to speed' and educated relative to the research science he (or she) was supposed to guide. As one might suspect, this initial period following the change in command was sometimes comical, sometimes frustrating, but always always interesting. The educational process varied depending on the personality type of director, ranging from informal conversations to formal 'classroom type' of lectures. In one particularly rewarding case, there was change-in-command just before AFRRI was scheduled for a major peer review with significant funding consequences. The new director being both bright and with an unassuming personality fully recognized his deficiencies in radiobiological research and problems that this impending review might bring to his new command. Much to his credit, he requested of me and several other senior researchers that he be given a series of tutorials designed to give the basics elements of radiobiology and essential 'talking points' to questions that might be asked of him during the forthcoming review. Over the course of several weeks we (the senior staff) did just that and the 'educational' process turned out to be quite successful- the director was happy with the results as we were, as he clearly learned a great deal of radiobiology in a very short space of time, essential to his job of managing and understanding the work of the institute. It's funny however how things turn out: although the director was intended to be only student and the chief beneficiary of the tutorials, we all benefited by his probing questions and demanding answers to often times very basic biological questions that required additional study from us. I guess you could call this a 'reverse Socratic' teaching process and proved to be very successful to participants.

I have to say however that this 'reverse mentoring' technique only worked in the right environment, with the right people. The majority of times I employed this technique, however, the final outcome was only partially successful and at rare times resulted in inconsequential or actually negative outcomes.

If one can learn from 'negative outcomes' it can indeed be beneficial in moving forward your career and in life in general. Although it is an obvious truism that not all life-experiences are positive and rewarding and that despite all of the planning and of all the 'best of intentions', sometimes things simply don't work out as one would hope for one reason or another. This is exactly what happened to me while employed at the Catholic University of America (CUA) here in Washington back during the 2003-2005 timeframe. In retrospect, I considered this to be a grand 'life experiment' that on the one hand failed in terms of my science, but on the other hand was highly successful in terms of my personal development. Here's the story ....here's what happened. I had spent nearly a decade earlier at AFRRI working radiobiological issues for the US DoD. My lab at the time was in full swing, highly productive and very well-funded. However, my longtime colleague and friend (and immediate supervisor) John Ainsworth (AFRRI's scientific director) retired to sunny California, leaving both a personal and scientific void in my life. I quickly tired under the new leadership and needed a change in my work environment. A long standing colleague, one Ted Letovitz, who was running a sizable research program focused on the physics of vitreous glass capture of spent radioisotopes suggested that I bring my biomedical research program from AFRRI to CUA. CUA offered great lab space and offices, along a group of supporting radiophysicists. The CUA setting was idyllic from both a physical setting and a collegial standpoint. However, despite the later niceties, the essential infrastructure needed to support my ongoing biomedical research was lacking, as were fellow biologists in residence. For all of the later essentials I had to go back and perform essential parts of my work at AFRRI anyway (the institute that I had just left) and to have meaningful dialogue with my colleagues who shared similar interests. In retrospect, it is hard for me to comprehend how I could have been so naïve as to think I could thrive scientifically without having these critical research components close at hand. The bottom line is that 'I did not' and I moved on after just a short two years. Regardless of this negative outcome, I did find my stay at CUA interesting and certainly challenging; but, most importantly, I did learn an invaluable lesson about just how critical it is to be located within a properly structured institution that is fully equipped and experienced in conducting and managing specific types of science and the need for collaboration.

These 'outcomes', positive and negative alike, have served to form the basis of a 'working model of collaborative interactions' that I tried to implement throughout my career. This 'model' is not a static one, but constantly evolving as I garnered different work experiences over time. I'll try to be brief and to the point in my explanation of this 'model', one that I've labeled the 'rocket launch' model. The essentials of this model (illustrated in figure 1) are the following: a) the ultimate target (goal) of the prospective launch; b) the rocket (primary research vehicle); c) the launch gantry, pad, and control center (the 'brick and mortar', lab-based facility/institution) and; d) the supporting cast of intra- and extramural personnel (scientists and technicians; and, of course, last but not least, e) the astronauts themselves, i.e., the primary investigators, the 'idea generator'). The message here is that that 'launching' a successful scientific endeavor is clearly a complex process requiring a mix of essentials in order for good basic ideas and novel concepts to be appropriately pursued and exploited and ultimately 'goals' achieved. These essential elements include, but are not limited to the following: a) extra- or intramural funds for the envisioned project, b) a supporting institution having the capacity and the track record to provide programmatic support, c) the availability of physical space- lab and office space, plus having core support facilities and critical and basic lab equipment, d) access to- and the availability of key scientific personnel, e) having institutional administrators who are both knowledgeable of the science being pursued and who can provide overarching guidance and oversight for the work; and of course f) the 'idea generators' and 1st line managers and promoters of the work effort, namely the principal investigator(s) along the co-investigators.

Shared challenges and successes in building collaborative teams.

It's hard for me to select and to highlight specific examples of 'shared challenges in the building of successful research collaborations': virtually all of what I done throughout my career and whatever modest successes achieved have come as a result of both intra- and extra-institutional collaborations. Nevertheless, I've picked out two situations that might serve as good examples of the 'trials and tribulations' of attempting to build major collaborative networks I've been involved with and that have transcended personal agendas and interests. The first of these was an international, collaborative effort for radiobiological research radiation science oriented research group within NATO. When I first started working for the DoD (AFRRI, NNMC, Bethesda, MD) in 1996, DoD directed AFRRI, a tri-service military organization devoted to the radiation sciences, to assist in the implementation of new radiobiology research task group for NATO. In turn, AFRRI's Director, along with the Scientific Director, tasked me with the responsibility of making this new research initiative happen. Although AFRRI had a long and distinguished history in the radiation sciences and in working within NATO, still this DoD directive was more than a bit daunting: various radiation research organizations within NATO's research realm (i.e., the stakeholders) needed to be brought into the planning process, lead researchers within the various laboratories of the different member countries needed to be contacted as well and consulted relative to their laboratories R&D programs and research requirements. Obligations and benefits relative to membership needed to detailed and conveyed to all potential members. Once a 'buy-in' was achieved and a consensus among the members as to process of formalizing the new 'Task Group', the 'Terms of Reference'(TORS) needed to be drafted and submitted for approval: first, to each of the participating laboratories within the various NATO aligned countries; and second, to NATO itself for final authorization. This was a prime example of the 'slow-motion' nature of a bureaucracy in action. As judged by the inordinately long time it took to do the essential consultations with all the stake-holders and prospective participants, 'time' apparently was deemed not a critical issue; despite the fact that advances in the biologic sciences, especially in radiobiology and its associated technology, were (and still are) moving quite fast, resulting in lost opportunities for the new task group to make timely and useful research advances on the organization's behalf. Countermeasures to military-associated nuclear/radiological events, whether they be physical or biological/medical in nature, can serve as effective deterrents and can be as useful strategically as having a new 'arrow in the quiver' (new weapons in the NATO's arsenal). However, this very basic point was largely missed by the military bureaucrats processing these research matters. Ultimately, the collaborative actions task group (so labeled TG006) proved to be quite successful in producing an array of novel medical countermeasures for possible radiological/nuclear contingencies facing NATO and its military operations. Without giving out specifics of these experimental medical systems, they included biodosimetric monitoring devices, systems to assess the extent and consequences of radiation exposures to personnel, and new pharmacological classes of medicinals shown either prevent or to mitigate serious bodily injuries stemming from field exposures. It needs to be emphasized however that these new 'countering' measures were 'experimental' by definition and in needed 'advanced development' prior to be placed into operational use (prior to fielding).

Before moving on to another example of the utility of building and executing broadly based collaborative network in order to attain specific research objectives, I need to stress the fact, i.e., stress the obvious, that the success of this NATO research group would never have been realized by individual laboratories of the various member countries, but only through a combined collaborative effort were primary goals reached. Each member enjoyed full benefit of this group's R&D, independent of effort and monies spent.

The next example is a little different by nature, although it involved work between several US government agencies and another European, non-NATO country, Russia. I'm not sure how helpful this collaborative work was for me personally or for my science, but it certainly was an interesting phase of my professional life. In any case, here's what happened: the US's Cold War adversary, the USSR, collapsed in the early 1990's due to the horrific economic state of the USSR; Soviet satellite countries wanting to 'break loose' and become independent, possibly as a consequence of the earlier 'perestroika' and 'glasnost' movements, the US government became exceedingly concerned about the potential catastrophic consequences of the 'unhinging' of Russia's vast complex of military laboratories devoted largely to the development of 'weapons of mass destruction' (WMD). It was a chilling thought that nuclear scientists within these facilities might be tempted to 'jump ship' and to start working for rouge nations with terroristic tendencies in order to improve their dire economic condition. The US wanted to assist in transitioning these military labs into R&D facilities for economic and peaceful purposes. So under the guise (I say this because this what I believed happened here, although there no absolute proof that this happened) of establishing purposeful and effective international collaborations between working scientists and their institutions, the US wanted above all to prevent Russian scientists from 'selling out' to the rogue nations for simple economic reasons and wanted to establish a legitimate mechanism (some might say a 'quasi-legitimate' research mechanism) for funneling monies to Russia in order to stabilize and secure its nuclear scientist work force. The principal way this was done was through a newly established 'International Science and Technology Center (ISTC)' (2) that had the principal responsibility of reviewing and awarding research contracts to Russian scientists and their collaborators. I was tasked by my DoD superiors while working at AFRRI as a senior civil servant.

Initially, Russia and the US had come to an agreement that would allow the exchange of scientists in order to visit specific laboratory sites and to open discussions concerning specific research programs. This of course was no big deal for the US research community; this type of scientific exchange was done all of time, for a good long time; however, for the Russians and their Cold War partners, this was a significant step for them to open up and allow access to their facilities by outsiders (especially those scientists from the US and from Europe) and allow the freedom to talk openly about ongoing research. During this period, I made several of trips to a number of the major Russian laboratories involved in nuclear research, including labs in Sarov, Obinsk, and Chelyabinsk, as well as to Kurchatov (the neighboring research city that originally supported the USSR's Semiplantinsk nuclear test site) in Kazakhstan. These trips were all quite different, although not easy, but they proved to be exceedingly interesting. The basic format for these 'collaborative site visits' were pretty much the same: first, there was administrative processing for lab entry; second, there were introductory meetings with principal administrators and researchers; third, standard research meetings with presentations made by both the visitors and by hosts; fourth, groups discussions followed and focused on possible areas of collaboration; fifth, this was followed by site visits to specific facilities and supporting laboratories; and finally, sixth, fairly formal exit meetings, with negotiations and the signing of 'memorandums of understanding' (MOUs) between the 'prospective research partners'. These were all very curious administrative 'dances', considering the fact that the 'prospective research partners' fully recognized the fact the ultimate objective was to get supporting funds to different Russian research groups in order to stabilize employment and to help these groups transition their work to R&D for more economically viable products and not 'Cold War'-type military products. Despite what one might think or say about the nature or quality of these 'collaborative' exercises, the ultimate objective of developing viable collaborations with western scientists and the securing new research funds via the ISTC was largely achieved. Further and most importantly, a sizable number of Russian research groups were able, with the collaborative support of US research groups, effectively move their basic or applied science forward into areas designed to yield more peaceful products.

For some time following this active 'collaborative' phase with several Russian groups, I remained involved in ISTC granting functions by scientific counseling and reviewing of grant proposals. What greatly impressed me about all of this was how few dollars it took to support rather sizable research groups in Russia as opposed to within the US. It was truly 'eye opening' in terms of the marked difference in the economics of the science being conducted within Russia and their satellites and in the west, the US and in western Europe.

Important influencers and mentors

Not unlike the vast majority of career researchers, my list of mentors is long and despite my 'retirement', the list continues to grow unabatedly. I hadn't given this much thought before, but this continuous 'growth' is not typically biologic by nature (living creatures are born, grow and when growth ceases, senescence ensues), but perhaps more akin to chemical processes. But I digress. It's easy to list my two principal mentors: my older brother, Dr J Richard Seed and my thesis advisor, Dr. Julius P Kreier. Without going into the details of their mentoring, let me just say that my brother showed me while I was still an undergraduate student what was possible in terms of developing a career in the biological sciences, while Dr Kreier instructed and guided me through the actual process(es) essential to this early career development period. Without these two individuals....my very able and trusted mentors....I doubt that I would have ever found my way into my chosen career as a biomedical researcher: for all of their patience, instruction and mentoring, I'll be forever grateful.

In addition to these two principal mentors, numerous other individuals served as mentors, encouraging and instructing me as to utility and 'the fine art' of collaboration. While I spent a very pleasant time in New Orleans during a summer research internship at Tulane University after my junior year in college, Dr Ed Risby was the first to demonstrate to me the usefulness of forming collaborative, intra-laboratory ties in order to more effectively achieve given research goals. A couple of years later, Dr. Bob Pfister at OSU and Chair of the Department of Microbiology, indirectly promoted the virtues of collaboration by getting a number of his students and technicians to assist me in learning specific technical skills in electron microscopy specifically and optical imaging in general. I had a similar collaborative experience in the electrophysiology lab of Dr. Phillip Hollander at OSU as well as I needed considerable assistance in my attempts to measure disturbances in ionic flux and associated changes in membrane potentials within malaria-parasite infected red blood cells. I personally found these collaborative interactions with both senior faculty and fellow graduate students alike to be wonderfully stimulating from an academic standpoint. I fully admit however that I didn't enter into these interactions for the sake of establishing a 'collaborative network' per se, but rather that I had specific research aims in mind and that I needed some outside help in achieving those aims.

Following my graduate work at OSU, I accepted a postdoctoral fellowship at Institute of Pathology at Case-Western University in Cleveland, Ohio, within the laboratory of Dr. Masamichi Aikawa. Dr. Aikawa was an anatomical pathologist by profession, but also an outstanding research microscopist with an international reputation in the area of cell ultrastructure of parasitic microorganisms. My stay at CWRU in the Aikawa laboratory was a wonderful experience, from both a personal and scientific standpoint. There was a specific element of Dr. Aikawa's mentoring that I think deserves mentioning and one that I personally had a hard time learning: Dr. Aikawa was a firm believer (because of his own professional history and the successes he achieved) in the concept of trying to be 'a big fish in a little pond', rather than 'a little fish in big pond'. He believed that it was far better for one's professional development and ultimately professional stature, to focus on a relatively narrow area of science, excel in that area and to be well recognized for that excellence by a limited number of scientists, rather than trying to cover too many scientific areas and to be less recognized (via dilution) in any given area. Still to this day, I have a hard time focusing on any particular subject for a prolonged period: too many subjects interest me, too many scientific questions are intriguing and all served to distract. I don't have any regrets about the pathway I followed and my 'jumping around' between subjects of interest, but I do believe that all young developing scientists need to come to grips about this dilemma (i.e., narrowing one's scientific focus and gaining local recognition or having broadly based interests that tend to minimize the chance of achieving significant recognition in any given area) and to be content with this professional choice.

My postdoc at CWRU was limited in duration by my own design and I moved on to my first 'real' job: The Blood Research Laboratory of the American Red Cross (ARC) in Bethesda, Maryland. To my surprise, my prior collaborative network did not collapse because of the change in work venue, but was simply pulled and stretched, encompassing a host of new colleagues, mentors and new collaborations that were necessitated by the basic work of my new employer. When I think back about my first job, it was an unbelievable opportunity that the ARC afforded me. Here I was right out of a postdoc and being given sizable lab space, sufficient 'startup' money for both basic- and very specialized types of microscopic equipment, and the authorization to hire some personnel. I was charged with the sole responsibility of developing (from scratch) a fully functional microscopy unit designed to support the microscopic needs of ongoing research within other ARC blood research programs. Except for the later, I was pretty much free to pursue whatever research interests I had. My point in telling you all of this was that the job and all of its challenges and obligations required that I form new intra- and extramural collaborations. My role in all of these collaborations involved 'microscopic imaging' of biologic targets of interest. This included work with Dr. Stephan Mironescu, a cell biologist, who had research interests in cryogenics and the nature- and mitigation of cell injury following cell/tissue freezing and with Dr. Marty Jett, another cell biologist/experimental hematologist with interests in structure/functions relationships of blood platelets during activation. There were also several immunologists, Drs. Jim Prahl and Roger Dodd, who were colleagues, along with a group of virologists within the experimental hepatitis detection laboratory who wanted help in screening and imaging isolated virus of interest in various blood plasma fractions. In addition, there were two individuals who provided significant mentoring during my stay at BRL/ARC: Dr Graham Jamieson, the Director of the BRL and my immediate boss and Dr. Len Friedman, a gifted bioengineer and a close colleague within the organization who ran a large, applied research operation with the BRL. I cannot say enough about the talents of these individuals and help they provided during these early, career-forming years. Dr. Jamieson was incredibly kind in his shepherding me through various administrative issues that I needed to handle in setting up and running my own laboratory, whereas Dr. Friedman was exceedingly knowledgeable about the needs and requirements of ARC in terms of its blood products, its R&D processes and, in general, the administrative structure of the ARC.

All of this wonderful mentoring that I received very early on in my career, helped me through more complex, more challenging situations that I found myself in later on: I am referring to specifically my next position at Argonne National Laboratory (ANL), a national DoE-funded research facility that is managed by the University of Chicago. In trying to spare you all the details of this employment, I was hired as an assistant biologist to both run a sizable microscopy unit with the Biology Division, as well as to establish my own experimental radiation hematology laboratory in support of one of the division's ongoing large animal studies of the health effects of chronic exposure to relatively low doses of ionizing radiation. In terms of my duties of running the microscopy unit (a core service facility for the division), I was basically on my own and expected to function independently in managing the sizable facility, that encompassed a suite of laboratories that housed a full array of both optical and electron microscopes, along with essential ancillary equipment transmission scopes). Although I 'inherited' a number of very competent and seasoned technicians, I was without the benefit of having 'in-house' mentors for this particular part of my job. Fortunately, I was previously well-schooled and reasonably experienced in managing and operating such a microscopy unit. By contrast, the other element of my ANL work obligation, involved a setting up and running an experimental radiation hematology laboratory. The later proved to be far more challenging, as I was on 'shaky ground' in terms of having specific work experience in this area of science. Fortunately for me, the ANL's Biology Division at the time was filled with very competent and renowned radiation biologists, many of whom kindly tutored and mentored me in various aspects of radiobiology and in selected areas of radiation hematology. The list of individuals to whom I owe a debt is long…long indeed…. but certainly includes Drs Michael Fry, John Ainsworth, Bill Norris, Tom Fritz, and Mr Dave Tolle. Dr Warren Sinclair, a stellar, radiation biologist was the director of the division when I first arrived at ANL, but soon afterward replaced by Dr Tim O'Conner, an equally well known viral oncologist. Both of these gentlemen provided a higher level of mentoring and support that proved to be extremely useful to me during the early part of my tenure at ANL. It was 'eye-opening' to me (and quite sad) to see how some 'missteps' relative to administrative decisions concerning senior personnel and science programs can be catastrophic in terms of one's career: I watched in awe and more than a little horror, Dr O'Conner run into a violent vortex of senior scientists who were opposed to some of the programmatic changes he wanted to implement in order to move the division's science forward into new areas. In the end, Dr O'Conner lost this administrative battle (and the war) and was forced to out of his position as director. Clearly, there was a 'lesson' to be learned here…… "Yah, be sure to 'watch your back' and 'know your enemies'"….but more seriously, good administrators need to establish a full dialogue with their staff in order to keep them informed, solicit input, and to educate them as to benefit of any new changes in program structure and content that one may wish to want to make administratively. On this point, the biology division's staff at ANL was by enlarge very well educated, highly competent and experienced group of employees who didn't take lightly to having their research programs altered and disrupted without good reason and without having the opportunity to weigh into the proposed changes. The instructional lesion here, i.e., the bottom line, is that as an administrator, you need to be 'inclusive' and 'open' with staff and get them to 'buy-into' any/all action plans that you might have in mind. In my mind, these are absolutely essential steps in maintaining a good working relationship between the staff and the administration, regardless of the institution involved.

This brings me to the next career stop, namely working at the Armed Forces Radiobiology Research Institute (AFRRI) within the National Naval Medical Center (currently called 'National Walter Reed and Naval Medical Center) here in Bethesda, Maryland for the US Department of Defense as a civilian employee. Again, this period in my career was clearly interestingly, filled with many new scientific opportunities and rewarding work experiences, but also at times (as in life) there were unpleasant situations that arose and had to be dealt with. As much of my AFRRI work has been described in part both above and in a previously published article (3), I'll spare you from the boring details. I would however like to comment on 'lessons learned' from my principal AFRRI mentor, namely Dr. E John Ainsworth. I mentioned previously that Dr. E John Ainsworth (EJA) was a long standing colleague of mine, stemming from our work at ANL and our common interest in radiobiology and animal models. John was a gifted and renowned and well-liked radiobiologist. However, as an administrator he was a bit autocratic….. benevolent… but autocratic all the same in his dealing with the AFRRI staff. His administrative style was contrary to what I had suggested earlier about the need of young administrators to be inclusive and to apply a 'soft-glove' in dealing with staff. In my view, John's administrative style was a 'justified' administrative approach in dealing with an older class of scientists who were 'civil' servants who viewed their employment as 'a birth right' rather than 'a privilege' and who failed to see the need…the obligation… to be scientifically productive. In a fear of my saying too much here, my old friend… E. John Ainsworth…. found a way to 'motivate' and to 'bring back to life' these relatively unproductive researchers, largely by insisting on intramural collaborations between the more productive scientists and those less so. Every time I think about this time spent under EJA's tutelage, I have to chuckle at all the truly novel ways.... the old school ways.... EJA administered his science program. Following my tenure at AFRRI and working within the DoD, I moved locally over to Catholic University of America (CUA) as a research professor and set up a new 'radiation countermeasure' research program within the 'Vitreous State Laboratory' and the Department of Physics. Once again, I found the move and my new work environment to be pleasing, but not terribly useful to me scientifically. I previously wrote about my experiences at CUA (3) so I won't retell this 'personal tale' other than to say the CUA didn't have the essential infrastructure and personnel needed to support the program that I had envisioned: all of my important collaborations were outside the university and I had no functional collaborators within CUA. I would be remiss in not mentioning however my interactions with Dr. Theodore (Ted) Letovitz, who was a 'founding father' of the VSL within CUA's Physics Department. It was instructive for me to see Ted in action and to see his patience, persistence and cleverness in growing a rather formidable science program from essentially scratch using largely private funding sources over a life-long career at CUA. The lesson learned here from Dr. Letovitz and my CUA experience is that while it is feasible to grow a viable and productive science program that is highly technology-dependent at small colleges and universities, it probably is not the most effective way to try to grow a research program or develop a lab-based science career. The reason for this is that public agencies that fund the vast majority of biomedical research within the US tend to disfavor funding research programs at the smaller schools that lack sufficient scientific infrastructure. Whether this is justified or not, or within the public interest, the difficulty of researchers at smaller, less well-recognized schools is real and substantial and presents problems to these researchers, despite their scientific acumen.

My final position prior to retiring in 2008 was as the Associate Chief of Research at the Radiation Effects Research Foundation (RERF) in Hiroshima Japan (http://www.rerf.jp/index_e.html). This was a US National Academies of Science (NAS) appointment, supported by both the US Department of Energy (DOE) and by the Japanese government. Before briefly describing my RERF work and my RERF-associated 'mentors', I'd like to acknowledge just how a wonderful an opportunity this was for me; not only from an administrative scientific standpoint, but also from a cultural perspective as well. It was enriching for me to work daily at a unique institution, within a major, storied Japanese city, that largely functioned under different sets of employment and cultural rules to which I had grown boringly accustomed. During my two years in country, every day would bring culturally unique situation that I hadn't previously experienced. As you might suspect, my getting by and functioning in this 'foreign land' required a host of new 'mentors' ......institutional as well as cultural mentors were needed. The first of these mentors was Dr. Charles Waldren, who was leaving the post I was about to step into and we had, by design, a bit of overlap at RERF. Within a few short weeks Charles graciously provided insights into how the institute functioned and who the 'players' were. This information turned out to be extremely useful in my acclimating to my new position. I should mention that I tried to pass this information forward to Dr. Roy Shore (a New York University professor), who, like me, was a neophyte in terms of the RERF culture and function, who arrived shortly after I did to assume a vacant Director's position at the institute. In additional to Dr. Waldren's mentoring, I was ably mentored in the financial affairs of the institute by Doug Solvie, an extremely likeably American expat who was working in the institute's business office and who gave me a rundown on the financial and funding aspects of RERF and its ties to NAS, DOE and to the primary Japanese funding agency. There were, in addition, senior Japanese administrators: Dr. Tohrue Okubo (RERF's Chief Officer and Director) and Mr. Takanobu Teramoto (Executive Director) who provided mentoring on a variety of topics, but mainly focused on RERF's scientific programs and general institutional culture. Both of these gentlemen I consider to be good friends and respected colleagues who taught me the nuances of Japanese biomedical sciences. In particular, I found Dr. Okubo's leadership qualities to be highly admirable, displaying a strong and determined hand needed in taking the right course in terms of staffing, but always fair and just. I need to acknowledge an additional Japanese colleague, Dr. Kei Nakachi, who saw to it that I was welcomed into his radiobiology group's activities. Without Kei's presence, my stay in

Hiroshima would have been far less pleasurable and certainly less productive scientifically. In any case, I owe all of these folks a great deal of thanks for their hospitality and kindness.

Advice to Millennials joining the workforce

Like the old adage "advice is always easy to give and to come by, but good advice....really useful, sage advice.... is an entirely different beast". In general, such 'good advice' is a much rarer commodity that's sometimes difficult to interpret initially and to act upon in an appropriate and timely manner. Accordingly, I am quite hesitant to say too much here, but I will suggest to the younger set of aspiring scientists that they should consider 'embracing the concept of collaboration'; this in order to leverage one's own creative talent, to garner in extended scientific expertise and associated resources. The practical advantages of such collaboration might be seen in terms of reaching scientific objectives, enhancing scientific productivity and ultimately, achieving personal career objectives.

In following up on the later point, despite what you might have 'heard-on-the-street' (and generally by people not directly involved in the sciences), reality runs somewhat counter to the thought that success in science is a personal event, driven solely by an individual's creative, ingenious ideas and hard-work and that you as an aspiring scientist, are the sole determinant of the success realized, as loosely defined by peer- and general media recognition' but rather, successful collaborations and collaborative networks generally are primary drivers of the successful scientific careers and associated achievements. Regardless, it's hard to deny the public's perception of what drives scientific accomplishment, but clearly it is not the whole story. Much of what you can or cannot achieve scientifically depends on your work environment and your associations with your peers. This is not to say that you as individual scientist cannot maintain your 'individualism' as a scientist and dictate the terms and directions, conditions and terms of your science, for surely you can and should, but be aware of the fact that your dreams and aspirations of having a 'successful' career in the sciences depends to a large extent on how successful you are in interacting with your peers: these 'interactions' that I speak of are by definition the very 'collaborations' that this chapter, this text attempts to describe and to discuss.

Here are few additional and final passing thoughts......some 'sound bits' related to advice...... that might prove useful in establishing a research career. First, try to maintain a strong and determined stance in pursuing your science, but also maintain a degree of flexibility in terms of considering new ideas and a willingness to change 'scientific direction' when results run counter to hypothesis-based expectations. Second, be consistent and true to your science. Third, achieving specific aims or goals of the scientific endeavor via the team effort should be your ultimate reward and not individual-based media attention that might stem from the work. Forth and finally, be cognizance and sensitive of research needs and goals of others and above all....... share the credit for any and all successes achieved.

Summary

The nature, type and consistency of scientific collaborations and associated collaborative networks are invariably different, depending on the science, the employment environment, and the individual researcher. In this regard, I consider my collaborative experiences over the course of a career to fairly typical and largely consistent with the rest of my colleagues and the scientific community at large. The point being is that due to this 'variability', there are no set rules and set guidelines to follow: I suppose that if there were such sure-fire guidelines available, the success rate of given collaborations would be one hundred percent and we certainly recognize the fact that a fraction of collaborations will fail for one reason or another.

I cannot stress enough, just how critical it is for young, developing researchers to develop strategic, functional collaborations with colleagues. As stated earlier, collaborations are essential to science and for those who pursue science in terms of leveraging individual ideas, expertise and limited resources in order to pursue given scientific objectives. Further, on the practical side, the process of successfully competing for and garnering in critical funding for projects should be considered…needs to be considered….as important benefit of the collaborative process. Not all collaborations will prove to be successful, but hopefully the majority will turn out useful. One needs to consider carefully who you plan on collaborating with and to what extent and try not to enter, 'willy-nilly', into new collaborative relationships without due diligence on your part. Useful collaborations can certainly be extended and the 'less-than-useful' collaborations that go 'south' than and should be jettisoned.

Although I offer no prescribed formulations or blueprints for successfully establishing collaborations, I have used from time-to-time a 'rocket model' (Figure 1) to introduce new collaborative efforts. The model attempts to make the proposed effort analogous to the NASA's space exploration program and associated rocket launches. Celestial targets (i.e., the scientific goal) are conceived by the principal manager (the principal investigator) and established in concert with the launch team (the co-investigators). The space rocket (physical vehicle or laboratory) is supported by the launch gantry (brick and mortar research plant/facility/institution), fueled by research money (grants) and guided by the operations team (PI, plus co-investigators) with oversight by the program manager(s). The successful launch and subsequent space projectory of the rocket to the final target requires continuous monitoring and control by the research team in order to reach space target (ultimate research goal). As in the space rocket analogy and in order to execute a successful mission and to achieve primary scientific goals, collaboration is essential, requiring a well-orchestrated and managed team effort, along with an appropriate level funding and proper institutional support.

My final word….. my 'bottom line' message…. to you is to 'embrace the concept of collaboration' and collaborative networking as primary and essential tools in achieving your personal goals and achievements of your scientific dreams.

I wish you the best and good luck in all of your future scientific endeavors. Be strong and keep the faith.

Acknowledgement

I'd like to thank Vicki, my dear wife and long-time English teacher, for kindly reading over, and editing and commenting on this text.

References

1. The Random House Dictionary of the English Language, Unabridged Edition, eds J Stein and L Urdang, p 289, Random House/New York, NY 1973.
2. ISTC. The International Science and Technology Center. https://en.wikipedia.org/wiki/International_Science_and_Technology_Center
3. Seed T. 2014, Seed Science: A personal study of growth and development. (eds) OJ Crocomo, Julius P Kreier, WR Sharp, In: Reflections & Connections. Personal Journeys through the Life Sciences, Vol II, Chp 12, 443-512, Science Tech Publishers, LLC.
4. Seed T. 2016. Journal Publications. In: Pub Med, NCBI. www.ncbi.nlm.nih.gov/pubmed
5. Seed Thomas M. 2016. Published/referenced science articles. Google Scholar. scholar.google.com/

Figures

Figure 1

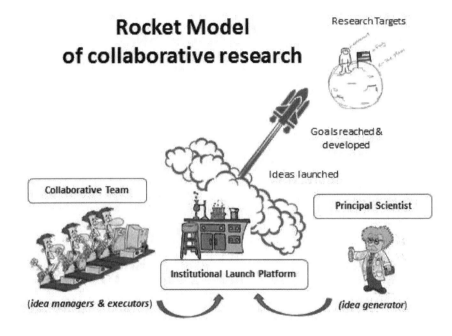

CHAPTER 21

Piracy and Its Impact Upon Creative Collaboration in the Independent Film Industry

Jeffrey Sharp
Award-Winning Independent Film and Television Producer

I have had the distinct pleasure of being a part of the genesis of this book from its earliest days. In fact, I remember the first moment when my father Rod Sharp told me that he was about to embark upon a new project with his distinguished colleagues from previous collaborations and a new generation of contributors from the worlds of academia, government, and private sector. We were walking along the bluffs of Santa Monica, California and I suggested the idea of Pathways to Collaboration as a theme, which ultimately became the title of the book.

As I had this opportunity to be part of this book from the beginning, I realized that I had been at the beginning of a, number of such collaborations over the course of my career. I've produced movies that started with the initial act of reading a book and deciding to option it only to watch it grow, in size with the addition of a screenwriter, director, cast, financier and ultimately upon green light, the crew which can range from fifty to hundreds of men and women working in the service of producing the motion picture. Once the film wraps, another community of post-production supervisors, editors, visual effects artists, composers, publicists, marketers, studio distribution execs and exhibitors all come on line and so on and so on... in fact, producing a film is arguably one of the most collaborative endeavors in the world. I've grown to love these collaborations over the twenty or so movies that I have produced over about as many years. There are extraordinary moments over the course the course of the film when the producer and the director find themselves working in service of the limitations of the crew size, the weather, actor schedules and finances to name a few. The infinite patience required and respect necessary for the film many contributors from star to craft service production assistant is key to running a successful production and that success often ends up on the screen.

As an independent film producer, I know that it takes years to develop a movie, months to film it, and another, many months to finish it. I know that films shoot out of sequence and that behind a mere three minutes of screen time can be a grueling 16-hour day — for literally hundreds of people.

The craft of filmed entertainment looks simple and easy to do. This presents misconceptions about the value of our work to audiences. Every day, consumers make economic choices about paying for movie tickets, subscribing to cable television, using over-the-top streaming services — or choosing not to pay at all and patronizing pirate sites. These decisions greatly impact our ability to receive the fair and appropriate reward for the time, money, and work that our cast, crews, filmmakers, and financiers have invested into our productions.

From 1996 to 2007, my producing partner, John Hart, and I ran Hart Sharp Entertainment, one of several prolific New York City-based independent film production companies at the time. Our budgets often, times averaged anywhere from two million dollars each in the early years of our careers to upwards of twenty million dollars, yet our films received outsized recognition for their artistry and achievement. And we made a living producing independent films such as "Boys Don't Cry," "You Can Count on Me," "Lift," "Nicholas Nickleby," "Proof," "A Home at the End of the World," "The Night Listener," "Evening" and "Revolutionary Road," among others. Our films earned Academy and Golden Globe awards and nominations, widespread commercial distribution, and often recouped their investment.

However, this thriving industry experienced a major disruption in 2008 with a marked decrease in box office for specialty films. The decline was brought on by many factors: the recession, new distribution technology, a shift away from DVDs to digital, and a global film industry downturn. At the same time, the indie film industry was competing with a growth in pirate sites that made illegal copies of our films available for free, sometimes the same day they opened in theaters.

While it is not entirely clear exactly how much online piracy has contributed to the decline of the independent film industry, piracy's impact has certainly been felt around the world which makes a big impact on our ability to finance indie films through international pre-sales.

Netflix and other legal streaming services have created exciting new business models for our industry. They bring seamless, high-quality access to many of our films and the works of new filmmakers to homes and devices — and serve the independent film audience by creating recommendation engines. However, recent reports show that even though a Netflix subscription costs as little as $8 a month, many of their top shows are among the most widely pirated.

Fortunately, the market is still quite robust for independent film. Over the past two years, I have produced four feature films and two TV shows including "The Yellow Birds" written by David Lowery, directed by Alexandre Moors and starring Alden Ehrenreich, Tye Sheridan, Jennifer Aniston, Toni Collette, Jason Patric and Jack Huston (which premiered at The 2017 Sundance Film Festival); "UFO" written and directed by Ryan Eslinger and starring Alex Sharp, Gillian Anderson and David Strathairn (in post-production for Sony Pictures Worldwide); "My Other Home" written and directed by Larry Yang and US basketball star Stephon Marbury and Loretta Divine (in post-production for Hay Bros. China) and "Crazy Alien" written and directed by Ning Hao and starring Huang Bo, Matthew Morrison and Tom Pumphrey (for Dirty Monkey Films, China).

While these films have not yet entered commercial release, it is difficult to predict how they will impact the investors and studios that financed production. In the past, I have been fortunate to have several films go into profit where the backend participation becomes meaningful for the creative team with payments into the many thousands of dollars per contributor. This return is dependent upon consumers going to the theatre and buying a ticket, buying or renting the film on a legitimate site like iTunes or Amazon, or streaming the film on an SVOD platform such as Netflix, Amazon or Hulu. Should the consumer not make a legitimate payment and decides to download or view the film on a pirated site, then the film risks not recouping and the creative team will not be paid out their rightful profit participation.

Currently there are organizations that advocate for the creative community and their rights to participate in the commercial success of their work. One such organization is Creative Future, an organization which advocates for artists' rights while promoting a new culture of respect for copyright, encourage audiences to choose responsible forms of consumption, and discourage advertisers from supporting pirate sites. I am proud to serve on the leadership committee along with other producing colleagues, directors, actors and studio executives and support copyright protections in order to empower creative artists to speak out against piracy and how it affects their ability to create and make a living.

After nearly 20 years in the content creation industry, I believe that we will always find ways to tell the stories that are important to us and to audience's eager for quality engaging commercial entertainment. My hope is that our industry can work together — and find support in Washington and internationally — to ensure that however people choose to watch creative content, the real people behind that creation can continue to be compensated. Collaboration in the film industry is dependent upon a financial model that provides a living wage to the team of creative that bring the story to life. That's essential for our industry in particular independent film, to continue being a career path for young and creatively minded people.

CHAPTER 22

Academic and Private Sector Collaboration Models

Spawning Interinstitutional Research and Spinoff Companies

William R Sharp
ScienceTechPublishers LLC

Introduction

The word "collaboration" according to Merriam-Webster, is defined *"to work with another person or group to achieve or do something"*. A group collaboration requires a collaborative team leader, usually defined as the person who leads or commands a group or organization. Today's fast changing world requires energetic team leaders armed with facilitation skillsets and state of the art technology knowhow with skillsets for sprinting across time zones in the delivery of new ideas leading to new products and/or services.

My contribution to *Pathways to Collaboration* builds on a series of stories encompassing my approach to building a collaborative career or more accurately a series of collaborative careers. Hopefully, Millennials will be able to harvest a few useful pearls of wisdom from the career collaborations documented in the pages ahead for charting successful collaborative career pathways of their own.

I reflect on an astonishing moment while being seated at the front table at The Ohio State University Phal Hall 04.15.2016 Arts and Sciences Alumni Awards Ceremony at the moment of my eightieth year on the planet after setting foot on The Ohio State University campus 62 years ago as a freshman. It was indeed an honor to have been selected as the recipient of The Ohio State University College of Arts and Sciences Alumni Society 2016 Distinguished Service Award. My table was populated by family and dear friends including author and educator sister Sally, integrated media executive and producer son Jeff and 6 year old student and grandson Jack along with Barbara Fergus, Founder, Owner/Partner of Midwestern Auto Group (MAG) and philanthropist, Roman Holowinsky, prize winning mathematician and Chair of the Ohio State University Steam Factory and Anna Gawboy, College of Music Scholar in Music Theory and Composition.

The banquet hall was a buzz with conversations, good cuisine and glowing comments from the podium while I nervously reviewed my three-minute recipient comments to be delivered to an overflowing crowd of alumni, faculty, colleagues and friends. My goal was to place emphasis on the importance of continuous collaboration with the university alumni groups and faculty. And the importance of participation in alumni volunteerism and venture philanthropy investment for the strengthening one's relationship with the Alma mater. My inspiration builds on the thoughtful words of Maya Angelo, "If You Learn - Teach and "If You Get – Give."

My Award Acceptance Comments 04.15.2016

Thank you, Executive Dean and Vice Provost David Manderscheid for being honored with the unexpected Alumni College of Arts & Sciences Distinguished Service Award.

Investing in The Ohio State University College of Arts & Sciences through volunteerism or venture philanthropy is comparable to an investment in a blue-chip stock portfolio providing potential lucrative dividends. Tonight, I would like to share the story about my lucrative dividends which parallels the experiences of many alumni.

My career evolved under the tutelage of The Ohio State University Professor Clara Weishaupt, my undergraduate biology advisor. I will always be thankful to Professor Weishaupt and The Ohio State University for the introduction to the biological sciences and providing so many important contributions to my career.

Following three years at Ohio State, I served in the US Navy/traveling the world/Afterwards, under the guidance of my OSU mentor, I pursued biology/biotechnology research programs at The University of Akron/Argonne National Laboratory/Rutgers University/Case Western Reserve University/The Ohio State University Department of Microbiology, the University of Sao Paulo, a blue chip food corporation and cofounder of several publicly traded biotechnology companies with exit routes to blue chip companies. This was capped with a professorship and deanship at Rutgers University.

The individual companies focused on different aspects of the biotechnology industry related to improved crop breeding, outcomes with consumer food benefits, functional foods, pharmaceuticals and industrial products with important global business and research partnerships in Brazil, China, Germany, India, Indonesia, Italy, Japan, Malaysia, Mexico, Venezuela and the UK.

These career opportunities were made possible because of the important inputs of the OSU faculty, engagement of former students and alumni serving roles as co-founders, employees, consultants, and advisory board members.

Currently, I am privileged to serve as a member of the OSU Arts and Sciences Advisory Committee, advisor to the OSU STEAM Factory and The Ohio State University/Rutgers University/University of Sao Paulo Tripartite Faculty, Student Research and Teaching Program.

Family collaborations reign at this point in my life with film producer, Integrated media Industry executive son, Jeff, author/educator sister, Sally and future Buckeye grandson Jack who is enrolled at the New York Science Tech School.

Thank you, David Manderscheid, College of Arts and Sciences faculty, staff, and alumni for your participation with me in a the remarkable 62-year collaborative partnership. And Go Bucks, Forever!

The Morning After

The morning after at an early breakfast, my sister, Sally, an educator, author and former radio host requested an interview about the importance of collaboration during the building of my career. This session served as an opportunity to reflect and summarize important collaborative stories contributing to my career or possibly more accurate a series of collaborative careers working backwards to graduate postdoctoral days.

Looking Forward and Backwards

My journey has indeed been fulfilled lightyears beyond expectation. I had the good fortune of being raised in a household of loving parents, siblings and grandparents followed by a tour of duty with the U.S. Navy, guidance by remarkable mentors at world class research institutions and opportunities for employment in world class academic institutions in Brazil and the United States, a blue chip corporation, start-up technology companies and a return to the academy in a leadership post.

The diversity of these continuous collaborative stories has prompted me to reflect on the lessons learned. These lessons have brought clarity to the importance of global collaboration among scientists employed by the academy and private sector institutions. Alexander Von Humboldt 1769-1859 communicated the importance globalization and collaboration during his extensive travels to South America more than 200 years ago which his colleagues have shared through the founding of the Humboldt Foundation.

It is of upmost importance that the academy, the private sector and state and federal governments embrace the importance of collaboration in science and technology along with collaborative partnerships with the arts and humanities as important drivers of the global economy. Collaborative partnerships between these entities are likewise important in providing financial resources for basic and applied research, and student support. This support is critical in allowing advances in science and technology along with the education of students with backgrounds in STEAM (Science, Technology, Engineering, Arts/Humanities and Mathematics). Federal immigration policy is another important factor ensuring that the human capital needs of academia, government and industry are satisfied. The best minds graduating from the research universities should be allowed by immigration services to adjust and seek employment (*Immigration and the Economy*, William R. Sharp, *Huffington Post*, The Blog, 04/08/2013).

This chapter will explore recent collaborative stories and work backwards to unveil the serendipitous beginning of my rewarding journey. Perhaps the word "Yes" was the important word allowing my transitionary movements across so many collaborative career stories and ignoring the obvious risk factors. Recently a story reported in the 09.09.2016 "BusinessInsider.com" about an interview with the Princeton Institute for Advanced Learning Emeritus Scholar Freeman Dyson reflecting on his career. Dyson expounded about his good luck in choosing next career steps because of his decision making process in which he always said "Yes" to the next crazy opportunity.

Important that I express my gratitude to Ahmad Hakim-Elahi, Ph.D. and Nicholas Madonia, CPA, two colleagues and friends who have been important collaborators and partners in exploration of the many initiatives that unfolded during my academic and business journey.

The Ohio State University Continuous Collaboration 1955 – 2016 and Beyond

The chapter will describe highlights of my collaborative relationship with The Ohio State University (OSU) stretching over fifty years from setting foot on the campus as a freshman during spring quarter 1955. Here my passion for the biological sciences evolved under the tutelage of classroom instructor and mentor Professor Clara Weishaupt which continued throughout service with the US Navy, graduate school, post-doctoral fellowship and appointment to the department of microbiology faculty. My department appointed me to an adjunct professorship following promotion to full professor and departure for the private sector which allowed for mentoring graduate students in our corporate laboratories. The University appointed me to the College of Arts & Sciences Advisory Committee (committee) on or about 2000. The Committee holds campus meeting twice a year along with numerous events in New York of which my son Jeff and I have sponsored a few in our respective areas of integrated media and science. The opportunity to continue a relationship with the university through the Committee members, faculty and students has been rewarding.

A serendipitous meeting with Roman Holowinsky, a founder and director of the Ohio State University STEAM Factory occurred at the Spring 2014 Arts and Sciences Advisory Committee Meeting with Guest Speaker, Dr. Roman Holowinsky, a founding director of the Ohio State University STEAM Factory. The organization was founded by a group of young faculty, postdocs, and staff in December 2002 with focus on the development of a diverse grass-roots network that facilitates creative, interdisciplinary collaboration across the university. It supports community outreach, increasing awareness of the relevance and diversity of Ohio State research and has become a dynamic presence both on campus and at its home 400 West Rich Street, a 1910 vintage manufacturing space and warehouse, converted into studios for artists, workspaces for entrepreneurial based startup companies, the Ohio State University STEAM Factory facility and home of the Stongwater Food and Spirits.

The meeting led to a tour of the 400 West Rich STEAM Factory facility and a lunch meeting at the New York Soho House with my son Jeff and me which led to much discussion, a collaboration between Jeff and Roman on an upcoming movie and my involvement as a member of an advocacy committee for the STEAM Factory. The involvement with Roman and the STEAM Factory has been explosive resulting in a major renewal of my relationship with The Ohio State University and the recent engagement with the Hasse Institute, a collaborative research relationship between Ohio State and sister research institutions.

Digital Publishing 1998 – 2017 & Beyond

My son Jeff Sharp and sister Sally Sharp were always there for me during the times of transition. And this transition was no exception. The three of us always shared a collaborative sense of adventure and travel. Jeff engaged me in his integrated media companies dealing with the acquisition and production of independent films, television series and pioneering digital books: Hart Sharp Entertainment, Sharp Independent at Harper Collins, Open Road Integrated Media, Hart Sharp Entertainment, Mining and Supply Company and current Sharp Independent. The adventures with Jeff included attending international book fairs highlighting books-to-film, movie shoots and movie appearances on the Silver Screen with Glenn Close in "Evening" and with grandson in "My Other Home", Stephen Marbury Life Story. And an appointment to the Open Road Integrated Media Advisory Board. My responsibilities included reviewing books and screenplays along with translation. These experiences provided me with the essential skillsets for storytelling, development and publication of digital and hard copy books. Some of our most creative moments occurred during walks along the beaches of Santa Monica and the New Jersey Shore along with endurance bicycle rides. These skillsets were further enhanced through collaboration with my author and television host sister. Sally and I likewise enjoy creative moments during walks along the New Jersey Shore and New York.

Storytelling was a totally new experience, in spite of being an experienced publisher of science/technology books and journal articles under the guidance and review of editors and editorial board managers for blue chip publishing companies and professional journals. Armed with these digital publication technical skillsets, understanding the importance of storytelling and the sharing of personal stories without the heavy-handed bias of the publishing houses offered new degrees of freedom for the collaborative publication of personal career stories with emphasis regarding the sharing diverse of approaches to collaboration and the building successful careers.

The initial collaborative book series entitled: "Reflections and Connections – Pathways Through the Life Sciences" edited by Otto Crocomo, Julius Kreier and William Sharp launched in 2012 with a 2014 publication date. The series engaged contributors reflecting on their academic and/or corporate careers in the life sciences with emphasis on the lessons learned. The purpose was to share the career challenges, triumphs and the lessons learned from the lives of thirty remarkable life scientists. The expectation was that these lessons would be of value to students considering a career in the life sciences as well as young scientists in the early stages of their careers. And possibly the casual reader interested in the making of scientists and their career navigational charts.

Our current project is a book series entitled "Pathways to Collaboration" which follows in the footsteps of the successful 2014 collaborative book series entitled: "Reflections and Connections". "Pathways to Collaboration" is a two volume book series with an expected 2017 release date. The book encompasses over 50 leading contributors from the world of business, art, music, science and technology. The chapters focus on the importance of collaboration in one's career achievement. Editors include Otto Crocomo, and Julius Kreier long time research colleagues from the University of Sao Paulo and The Ohio State University respectively and three younger colleagues: Jim Fowler and Roman Holowinsky, The Ohio State University and Austin Channell, Vanderbilt University

The publishing projects have provided an astonishing new career with a focus on storytelling and the opportunity to continue collaborative relationships with long-term colleagues, family and friends as well as reaching out to new colleagues and friends.

University Spin-Off Companies 1998 – 2014

Prior to stepping down from a deanship at Rutgers University, I was contacted by a group of former colleagues about forming Gladstone New York Partners LLC (GNP), a LLC (Limited Liability Corporation) in New Jersey for the purpose of assisting university spin-off company entrepreneurs. Our collaborative team consisted of a group of seasoned individuals: a small business owner/former president of the New Jersey Farm Bureau, a lawyer/scientist with a background in biotechnology and senior licensing positions at research universities, a CPA, who possessed extensive experience working with start-up technology companies and a former biotechnology research director. The fledging new ventures included: Jersey Flora Inc.- a floriculture product company, MedTower Inc.- a digital health system, A Sickle Cell Anemia Company, the Norman Borlaug University – digital education company, and Jersey Flora, Inc. – value added horticulture company. Another company, Wellgen, Inc. – a medical food company formed with former business associates and a fellow alumnus. Our team was essentially giving back and linking entrepreneurs to our personal business and technology networks. The companies were incubated mostly at research universities and secured initial funding from the New Jersey Commission On Science and Technology, angel investment and corporate investors.

The companies had access to university resources but differed from the companies spawned during my earlier career which were built on existing research, development and commercialization platforms. There will be no extensive elaboration on the stories associated with the university startup companies because of the importance of adhering to the editorial chapter page guidelines and noting that my involvement was restricted to board positions which placed me outside the day-to-day management. Board members however are important decision makers regarding fiscal and human resource policy issues.

The fledging companies achieved successes ranging from recruitment of senior management, startup government grant awards, successful corporate financing, and acquisitions. Herculean challenges however faced our managements as with all startup enterprises. These challenges: included the death of a CEO, dismissal of a senior employee, a technology transfer dispute, political seizure of government grant funds, and a litigation issue.

The opportunity for working with the GNP team and the company managements was indeed rewarding and served to enhance my business/technology network. These experiences related to true startup companies have enhanced my business and technical knowhow and provided an opportunity to continue collaborative relationships with colleagues and friends. One day I hope to elaborate on this interval of my career when the appropriate publishing opportunity surfaces. Special thanks are due to Stephen George, former President of the New Jersey Farm Bureau. And longtime colleagues and friends Ahmad Hakim-Elahi, Ph.D., J.D. and Nicholas Madonia, CPA. Ahmad and Nick have collaborated with me during my career in the biotechnology industry and their contributions are treasured.

Transitioning to Academia Following 14 Years of Biotechnology Industry Experience
Rutgers University
1993 – 1998

In early January 1992, a former colleague called me at my office at PhytoPharmaceuticals Inc., a subsidiary of EscaGenetics Corporation in San Carlos, California to urge me to consider the position of Dean of Research at Cook College/ Director of the New Jersey Experiment Station at Rutgers University. I politely responded that the opportunity was intriguing, but the timing unfavorable. One year and one phone call later, I agreed to a meeting in New York with a member of the Rutgers Search Committee. Subsequently, I was invited to Rutgers for present a seminar and attend meetings with the search committee, faculty groups and administrators. Seven candidates were in the process of being interviewed for the position.

Preparation for the Rutgers visit required research and information gathering about Cook College, the New Jersey Agricultural Experiment Station, the New Jersey Marine Ecosystem and the New Jersey Pinelands National Reserve. This information provided important background for preparation of a seminar based on the prospects for Rutgers University providing national leadership for an interdisciplinary collaborative biodiversity research and teaching leadership program across all academic departments and the New Jersey Agricultural Experiment Station.

My visit to Rutgers was met with enthusiasm by the faculty and members of the search committee although no correspondence occurred after the return to San Carlos. My assumption was that the administration favored one of the other candidates. Daryl Lund, the Executive Dean, phoned me during late August to inform me that the search committee had decided to appoint me to the position of Dean of Research and Director of the Experiment Station. I requested a week to think over the opportunity, and to discuss it with my associates.

ESCAgenetics at the time of the invitation at Rutgers was in discussions with Pulsar SA, a Mexican company for acquisition of the agricultural subsidiaries while the Korean pharmaceutical company, Samyang Genex Co. Ltd. was in discussions about acquisition of the Phytopharmaceutical assets. The reality of the situation was that time was perfect for me to transition, considering that PhytoPharmaceuticals had been successfully launched. My equity position in the company would allow me to enjoy the upside of the company's future success. With this in mind, I informed Ray Moshy, CEO, ESCAgenetics, Corp. about my decision to return to academia and willingness to continue a relationship with the company as a consultant. He endorsed the plan and congratulated me.

The following weeks were hectic. I was busy packing, arranging the move for transportation of furniture, books, files and automobile to the east coast. Fortunately, I discovered beautiful living quarters in Highland Park, a lovely suburb of New Brunswick, within walking distance to all five of the New Brunswick campuses, including the Cook Campus College. My office suite was located on the first floor of Martin Hall, the administration building that had formerly housed the laboratories of Selman Waksman, the Nobel Laureate and his graduate student, Albert Schatz, the co-discovers of streptomycin.

With a faculty and staff of 350 and a student body of 3,500 undergraduates and about 800 graduate students, the opportunity at Rutgers Cook College (Now – SEBS, School of Environmental and Biological Sciences) was both challenging and exciting. The total student population of the university undergraduate population was about 40,000 and total university student population was over 52,000. The academic departments at Cook College during my time consisted of Agricultural, Food and Resource Economics, Ecology, Evolution and Natural Resources, Animal Science, Biochemistry and Microbiology, Entomology, Environmental Sciences, Food Science, Landscape Architecture, Marine and Coastal Sciences, Meteorology, Natural Resources, Nutritional Sciences, and Plant Biology and Pathology. The departments were complemented by several research centers and institutes including the Center for Advanced Food Technology, the Agricultural Biotech Center, the Center for Environmental Prediction, Institute for Marine Biology and Coastal Science, Center for Remote Sensing, Center for Turfgrass Science, and the National IR-4 Project.

My first few months were committed to on-site visits with faculty members, departmental chairs and research center/institute directors for developing an understanding of their research and teaching programs and to explore possibilities for cross-campus collaborative programs. It was crucial to devise a strategy as to the appropriate approach to catalyzing collaborative faculty research and teaching as well as sources of funding. The laboratory visits were augmented with important social events bringing the faculty together including a research dean early evening seminar program including a buffet dinner and beverages, office lunches, dinner events at the Frog and Peach in New Brunswick and Charlie Browns in Highland Park. Jeff joined on numerous occasions at Charlie Browns. The same approach was implemented for the New Jersey Experiment Station (NJAES) Board of Managers – an important advocacy board responsible for linkage of NJAES to the various county boards of agriculture My colleague, Zane Helsel, Dean of Outreach and I hosted monthly buffet dinners and faculty research updates at our Martin Hall Office Suite.

I must say, that these first months were among the most memorable of my lifetime. Regular meetings with the faculty, staff and stakeholders provided me with an eagle eye view of new possibilities for the catalysis of academic research and teaching programs. It was an opportunity to envision interdepartmental, government, and industry collaborative opportunities among the Cook Campus academic departments and research centers and sister campuses in New Brunswick, Newark and Camden along with the sister academic institutions.

Our Martin Hall research leadership served as a catalyst for drafting collaborative faculty grant proposals. The proposals were drafted for the usual government science agencies, e.g., DARPA, EPA, NSF, NASA, USDA as well as New Jersey County, State Department of Agriculture, Commissioner of Commerce, Commissioner of Education, Department of Environmental Protection, Commission of Science and Technology and the Port Authority Agencies. The resultant grant awards led to creation of a number of new research centers, including, the Rutgers EcoComplex focusing on new-use technology research and product development. The Rutgers EcoComplex founding was based on collaboration between the Cook College, Rutgers Cooperative Extension Service, Burlington County Resource Recovery Complex, the New Jersey Department of Environmental Protection, Stevens Institute of Technology; NASA, and the New Jersey Department of Commerce. Other successful outcomes included the Biodiversity Center, the Nutraceuticals Institute, the Center for Environmental Prediction, the Equine Research Center and the EcoPolicy Institute which later evolved into the Food Policy Institute under a successor administration led by Dean Soji Adelaja. The Nutraceuticals Institute led to a collaborative nutraceuticals teaching program between the Department of Food Science and the College of Pharmacy. And the founding of Wellgen, Inc. in partnership with the Center for Advanced Food Technology, Department of Food Science and the Robert Wood Johnson Medical School launched by a substantial grant from the New Jersey Commission On Science and Technology.

A number of global collaborative research programs were launched during this period, including a natural products collaborative research program with the world-renowned scientist Monroe Wall, Research

Triangle Park, leading to the Monroe Wall Research Colloquium Series in New Brunswick and Simon Bolivar University, Venezuela. The Tripartite Biotechnology Collaborative Research and Teaching Program between Rutgers, Ohio State University and the University of Sao Paulo. The Program provided a new and innovative model for undergraduate, graduate, faculty research and teaching exchanges. Other initiatives included research partnerships with institutes of the Chinese Academy of Sciences, European Research Council Research Facility in Todi, Italy and National Autonomous University of Mexico.

Looking back on my life, the five years at Rutgers were among the highlights of my career. Nonetheless, I decided to step down and turn the responsibilities over to younger colleagues and pursue other interests in the biotechnology sector. The pace at Rutgers required appearances at wall-to-wall meetings during the week and weekends in New Brunswick and numerous award dinners at statewide venues. An aging body can withstand only so much rubber chicken.

Three years into my tenure at Rutgers, Daryl Lund, the Executive Dean, accepted a parallel position at Cornell, which precipitated successive changes in the leadership. This was a playback consistent with other experiences at Case Western Reserve University, The Ohio State University and the Campbell Soup Company. In all cases, my immediate supervisor departed early in my employment, creating new organizational and programmatic challenges. I was asked to serve as the interim executive dean after Daryl Lund's departure, but I turned down the offer. My hearing disability would have compromised my performance and made the position too demanding. The Executive Dean must make regular appearances at the State Board of Agriculture and the General Assembly to review the budget for the New Jersey Agricultural Experiment Station. Afterwards, Cook College was led by an acting dean, who was followed by an older non-tenured administrator.

I took stock of the situation and came to grips with the fact that the first five years of my tenure were coming to a close. The enhancements to the research establishment that I had planned had for the most part been accomplished. Moreover, our team consisted of a group of capable young individuals who were destined to move on to positions of greater responsibility. After making the decision to resign, a consultancy was offered involvement with the W.K. Kellogg Mid-Atlantic University Collaboration, a successful collaborative research and teaching program among the mid-Atlantic universities and with several international program initiatives. The international programs included the Rutgers/Ohio State/University of Sao Paulo Tripartite Research and Teaching Collaboration and the Global Institute for Bio-exploration (GIBE).

The Tripartite program was most innovative and supported annual undergraduate research scholars participating in one another's annual undergraduate research symposia that involved a one-week campus visit and presentation of research programs at poster sessions, lectures or roundtables. The Tripartite program also encompassed collaborative faculty research, an undergraduate foreign exchange and a double diploma Ph.D. program, involving faculty on two campuses.

Collaboration with the Institute for BioExploration was likewise rewarding with travel and participation in workshops in Botswana, Ghana, Nigeria, and South Africa and at Rutgers. The research and teaching efforts of the program focused on the exploration of natural products from native flora for the development of dietary supplements, functional foods, nutraceuticals and ethical drugs. The program was an extension from a successful collaborative NIH grant held by Dr. Ilya Raskin involving a group of countries in Central Asia.

The Rutgers opportunity served to expand my academic leadership skill sets and to gain knowledge in a smorgasbord of disciplines including extensive travel to Africa, Brazil, China and Mexico. The most satisfying rewards resulted from the successful outcomes of the collaborative interdisciplinary collaborations.

California PhytoPharmaceuticals Inc. 1991 -1993

In August 1991, after the sale of the DNA Pharmaceuticals Inc. assets to Cibia-Geigy, I received a phone call from a senior vice president of ESCAgenetics Corporation, San Carlos, California, a successor to one of the first U.S. biotechnology companies - International Plant

Research, about my potential interest in assuming leadership position for a research and development project for the anticancer drug Taxol from *Taxus* cell cultures grown in bioreactors. The inquiry led to a trip to San Carlos in late 1991 during which I was offered an opportunity to launch PhytoPharmaceuticals, Inc., a spin-off company from ESCAgenetics Corporation to development plant based pharmaceuticals. I decided to occupy the number two slot as always and focus on the creative aspects of business development and research. My title was Vice President of Business Development.

Integrated media executive son, Jeff, who at the time was located in Santa Monica, was engaged in a San Francisco project mapping locations for a future film project. He assisted me in finding a beautiful residence on California Street overlooking Chinatown and the magnificent Embarcadero. I moved to San Francisco during the morning hours of January of 1992 to assume responsibilities related to the launch of PhytoPharmaceuticals Inc., the drive to San Carlos from the San Francisco was about 25 – 30 minutes.

Life was hectic with the recruitment of a management and technical team to complement the scientific team already in place at ESCAgenetics. I collaborated with the Vice President of Research at ESCAgenetics Corporation to structure a pharmaceutical research team. This involved reassignment of the engineering unit and select members from the cell biology and chemistry units. I employed the usual socialization process for development of congeniality among the diverse members of the group including lunches, dinners, Karaoke nights and Sunday brunches for the research teams and families at my apartment on California Street above San Francisco Chinatown and the Embarcadero. Beverages and hors d' oeuvres were served while scientists chatted and children played with toys and games. Afterwards, we would walk to the Embarcadero Outdoor Restaurant on the waterfront and enjoy brunch. Our visitors were encouraged to spend the weekend and join our Sunday events and sometime walk the Golden Gate Bridge to Sausalito for brunch. A number of important collaborations resulted from the walk and talks.

Dr. Tom Glenn, a longtime colleague, was appointed to the CEO position because of his business and research leadership background.

He had served as Vice President of Research for both Ciba-Geigy Corporation and Genentech and held CEO positions at several start-up pharmaceutical companies. Peter Hylands, a former biochemist professor at the London Kings College of Pharmacy and director of chemistry at Xenova Group PLC was hired as the Chief Scientist. I collaborated with the pharmaceutical team to finalize the business plan and marketing prospectus. In addition, I co-chaired the weekly research team meetings.

Tom Glenn was totally dynamic. His work hours commenced at 4:30 A.M., requiring a change in my work schedule and the resetting of my biological clock, which remains unchanged to this day. I usually left my residence on California Street at 4:00 A.M., which allowed me to meet with Tom prior to the employee foot traffic, meetings and ringing telephones. I enjoyed the solitude of the early hours and the ability to organize and focus my thoughts on the projects of the day.

The company negotiated collaborative research and development agreements with the Shanghai Institute of Materia Medica, Beijing Institute of Botany and the Chengdu Institute of Biology (all members of the Chinese Academy of Sciences) for evaluating plants used in traditional medicine in the state-of-the-art High-throughput pharmaceutical screens. A parallel agreement was negotiated with the Agricultural Biotech Center, ESALQ-University of Sao Paulo, Piracicaba, Brazil, with Professor Otto J. Crocomo. Important to note that the leadership of the Chinese and Brazilian institutions were colleagues and partners from earlier collaborations. Important to emphasize that colleagues and associates from former collaborations are invaluable business and technology network treasures.

Our talented chemical engineering team successfully developed a bench-top bioreactor process for Taxol production and were subsequently awarded a substantial grant from the National Institutes of Health (NIH). The Company entered into a collaborative business relationship with Genencor, a Dupont subsidiary for the scale-up and fine-tuning of the production process at the company's Rochester, New York, facility. Dr. Roy Stalhut, a senior scientist, was reassigned to the Genencor Team and I assumed responsibility for managing the project, requiring weekly management meetings in Rochester on Monday mornings and to return to San Francisco on Monday afternoons. My usual itinerary was a red eye flight on Friday to New York to visit family over the weekend and travel to Rochester on Monday mornings. Then Samyang Genex Co., Ltd., invested in the Taxol project and a collaborative ethical drug development program. The company had collaborative research agreements with the Chinese Academy of Sciences - the Beijing Institute of Botany and Shanghai Institute of Materia Medica.

Samyang Genex Co. assumed a substantial equity position in PhytoPharmaceuticals Inc. and the Taxol process was transferred to Samyang Genex Co., Seoul, Korea for commercial scale-up Taxol following successful development of the production process at Genencor. The Samyang Genex Company has a relationship with Rutgers during my tenure and the management often visited. My regret was that time did not permit me to visit the Taxol production facility in Seoul.

The opportunity to build PhytoPharmaceuticals Inc. on the backbone DNA Pharmaceuticals Inc. and develop a pharmaceutical product production process in collaboration with Genencor and subsequently forge a collaborative relationship with Samyang Genex Co. was indeed a moment celebration for our business and research and development team.

DNA Pharmaceuticals, Inc. 1988 -1991

One of the most exhilarating corporate career moments was the opportunity to collaborate with the Chinese Academy of Sciences (CAS) and several of the CAS research institutes. A few words about CAS, Retrieved August 5, 2013 from The Chinese Academy of Sciences (CAS), formerly known as Academia Sinica, is the national academy[14] for the natural sciences[15] of the People's Republic of China[16]. It is an institution of the State Council of China[17], functioning as the national scientific think-tank, providing advisory and appraisal services on is-

---

14 https://en.m.wikipedia.org/wiki/National_academy
15 https://en.m.wikipedia.org/wiki/Natural_science
16 https://en.m.wikipedia.org/wiki/People%27s_Republic_of_China
17 https://en.m.wikipedia.org/wiki/State_Council_of_the_People%27s_Republic_of_China

sues stemming from the national economy, social development, and science and technology progress. It is headquartered in Beijing[18], with institutes all over the People's Republic of China. It has also created hundreds of commercial enterprises, Lenovo[19] being one of them

Diyoung Wang, a former colleague from DNA Plant Technology Corporation and I visited China on several occasions and met with Dr. Zhou Guangzhao, the President and Dr. Hu Hesheng, the Executive Vice President of the Chinese Academy of Sciences (CAS) and two of the CAS Institutes: Shanghai Institute of Materia Medica and Beijing Institute of Botany. The meeting occurred at the headquarters of the Chinese Academy of Sciences in a formal palace-like chamber furnished with large sitting areas. The seating was arranged in a hierarchical pattern with Drs. Hu and Zhou seated in the center and the guests of honor on either side. We were served tea and biscuits.

Our conversation was relaxed, doubtless, because of our mutual backgrounds in academia and research histories. We informed one another with a brief account of our academic backgrounds. Dr. Zhou was a world class physicist who escaped death during a visit to Moscow with two fellow leading nuclear physicists from China during the Nikita Khrushchev regime in the USSR. President Khrushchev told Chairman Mao that the USSR would assume leadership in nuclear energy research for both China and the USSR and invited three leading CAS physicists to Moscow to initiate the collaboration. During the meetings, disagreement arose over the USSR's assumption of leadership of the Chinese nuclear energy research and development program. Dr. Zhou decided to return to China a day early by train to attend a meeting in a remote part of China while his two colleagues returned by plane. The plane exploded shortly after takeoff, killing the two Chinese nuclear scientists while Dr. Zhou, was safely in Chinese territory at the time of the explosion. Dr. Hu Hesheng was a renowned mathematician and former president of the Shanghai Mathematical Society and specialized in differential geometry. She led a group at Fudan University in the 1980s and 1990s. Her husband, Gu Chaohao,

---

18 https://en.m.wikipedia.org/wiki/Beijing
19 https://en.m.wikipedia.org/wiki/Lenovo

also a renowned mathematician, served as president of the University of Science and Technology of China.

Drs. Hu and Zhou agreed to consider participation of the two institutes of the Chinese Academy of Sciences (Chinese Institute of Materia Medica in Shanghai and the Chinese Institute of Botany in Beijing) in a collaborative research program with the proposed startup company, DNA Pharmaceuticals Corporation for evaluation botanical materials used in traditional medicines in for discovery of new lead pharmaceutical compounds using state of the art high throughput pharmacological screens. The proposed collaborative relationship was to include an equity position for CAS in DNA Pharmaceuticals Inc. Dr. Hu agreed to assume leadership in negotiation of the business and technical relationship. CAS after completion of negotiations acquired a significant equity stake and a Board of Directors seat.

My role was to serve as a facilitator for organization of the company since this was my first entry into the pharmaceutical industry. A first step was engagement of consultants Professor Douglas Davidson from McMaster University and Dr. Bryce Douglas, former Vice President of Research for Smith Kline Corporation in Philadelphia. Dr. Douglas had led a major research operation at Smith Kline Corporation for evaluating botanical materials for drug development. Subsequently, we had the good fortune to appoint a senior business development and officer and research scientist from the neurobiology unit at Ciba-Geigy because of shuttering the U.S. neurobiology unit and consolidation of the unit within the corporate research headquarters in Switzerland. We now had in place, a team to develop a business plan and specific collaborative research programs with the Chinese Academy of Science and the two institutes.

DNA Pharmaceuticals Inc. was founded in 1988 in partnership with the Chinese Academy of Sciences. Don MacKinnon, who had just retired as president of Ciba-Geigy U.S.A., was appointed to the CEO position. We celebrated the launch of DNA Pharmaceuticals Inc. at the "Windows on the World" at the World Trade Center in New York attended by CAS President Zhou Guangzhao, CAS Executive Vice President Hu Hesheng, the DNA Pharmaceuticals Inc. officers and board of directors. Our offices were originally located in

Cinnaminson, N.J. and later relocated to Stamford, Connecticut. Our trips to China were frequent for the managing the drug development projects. Genentech and Ciba-Geigy kept a close eye on our progress with frequent meetings and invitations to attend the Friday afternoon social gatherings called "Ho-Hos" with the Genentech team prior to our travel to China for collaborative sponsored research between DNA Pharmaceuticals, Inc., and the Institutes of CAS.

Genentech proposed forging a relationship with DNA Pharmaceuticals, Inc., that would allow investment and collaborative research, and relocate DNA Pharmaceuticals, Inc., to Genentech's headquarters in South San Francisco. The opportunity created excitement in the venture capital community. However, enthusiasm abruptly ended with the Tiananmen Square protests on April 15, 1989, and plans for collaboration and for financing by the venture capital community were cancelled. We scheduled a meeting in China following Tiananmen Square to request approval of merging the company with another company or selling the assets. The Chinese colleagues were in agreement.

Xenova Group PLC, Slough, United Kingdom entertained a possible merger with DNA Pharmaceuticals Inc. based on an earn-out proposition on achievement of successful clinical trials and commercialization of compounds in the Company's pipeline. After rejection of the offer, Xenova offered me a senior position as opposed to merger of the two companies. Don Mackinnon and I had a number of meetings with the executive team. Once again, I was worried about possible litigation in regard to closing on such a proposition because of my equity and officer role although I did like the company.

Ciba Geigy acquired the assets of DNA Pharmaceuticals, Inc. including the collaborative research agreements with the Chinese Academy of Sciences and the institutes. The transaction allowed for payment of creditors and distribution of monies to the shareholders. The successive collaborative relationship with the two institutes of the Chinese Academy of Sciences evolved and continued through the merger of Ciba Geigy and Sandoz which resulted in the creation of Novartis, a 30-billion USD pharmaceutical company. Subsequently, Novartis invested $100 million dollars in the

CAS research collaborations during 2006 and more recently over $1 Billion Dollar investment in research facilities during 2009. DNA Pharmaceuticals, Inc. was dissolved the early 1990s, and I was uncertain in regard to the next opportunity. Or perhaps this had been the last dance for me until the phone rang about the next collaborative opportunity in California to join ESCAgeneics Corporation and lead the founding of PhytoPharmaceuticals Inc.

DNA Plant Technology Company 1981 -1988

1981 was my forty-fifth year. I somehow thought that I had done it all and seen it all. Never did I believe while growing up in Akron that I would be appointed to a leading research position at a blue chip corporation as Director of the Pioneer Research Laboratory for Campbell's Soup at the Cinnaminson, New Jersey research complex with the role of creating a vibrant biotechnology research program. Basically, I was offered a remarkable opportunity to build a biotechnology program on a platform of conventional research programs geared to food chemistry, food technology, genetics, plant breeding and plant physiology. Our biotechnology team successfully integrated the conventional research team and within one year conducted the first biotechnology crop field trials for selection of value added consumer and processing traits.

And little did I know that the most exciting and rewarding roller coaster ride was about to begin. These opportunities arose from past associations with Bill Jacobs, Princeton Professor and Bill Wardell, University of Maryland Professor, who happened to be sitting next to me and my graduate students on a bus from Helsinki to Leningrad for the July 1975 12th International Botanical Congress in Leningrad. I had known Bill Jacobs from graduate school days at Rutgers when he and my mentor, Jim Gunckel held joint research meetings for their graduate students. Bill Wardell had visited my laboratory at Ohio State University on a number of occasions as part of a collaborative recombinant DNA research program. Bill Jacobs and Jim Gunckel, my mentor at Rutgers had been classmates at Harvard.

On or about Friday, April 3, 1980 in the late afternoon, my secretary announced that a gentleman by the name of Myer Blech from the Wharton Group in New York was on the phone. The assumption was that he was bothering me about opening a brokerage account. I requested Karen to inform him that I had no interest. She returned to report that he was calling about a new venture in agricultural biotechnology. I accepted the phone call and the roller coaster ride began.

Myer informed me that his sons, David and Isaac, had recently founded Genetic Systems Corporation with scientist, Robert Nowinski, the former research director at the Hutchinson Institute in Seattle, and they were currently exploring the possibility of forming an agricultural biotechnology company on the eastern seaboard. I inquired as to how he had come across my name and he told me that I was referred to his sons through Lloyd Schoen, a biochemist, at the Memorial Sloan-Kettering Cancer Center in New York. Apparently, Lloyd was a consultant to the Blech brothers and had known Bill Wardell during postdoctoral days at the University of Wisconsin. Myer asked if I could act as a consultant to his sons. I politely declined and informed him that my engagement as a consultant would impose a conflict of interest issue with my employment at CSC. I would, however, be pleased to recommend potential candidates for a chief scientist position.

The frequent phone calls continued during the following months, but usually my schedule for Friday was filled with meetings at Campbell Place in Camden or in Cinnaminson. In late May, I agreed to meet Myer, Lloyd Schoen and Meyer's sons in New York for a 6:00 P.M. Sunday dinner at Siegel's, a Kosher Restaurant, in midtown New York. Myer and I arranged to meet in front of the Park 'N Lock Garage across from the Lincoln Tunnel exit onto 42nd Street. I waited and waited but Myer didn't appear. After thirty minutes, I phoned the restaurant and spoke with Lloyd Schoen. Lloyd. He said that Myer had mistakenly thought that I was parked at the nearby Port Authority Garage and he would contact Meyer shortly. A few minutes later, a twelve-year old Cadillac pulled up to the curb and stopped. Myer stepped out of the car and shook hands. I immediately liked him. Because of the months of phone conversations, he was like an old friend. He reminded me of my father. On the way to Siegel's Restaurant, just a few blocks away,

Myer mentioned that he had been driving the Cadillac and wearing some of the same clothing since he closed on his first big deal. He was afraid that lady luck would abandon him if he departed with the precious automobile and clothing possessions. Myer replaced the car engine a few years earlier and maintained the car in mint condition. My father was likewise superstitious and followed behavioral patterns quite similar to Myer.

But, I must tell you a bit more about Myer before moving on with the story. Myer at one time was rejected for admission to the Wharton School MBA Program at the University of Pennsylvania. He sought revenge by naming his New York brokerage firm the Wharton Group. The idea was to keep the Wharton School from opening offices in New York. He was passionate about the founding of Israel in 1948 and volunteered to serve as a rabbi after completion of his service in the Chaplain Corps of the U.S. Army during World War II. He was notified that Israel was interested in immigration of individuals with background in business, education, engineering, law, medicine, science and the trades, but unfortunately for Myer, Israel had more than enough rabbis. Myer immediately enrolled in auto mechanic school, but his wife Ester and family discouraged emigration to Israel. The young family stayed in Vineland for a while longer and then moved to Brooklyn for the launch of the Wharton Group.

We arrived at Siegel's Restaurant at about 7:00 P.M. The restaurant was quite noisy with a Sunday evening family crowd. Myer introduced me to Lloyd Schoen, David and Isaac, and after exchanging the usual niceties, Myer requested the Maître 'D to seat us in a quiet corner. Lloyd and I hit it off immediately because of our research backgrounds. Lloyd told me that he and Bill Wardell had been roommates during their postdoctoral fellowship days at the University of Wisconsin. He had recently spoken with Bill regarding possible candidates for a research director to provide leadership for an agricultural biotechnology company. Bill mentioned my name and our recent trip to Leningrad for the International Botanical Congress, and the research collaboration between our laboratories at Ohio State University and the University of Maryland.

David and Isaac were a bit shy at first. David informed me that he had put his dad up to calling me at the Campbell Soup Company out of fear that I would not respond or take him seriously because of his age and lack of scientific background. He was 25 at the time and Isaac was 31. David and Isaac were Baruch College graduates with majors in music and film, respectively. After Baruch, David earned a MFA in music from Columbia University and assumed a position at the Wharton Group with his father. Isaac held a position with a marketing research firm in New York. The two brothers recorded over five record albums with Shanghai Surprise topping the charts in Hungary. David wrote the music and Isaac penned the lyrics. David told me about the founding of Genetic Systems Corporation in Seattle with Robert Nowinski, former scientific director at the Hutchinson Institute, and securing an investment from the Schroder Bank in New York. The way the deal was inked by David was quite brilliant. Bob Nowinski and colleagues had an offer to join a blue-chip pharmaceutical company in New Jersey when David proposed forming Genetic Systems Corporation in Seattle and allowing the scientific team to remain in Seattle. David's offer cinched the deal and Genetic Systems Corporation was born.

David proposed that I resign from the Campbell Soup Company and join he and Isaac in founding an agricultural biotechnology company in New Jersey. I reminded David that I was a scientist not a businessman and my skill sets were inappropriate for the CEO task. He proposed a lunch meeting the following week to explore the possibility further with John Connor, Chairman of the Schroder Bank on Wall Street in New York. I agreed and requested bringing along my colleague, David Evans.

The following Monday, David Blech phoned to confirm a lunch meeting on or about Thursday May 28 at the Schroder Bank with John Connor and associates. David Evans and I were excited about the opportunity and discussed it at length. As mentioned earlier, CSC was in fact exploring the possibility of investing in one of the newly minted agricultural biotechnology companies. We prepared a presentation for the Schroeder Bank with care not to disclose CSC proprietary information.

Thursday morning was a bit hectic because of an early meeting at CSC Headquarters at Campbell Place. I returned to Cinnaminson at 9:30 A.M. and picked up Dave. Fortunately, the turnpike traffic was light and we were on time for the 12:30 P.M. lunch meeting. We were received by Mr. John Connor, Stephen Petschek, the President of J. Henry Schroder Corporation, Jeffrey Collinson, Managing Director, David Blech and Isaac Blech. The dining room was much like a fish bowl with an amazing panoramic view of the battery, Ellis Island, the Statue of Liberty and assorted maritime vessels.

John Connor was a seasoned senior business icon having served as President and CEO of Allied Chemical, Merck & Co. and U.S. Secretary of Commerce under LBJ. He had been very friendly with William Murphy, former CEO at the Campbell Soup Company during his tenure at Merck and Company in the 1970s. John Connor had been a pioneer in the implementation of strategic planning and during a golf match, advised William Murphy to consider the same, for the Campbell Soup Company. Mr. Murphy heeded the advice and encouraged basic research and vertical integration at CSC. The emphasis on basic research was the basis for the Campbell Institute for Agricultural Research and the hiring of me and Dave Evans. Dave and I enjoyed sharing our thoughts with Jack Connor. After lunch, we were invited to Jack Connor's enormous office suite. An endless display of awards including championship golf plaques and trophies, hung on the walls and filled glass cases. We were regaled with stories about his time in Washington, D.C. as Secretary of Commerce. One day, LBJ approached Mr. Connor about his passion for golf and requested that he retire from the sport. Mr. Connor offered to resign from the cabinet if his playing were going to create a problem for the White House, but the President didn't pursue the issue. One weekend, he was in the finals of a championship golf tournament located in a remote area of Bermuda when the President tried to telephone him. The White House aides had tracked down a local restaurant in proximity to the golf course.

The White House placed a phone call to the restaurant and the proprietor responded, "Ha, Ha, the President."

After numerous phone calls, Mr. Connor was told of the call from the president and responded, "Please inform the president that I will return the phone call in about 20 minutes."

Mr. Connor phoned the White House and the President said, "Jack, it must be nice to be relaxing on the greens while my team is solving the nation's problems."

Mr. Connor then returned to the business at hand and said, "Rod, next time you visit, please bring a presentation on your science for us to discuss."

I replied, "Turns out that we brought a brief presentation to share with you today."

Dave and I shared a twenty-minute presentation on the biotechnology opportunities for the agriculture, food and industrial sectors.

Mr. Connor asked thought provoking questions after summarizing the conversations of the afternoon, said, "Let's form a new agricultural biotechnology company and make it all happen."

I replied, "Wonderful opportunity, however, I do not have the business experience to make it happen! If we had a seasoned businessman like you to handle the business aspects, we could make it work!"

Mr. Connor immediately replied, "What if I serve in the Acting CEO capacity while we search for an appropriate CEO candidate?"

I agreed and we all shook hands on moving forward with the deal.

The Transition

The meeting at the Schroder Bank led to a surge of activity followed by a series of collaborative meetings at law offices in New York and drafting a prospectus. Then came meetings in New Jersey related to drawing up employment agreements for David Evans and me. I was fortunate at the time to have a tenant in my duplex residential dwelling in Haddonfield. The tenant, a vice-president of the Bank of New Jersey, was so kind as to recommend a law firm in Haddonfield to represent David Evans and me in negotiating the employment agreements. The law firm drafted five-year employment agreements requiring that the company provide zero interest loans for the purchase of founder's stock and establishment of an escrow account at the Bank of New Jersey for deposit of one year's compensation. The Company was incorporated on June 11, 1981 as the DNA Plant Technology Corporation (DNAP). On Monday June 15, David Evans and I resigned our positions at the Campbell Soup Company.

I had some hesitation about leaving the Campbell Soup Company, but saw the new company as an extraordinary opportunity to pioneer and expand applications of biotechnology for the agriculture, food, and plant based chemical industries. The severing of ties with the Campbell Soup Company was a stealth operation that involved leasing a Hertz moving van to remove personal effects from the Pioneer Research Laboratory under the cover of night during an early summer weekend. I joined forces with Dave Evans, his wife, Kitty, my son Jeff, and my sister Sally, to mastermind and execute the operation. We carefully, sorted through files and books to remove personal effects and leave behind corporate materials. We were nervous about being challenged by security forces and a possible arrest. These extreme measures were taken because only a few months earlier the personal effects of the former vice president of research were confiscated when he resigned from the company. In those days, research scientists accumulate massive paper files of scientific reprints and books. Today of course the files would be stored in electronic databases.

Dave Evans, and I, officially resigned from the Campbell Soup Company on the morning of June 15, 1981. That evening, I received a phone call from our CSC group vice president and Gordon McGovern, the CEO, to schedule a lunch meeting with our bankers and other investors in DNA Plant Technology Corporation. Arrangements were made for the bankers and other investors to meet at the Campbell Place Office of the President the following Thursday for a lunch. Dave Evans, David Blech, Issac Blech and I put our thoughts together and drafted a prospectus in preparation for the meeting. The named participants included John Connor, Jeffrey Collinson, David Blech, Isaac Blech, Dave Evans and Rod Sharp.

On Thursday June 25, the bankers and other investors arrived in two stretch limousines at the Campbell Place Headquarters in Camden, while Dave Evans and I arrived by car and were escorted to the president's dining room, Gordon McGovern was most gracious to me. He and I were seated at opposite ends of the dining room table. The lunch meeting began with Gordon McGovern and Jack Conner recounting their experiences together at Harvard playing touch football and their early career acquaintances and milestones. The drafting of a final business plan for the DNA Plant Technology Corporation and the recruitment of a senior executive from the food industry for the CEO Position were the topics of discussion. Gordon McGovern informed John Conner that Campbell Soup Company was interested in taking a lead investment position in the new company and would invest a combination of cash and the Cinnaminson, N.J., laboratory facilities. Moreover, the Campbell employees would have an option to continue employment at the Campbell Soup Company or to join the new company. The next step was to move beyond a handshake to draft a definitive investment agreement, to conclude final negotiations and execute a formal investment agreement. Mr. Connor agreed to provide leadership to DNAP during the negotiation process.

It was apparent to all that the CSC investment of capital and the Cinnaminson New Jersey research complex, and the opportunity to retain the former Campbell Soup Company Pioneer Research Division personnel provided the new company with crucial momentum from Day One. We started off as a full-fledged biotechnology company with highly skilled staff, farms, financial resources, greenhouses, and research laboratories. Most important was that a collegial relationship existed among the research team.

There was much more work to be done prior to closing with CSC and other investors on a private placement. The important task of constructing a business plan lay ahead of us. This process began with regular meetings with Evelyn Berezin at her pied-a-terre in Greenwich Village. Dave Evans, Kitty Evans and my son Jeff would book hotels for the weekends in New York. Dave and I would meet at Evelyn's place to work on business plans while Jeff and Kitty hung out in Greenwich Village. Evelyn's husband Israel Wilenitz was always wonderful to us and often joined us for lunch.

Evelyn was a physics graduate from NYU who pioneered the word processor during graduate school at NYU by hooking up an IBM typewriter to an oscilloscope. She also developed appropriate software and demonstrated the word processing process. She was awarded a number of patents and founded Readactron, which designed, developed and manufactured word processing systems worldwide. She subsequently sold her company to the Boroughs Corporation (now Unisys) and was appointed to a vice president position. She served as president of Greenhouse Management Company and as General Partner of a group of venture capital funds and held a number of key positions at SUNY Stony Brook. Evelyn was named to Business Week's list of the top 100 Business Women in the United States.

John Connor assigned two of his senior vice presidents at the Schroder Bank to negotiate the investment deal with CSC. The stumbling block had to do with the biotechnology research program rights for CSC. Finally, an agreement was reached by which DNAP would provide quarterly options to CSC for investment in two major food crop biotechnology research and development programs with an appropriate review period. If CSC turned down an investment opportunity, DNAP was granted the technology and was free to negotiate a research development and or license agreement in the field with other major agricultural and food companies.

The negotiation process between the Campbell Soup Company (CSC) and DNA Plant Technology Corp (DNAP) to reach a final agreement for a private placement was time consuming. The joke at the time was that we would be closing in two weeks, but the two-week closing date never seemed to happen. At one point, John Connor mentioned the possibility of renting incubator space at Rutgers University. On a handshake with Gordon McGovern, Dave Evans and I received permission from CSC to move back to our offices with continued access to our administrative assistants and support staff.

The final step was negotiation of a multiyear, multimillion dollar tomato research and development agreement that was essentially a continuation of the programs in progress prior to the formation of DNAP. On a late Thursday afternoon in March prior to closing time, a meeting was scheduled by the Chief Financial Officer for early the next morning to discuss financial aspects of the proposed research and development agreement. I showed up for the appointment Friday and the CFO explained to me that CSC would agree to a two year, two hundred thousand dollar contracts on a yearly basis on a take it or leave it basis. I hesitated for about thirty seconds, shook hands, and agreed to accept the CSC offer on behalf of DNAP. There were clearly forces within CSC that disagreed about the proposed DNAP investment. The expectation had been that CSC would enter into a multi-year 1-2 M million-dollar research agreement.

Finally, on March 23, 1982 all negotiations were complete. David Evans, David Blech and Isaac Blech and representation from the Schroder Bank Counsel met at the offices of Drinker Biddle & Reath at Broad and Chestnut Streets in Philadelphia and proceeded to sign hundreds of multiple original documents pertaining to the closing, a process that took about five hours. The transaction included title to the Cinnaminson New Jersey Research Complex which was the former Dorrance Family summer estate. John Dorrance II at the time was chairman of the board for CSC. Our former CSC forty-five-member research and technical support team was given an option to join the new company or to relocate to corporate headquarters at Campbell Place, Camden, New Jersey. All but two members of the team decided against joining the new company. Gordon McGovern, president and chief executive officer, offered all services of CSC's services to help the new company get up and running including access to the CSC health insurance plan. Our board of directors was stellar and included John Connor, Chairman, Schroder Bank and Acting DNAP CEO, Jeffrey Collinson, Senior Vice President, Schroder Bank, Henry Roberts, Retired Chairman & CEO, Connecticut General, Evelyn Berezin, CEO, Greenhouse Ventures and pioneer in word processing, Gordon McGovern, President & CEO, Campbell Soup Company, the Blech brothers and Rod Sharp.

Our team at DNAP began the process of reaching out to industry for additional investment and securing collaborative research and development agreements. In tandem, I worked closely with Gordon McGovern and John Connor in search of a CEO for DNAP. A number of candidates were interested in the position but were not quite suitable because of the lack of a science and engineering background. Finally, Henry Roberts, a DNAP board member and former Chairman and CEO of Connecticut General identified the perfect candidate. Henry was a member of the board of directors of General Foods Corporation (GFC) and a friend of Richard Laster, the executive vice president who was just retiring.

Henry Roberts tried unsuccessfully to reach Richard Laster by phone to discuss the DNAP CEO opportunity. He decided to drive to the Laster Home in Chappaqua and meet with Richard. Henry saw an airport transport vehicle in the driveway as he approached the house. Richard and his wife Lee were off on a trip to Europe and would not return until the later part of April. Richard agreed to phone Henry after his return to discuss the opportunity.

In the later portion of April, Richard Laster and Henry Roberts visited DNAP Headquarters in Cinnaminson, NJ. We arranged a meeting with the scientific team, brief research presentations and a tour of the facilities. Richard and, I knew of one another through the research team at GFC and hit it off immediately. Richard had begun his collaborative career at GFC at the Tarrytown Research Laboratories. Overtime, he received awards and honors for his innovative research and contributions to key GFC product lines. GFC had a portfolio of important consumer brand names including Crystal Lite, Entenmanns, Kool-Aid, Maxwell House, Minute Rice, Oscar Meyer, Post Cereals, Sanka Coffee, Shake N'Bake, and Tang.

Richard Laster agreed to join our management team as CEO and President. We were off and running. Dick was a marketing genius and brought invaluable creative energy in crafting research and development proposals for key companies. Under Richard Laster's leadership we began to explore aggressively joint ventures with blue chip agricultural and food companies.

Dick Laster and I met with Jim Imshoff, the Vice President of Strategic Planning and formerly a colleague of mine at the Campbell Soup Company, about consultants for business plan development. Jim had been a professor at the Wharton School and recommended, a former colleague, Peter Davis. During the next few months, Dick, Dave and I met with Peter and a team of undergraduates to develop a definitive business and financial plan, which was necessary for development of a prospectus to be used for both the IPO and Secondary Public Offering.

Within a short period, the company had inked important collaborative agreements with the American Home Products Corporation, Brown & Williamson Tobacco Company, CPC International Inc., DuPont Company, Farms of Texas, Fermenich Incorporated, General Foods Corporation, Hershey Food Corporation, Koppers Company Inc., Kraft Inc., Knorr and Maxwell House, a division of GFC. Under Richard Laster's leadership, the Company developed a creative approach to alliances with corporate partners for collaborative research, development and commercialization agreements with a joint venture. Upon successful development of product prototypes for commercialization, DNAP and the corporate partner would enter into a joint venture for market testing and subsequent product launch.

We expanded the board membership to include Frank Carry, CEO, IBM Corporation, and Edward Hennessy, Jr., CEO, Allied Chemical Corporation, and completed the initial public offering (IPO) in January 1984 and a secondary offering in April 1986. We named a scientific advisory board that included the most prominent scientists in plant biology including the preeminent Nobel Laureates Norman Borlaug, Melvin Calvin, and academics from The Ohio State University, The University of Florida, Institute Agronomico de Campinas, CEPEC/CEPLAC Cocao Research Institute.

Shortly, thereafter, Dr. Maro Sondahl, brilliant graduate student from my lab at Ohio State, senior research scientist at Agronomico de Campinas, Sao Paulo, Brazil along with a number of key Ph.D. scientists from The Ohio State University including David Grothaus, Willie Loh, Sally Miller and Donald Styer, were recruited to join the research team at DNAP. The Company forged collaborative research agreements with the University of Sao Paulo-ESALQ Campus and the University of Campinas in Brazil.

My business skill sets were continuously being fine-tuned under the tutelage of David and Isaac Blech, John Connor, Jeffrey Collinson, and Richard Laster, but especially I am indebted to Richard Laster for his patience in the sharing of his comprehensive knowledge of the food industry. Dick Laster made contact with Leslie Misrock, senior partner at the Pennie and Edmonds Law Firm about representing DNAP. Leslie Misrock was the biotechnology intellectual property guru and

Dick Laster's neighbor in Chappaqua, who had prosecuted the groundbreaking patent on the patenting of life. Our team at DNAP enjoyed a productive relationship with Leslie Misrock and his team of intellectual property lawyers. Leslie opened the first biotechnology law practice and was known as the father of biotechnology law. Because of Leslie and team, the Company was successful in the prosecution of an impressive portfolio of plant biotechnology patents. Under his tutelage, I learned effective leadership skillsets in the management of the company's intellectual property which have been invaluable for future ventures.

Arnold Jacobs, who, at the time, was a senior partner at Shea-Gould, served as the DNAP legal counselor. He provided leadership to DNAP and collaborated with Lehman Brothers, our lead investment banker, management teams, during both the IPO and secondary offering. The preparation for an initial public offering is a very time-consuming process involving drafting a prospectus and preparing an assortment of regulatory documents. Arnold Jacobs and Shea-Gould guided us through the process smoothly. Arnold Jacobs is a world class business law genius with an understanding of both business law and technology. He holds degrees in engineering and law and has authored of a multivolume comprehensive treatise on business law. I have had the good fortune to enjoy a continued friendship with Arnie over the years. He is known as the "dean of securities law" by Crain's New York Business. He took Donna Karan International and Bear Sterns public, defended William Casey in a securities fraud case, when Casey was head of the CIA, in a securities fraud matter. He represented the biotech company Celgene in a more than $1 billion equity public offering and set a world record by writing a law review article with 4,824 footnotes. Today, he advises my son, Jeffrey, in his business endeavors.

Lehman Brothers, our lead investment banker organized numerous road show meetings with potential investors in major U.S. cities and European capitals, including with Atlanta, Boston, Chicago, Los Angeles, Miami, New York, and San Francisco along with European Trips to Dublin, Edinburgh, Frankfurt, London, Munich, and Paris. We were much like an athletic team with events in multiple cities. Truly we were on a treadmill with a blur of airports, air-train travel, hotels and limos. We participated in two or more road shows each day along with assorted breakfast, lunch, and dinner meetings. I marveled at the expertise of Lehman Brothers in processing the investor subscriptions and the launch of the IPO. When, the big day finally arrived, it seemed anticlimactic. The key people that participated in making the IPO happen joined the DNAP management at 21 Club in New York for the victory celebration.

DNAP slowly matured into a top echelon of agricultural biotechnology company in the development of plant-based products for consumers and industry. The Company applied its pioneering work in plant cellular genetics led by David Evans and myself resulting in the pioneering patents entitled: Generation of Somaclonal Non-Mendelian Variants and Gametoclonal Variation. These approaches allowed for the creation of new plant cultivars with characteristics desired by consumers, food processors, and industrial users and did so in less time than could be achieved by traditional breeding methods alone or by molecular genetics alone. The research and development focus was on products at the high value end of the agricultural chain. For instance, the Company was involved in developing tomato cultivars with improved eating or processing characteristics, rather than tomato seed with improved agronomic properties. The Company identified such properties by conducting preliminary market research and analyzing its technological ability to develop new or improved products to satisfy the needs of the consumer market place. The principal considerations in choosing product candidates for commercialization were market size, competition, and the length of time until revenues could be generated. Of course, another requirement was the availability of the funds for successful commercialization. The lead products in development and near production at the time were branded vegetables such as carrots and celery to be marketed under the name VegiSnax, agricultural disease diagnostic kits, enhanced processing and fresh market tomatoes, improved consumer traits in coffee and popcorn, polyunsaturated cooking oils from canola, and enhanced plant derived raw materials for the flavor and fragrance industry.

A few unlikely challenges arose along the way. Production of the biotechnology-derived tomatoes were placed in a major field trial in

Mexico with a contract farmer frequently used by the Campbell Soup Company and under the supervision of a Mexican Ph.D. plant breeder graduate from the University of California Davis. Our research team went to evaluate the tomatoes and discovered that the tomato fields had been plowed under by the farmer and that our supervising breeder consultant had been hired the week before by the Campbell Soup Company Research Station in Davis California. Neither the consultant nor the Campbell Soup Company had informed us of the hiring. For the record, the director of the Campbell Research Station in Davis had been a plant breeding professor at the University of California Davis. Our collaborators at the Campbell Research Station in Davis, CA and the consultant denied any knowledge of the matter. The farmer informed our team that he was ordered to plow under the tomatoes by an official who he assumed was affiliated with DNA Plant Technology Corporation.

The situation was sensitive because CSC had a significant equity position in the company at the time. Word of the incident would have been devastating to a public traded biotechnology company. It is amazing what actions are taken by individuals within the corporate world who view advances in science and technology as threat to their corporate existence and livelihoods.

But commercial success takes more than good science to complement the Company's scientific capabilities with manufacturing, marketing and distribution resources of major consumer and industrial companies. The Company entered into an array of joint venture and licensing agreements with such companies as American Home Products Corporation, Brown & Williamson Tobacco Company, Campbell Soup Company, CPC International Inc., E.I. du Pont Nemours and Company, Firmenich Incorporated, General Foods Corporation, Hershey Foods Corporation, Koppers Company, Inc., and Kraft, Inc.

In 1988, DNAP merged with Advanced Genetic Sciences, Inc. (AGS), an important agricultural molecular biology company to become the largest public plant biotechnology company. AGS was under the leadership of Joseph Bouckaert, the President and Chief Executive Officer, and John Bedbrook, Scientific Director. The new company was incorporated into DNAP Plant Technology Corporation under the leadership of Richard Laster and Joseph Bouckaert resigned and the boards of the two companies merged.

In the later DNAP years, a collaborative opportunity developed through Diyoung Wang, a DNAP scientist, Chinese Citizen, and Green Card holder. I gained support from our scientific advisory board regarding the filing the essential documents with the immigration officials. The opportunity for Diyoung and me was the evaluation of Chinese traditional medicinal plants for pharmaceutical active compounds and the subsequent development of ethical drugs. We visited China and entered into collaborations with the Chinese Academy of Sciences (CAS) and two CAS Institutes: Shanghai Institute of Materia Medica and the Beijing Institute of Botany. Prior to joining DNAP, Diyoung had been a senior scientist at the Institute of Genetics a member organization of the Chinese Academy of Sciences. Diyoung and I decided to resign from DNAP because the consolidation of the two merged companies in Cinnaminson and Oakland did not allow time for consideration of another investment opportunity. DNAP had capable leadership, which made me feel comfortable to explore new venture opportunities. I always made certain that a number two person was in place to assume my position. Diyoung, three former executives from the Ciba-Geigy Company, including the former president of the U.S. operations, joined forces with me in the founding DNA Pharmaceuticals Inc.

The DNAP operations were eventually consolidated and located in Oakland, California. The company was later acquired by the Pulsar International SA (Pulsar), a Mexican company. Pulsar made a decision to divest their tobacco business and invest in agricultural biotechnology leveraging their management expertise in agriculture. Subsequently, in addition to DNAP, Pulsar acquired a collection of vegetable seed companies under the umbrella of the Seminis Seed Company. Seminis is the world's largest development, production and marketing vegetable seed company. Their hybrids improve nutritional quality, increase yields, limit losses from pests and reduce the need for agrochemicals. In 2005, Seminis became a wholly owned subsidiary of Monsanto Company.

The DNA Plant Technology Corporation years expanded my skillsets and future horizons. Highlights were the introduction to marketing, negotiation of collaborative research, development and commercialization deals and the management of intellectual property on a collaborative basis with blue the chip law firms. This background provided me with the confidence to lead future startup ventures for exploration of plant based pharmaceutical discover

The Campbell Soup Company
The Blue-Chip Corporate World
1979-1981

Our lab phone at Ohio State University began ringing with consulting opportunities and in the late autumn an invitation was received to present a seminar at the Campbell Soup Company in Camden, New Jersey. This invitation was a follow-up from the recent visit of the Company's vice president for poultry research, who had participated in our weekly departmental seminar program and for which during autumn quarter the theme was corporate research. I remember at the time, his request to visit our laboratory and the graduate students and him mentioning that the Campbell Soup Company should be interested in our research programs. However, as much as I appreciated the seminar invitation, I was unable to accept because of the end of the quarter demands of examination grading, graduate student exams and research grant submissions.

Finally, an agreement was in place for a brief trip to the Campbell Soup Company (CSC) in Cinnaminson, NJ for a seminar presentation. I quickly, assembled a slide show and packed my luggage for the trip. Rapid Rover Van Services shuttled me from the Philadelphia International Airport to the Cherry Hill Inn. Bill Ramer, the Research Vice President of the Campbell Institute for Agricultural Research, invited me and members of the research team from the nearby the Pioneer Research Laboratory in Cinnaminson, N.J., to his home for a reception. Bill and I had previously met at scientific meetings and at the recent research colloquium entitled *Plant Cell and Tissue Culture: Principles and* Applications held at Ohio State University on 6-9 September 1977. After the reception, we dined at a Hanover Trails restaurant, the CSC restaurant chain. Bill and his team provided me with a comprehensive understanding of the company and the research and development goals. Bill had been a senior scientist at the USDA Beltsville research facility in Maryland prior to joining the CSC and was quite interested in moving the company into biotechnology research. The evening had been quite enjoyable and I appreciated the hospitality. Little did I realize what the following day had in store! My feelings were that Bill was appreciative of the meetings at Ohio State and wanted to thank me and possibly engage me as an advisor in the future. The company provided my travel, lodging and a thousand-dollar honorarium.

My seminar was scheduled for 9:00 A.M. the following morning at the Pioneer Research Laboratory in Cinnaminson, New Jersey. The Pioneer Research Laboratory research team and a few corporate vice presidents from Campbell Place Headquarters in Camden, NJ attended. The seminar session was followed by a stimulating question and answer session, and a tour of the facilities, and meetings with the senior research scientists. The Pioneer Research Laboratories conducted research related to basic research, development and commercialization of vegetable cultivars with improved processing characteristics. A nearby facility in Moorestown conducted research on advanced packaging and developed plastic soup containers used by CSC today. The Pioneer Research Laboratory Complex was situated on a beautiful campus in Cinnaminson, New Jersey consisting of three main research buildings, state-of-the-art laboratories, an electron microscopy facility, a tomato processing facility, a research greenhouse facility, two residential houses for the grounds keepers, miscellaneous storage sheds and a nearby 100-acre vegetable farm for breeding trials. The farm, which was about a fifteen-minute drive from the Pioneer Research Laboratory, also had several research buildings. It was interesting to note that the Pioneer Research Laboratory campus had been the former summer home for the founding family of the Campbell Soup Company, the Dorrance family. John T. Dorrance was Chairman of the Board at the time. The family owned over fifty percent of the company even though CSC was a publicly traded company.

Lunch was scheduled in Camden at the Campbell Place Corporate Headquarters with additional corporate leaders in marketing, product development, agricultural research and strategic planning. We ordered lunch using individual order cards and of course, I ordered the Campbell Soup Special of the Day and a sandwich. Food was served and I observed that the soup was solidified. I proceeded to eat the sandwich and the product development executive asked if I enjoyed the soup. I answered that I did and was waiting for the soup to cool. As we finished lunch, I covered the small soup bowl with my napkin to avoid any embarrassment. Lunch was followed by a meeting with Harold Shaub, CEO, and the vice president of human resources in the president's office suite. Much to my surprise, after the introductory niceties, Mr. Shaub offered me the Director of Research position for the Pioneer Research Laboratory, Cinnaminson, NJ, a division of the Campbell Institute of Agricultural Research, which included other laboratories in Arkansas, California, Maine, New Jersey and Ohio. My responsibility was to lead the development of an agricultural biotechnology research program. The employment package more than doubled my compensation and offered many perks including stock options. I was flabbergasted and requested two weeks to consider the offer. There was much to contemplate during the return trip to Columbus regarding my career, family, colleagues and obligations to my graduate students and colleagues.

The job offer was indeed a marvelous opportunity to leverage knowledge that had been gained over the past decade in my laboratory and around the world in plant biotechnology for enhancement of consumer products and food processing. Biotechnology, the new focus of the biological sciences was not a basic discipline, but rather represented a consolidation of disciplines, i.e., agronomy, cell culture, horticulture, plant biology, pathology, physiology, biochemistry, plant genetics and breeding, horticulture and molecular biology related to production of innovative goods and services.

On arriving home, I spoke with my son, Jeff, and Virginia, my former wife, about the opportunity. I invited Jeff to join me the following weekend in Philadelphia and before I knew it, we were off to Philadelphia. Snow and ice made the trip difficult. We lodged at the Holiday Inn on Market Street and visited the Campbell Place Corporate Headquarters, the Pioneer Research Laboratory in Cinnaminson, N.J., and enjoyed the environs of Philadelphia. We walked and talked about the future. Jeff was age 14 at the time, but quite mature for his age with many interests including acting, books, music, travel and track.

I remember, Jeff saying, "Dad, you know the opportunity would be good for both of us. Air tickets are inexpensive and I can visit you on weekends, during my school holidays and summer vacation." The salary increase made all things possible and sealed the deal between Jeff and me. Following the return trip home, Virginia and I negotiated an arrangement to allow Jeff to fly to Philadelphia for weekends and vacations.

The following week, I was busy with final examinations and grading, but managed to find time to talk with my graduate students about the opportunity. I promised to remain involved with their research programs and studies. Arrangements were made with the deans and departmental chairs in the Colleges of Agriculture and Biological Sciences for a seamless transition of the student's graduate programs. One of the students moved to CSC with me to complete her graduate studies because her husband had accepted a position at Hahnemann Medical School in Philadelphia. The chair of my department and the dean of the college requested that I remain at Ohio State University and offered a significant increase in compensation in a display of generosity that I greatly appreciated. I will always be indebted to Patrick Dugan, the dean, and Robert Pfister, the departmental chair for their considerate efforts on my behalf. The career disruption was painful but deep down, I knew that I had to accept the new challenge and move on.

January 1978 was the start of a new life for me as Director of the Pioneer Research Laboratory at the Campbell Soup Company. I took up temporary residence at the Cherry Hill Inn while waiting to close on a home in Haddonfield, New Jersey. I signed a contract to purchase a duplex in Haddonfield, NJ adjacent to Cherry Hill, NJ, but was not able to close because the banks were waiting for approval of the new financing interest rates. The higher interest rates for financing were approved two months later and a closing was scheduled. The Campbell Soup Company director position was going to provide an important experience in linking the research laboratory to the marketplace. The experiences of working at CENA and the University of Sao Paulo-ESALQ in Piracicaba, Sao Paulo, Brazil had provided me with important background in applied research, but industrial research added the dimension of commercialization, which was the final link between the laboratory and the end user.

I landed on the ground in Cinnaminson New Jersey running and developed an excellent rapport with Bill Ramer, Vice President of Research and the director and vice president of potato breeding and miscellaneous crops, Charlie Cunningham, a former university professor. Over the holidays, I worked on a biotechnology research plan that was tweaked by Dr. Bill Ramer, the group vice president at the Campbell Institute for Agricultural Research and Dr. Bud Denton, the Corporate Vice President for Research. We developed concise research and development goals and a budget for a five-year program. The proposal allowed recruitment of five Ph.D. scientists with appropriate technical support to augment the research team at the Pioneer Research Laboratory. The CSC graphics unit was a superb creative team. The director of the CSC graphics unit provided invaluable assistance in preparation of the biotechnology research program slides for the upcoming research program presentation about providing a biotechnology focus for the Pioneer Research Laboratory. I had been advised to limit the presentation to fifteen minutes, which meant ten minutes for slides and five minutes for discussion. I rehearsed the presentation with Bill Ramer and Bud Denton several times prior to the meeting with Mr. Shaub.

The meeting in Mr. Shaub's office was interesting. All, seemed to be going well, until five minutes into my presentation, Mr. Shaub pulled out his car keys and began jiggling them. I said, "Mr. Shaub, please allow me to show the final slide. Afterwards, he responded, "Dr. Sharp, please don't ever do this again! I'm a busy man and time is of the essence to me. Please in the future limit presentations to five minutes! I hired you for your expertise. All you need to provide me is a brief plan and budget. Moreover, all letters and memos to this office should be limited to one paragraph or, better yet, one sentence. Do you understand?" "Yes, Mr. Shaub, I will comply. Thank you." This was my CSC baptism, but there was much more to come. Mr. Shaub approved the biotechnology research program and budget for the Pioneer Research Laboratory, which allowed me to begin implementation of the research plan and organization of the research team.

Meetings were scheduled with the plant breeders to better understand their programs and the important traits being bred into the CSC processing vegetables for the U.S. and overseas field production operations. Our strategy was to use the cell biology tool of Somaclonal variation, which involved test tube culturing tissues from commercial processing vegetable cultivars, for the purpose, of, inciting genetic variation and subsequently selecting genetically modified cultivars of with improved processing traits from the field. The idea at the time was to marry the Somaclonal variation process with conventional breeding programs to shorten the time lines for releasing improved commercial vegetable cultivars. Conventional breeding usually required seven to eight years for development of new processing cultivars.

The next steps required the development of a collaborative relationship with the plant breeders in which the outcomes of the biotech program could be integrated. This required additional meetings at our Cinnaminson headquarters and at Campbell Place Headquarters in Camden over lunch and holed up in conference rooms. After receiving a greenlight, we immediately installed tissue culture growing racks in the laboratories and began to isolate and establish cell cultures from leaf explants from the CSC commercial tomato cultivars along with carrot. Our goal was to have seed from greenhouse grown tissue culture-derived tomatoes for field trials in the summer of 1979.

David Evans a faculty member at SUNY Binghamton with a Ph.D. in genetics at Ohio State University joined the Pioneer Research Laboratory team. In addition, we recruited a first-rate Ph.D. molecular biology fungal geneticist from Ohio State to head a program on improvement of cultivated mushrooms.

One morning, a memorandum was circulated from corporate headquarters that a hiring freeze would immediately be implemented and only critical hires approved by the office of the president could be approved. At once, I knew that I must spring into action and requested permission to engage graduate students, postdoctoral fellows and visiting scientists to enable us to reach a full research team complement without using permanent positions. Approval was granted and within six months two world class plant scientists joined the company. Visiting scientists from Italy and Venezuela were appointed along with graduate students from Ohio State University and Rutgers University.

Our research team was highly motivated and worked late and weekends. As usual, I embraced socialization activities. Dave Evans home was in shouting distance for basketball pick-up games, board games, Super Bowl parties during the week with food and drinks. Seminar speakers were often hosted at my home in Haddonfield along with buffet dinners and drinks in Philadelphia. These activities were important to the bonding of our research and business teams.

Another bomb was dropped within a few months into my assumption of the research directorship at CSC. The group vice president was departing the company for unknown reasons and would no longer be allowed on the premises. Shortly afterwards, I ran into Bill Ramer at the Philadelphia International Airport on his way to St. Louis to interview for an executive position with Ralston Purina to which he was later appointed. He requested that we return his personal books and files in storage at the Pioneer Research Laboratory. Understanding the value of personal research papers and books to the career of a research scientist, we immediately complied with his wishes.

After the announcement of the departure of Bill Ramer, my immediate report, I made an appointment with the CEO, Mr. Shaub, to ask if he would like me to submit my resignation. He requested that I remain with the company and report to him until the research operation reorganization was completed. I subsequently reported to Dr. Bud Denton and very soon afterwards to Dr. Charles Duncan, a former microbiology professor from the University of Wisconsin. We had an immediate rapport and the reporting arrangement was superb. We were always on the same wavelength.

Much excitement was created during the 1979 field trials demonstrating Somaclonal Variation for improving processing traits. The Vice President of Strategic Planning, Jim Imshoff and his team took a special interest in our work and recommended that strategic plans be devised for our research and development programs. This was an important experience for me in sharpening my business skill sets. The bean, carrot and mushroom programs were likewise taking shape with early successes. CSC acquired Lexington Gardens and soon we had improvement programs in place for herbs, spices and ornamental plants. The link to the strategic planning group kept us at the forefront of the CSC business aspirations.

Following Harold Shaub's acquisition of the Domsea Farms Inc., a sea farming, sea ranching and aquaculture operation in Seattle, Jon Lindbergh, the research vice president and son of Charles Lindbergh visited the Pioneer Research Laboratory to discuss possible collaborative research. He was clearly a world class underwater explorer and aquaculture pioneer who aspired to feed the world's people by harvesting the bounty of the oceans. He followed in the footsteps of his famous aviator father. Our research team enjoyed meeting Jon Lindbergh and developing a better understanding of the Domsea Farms Inc. research, development and production programs. The CSC Hanover Trails Restaurant chain began offering salmon from the Domsea Farms Inc. operations. Jon Lindbergh was enthusiastic about our work and said,

"Rod, you are a pioneer much like my father in ushering in new technology for the betterment of humankind. Your new approaches to the development of improved plant cultivars will no doubt be important to the world food challenges."

In 1980, Gordon McGovern, former president of Pepperidge Farms, the Campbell Soup Company subsidiary, succeeded Harold Shaub as the new President and CEO of the Campbell Soup Company. He was quite interested in our work, as were several BOD (board of director) members, including Dr. Sterling Wortman, President of the Rockefeller Foundation, who met with our research team on a regular basis and fine-tuned our research programs. Sterling Wortman (1923-1981) was an eminent agricultural research scientist who made significant contributions to world food production.

Gordon McGovern visited quite often and promoted fresh market opportunities that built on the Farm Fresh Mushroom Brand, such as farm fresh tomatoes, ready-to-eat pastas and salads. The pioneer Research Laboratory was green lighted to engage in research and development programs geared to the development of value-added fresh market products, including tomatoes and possibly Shitake mushrooms, other exotic mushroom cultivars, and strawberries. We scoped out a worldwide study of successful hydroponic operations in Holland, Japan, U.S. and the U.K. This was based on our contacts in Holland and the U.K. and collaborative relationships between the agricultural engineering department at Ohio State University and Professor Yasuyuki Yamada, Kyoto University. In the U.S., we relied on Merle Jensen and Paul Hodges, leading horticulturists and engineers at the University of Arizona and the Disney Epcot Land Pavilion. Our team worked with the engineering and strategic planning groups to development of an experimental hydroponic tomato production feasibility program.

The CSC experience along with the research background gained during the years at USP-ESALQ – School of Agronomy in Piracicaba provide me with the applied research and commercialization for leading a world class startup agriculture biotechnology company in collaboration with the Campbell Soup Company.

The Ohio State University 1969-1979

The Ohio State University's roots go back to 1870, when the Ohio General Assembly established the Ohio Agricultural and Mechanical College. The new college was made possible through the provisions of the Land-Grant Act, signed by President Lincoln on July 2, 1862. This legislation revolutionized the nation's approach to higher education, bringing a college degree within reach of all high school graduates. The Ohio State University's main Columbus campus is one of America's largest and most comprehensive. More than 56,000 students select from 170 undergraduate majors and more than 250 graduate and professional degree programs. As Ohio's best and one of the nation's top-20 public universities, Ohio State is further recognized by a top-rated academic medical center and a premier cancer hospital and research center[20].

Following the mass exodus of senior faculty from the Department of Biology at Western Reserve University (Now Case Western Reserve

---
20 Ohio State University History, Retrieved August 5, 2013 from http://www.osu.edu/news/history.php

University), an opportunity surfaced at The Ohio State University for appointment to an unconventional lectureship. The process began when at the request of the department chair, my wife and I represent Western Reserve University an open house at the Ohio State University College of Agriculture Research and Development Center in Wooster, Ohio. We were briefly introduced to the dean and associate dean of the newly formed College of Biological Sciences in Columbus. Dr. Don Dougall, the associate dean, had formerly been a research scientist at the Ohio Research and Development Center in Wooster Ohio, a division of the College of Agriculture at The Ohio State University, where he conducted plant biochemical research with plant cell cultures. We knew one another through our research papers and presentations at scientific conferences. The week after the open house, a secretary phoned me to schedule a visit to Ohio State to meet with the two senior administrators at the College of Biological Sciences.

The meeting and tour of facilities was impressive and, much to my surprise, I was offered a position as a lecturer beginning January of 1969 in the Faculty of Microbial and Cellular Biology of the College of Biological Sciences. The employment offer was a bit confusing because during the visit with the chair and a group of departmental faculty members, I was told that for budgetary reasons the department expected to make no additional faculty appointments in the current academic year. The verbal job description was to develop a plant based cell biology research program, participate in a course in general cell biology for upper division and graduate students and eventually develop an upper division advanced course in cell biology. Furthermore, I was told that the following autumn my appointment was to be converted into a tenure track assistant professorship with appointment to the graduate faculty.

The faculty at the time of my appointment was top heavy with tenured professors and had no tenure track assistant professors. In spite of the confusion in regard to the academic appointment, I was confident that I could win the support of the faculty because of the commonality of microbiology and plant cell biology research in employing *in vitro* approaches to the study of cellular genetics, physiology and development and the department's responsibility for teaching courses in general cellular biology. Two of the microbiology faculty members teaching general cellular biology had research expertise in protozoology and a third member with expertise in plant cell biology and biochemistry.

The laboratory space assigned to me was on loan from the Botany and Plant Pathology departments because of the lack of space in Edith Cockins Hall – Headquarters for the Faculty of Microbial and Cellular Biology. The laboratory space was shared with Donald Dougall, the Associate Dean of the College of Biological Sciences, and a faculty member of the Faculty of Microbial and Cellular Biology. The laboratory consisted of two interconnected laboratory spaces, an office, aseptic transfer room, and carrels for the graduate students. Autoclave rooms, growth chambers and a greenhouse complex were located nearby. Don Dougall had three graduate students and a technician at the time, including two students from Brazil, a student from Maine and a talented technician with credentials from a laboratory technical school in the U.K. Dr. Dougall introduced the team and an instant repertoire was established. The timing was fortuitous in that publication of three of my research papers in the Journal of Plant Physiology during the next two months gave me credibility. My teaching responsibilities didn't commence until the following autumn, providing me time to prepare my lectures. I had the time to meet the departmental and neighboring faculty in the Botany and Zoology Building and to initiate a research program.

I enjoyed a spacious faculty office adjacent to the two connected laboratory spaces that had been occupied by Don Dougall prior to his appointment to the deanship. Case Western Reserve University allowed me to borrow some key pieces of equipment that enabled me to continue my ongoing research program. In addition to this, the departmental chair gave me permission to continue my collaboration relationship with the Argonne National Laboratory. Quickly, I immediately set to writing research proposals and submitting grants applications. Meeting members of the Faculty of Microbial and Cellular Biology was somewhat challenging because of my unconventional appointment. Nevertheless, meetings were scheduled with each faculty member. I also arranged to monitor the winter quarter's course in general cellular biology for which I would assume responsibility in the autumn quarter.

The chaos of departmental reorganization worked to my advantage. The College of Biological Sciences was undergoing a revolutionary change in which the departmental administrative units were replaced by faculties under the direction of faculty administrators. All administrative fiscal responsibilities were thereafter assumed by the college administration. The former Department of Microbiology had evolved into the Faculty of Microbial and Cellular Biology. After my meetings with the faculty, the opportunities for collaboration with fellow faculty became evident.

Dr. Julius Kreier, a professor and expert in pathogenic protozoology with doctorates in veterinary medicine and immunology and originally appointed to the College of Veterinary Medicine, transferred his appointment and laboratory to the Faculty of Microbial and Cellular Biology. Dr. Kreier reached out to me and organized lunch meetings with fellow faculty members and invited me to participate in organizing the departmental weekly seminar program. He administered a large research operation with a global population of graduate students and postdoctoral fellows. He served as my mentor for recruitment of graduate students, grant writing, publications, committee work, organizing colloquium/symposium and development of a monograph series.

In the spring quarter, I was invited to present a research seminar to faculty and students. Knowing that a seminar was usually required of candidates for university academic appointments during the recruitment process, I was quite nervous. Apparently, the lecture was well received because shortly thereafter, the departmental chair informed me that I would be reappointed to a tenure track assistant professor position, which would allow me to be considered for a tenured appointment. Thus, began a probationary period that could eventually lead to a vote for appointment to a tenured associate professor and thereafter professor. Tenure track assistant professors are expected to hit the ground running and demonstrate scholarship with publications in referred journals. Publication establishes the reputation of a scholar in his or her chosen field. The dissemination of knowledge through publications and teaching is the primary basis of national and international recognition and distinguishes the research university. Publication is a gauge that determines career mobility, national and international recognition. During the tenure approval process, an academician's record is evaluated by departmental senior faculty and panels of national and international experts in the field of specialization. The quality of the original research is judged based on originality, publication in leading journals and science index rankings. Other important factors include successful grantsmanship, graduate program participation, editorial review, and teaching. Congeniality and collaboration with senior academicians in the academic unit and the field are also important. Recently, intellectual property, patents and collaboration with the private sector have been included in the tenure evaluations.

The graduate students, Donald Dougall and I participated in weekly collaborative research meetings in which we reviewed our research programs and relevant journal papers. Don and I developed a few collaborative projects that proceeded well and we often traveled together to the annual research conferences and presented papers. The three graduate students were talented. Ruy Caldas was from a rural town in the state of Minas Gerias situated in the interior of Brazil and Henrique Amorim resided in the city of Piracicaba of the state of Sao Paulo. Ruy and Henrique graduated respectively from Versosa University and the University of Sao Paulo – ESALQ Campus both premiere research universities. Ruy's family had an agricultural background while Henrique's father was a medical doctor and his father and uncles were businessmen involved in a number of agriculture ventures. Harry Sommer, a graduate of the University of Maine delayed graduate school until fulfillment of his ROTC military obligation. He had been assigned to a biological warfare unit with the U.S. Army that he couldn't discuss because of secrecy issues. All three graduate students were passionate about their studies and research. Don had an invitation to conduct collaborative research in Australia in the summer months and departed at the end of spring quarter.

My wife, son and I held frequent social events at our home on Highland Street, a skip and jump from our research laboratories in the B & Z Building. And weekend social events at popular diggs in the German Village, e.g. Max and Irma's and the Ratskeller. Students and postdoctoral fellows were invited to attend all fireside social events for visiting seminar speakers. Colleague Julius Kreier and family held firesides often at their Worthington home for faculty, visiting scientists, postdoctoral fellows and graduate students. Later following the separation from my wife, my grandmother and I hosted firesides often. She was among the most informed humans on the planet.

The summer was spent in the laboratory, writing papers for scientific meetings and preparing lectures for autumn semester. The autumn cell biology course included morning lectures and four afternoon teaching laboratory sections, each of which accommodated 25 students. The teaching laboratory was equipped with state-of-the-art lab benches, microscopes, balances, spectrophotometers, and accessory equipment. My wife and son accompanied me to conferences at which I presented research papers and that afforded opportunity for all of us to travel together.

Summer passed quickly. I soon was standing in a lecture hall, a bit overwhelmed, by the expectant faces of 100 upper division undergraduates and first year graduate students. The routine included daily lectures scheduled each morning at 8:00 A.M., afternoon teaching laboratory sessions, graduate student laboratory assistant meetings, student meetings and lecture preparation each evening. Tom Byers and Don Dougall were both helpful to me during the orientation period, as I had never been an instructor. My graduate school and postdoctoral fellowship activities had been limited to laboratory research funded by fellowships with no teaching requirement.

The Microbiology Graduate Program

I was fortunate to have served on the graduate committees of Dr. Donald Dougall's three graduate students along with some of the students from the laboratory of Dr. Julius Kreier. This experience prepared me for acceptance of my first graduate students. I learned that not only should candidates for graduate school be academically qualified, but must possess a passion for conducting basic research and contributing to the body of scientific knowledge.

Rosa Raskin, a young attractive student with an exceptional academic background in the biological sciences, was my first graduate student. She had the advantages and disadvantages of working with a young assistant professor recently completing his Ph.D. degree and a postdoctoral fellowship. Shortly thereafter, John Peters, an honors student from Otterbein College in Westerville, Ohio joined the laboratory. John and Rosa were in the process of learning how to become effective independent research investigators while I was learning how to become an effective mentor. It is essential to teach graduate students with the importance of reading the scientific literature, observation, experimental design, data collection, analysis, and the drafting of scientific communications and manuscripts. Communication of discoveries through mass media was also vital. I always emphasized the importance of linking the laboratory bench to the pages of *The New York Times* and *Wall Street Journal*.

The important question is how laboratory research results might be translated into the development of products or services for the betterment of humankind. The goal is for graduate student to become independent and productive scholars and join the ranks of the professor's colleagues. I always followed the pattern set by my graduate school mentors, in allowing graduate students flexibility in determining their own research program within the guidelines of the funding agencies which dictate the parameters of a particular research program.

The years at Ohio State University were important to the development of a platform for launching my subsequent corporate career. I developed a friendship with Dr. Clyde Allison, a senior faculty member from the Department of Plant Pathology, who had an office and laboratory adjacent to mine. He was an expert in tropical plant pathology research and a veteran of global collaborations, particularly Brazil. He expressed interest in our laboratory's plant cellular research programs and suggested contacting a Brazilian scientist working in the field of coffee genetics. At the time, Coffee Rust, a fungal disease, was becoming a threat to coffee growing regions in the northern part of South America and quickly moving southward. He encouraged me to apply for a Fulbright-Hays Fellowship for the genetic improvement of coffee using plant tissue culture technology. Further encouragement came from Henrique Amorim and Ruy Caldas, the Brazilian graduate students.

I applied for a fellowship and, during the last week of May, I was surprised to receive a telegram from Washington D.C. stating that I was one of two Fulbright-Hays Fellowship Awardees selected for the Brazil program and that I should report to Washington D.C. for participation in a three-day orientation program. The recently appointed chair of my faculty, Patrick Dugan, approved my acceptance of the fellowship. Dr. Dugan told me that although I was a recent hire, collaboration with the University of Sao Paulo and the Brazilian Nuclear Energy Commission would provide an important opportunity for the department. I was pleased by Dr. Dugan's forward thinking and for the opportunity for both the department and my career. About the same time, a new dean of the College of Biological Sciences was appointed who issued a mandate to regroup the various faculties into departments. The Faculty of Microbial and Cellular Biology was renamed the Department of Microbiology with a chair responsible for undergraduate education, faculty teaching responsibilities and budgetary matters.

Fulbright-Hays Brazil

My Grandmother Mary Garrison who invited me to reside at her home in Clintonville following separation from my wife accompanied me on my first visit to Brazil in mid-June. We were greeted at the Viracorpos Airport, by Dr. Otto J. Crocomo, who at the time was the research coordinator of the Plant Biochemistry Sector of CENA (Center for Nuclear Energy in Agriculture), A National Atomic Energy Commission Laboratory situated on the University of Sao Paulo ESALQ Campus in Piracicaba, S.P. We travelled to Piracicaba from the airport for an extraordinary welcome dinner hosted by Otto, Diva Crocomo and family. Our drive to Piracicaba provided a firsthand look at the Sao Paulo environs, the heart of the city and Piracicaba, which is a beautiful city located in the Brazilian state of Sao Paulo. The warm reception and spectacular setting immediately made us feel at home with the Crocomo family.

My appointment was at Centro de Energia Nuclear na Agricultura (CENA) which is situated on the ESALQ Campus of the University of Sao Paulo in Piracicaba although in subsequent years my appointments at CENA were held jointly with ESALQ and the Agronomic Institute in Campinas, Sao Paulo. CENA was established by a group of ESALQ faculty members who envisioned the potential agricultural and environmental applications for nuclear techniques. Studies with radioisotopes and radiation were conducted by these faculty in collaboration with other research centers, e.g., IEA, currently IPEN) and USP Units after 1955[21].

The Fulbright-Hays Fellowship Grantee Award inaugurated a forty-five-year research collaboration and friendship with Dr. Otto Crocomo and the University of Sao Paulo. I must say that many others were important to the melding of my relationship with Dr. Otto J. Crocomo including Drs. Henrique Amorim and Ruy Caldas, both graduate students in my laboratory at Ohio State University who returned to Brazil to assume professorship positions at the University of Sao Paulo ESALQ Campus in Piracicaba and the University of Brasilia in Brasilia. Dr. Amorim led successful programs in the improvement of consumer based coffee quality and subsequently pioneered the Brazilian ethanol program with the founding of Fermentech S.A. Today as CEO of Fermentech, he has developed a global technology company consumer based products. Henrique Amorim possessed excellent business skill sets and advised me on numerous occasions on important business decisions.

Under Dr. Crocomo's direction, we equipped the plant cell culture laboratory and developed collaborative initiatives with colleagues at the University of Sao Paulo and other leading Brazilian research laboratories. Ruy Caldas, Otto Crocomo and I constructed cell culture transfer facilities because laminar flow hoods were not yet standard laboratory equipment. The carpentry skills developed from Soap Box Derby days and constructing tissue culture transfer chambers with my

---

21 CENA History Retrieved August 5, 2013 from http://www.iaea.org/Publications/Magazines/Bulletin/Bull180su/18005493338su.pdf

father came in handy. We immediately launched a program developing cell cultures for the important cultivars of tropical crops with special interest in citrus, cocoa, coffee, beans, palm, and sugarcane. These programs were initiated in collaboration with geneticists and plant breeders at the University of Sao Paulo/ESALQ Campus and the Institute of Agronomy in Campinas, Sao Paulo. Social events at the home of Dr. Otto Crocomo, wife and family along with frequent evening drinks and dinner at Café Flamboyant on the Piracicaba River, an unpretentious restaurant and bar attracting a diverse cliental ranging among professors, students, medical doctors, politicians and local fishermen. This led to phenomenal conversations. Henrique Amorim, colleague and friend from Ohio State, he and family often participated in these events. These social events were important in cementing collaborative relationships with the scientists affiliated with CENA and the adjacent university academic departments in biology, chemistry, forestry and genetics.

A few words need to be mentioned about the importance of the unique Brazilian family culture in building deep rooted lifelong collaborations and friendships. Family celebrations and social club events are all inclusive with the incorporation of children, grandparents, extended family, friends and business colleagues with activities geared to all ages. I experienced this life changing culture during all my collaborative relationships across Brazil. The Brazilian family culture influenced my understanding about the importance of the socialization process in the bounding of collaborative research and business teams. The family culture was reinforced during my collaborations with academicians in Campinas, SP, Brasilia, S.P. Itabuna, Salvador, and Rio de Janeiro.

The laboratory work proceeded extremely well. Otto and I developed a number of research projects which included scientists, undergraduate/graduate research scholars and submitted a two-year training course proposal to the Organization of American States beginning in the summer of 1972. We cemented plans for continuing our collaboration after my return to Ohio State University. I confess, very happily, that my eagerness to apply plant tissue culture to agricultural problems was encouraged and sharpened during the years at CENA and the University of Sao Paulo ESALQ Campus. I was among the fortunate individuals to have the opportunity to travel abroad and forge lifelong collaborative relationships. I learned that successful research and teaching programs benefited from collaboration with colleagues at home and abroad. I have often discussed with Drs. Otto Crocomo and colleague and friend Henrique Amorim about the value of the US/Brazilian collaboration in regard to globalization and development of new opportunities for our colleagues and students.

On my return to Ohio State in November, I became engaged with my graduate students and in the team teaching approach to the general cellular biology course with daily lectures and afternoon student laboratory sessions. The course was quite popular with students from a number of colleges because of growing interest in the advances of cell biology and the importance to technology to multiple disciplines. My autumn lectures were delivered during November and December in the winter quarter. I assumed administrative responsibilities for the course and delivered about two-thirds of the lectures. I slowly improved my classroom m lecture delivery performance.

In the spring quarter, I organized an advanced course on current topics in cell differentiation based on the mitotic cell cycle and differentiation, cancer, and animal and plant embryogenesis. I also had the good fortune to co-chair with Julius Kreier, the weekly departmental seminar series, the largest such series on campus with an enrollment of over 150 students. The seminar series evolved into a one-hour course and included lectures by world class scientists in various fields of cellular and microbiology. Julius and I were successful in attracting funds from major granting agencies and foundations for providing honoraria, lodging, and travel funds for visiting scientists. We invited students from the department and those in our classes to participate in evening fireside chats. Both faculty and students found these sessions to be most worthwhile. My cell differentiation course for upper division undergraduate and graduate students was taught at 8:00 A.M. (Monday thru Friday). Students were required to write research papers and attend the late afternoon and evening fireside chats for the visiting guest lecturers. The teaching assistant and I ordered coffee, tea, water, donuts and bagels for the students each morning, a custom that improved the quality of life for all as well as classroom participation.

In 1974, a second advanced course was added entitled, "Advances in Plant Cell Culture and Differentiation," which included a laboratory session. The course drew a sizable audience of students from a number of colleges. The two advanced courses provided ideas for updating a number of the lectures contributed in the general cellular biology course and for the introduction of new laboratory exercises. These advances gave me more confidence regarding my professional abilities.

In the summer of 1972, Dr. Crocomo, Dr. Linda Caldas, a recently minted Ph.D. from Ohio State University, and I, conducted a four-week training course in plant cell culture sponsored by the Organization of American States for about 30 students throughout the Americas. We authored and published a handbook for the students. Morning, noon and night, we taught classes, held laboratory sessions, supervised student research projects, and led seminars and informal discussions on the potential of cell culture for basic and applied research. Two of the students from this training course were selected for participation in a two-year research fellowship program. Maro Sondahl, the top performing student, accepted an offer to complete the Ph.D. degree in my laboratory at Ohio State University and continue to pursue the cellular genetics research program that he initiated at the Agronomic Institute, where he held the position of research associate.

About the same time Dr. Henrique Amorim and his wife Vera Amorim from the University of Sao Paulo and Dr. Vasantha Padmanaban, a postdoctoral fellow from India joined our laboratory as visiting faculty members. A number of superb graduate students joined our research team including Antonio Goncalves, Willie Loh, Sharon Maraffa, Marinez Molina, Bob Reisner, Wei Shen, and Karen Templeton. The students all launched successful careers in academia, medicine and industry. They all became leaders in their respective fields.

The visits to Brazil continued throughout 1972, 1993, 1974, 1975 and 1976. Grant support was provided by the Brazilian Nuclear Energy Foundation. Otto Crocomo and I generated a number of refereed journal papers and several books. The CENA laboratory at USP-ESALQ resulted in the education of a number of scientists from Brazil and the Americas who assumed senior positions in academia, government research laboratories and industry. Our collaboration expanded and included exchanges of a number of scientists from one another's institutions.

In 1974, the faculty and university promoted me to the level of associate professor with tenure. The process of promotion was becoming quite rigorous requiring extensive documentation that included prospectuses of courses taught, student evaluations, updated *curriculum vitae*, letters of recommendation from colleagues at leading U.S. research universities and institutes and recommendations from scholars at leading U.S. and foreign research universities and institutes and science citation index data on publications. Science citation index searches provided information on the significance of scientific papers by documenting the number of times the paper was cited in the scientific literature. Appointment to tenure provided a faculty member with more involvement in decision-making at the departmental and university levels, because many important departmental and university wide committees was restricted to tenured faculty members.

Received an invitation from the organizing committee of the twelfth International Botanical Congress, Leningrad, July 1975 for participation and chairing one of the major sessions. The invitation resulted from a friendship with colleague Professor Raisa Butenko, Director of the world esteemed Moscow Komarov Botanical Institute. This was a remarkable life moment in which two of my graduate students accompanied me. Professor Butenko invited me to attend a celebrity banquet in which I represented the United States scientific community along with colleagues from other countries of the world including dignitaries for the Russian Academy of Sciences. Each international guest was asked to recite a poem and sing a song representative of their country followed by a toasting of Vodka shots. As the evening progressed, I nervously wondered how I would manage to chair my session scheduled for the following morning? I poured the contents of the shot glass on the floor using the camouflage of a napkin covering my mouth and concluded the evening in a sober state. The next challenge was the late-night difficulty in haling a taxi. A group of four young Russian men and women offered to share their taxi and return me to the hotel. They were fluent in English and requested information about my purpose for traveling to Leningrad and my country of origin? I provided answers and inquired about their backgrounds which were in economics and engineering. The young woman challenged me about the problems facing the United States and stated that she would never travel there. My answer was, Yes, we have our share of challenges as do all countries. I mentioned that I enjoyed the beauty of Leningrad and the people.

I offered to settle the fare after arriving at the hotel but they intervened and picked up the fare. The four of them exited the taxi and gave me hugs and we said our goodbyes before they departed to their destination. Always interesting to mingle with the local people.

In September 1977, an opportunity occurred for collaboration with three other faculty members at Ohio State University from the departments of botany, genetics and plant pathology to organize an international colloquium entitled "Plant Cell Culture – Principles and Applications." David Evans and Maro Sondahl, Ph.D. candidates at Ohio State at the time and my Brazilian colleagues contributed to the success of the colloquium. The colloquium was financed by corporate donors and major research foundations and attended by 350 scientists from around the world. It became clear that plant cell culture had come of age and would become one of the cornerstones of the age of biotechnology. Although, I was unable to visit Brazil in 1977 because of the colloquium, the Brazilian Nuclear Energy Commission nevertheless paid my summer stipend, which was crucial to my financial situation at the time. The outcomes of the colloquium were publication of the proceedings, academic promotion, publication of a monograph series and a career in the private sector.

1977 was a surprising year with the chair of the department requesting that I submit credentials for consideration for promotion to full professor. Shortly thereafter, our laboratory research team moved to the top floor of the biological sciences tower in one of the three laboratory suites designated for Nobel Prize Laureates in the design of the building. The Department of Microbiology had a distinguished faculty but lack of funding prevented recruitment of the

Nobel Laureates. Our research team was overjoyed with the new laboratory facilities and quickly resumed our research activities.

I will always be indebted to the faculty, administrative leadership, students, alumni and stakeholders of The Ohio State University for providing me with the opportunity to launch a career in cell biology leading to my leadership in advancing the biotechnology industry.

Case Western Reserve University 1967-1969

Graduate school was followed by a post-doctoral fellowship at Case Western University from 1967-1969. Here I continued to study the regulation of plant tumor development and growth. Western Reserve College was founded in Hudson, Ohio, in 1826, about 30 miles southeast of where the campus stands today. In 1882, the college moved to "uptown" Cleveland and assumed the name Western Reserve University. The merger of the Case Institute of Technology during 1967 created a leading institution for academics and research, as well as one the nation's top-ranked universities[22].

My time at the university was especially opportune because of the world-class faculty in the Department of Biology and the Developmental Biology Center. Dr. Howard Schneiderman, an eminent developmental biologist, academician, and university administrator, provided leadership for a multimillion dollar grant from the Ford Foundation to attract leading scientists in the biological Sciences to Western Reserve University. Dr. Schneiderman's proposal to the Ford Foundation provided the blueprint for the eventual merger of Western Reserve University and the Case Institute of Technology. The scientists recruited included Roger Bidwell, Douglas Davidson, Boris and Harriett Ephrusi, Michael Locke, Bodil Schmidt-Nielsen, Clifford Slayman and Carolyn Slayman. Howard Schneiderman invited me to attend his laboratory's weekly insect developmental research meetings broadened my background in cellular and developmental biology. The laboratory investigations focused on silkworm and *Drosophila* developmental genetics.

---

22 Information Retrieved from http://ech.case.edu/cgi/article.pl?id=CWRU

My approach to understanding the plant tumor problem was influenced by two faculty members with different approaches to development: Dr. R.G.S. Bidwell, a plant physiologist, and Dr. Douglas Davidson, a cytogeneticist and developmental biologist. My interaction with them reinforced the importance of collaboration and continued learning. During this time, I developed expertise in thin layer chromatography and deeper understanding cell genetics and plant physiology. Among the highlights was the visit of Ruth Sager, a leading research scientist from Hunter College in the field of organelle genetics. She delivered a lecture series based on her course in organelle genetics at Hunter College. Cell biology lectures by Dr. Douglas Davison also were memorable. He was a superb lecturer and mentor. In addition to being eminent biologists, and prolific contributors to the scientific literature, Roger Bidwell and Douglas Davidson entertained many other diverse interests. Roger Bidwell was a master at Bridge, collected antique automobiles, played both the harpsichord and piano, and participated in several musical groups. Douglas Davidson appeared on the London stage with Maggie Smith during his graduate school days at Oxford, collected prints and organized a print group for collectors at Western Reserve. Lunch hours were spent at bridge tables throughout the laboratories. Graduate students, postdoctoral fellows and newly appointed faculty members were required to participate with the tenured faculty. Our lunches were ordered from a local delicatessen and consisted of bagels, cream cheese and lox. Roger Bidwell told us that playing bridge was an exercise in mental gymnastics important for improving our scientific thought process.

In 1969, the institutional grants and Ford Foundation grants were not renewed precipitating the departure of the best scientists. Howard Schneiderman's went to the University of California at Irvine to head the Department of Cellular and Developmental Biology to become the 3rd Dean of the School of Biological Sciences. Roger Bidwell moved to Queens University, Douglas Davidson to McMaster University and others assumed academic positions in Europe. I was offered a lectureship in the Department of Microbiology at the Ohio State University in Columbus.

Rutgers University
1964-1967

The institution was chartered in 1766 as Queen's College, Rutgers is the nation's eighth oldest institution of higher learning and has a centuries-old tradition of rising to the challenges of each new generation. Soon after opening in New Brunswick in 1771 with one instructor and a handful of students, the college was caught up in the struggle for independence.

During the war, classes were suspended on several occasions as students, faculty, and alumni joined the fight for freedom. That revolutionary legacy is preserved today in the university's name in 1825, Queen's College became Rutgers College to honor trustee and Revolutionary War Veteran Colonel Henry Rutgers. Rutgers is a leading national public research with more than 56,800 students from the 50 states and 125 countries including 42,300 undergraduates and 14,500 graduate students and more than 13,000 faculty and staff[23].

In the autumn of 1964, I entered graduate school at Rutgers University with a NASA pre-doctoral fellowship under the mentorship of Dr. James E. Gunckel. Jim was born and raised in Dayton, Ohio, graduated from Miami University, Oxford, Ohio, in 1938 and received his doctorate from Harvard in 1946, where he studied under Dr. Ralph Wetmore. He did his postdoctoral research with Dr. Kenneth V. Thimann.

At Rutgers, for many years, Dr. Gunckel chaired what was then called the Botany Department and did pioneering work in two important areas of study: tissue culture (plant cloning) and radiation biology, where he conducted benchmark studies on the effect of radiation on a variety of plant species. A prolific publisher of scientific articles, he presided at many national and international botanical meetings served as the translating editor of the seminal German botanical text, *General Botany* by Wilhelm Nultsch edited the textbook, *Current Topics in Plant Science*. A former president of the Torrey Botanical Society, the oldest botanical society in America, he also served many years as editor of *The Bulletin of the Torrey Botanical Society*, a refereed botanical journal.

---

23 Rutgers University History Retrieved from http://www.rutgers.edu/about-rutgers/rutgers-history

In 1959 having been awarded a Waksman Foundation Fellowship, he pursued meristem culture (plant tissue cloning) research at Station Centrale de Physiologic Vegetate, Versailles, France, under the tutelage of Dr. Georges Morel. His unequaled knowledge of radiation biology, much of it gained through his many summers of research in collaboration with Dr. Arnold Sparrow at the Brookhaven National Laboratory, led to his being called upon to provide expert testimony in a legal case pertaining to the Three Mile Island nuclear power plant accident.

Dr. Gunckel, my mentor, who became a lifelong friend, believed in the importance of cell culture technology as a tool for unraveling the mysteries of plant development. At Rutgers University, I continued the NASA-related work and investigations on the developmental physiology of plant tumors. During these graduate school years, I was privileged to know Armin Braun at Rockefeller University and meet with him often. He was an invaluable resource and the friendship with him continued during my professional career.

My classes at Rutgers provided an understanding of cellular and developmental biology. The study of organelle genetics was in its infancy. Dr. Charlotte Avers offered a graduate lecture and laboratory course in organelle genetics that significantly broadened my knowledge of cell biology. Another important course in advanced plant physiology that involved the isolation and study of organelles was taught by Dr. Carl Price. Dr. Gunckel and his colleagues nurtured a most unique environment for graduate students to interact with faculty and students in journal clubs, departmental seminars, and meetings with Dr. Bill Jacobs, a professor at Princeton University, and his research team. Dr. Jacobs had been a graduate school colleague of Dr. Gunckel at Harvard. In addition, Dr. Gunckel service as president of the Torrey Botanical Society, the oldest botanical society in the Americas. The Torrey Botanical Society was founded in the 1860s by John Torrey. The Society promotes the exploration and study of plant life, with particular emphasis on the flora of New York City and metro areas and until 1997 published the Torrey Botanical Bulletin. The Society was celebrating a 200-year anniversary and organized monthly meetings at important research universities, research centers and institutes including Boyce Thompson Institute, Brooklyn Botanic Garden, Columbia, Lehman College, New York Botanical Garden, New York University, Princeton, and Rockefeller University. This provided an opportunity for the graduate students to network with the leading scientists in the field which was important to their future careers.

The highlight of the Rutgers experience was the 1965 birth of our son Jeffrey William during October. Pregnancy is a sobering moment for a young married couple and even more so for me being a cellular and developmental biologist. Spouses develop great empathy for women undergoing the discomfort and distortion of their bodies during the pregnancy development process. I remember our nightly walks in Johnson Park during the final weeks and the joy of driving to Princeton Hospital for the delivery of our new born son. The birth of a child and transition into a parent is a life changing moment. A moment for assumption of new responsibilities for Ginny, my wife and me and at the same time the making of a lifetime friend. Today my son and grandson are my treasured best friends. Sadly, my former wife and Jeff's mother transitioned prior to the birth of our remarkable grandson who enjoys a treasured friendship with my son.

Dr. Gunckel was an important mentor to newly hired tenure-track assistant professors who received nine month appointments. He aggressively identified summer support to fund their summer research and travel which was key to contributing top quality research publication to the premiere refereed scientific journals. These resources and opportunities facilitated the professional development of young faculty members and resulted in their successful promotion and tenure. The result was the emergence of a world class academic department.

The first draft of my dissertation was completed during the summer of 1966. Dr. Gunckel gave me permission to accept a postdoctoral position at Western Reserve University (Now Case Western Reserve University) beginning in June 1966 with return trips to New Brunswick for revisions. Virginia, Jeff and I would usually lodge at the Gunckel's magnificent home in Somerset New Jersey during these sessions. I spent the time in the basement apartment with my typewriter and in the evenings, I would work with Dr. Gunckel during editing sessions. These sessions were most important for developing my writing skills. I will never be able to thank him enough for his vitally important investment in my career. The dissertation was completed toward the end of summer but the defense was delayed until early autumn because one of the committee members was away on sabbatical leave in India. I graduated at the spring commencement of 1967 with U Thant, a Burmese diplomat, and the third Secretary General of the United Nations awarding my diploma. Virginia, Jeff and my grandmother from Columbus attended the ceremony. My parents were unable to attend because of my mother's illness.

Argonne National Laboratory 1967 – 1971

At the end of the semester, Virginia and I packed our possessions for storage and shipment to New Brunswick, N.J. and headed for Downers Grove, Illinois for the summer internship at Argonne National laboratory. Argonne was an amazing place. Here I had the opportunity to apply my knowledge in cell culture to understanding cell growth and differentiation in zero gravity environments. I had the opportunity to work with Drs. Richard Dedolph, Solon Gordon, and Jane Shen-Miller, all prominent researchers in plant physiology and plant biochemistry. Dr. Solon Gordon was director of the Division of Biological and Medical Research. Studies in plant growth and differentiation were of high priority for NASA at the time because of the need to understand the effects of gravitational-free environments on living organisms during prolonged space travel. I conducted experiments on carrot tissue explants grown in Erlenmeyer cell culture vessels clamped onto clinostats placed in gravitational free chambers. Interesting effects on organelles clumping and respiration were observed. My first research paper was published with Drs. Jane Shen-Miller and Solon Gordon. The Argonne internship lasted for three months but evolved into an academic visiting research fellowship during my years at Case Western Reserve University and Ohio State University. The opportunity to work with a world class team of scientists was invaluable to me in learning about experimental design, data crunching, the maintenance of laboratory notebooks, monthly/quarterly research reports and the importance of intellectual property.

Argonne was leading the quickly evolving field of cell biology and advances in microscopy, the electron microscope and cytology. The laboratory is situated on 1,500 beautiful, wooded acres and surrounded by the "Waterfall Glen Forest Preserve", Argonne is one of the nation's leading federally funded research and development centers and is the U.S. Department of Energy's oldest and largest national laboratory for science and engineering research. The facility employs about 3,200 employees including 1000 scientists and engineers, three quarters of whom hold doctoral degrees. The annual operating budget is about $630 million and supports 200 research projects. Since 1990, Argonne has developed collaborations with more than 600 companies and numerous federal agencies and other organizations[24].

University of Akron
1962 -1964

After my discharge, I enrolled at the University of Akron. I soon became engaged to Virginia, and marriage plans were set for June of 1962. My family applauded the decision that I was going to return to the university and complete a degree program.

I chose to attend the University of Akron because at the time Ohio State University adhered to the quarter system which was already in progress at the time of my discharge. This decision turned out to be a blessing in disguise as to my choice of scientific research focus.

Following my return to Akron an appointment was scheduled with Dr. Roger Keller, Chair of the Department of Biology at the University of Akron and a geneticist with a doctorate from Indiana University. The meeting with Dr. Keller was encouraging. Also, having served in the military, he understood my situation. My credits from Ohio State University were accepted by the University of Akron and I was granted senior student status. The remaining courses were planned for

---

24 Argonne National Laboratory History Retrieved August 5, 2013 from http://www.anl.gov/about-argonne/history

completion of the B.S. and potential M.S. Degree in Arts and Sciences during spring, summer and autumn semesters with courses in advanced genetics, geology, literature, microbiology, micro-technique, plant anatomy, plant morphology, plant physiology, plant taxonomy, physics, independent studies and comprehensive German.

Dr. Keller and I discussed future career possibilities for me along with graduate school. I told him about Dr. Weishaupt from Ohio State University and her mentoring through my Navy years and the following years in Akron. Dr. Keller suggested it was time for me to get serious and focus on the academics and pursue graduate school, and a career in academia. I mentioned that I would probably seek a part time job and he offered me a position in the department that entailed managing the greenhouse facility, cleaning laboratory glassware and doing preparatory work for the introductory undergraduate classes. I was most grateful to him. After our meeting, he kindly drove me home and making the beginning of a lifelong friendship.

Dr. Roger Keller led me though the many hurdles toward the B.S. degree in the Biological Sciences followed by a MS degree. Dr. Keller and fellow faculty member, Dr. Paul Acquarone, were important in my scientific development. Dr. Acquarone and I had several discussions about my potential interests in plant biology and cell culture. He encouraged me to review the dissertation of Dr. Samuel Caplin, one of his former students. Dr. Caplin was a leading researcher in plant cell biology and cell culture. He earned a Ph.D. degree at the University of Chicago under Dr. F.C. Steward after completing his M.S. Degree at the University of Akron. I checked out the library both his dissertation and "The Handbook on Animal and Plant Cell Culture," by Philip White, a scientist at the Bar Harbor Institute. Drs. Acquarone and Keller encouraged me to undertake a special project in plant cell culture, helped me equip the laboratory appropriately, and persuaded me to remain at the University of Akron for an additional year to pursue the M.S. degree. Their support was critical to my eventual pursuit of the Ph.D. degree. Two other professors who were very important were Dr. Eugene Flammenhaft and Dr. Grace Kimble, both microbiologists and key to my involvement in plant cell culture research.

My dad and I bonded again and spent a weekend employing our skill sets from the soap box derby days to purchase lumber, craft and paint a sterile transfer chamber for the lab. This was before the availability of commercial laminar flow hoods with positive pressure for manipulating organisms under aseptic environmental conditions. I was especially interested in plant cancers, which mimicked animal cancers, and quickly developed skills in aseptic culture technology and succeeded in the culture of a number of plant-based cancer cell strains. I was surprised to discover that Dr. Acquarone was a classmate of Philip White at Johns Hopkins University and had been in a postdoctoral program with him at the United Fruit Company. Dr. Acquarone introduced me to Philip White and Samuel Caplin, two giants in the world of plant cell biology, who in turn recommended graduate program opportunities for me.

The First International Plant Tissue Culture Conference was held in 1963 at Penn State University while I was in undergraduate studies at the University of Akron. I was awarded a travel grant by the Akron Chapter of Sigma Xi to attend the Conference. Sigma Xi is a scientific research society, founded in 1886 to honor excellence in scientific investigation and encourage a sense of companionship and cooperation among researchers in all fields of science and engineering. The conference marked the 30th anniversary of the publication of Philip White's paper on the continuous aseptic cultivation of tomato root cultures (1933) and was organized by Philip White during his sabbatical leave at Pennsylvania State University. The gathering was attended by 40 to 50 dedicated scientists from around the world who spent the week discussing technical problems, successes and the future of this very young and promising field of plant biology. After the meeting, the scientists returned to their respective laboratories and the field began to blossom.

My professors supported my request to undertake an independent research project during the senior year using cell culture to develop a better understanding of crown gall bacterial-mediated plant tumors and genetic tumors occurring in certain interspecific genetic tobacco hybrids. It was my belief that plant cell culture held promise as a key research tool in unraveling the mysteries of plant cell differentiation and plant development, as well as having practical applications in genetics and plant breeding. This senior research project set the stage for my M.S. and Ph.D. dissertation research programs. I could not believe that I would soon be graduating with a B.S. degree. During the same week that I completed the form for graduation, a letter arrived from the Dean of the Graduate School that I had been admitted to the M.S. Biological Sciences Graduate Program at the University of Akron under the supervision of Drs. Paul Acquarone and Roger Keller.

I met with the members of the Graduate Committee to obtain approval of a graduate degree research proposal to study the influence of minor inorganic elements on the growth and differentiation of carrot cell cultures. Dr. Keller assisted me to procure the necessary scientific instrumentation, laboratory supplies and important analytical chemical assay protocols. My graduate committee included professors with expertise in minor nutrients from the Department of Chemistry. The experimental work progressed on schedule and provided me with good laboratory skill sets. The laboratory research experience was an important step in allowing me to become an independent researcher. I will always be appreciative of the mentorship of my professors who were so kind as to take an interest in my career building efforts

Coming to Grips
US Navy
1958 -1962

A self-appraisal during 1958 brought me to the realization that I was quite immature for my age and not yet ready to make decisions regarding an area of concentration at the university or a potential career. Therefore, I decided to enlist in the U.S. Navy and to attend the Navy Technical Schools and tour the world. The decision was precipitated by a recruitment billboard for the U.S. Navy. As you may recall, I was somewhat familiar with the U.S. Navy from the stories told by my aunt and uncle about their tours of service as officers. The morning, after making my decision, I went to the naval recruitment office at the main post office and enlisted. Virginia was quite disappointed, but we agreed to continue our relationship. Although, I felt remorse about disappointing Virginia, I wasn't yet ready for marriage. My grandparents gave their instant approval, as they always did to my decisions, and assured me that the experience would be worthwhile. I purchased a Greyhound ticket and rode the bus to Akron for a weekend visit with my parents to say goodbye and to inform them that I was heading to the Admiral Nimitz Naval Base in San Diego for basic training early during the next week. My father was in disbelief but the other members of the family were supportive of my decision. I believe that my father thought that entry into the military as an enlisted man was a dead end in regard to my education and career, and he could have been correct. Although as a young man during World War II, my dad had wanted to enlist in a pilot training program with the U.S. Air Force. However, my father was denied enlistment because of a health issue relating to a kidney infection which required surgery. My uncle was drafted into the U.S. Army toward the end of World War II for a short period of time.

The following Tuesday, I returned to Columbus, Ohio and my grandparents and Virginia drove me to Port Columbus and wished me well with hugs and kisses as I boarded a TWA flight for Chicago connecting to San Diego. Our treatment on arrival at the Admiral Nimitz Naval Base was a bit inhuman. We were herded much like prisoners of war, stripped for a medical examination, heads shaved, measuring and allocating uniforms. Groups of 60 recruits were assigned to individual squadrons and marched off to the barracks that was to become our home for the next eight to nine weeks.

A squadron commander and a recruit commander were assigned to each squadron. I served as recruit commander for three to four weeks until sickness with pneumonia from the damp weather and limited sleep put me in the hospital. After three weeks in the hospital, I was assigned to a new squadron and completed my basic training. The training was rigorous with emphasis on physical fitness, seamanship, firearms, firefighting, shipboard damage control, core values, teamwork, and discipline. Above all, emphasis was on cleanliness and organization. The rigorous training at times was life threatening because some squadron commanders were naive about the vulnerability of the human condition. Graduating recruits were required to take an examination covering all aspects of the boot camp training, including the U.S. Navy military history. I scored the highest grade among all recruits in the graduating class. My squadron commander asked if I was planted by the C.I.A. and I replied, "I wish that was true because my understanding is that they enjoy a higher pay grade." I took away lifetime lessons in leadership, collaboration, organization and the importance of cleanliness which continue to be part of my character. During basic training, I had a few opportunities to visit my aunt, uncle and family. On one of the visits, they took me on an immensely enjoyable trip to Tijuana. On the Gold Coast of Baja California, Tijuana is the municipal seat, cultural, and commercial center of Tijuana Municipality. I have since visited there many additional times for business and vacation.

After, Navy Boot Camp, I was assigned to the Great Lakes Naval Base for enrollment in Fire Control School which was to provide background in electronics and mechanical computers. I flew to Chicago and boarded the train to the Great Lakes Naval Base. I enjoyed the classes and getting to know Chicago, Waukegan and Milwaukee. I especially liked Chicago, and many years later, my wife, son and I had an opportunity to visit Chicago often during my adjunct research appointment at Argonne National Laboratory.

My track record at Ohio State had been mediocre with the exception of the required classes in chemistry and biology. I elected to satisfy the biological sciences requirement by enrolling in botany classes. I had the good fortune to enroll in a general botany course taught by Professor Clara Weishaupt, a brilliant professor, with a superb understanding of plant anatomy, plant development and physiology. Professor Weishaupt was regarded as an expert in the *Gramineae* (grasses), served as curator and director of the Ohio State University Herbarium, developed a teaching manual and field book guide to Ohio plants, and co-authored an authoritative guide to Ohio plants.

Professor Weishaupt's classrooms of thirty students seated at laboratory benches were alive with scientific curiosity and excitement. She conducted science demonstrations and experiments in front of the classroom and/or had us make observations using microscopes at our laboratory benches. I was passionate about attending her courses and received top grades. She unselfishly opened up and shared her world of plant science with her many students. She voluntarily served as my academic mentor for many years and encouraged me to complete the B.S. Degree and attend graduate school. She was one of the important influencers of my future career. One could feel her passion for the plant sciences, the herbarium, and her office. My only wish was that somehow, I could have reciprocated and bestowed appropriate honors and recognition on her for her commitment and passion to mentoring and providing career guidance to me and so many other students. Maybe, I will still find an opportunity to honor her in some way at Ohio State University.

Navy service followed a positive track and accelerated my coming of age and development of the ability to make important decisions regarding my future. The Navy was both a refuge and training ground. I was delighted to have had the opportunity to attend the U.S. Navy technical schools in fire control which provided background in electronics and mechanical computers that were central to the operations of a military ship fire control systems for air and sea defense. I advanced rapidly though basic training at the San Diego Naval Base and the technical schools located at the Great Lakes Naval Base. Thereafter, I was assigned to the U.S.S. Compton (DD 705) at the Naval Station Newport, Rhode Island and again the importance of teamwork and collaboration was emphasized, Newport was the homeport for Cruiser Destroyer Force Atlantic (COMCRUDESLANT) until 1970.

My responsibilities on the USS Compton related to operations and maintenance of one of the advanced fire control systems. I reported to George Nicky, a senior non-commissioned second class petty officer from Ohio. He was bright and possessed superb engineering talents. He returned to Ohio following completion of his enlistment and enrolled at Ohio State University. He attended my wedding and served as an usher. I enjoyed the shipboard operations in the Caribbean, Europe and the Middle East. Captain Zimmerman, the commanding officer, mentored and encouraged me to apply for special programs and merit salary bonuses. I was granted leave during visits to the Italian cities of La Spezia, Naples, Rome and the Middle East for Amman and the Jerusalem Old City, Jordan (at the time), Damascus, Syria and Jerusalem. Our multiple port calls included Beirut, Cannes, Istanbul,

La Spezia, Lebanon, Naples, Piraeus and Sicily. The time aboard ship, especially during evenings when alone in the fire control operations room or on the deck during good weather, gave me time to read, write letters and give thought to my return to civilian life.

The service with the US Navy opened my eyes to the importance of collaboration among the many individuals contributing to the success of the US Navy fleet operations. Such a remarkable sight to view an operation of US Navy ships in formation at sea incorporating a diverse group of aircraft carriers, cruisers, destroyers, submarines, destroyer tenders and supply ships. And realize that the operations mimic a multicellular biological organism. Success of these complex naval operations and the well-being of the shipmates are dependent on the competence and collaborative abilities of the operation personnel.

Dr. Clara Weishaupt, my former professor and mentor from Ohio State wrote to me often and I in turn shared my insights and sent her postcards from port calls. She always encouraged me to return to academia and complete the B.S. Degree following my tour with the Navy. The letters from my grandparents and parents were likewise encouraging. Our Division was known as the Fox Division and I was assigned to a compartment below the Mess Deck that served as our living quarters. Each of the sailors was assigned a bunk and storage space for his gear. Members of the Fox Division included Electronic Technicians, Fire Control Technicians, Torpedo Technicians and Sonar Technicians. My two closest friends were Don Brown and Bill Bradford, both of who were Sonar Technicians. We had many good times together during port visits seeing the tourist attractions, visiting the clubs and meeting the young local women. Unfortunately, after leaving the Navy, we lost track of one another, something that would not have happened in today's world of e-mail, text messaging and social networking.

Captain Wertheim, succeeded Captain Zimmerman, of the USS Compton, as commander, after an unfortunate accident at sea in which the USS Compton rammed the fantail of another ship in our squadron just off Block Island on its return to the Newport Naval Station from an exercise at sea. Captain Zimmerman was assigned to shore duty following a US Navy Board of Inquiry by a panel of admirals. Captain Wertheim encouraged me to apply for Class B Fire Control School at the Great Lakes Naval Base and then to the Submarine Service. The Class B Fire Control School provided advanced training for the next generation of electronic and computer based fire control systems.

My division officer and shipmates organized a ceremony on the deck for my sendoff to the Great Lakes Naval Command. It was indeed one of life's bittersweet moments, because duty on the USS Compton had been a rewarding period of my life. It had provided me with opportunities to visit ports in Europe and the Middle East and to attend the Navy Technical Schools where I establish new friendships.

The next step was a train from Providence to Chicago connecting to the Great Lakes Naval Base where I settled into barrack living quarters adjacent to the Class B Fire Control Training School. Shortly after classes began, I took the Submarine Service Interview and physical examination. The process proceeded well except for the physical examination which disqualified me for the Submarine Service. An explosion had occurred earlier in the year from a misfire while two shipmates and I were loading ammunition for the aft gun turret, puncturing my ear drums which resulted in stone deafness. Gradually, my hearing returned, but it was never quite the same because of nerve damage. The combined damage to my hearing resulting from the shipboard accident and a childhood illness caused challenges during my subsequent academic and career pursuits. The hearing loss abruptly terminated my naval career and I was subsequently transferred to the U.S. Naval Hospital in Philadelphia for discharge effective January 1.

University of Akron & The Ohio State University 1955 -1959

High school was concluded uneventfully without any profound ideas about college programs or career choices. At the last minute, I registered at the University of Akron for the beginning Autumn Semester of 1954. I began my first university semester while continuing my job at the Saveway Supermarket. The required freshman courses were held in huge lecture halls and, although somewhat enjoyable, provided no clue as to my future career might be. During the semester, I visited my grandparents several times to discuss the possibility of enrollment at the Ohio State University beginning in January 1955 to continue a liberal arts curriculum with a science major. I thought that the move away from home would be beneficial to me by providing greater independence. After some deliberation, I decided to move to Columbus and live with my grandparents, who offered me a furnished third floor apartment in their home which was a wonderful place to sleep and study. I was fortunate to gain employment at the local A & P Supermarket which provided income to supplement the assistance that my parents and grandparents always willingly gave me.

Ohio State was a huge place with a smorgasbord of academic programs and courses, enabling me to enroll in an assortment of required classes in the humanities, social sciences and sciences. I decided to join a fraternity to enhance my social life. The fraternity offered opportunities for me to assume creative leadership and collaborative opportunities for developing and directing charitable events, sponsorship of dance bands, the annual rush program for membership recruitment, and designing and publishing marketing materials. Fraternity membership was no doubt a distraction from my studies, but instilled confidence in my abilities to be at the "tipping point" in development of important collaborative teams for the nurturing business and not-for-profit programmatic initiatives. I was fortunate to have a fraternity brother introduce me to Virginia Sue Riebel, a younger, smart and beautiful woman from Columbus enrolled in the College of Education at Ohio State University. We dated often and discussed our goals and aspirations. Our relationship evolved quickly but neither of us was quite ready for engagement and marriage. The relationship continued after I dropped out of college from Ohio State University and enlisted in the U.S. Navy. We wrote letters and talked by phone often when my ship was in port and saw one another during my weekend and annual leaves in Ohio and New York.

The Beginning

It all began in Akron, Ohio, on September 13, 1936, followed by moves to other cities and towns tracking my father, William John Sharp's early career in the retail division of the Goodyear Tire and Rubber

Company. Our city name, Akron, is derived from the Greek word "Acropolis, meaning city at high point. The fifth largest city in the state of Ohio and the county seat of Summit County, it is located in the Great Lakes region approximately 39 miles south of Lake Erie along the Little Cuyahoga River. Akron is today part of the larger Cleveland-Akron-Elyria combined statistical area with a population of 780,440 according to Ohio Central History, Retrieved August 4, 2013 from

Our family returned to Akron following my father's promotion to a corporate position at Goodyear headquarters during the summer of 1947. We purchased a beautiful home on Kenilworth Drive adjacent to the homes of the Rubber Barons – The Harvey Firestone Estate and the Charles Seiberling Estate. I enjoyed our home and the relationship with my siblings and visits to the home of my aunt and uncle who lived on Castle Boulevard, a beautiful tree lined boulevard, adjacent to Kenilworth Drive. My hobbies during the early years were collecting coins, stamps and building model airplanes. I was a fan of the radio serials: *Batman, Captain Midnight, Jack Armstrong, the Shadow, The Thin Man, The Fat Man, Sam Spade, Tom Mix*, and subscribed to all the radio program special offers which required remittance of cereal box tops and small change. I was a big-time fan of the Cleveland Indians and in pursuit of my great dream of becoming a batboy for the team, participated in the batboy lottery for a number of years.

My time during coming of age was occupied with school and an obsession with reading newspapers and magazines page to page. I invested my allowance and monetary gifts in subscriptions to dozens of magazines including *Life Magazine, National Geographic, Popular Mechanics, Popular Science, Readers Digest, Saturday Evening Post, Time Magazine*, and many others. My dad ended his career with Goodyear during 1948 after he and his brother, John William Sharp received substantial funds from a trust fund established by their deceased father. Some of the funds were used by my father for founding the Sharp Sporting Goods Company and in tandem with my uncle launched the Highland Square Hardware Store. Sharp Sporting Goods was housed in about 5,000 sq. ft. of retail space in a new shopping center located in an affluent section of Akron. The company, retailed fishing and hunting gear, HO scale model trains, model airplanes, u-control airplanes and accessories and sports equipment and toys. Sharp Sporting Goods Company was a frequent sponsor of county-wide competitive u-control airplane meets with divisions for different age groups in which my siblings and I often participated. Winners were awarded trophies and merchandise prizes. Several times my siblings and I were subjects of articles appearing in the *Akron Beacon Journal* Newspaper along with our father. Our parents were forward thinking and believers in family collaboration with the founding of a family circle allowing for my siblings and I input regarding important family decision maters and responsibilities ranging from menu planning, homework, daily chores, weekend activities and summer holidays. The family circle experience proved to be an important toward preparing the four of us for successful collaborative academic and career journeys.

My parents encouraged my collaborative participation in all facets of retailing at the Sharp Sporting Goods Company beginning at age seven, which allowed me to evolve into an experienced salesperson. I was permitted to accept payment from customers for construction of model airplanes and HO scale railroad cars and for maintenance of model airplane engines. These experiences were important in molding me into the person that I ultimately became.

I attended the Akron public schools of my parents including my Dad's King Elementary School and both parent's John R. Buchtel High School. My academic progress varied according to my interest in subjects and focused on science and the social sciences with no clear career goal. My academic performance was slightly better than average and I bonded minimally with my teachers. Elementary school was somewhat of a calamity in grades one through four. The teacher during my 2nd, 3rd and 4th grades was considered at the time to be a forward-thinking educator. She segregated our class of thirty students into six units of five students each and introduced the concept of collaboration. The student groups had elected leaders and were organized in semi-circles based on academic achievement. The group members were encouraged to embrace the spirit of collaboration.

Among my early collaborative activities was the construction of a soapbox derby racing car and entry into the Akron All American Soap

Box Derby in my hometown of Akron. I did this under my dad's supervision. This was a big deal because Akron was the headquarter and home for the All-American Soap Box Derby competition. The Soap Box Derby building and entry in the race car completion occurred over a five-year period for boys age 8-12. The Soap Box Derby provided me with experience in collaborative project management with my dad and the thrill of participating in a competitive event. I had the good fortune of participating in the runoff competition during my final year and almost winning the Akron All American Soap Box Derby.

The weekly bonding and conversations with my father in our basement workshop were enjoyable and important during the Soap Box Derby years and doubtless to say, this also sparked my interest in science and technology. My father was committed to the father and son bonding opportunity, probably because of the lack of a father figure during his early childhood. He and his brother were raised by their mother and shuttled off to the Great Lakes Summer Camp for Boys every summer. They were hired as camp counselors during their high school years. Their father, William Walter, died of pancreatic cancer when my dad was seven years old. However, he remembered some of their important times together and a few pearls of wisdom bestowed upon him by his father during the brief time they shared together. Some of these pearls of wisdom were passed down to me.

One of those lessons was imparted when my dad and his father were flying a kite together on a weekend afternoon and the kite and string became tangled in a tree. His dad removed the kite and tangled string from the tree and requested that my father untangle the string. My dad said, "Untangling the string is impossible." "Nothing is impossible in this world," his father replied to him. "You must untangle the string before you return to the house." My dad spent considerable time untangling the string before returning to the house to acknowledge that all things were indeed possible.

Family Life

Together my dad and I purchased construction materials for building the soap box derby racecar, learned about the use of shop tools, explored the principles of tear drop race car design for reduction of wind resistance, selected paint color for maximum absorbance of solar heat, developed expertise for conditioning the ball bearing based wheel mounts with graphite and various lubricants, plus, and selected the wheels for rubber hardness. A rubber gauge was used to measure the hardness of rubber and selection of appropriate racecar wheels. My dad and I would scout retail outlets and examine hundreds of race car wheels to inspect the ball bearing wheel mounts and hardness of the rubber tires prior to the purchase of the multiple wheel sets. My dad's university education was business oriented; however, he possessed superior intellect and the mindset of a scientist and/or engineer. Our conversations in the basement shop between us while constructing the race car dealt with science and engineering topics and beyond. I'm certain, if my paternal grandfather had lived, that he would have encouraged my father to enroll in engineering school. Topics of our discussions with my dad, ranged from the origin of life to the peaceful applications of nuclear energy. In addition to science, and engineering, both my dad and mom, were interested in the political and social science aspects of current events with a special concern for human rights issues.

My early interests, as mentioned earlier, included model airplanes, soapbox derby race cars, reading magazines, working in my parent's store, swimming at the YMCA, and collecting stamps and coins. Gardening was always an important activity for me at home and at my grandparent's home in Columbus. This interest probably began at my great grandparent's farm, where I spent summers of my early childhood. My grandmother was an expert gardener and had a large backyard with an expansive array of huge gardens planted with exotic ornamental plants and vegetables. She belonged to garden clubs and was knowledgeable about all the new varieties of vegetables and ornamental plants. I was fascinated by the diversity of color patterns, shapes, and sizes of gourds. My grandmother encouraged collaboration and urged me to subscribe to gardening books and seed catalogues about gourds, pumpkins, squashes and tomatoes. I learned that gourds were members of the *Cucurbitaceous* family and enthusiastically ordered an assortment of diverse cultivars and embarked upon breeding experiments. I learned how to pollinate using small hobby paint brushes and developed novel cultivars that, with my grandmother's encouragement were exhibited at the County and The Ohio State Fair in Columbus and won a few prize ribbons. I had the good fortune to meet an Ohio State University graduate student contest judge from the Botany and Plant Pathology Department at The Ohio State University. We discussed the breeding experiments that produced the prize gourds and tomatoes. The graduate student encouraged me to pursue my breeding interests and to consider plant biology as a major in college and even to undertake graduate work in preparation for a career in research. I appreciated his encouragement and filed away the possibility of a research career in the back of my mind at that time. My grandmother was always my loving guardian angel and there is little doubt that she continues to watch over me today. And I will never be able to thank her enough.

CHAPTER 23

Fascinated by Plants

Judy Lyman Snow
Former Associate Director Biotechnology Center
for Agriculture and the Environment
Rutgers University

Coming of Age

I remember having an interest in plants from a very early age, no doubt absorbed from my mother, who loved to garden. I was born in New Jersey in the early 1950's, and then moved with my parents and younger sister to a suburb near Rochester, New York, where I started school. There were large fields behind the house where my sister and I walked to and from school, and where I spent much time observing the variety of meadow plants. The first spring there, my mother gave me a couple of seed packets in my Easter basket and some space in the garden to plant radishes and lettuce. How proud I was of my first garden produce! I went on to try a variety of herbs and vegetables, help plant bulbs and annuals, and learn about propagation. It was the start of a life-long love of plants and gardening that has given me endless hours of pleasure and helped shape my career.

Developing an Interest in the Sciences

When my family moved to the Detroit area during my middle school years, I was thrilled to find that our retired next-door neighbor had a large greenhouse and an extensive garden. He was happy to share his knowledge with me, and by high school I was allowed to design and plant a section of his garden with annuals raised from seed. Transplanting the seedlings into flats was my particular job since his fingers were stiffened by arthritis. By this time I was reading horticulture magazines and was definitely bitten by the gardening bug.

The idea that a small packet of seeds could result in a riot of colorful flowers and vegetables seemed to open limitless possibilities to me. At some point I had also developed a parallel interest in fungi, probably because of their endless variety and colorful habits. I collected them in my rambles through the fields and woods, and brought them home to identify them and sketch them. My parents encouraged me in this interest as well, and even provided me with silica gel in which to dry and preserve my specimens. This unusual hobby attracted the attention of a friend of theirs, a botanist named Jim Wells who taught at the prestigious Cranbrook Institute of Science, not far from where we lived. He took me to the University of Michigan to meet Dr. Alexander Smith, a renowned mycologist, who kindly showed me around the herbarium and signed my copy of his book. That summer Dr. Wells arranged a part-time job for me at Cranbrook, cataloging the specimens of fungi in their herbarium. He also encouraged me to take a couple of summer courses in mycology at Douglas Lake, a biological station in northern Michigan run by the University of Michigan. No doubt he pulled strings to gain admission for a high school student to courses normally open only to undergraduate and graduate students. Because I already knew quite a bit about fungi, I did well in the lab courses, which helped my self-confidence tremendously when I went on to college. Very recently, I came across a list of my classmates from that summer, and among them to my amazement was the name of a long-time faculty colleague at Rutgers University. Neither he nor I remembered the other, but we both had vivid memories of the class.

As an aside, I should mention that I had a number of other interests that took me in different directions. I started violin lessons in grade school and continued to play throughout high school. When it was time to apply for college, I reluctantly decided that my talents were not enough to make a career of music, and that a career in science held more opportunities. However, music continues to be an important part of my life to the present day.

Meanwhile, I was also intrigued by other cultures and languages beyond the U.S. My mother, who had spent a year studying in Europe during college, belonged to an organization in Detroit that hosted international visitors. A procession of guests from all over the world came to dinner at our home during my high school years. So when I had the chance to go to Japan as a summer exchange student, I didn't hesitate. That was the first of many international adventures that I was fortunate to enjoy. Throughout my life, my parents were always supportive and very proud of my achievements. They encouraged me and followed my career with interest, so I always felt that I had a strong team behind me. As time went by and I learned about the struggles of others, I came to realize how lucky I was.

Choices of Undergraduate and Graduate School

When I began looking at college choices, my friend and mentor Dr. Wells did me another good turn by recommending that I consider Duke University, which had a strong Botany program at the time. I visited there and was warmly welcomed by the department chair, so I applied and was accepted through the early decision program. I enjoyed my years at Duke, with its mild climate and Piedmont ecology. I made a little extra money doing botanical illustration for one of the professors who studied mosses. This brought me into contact with the graduate students, who were friendly and encouraging to a new undergraduate. Since I had extra credits from advanced placement courses and summer classes, I was able to graduate in three years. However, I knew that I was not finished with my education and ought to continue through graduate school. Recognizing that there were not a lot of job opportunities in botany, my father suggested agriculture as a practical application for my interest in plants. This wise advice put me on a new path that led to many new adventures and challenges.

I decided that plant breeding was the direction I wanted to pursue, and applied to several universities with strong programs. Cornell University was high on my list because it had not only a strong plant breeding program, but also a long history of international efforts. I was thrilled when Cornell accepted me with the offer of a graduate assistantship—but in horticulture, not plant breeding! They pointed out that I had had no undergraduate genetics courses. That was the down side of rushing through my undergraduate years so quickly. Nevertheless, I accepted the offer and headed to upstate New York in 1974.

Cornell's Horticulture Department was also a strong one, and Dr. Harold Tukey, Jr. became my advisor for a master's degree project that focused on plant physiology and propagation. Still thinking about plant breeding, I took genetics classes and other prerequisites for the plant breeding graduate program. In hindsight, I am surprised that my love of gardening did not seduce me into staying with horticulture and pursuing a career in landscape gardening or public garden management. When my master's degree was completed, I took a year off to consider my options.

Dr. Jerry Grant of the Rockefeller Foundation, who had recently retired as director of an international agricultural research center in Colombia (CIAT), arrived in Ithaca for a sabbatical year. He gave a seminar about the research underway at CIAT, with its focus on breeding beans, maize, rice, and pasture grasses for Latin America. When I talked with him afterward, he offered me a job as his assistant while he was in Ithaca. While this was an administrative position rather than a research position, it gave me the opportunity to learn about the world of international agricultural research. This convinced me that plant breeding in an international setting was still what I wanted to do. So I applied to the Plant Breeding Department to continue for a Ph.D. and was accepted. Dr. Henry Munger, a renowned vegetable breeder, agreed to take me on. After two years of coursework and participation in Dr. Munger's breeding projects on melons, cucumbers, and onions, I came up with a thesis project focused on breeding lima beans for tropical conditions, based at CIAT in Colombia.

CIAT, which I had visited with Dr. Grant, held the world collection of Phaseolus beans in its gene bank. The center's bean breeding program focused on *Phaseolus vulgaris*, but little attention had been given to the samples of *Phaseolus lunatus*, or lima beans. My thesis project evaluated the lima bean collection for disease and insect resistance in order to select promising lines for a breeding program. The presence of cyanide in the seeds was also checked, as some varieties had levels that might be toxic. I grew trial plots in several different locations and learned a great deal about field research during two busy years, from 1978-80. In hindsight, it was not the best arrangement to conduct my field research so far away from my major professor, as this was well before the advent of email and Skype. However, I got help from Dr. Mark Hutton, a retired professor and experienced breeder visiting from Australia, who very kindly spent time showing me some of the practical aspects of bean breeding.

One positive impact of my stay in Colombia was the exposure to team-based research programs with clearly stated goals. It was a very different strategy from the single-scientist approach that was then the model at most universities, and seemed to produce measurable results much more quickly—new varieties, better agronomic practices, and more effective economic policies. Now, of course, multi-disciplinary research teams are required for major grant-funded research projects.

I also met a diverse group of talented young scientists from around the world. They all spoke English, which was the common language at the research station, even among the staff. Nevertheless, I was determined to learn Spanish so I could communicate with the people outside the center walls. I had studied French for years all the way through college, but had only six weeks in which to take a few Spanish classes before heading to Colombia. CIAT employed a Spanish teacher who gave regular classes on site, and I became fairly fluent after a few months. I was proud that I gave a final seminar on my research in Spanish, rather than in English.

My project at CIAT was basically self-financed, since my assistantship at Cornell was state-funded and not available for international work. However, because of my experience working for Dr. Grant, I got a job as assistant to CIAT's director of research, Dr. Ken Rachie, also a Rockefeller Foundation employee. Although once again it was an administrative job rather than a research position, it gave me an inside view of the management of an international research station. I recorded the minutes for board meetings at which members from around the world debated the merits of research objectives, as well as budget constraints and priorities. It was a priceless experience that piqued my interest in the bigger picture of how international programs were organized, priorities determined, and funding obtained to carry out the vision.

Since the Rockefeller Foundation was one of CIAT's founding donors, the director of its agricultural sciences program, Dr. John Pino, was a member of CIAT's board. During one of the breaks in the board meetings, he asked me what I planned to do after completing my Ph.D. thesis. At that time the Foundation was concerned about plant genetic resource issues and the loss of diversity among crop plants. My experience with the bean germplasm collection at CIAT was very relevant, so Dr. Pino suggested that I come to the Foundation's New York headquarters as a junior scientist to work on these issues and help the Foundation determine where its funding should be focused. My decision to accept his offer was an important one, as it led me away from field research into the administration and management of research programs. I never regretted the move, which led onward to several long-term and rewarding positions.

People Influencing One's Career Pathway

I arrived at the Rockefeller Foundation in 1980, when the network of international agricultural research centers had expanded to build on the successful approach of the Green Revolution (and to address some of its shortcomings). The Foundation's Agricultural Sciences program, led by Dr. Pino, had more than 60 staff members stationed in centers around the world. The funding requirements for these centers, initially established by the Rockefeller and Ford Foundations, had grown dramatically. The Consultative Group on International Agricultural Research (CGIAR) was established in 1971 to manage the centers and provide coordination for the donors, and was a very complex organization. Dr. Pino was one of the visionaries who had played a key role in founding the CGIAR, and was naturally still very much involved as a member of its executive committee. How fortunate I was to learn about the critical issues facing the CGIAR from one of its architects, and to contribute to policy papers and proposals for deliberation at its meetings. Working with John was exciting. He would often have me write down ideas that flowed quickly as he talked. Then it was my job to fill in the details and edit the draft into a cohesive whole. It was good training for a young staffer and a steep learning curve.

My primary focus was on plant genetic resource conservation and management. The Rockefeller Foundation was providing some funding to a non-profit journal called *Diversity*, which reported on genetic resources issues. Bill Brown, President of Pioneer Hi-Bred, had helped establish the journal, and I became friendly with its editor, Deborah Strauss. Although there were a number of international agencies working on plant genetic resource issues, *Diversity*'s reporting focused attention on the subject in a sustained way and got the message out to a very broad audience. Along with the Keystone Conferences, which brought together the leaders in the field, *Diversity*'s efforts spurred a global interest in collection, preservation, use, exchange and other facets of this natural resource. Years later I served several terms on the board of *Diversity* as Secretary/Treasurer. This afforded me the privilege of meeting and working with Bill Brown's wife, Alice, and son Bill, who had come on the board after his father passed away. Both John Pino and Peter Day served many years on the board. In the meantime, I also contributed a couple of chapters to the book "*Managing Global Genetic Resources: Agricultural Crop Issues and Policies*," which was published in 1990 by the National Research Council of the National Academy of Sciences, Washington, D.C. These efforts were the fruits born after I had left the Foundation in 1984, but they originated in friendships and connections made during my tenure at the Foundation.

The Rockefeller Foundation's Agricultural Sciences staff in New York consisted of a small group of senior scientists who had come up through the international research system, supported by a few younger staff members and several post-docs, of which I was the most junior. Dr. Gary Toenniessen, then a junior staff member, had an office right next to mine and was a great help in showing me around and explaining how things functioned. I appreciated his friendliness to me and was very pleased to see years later that he was eventually promoted to become Director of Agricultural Sciences—a well-deserved reward for his long experience and loyal service.

Another valuable experience I gained while in New York was learning how a foundation functions: how it sets its priorities and organizes its programs, how it crafts a call for proposals, and how it evaluates the proposals it receives. Reading a wide variety of proposals—from crude to highly-polished—was extremely valuable training for me which contributed directly to a major part of my responsibilities subsequently at Rutgers University.

Many people visited the Rockefeller Foundation officers in New York, hoping to persuade the Foundation to fund their efforts. Among them were two scientists I had met at CIAT—Dr. James Brewbaker and Dr. Jake Halliday. Both of them were then located in Hawaii, the former a distinguished plant breeder of maize and leguminous tree crops, and the latter a young microbiologist who headed the University of Hawaii's NifTAL program (Nitrogen Fixation by Tropical Agricultural Legumes). They successfully argued for support to organize an international conference on the genetic resources of nitrogen-fixing trees, at the Foundation's fabled conference center at the Villa Serbelloni in Italy. I was brought in to help coordinate the conference and produce the report. The event was one of the highlights of my tenure at the Foundation.

During the time that I worked at the Foundation, Dr. Pino and the senior agricultural scientists were already looking beyond the achievements of the Green Revolution for the next breakthrough. Biotechnology was in its very early stages, and they were debating how its potential could be applied to the problems of agriculture in developing countries. Along with Dr. Pino, I attended a meeting led by Pioneer Hi-Bred's President Bill Brown. The meeting brought together many leading scientists to discuss which directions biotechnology research should take, which crops could serve as model systems, and whether the results would have a practical impact on the needs of the developing world. Once again, I was privileged to listen and learn from some of the key people involved in the early days of the technology.

Back in New York, I did a lot of literature research on the potential of biotechnology as background for position papers that the staff used in its internal deliberations. I no longer recall how it came about, but I received an invitation to participate in a small workshop in Rome at the Vatican. The purpose was to present recommendations to the Pope on the potential of the biotechnology and how it might contribute to society. Accordingly I prepared a paper and presented myself in Rome for a dream-like week of meetings in a small room inside the Vatican walls. It was hard to focus on the papers due to the beautiful frescoes decorating the ceiling and walls, but we managed to produce our report as charged. One of the other participants was Dr. Peter Day, then head of the Plant Breeding Institute (PBI) at Cambridge, England, which was in the forefront of plant molecular biology research at the time. Later I went to a research conference hosted by Dr. Day at the PBI, since the Rockefeller Foundation was funding some of their research. Dr. Day and his wife kindly invited me to stay at their home, which I later learned was just one example of their generous hospitality to visitors. Little did I know that as a result of that brief stay, Dr. Day would recruit me to a position as his associate that would last more than 20 years!

However, there were many other changes underway in the meantime. There was a new president at the Rockefeller Foundation, and a feeling that the Agricultural Sciences division with its large and costly field staff should downsize to support more lab-based research in biotechnology. Dr. Pino left for a position in Washington, which was a big blow to me. Losing one's mentor is always unsettling. Fortunately, my personal life took a lucky turn at that time when Jim Snow, a fellow Cornell graduate student, asked me to marry him. By coincidence, he had taken a job not far from my parents' house in New Jersey at the United States Golf Association. We married in 1984, and I embarked on a new path familiar to so many women who have to learn how to juggle family lives and careers. I am lucky that my husband has been so supportive through the years, and we will soon celebrate our 30th anniversary.

Between the downsizing underway at the Rockefeller Foundation and a new home with my husband in New Jersey, it was clearly time to look for another job closer to home. However, the options in the metropolitan area for someone with international agriculture experience were limited. I had a couple of interviews with big agricultural chemical firms, but they were not a good fit. Fortunately, I found Dr. Reed Hertford, an economist and former Ford Foundation staff member who headed the International Agriculture and Food Program (IAFP) at Rutgers University. He offered me a staff position split between the IAFP and a new biotechnology initiative that was underway. At that point I recognized that I was heading for an administrative career, rather than a faculty position of research and teaching. It was not a decision to take lightly, but the exposure I'd had to research policy-making at CIAT and then at the Rockefeller Foundation had been intriguing, so I accepted the offer and started a new chapter at Rutgers in late 1984.

Like most university-based international agriculture programs, Rutgers' IAFP operations were funded through contracts from the U.S. Agency for International Development (USAID), other government agencies, and some non-profit foundations. Dr. Hertford had won a contract for a field project in Panama, helping the ministry of agriculture evaluate its policies and improve the effectiveness of its national agricultural research stations. I spent several weeks in Panama on a couple of occasions with a multi-disciplinary team, visiting research stations and talking with the Panamanian scientists. Back at Rutgers we sifted through large amounts of economic data and wrote a lengthy report. It was a challenging assignment and good experience. That contract and some smaller projects kept me busy for about two years, but it was becoming more difficult to land contracts as USAID funding dried up.

In the meantime, Rutgers had convened a committee to develop a biotechnology center at Cook College, where the New Jersey agricultural experiment station was located (as well as the IAFP). The groundwork had been laid for support from the state legislature through a series of bond issues. As the plans matured, Peter Day was recruited from the Plant Breeding Institute in Cambridge, England to lead the new center. When he visited Rutgers in late 1986 to finalize his appointment, he stopped by my office at the IAFP and offered me a position to work with him in getting the new center off the ground. Naturally I was delighted to see him and both flattered and excited by the offer. However, there were two issues to grapple with. The first was that I felt I owed Reed Hertford some loyalty for his help in creating a position for me, and the second was that I was then pregnant with my first child. After much deliberation, I realized that the IAFP was on a downward path, while the biotech initiative was about to take off. Another deciding factor was that Dr. Day was willing to let me work part-time after my baby was born. While it was difficult to tell Dr. Hertford of my decision, subsequent events proved that I had made the right choice. After another year or so, he moved on as well.

Accepting the position with Peter Day in the Biotech Center in 1987 was the start of a long and exciting trajectory that would continue more than 20 years. I had the good fortune to be in the right place at the right time, and to have such a great boss. Peter was already a senior statesman in his field and a real gentleman--it would be hard to imagine a more considerate person. His style was to lead by expecting great things of his staff and faculty, and no one wanted to let him down. He was genuinely interested in the personal lives of his staff, and always asked about family members. He was also willing to help when the chips were down. Several times when I was working late to get out a grant proposal, he offered to stay and help copy and package the documents. I just naturally wanted to do my best for him.

In the beginning, there were three of us sitting in a small office in the college administration building—Peter, myself, and Phyllis Telleri, the executive secretary. My title was something like Program Associate at the time. We prepared endless documents and budgets for the university and the legislature, held many meetings within the university, visited New Jersey companies interested in biotechnology, and finally began recruiting faculty. The first few hires were placed temporarily in labs in other units of the university until we could build our own space. In 1989 an extra floor was added to a new wing of the Environmental and Natural Sciences building, so our growing center could be housed together. The dream was becoming reality.

After some debate, the name chosen for the new initiative was the AgBiotech Center. Our mission was to "pioneer in agricultural and environmental biotechnology research; educate and train students to build a high-tech workforce; and to share knowledge and technologies that improve the quality of life." As the center expanded, some of the areas the faculty worked in were agricultural and environmental applications of genomics, mechanisms of gene regulation, bioprospecting for useful microbes and plants, discovering novel plant pharmaceuticals and nutraceuticals, disease resistance in plants, bioremediation of contaminated environments, endocrine regulation of animal development, animal models for gene therapies, and ethical issues associated with biotechnology.

Another important team member came on board at that time—Roger Grillo, who was our financial and administrative guru. He was also our resident computer and equipment expert. In fact, he did just about anything except wash lab glassware during those early days when our staff was so small. One Thanksgiving weekend he was on call when the building water system developed a leak, and he and Peter had to come in to stop the leak and mop the floors! Roger was a terrific colleague and a great person to work with—again, a lucky break for me. With Peter at the helm and Roger and Phyllis to work with, it was a "dream team" for me. They helped me keep all the balls in the air when my second child was born in late 1991. I was still working part-time, but tried to be flexible and come in for meetings even if they took place on my "off" hours. My husband traveled extensively, so it was a challenge to keep all the bases covered. My parents had moved to Massachusetts some years before and were not available to help with daycare, but I found a wonderful woman (a former teacher) who took care of kids in her home and remains a close friend to this day. Many times I realized how critical it is for women to have a supportive husband, a flexible boss, and good day care for their kids in order to pursue their career. I was very fortunate.

Back at the office, Peter, Roger and I were working on a major proposal to the US Department of Agriculture (USDA) for funds to help construct the center's eventual home. Most of the funds came from New Jersey state bond issues, but an additional $10 million was awarded by USDA. With that in place, planning for the building could go forward. In 1992 we held a ground-breaking ceremony, inviting all the leaders from the legislature, the university, industry, and government agencies who had helped move the project forward. I was in charge of coordinating the event and had to write speeches for Rutgers' president, the Cook College dean, and for Peter Day. Naturally the timing was carefully worked out. Imagine my dismay when the president began ad-libbing and strayed far off-script! However, all ended well.

Although located at Cook College (the ag school), the AgBiotech Center reported directly to the university's Vice President, Joe Seneca, who was a key backer and gave us much of his time. A number of college deans held office during the life of the center. Initially they were supportive and worked with the center on college-wide efforts. Dr. Rod Sharp, with a background in molecular biology and corporate experience with DNA Plant Technologies, was hired as the Dean for Research in 1993 and was especially enthusiastic about the Center's work. He was very encouraging and took the time to get to know the AgBiotech center staff. It always made a big impression on me when senior administrators had time for staffers.

At Rod's request I coordinated a weekend event at Cook College in 1994 with Johns Hopkins for 500 talented middle school students and their parents, introducing them to biotechnology research through lectures and hands-on lab exercises in labs around the campus. I solicited volunteers from the faculty and students to help with the labs and logistics. There was a student biotechnology club called Designer Genes, which offered to help. Just before one of the club's meetings in the AgBiotech Center's conference room, someone threw butyric acid (which smells like vomit) in the halls of the building. It reeked for days. Around that time there were protests nationally against biotechnology and "Frankenfoods," and I was worried that whoever had vandalized our building might try to do the same at the Johns Hopkins event. I could imagine the reports on the evening news! So in addition to all the other planning to take care of, I had meetings with the campus police, who did some investigation and learned that the perpetrator was the disgruntled boyfriend of a female student who worked in our labs. They warned him off and sent a plainclothes officer to the event. Thankfully it went off without incident, but it was a nerve-wracking experience that I will never forget!

Meanwhile, Peter and Roger spent untold hours from 1992-1995 with the architects, poring over building plans, and then with the contractors as the new building went up. In 1995 it was finally finished, and we moved all of the faculty and staff into 34,000 square feet of labs and offices in our three-story wing. The building housed not only the AgBiotech Center, but also the Plant Science and Plant Pathology Departments, and a new science library named for donors Stephen and Lucy Chang. Ultimately the Biotech Center had around 13 core faculty, and a staff of about 100 that included postdocs and graduate students.

When the building was nearing completion, I asked if there would be a plaque in the lobby honoring Walter Foran. I was told that yes, there would be a plaque with a date and the names of the President and Board of Governors at the time. But what about Walter Foran? I was told I would have to take care of that. So I called the Dean's office, who contacted Mrs. Foran. She graciously agreed to fund the plaque and provided some photos of Senator Foran. I worked with a local business to design the plaque, which included a bas-relief bust of Mr. Foran and a description of his important role in siting the biotechnology initiative at Cook College. I took pleasure every day in seeing the plaque, just to the left inside the main entrance, as I came and went from the building.

The new building was dedicated in October 1995 and named in honor of the late Walter Foran, a New Jersey Senator who had been a key supporter. Guests included Senators Frank Lautenberg, John Ewing, Mrs. Foran, and other dignitaries. There were 400 guests and many speakers to include. Naturally the planning for this event was another major project! It was a festive day and a major milestone reached in the growth of the Center.

Up to this point, I have related some of the highlights and big events that took place in the life of the AgBiotech Center, but I haven't described what occupied most of my time on a regular basis. My role and responsibilities changed as the center grew, but there were always reports and proposals to write. In the beginning these were focused on funding to get the center up and running. Then we worked on recruiting faculty, which required the drafting of position descriptions and policy statements. As the faculty came on board and began their research, I devoted more time to helping them with grant proposals and preparing budgets. Grant development became my specialty, and I worked closely with the university's grants office to streamline the Center's submissions. In addition, I wrote annual work plans to accompany budget requests to the New Jersey Commission on Science and Technology (NJCST)—our state sponsor--as well as annual reports documenting results. I found that my science training was essential to understand the faculty's research initiatives, and to summarize them in terms intelligible to a broader audience. Eventually, over a period of more than 20 years, those reports filled a whole shelf in my office.

Working with the faculty and the graduate students was very satisfying. It was intriguing to hear their ideas for new projects as I helped them with grant proposals, and then follow their progress when the grants were awarded. There were a number of international projects that were challenging to administer, particularly one led by Dr. Ilya Raskin that had partners in four Central Asian countries. There was also a tripartite exchange program between the Universities of Sao Paulo/Brazil, Ohio State, and Rutgers with annual meetings that rotated between the participating universities. Rod Sharp was the key person who brought Rutgers into the exchange. Graduate and undergraduate students participated, along with the faculty. It was exciting to see the sparking of new ideas during the discussion following research presentations, and to get to know the Brazilian researchers. Later Dr. Raul Machado, Dean of Escola Superior de Agricultura "Luiz de Queiroz" (ESALQ), the agricultural college of the University of Sao Paulo, Brazil, spent a sabbatical year at Rutgers in an office across from mine, and I was privileged to work with him daily.

Tours and outreach efforts were another of my responsibilities. The Center hosted a number of annual workshops and events for high school students in cooperation with other units at Rutgers. I coordinated with the faculty to run hands-on lab experiences for the kids, as well as tours through the center. As I gave each group a welcome and brief summary of the center's activities, I always encouraged them to ask the faculty and graduate students about their careers, and what got them interested in science. I also urged them to think about other applications of biotechnology beyond medicine (their usual interest), and gave examples that they would see during their visit.

Sometime after the AgBiotech Center had moved into Foran Hall and its programs were expanding, funding from NJCST--the key state sponsor--began to dwindle, and eventually to dry up. The rationale was that the state funding was intended to get the Center up and running, and then the agency would move on to other new initiatives. Fortunately, the faculty had developed successful grant programs that funded more than 50% of the center's budget. The university agreed to pick up some of the building expenses which had been paid by the NJCST. Around the same time, the Center's name was changed to the Biotech Center for Agriculture and the Environment, to better reflect the focus on environmental microbiology that was a major part of its programs.

Meanwhile, family life continued to present its rewards and challenges. My kids moved on to elementary school, which meant finding afterschool programs and summer camps. In many ways, that required more juggling than when they were in year-round preschool care. More serious was the bad news that the cause of my mother's increasing difficulties was diagnosed as Alzheimer's disease. I encouraged my parents to move back to New Jersey so that I could help. Amazingly, there was a house for sale on my street that fit their needs, so they were close by. With Peter Day's blessing, I shuffled my schedule to spend more time with my mother. It was very difficult to see someone so smart and talented struggle with such a debilitating disease, but despite that, I have some good memories of the time we spent together. Later, when more care was needed, we found some wonderful caregivers from Kenya, and I helped my Dad coordinate with them for my mother's care.

Life was moving on at Cook College and the Biotech Center as well. Rod Sharp had left around 1998 when the college administration changed once again. Peter served as Acting Dean of Research and Director of the Experiment Station from 1999-2000 after Rod's departure, while continuing as Director of the Biotech Center. Finally the day came that all of us had been dreading: Peter announced his retirement. He must have been in his mid-70's at the time, and still working at a pace that would have exhausted someone half his age. However, he told us that his wife, Sue, was getting tired of waiting! Naturally the faculty and staff wanted to honor his contributions, so planning got underway for a retirement event in October 2001.

In the late summer and fall of that year, my mother—who had developed cancer in addition to Alzheimers—slipped into a coma. She wanted to stay at home, so we had the support of a hospice program. On top of it all, the 9/11 event shocked everyone, particularly in my town, which lost 19 people in the disaster. It was a very emotional time. I was working from home and going in to the office for essential meetings leading up to the retirement event. I was hoping that my mother would hang on a bit longer, but she passed away the day before Peter's retirement program. Naturally Peter was very sympathetic and said that he did not expect me to come, but I wanted to see him honored and his contributions celebrated. So I went and told no one else that my mother had died, because I didn't want to distract attention from Peter's well deserved send-off. It was a double blow, losing my mother and my revered boss and mentor.

As years went by, resources for Cook College (and the university) were strained, and later deans wanted more control over the Center's resources. With Peter Day's retirement in 2001, and Joe Seneca's departure from the central administration in 2003, it became more difficult to maintain the Center's autonomy. Eventually the Center's reporting line was shifted from the VP's office to the Cook dean, who began moving personnel and funding away from the Center to start a new initiative. It was a shame to see the Biotech Center's programs dismantled after all that had been accomplished. My position was eliminated, and after a short and frustrating stint in the college's central administrative office, I took an early retirement. It was not the way I would have chosen to end my career, but the outpouring of appreciation from the faculty was uplifting and proved that my efforts through the years had been valued.

Proudest Achievements and Lessons Learned

I was very fortunate to have found such able and supportive mentors throughout my career. They were all men, as there were few senior women at the time in the settings where I worked. I attribute my good fortune to showing an interest in the careers of others, and a willingness to ask questions and talk to people more senior than I. They were usually pleased to talk about their careers and their current responsibilities, so I could learn from their experiences or at least judge whether or not they were relevant to my interests. I was lucky to find positions where I could learn and contribute in exciting and challenging programs and institutions. It was important to me to be in a stimulating academic setting where learning goes on every day, and every day brought some new challenge.

As the years passed, I wanted to do what I could to help younger people get started in their careers, particularly the young women. There was a young Chinese woman who came in as a postdoc, and then took a technician's position where she seemed to get stuck, even though she was basically running the lab. She was an extremely productive worker and full of ideas—it was interesting to listen to her talk about her research plans. I encouraged her to publish more and look for a tenure-track assistant professorship. She took on more and more initiatives and made herself indispensable in a new lab where she is making better progress. I look forward to following her career. Another opportunity came along when one of my daughter's high school friends was looking for a summer lab internship. I went back to my Chinese friend, who agreed to take the high school girl on and gave her a couple of interesting projects to work on. I was gratified that she, in her turn, was helping a younger woman get a start.

After my early experience in Colombia, where I was able to travel through the rural countryside and observe the poverty and limited opportunities, it was natural to feel sympathetic toward the plight of the immigrants in the United States. Through the years I have become good friends with several of my Hispanic cleaning women, and helped them out with references for other jobs, tuition for classes, and legal issues. The same rapport developed with the Kenyan ladies who helped care for my mother, and later for my grandmother as well. I was grateful for their loving care, and they appreciated having a job where they were respected and well treated. I have always believed in the old adage, "Treat others as you would have them treat you."

There were many other experiences in the work environment that helped me grow along the way. One was learning to find some common ground with people who were from very different backgrounds than mine, so that we could work comfortably together. The diversity of cultures added richness and also complexity to the work environment, and was a good reminder that there are many ways to look at problems. One behavior that I had no tolerance for was the backstabbing that went on at all levels, but was worse in some units than in others. I have never understood the attitude that you have to step on others in order to get ahead. I often observed that the leadership of the unit set the standard for the rest of the group, and was grateful once again to work in an office where civility and consideration were the norm.

Of course, affairs did not always go smoothly, and there were pressures both internal and external that led to considerable stress. Learning to handle stress was probably the most difficult of all the challenges I faced. When it was possible to take action to resolve the problem, even if it meant extra work or disagreeable tasks, that seemed better than doing nothing at all and letting the problem fester. At other times, having the patience to let things work themselves out without interfering was the best approach, but that was also difficult. And there were many times when there was nothing at all that I could do to remedy the situation—they were the most frustrating. That's where relaxation techniques come in: deep breathing, a long walk, or a soothing cup of tea.

This brings me back to gardening--always an absorbing and soothing activity for me. I have had plants around me ever since childhood, and now that I am no longer working I have more time for serious gardening. My husband and I have developed extensive gardens around our current home, where there was almost nothing aside from foundation shrubbery when we arrived 15 years ago. Now there are hundreds of different varieties of trees, shrubs, perennials and annuals. We support a nearby arboretum, visit gardens in the U.S. and abroad, and go to conferences for serious plant geeks. I have also designed and planted gardens for a couple of friends. It's the ideal hobby because it gives pleasure to yourself, your family and friends; it beautifies your home; and it provides lots of physical activity. There is always something to do--and a new plant to add to your collection. What's more, I have met many interesting friends through gardening, so it's a nice social connection as well. Last but not least, a friend of my daughter's has been helping me recently, so I am able to teach her some skills and hopefully pass on a love of gardening to her.

I will add a few thoughts on retirement to these reflections, as it seemed like uncharted territory since I had not expected to get there so soon. Advertisements that show pictures of laughing seniors enjoying a carefree life make you think that retirement will be like embarking on a very long vacation. Obviously financial planning is essential, particularly in the current economic circumstances. I was surprised by the number of decisions to make and the mountains of paperwork required to set our affairs on the new track. Not to mention health insurance options, health issues, related paperwork and online screen time. It's a good thing I was a professional administrator!

However, there is certainly a much greater degree of freedom to choose how you want to spend your time. Some people elect to downsize their homes and move somewhere completely different, or to begin another career. Volunteer options are numerous and can be very rewarding, as well as connecting you to a new network of friends. I volunteer in the book department of a huge semi-annual rummage sale, which affords me an unlimited supply of reading material. I am also playing in a chamber music group during the winter and taking piano lessons. Travel is another mind-expanding option, and an opportunity to reconnect with family and friends. In short, time is flying by and the days are never long enough for all that I want to do. With a little luck, I hope that the next chapter in my life will be as full and rewarding as the ones already completed.

UPPER LEFT: In the garden, 2012.
UPPER RIGHT: Judy Snow and John Pino at a *Diversity* event, 2001.
BOTTOM: Peter Day, Judy Snow, Roger Grillo, and Phyllis Telleri, 2003.

CHAPTER 24

A Boy Who Loves Flowers Can't Be All Bad

Roy Stahlhut
General Manager Pacific Berry Breeding

Where do I begin to attempt to write something about my career and my life because, for better or for worse, the two have been inseparable. First, I need to acknowledge a person who I met too late in his life and fairly-late in my life, but early enough to have had a lasting influence on me…and the person who inspired the title of this chapter. I met Jerry Twomey when he was already in his eighties. At the time, I was managing a micropropagation lab and breeding carnations at California Florida Plant Company in Salinas, California. Jerry started breeding roses when he was about 65 years old after the death of his first wife from cancer. As he told me, he was moping around feeling sorry for himself after her death and needed to do something to keep himself from going crazy. After a few years of research figuring out rose family trees, contacting and meeting with all the eminent rose breeders of the time and collecting breeding germplasm, Jerry made some crosses and within a few short years, one of his varieties won the All-American Rose Selection prize for the year. This honor was repeated a couple of years later with another of his varieties. It was several years later that we became acquainted when he was looking for someone to propagate his rose varieties. A working relationship led to a friendship and mentorship. I think I realized early on that Jerry was the first, and until this point in my life, last true genius that I ever met.

In addition to acknowledging Jerry as the inspiration for the title, I have related this abbreviated account about him because it is a recurring story throughout my career. While I feel various levels of pride or self-satisfaction as I think about some of my professional accomplishments…which are insignificant in the big picture of scientific endeavor…it is the people I have met and who have blessed me with their knowledge and friendship that overwhelms me. As I am just starting to put something down on paper for this chapter, I think it will be these people who will be the focus of my story…or the glue that binds the story together.

So, what about the boy who loves flowers? Just as I wasn't the child prodigy that sat down at a piano at three years and began to play Beethoven, I wasn't a natural inventor, naturalist or scientist. I just had an intense interest in nature and geology and I had the good fortune to have met people throughout my life that have fostered this interest.

I guess the first mentor that nudged me in the direction of a life in the plant world was my mother. As an avid gardener and plant lover, my earliest memories were of digging in the rocky soils of Connecticut and visits to the local garden center to purchase flowering plants for the ever-expanding flower gardens my mother created around our house. Flowering plants and rocks were my two earliest passions and ones that have followed me throughout my life. I had a serious rock hound hobby that started at an early age and I had considered studying geology at various times through my early teen years. Landing a job while in high school at a local retail nursery and garden center solidified my love for plants and gardening, but did not convince me that I should pursue this love in college. That's the next part of the story.

High School for me isn't a great memory as it is for many. I really hated academics, except for biology and chemistry classes. Again, it was the people in my life, in this case Brother Lovito (I went to a Catholic school taught by the Brothers of Holy Cross), my biology teacher and Mrs. Williams, my chemistry teacher at Notre Dame High School in West Haven, Connecticut, who had the most lasting influence on me during my miserable years in high school! As much as I enjoyed their classes, by senior year, I had firmly decided to do anything but go to college. I toyed with going on a motor cycle tour of Europe or hitchhiking the US, but a military recruiter got his claws into me and I ended up in the Air Force. To get me to sign the enlistment papers, I was promised what seemed like a cool job at the time; interpreting spy satellite imagery. Of course, once I was enlisted, they pointed out that my corrected eyesight disqualified me for this field! So, the kid who was running as far from any type of academic situation was offered a choice; get thrown into a pool of people who would be put into jobs that no one else wanted OR take a test for language aptitude to qualify for linguist school...which was about the most academic field offered by the Air Force outside of the Air Force Academy! I chose the latter, obviously. So off to California I went to the Defense Language Institute in Monterey to study Mandarin Chinese. Not wanting to find out what happens to students who flunk out of the language school, I learned the study skills I needed to make it through the class and graduate, skills that would serve me well when I finally committed myself to pursue academics.

During my time in the military, I was stationed in Thailand and Taiwan. Rural Thailand opened my eyes to the concept of subsistence agriculture. I wasn't thinking in those terms at the time I was living there, but it made a deep impression on me that came back into focus when I was studying agronomy a few years later at university. In Thailand, I had the good fortune of being supervised by a sergeant who took every opportunity to encourage me to pursue my growing interest in agriculture and plants by applying for the university. My interest in the Chinese language and Asian culture enticed me enough to extend my enlistment for an additional year in order to return to an intermediate Chinese language course at the language institute. Upon graduation, I was sent to Taiwan where I was again exposed to agriculture in the countryside surrounding our small air station. It was at this point in my life that I had a major choice to make; extend my enlistment in order to return for an advanced language course and a likely lifetime career in the Air Force or apply for Agronomy School at the University of Connecticut. The influence of my sergeant during the time in Thailand won the day and I applied and was accepted at the University of Connecticut…all expenses paid by the State of Connecticut because I was a Vietnam era veteran and a monthly stipend from Uncle Sam's GI Bill. Not a bad deal! The five-year hiatus between high school and discharge from the military wet my appetite for learning everything I could about agriculture and plants. Armed with the good study skills I picked up at the language school, the maturity I gained in the military and my eagerness to learn, classes turned out to be a joy.

Stepping back a bit to the first day I started at the University of Connecticut and how green I was. In order to assign me an academic advisor, the head of the department asked me whether I was pursuing a soils or plants major. I guess I hesitated a bit because I was thinking to myself, "I'm an agronomy major…don't you need to learn both?" That hesitation resulted in me being designated a soils major, something I remedied a few days later after asking a few more questions. I was now a plant major student.

Greenness continued in another form; youthful zeal to save the world from the impending starvation that was being predicted for the end of the 20th century. One miracle plant that was being touted as the solution to this problem was the winged bean *(Psophocarpus tetragonalobus)*. I latched on to this and asked to do a senior project related to rhizobium inoculation of winged bean seedlings. This set me on a path with a desire to continue working on this plant as a master's student. I applied to UC Riverside, Cornell and the University of Illinois. In particular, the University of Illinois had a professor, Ted Hymowitz, who had published some reviews about the winged bean. He replied to a letter I wrote him inquiring about the possibility of working on the winged bean in his lab. He replied encouragingly that there were a few more acres of soybeans than winged beans in Illinois! He had ample funding to work on soybeans and anything I learned about soybeans could be applied to winged beans or any other plant I might chose to work on in the future. I was offered a research assistantship in his lab to work on soybean genetics.

I should mention here that another area of his research was the wild germplasm of soybeans, which happens to be centered in China… and that he had been invited by the Chinese Ministry of Agriculture to tour major soybean growing areas in the Northeast of China...and that he needed a translator for his trip...and I happened to speak and read Chinese fairly-well. Who could have known that my Chinese studies would take me on a month-long agriculture-focused tour of China shortly after starting my studies for a Master Degree. What's the lesson here kids? Just about any subject you study or experience you have may come in handy one day in a most unexpected way. The more tools you have in the tool chest, the better able you'll be able to handle any situation.

The Agronomy department at the University of Illinois was a wonderful place to learn from all the great teachers and their practical experience. The most lasting impression and something that comes to mind often were the corn and soybean breeders who were the first to the office in the morning and the last to leave at night. Several of them were emeritus professors already 'retired' for many years, but they couldn't stay away from the field and their breeding efforts. That passion was something that has had a lasting impression on me and has infected me during my career.

Despite passion for a career, a job or a research project, of which I have an abundance, there are aspects of any of these that are rather mundane. A good many of the hours I spent in the laboratory during my Masters studies were involved in screening thousands of individual soybean germplasm accessions for seed proteins. It turns out that the skills and patience I developed during this process would come to my assistance several additional times during my later career.

By the time, I had finished my Masters, that old uneasiness with academics returned and I decided to look for employment rather than continue-on in a doctorate program. It was my good fortune that a fairly-new plant biotech startup was looking for someone with soybean experience...and tissue culture experience, of which I had a little from some after-hours playing around that I was permitted to do in the lab of one of the professors in the biology department at the University of Connecticut. I never really accomplished anything other than getting a feel for aseptic technique and how carrots and tobacco could be regenerated from somatic tissues, but that...and mainly my soybean field experience...was enough to get an offer to work for Dr Oluf

Gamborg, the head of the tissue culture lab at the International Plant Research Institute (IPRI) in San Carlos, California. Dr. Gamborg was a well know early pioneer in the plant tissue culture field. He had been recruited away from a university career in Canada. In fact, IPRI, with the help of millions in venture capital dollars, recruited some of the biggest names in genetics, plant breeding, pathology, chemistry and molecular biology to form research teams. The labs were equipped with the latest equipment and no money was spared on social events to keep employees happy. As a result, within about 9 month of starting to work there, the venture capital money well dried up and the majority of employees were laid off, including me.

Fortunately, more soybean grant money was available at the University of Illinois, this time in the lab of Dr. Jack Widholm. Because of my nine months of soybean tissue culture experience at IPRI, I had the right background to apply for a research assistantship in his lab using this money. What I wanted to work on was largely left up to me. I don't remember why, but I discussed doing research on nitrogen metabolism related to nitrogen fixation using soybean cells growing in vitro as a model system. Dr. Widholm agreed to be my major advisor, but with the condition that I invite several faculty members who were actively studying nitrogen metabolism to be on my doctoral committee. So back to the University of Illinois I went.

What an academic…and cultural…experience it was in Jack Widholm's lab. He was one of the most kind and open-minded people I have ever met and was very, very fond of international students. We had students, post-docs and visiting scientists from all over the world. Jack and his wife would host regular get-togethers and encourage us to share cultures and foods. I was extremely busy during my doctoral studies and the time flew by. I had arranged to continue my studies as a post-doc at the University of Missouri when another of those turning points appeared in my life. After finishing the defense of my thesis, the family and I planned a train 'adventure' from Illinois to Los Angeles via Seattle to visit my wife's family. While in California, I called up a former colleague from my time at IPRI in the San Francisco bay area. It turns out, a bankrupt IPRI reincarnated itself as Escagenetics. Several of the same people that had worked at IPRI remained behind because of an irresistible financial incentive to do so. As it turned out, the company was looking for someone with my background and made me a reasonable offer. I backed out of my post-doc and we moved back to the San Francisco bay area. The new focus of my research would be secondary metabolites in plants, specifically, vanilla flavor components in suspension cultures initiated from the vanilla orchid. While I and several other scientists had doubts about the business value of a 'natural' vanilla flavor produced by plant cells in fermenters, we were all driven by the possibilities of the systems we were developing to produce pharmaceuticals. The desire by most of the scientific staff to begin investigating pharmaceuticals was repeatedly quashed by upper management mainly because most of the money they raised to resurrect the company came from investors with interest in food products.

Money speaks! When further investment money for food research dried up, management went hunting for other investors and not surprisingly, money for pharmaceutical research was readily available. The vanilla research program quietly faded into oblivion without a product ever being developed. About the time the vanilla research effort was waning, I read that Dr. Rod Sharp was working on starting a company to work on production of pharmaceuticals by plant cells grown in tissue culture. Dr. Sharp was an early and important figure in the developing plant biotechnology industry. I contacted him to see if he was recruiting people for his new company and conveyed my interest in working for him. He contacted me immediately and said he was still in the process of organizing the new company and would be back in touch when he was ready to hire. Not many month after that, I heard the news that Escagenetics had brought him in to organize a new company to work specifically on pharmaceuticals produced by plants and plant cells. After some wrangling with the management of Escagenetics, the company Phytopharmaceuticals was born and I was now working for Rod Sharp. It was the beginning of a long working relationship and friendship that I treasure to this day.

The main research effort at the newly established company was to develop a reliable source of the anticancer drug taxol. Everyone assigned to this new effort was energized to be working on such a promising project and real progress was made early on by the group. Scaling up the process that we were developing in flasks, bioreactors and small fermenters led us to establish a relationship with the company that was then called Genencor located in Rochester, New York. Despite the promising research results we were seeing, the biggest problems we were running into were interpersonal relations within the group and between us and our new collaborator in Rochester. The problem with Genencor escalated to the point where we were in danger of losing them as a contractor and potential collaborator in the future. It's worth a moment here to mention the reasons for this breakdown in a relation that started out very positively. The PhD scientist in charge of developing this relationship, transferring the technology and advising the crew at Genencor went into this relationship with the attitude that we are the experts and we have contracted you to execute for us. It was a mistake that I have seen several more times in my career with a similar result. Arrogance and the failure to recognize the university of life that produces experts without letters after their names, but immensely important experience and skills that complement academically trained scientists.

Rod Sharp cut through some internal politics and brought in a highly respected former Senior Vice President from Ciba Geigy, Gastone Bello, as a consultant to smooth things over with Genencor and prevent future problems. Gastone acted with swiftness to remove the problems from our side and as a result, I found myself in charge of the plant biology group and directly responsible for our collaboration with Genencor and the transfer and scale-up of our technology at their facility…which meant bi-weekly coast-to-coast trips to Rochester, NY. I already had a good relationship with the crew at Genencor and it only improved, especially after they introduced me to the local hotel/brew pub where we spent many an evening…and where I stayed during the many days and nights in Rochester!

The work we did together at Genencor was really challenging and we had many long nights in the fermentation plant, but the ultimate success of what we did was the result of developing a respect for each other's experience, abilities and opinions. We all learned a lot from each other and long after the collaboration was over, we stayed in touch. This same recipe for success based on respect and teamwork has yielded the same result many times in my career.

I thought frequent cross-country trips were challenging. Based upon the results obtained at Genencor to develop a fermentation system to produce Taxol, a Korean Company, Samyang Genex, licensed our technology and I found myself flying back and forth to Korea on a regular basis. Realizing that technology transfer of the process and development of the supporting infrastructure would require extended stays in Korea, I was provided an apartment by the Korean company. Things were going well in Korea but less so back at the headquarters of Phytopharmaceuticals. During one of my extended stays in Korea, I was informed that cash flow had become critical and Phytopharmaceuticals would be laying off all of my colleagues in the US and closing operations. I was ordered by executives in Escagenetics, the mother company of Phytopharmaceuticals, to return to the US and cease all transfer of knowledge and technology to Genex. At that point in time, I had already transferred all technology to Genex in documents I had prepared detailing the processes we were using. At that same time, the person I had been working most closely with and the general manager of Samyang Genex offered to hire me at the same salary I was making in the US, provide me with housing, a car, a meal allowance and regular visits to my family back in the US. So, the choices were to stay in Korea and continue working on the development of a project I had worked on for several years already…and get paid to do it…or return to the US and get laid off with everyone else. It was an easy decision!

My time in Korea was very rewarding. I was able to immerse myself in the culture, food and scenery of a country that as an economic powerhouse, has only recently emerged from an agrarian society. The contrast between the major cities, especially Seoul and the rural countryside is startling. I fit in well with the Korean work ethic and found myself busy and working six days per week. The time went by very quickly and the scale-up of the Taxol fermentation process in ever larger scale fermentors toward a commercial process became a reality. At this point after almost two years in Korea, I felt it was time for me to pursue something back in the US to be closer to my family.

Networking. It's not something that I excel at in the technical sense of the word. I've never been someone who makes a conscious effort to connect professionally…or socially with lots of people. All my connections are and have been with people I enjoy working with and when the opportunity arises, socializing with. I'm bringing this up now because objectively speaking, my approach is not the one I would recommend professionally. It fits my own personality, but I would recommend a more proactive approach professionally. What has worked for me professionally and socially is to make every effort to help any contact you have when they are in need. When the time comes, many of these contacts will either help you directly in return or put in a kind word about you that may be helpful in your time of need.

I brought up the subject of networking because how I found my next job after leaving Korea is a great example of how this worked for me. While I was at Escagenetics/Phytopharmaceuticals, I was acquainted with a colleague who originally came from Korea but had been living in the US for many years. He hadn't been back to Korea or had contact with his family for almost 30 years. While I was living in Korea, I invited him to visit and stay with me which led to a reunion with his family and reconciliation with his elderly father. We had a good relationship and stayed in touch after I returned from Korea. He was working for an American seed company and through his contacts, recommended me to an Australian company with operations in the US. I met the president of ForBio America at San Francisco International Airport while he was on route to Australia. We had a good conversation and it led to a job offer to run their tissue culture lab in Watsonville, California.

I was now working for ForBio which was based in Brisbane, Australia. The name was derived from an abbreviation for what the original main-focus of the company was when founded; Forest Biology. The company brought together teams of plant biologists, molecular biologists, tissue culturists…and hardware and software engineers, roboticists and mechanics. The company's mission was to develop robotic technology to micropropagate millions of tropical forest trees for reforestation and commercial forestry. In order to develop and demonstrate this technology, the company purchased a company producing seed potatoes in Watsonville, California. The operation included a small tissue culture laboratory to produce clean mother stock from which to begin greenhouse production of seed potatoes. A prototype of a robot developed in Australia was shipped to the US and installed in the tissue culture lab. Why potatoes if forest trees were the focus of the company? As it turned out, potatoes growing *in vitro* are very easy to manipulate in a robotic system which relies on imaging of the plant and subsequent handling robotically. It was a very clean model system with which to demonstrate the potential of the micropropagation robot to the US market.

My time at Forbio was fantastic from the point of view of working on very interesting projects with a variety of even more interesting people! Combine that with my interest in tinkering with mechanical things and it was a dream job. I had an opportunity to visit Australia several times and on one occasion, spent a couple of months working in their laboratories in Brisbane with engineers and biologists and in Gosford near the central coast in their commercial micropropagation laboratory. Forbio was a dynamic company with grand visions, but unfortunately, the visions increasingly out-paced the reality of what we were finding to be possible biologically and mechanically. The goal in the company was for the biologists and roboticists to develop each of their technologies to a point where they would meet midway, or at least somewhere in between, in order to develop a viable automated micropropagation system. This turned out to be an elusive goal for the most important forest trees we were trying to propagate robotically. In the meantime, the company was expanding by purchasing existing or establishing new operations in other parts of the world. At about the same time as this rapid expansion was occurring, the Asian financial crisis hit and had a very significant impact on the value of the Australian dollar. This was the beginning of the end for the company and the first casualties were operations in the United States and Europe. I and the small group producing potato minitubers found ourselves out of a job.

Hopefully anyone reading this never had and will never have to experience losing their job. I have had the experience of losing jobs for assorted different reasons during my career. Agony is supposed to love company, but losing your job simultaneously with all your former colleagues is more agonizing than getting the boot individually. It affects each person differently, some in very drastic ways. As a manager who got to know each of my employees in the laboratory, I found it a particularly painful experience, one that I would experience again later in my career.

I had quite a bit of moral support during my time unemployed and I was also able to pick up a couple of small consulting opportunities. Again, through a wonderful guy I got to know, Stan Iverson (now deceased) at Suncrest Nurseries in Watsonville, I was introduced to the manager of California Florida Plant Company in Salinas, California. I guess for a boy who loves flowers (and had experience in tissue culture), this was a dream job. They were looking for someone to manage their plant micropropagation laboratory AND carry on the carnation breeding program of the breeder who was planning to retire in about 5 or 6 months. I was ready to start work on the spot, but was told that they would wait until the current breeder retired in November before hiring me. I was also told that after retirement, he would be available to mentor me on his experience in carnation breeding as a part time consultant. So, about a week or two prior to my official start date… and after waiting impatiently for several months, I received a call informing me that the breeder and my future mentor had passed away! I started work the next week.

My first task, absent a mentor, was to go through his breeding records and notes. I quickly discovered that these were practically nonexistent or had entries which read "flowers similar to red robin but plant form like coronation". Of course, there were no records of any of the old varieties he referred to and for the most part, he had stopped taking notes in later years and held everything in his head. I was basically starting from scratch other that having the breeding material and current varieties held over in the greenhouse and in tissue culture. I had already been reading any information I could get my hands on about carnations so I had a fairly-good academic knowledge of the crop starting out, but so much of breeding is an art and only the artist can pass on his knowledge and feeling for a crop.

I'm sure some time was lost during my learning phase with carnation breeding, but I also think a fresh set of eyes, some naiveté and the freedom to try wild ideas can be a powerful force for innovation...and innovate we did! For the most part, all the wonderful fragrances found in the Dianthus ancestors of commercial cut carnations had been lost to breeding efforts to increase production, flower shelf life, disease resistance and other economically important traits just as the fragrance of old garden roses had been bred out of cut-flower roses. My breeding efforts initially were divided between standard cut carnations and a newer line of dwarf carnations grown as live plants in small pots for retail sale. Further efforts on standard cut flower carnations ceased early on due to diminished demand in the market. I focused all my efforts on our dwarf potted carnations which were unique to our company at the time. My goal was to introduce fragrance, novel color and color patterns, increased petal laceration and cutting propagation productivity. Because of the novel Dianthus genetics I was introducing into our breeding base, I also started to evaluate all selections for garden performance. We ended up introducing a highly lacerated, very fragrant and very productive selection which also performed well in gardens. We also developed a green, mildly fragrant selection and many pastel and blush-colored varieties that were particularly popular in the Japanese and European markets.

At the same time, in an effort, to support the operation of the micropropagation lab, we worked on contracts with a wide variety of agricultural companies on commercial production, breeding programs and clean stock maintenance on plants such as fruit and nut trees, berries, vegetables, ornamentals, grapes, cactus and many others. Besides acquiring broad experience with growing many types of plants in tissue culture, I established many new contacts in the plant business that I am still in touch with on a regular basis to this day.

Although I thoroughly enjoyed the work that I was doing at California Florida Plant Company and had a great amount of excitement about the new plants that were coming out of my breeding program, a series of layoffs in the company, the likelihood of more to come and rumors that the land the operation was located on would be sold off to developers sent me looking for another opportunity. As all this was unfolding, one of the contacts I mentioned, a plant breeder at

Driscoll Strawberry Associates encouraged me to apply for an opening as their tissue culture lab and propagation nursery manager.

I was offered the position as lab and nursery manager, but it also included responsibility for designing and supervising the construction of a new tissue culture laboratory, renovating an existing range of greenhouses and new construction of additional greenhouses and outside growing areas. This was occurring at the same time as plant orders were rapidly increasing to meet the greatly increasing demand domestically and internationally for Driscoll's raspberries and blackberries. The propagation nursery not only produced plants for commercial orders and orders for field nurseries, but we also supported four breeding programs supplying clean stock of new selections for further evaluation and maintenance of breeding material. Driscoll's was an incredibly dynamic and exciting place to work. It was definitely a classic example of working and playing hard with a strong sense of comradery. We all had great passion for what we were doing and what the company was accomplishing and there was incredible support by the company for professional and personal development and recognition of accomplishment. At the same time, the rapid growth in the company really began to put strains on everyone from the top down. We were all being asked to do more with the same resources. That said, when you work in a tight-knit group that enjoys working together, everything can be looked at as a challenge and not a burden. Extra hours on Saturday to fulfill numbers for an important order deadline became an opportunity to celebrate with a pizza party.

Driscoll's was another great opportunity for me to work with and learn from a wide variety of incredibly talented people here in the US and internationally. I travelled to Mexico several times to visit nursery operations, attend company meetings and visit potential collaborators for micropropagation of our varieties. I toured nursery operations in Europe with local Driscoll's agronomists and learned about the latest techniques being used for propagation and fruit production in substrate (hydroponic) systems. I visited the AQIS quarantine facility, our nursery supplier and the Driscoll's laboratory in Australia. I benefited immensely from these visits and all the information and ideas I brought back with me to our lab and nursery in the US. And of course, there was the continuing collaboration and in many cases friendships that developed and have carried on long after these short trips.

Up to this point in my career, it had been the shutdown or imminent shutdown of the company I was working for that had me moving on to the next chapter. In the case of Driscoll's, it was an untenable situation involving personalities. As in nearly any situation involving interpersonal relationships, each side deserves some of the responsibility…or blame. I'll leave it at that and only say that one of the morals or lesson of this chapter is to try to be objective and introspective, size up a situation early and be as proactive as possible to either change the existing situation where you are (if possible) or start looking at what other options are available. I held on too long thinking that the situation I was in would somehow resolve itself. It's obvious now, looking back, that this could never have happened.

Trying to find another job when you are out of work is never easy… unless you are in a profession in high demand and not dependent on location…an accountant or nurse for example. Finding another job when you're in your fifties or older is orders of magnitude harder! I decided after leaving Driscoll's that I wasn't interested in changing locations for my next chapter…the Monterey Bay area of California is a great place to live. And the rule about giving yourself one month for each $10,000 in salary expectation to find your next job wasn't working out for some of my former colleagues. I had some projects around the house that had been waiting for some time, but those weren't going to fill all my hours, day, weeks, months…and hopefully not years…until my next job.

The story I'm going to relate now is one that could be called inspirational for anyone reading this while out of job and hoping something comes along soon. It illustrates how decisions we make every day can impact our lives and the lives of others in unimaginable ways. Maybe it's an example of the butterfly effect in a more tangible short-term career way. You know…the flapping of a butterfly's wings in your garden can eventually affect weather on the other side of the planet.

For a number of years before, and during my time at Driscoll's, I had been interested in volunteering at CASA (Court Appointed Special Advocates), an organization that pairs adults with kids in the foster care system. I never took the first step because my excuse always was that I would be too busy to dedicate the time needed for a foster kid. Now I was out of a job and that excuse no longer held water so I dove in head first. A background check, interviews and several weeks of training found me and my fellow trainees being sworn in by the court as advocates. I was ready for the most challenging case they had and the staff at CASA obliged! I was going to march in and 'save' a fifteen-year-old boy, turn his life around, go to his college graduation…well maybe my aspirations weren't that lofty. As it turned out, this particular teenager and probably most kids his age didn't want to have anything to do with a well-intentioned adult. I was rejected! But not to worry! His eight-year-old brother was ready to fill his role! So, began a-two-and-a-half-years of challenges and rewards that changed my life…and the life of the kid I advocated for.

So how does this experience in my life relate to my career? I had been out of work for over a year and deeply involved with my kid and his family when I was asked by CASA to make a small presentation to a meeting of prospective future advocates. As people were introducing themselves, I recognized the last name of one of the attendees as a long-time local flower and berry grower. After the presentation, I introduced myself to her husband who was also in attendance and let him know I was in the job market. He was fairly-positive but non-committal about some new business developments at Naturipe Berry Growers, the company he was vice president of, and said he would get back to me. A few weeks passed and I followed up with him. To my surprise, he asked if we could meet the next day. I met him and a consultant to the company for coffee, chatted for a while and left feeling fairly-positive. I didn't hear a thing for a few weeks and figured that I had made a bad impression at the meeting. Not so! I received a call asking me if I was still interested and whether I could be available at the beginning of February…which was only a few weeks away. And that's the story of how all my direct efforts at job hunting, all the things they tell you to do when you are out of a job (and you really should do!), were for naught, but by a series of unrelated life decisions, circumstances and luck, I found my next job. Maybe it was karma, if you believe in that sort of thing!

And here I am at Pacific Berry Breeding (part owned by Naturipe Berry Growers) in Watsonville, California having just reached my third anniversary at the company. I'm working with a wonderful group of people here in the United States and internationally in Mexico, South America and Europe who are dedicated to bringing berries to the market 365 days a year and supporting the growers who make this happen.

So, the boy who loved…and still loves flowers has been working with flowers…and berries…and numerous other plants…and plant cells in fermenters for over 40 years now. When he was digging in the rocky soils of New England, he never could have imagined where this love would lead him and who he was going to meet and the places he was going to go along the way. None of this would have played out the way it did without the people he was fortunate enough to have encountered in his life and in many cases who have been a part of his life until this day.

A gentle nudge in one direction or another either by advice given or by good example demonstrated can have a profound and long-term effect. Keeping in touch with the people you love and respect (or using the buzzword, 'Networking'!) either as a beneficiary of their mentorship or as a mentor to them will enrich your life in ways that will continue to be beautiful and unpredictable.

CHAPTER 25

A Systems Approach to Collaboration

K.C. Ting
*Vice Dean for Academic Affairs and
Strategy Zhejiang University
International Campus, Haining, Zhejiang, China.*

Early Collaboration Experiences

My educational experience from kindergarten through university was mostly in an environment that rewarded individual achievements. Most performance assessment methods measured the students' ability to memorize facts that were provided in classes and/or through assigned reading materials. Public schools at all levels, especially beyond the elementary education, were viewed as the more desirable choices. There were a number of major government administered examinations at several critical schooling stages that were designed to determine an individual's qualification to advance in the educational system. One had to pass examinations to enter a middle school, a high school, and then a university/college. The competition was fierce. For example, when I was taking the nation-wide joint college entrance examination, less than 20% of the people who took the examination would have an opportunity to enter a college of any kind. People who were highly capable of retaining standard answers to standard examination questions had a better chance to enter the schools that were high on their preference lists. Under this reward system, it was natural to understand that collaboration in academic work was not encouraged or even considered useful. This kind of mentality and work style was frequently carried on into other work places. Opportunities to collaborate did exist through participation in extracurricular activities or team sports. However, students of good academic standings were mostly discouraged from participating in those activities. It was a rarity to have students who exceled both in and out of classroom activities.

During my early years of mandatory military service, I started to learn the concept and skills of collaboration and leadership as part of the officer training. It was quite an enlightening experience for me. I began to realize that there was "written" information on collaboration and leadership, as well as the useful information in daily tasks that were assigned to me. I also started to understand that this kind of information tended to be most helpful if more people (especially the members of a team) had been exposed to it, since collaboration and leadership could not be a solo act. I have been fortunate to have opportunities not only to acquire more knowledge about collaboration and leadership throughout my professional life, but also to practice what I learned and develop my own philosophical view from my leadership roles in various occasions. Leadership and collaboration are inseparable aspects of team work. It is important that leaders must enable themselves and others to lead; then collaboration will occur.

Collaboration in Research Initiatives

Many of us, in academia, are in the business to empower human capacity with knowledge and wisdom for life, which is a great business to be in. Our activities are mostly in the forms of education, research, service, and engagement. Almost all these activities require some degree of collaboration to be effective. After having conducted many research projects on a wide range of topics within my technical discipline of agricultural and biological engineering, I have devoted much of my effort in studying how to make things work together as functional systems, in addition to studying how to make individual things work better. This field of study is called systems analysis, systems engineering, systems integration, or systems informatics and analytics. Its emphasis is to investigate how behaviors of individual parts and their interactions affect the overall performance of the system as a whole. Combining my scholarly interest and administrative responsibility, I have become convinced that the systems thinking approach and leadership skills complement each other in a very enlightening way. Collaboration is certainly a systems type phenomenon.

More and more research projects that provide solutions to real world challenges require collaboration by individuals across a wide range of backgrounds. While collaboration is needed in addressing challenging issues for the society, there are inherent challenges in collaborative activities. However, the opportunities for success through collaboration beyond the simple sum of what individuals can achieve are also significant and exciting. Here is some of my own experience in challenges and opportunities from participating and leading collaborative research efforts.

There seems to be a lot of information and publicity on the critical problems that our society is facing. While it is easy for the majority of people to agree on the "grand challenges," it is not always obvious how to identify the right problems that are worthy of solving. Identifying correct problems to solve certainly requires collective efforts. Once a researchable problem has been clearly laid out, a series of actions will need to effectively carried-out: frame the pathway to solutions, assemble a collaborative team, build an effective team, obtain and deploy resources, establish effective communication mechanisms, encourage continuous interactions, set decision points, make informed changes, capture and document the collective wisdom, share credits, and celebrate successes.

Leadership in Collaboration

As mentioned above, collaboration is a system level phenomenon. Leaders lead systems and system thinking informs leadership. System and leadership are two widely used words in the literature, as well as in formal presentations and casual conversations. Most people understand the meaning of these words; however, everyone seems to interpret the words somewhat differently. On the other hand, it is interesting to observe that almost all believe both systems approach and effective leadership are essential to the success of an organization. It is, therefore, important to build the capacity among leaders to have a truly "system level emphasis" in their approaches to addressing relevant issues when leading their organizations.

The term "system" has been used in a wide range of contexts. It mostly represents two things: a form or a methodology. Although both form and methodology are equally important, it appears that more attention has been paid to systematically understand and describe the form than to apply the methodology to address systems level concerns. Often times this systems level methodology is of critical importance for decision makers to reach "well-founded" and "well-balanced" conclusions. Since leaders must lead, a leadership style that emphasizes systems level questions (as opposed to only focusing on component or local level issues) is necessary in handling the complexity of an organization.

Many books have been, and will continue to be, written on the subject of leadership. In many book stores, it is common to see shelves that are dedicated to displaying books dealing with leadership and related topics. I have benefitted in many ways from reading a good number of those books. I have learned how to identify and describe situations when leadership skills, such as visioning, strategic planning, motivating, team building, etc., are needed. I have gained a good understanding of well-researched and textbook style methods in carrying out leadership tasks.

I have been fortunate to be given the opportunities to lead several academic departments at four different universities over the past 23 plus years. I have been told by many experienced high level university leaders/administrators that academic department heads/chairs are the most stressful, although not the most difficult, positions on the campus. I fully agree with this assessment. Frequently, a department head needs to simultaneously play multifaceted roles, excel in scholarly contribution and administrative effectiveness, balance in promoting academic advancement, exercise good business sense, interface between the departmental faculty and the department/college/university administrators, and interact with the stakeholders. In addition, a department head needs to be visionary on the one hand and to be able to handle detailed work on the other hand. Frequently, the available "staff" support at the department level is inadequate. Parallel processing and multitasking to directly satisfy a large clientele and solve problems that do not have obvious answers are typical in a department head's very long work day. On top of all these, an academic department head has to face the consequence of his/her decisions directly and immediately. In the end, the success of a department, just like any organization, is measured by the collective performance of all its members.

Implementation of collaborative teams may benefit from following a systematic approach that has three essential aspects: systems, system thinking, and system analysis steps. The simple definition of a system is a group of interrelated components integrated to function/behave in certain ways and/or serve certain purposes, normally under certain constraints and/or external influences. "System" and "component" are relative terms. A system may be a component of a larger system and a component may be a system of smaller components. For example, an academic unit is a system that consists of students; faculty; staff; education, research, and outreach programs; offices; laboratories; equipment; by-laws; administrative structure; etc. An academic unit can also be a component of a campus system.

System thinking is a holistic approach emphasizing the performance as a whole based on the understanding of all components in the system and the interrelationships among the components. The overall purpose is to make things work better, as well as make things work together. The reasons why system thinking is important are (1) individually functioning components do not necessarily make up a workable system, (2) piece-wise knowledge about individual components does not automatically provide a complete understanding of the overall system, and (3) necessary yet missing components can be detected after observing/analyzing the system as a whole.

Tasks may be carried out and problems may be solved by a team in many different ways. One proven set of problem solving system analysis steps is as follows:

1. Define system's scope and objectives – set system boundaries for the purpose of analysis, specify required system functions, describe relevant system considerations, state system level issues and question, etc.
2. Identify system constraints – consider resource limitations, social acceptance, regulatory policies, etc.
3. Establish indicators of success – investigate minimum cost, maximum return on investment, maximum productivity, minimum undesirable consequences, maximum social benefit, etc.
4. Conduct system abstraction – state key components and their descriptors, interrelationships and interactions among components, initial condition (current situations), boundary conditions (external factors), etc.
5. Obtain data and information – identify data needs and sources, establish data protocols, etc.
6. Handle uncertainty and incomplete information – commonly seen techniques include stochastic simulation, heuristic reasoning, fuzzy logic, gap analysis, etc.
7. Incorporate heuristic and fuzzy reasoning – consult with experts, obtain input from diverse viewpoints, practice experiential learning, etc.
8. Develop system model – quantify information and/or process, correlate data mathematically or logically, etc.
9. Verify and validate model – ensure the model performs algorithmically and/or computationally as designed, evaluate the closeness of the model output to the reality, etc.
10. Investigate what-ifs – conduct scenario simulation, determine the optimum solution, etc.
11. Draw conclusions – determine technical workability and reliability, resource requirements, environmental impact, economic viability, sustainability, etc.
12. Plan and execute actions – take the advantage of the power of strategic intent, balance planning and actions, map short-term success versus long-term goals, assemble effective task forces, etc.

13. Communicate outcomes – provide decision support, support system planning, facilitate system management, enable system operation, monitoring, and control, etc.
14. Continuous monitoring and improvement – identify metrics for performance measurement, establish feedback loops for calculated changes, understand the effect of changes, etc.

Leadership in collaboration may be expressed in a variety of forms. In order to create an environment that is favorable for collaboration, my personal experience has shown me that the following leadership actions are essential:

Think systems – Problems and issues that are worth a leader's effort to solve and resolve are those without obvious solutions. As mentioned above, an effective way of analyzing problems and formulating solutions is system approach. System thinking also facilitates big-picture views.

Pay attention to details – It is a common saying that the devil is in the details. It is important to avoid vacuum behind big ideas and communicate expectations clearly. Delegation is effective leadership; however, it requires periodic follow-ups. Every team needs at least one detail person.

Make things happen – Leadership is essential in charting directions and managing changes. Leaders need to have skills in persuasion, motivation, and consensus building; consolidation of ideas; and conflict resolution. It is important for leaders to understand the power of a first draft.

Get things done – Leaders need to be very skillful at multi-tasking and parallel processing, delivering high quality results in a timely fashion, practicing the art of delegation, mobilizing taskforces with clear expectations, and allocating resources towards strategic goals and tasks.

Enable people to succeed – Leaders recognize talents, help set goals, provide mentoring and role models, help with networking opportunities, provide enabling work environment and resources, provide leadership and succession opportunities, provide professional development opportunities, and recognize achievements.

Lead, follow, support, cheer, and celebrate – Leaders must lead. They also know the importance of team work, pay attention to cultivate future leaders, provide leadership opportunities to others, promote graceful effectiveness, and give/share credits.

Challenges and Successes in Building Collaborative Teams

In the process of becoming an experienced leader, several core competencies are very likely to be acquired. Although everyone may place a different emphasis on what the most useful skills are for a leader that is charged to build effective collaborative teams, it is worthwhile to highlight some indispensable ones.

Communication - It is probably a cliché for many people to hear that communication is very important to effective leadership and team building. The benefit of proactive communication is to ensure that a leader will have well-informed colleagues to work with. It is easy to agree that well-informed colleagues are an invaluable strength of an organization. Communication is not just disseminating information in a one-way fashion. It requires a careful attention to who the audience is, what message to convey, how to deliver and receive the message, when to follow up if actions are needed, and how to evaluate and improve the effectiveness of communication.

Vision - We all know that change is constant. It is especially true for a sustainable and competitive organization. One of the leader's main tasks is to lead the processes of change. Contrary to common belief, most of the members of an organization do not mind changes. What they may be concerned about is the uncertainty of what the organization is changing into. Therefore, it is important that a leader is visionary; i.e. having the ability to chart a viable vision for the organization and to clearly communicate the vision internally and externally. Without this ability, it will be difficult for the leader to motivate the members of the organization to follow his/her leadership.

Making decisions – Decisions trigger actions. Leadership requires problem solving skills. Problem solving processes frequently include a series of decision making steps. Making a decision is not necessarily a difficult task if the outcome is expected to be only an actionable decision. What becomes more challenging is to always bring about an optimum decision. In many cases, how and what decisions are made are equally important. The ability to effectively identify information and people for supporting the decision and managing the decision process is highly valuable in a leader. Transparency and inclusiveness in decision making, except for sensitive or confidential matters, are highly advisable.

Fostering leadership – Changes will be constant and, therefore, leaders will always be needed to lead changes. There are many ways leaders are needed. Every organization needs to have a sustained ability to identify and attract the best people in its effort to continuously advance its goals. The best people to assume the leadership roles may be recruited externally. It is equally important to develop future leaders internally. There is an intrinsic value for an organization to nurture leadership among its members. A long term impact to an organization that fosters leadership, as well as administrative skills, is its continuity in pursuit of excellence. Immediate benefits will come from the fact that people who understand leadership are not only good leaders but also good team members. Staying abreast of new concepts and continuing improvement of skills for current leaders are obviously very important for a successful organization. Leadership development opportunities may be provided through training programs and assignment of leadership responsibilities. It is also extremely helpful to have an organizational culture that values leadership ability, engages in leadership development, and encourages leadership actions.

Enhancing productivity – Organizations are established to collectively develop, achieve, and advance their goals. Their effectiveness is frequently measured by their productivity, i.e. the ratio of accomplishment (output) versus effort (input). The success of leadership is judged by how productive the team is. It should, therefore, be an effective leader's task to constantly enable the highest possible productivity of his/her team. The definition of productivity should be developed by the participation of the team members and the clientele. Many factors may affect the productivity of a team. It is important to have the "best people" on the team; however, in many cases, it is even more productive to have team members who have the synergy to work together. Effective leaders need to work with their team members to create a clear expectation at the organizational level, facilitate the alignment of personal goals with the organizational goals, and seek ways to optimize how things are getting done.

Measuring effectiveness – It is well-known that monitoring and control are essential in ensuring the proper functions of physical systems. It works the same way for an organization. It is very common for organizations to use certain metrics to evaluate the performance of their units and employees. Normally, quantitative and/or qualitative goals and objectives are identified by an organization as an outcome of its planning process. Although quantitative metrics are conceptually easier to measure, certain qualitative indicators are very important for some organizations. The measurement of effectiveness is a continuous process since continuous improvement is very important to an organization, especially in a constantly changing environment. One useful consideration in designing the measurement method is to generate actionable insights, i.e. the kind of information that will help decide what, if any, changes need to be made.

Developing human resources – A seasoned leader would agree that the most critical element of an organization is its people. Almost all things evolve around people. Issues related to people could be the easiest to address or the most challenging to deal with. It all depends on whether the people have the right skills, attitude, and support to carry out their tasks and fulfill their responsibilities. Therefore, human resource development is a central job function of a leader. He/she is required to carefully develop hiring plans, recruit the best people, and enable them to succeed. It is obvious that no leader would purposely bring someone into his/her team to fail. Since a leader is most likely to have the responsibility of creating productive and pleasant dynamics among the people he/she works with, he/she needs to be prepared to help align personal goals with the organization's goals, deal with people who have poor interpersonal skills, and resolve conflicts. On the positive side, leaders are uniquely positioned to have the pleasure of rewarding high performance and celebrating success of their team members.

Formative Process of Approach to Collaboration

Through my many years of working with people from a wide range of backgrounds, I have found that certain professional and personal traits, styles, and behaviors are easily recognized and much appreciated by others, including collaborators. Here is a list of them:

Quality work – We are frequently judged by how we do things and what we produce (in terms of quantity and quality). Almost all of us put considerable effort into getting things done every day. We always have a choice: accomplishing the tasks in an "acceptable" manner or striving to produce the results of the highest quality possible. The criteria used to evaluate the quality of work in different organizations are expected to vary. In any case, for an organization, high quality work may contribute to saving cost, increasing profit, reducing risk, establishing reputation, recruiting and retaining the best people, attracting better business opportunities, creating a productive and pleasant work environment, and enhancing sustainability and competitiveness of the organization. At the personal level, sustained high quality work shows attention to professionalism, respect for others, and a high performance standard. It also helps build self-confidence, professional credentials, and external recognition.

Be responsive – With the current technology, communication occurs at lightning speed in most parts of our daily life. It seems that the initiators of communication always expect to receive a response at almost a near real-time level. Most of us have a genuine intention to be prompt in our correspondence with others; however, we also feel the challenge in managing our time and energy every day. Nevertheless, there are significant benefits from being responsive. It sends a clear message that a person puts a strong emphasis in engaging and working with others. People really appreciate the attention they receive when the replies come promptly. Responsiveness helps sustain and enhance networking and collaboration. The perceived accessibility increases people's assurance of closing the loop in a timely fashion. Also, it in effect helps smooth out the workload over time for everyone involved. Although responsive individuals are frequently requested and trusted to help deal with urgent matters, they are also more likely to be offered opportunities to engage in exciting activities.

Meet the deadlines – Work being conducted as part of a complex system requires effective interfaces with the work of many others. The successful coordination of work done by a team, simultaneously and/or sequentially, depends heavily on the timely progress of each team member's tasks. To prevent from being a bottleneck or becoming a hurdle in achieving a team's planned goals, it is extremely important that all team members are able to meet their deadlines. In fact, not being responsive or not making the deadlines is frequently a major deterrent of effective collaborations.

Think globally, act locally – There is a Chinese saying that advises people to "look at the big picture and take care of small details." Our work is getting more and more locally operated and globally connected. A leader needs to be able to think globally in decision making and act locally in execution. The ability to map the two is highly valuable. This concept and methodology is discussed in the Leadership in Collaboration section above.

Honesty and integrity – Simply put, honesty is "say what you do" and integrity is "do what you say." (Note: This does not suggest that we openly disclose confidential and sensitive information). An effective leader is frequently a trusted individual. This kind of trust is mostly built upon telling the truth and following through with the promises. Many people are depending on leaders to provide guidance and support. When (mutual) trust ceases to exist, the desirable productive and pleasant work relationship can easily become non-sustainable. In addition, keeping honesty and integrity as core values in our operations tends to minimize complications in the long run.

Team work (lead, follow, support, cheer, and celebrate as described above) – Leaders are most needed in addressing and solving complex problems that require a significant amount of teamwork. A leader's role in facilitating teamwork has many facets. It is obvious that a leader must lead. It is equally important that a leader knows when and how to follow, support, cheer, and celebrate in a team setting. (The only thing a leader should not do, if at all possible, is to stay out of the way). A team can be a small group or a very large organization. Regardless the size of the team, it is the team leader's responsibility to make sure the goals of the team and team members are aligned and the ability to succeed as a team and as individuals is enabled and empowered.

Be part of the solution – It is part of the human nature to air our disappointment and/or frustration when things have not gone well, and it is fine to do that in a constructive way. One sign of an effective team is to be able to quickly recover from the setback and redirect the energy towards solving the problem together. A good thought and action to have in dealing with challenging situations is to ask the question: "How can I help?" This kind of attitude is very valuable in strengthening the resiliency of the team. A leader needs to always be part of the solution. Also, it is his/her responsibility to create an environment that encourages the team members to exhibit this kind of behavior.

Collegiality – The climate of a work place should enable people to be productive in a pleasant way. Many of us spend a very big portion of every week at a work place. We all contribute to the creation of the climate of our work place. Collegial colleagues make our time at work more enjoyable. Collegiality does not mean we always agree with each other on every issue. It is the respect and friendliness we extend to our co-workers. Our concern for and interest in other's feelings makes us a good person to work with. This will in turn shape how we interact with each other and build a functional and effective team.

Interpersonal skills – Many of the above mentioned traits are ultimately expressed by how we relate and interact with others. We all come from a wide range of cultural and educational backgrounds. What professional and personal styles we carry to our work place will need to be interfaced with what others bring. I think we all can recognize the difference between good and bad interpersonal skills. However, we continue to see some individuals treating others in inappropriate ways. Interpersonal skills can frequently drive whether or how things get done in an organization. We already talked about how an organization can benefit from having collegial co-workers. On the other hand, individuals with poor interpersonal skills can put a huge burden on their organization's daily operations.

Be patient – We all want things to happen at a pace to our liking. Unfortunately, in a complex world, complications frequently occur. Being patient is not to just sit back and wait for things to come around.

It is to understand that being unnecessarily anxious about something beyond our control may not be helpful at all; especially if we let the situation become the source of our frustration. Proper ways of handling patience can keep a person calm, which can be projected as a strength of a leader. Patience can often time serve as a mental buffer for someone whose dynamic work pace requires multi-tasking and parallel processing.

Strategic framing – I would like to quote another old Chinese saying: "One who has no long-term plans will definitely have short-term worries". It is beneficial for everyone, especially the leaders, to know how to plan for the future. Some kind of strategy is commonly used as a future plan. How to develop a strategy that includes effective actions is a learnable skill. Leaders must have this strategic framing skill, or be closely supported by people who have the skill. Furthermore, this skill must be put into use to constantly provide clear direction for the team the leader is leading. An organization that has an effective and actionable strategy to advance its future goals will be able to motivate its members to feel the excitement of their contribution to the organization. On the other hand, the atmosphere of a strategy-less organization can be quite stale. The commonly known items in a strategic frame of an organization are vision, mission, values, domains, goals, objectives, indicators of success, and actions.

Advice for Building Successful Collaborative Teams - Systems Approach to Collaboration

By this time, we have emphasized that system methodology and leadership ability are a powerful combination of skill sets for leaders that enable and empower collaborations among team members and beyond. Some core competencies of an effective team are as follows:

Manage feedback and feedforward change loop – Figure 1 shows the concept of managing changes using feedback and feedforward mechanisms. When a team needs to develop a vision, address issues at hand, and solve critical problems (stage 1), one immediate task is to come up with expectations and indicators of success (stage 2). The leader(s) of the team will work with the team to fulfill the expectations (stage 3). Strategic change actions (stage 4) implemented by the organization(s) undergoing the change (stage 5) will be executed. The stakeholder(s) and customer(s) of the organization(s) will evaluate the outcomes of the change (stage 6). Before the change actions are taken, a model may be used to predict the outcomes of the change (stage 7). Both or one of the results of model prediction (i.e. feedforward) and stakeholder/customer evaluation (i.e. feedback) may be used to measure the success of the change (stage 8). This outcome assessment may then be used to modify the vision, issue, and problem, as well as to advise change leaders (point A) in formulating new change strategies. External to this change loop are possible external factors (point B) that may influence various stages of the loop. This loop may have to be carried out iteratively.

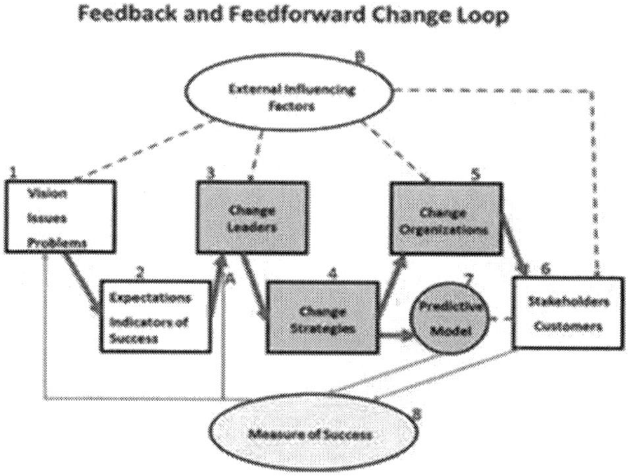

Figure 1. Schematic diagram of feedback and feedforward loop in managing changes

Formulate decision support – Effective decision making needs to have sound information support. The process in gathering decision support starts with defining the scope of the problem followed by formulating required analyses and/or solutions. It is frequently helpful to connect the problem at hand to a bigger picture to see the "global" impact of "local solutions." After that, the needed information may be determined. The next step will be to identify sources of information and methods of information gathering. Several worthy things to consider are asking good questions, following "science based" methodologies in data/information analysis, communicating the proper use of the outcome of analysis, and being mindful of the power of the first draft.

Conduct strategic planning – Various strategic planning processes have been practiced by many organizations. Here is a step-by-step example:

1. Prepare for a brainstorming session
    ii. Determine when and where
    iii. Select participants (facilitator, support staff, integration leaders, discussion leaders, discussants, etc.)
    iv. Perform strengths, weaknesses, opportunities, and threats (SWOT) analysis
    v. Distribute or present the result of SWOT analysis
    vi. Formulate and distribute brainstorming session agenda
    vii. Arrange logistics (meeting and breakout rooms, audio/visual equipment, name tags, refreshments, lunches, dinners, etc.)
2. Conduct brainstorming sessions
3. Summarize information gathered during the brainstorming session
4. Prepare a draft report
5. Review and revise the draft report with the integration leaders
6. Distribute the draft report to the discussants and request input
7. Finalize the draft report into a strategic plan by considering the input
8. Prepare and distribute various versions of the strategic plan
9. Implement the strategic plan
10. Monitor, evaluate, and modify the strategic plan

Perform concurrent analysis – This is the process of integrating information, knowledge, and wisdom related to the problem from various sources in a (near) real-time fashion. The concurrent analysis is particularly useful in evaluating solutions to system level questions. It will facilitate delivering the results of analysis based on the most current situation, also in a (near) real-time fashion.

Make decisions – As alluded to above, decision making is one of the most important responsibilities of a leader. Perceived or real inability of a leader to make decisions is a major cause of frustration for his/her team members. High quality decision support is invaluable in decision making. A sound "philosophical" backing help maintain the consistency and transparency of decisions. The processes used to derive decisions are often times as important (if not more than) as the decisions themselves. Negotiation, conflict resolution, crucial conversation, and consensus building skills are frequently needed. Efforts should be made to avoid any local optimum that causes system level problems and/or unexpected consequences. Leaders should not be satisfied with only workable solutions and should strive for "optimum" solutions. Ideally, any decision should not prevent a leader from making good decisions in the future.

Facilitate simultaneous planning and implementation – This process demonstrates the leader's strong interest in implementing the outcome of planning. Short-term wins towards long-term goals keep team members motivated. Implementation could provide feedback to planning. Task forces with volunteered membership and elected leaders are frequently used for identifying implementation activities, responsible parties, and timelines. Properly executed, this process helps build a "culture of experimentation" for the organization.

Balance analyses and actions – It is easy to understand that action without analysis is not wise and analysis without action appears to be indecisive. Properly set scope, purpose, and depth help balance the analysis and action. Frequently, analyses do not have to reach "perfection" to be useful. Many analyses require reasoning with uncertain and incomplete information. Leaders are expected to exercise good judgments in deciding the corresponding courses of actions. Outcomes of actions are valuable in refining or enhancing future analyses.

Promote graceful effectiveness – There are usually many ways to get things done and goals accomplished. Collegial and cooperating environments promote system wide effectiveness. Every member of an organization deserves to be in a productive and pleasant environment at his/her work place. The "being part of a solution" mentality is worth cultivating within an organization. System level optimum (as opposed to local optimum) is easier to achieve when things are done with graceful effectiveness.

Build knowledge and wisdom – A learning organization is very good at systematically capturing, sharing, and utilizing knowledge and wisdom from the information gathered, analyses performed, creativity generated, success achieved, and lessons learned. Success breeds success; especially for organizations that are effective in building their knowledge and wisdom. Building knowledge and wisdom is a continuous process.

Empower with knowledge and wisdom – Leadership intelligence relies heavily on information, knowledge, and wisdom. Sharing of accumulated knowledge and wisdom should be strongly encouraged in an organization. Organizational knowledge and wisdom enhance the organization's sustainability and competiveness; simply put, sustainability is "continue to do well" and competitiveness is "positioned to win." The sustained wellness and short-term and long-term wins of an organization are better collectively defined by its members as a team.

Summary

Collaboration is a powerful way of achieving and advancing goals of an organization when working as a team. Everyone's experience from working collectively with other team members can be very different. Leadership ability and skills are essential to enable and empower proactive and effective collaboration among members of a team. An organization or a team is a system. Issues, problems, and tasks that an organization needs to address, solve, and execute are mostly of system level scopes as opposed to individual focus. In this article, we have touched upon the topics of necessary elements for leadership development and generally appreciated traits of a leader, as well as how leadership can be made exciting and effective. We also discussed how leaders can solve complex problems using systems methodologies and how we can integrate systems methodologies and leadership.

CHAPTER 26

STEAM Business Collaboration

STEAM Education Key to Creating an Innovative Workforce

Harvey White
Founder and Former Chairman of Leap
SHWX2

My childhood and formal education did not dwell on, overtly encourage, or have any recognizable collaboration included in its curricula. I was born in the middle of the great depression into a family that had minimal education, but was lucky to have found jobs so that our economic situation was hard but not crushing. I was raised in a family and community where cultural discussion of diverse issues was not prevalent.

My father was born in Sweden, stowed-away on a ship – was caught en-route to America and finished the voyage working at menial tasks. I would surmise that his vetting at Ellis Island was minimal. He was a true salesman. My mother was born and raised in West Virginia on the Ohio River. Unlike many within her community, she and her family were not raised in the coalfields. She had been living in New York City working in a department store and enjoying the roaring twenties where she met my father. They married just before the great economic crash and divorced soon after I was born. My mother and I returned to

West Virginia when I was almost one or two years old and we moved in with my grandparents. Afterwards she met my stepfather, also a true salesman and a local piano musician, and they married when I was five.

Education and Related Items

My education was all in West Virginia except for 4 grade school years in South Carolina. When we returned to West Virginia, I entered 7th grade in the local public school system. I played some sports in junior high, but other than that, I did not look for or get very involved in any significant extracurricular activities. I graduated right after I turned 17 with a B+ average.

I chose to attend a small private college that had a strong reputation as having the best chemistry department in the area. I was a chemistry major and did very well as a freshman. I was the first sophomore ever selected to run the freshman lab. In my sophomore year, the department head told me he would help me obtain a scholarship or grant to get a masters and doctorate if I continued to perform well. He painted a picture of a career in research and/or teaching. I did not picture myself doing either of those. I liked being with people and instead saw myself in a lab full of bubbling retorts, beakers and flasks.

So, after 2 years I transferred to a large state university and finished with a BA in economics. It also happened to greatly reduce the cost of college, which was not why I chose to go there, but was a nice side benefit. I had my first paper route when I was 12 and worked every summer from age 14 to college graduation. As a result, I paid for almost all of my college expenses up front and graduated with very little debt.

During my first semester in college I joined a fraternity and was a chapter officer by the end of my freshman year. I had met my first girlfriend and went to a lot of chapter events and parties. When I transferred to the large state university, I found that my fraternity chapter at the university was in terrible shape, with no chapter house and few members (I would have black balled most of them had I been there). It was seen to be among the worst fraternities on campus.

I tried to join another fraternity but found out that this was not allowed. I had a choice to make. I could either miss out on the fraternity party-world entirely or fix the fraternity chapter – I decided to do the latter. This was my first opportunity for collaboration with others and it was very successful. I worked with the Student Government and the other fraternities in the Inter Fraternity Council (IFC) participating in numerous projects. I found that if I helped someone or an organization to reach an objective they had, I would also earn their commitment to help me when I had an important objective or needed their support. Through this collaboration with IFC and our alumni, we were able to get a chapter house, had great pledge classes, and by graduation our fraternity was rated one of the best chapters on campus. I also benefited personally from all of this hard work. I got to be a "player" on campus as VP of the fraternity and the IFC, a Student Senator, Student Judge, and a member of the University's student leadership Honorary.

Seeing America

Two of my fraternity brothers and I were elected as delegates to the national fraternity convention in San Francisco during the August after I graduated. Due to the gas rationing in WWII, my parents' jobs and financial constraints, we did very little traveling as a family when I was growing up. Most of our travel was restricted to visiting family in other parts of West Virginia. We did not get to do much sightseeing, or visiting of historical sites, etc.

This trip with my fraternity brothers was a brand-new type of adventure for me. So, when we entered Alabama, it was the farthest west that I had ever been before. Fortunately, we did not have to pay for a single room rental until we reached Las Vegas. We lodged from fraternity chapter to chapter and spent a couple nights at the homes of relatives as we went west on the drive across the south and southwest on the way to San Francisco. San Francisco was the largest city I had ever spent time in and the bustle of the city, the Golden Gate Bridge, and the view from the Oakland hills to the ocean were all new experiences for me.

Seeing the topography and sires in the actual trip was a real eye-opener of what our country really looked like. On the way back, we drove across the plains states without stopping except for gas, changing drivers and food. We arrived back home at the end of August quite impressed, happy, and tired.

Business – And the Luck of the Draw

Upon returning from the convention, I started looking for a position in the fall of 1955. Most jobs for graduates had been filled during the summer, but I got a job as an Industrial Engineer at a plant of a cost-driven producer of rayon. The company wanted to hire a graduate chemist without paying the going salary. They settled for my 2 years in chemistry and paid me more than BA's in economics were getting. The plant was started in the depression and did very well because rayon was cheaper to make than nylon. It also did well during WWII, because airplanes had a growing impact on warfare and therefore nylon was essential for parachutes. Rayon was a good substitute material for parachutes other uses that nylon had served.

I spent most of my days in the factory. Most hourly employees were paid, based on time studies like mine, piece-work amounts for tasks done. I was doing studies for the maintenance tasks. These were men who were the bread-winners for their families. They were the base of a manufacturing company and the dedicated workers who wanted to do a good job and raise a family that were, and are, the heart of our country. I saw what a manufacturing company looked like and how it operated. I had exposure to manufacturing processes that were invaluable assets for the first position of my career.

Two years later, I was recruited to join a team of 3 Harvard MBA's and a CPA that reported directly to the CEO and was tasked with turning around the company for new owners. Now married, we packed up and moved to Richmond where the head office was located. I did a wide range of tasks from operational and personnel reviews to financial analyses and budgets. We uncovered a lot - fixed or closed some divisions, and made systems and operating improvements. Learning how companies are structured and the various manager's roles and how they impacted performance was a very different view than the one on the factory floor - but equally valuable for me.

I found that I could deal with, and hold my own with, executives and other college graduates, with all kinds of degrees and titles. Regarding degrees and titles, I felt that one of the three MBAs was great, one was so-so, and one was not very good. If they had not been Harvard MBAs, then one would have been great, one so-so, and one not very good.

The company had many problems and was headed towards closure or sale, so I started looking for my next job and planning my career. I had gained valuable business experience at all levels (from floor to CEO) which assisted me in my career planning. I had seen that whether it was sales pricing, or volume, or products cost, or people's wages, etc. – all the results, ended up being reported as dollars.

There are two paths to a career in finance - the CPA path of reporting results or the Control path of using the reported data for planning, developing systems, and controlling costs and effort. I much preferred the latter. I included my recent budgeting and financial analysis tasks in my resume and it worked.

Finance as A Skill and A Career

I was hired by a large, Boston headquartered, technology company as the Budget Manager of their Bristol Tennessee/Virginia missile components plant. This was my first job managing people. It was a small staff of budget analysts. The much larger Cost Accounting Department, whose staff of largely clerks, was then added to my department and that required me to expand my management skills.

I was transferred and promoted to the Boston Area. I assumed, a number of positions as a Finance Department Manager or a Controller of a plant. This culminated as the Plant Controller for a large missile engineering and production facility. In the expanse of 5- years, I had run financial responsibilities for increasingly larger single site operations.

I wanted to run a business or a plant. I found that the company had only technically degreed personnel as business managers. I began a search and a headhunter I knew got me a position as the Operations Manager, responsible for production, customer service, personnel, finance, purchasing, i.e. all functions (but Sales), for a privately-owned mattress company serving Southern Connecticut and the New York City area. I found that selling to sleep shops was fascinating. This provided valuable lessons in consumer customers and marketing that later helped me run my consumer business.

When I joined, I asked for, but got no options or stock. I was told they could come if I did well, and I did well, but still no stock. Slowly it dawned on me that I was there to "keep the seat" warm for the owner's son to graduate and I would never see stock.

Go West – Young Man

Over Thanksgiving, I called a friend for a reference – he said *"reference no – get your (blank) out here now- I have a new job and I need you to help me"*. Also, moving to LA sounded neat and I started working for him on January 1st

Working for the next 4-years at large multi-product companies provided me with a lot of experience in varied industries that helped me eventually move into running them.

My friend was the Controller of a large public company that was rapidly acquiring companies with a wide variety of products and located across the country - based on the idea that "Synergism" (from using a single financial reporting, and control system) would reduce costs and streamline operations. I was to build the team to define, establish, and operate that system. This was the time period when key punched cards were the input for the system. I set up regional data centers at locations that had the fewest days of air service lost to storms. Unfortunately, this required extensive travel virtually every week. Having a family with 3 young kids, this was not acceptable.

I then accepted a position as Group Controller of a large technical company. I reviewed monthly performance with all division presidents and their controllers at locations across the company, as travel did not slow down much.

I responded positively to a new opportunity when a headhunter contacted me.

Sun, Sand and Success –

This was when I joined a Fortune 500 company as Asst. Corporate Controller. Turned out to be my path into corporate management. We moved to San Diego – and I have not left since!!

The company consisted of three groups - the Aerospace Group ASG that designed and built airplane parts, the Transportation Group TSG that designed and made subway cars and people movers, and the Industrial Systems Group ISG which consisted of a number of small companies. I was the Controller for both ISG & TSG

My responsibilities expanded rapidly. Within 6 months I was the Corporate Controller and before the end of the first year I was the EVP of ISG. In another year, TSG was struggling with its 300-subway car order for WMATA and the EVP was let go and combined with ISG. As a group EVP, I negotiated national telecom deals for antennas, a joint venture with a British firm for bulk mail systems for USPS. I dealt with the WMATA Board of Directors on major engineering issues with their cars. Also, I acted as the CFO to negotiate a 4-bank debt restructuring. (I say I may be the only CFO of a Fortune 500 company who never set foot in an Accounting Class.)

Due to WMATA in-fighting by officers, replacement of the retired president, and other horrific politics, I couldn't stand being there anymore so I negotiated a deal and left.

Joining The Local Economy

A friend and I bought two distributors - one for fishing tackle and one for Christmas ornaments. The products worked well together as October, November and December are not great fishing tackle months. We sold to individual stores but our main customers were the Sears stores for fishing and the Military PX's for both.

After a while, we saw that both of us weren't needed to run the company and we decided that each of us would look for a new job with the other remaining. I was the first to find a new job and as the CFO of Linkabit, a small private technology company that is the progenitor of the telecom industry in San Diego, due to the number of people who left and started or who lead successful telecom companies in San Diego.

Linkabit was a significant supplier of sophisticated (often classified) communication systems for DoD. We expanded to develop commercial products such as a Video-cypher that allowed satellite TV networks to stop free poaching of their programs.

As we grew, we restructured management by forming an Office of the President that included the CEO and me as COO. This allowed the CEO to concentrate on the technology and for me to handle the non-technical areas and issues. (We collaborated in that structure for 20 years.) I was also named a director. I set up a plant in Puerto Rico, negotiated with the government, commercial customers, DoD agencies, and suppliers. We merged with another company, but that ultimately did not work out as it greatly impacted our culture. Seven of us left. The merged company was then later acquired.

In 1985, the seven of us who left founded Qualcomm, thus creating the first mobile wireless data service. Qualcomm is now a multi-billion-dollar company that dominates inventing, designing and licensing its proprietary CDMA technology, and the sale of chips for the ever higher-speed and capacity needs of wireless users. It is still growing and creating new products with facilities and sales worldwide.

In 1998, I left Qualcomm and was the founding Chairman and CEO of Leap Wireless. We built cellular systems in Latin America and the US where our Cricket wireless became a nationwide service. We introduced the "all you could use" pricing model that is the base of all bundled pricing today. Leap was bought, by AT&T for $1.2 billion after I retired in 2004.

Freedom to Pursue Other Interests

I served as an employee in all the companies that I worked with the exception of the last three.

In those three companies, I was also an owner, which changes the economic returns that owners experience. Because we were successful it allowed me to retire comfortably.

As a result, of stepping down, I have had time to my experience and contacts to address a range of areas including my interests like STEAM.

Owners also see how companies develop, innovate, grow and prosper - rather than just survive – and that knowledge can be applied to areas other than business.

Community, Arts, Education and Philanthropic Involvement

My first arts board was the Old Globe Theater - one of the most highly regarded regional theaters in the US with many shows that go to Broadway – and then go on to win Tony's.

The Globe is special to me and makes my retirement more fun and exciting. It is where I met my wife, Sheryl, who retired as a top executive for a large regional bank. She has served on several theater and other boards. We support the Arts locally – and grew concerned about their removal from public school systems.

When working, I participated in business leadership groups. The San Diego business base was moving from tourism and the military, to technology. I was asked to join the Economic Development Corporation (EDC) whose members are the business leaders in the San Diego region. I also co-founded the San Diego Telecom Council.

STEAM - And Why Was I Involved?

My grandchildren were progressing through school and college and I had a concern about how our country's economy was doing and what that would mean relative to their future. That made me want to know more about innovation. I had seen this quote in a newspaper that summed up where we were and the country's economic future:

> *"The strength of the US economy in the future will be determined by our success in innovation versus the existing developed nations and their economies and, probably more importantly, the emerging nations and their rapidly developing economies."*

Manufacturing jobs were declining, not only because of international wage disparity, but also because automation would continue to expand. The US would not regain superiority.

Data on innovation rankings said that, for years, the US was the most innovative economy in the world. However, the US had dropped to 6th in many rankings and slipped to 8th in one. For a while the US got back to 3rd, but as other countries added emphasis on innovation, the US dropped back to around 5th - the last time I looked.

Bill Clinton's former Secretary of Education, Richard Riley, In the early 2000's, had summed up this need for innovation to drive our future by predicting that –

> *"The jobs in the greatest demand in the future don't yet exist and will require workers to use technologies that have not yet been invented to solve problems that we don't yet even know are problems"*

I agreed – innovation was key to success and it was necessary for us address it. The pace of new technologies and innovation is probably growing even faster now.

I decided I needed more information on innovation. Someone suggested I read this book: *A Whole NEW Mind* by Daniel Pink - sub titled "*Why right-brainers will rule the world*".

Pink writes that substantial research has been done to determine the tasks and processes that each side of the brain concentrates on and how each half works (i.e collaborates) with the other half to get the best results. That using both halves of the brain is what drives innovation and it is necessary, important and doable. This calls for a STEAM education system for us to have an innovation based economy.

But we don't have such a system – we have a 150+ year old system that was designed to deal with a basic change in the economy - from an agriculturally based one to a manufactured product based one. We face the same need to design a system to deal with a basic change in the economy – from a manufacturers product based one to an innovation based one.

The basic education system was founded to train boys to read, write, and do the simple math necessary to do the factory jobs and who were strong enough for the work too. Some teachers were needed so a few "Normal Schools" existed to train women to be the teachers for the boy's classes. It was well designed and worked pretty well, but the manufactured product business economy has changed – and our education system has not. It is not bad or broken, it's just too old.

An Unsuccessful Odyssey

I reengaged with the EDC, to get a sense on how others felt about the innovation need. During a presentation about STEM education, which I agree is needed, but feel is not sufficient, I was credited with coining the acronym STEAM as being the answer.

I decided that I would try to advance STEAM. I started with government officials because I had seen that STEM had been very successful largely to the President's support and the "cover" it gave politicians to support it when money issues were raised - and with the press it therefor garnered. So why not STEAM too?

Over the next year or two I met at least twice with both the Secretary of Education, Arne Duncan, and with the head of the NEA, Rocco Landesman, and several times with their staff. Both talked positively, but neither were really able to have a positive effect on STEAM as a necessity. Neither connected it with innovation. I also met once with the chairwoman of a special department set up by the Obama administration concerning arts and education who appeared to be uninterested and was not useful.

I was invited to a Sundance meeting of arts and business leaders. The arts leaders have the PTA mother's approach –which is "the school board should reinstall the school band because my daughter (or son) got so much out of it". I met several times with Bob Lynch of Americans for the Arts and addressed its national convention.

I met with the board of trustees with a major university and spoke at others. I was on TV forums and talked with business executives and others etc. etc. without any positive traction, though some STEAM based schools are beginning to spring up.

None of the above had connected STEAM and innovation at that time. I do see now that some schools have adopted STEAM as a better curriculum – not sure they have connected it as a national economic priority.

If There Ever Was a Need for Collaboration – It Is Here and Now!

Collaboration is the process of two or more people or organizations working together to realize or achieve something successfully.

I see the issue to be - getting agreement on anything in our very divided country today is really-hard, if even possible. However, I think that both sides of this division believe in a stronger economy – and that seems to me to equal "Collaboration".

My "collaborations" were many but were mostly called "negotiations" to reach a mutually sought goal. So, I don't have advice on how to get collaborations started. But the following are some of my thoughts or ideas on the collaborations that are needed.

- STEM proved that having "cover" for politicians and government personnel is critical. All of them, from the president to the local school board officer needs to see STEAM as a national economic priority.
- Business leaders collaborated in founding the existing 150-year-old system and they need to do it again for the new STEAM based education system. Therefore, collaborations at the federal, state and local agencies level as well as between all of them are important I think. I have no idea how to facilitate that task but perhaps they will listen to academic leaders like the authors of this book series "Pathways to Collaboration". A kind of "weird example" I thought of was - could the government (mainly IRS) let businesses "capitalize" funding for the needed STEAM educated innovative talent in the same way they currently allow companies to do for building a new plant that is required? They then would be able to spread the cost over years instead of impacting quarterly earnings and instead of government funding.

- Collaboration between scientific, neurological, and humanity entities to do a test or a study to show that the use of both sides of the brain really does make a quantitative improvement in innovation. This could answer the criticism that the studies that showed that many innovators also had an artistic skill may be coincidental or not. In other words -does using both sides of the brain really improve innovation? A similar study of how current graduates from the new STEAM based schools are doing in college or industry on innovation vs. other non-STEAM graduates would also be useful.

Epilogue

"The end of one collaboration is the beginning of another." This is true in the practical sense that a common reason for wrapping up one collaboration is the time demand of a new collaboration's beginning. But it is also true in the teleological sense of an "end" or "purpose." *The purpose of collaboration is to generate more collaborations.* It's how we know that a collaboration is alive and thriving; as life begets life, so too does a collaboration give rise to more collaborations.

While wrapping up the story of so many great collaborations, it is appropriate to think about the new collaborations that will grow out of what has been presented in these *Pathways to Collaboration*. What does the future look like for collaborations within and between academia, industry, and government?

The preceding stories provide hints as to what the future might bring. A common tension is the tension between serendipity and intention. Some collaborations were intentionally planted and grown over a long period of time before they bore fruit, but other collaborations arose seemingly out of nothing. Was it really from nothing? Exploring these *Pathways* is not only to celebrate collaborations, but also to better understand the genesis of great collaborations, to search out how best to encourage collaborations to flourish. What common features have we seen in these stories of success? Are these stories of great people or stories of great institutions? Luck or hard work?

It's easier to be lucky when betting on a biased coin, and it's easier to be a great person when the institution is supportive. The hope is that these *Pathways* might be a lesson for our institutions as to how they might "engineer serendipity" and how they might identify and support their "orchestrators of the organic." Many of these successful collaborations arose in environments that explicitly valued collaboration, which trained people to work with people who aren't like themselves. This is hard. It takes time and is risky. But figuring out how to build capacity for collaboration promises big payoffs for all our projects, and ultimately creates a virtuous cycle of collaboration begetting collaboration.

These stories are, admittedly, stories of *Pathways* and not of *Highways*. Perhaps instead of today's too-hidden trails connecting academia, industry, government, a future volume will highlight deeper and more permanent connections to be made between teams looking at the world in quite different ways. For today, the invitation is to be trailblazers, and to start from these collaborations to create even more.

Jim Fowler and Roman Holowinsky
The Ohio State University

About the Contributors

Andy Burnett

Andy Burnett is a recovering academic with a passion for creativity and technology. Over the years he has run software companies, taught at various universities, got degrees, and consulted for organizations both large and small. In other words, just like lots of other people, he has done stuff. However, along the way he was fortunate to discover that what really excites him is the potential to massively increase human creativity by harnessing the internet to build networks of creative minds. Given half a chance, he will launch into long tirades about how amazing this will be, when it finally comes together. Not surprisingly, Andy leads the KI work on Virtual Innovation Labs.

Otto J. Crocomo

Otto J. Crocomo was born in Piracicaba in the state of São Paulo in Brazil on September 23rd 1932 the eighth son of Giovani Crocomo and Thereza Vidili Crocomo. Married to Diva Lovadino Crocomo for 55 years, they have 5 children Marco Augusto, Adolfo Egídio, Maria Paula, Carla Maísa and Daniel and 1 grandchild Pedro Augusto. From a very early age he became interested in literature and, in high school in Chemistry, having participated in five Chemistry Debates as team leader, winning all debates. In, February 1953 he began his studies at "Luiz de Queiroz" School of Agriculture (ESALQ), University of São Paulo (USP), in Piracicaba. Still as an undergraduate student, he published 5 scientific papers and participated in three Congresses of Students of Agronomy (1954, 9155, 1956). Crocomo graduated as an Agronomist in 1956. In 1959 Crocomo obtained the academic title of "Free Lecturer" at ESALQ after four days of theoretical and practical examinations and the defense of his thesis on the metabolism of urea-14C in coffee leaves. Between the years 1959 and 1960, he was Assistant Professor of Biochemistry at the Faculty of Dentistry of Piracicaba and in 1960 was hired by ESALQ / USP as Assistant Professor of Organic Chemistry and Biological Chemistry. In 1966 Crocomo was appointed as Associate Professor of Organic Chemistry and Biological Chemistry and in 1975, after two days of public exams, became Full Professor of Biochemistry of the Department of Chemistry at ESALQ. Crocomo was Head and Vice-Head of that Department from 1971 to 1989.

Crocomo collaborated in the creation of the Center of Nuclear Energy in Agriculture (CENA) in 1966 and was responsible for development of the Plant Biochemistry Section between the years 1966 and 1988.

Between the years 1961 and 1962 Crocomo, he served as Professor of Chemistry and Biochemistry at the Faculty of Agronomy of the University of Zulia, Maracaibo, Venezuela. Between 1964 and 1965 Crocomo was a Fellow Researcher at the University of California, Davis campus (Prof. C. C. Delwiche) and from October 1968 to February 1969 at the University College London at Gower Street, London, England (Prof. L. Fowden). In 1976 Crocomo was a visiting Professor at the Botany Department of Durham University, Durham, England (Prof. Donald Boulter).

In 1971 with the collaboration of William Rod Sharp (The Ohio State University/USA), he introduced in Brazil at CENA the use of the techniques of plant cell, tissue and organs cultures in agriculture. In 1973 he was a member of the International Association of Plant Tissue Culture (IAPTC). Between 1973 and 1986 Crocomo was representative of Brazil in that Association. Crocomo attended International Congresses of the IAPTC in 1973, 1976, 1980, 1984, 1986, 1990 and 1994. In 1983 he was one of the founder of the Brazilian Association of Plant Tissue Culture (ABCTP) and its first president.

In 1978 Crocomo became a member of Academy of Sciences of the State of São Paulo; In 1981 Crocomo received the CNPq Medal/Brazil, in 1986 he received a DNAP Medal/USA, and in 2001 Crocomo received the Rutgers University Award/USA. In 2001 Crocomo was awarded the Scientific Merit Government of the State of São Paulo Medal/Brazil. In 2003 Crocomo was recipient of the ABCPT Award. In 2011 Crocomo received the Piracicaba Rotary Club Medal, and in 2012 he was awarded the Fernando Costa Medal from the Agronomic Engineers of the State of São Paulo Association. From 2009 to 2013 Crocomo was president of the ESALQ Retired Professors Association (ADAE).

In 1981 Crocomo idealized and founded the Center for Agricultural Biotechnology (CEBTEC) at ESALQ. In 2012 CEBTEC became Laboratory of Agricultural Biotechnology "Prof. Otto Jesu Crocomo".

From 1962-2003 Crocomo was a mentor to dozens of students and professionals in plant biochemistry and biology and collaborated with private companies in the use of *in vitro* culture of plant cells and tissue for plant propagation. In Brazil and abroad he as been a prolific publisher of refereed scientific articles and books, promoted and attended Symposiums, Congress and Scientific Meetings.

Patrick R. Dugan

Patrick R Dugan is an emeritus professor of microbiology at the Ohio State University in Columbus Ohio and is also a retired Science Fellow from the Idaho National Laboratories in Idaho Falls Idaho. Dugan holds B.Sc, Master of Science and PhD degree from Syracuse University. He spent eight years as an associate research scientist at the Syracuse University Research Corporation, investigating environmental and food related problems.

In 1964 he joined the faculty of the Department of Microbiology at the Ohio State University where he taught and conducted research on various aspects of environmental contamination. During this period Dugan served as a Department Chairman and later as the Dean of the College of Biological Sciences. He also served as a trustee of the Columbus Zoological Association and Zoo and was president of the Ohio Chapter of the American Society for Microbiology from 1968 to 1970

In 1987 he retired from the Ohio State University and joined the Idaho National Laboratory where he became a Science Fellow and Director of the Center for Bio-processing Technology; conducting research on a variety of projects of interest to the United States Department of Energy, while continuing the graduate faculty of the University of Idaho and the Ohio State University. In 1990 to 1991 he was an Association of Western University's Distinguished Lecturer. Dugan's published work as author and coauthor includes over 150 articles in peer reviewed journals, book chapters, and the book *Biochemical Ecology of Water Pollution* published in both English and Japanese.

Erich Grotewold

Erich Grotewold received his B.Sc. in Chemistry and Ph.D. in Molecular Biology/Biochemistry at the University of Buenos Aires, Argentina. Following a 3-year postdoc at Cold Spring Harbor Labs, he became a Staff Investigator at the Labs. In 1998, he moved to The Ohio State University, and is currently a professor in the Dept. of Molecular Genetics (College of Arts & Sciences) as well as in the Dept. of Horticulture & Crop Sciences (College of Food, Agriculture & Environmental Sciences). Dr. Grotewold's research focuses on plant systems biology, and main research projects include understanding the control of plant gene expression, establishing the architecture of plant gene regulatory networks, engineering plant metabolism using transcription factors, studying the transport of phytochemicals, and identifying cellular targets of natural products in plants and animals. Dr. Grotewold was elected AAAS Fellow in 2009, is the Director of the Arabidopsis Biological Resource Center (ABRC) as well as the Director of the Center for Applied Plant Sciences (CAPS) at OSU.

Alan R. Knight

Alan R. Knight (1946) was raised on a small farm in Rhode Island, where he also worked as a summer camp counselor, golf caddy, farm laborer, and life guard before attending the University of Rhode Island, where he graduated with a degree in agricultural technology and an ROTC commission in the U.S. Army. After a tour of duty in Germany as a communications intelligence company commander in the Army Security Agency and a sideline assignment as Rod and Gun Club manager and hunting-license instructor for U.S. soldiers, he returned to the USA and went to work for Cornell University as a county agricultural and community development agent.

During his eight years with Cornell, he also served as interim State Program Leader for Community Resource Development, communications specialist with the Cornell Farming Alternatives Program, and Science Writer with the Cornell News Service, and earned a Master of Professional Studies in Agriculture, involving a multi-disciplinary study of land resources.

After creating a new magazine for the New York Forest Owners Association, he was invited to become Associate Editor of *American Agriculturist* magazine, where he served for ten years, followed by short-term assignments with Rodale's *New Farm*, *Vineyard and Winery Management*, and *Farm Journal*. He also served as editor-in-chief and general manager of *New England Farmer* magazine.

His final career stop, before retiring in 2012, was a ten-year assignment with New York Farm Bureau, where he created the largest circulation farm newspaper in the state, designed a set of award-winning agriculture-promotion posters, and built a statewide program through which farmers donate more than 8.4 million pounds of surplus food to food pantries every year.

He also served as Chairman of the New York State Rural Safety Council and founder of both the Fred C. Waterman Conservation Education Center and the Ithaca Press Club.

Together with his wife, Nancy, Mr. Knight operated for many years both a sheep farm and a tour company that organized overseas study tours.

Julius P. Kreier

Julius P. Kreier, Professor Emeritus, Department of Microbiology, The Ohio State University, Columbus Ohio; Birthplace: Philadelphia, PA 1926; Education. Philadelphia Public Schools, 1932- 1945. Temple University 1945-1948, University of Pennsylvania, 1949-1953, V.M.D. University of Illinois, 1956-1962, MSc. Ph.D.; Employment. Veterinarian, Cooperative Mexican American Commission for the Eradication of Foot and Mouth Disease, Mexico 1954-1955. Veterinarian, Tuberculosis and Brucellosis Eradication Campaign, 1956 Maryland, USA. University of Illinois, Urbana Illinois, Research Associate 1956-1962. Ohio State University, Assistant Professor, Associate Professor and Full Professor of Microbiology 1962-1989; Professor Emeritus of Microbiology, 1989 to present. Publications 150 in reviewed journals. Books 22; Teaching. Parasitic Protozoology, Rodent Surgery, Introductory Immunology, Infectious Diseases; Mentoring of graduate students: PhD students 24, MSc students 38, Postdoctoral fellows and visiting professors 4; Fulbright Award University of the Republic of Uruguay, invited lecturer, Campinas University Brazil, Veterinary College, Ankara Turkey, Institute of Parasitology Shanghai China, Haryana Agricultural University, Madras, India; My research was primarily on the pathogenesis of infectious diseases of the blood. These were primarily caused by protozoa although some were caused by Rickettsial type organisms. From my work the greatest pleasures I had were from teaching. In fact I also believe that my greatest contribution to science was the students trained. My students are now scattered around the world and most are continuing to carry out scientific investigations.

David Lee

David Lee is Emeritus Professor of Biology at Florida International University and resides in Crestone, Colorado. He was born in Wenatchee in 1942 and raised in Ephrata, on the Columbia Plateau of eastern Washington State. He attended Pacific Lutheran University (B.S. in Biology, 1966) and Rutgers University in New Brunswick for graduate work in Botany (M.S. in 1968, Ph.D. in 1970, in biochemical plant systematic under the direction of David E. Fairbrothers). Following postdoctoral research in plant cell biology and tissue culture with Rod Sharp and Donald Dougall at The Ohio State University (1970-1972), he and his wife Carol moved to Malaysia, where he worked as a Lecturer at the University of Malaya, in Kuala Lumpur, 1973-76. There he developed life-long research interests in the functional ecology of tropical plants. He then worked with Francis Hallé at the University of Montpellier, 1977-78. Following a couple of years of work as a carpenter and landscaper in upstate New York, he moved to Miami to work as Assistant (and then Associate and Full) Professor at the young Florida International University. There he developed a research program in tropical botany, and he helped the institution develop strength in tropical biology, partly through collaboration with local institutions, particularly Fairchild Tropical Botanic Garden. He conducted field work in tropical Asia, Latin America and West Africa. He is best known for discoveries concerning the basis and function of color in vegetative organs (as autumn coloration in temperate trees and structural colors in tropical plants), and the plastic developmental responses of plants to understory shade. This research has resulted in the publication of 89 peer-reviewed articles and book chapters, and 10 books (three edited). His 2007 book, Nature's Palette (University of Chicago Press) won the AAP award for scholarly publication in the life and biomedical sciences for that year. A companion book, Nature's Fabric, about leaves, by the same publisher appeared in 2017. He received the Bessey Award for Excellence in Teaching by the Botanical Society of America in 2005, and the Alumni Association Outstanding Faculty Award at FIU in 2007. Just prior to his retirement in 2009, he served as Director of The Kampong of the National Tropical Botanical Garden, in Coconut Grove, and recently published a book about its founder, The World as Garden. The Life and Writings of David Fairchild (CreateSpace, 2013). Email: leed@fiu.edu.

Raul Machado Neto

Raul Machado Neto, lives and works in Piracicaba, his hometown, and the current institutional address is – Universidade de São Paulo, Escola

Superior de Agricultura Luiz de Queiroz (USP/ESALQ), Av. Pádua Dias 11, Piracicaba, São Paulo, CEP 13418260, Brazil. Higher educational training includes BS in Agricultural Science (1973), MS in Animal Science (1977), both at Escola Superior de Agricultura Luiz de Queiroz, the College of Agrculture of Universidade de São Paulo, USP/ESALQ, Piracicaba, São Paulo, Brasil, PhD in Animal Physiology, University of Illinois at Urbana Campaign, USA, in 1980, and Postdoctoral Fellow at Agricultural and Food Research Council-AFRC, Institute for Animal Health, England, (1989-1990). About the professional career, always at USP/ESALQ, started in 1974 in the position Assistant Professor of Universidade de São Paulo/Escola Superior de Agricultura Luiz de Queiroz, USP/ESALQ USP/ESALQ (1974-1980), Doctor Assistant Professor (1980-1985), Associate Professor (1985), and Full Professor (1997). He received in 2001 the Scientific Merit Medal of State of São Paulo Governor, is currently Research Fellow of CNPq (National Council for Scientific and Technological Development), has delivered numerous lectures and published sixty two papers in scientific journals. Dr. Machado currently serves as Provost for International Cooperation. His email is raul.machado@usp.br

Sally A. Miller

Dr. Sally A. Miller is a Professor of Plant Pathology at The Ohio State University (OSU) and state Extension specialist for vegetable crop disease management. She was born in Canton, Ohio, the third of seven children of Eileen and Stanley Miller. She received her B.Sc. in biology with Honors and with Distinction from OSU in 1976, and M. Sc. (1979) and Ph.D. (1982) degrees in plant pathology at the University of Wisconsin-Madison. Dr. Miller's first postgraduate position was as a Research Scientist at DNA Plant Technology Corporation in Cinnaminson, New Jersey, from 1982-1983, where she worked in the area of plant disease resistance. She transitioned from DNAP to Agri-Diagnostics Associates, a DNAP affiliate, and served as Manager, then Senior Manager of the plant pathology program from 1984-1991. At ADA Dr. Miller collaborated with internal teams on product development and marketing. She also led plant disease diagnostic product applications development, as well as product testing with corporate sponsors and academia. Dr. Miller joined OSU at the Ohio Agricultural Research and Development Center in Wooster in 1991. Her research and extension programs focus on disease diagnostics and sustainable management of vegetable crop diseases in conventional and organic open field and protected environment production systems. Her lab provides clinical diagnostic services to vegetable producers throughout the state of Ohio, nationally and internationally. She teaches courses in vegetable disease management and diagnostics and has mentored 25 graduate students and numerous postdoctoral associates, international scholars and visiting scientists. Dr. Miller has led and/or participated in collaborative projects on integrated pest management (IPM), microbial food safety, the interaction of plant and human pathogens on produce, the pathology of plant pathogenic bacteria on vegetable crops, and antimicrobial identification, among others. She has led or participated in the USAID-funded IPM Innovation Laboratory programs since 1995, with projects in South and Southeast Asia (The Philippines, Cambodia, Nepal, Bangladesh, India), East (Kenya, Uganda, Tanzania, Ethiopia) and West (Benin, Mali, Senegal) Africa, and Central America (Guatemala, Honduras). She has also conducted collaborative research and outreach programs with the USAID Horticulture Innovation Lab in Nigeria and Kenya, Pest and Pest Management Program in Ukraine, and iAGRI in Tanzania, as well as consultation on vegetable diseases and management in Egypt, Mexico, and Turkey. Dr. Miller was elected Vice President of the American Phytopathological Society (APS) in 2013 and served as President in 2015/16. She is a Councilor of the International Society for Plant Pathology and Executive Vice Chair of the International Congress of Plant Pathology 2018. Dr. Miller was named an Honorary Professor, D'nepropetrovsk State Agricultural University, Ukraine (1997) and is the recipient of the OSU-OARDC Multi-Disciplinary Team Research Award (2013), the International IPM Excellence Award (IPM IL Team, 2009), the Gamma Sigma Delta International Award of Merit (2007), the APS International Service Award (2002) and APS Fellow (2010). She has been married to Chip Styer since 1976; they have two daughters and a son.

Mark Mueller

Dr. Mark Muller joined the faculty at The Ohio State University in 1980, initially in the Department of Microbiology. In 1988, along with several colleagues, he helped create the first Department of Molecular Genetics in the country. Dr. Muller was Professor of Molecular Genetics until 2004 when he was recruited to join the Biomolecular Science Program at the University of Central Florida in Orlando. Dr. Muller was involved in forming a new College of Medicine at UCF and joined the Medical School faculty in 2007. He is currently Professor of Medicine at UCF and runs a cancer research group. The laboratory is an established group of researchers working on the molecular biology of cancer and gene regulation. Specific research focus areas include studies on epigenetics, gene silencing, DNA repair and telomerase regulation. Dr. Muller has nearly 100 publications in the fields of cancer and virology and multiple patents (H-index >30). In addition, he has over 400 national and international presentations and abstracts. Dr. Muller currently has national collaborations with researchers at NIH, Mayo Clinic, MD Anderson, as well as international collaborations with the University of Napoli (Naples, Italy) and the University of Kwazulu-Natal (Pietermaritzburg, South Africa). Dr. Muller has started several for-profit biotechnology companies, including TopoGEN, Inc., Visual Genomics, Inc., Methylation, Ltd., DNA Protein, Ltd., and is active on Scientific Boards in the US and EU. He has worked with Nobel Laureates including Howard Temin (University of Wisconsin) and Michael Smith (University of British Columbia). Dr. Muller is an active member of the American Association for Cancer Research, American Society of Molecular Biology and Biochemistry, and American Association for the Advancement of Science. He reviews manuscripts for multiple journals and grant applications and is a member of the editorial board for The Journal of Plant Pathology and Microbiology. Email contact: Mark.Muller@ucf.edu, Facebook:https://www.facebook.com/mark.t.muller, LaboratoryWebsites:www.biomed.ucf.edu/mtmuller (general public), http://med.ucf.edu/biomed/directory/profile/dr-mark-t-muller/ (scientific), Current Address: Dr. Mark T. Mueller, Ph.D., UCF, College of Medicine, 6900 Lake Nona Blvd,, Orlando, FL 32127.

Professor Tsai Siu Mui

Professor Tsai Siu Mui currently serves as Director of the CENA/USP. Member of the Managing Committee of the Sectorial Fund of agribusiness as a representative of the academic and scientific sector of MCTI-DF. Container of scientific and technological Merit Medal, Scopus Award 2008 and 2050 Challenge Award in agribusiness (FAO). Elected member of the Brazilian Academy of Sciences in May 2008. Fields of study: Agronomy, with emphasis in microbiology and Microbial Molecular Ecology, working mainly on the following themes: plant interaction, symbiosis, molecular markers, sequencing of genomes, genes in defense plants, microbial biodiversity, with emphasis on analysis of structures of microbial communities, bioindicators of soil quality as a function of land use conversion with focus on biogeochemical cycles. Bean studies focus on determining the tolerance to water stress in elite genotypes in association with microsymbionts

Academic Training: Agronomy | 1971 | ESALQ/USP, Master's degree | 1974 | ESALQ/USP, PhD | 1978 | ESALQ/USP, Postdoctoral | 1989-92 | UC-Davis-USA, Habilitation | 1997 | CENA/USP, Associate Professor | 1997 | CENA/USP, Professor | 2006

Quantitative genetic research areas: Plant Genetics, Molecular Markers, Applied Microbiology, Molecular Markers, Microbiology and biochemistry of Soil

Professional experience: Biochemical and molecular basis of plant-microorganism interaction, Quantification of the processes associated with microorganisms of the soil and water, using conventional and isotopic techniques, Phylogeny and paternity analysis using molecular techniques, Genetic mapping using molecular markers (RAPD, RFLP and microsatellites), Genetics and improvement of nitrogen fixation in legumes; with emphasis on bean

Scientific Production: 311 publications prior to 2017

Thomas M. Murnane

Tom Murnane has successfully provided strategic advice and direction to senior executives of Fortune 500 companies for more than 30 years, focusing primarily on revenue growth through integrated merchandising, branding, marketing and operating initiatives designed to achieve competitive advantage. Through his broad-based industry experience with apparel, retail and consumer products companies, Murnane has emerged as a leading authority in the development of highly effective business and brand positioning strategies in these industries.

- A retired partner from PricewaterhouseCoopers Consulting, New York, where he held several high-level global and national strategic consulting positions, his clients have included the senior managements of many of the largest and most successful retail chains and their key vendors.
- Founder of ARC Business Advisors, a firm that provides strategic advisory services and transaction management support to investors in the apparel, retail and consumer industries.
- Director – Blain Supply, a privately held general merchandise wholesaler/retailer, headquartered in Janesville, Wisconsin
- Director – Goodwill Southern California, one of the largest Goodwill organizations in the world
- Director – President's Alumni Advisory Council, The Ohio State University, Columbus, Ohio
- Director – Retired Partners Advisory Committee, PwC, Los Angeles, California
- Former Director – Pacific Sunwear (PSUN), a $900 million specialty retailer of apparel, footwear and accessories, targeted to teens and young adults, headquartered in Anaheim, California.
- Former Director – The Pantry (PTRY), a $2.5 billion convenience store chain, headquartered in Cary, North Carolina.
- Former Director – Finlay Enterprises (FNLY), a $1.0 billion lease operator of jewelry departments in most of the major U.S. department stores, headquartered in New York City.
- Former Director – Captaris (CAPA), a $150 million technology company, headquartered in Bellevue, Washington, that was recently sold; Captaris is a leading provider of business information delivery solutions that integrate and automate the flow of messages, data and documents.

Professional Experience

ARC Business Advisors, LLC New York, NY/Los Angeles, CA
Principal/Owner (www.arcbusinessadvisors.com)

Founder of strategic advisory firm focused on the apparel, retail and consumer industries. Its mission is to provide highly informed advice on strategy and operations to executive management, boards of directors and financial investors. Clients include consumer-oriented enterprises (wholesale, retail and direct) at every stage of development from emerging growth to turnaround, in addition to advising financial firms that actively invest in these businesses. Some recent consulting projects:

- For a major men's apparel chain, conducted a comprehensive strategy and operations review culminating in recommendations for fine tuning both strategic positioning and retail mix variables.
- For a national, high-end, off-price retailer, performed a complete strategy review including extensive consumer research specifically aimed at repositioning their approach to merchandising and customer service.
- For a highly specialized, high-end, national eyewear retailer, reviewed and recommended modifications to brand positioning and various operating components of the business to drive enhanced revenue generation.
- With a private-equity firm, conducted strategic and operational due diligence of a highly specialized, national retailer of personalized gifts culminating in a successful closed transaction.

PriceWaterhouse Coopers New York, NY/Los Angeles, CA
Global Director of Marketing and Brand Management, Director, Manager, Consultant

Retired in 2002 as a Senior Partner of PriceWaterhouse Coopers Consulting where he held several high-level global and national strategic consulting positions. His clients have included the senior managements of many of the largest and most successful retail chains and their key vendors.

- Worked directly with many of the largest and most notably recognized companies in the United States and around the world to develop and implement highly effective strategies with demonstrated results
- Managed the retail strategy consulting practice for Management Horizons, Division of PwC, Columbus, Ohio
- Developed, launched and managed the West Coast retail practice for Management Horizons, Division of PwC, Los Angeles
- Managed the national retail strategy consulting practice at PwC Consulting, New York City
- Directed the East Region general strategy consulting practice at PwC Consulting, New York City
- Served as global director of marketing and brand management and was named to the executive committee for PwC Consulting, New York City.

The Ohio State University, Columbus, OH
Graduate Fellow, Director of Professional Practice Program, Instructor (taught undergraduate, senior-level, Marketing Research classes)

BancOhio Corporation, Columbus, OH
Director of New Product Development, Director of Marketing Research, Staff Officer, Management Trainee

Education
The Ohio State University, Bachelor of Science in Business Administration and Master of Business Administration

Neftalí Ochoa-Alejo

Born in Pajacuarán, Mich., Mexico, on January 27th, 1951. B. Sci. degree from Escuela Nacional de Ciencias Biológicas del Instituto Politécnico Nacional, Mexico City. 1977. M. Sci. degree from Escola Superior de Agricultura "Luiz de Queiroz", Universidade de São Paulo, Brazil. 1981. Ph. D. degree from Instituto de Química, Universidade de São Paulo, Brazil. 1983. Research Assistant, Unidad de Biología Experimental, Facultad de Medicina, Universidad

Nacional Autónoma de México (UNAM), 1972-1975. Full-time researcher, Centro de Investigaciones Biológicas de Baja California Sur 1975-1977, 1983. Full-time researcher, Departamento de Ingeniería Genética, Unidad Irapuato, Centro de Investigación y de Estudios Avanzados del Instituto Politécnico Nacional, (Cinvestav-Unidad Irapuato), 1984-present day. Academic coordinator, Cinvestav-Unidad Irapuato, 1992-1997. Head of the Biotechnology and Biochemistry Department, Cinvestav-Unidad Irapuato, 2010-2018. Member of the National Research System, 1984- present day. Level III. Member of the Mexican Academy of sciences. President of the Mexican Academy of Sciences, Central Section, 1999-2001. Member of the Mexican Society of Biochemistry. Member of the American Society of Plant Biologists. Member of the International Association for Plant Biotechnology. Associate editor of In Vitro Cellular and Developmental Biology-Plant.

Enio Tiago De Oliveira

Enio Tiago de Oliveira began his scientific career at the age of 18 as an intern in 1977 in the Plant Biochemistry Section of the Center for Nuclear Energy in Agriculture (CENA / USP), in Piracicaba, Brazil. In 1980 he was hired as a laboratory assistant and, for over 40 years of activity at the University of São Paulo, he has evolved from lab assistant to Academic Assistant, Laboratory Technician, Higher Level Technician and currently performing duties as a Biologist Researcher. In 1986, he was transferred from CENA / USP to the Department of Chemistry of "Luiz de Queiroz" College of Agriculture (ESALQ/USP) to work at the Center for Agricultural Biotechnology (CEBTEC). Currently de Oliveira serves as Research Biologist and participates in scientific projects at CEBTEC, which has become an academic unit of the Department of Biological Sciences of ESALQ.

In 1982, he finished high school/technical school as Industrial Chemistry Technician with Full Qualification in Chemistry. In 1987, he graduated in Biological Sciences from the Methodist University of Piracicaba. In 1995, oriented by Prof. Otto J. Crocomo, he completed a

Master's Degree in the Program of Plant Physiology and Biochemistry at ESALQ / USP with the work "Specific activity of the glutamate dehydrogenase enzymes, glutamine synthetase and glutamate synthase in bean embryo axes (*Phaseolus vulgaris* L. cv. Carioca SH 80) *in vitro* in the presence of different nitrogen sources ". In 2007, he completed his PhD in the same postgraduate program with the work "Micropropagation and biochemical, physiological and nutritional monitoring of *Aloe vera* (*Aloe vera* (L.) Burm)" cultivated in different doses of nitrogen.

Throughout 40 years of activity he collaborated with undergraduate and graduate (master and doctor) students in the development of their scientific works. He has participated in dozens of scientific projects in the areas of Plant Biochemistry & Biotechnology.

Thomas J Orton

Dr. Orton attended Michigan State University, where he earned a Ph.D. in Botany and Genetics in 1979. From 1978 to 1994, he was a faculty member at UC Davis, a Group Leader at Agrigenetics Corp. and a Senior Director at DNA Plant Technology Corp. In 1995, he joined the faculty of the School of Environmental and Biological Sciences at Rutgers University, where he served as a department Chair and Assistant Director of Rutgers Cooperative Extension until 2002. Following two years as an Interim County Agricultural Agent in northern NJ, he assumed his current position, Professor and Extension Specialist in Vegetable Horticulture in 2004, and is located at the Rutgers Agricultural Research and Extension Center in Bridgeton, NJ. His research, teaching, and extension programs currently focus on fresh market and processing tomato genetics and breeding, new ethnic pepper breeding, season extension in asparagus, and new product development in perishable commodities. Dr. Orton has authored or co-authored over 50 research publications and over 20 monograph chapters during his career, and is currently developing a textbook entitled Horticultural Plant Breeding.

Amanda Perrin

Amanda Perrin is an Organizational Development and Talent Management consultant. For nearly a decade Amanda worked on Wall Street, and served as Head of U.S Talent Management at NYSE Euronext - a leading global operator of financial markets. There she was responsible for all Human Capital and OD practices within the United States and globally. In this role, she oversaw a broad portfolio of programs to build talent pipelines, augment culture and foster organizational effectiveness. In 2013 NYSE Euronext awarded her their Global Award for Innovation, for creating a digital and scalable solution for Leadership and Emerging Talent Development.

Amanda has deep expertise in driving complex change initiatives, and she approaches her work with passion and creativity. Currently Amanda works with a range of clients across various industries -- from Art to Private Equity -- and helps individuals harness their strengths to overcome considerable business challenges and more effectively realize their goals.

Prior to Wall Street, Amanda worked in management consulting at several leading companies in the U.S. and Canada. Amanda holds an M.A. in Culture, Education and Human Development from New York University's Steinhardt School of Education, and is a graduate of Queen's University in Ontario, Canada.

John E Peters

John grew up in Dover, Ohio as the oldest of three children. In 1971 he graduated from Otterbein College majoring in Life Sciences. Upon graduation, he was commissioned as a Second Lieutenant in the United States Air Force. He obtained an educational delay from the Air Force to pursue a Master's degree at The Ohio State University where he became a member of Dr. William R. Sharp's laboratory performing plant tissue culture studies. In 1973, he received his Master's degree and entered active duty in the Air Force. After a brief period working in radar and air defense, John was selected to cross-train to become a Biomedical Laboratory Officer. Upon completion of certification as a Medical Technologist, he managed a hospital clinical laboratory for three years before being selected to teach in the Biology Department faculty of the Air Force Academy. He taught courses in Introductory Biology, Microbiology, Molecular Biology, and Developmental Biology. Following completion of this assignment, he was sponsored by the Air Force to return to The Ohio State University to complete a Ph.D. program. Working in Dr. Darrell Galloway's laboratory, he discovered a new enzyme that greatly enhances the tissue destruction of certain flesh-eating bacteria. John completed his Ph.D. in 1990 and became the director of the Air Force's largest clinical microbiology laboratory at Lackland Air Force Base, San Antonio, Texas. In 1994, John retired from the Air Force as a Lieutenant Colonel and began a second career as a biology faculty member at McHenry County College in Crystal Lake, Illinois. During his tenure at McHenry County College, he taught courses in Introductory Biology and Microbiology for biology and allied health majors and served as the departmental chair. At the end of 2014, he retired from this position to return to Columbus, Ohio to be close to family and grandchildren.

Robert M Pfister

B.A., (1957) M.Sc. (1960), PhD. (1964) Syracuse University. Inspected and tested for bacterial contamination in all paper cup products and converting plants and a number of paper producing plants as part of the Syracuse University Research Corporation contract with the National Paper Cup Association. Teaching Assistant in the Department of Bacteriology during last year as an undergraduate. Supervisor of the Paper Testing (microbiology) laboratory at The Syracuse University Research Corporation. 1960-1964. Post-Doctoral Fellow at Lamont Geological Observatory with Paul Burkholder PhD studying microbes from the sea and their antibiotic potential. Developed and published computer numerical taxonomy program to identify organisms from the Antarctic Ocean. Joined the Department of Microbiology at the Ohio State University in 1966. Supervised more than 60 graduate students toward their advanced degree. Published 50 articles in scientific journals and presented more than 60 papers at various meetings.

Member of The Society of Microbiology 1963-1993. Contributed chapter in "Reflections & Connections Vol. II, Crocomo OJ, JP Kreier, and WR Sharp. Science Tech Publishers 2014. Chairman Department of Microbiology 1973-1985. Professor Emeritus, The Ohio State University 1993-present.

Carl Arthur Price

Carl Arthur Price was born in Long Beach, CA, educated at the California Institute of Technology and Harvard University. After a post-doctoral fellowship with Sir Hans Krebs in Sheffield, England, followed by additional training at Purdue University and Massachusetts General Hospital, Carl accepted a tenured position at Rutgers University in New Brunswick, NJ.

In the forty plus years that Carl remained at Rutgers, he taught thousands of undergraduates and mentored graduate students, post-docs and visiting scientists. His active research program may have owed its success to the centrifuge rotors he designed: some of which answered specific questions whereas others proved generally useful. One rotor allowed the separation of intact chloroplasts from stripped thylakoid membranes. The raw silica sol medium used to achieve that separation proved to be the precursor to a now commercially available product, Percoll.

The advent of physiologically functional plastids allowed Carl and his laboratory to look at other subcellular organelles: amyloplasts and chromoplasts. All these cellular components are capable of making some, but not all, of their own proteins, some functions of which are specific to the cell type, stage of development.

It was during this very active stage of his research career that Carl took on the responsibility of editing the fledgling *Plant Molecular Biology Reporter*. The Reporter was the house organ of the International Society for Plant Molecular Biology and tenderly nurtured as a typewritten, photocopied handout by Maureen Hanson in 1980. Over the next two decades Carl took this to the status of a computer-generated, color enhanced publication and broadened its exposure worldwide.

Upon retiring in 1999, Carl retreated west to his favorite ocean and enjoyed swimming, walking the beach, collecting sand dollars and travel.

Friends always marveled at his sense of humor and genuine kindness. He remained a proponent of scientific education by directing a program on science and medicine at UCSD for interested and mostly retired members of the local community. To the end, Carl Price remained a cheerful and happy role model for gracious aging.

Ellen Moore Reardon

Ellen Moore Reardon was born in Atlantic City, NJ, educated at Elms College, Chicopee, MA and Rutgers University, New Brunswick, NJ. I married my college sweetheart, Ned Reardon and raised four outstanding children. When my husband became terminally ill, I started working for a major pharmaceutical company and I realized that I needed to catch up on my education.

My liaison with Carl Price began in 1975 when I became his graduate student, then following my Ph.D., his research associate and laboratory coordinator. My research was in the area of photosynthesis, specifically, light/harvesting proteins of chloroplasts and also contrasting the similarities and differences among sub-cellular organelles.

Following post-doctoral fellowships at the University of Arizona, Tucson, and the USDA in Beltsville, MD, I returned to Rutgers as Laboratory Operations Coordinator for microbiology, molecular biology and physiology. I was associate editor of Plant Molecular Biology Reporter as Carl was a superb and devoted editor. Scarlett was associate editor of Probe as I edited that journal.

Carl and I subsequently married when we lost our spouses. Upon retirement, we divided time between travel to scientific meetings and our homes in California, Arizona and New Jersey. I am currently enjoying grandchildren, photography and travel.

Charles B. Redington

Thomas Mann made a prophetic statement that "No Man is an Island." No person nor living organism stands alone from the biological point of view. In order, to survive, organisms interact in ways positive and negative to themselves and those they interact with. Collaboration is a form of biological interaction. For example, some collaborations are mutualistic, others competitive, some predatory, and still others cooperative. I'd like to focus on the positive aspects of collaboration. It can be seen, as working together through such things as partnerships, team work, delegation, reflection, and other means of accomplishing an endeavor. In the "Redington Field Guides to Biological Interactions," we find that the common cattail, *Typha latifolia*, joins forces (collaborates) with over 100 different organisms, including birds, amphibians, reptiles, fish, mammals, insects, spiders, and humans, affecting the survival of these organisms and themselves. Well, as I reflect upon my life, it is quite clear to me that collaboration is what got me through life's challenges and to where I am today.

I am a WW II baby born in 1942, spending the war years as a small boy in Pittsburgh, PA, with my mother and her parents, while my father, a Merchant Mariner, was onboard two different ships sunk, one in the Atlantic and the other in the Mediterranean. After the war, we moved to Elyria, Ohio. My father was a wounded (physically and emotionally) veteran. I mention this because it was a factor in my being raised by a gregarious, yet at times, quick-tempered and violent father. This behavior affected me by my being scared, on guard, and feeling unsure of myself. He did want me to do the best I could but would confront me with the successes of other young boys in our neighborhood who were outstanding students or great athletes and tell me to be like them. I suppose in the end this approach did have a positive effect on me because I have always had a competitive personality. I would affirm myself by thinking, "If so and so can do such and such, well then, so can I."

Overall, I made sure I had a fun and adventure-filled childhood, replete with camping, fishing, biking, shooting, playing baseball (even pitched tryouts for the Cleveland Indians), scouting, model building, stamp and coin collecting, astronomy, you name it. I did well academically in high school, attended the University of Michigan Biological Station, graduated from Baldwin-Wallace College (now University), was married and then attended graduate school at Rutgers University where I earned my Master of Science degree from the Biology Department and Ph.D. in Plant Pathology and Physiology at the Rutgers College of Agriculture and Environmental Science (CAES). From there, my wife and I moved to East Longmeadow, MA, with our 2 1/2-year-old son Chuck and 3-week-old daughter Laurel, where I began my forty-four-year career as a Professor of Biology and Environmental Science at Springfield College, the birthplace of basketball. I wore many hats at the college including chair of the Bio/Chemistry Department., appointed Springfield College Distinguished Professor of Humanics and upon retirement, appointed Professor of Biology, Emeritus. During those forty-four years, I also worked as a state recognized senior environmental analyst with the Baystate Environmental Consultants of East Longmeadow, MA. As I reflect, on these things and more, I realize without collaboration along the way, none of this could have been accomplished.

Today, I am retired happily in Florida with my wonderful wife Carolyn Frances and our regal Beagle Button. Here we enjoy new friends, fishing, boating, biking, tennis, pickle ball, etc., we make sure to get all the screenings and tests from the medical profession that people our age should, and enjoy visiting with our children and grandchildren.

Laurie Repko

Laurie Repko, has taught in two school districts in Ohio for a total of 22 years at both the middle and high school levels with a BS in Education and MA in English both from Youngstown State University. She has earned professional regard for building community among her peers, students, and their families by modeling and instructing collaboration. Recently her efforts were written about in a chapter for a book called *The Best Teacher in You*. She has been teacher of the year in her building, and was recognized as a Battelle for Kids Distinguished

Educator for two consecutive years. She lives in Lewis Center with her husband, Ed, and her son, Danny.

Donnalyn Roxey

Donnalyn Roxey received her B.Sc. in Biological Sciences from the University of Maryland, College Park. After graduation, she began a career in research administration at The Ohio State University. She has served as a sponsored program officer, clinical trial contracts and budget analyst as well as a senior grants manager within Ohio State's College of Medicine. Most recently at Ohio State, she led the administrative side of two PhD Graduate Programs and a multi-college, interdisciplinary center, The Center for Applied Plant Sciences (CAPS). Donnalyn's passion for creativity, coupled with her long-standing involvement in biological research, has led to her focusing her energy on the science of team science. After five year in CAPS working closely with teams of scientist, she is fascinated by how research teams are formed, operate, can be supported and recognized, and how they can work even more effectively. After ten years in academic administration, Donnalyn left the university to pursue her passion in facilitating scientific innovation and to goals in pursuing her education. She is currently finishing her Masters of Science in Creative Studies from SUNY's Buffalo State College and serving as a co-chair for the National Organization of Research Development Professionals' committee on professional development (NORDP-PD).

Richard Sayre

Dr. Richard Sayre is currently a Senior Research Scientist at Los Alamos National Laboratory (LANL) and the New Mexico Consortium (NMC). Dr. Sayre's research interests include; characterization of primary processes in photosynthesis, algal and plant biotechnology, and nutritional biofortification of crop plants. Dr. Sayre completed his undergraduate degree in biology at Humboldt State University, his Ph. D. at the University of Iowa, and did postdoctoral work at Harvard University. From 1986-2008, Dr. Sayre was a faculty member and later Chairman of the Department of Plant Cellular and Molecular Biology at Ohio State University. Prior to coming to LANL/NMC in 2011, Dr. Sayre was the Director (2008-2011) of the Enterprise Rent-A-Car Institute for Renewable Fuels at the Donald Danforth Plant Science Center in St Louis. He has also been engaged in several start-up companies including: Phycotransgenics, Phycal, and more recently Imugenix.

Dr. Sayre has directed a number of major research consortia including:

- Principle Investigator (2005-2010) of Phase I of the BioCassava Plus Program funded by the Grand Challenges in Global Health Program of the Bill and Melinda Gates Foundation. The BioCassava Plus program focused on developing enhanced cassava cultivars to provide complete nutrition for subsistence farmers in sub-Saharan Africa.
- Principle Investigator (2009-2011) for the Center for Advanced Biofuel Systems, a Dept. of Energy (DOE) Energy Frontier Research Center focusing on generating advanced biofuels from algae and plants
- Scientific Director (2010-2013) of the National Alliance for Advanced Biofuels and Bioproducts (NAABB), the largest DOE-sponsored algal biofuels consortium funded to date.
- Principle Investigator (2016-2019) of the US-DOE sponsored PACE targeted algal biomass and bioproducts program.

Dr. Sayre has received several honors including:

- Distinguished Professor in the College of Biological Sciences, Ohio State University (2005)
- Honorary member of Phi Beta Kappa (2006)
- Fulbright Scholar at the Inst. Quimica, University Sao Paulo, Brazil (2007)
- Selected by *Nature* as one of "Five Crop Researchers Who Could Change the World"; *Nature* 456: 563-569 (2008)

- Invited attendee at Google/Nature/O'Reilly SciFoo Camp for Innovators (2009)
- Elected a Fellow of the American Association for the Advancement of Sciences (2011)

Thomas Michael Seed

Thomas Michael Seed. <u>DOB & Place</u>: December 8 1945, Paterson, NJ. <u>Current residence</u>: Bethesda, MD, USA. <u>Communication address</u>: tmseed@verizon.net . <u>Education</u>: *1964-1968* – University of Connecticut, Storrs, CT, BSc (Bacteriology); *1968-1972* – Ohio State University, Columbus, OH, MSc (1969 - Microbiology), PhD (1972 – Microbiology; *1972-1973* – Case Western Reserve University, Institute of Pathology, Cleveland, OH, (Postdoctoral Fellowship in Cellular Ultrastructure). <u>Positions & Institutions</u>: *1998-present* – Consultant, Tech Micro Services Co., Bethesda, MD; *1995-1997* - Associate Chief of Research, Radiation Effects Research Institute, Hiroshima, Japan; *1993-1995* – Research Professor, Vitreous State Laboratory, Department of Physics, Catholic University of America, Washington, DC; *1996- 2003* – Senior Scientist/Group Leader, Radiation Casualty Management, Armed Forces Radiobiology Research Institute, Bethesda, MD; *1975-1995* – Research Biologist & Group Leaders for Radiation Hematology (1982-1995), Radiation Leukemogenesis (1979-1981), Cellular Indicators (1977-1978), Electron Microscopy (1975-1995), Divisional of Mechanistic Biology and Biotechnology, Argonne National Laboratory, Argonne, IL; *1973-1975* – Assistant Biologist & Head, Ultrastructure Group, Blood Research Laboratory, American National Red Cross, Bethesda, MD. <u>Professional works</u>: Journal articles (107 as per 'Pub Med' listing; 4); Total cited publications, including books, book chapters, guidance documents, etc (~186 publications cited ~2800 as per Google Scholar listing; 5); <u>Patents</u>: 3 patents- 'Radiation Countermeasures' (US Patent US 7,919,525 B2; US Patent 7,665,694 B2; EP Patent EP 1,767,215); <u>Awards/honors (select listing)</u>: Appointed, The Ohio State University Research Fellowship, 1971-1972; Appointed Head, US Delegation, NATO Research

Study Group-23, 1996-1998; Elected, Chairman, NATO Research Task Group TG-006 (1999-2001); Awarded, Distinguished Seminar Speaker (2006); Elected, Council member (2005-2010) & Consociate member (2010-present), National Council on Radiation Protection and Measurements; Professional affiliations: American Association for the Advancement of Science (AAAS- emeritus); Microscopy Society of America (MSA- emeritus); American Society for Microbiology (ASM- emeritus); International Society of Experimental Hematology (ISEH- emeritus); Radiation Research Society (RRS- retired member). General research interests: Nature and mechanisms of radiation injuries; Medical countermeasures; Hematopoiesis (structure/function/pathologic mechanisms); Leukemogenesis (nature/mechanisms); Low level radiation/chemical toxicity.

Jeffrey William Sharp

Jeffrey Sharp is an award-winning independent film and television producer working in New York, Los Angeles and Beijing. As a producer, Sharp is in post-production on "UFO" written and directed by Ryan Eslinger and starring Gillian Anderson, Alex Sharp, and David Strathairn; The Yellow Birds written by David Lowery, directed by Alexandre Moors and starring Jennifer Aniston, Toni Collette, Jack Huston, Tye Sheridan, and Alden Ehrenreich; My Other Home written and directed by Larry Yang and starring Stephon Marbury for China's Hairun Pictures and Huayi Bros; and Wanderer directed by Jin Liu for Tianyi Movie and TV Co, China. Sharp is currently in pre-production on Crazy Alien written and directed by Ning Hao for Dirty Monkey Films, China.

Sharp has produced a series of Academy Award® and Golden Globe® winning and nominated films such as: *Boys Don't Cry, You Can Count on Me,* Nicholas Nickleby, and *Proof.* With those movies, as well as other renowned adaptations, including *A Home at the End of the World, The Night Listener* and *Evening,* Sharp has worked to better integrate the publishing and film industries. Sharp co-founded the digital publisher Open Road Integrated Media with former HarperCollins CEO Jane Friedman, which has become a leading independent e-book publisher in the US. At Open Road, Sharp looked for new ways to option film and TV rights as part of the publishing process, which led to the formation of Story Mining & Supply in Los Angeles in 2012 where Sharp, as President and CEO, oversaw the development and production of several feature films and TV shows from Open Road and other publishing properties including Outlander (nominated for three Golden Globes®). Sharp currently serves as Chairman of the Hamptons International Film Festival Advisory Board, member of the Board of Literacy Partners, Special Advisor for the Book-Meets-Film Forum at the Taipei International Book Expo, as well as a member of the Advisory Board of BookExpo of America. He is a member of Academy of Motion Picture Arts and Sciences, BAFTA (British Academy of Film and Television Arts) and the PGA (Producers Guild of America). Sharp graduated with an MFA in Film Studies from Columbia University and a BA Colgate University.

William Rodney Sharp

William "Rod" Sharp's background resides in biotechnology, translation of science into business ideas, spawning start-up companies and extensive technology transfer experience in the Americas and Asia with important corporate research and development collaborations with the University of Sao Paulo and institutes of the Chinese Academy of Sciences. He has authored over seventy original research papers, abstracts and books in the field of plant cell biology including the coediting of the five-volume series *Handbook of Plant Cell Culture*, two volume *Reflections and Connections – Journeys Through The Life Sciences* and the pending two volume *Pathways To Collaboration* series. Positions held include: Dean of Research/Professor of Plant Science, Cook College and Director of Research, New Jersey Agricultural Experiment Station, Rutgers University; Vice President, Business Development, PhytoPharmaceuticals Inc., Executive Vice-President, DNA Pharmaceuticals, Inc.; Executive Vice-President for Research, DNA Plant Technology Corp; Research Director, Pioneer Research, Campbell Institute for Agricultural Research & Technology, Campbell Soup Company. The biotechnology companies subsequently exited into

Groupo Pulsar/Savia. S.A. de C.V.; Ciba-Geigy Corporation (Novartis-Geigy-Sandoz following merger); and Samyang Genex. Prior academic appointments include: Professor of Microbiology, The Ohio State University; Fellow, Argonne National Laboratory, Eminent Professor, University of Sao Paulo and Fulbright Grantee during 1971 and 1973.

Honors include the following: The 1999 University of Sao Paulo Luiz Queiroz Distinguished Service Medal, Ohio State University Board of Trustees 2007 Distinguished Service Award, naming of the William Rodney Sharp Conference Facility at the University of Sao Paulo/ Escola Superior de Agricultura "Luiz de Queiroz" Center of Agricultural Biotechnology (CEBTEC), Sao Paulo Academy of Sciences Foreign Correspondent Membership and The 2016 Ohio State University College of Arts and Sciences Distinguished Services Award.

Currently, Rod Sharp serves as a member of The Ohio State University College of Arts and Sciences Advisory Committee, Chairs the ASC Resource Subcommittee and serves as an advisor to the Ohio State University/Rutgers University/University of Sao Paulo Tripartite Faculty/Student Research/Teaching Program and Advocacy Committee for the Ohio State University STEAM Factory and Erdos Institute.

Rod Sharp attended The Ohio State University and University of Akron, holds a Ph.D. in Plant Cell Biology from Rutgers University and completed a postdoctoral fellowship at Case Western Reserve University.

Judy Lyman Snow

Judith Lyman Snow, Basking Ridge, NJ, Judysnow99@gmail.com,

Employment

Rutgers University, Cook College--1985-2011, Biotechnology Center for Agriculture and the Environment (AgBiotech); Rockefeller Foundation, Agricultural Sciences--1980-1984, *Education*, Cornell University, MS in Horticulture--1976, PhD in Plant Breeding—1980

Duke University, BA in Botany, Magna cum Laude—1974, *Publications:* Author, annual reports and work plans for the AgBiotech Center at Rutgers for over 20 years, Author/co-author/editor of 2 books, 4 book chapters and 7 journal articles, Editor, Cook College *Grants Alert* weekly email newsletter 1993-96, *Awards:* Junior Science & Humanities Symposium Service Award, Rutgers University—2002 Cook College/NJAES Individual Impact Award, Rutgers University—1996 Rutgers University Merit Award—1994, *Associations/Affiliations*: Missouri Botanical Garden, William L. Brown Center for Plant Genetic Resources: Secretary of the Advisory Board—2002-2008, *Diversity* journal for plant genetic resources: Secretary/Treasurer—1996-2002

Roy Stahlhut

Roy Stahlhut, General Manager at Pacific Berry Breeding, a company dedicated to the breeding of improved raspberry and blackberry varieties. Prior positions: Senior Manager, Propagation Nursery at Driscoll's, Research and Development Manager, California Florida Plant Company, Senior Scientist ForBio America, Plant Cell Biology Group Leader at Samyang Genex Corporation.

Education: Ph.D. Agronomy and Crop Science, University of Illinois at Urbana-Champaign.

Donald "Chip" Styer II

Dr. Donald "Chip" Styer II was born in El Paso Texas to Col. Donald James Styer and Carol Hancock Styer in 1954, the youngest, and only son, among five siblings. He moved frequently with his military family, attending high school in Annandale, VA, where he was a valedictorian in his class of 700. He was a volunteer tour guide at the Smithsonian Air & Space Museum in Washington D.C. during high school, and met Sally Miller at The Ohio State University where he received a B. S. in Microbiology with Honors and with Distinction in 1976. He earned a Ph.D. degree in Plant Pathology from the University of Wisconsin-Madison in 1982, then joined DNA Plant Technology as a Research Scientist. At DNAP he developed bioreactor systems for a number of tissue cultured plant species, but his career path was altered irrevocably when he obtained an early personal computer, the Macintosh Plus. He developed a laboratory data acquisition system and started computer analysis of the data, which led the development of an interest in data analytics. After moving to Ohio in 1991, he worked as an IT consultant, and in computer sales. He joined The Ohio State University in 1999, where he was instrumental in the development of faculty reporting systems for the College of Food, Agricultural and Environmental Sciences. He now conducts data analytics as a Resource Planning Analyst. His most significant collaboration is with Sally Miller, which has produced three wonderful children and an amazing adventure.

K.C. Ting

K.C. Ting is currently Vice Dean for Academic Affairs and Strategy Zhejiang University International Campus, Haining, Zhejiang, China. He formerly served as Head, Department of Agricultural and Biological Engineering, University of Illinois at Urbana-Champaign from 2004 to 2016. He has been leading research teams to develop and implement the Automation-Culture-Environment-Oriented Systems (ACESys) analysis methodology and Concurrent Science, Engineering, and Technology (ConSEnT) decision support computational platform. The methodology and platform have been applied to develop and deliver system scoping techniques, computer models, simulation and optimization results, and decision support systems for agricultural production and intelligent food systems, as well as to study the related issues of energy efficiency, environmental impact, and economic feasibility. He has participated, by contributing his intelligent agricultural/food systems expertise, in proposal developments for four large successful research programs: NASA New Jersey Specialized Center of Research and Training, BP Energy Biosciences Institute, ADM Institute for the Prevention of Postharvest Loss, and USAID Sustainable Intensification Innovation Lab Appropriate Scale Mechanization Consortium. He has published over 290 articles, papers, monographs, presentations, and reports and delivered over

125 invited presentations in 17 countries. His research funding includes PI and Co-PI for over $12 million. He served as an Editor-in-Chief for Computers and Electronics in Agriculture during January 2007-December 2010 and Honorary Theme Editor, UNESCO Encyclopedia of Life Support Systems, for the theme "Systems Analysis and Modeling in Food and Agriculture" during February 2004-2007. He was a fellow of Food Systems Leadership Institute in 2006-2008. He was a participant of ESCOP/ACOP/USDA Leadership Development Program (currently Lead 21) in 1993-1994. He has participated in and led a good number of external review committees to assess academic and research units and programs, as well as strategy formulation meetings to develop visions and action plans in the areas of agriculture and food systems in several countries. He has conducted workshops on academic leadership in China, Japan, Taiwan, and the U.S. He served as a member of the American Society of Agricultural and Biological Engineers (ASABE) Foundation Board of Trustees during 2009-2015. He co-chaired the Conference Program Committee for the ASABE Global Food Security Conference held on October 24-27, 2016 in Stellenbosch, South Africa. His awards and recognitions include: Illinois Land Improvement Contractors of America Shiny Shovel Award, January 2013; ASABE James R. and Karen A. Gilley Academic Leadership Award, August 2011; ASABE Kishida International Award, July 2008; Guest Chair Professor, College of Biosystems Engineering and Food Science, Zhejiang University, Hangzhou, China, April 2006; Fellow of ASME elected in July 2002; Fellow of ASABE inducted in July 2001; and Cook College/Alpha Zeta Professor of the Year, Rutgers University, 1997.

Email: kcting@illinois.edu

Harvey P. White

1934 Born Sven Harvey Philip in Providence RI. Father a Swedish Immigrant. Parents divorced when I was 2.

and I moved to West Virginia. She remarried in 1939. Step-father adopted me. I became Sven Harvey Philip White.

Education
Raised and educated in West Virginia - except for 4-years in South Carolina.

1951 West Virginia Wesleyan College in as chemistry major. Transferred to Marshall University in 1953. Graduated in 1955 with a BA in Economics.

Wesleyan Trustee and a Marshall commencement speaker. Honorary PhD's, from, both schools.

Business career
1955 American Viscose Corporation - local rayon manufacturer. As industrial engineer setting time standards on factory floor I saw manufacturing close- up

1957 Virginia Carolina Chemical Corp. – multi product agricultural firm. Member of 5-man team hired to evaluate status and help turn-around company. Did financial analyses and forecasting projects. Reported to CEO, saw business from the top

Decided on finance Career
1959 Raytheon Corp, – aerospace and technology company. Started in Bristol Tennessee/Virginia plant as budget and cost accounting manager. Transferred to Boston area and held several positions ending as Controller of major facility.

Could not enter general management unless an engineer.
1966 Sealy Mattress – privately held Franchisee for NYC. Operation Manager responsible for all functions except sales with promise of equity in future. Left when obvious equity would not happen.

1968 Whittaker Corp – rapidly growing (through acquisitions) conglomerate in LA. Asst. Corporate Controller hired to establish a corporate-wide financial control system for entities in all parts of the country. Travel was nearly every week. With three young children, this was not tolerable.

1970 TRW Electronics Group –Group Controller with Controllers at multiple locations across the US. Major travel required also.

1972 Rohr Industries – Fortune 500 Company. Asst. Corporate Controller – promoted to Controller and then named EVP for group with products ranging from pre-stressed concrete to software systems and second group that made subway cars for WMATA added –found WMATA had engineering issues and a large projected loss. Internal politics and back-stabbing was huge. As CFO negotiated 4 bank debt restructures.

1976 Burned out - bought, with a friend, 2 distributorships. After 2 years we decided it did not need both of us - I found another job.

1978 Linkabit Corp. a rapidly growing private company - Joined as CFO and became director and COO when we established Office of the CEO to support growth from delivery of sophisticated communications products for DoD. Wanted to add commercial products and merged to help us. Merger failed and 7 of us formed a new company and resigned.

1985 Qualcomm - Director, EVP and COO. We had early success with DoD. Qualcomm's Omni-TRACS was the first mobile communication system for trucks. Our CDMA technology made cellular systems successful because they could to grow to meet user demand. Was heavily involved in initial private funding, going public, financing rounds and interface with banks and financial analysts. Active in international expansion of Omni-TRACS and CDMA.

Founder and Chairman of Leap. Built cellular networks in Latin America and the US. Our Cricket brand, with its "all you can talk" for a fixed price, established the bundled pricing system used by cellular carriers today, AT&T acquired Leap for $1.2 Billion after I retired in 2004.

Post Corporate world

1999 and 2000 my wife and I divorced. In 2001, I married my wife - a retired bank officer. She has invented and manages a fashion accessary product. I see manufacturing is done on a timely and cost-effective way.

2004 formed a personal business (SHW)2 to do consulting and working with, and occasionally investing, in new companies. Am on a public board, 2 private technology boards and several arts boards.

I see that emphasis on changing the existing curricula to match the need for innovation by having it STEAM based– not manufacturing based - as is true now. Our country's future relies on innovation. STEAM is a national economy priority!

Susan S. Williams

Susan S. Williams is Professor of English at Ohio State University. A specialist in nineteenth-century American literature, she is the author of *Confounding Images: Photography and Portraiture in Antebellum American Fiction* and *Reclaiming Authorship: Literary Women in America, 1850-1900*. She is a former co-editor of the journal *American Periodicals* and, with Steven Fink, co-edited *Reciprocal Influences: Literary Production, Distribution, and Consumption in America*. Williams is the recipient of the OSU Alumni Award for Distinguished Teaching, the OSU Distinguished Faculty Service Award, the Founder's Award of the OSU Academy of Teaching, and of grants and fellowships from the American Antiquarian Society, the National Endowment for the Humanities, and the American Council for Learned Societies. She served as Vice Provost in Ohio State's Office of Academic Affairs for five-and-a-half years before assuming her current role as Vice Dean in the College of Arts and Sciences. There, she is responsible for coordinating faculty affairs across the college and works with the executive and divisional deans to support college-wide initiatives and collaboration.

About the Editors

Jim Fowler

Jim Fowler, Ph.D. is an Assistant Professor of Mathematics at The Ohio State University and is the Director of Outreach for The STEAM Factory. His research interests broadly include geometry and topology, and more specifically focus on the topology of high-dimensional manifolds and geometric group theory. In other words, he thinks in depth about highly symmetric geometric objects. He's fond of using computational techniques to attack problems in pure mathematics. Prior to working at The Ohio State University, he received an undergraduate degree from Harvard University and received a Ph.D. from the University of Chicago.

In terms of teaching, Jim Fowler is at the forefront of educational technology. Through MOOCulus (a massive open online calculus course), Jim has made calculus more engaging for hundreds of thousands of Coursera students who have enrolled in his online courses. His YouTube channel has now received more than 1 million views. Forbes magazine recently called him "the prof that is making calculus go viral."

Roman Holowinsky

Roman Holowinsky, Ph.D. is a mathematician known for his work in analytic number theory, and in, the theory of modular forms. He is currently an Associate Professor with tenure at The Ohio State

University and Managing Director of the Erdős Institute. He is also Chair Emeritus and Cofounder of The STEAM Factory, a grassroots interdisciplinary collaboration facilitator in the Ohio State and Columbus community.

Holowinsky received a Bachelors in Science Degree in Mathematics and Computer Science from Rutgers University in 2001. Afterwards, he continued his studies at Rutgers and received his PhD in 2006 under the direction of Henryk Iwaniec. Holowinsky was awarded the SASTRA Ramanujan Prize in 2011 for his contributions to "areas of mathematics influenced by the genius Srinivasa Ramanujan", for proving, with Kannan Soundararajan, an important case of the Quantum Unique Ergodicity (QUE) conjecture. In 2011, Holowinsky was also awarded a Sloan Fellowship. In addition to research and teaching, Holowinsky is highly active in service to The Ohio State University and the greater Columbus community.

Austin Channell

Austin Channell is a rising senior at Vanderbilt University in Nashville, Tennessee and is double-majoring in Engineering Science and Communications of Science and Technology (a Vanderbilt-specific major which pairs a strong background in the natural sciences with development of public speaking, writing, and media skills). At Vanderbilt, Austin has been involved in a wide range of groups, including Vanderbilt Symphonic Choir, Jazz Choir, American Society of Civil Engineers (ASCE), and Vanderbilt Student Volunteers for Science (a group which teaches science lessons in local elementary schools). Austin has been involved in research with Dr. Jonathan Gilligan (Earth and Environmental Science), and was selected as a recipient of a Vanderbilt University Summer Research Program grant in the summer of 2016. The end product of that summer, "Greenhouse gas reduction through individual and household behavioral change" won the 2016 Vanderbilt University Undergraduate Research Fair.

Additionally, Austin was selected in his freshman year to be a part of the Vanderbilt Curb Scholars Program in Creative Enterprise and Public Leadership, due in part to the success of his 2013 TEDxColumbus talk, "Why taking choir kept me from being Valedictorian." It was at this TED event that Austin met Roman Holowinsky, chair of The STEAM Factory, a faculty collaboration group at The Ohio State University. In summer of 2015, Austin worked as a student intern for The STEAM Factory where he created policy documents for the organization, learned about its operations, and helped to organize a hackathon between Columbus, Ohio and Cherkasy, Ukraine.

In fall of 2015, Austin co-founded Vanderbilt Theater Lab, a student organization dedicated to producing original theatre pieces via a collaborative process. He served as the organization's president for four semesters, and has overseen the development of three theater pieces. The first, *Mass Cycle: A Meditation on Cancer* was inspired by the story of a fellow Vanderbilt student who received a stage IV ovarian cancer diagnosis. The second show, *Shift Happens: A 60(ish) Minute History of U.S. Politics* featured collaborators from Vanderbilt's history and theater departments, while the group's third work, *Fear Itself*, showcased the talents of several groups of young student writers exploring the concept of fear in the 21st century. Building on his involvement with Vanderbilt Theater Lab, Austin was selected as the Artistic Director of Vanderbilt Off-Broadway, where he will direct a production of *American Idiot* which will open in January of 2018. He also serves as the Campus Outreach Chair of the Vanderbilt Performing Arts Community, an umbrella organization for arts at Vanderbilt, where he is responsible for fostering artistic collaborations between campus organizations.

Otto J. Crocomo

Otto J. Crocomo was born in Piracicaba in the state of São Paulo in Brazil on September 23rd 1932 the eighth son of Giovani Crocomo and Thereza Vidili Crocomo. Married to Diva Lovadino Crocomo for 55 years, they have 5 children Marco Augusto, Adolfo Egídio, Maria Paula, Carla Maísa and Daniel and 1 grandchild Pedro Augusto. From a very early age he became interested in literature and, in high school in Chemistry, having participated in five Chemistry Debates as team leader, winning all debates. In, February 1953 he began his studies at "Luiz de Queiroz" School of Agriculture (ESALQ), University of São Paulo (USP), in Piracicaba. Still as an undergraduate student, he published 5 scientific papers and participated in three Congresses of Students of Agronomy (1954, 9155, 1956). Crocomo graduated as an Agronomist in 1956. In 1959 Crocomo obtained the academic title of "Free Lecturer" at ESALQ after four days of theoretical and practical examinations and the defense of his thesis on the metabolism of urea-14C in coffee leaves. Between the years 1959 and 1960, he was Assistant Professor of Biochemistry at the Faculty of Dentistry of Piracicaba and in 1960 was hired by ESALQ / USP as Assistant Professor of Organic Chemistry and Biological Chemistry. In 1966 Crocomo was appointed as Associate Professor of Organic Chemistry and Biological Chemistry and in 1975, after two days of public exams, became Full Professor of Biochemistry of the Department of Chemistry at ESALQ. Crocomo was Head and Vice-Head of that Department from 1971 to 1989.

Crocomo collaborated in the creation of the Center of Nuclear Energy in Agriculture (CENA) in 1966 and was responsible for development of the Plant Biochemistry Section between the years 1966 and 1988.

Between the years 1961 and 1962 Crocomo, he served as Professor of Chemistry and Biochemistry at the Faculty of Agronomy of the University of Zulia, Maracaibo, Venezuela. Between 1964 and 1965 Crocomo was a Fellow Researcher at the University of California, Davis campus (Prof. C. C. Delwiche) and from October 1968 to February 1969 at the University College London at Gower Street, London, England (Prof. L. Fowden). In 1976 Crocomo was a visiting Professor at the Botany Department of Durham University, Durham, England (Prof. Donald Boulter).

In 1971 with the collaboration of William Rod Sharp (The Ohio State University/USA), he introduced in Brazil at CENA the use of the techniques of plant cell, tissue and organs cultures in agriculture. In 1973 he was a member of the International Association of Plant Tissue Culture (IAPTC). Between 1973 and 1986 Crocomo was representative of Brazil in that Association. Crocomo attended International Congresses of the IAPTC in 1973, 1976, 1980, 1984, 1986, 1990 and

1994. In 1983 he was one of the founder of the Brazilian Association of Plant Tissue Culture (ABCTP) and its first president.

In 1978 Crocomo became a member of Academy of Sciences of the State of São Paulo; In 1981 Crocomo received the CNPq Medal/Brazil, in 1986 he received a DNAP Medal/USA, and in 2001 Crocomo received the Rutgers University Award/USA. In 2001 Crocomo was awarded the Scientific Merit Government of the State of São Paulo Medal/Brazil. In 2003 Crocomo was recipient of the ABCPT Award. In 2011 Crocomo received the Piracicaba Rotary Club Medal, and in 2012 he was awarded the Fernando Costa Medal from the Agronomic Engineers of the State of São Paulo Association. From 2009 to 2013 Crocomo was president of the ESALQ Retired Professors Association (ADAE).

In 1981 Crocomo idealized and founded the Center for Agricultural Biotechnology (CEBTEC) at ESALQ. In 2012 CEBTEC became Laboratory of Agricultural Biotechnology "Prof. Otto Jesu Crocomo".

From 1962-2003 Crocomo was a mentor to dozens of students and professionals in plant biochemistry and biology and collaborated with private companies in the use of *in vitro* culture of plant cells and tissue for plant propagation. In Brazil and abroad he as been a prolific publisher of refereed scientific articles and books, promoted and attended Symposiums, Congress and Scientific Meetings.

Julius P. Kreier

Julius P. Kreier, Professor Emeritus, Department of Microbiology, The Ohio State University, Columbus Ohio; Birthplace: Philadelphia, PA 1926; Education. Philadelphia Public Schools, 1932- 1945. Temple University 1945-1948, University of Pennsylvania, 1949-1953, V.M.D. University of Illinois, 1956-1962, MSc. Ph.D.; Employment. Veterinarian, Cooperative Mexican American Commission for the Eradication of Foot and Mouth Disease, Mexico 1954-1955. Veterinarian, Tuberculosis and Brucellosis Eradication Campaign, 1956 Maryland, USA. University of Illinois, Urbana Illinois, Research Associate 1956-1962. Ohio State University, Assistant Professor, Associate Professor and Full Professor of Microbiology 1962-1989;

Professor Emeritus of Microbiology, 1989 to present. Publications 150 in reviewed journals. Books 22; Teaching. Parasitic Protozoology, Rodent Surgery, Introductory Immunology, Infectious Diseases; Mentoring of graduate students: PhD students 24, MSc students 38, Postdoctoral fellows and visiting professors 4; Fulbright Award University of the Republic of Uruguay, invited lecturer, Campinas University Brazil, Veterinary College, Ankara Turkey, Institute of Parasitology Shanghai China, Haryana Agricultural University, Madras, India; My research was primarily on the pathogenesis of infectious diseases of the blood. These were primarily caused by protozoa although some were caused by Rickettsial type organisms. From my work the greatest pleasures I had were from teaching. In fact I also believe that my greatest contribution to science was the students trained. My students are now scattered around the world and most are continuing to carry out scientific investigations.

William Rodney Sharp

William "Rod" Sharp's background resides in biotechnology, translation of science into business ideas, spawning start-up companies and extensive technology transfer experience in the Americas and Asia with important corporate research and development collaborations with the University of Sao Paulo and institutes of the Chinese Academy of Sciences. He has authored over seventy original research papers, abstracts and books in the field of plant cell biology including the coediting of the five-volume series *Handbook of Plant Cell Culture*, two volume *Reflections and Connections – Journeys Through The Life Sciences* and the pending two volume *Pathways To Collaboration* series. Positions held include: Dean of Research/Professor of Plant Science, Cook College and Director of Research, New Jersey Agricultural Experiment Station, Rutgers University; Vice President, Business Development, PhytoPharmaceuticals Inc., Executive Vice-President, DNA Pharmaceuticals, Inc.; Executive Vice-President for Research, DNA Plant Technology Corp; Research Director, Pioneer Research, Campbell Institute for Agricultural Research & Technology, Campbell Soup Company. The biotechnology companies subsequently exited into Groupo Pulsar/Savia. S.A. de C.V.; Ciba-Geigy Corporation (Novartis-Geigy-Sandoz following merger); and Samyang Genex. Prior academic appointments include: Professor of Microbiology, The Ohio State University; Fellow, Argonne National Laboratory, Eminent Professor, University of Sao Paulo and Fulbright Grantee during 1971 and 1973.

Honors include the following: The 1999 University of Sao Paulo Luiz Queiroz Distinguished Service Medal, Ohio State University Board of Trustees 2007 Distinguished Service Award, naming of the William Rodney Sharp Conference Facility at the University of Sao Paulo/ Escola Superior de Agricultura "Luiz de Queiroz" Center of Agricultural Biotechnology (CEBTEC), Sao Paulo Academy of Sciences Foreign Correspondent Membership and The 2016 Ohio State University College of Arts and Sciences Distinguished Services Award.

Currently, Rod Sharp serves as a member of The Ohio State University College of Arts and Sciences Advisory Committee, Chairs the ASC Resource Subcommittee and serves as an advisor to the Ohio State University/Rutgers University/University of Sao Paulo Tripartite Faculty/Student Research/Teaching Program and Advocacy Committee for the Ohio State University STEAM Factory and Erdos Institute.

Rod Sharp attended The Ohio State University and University of Akron, holds a Ph.D. in Plant Cell Biology from Rutgers University and completed a postdoctoral fellowship at Case Western Reserve University.

Made in the USA
Middletown, DE
17 January 2018